CW00530865

The Ultimate Air Fryer Cookbook

1200 Easy Air Fryer Recipes for
Beginners and Advanced Users

Delois Townsend

Table of Contents

Vegetables and Sides Recipes 50

Fish and Seafood Recipes 75

Beef, Pork, and Lamb Recipes 132

Dessert Recipes 159

Introduction

Air Fryers are the new sensation in the market nowadays and this revolutionary appliance makes its way on top at our kitchen top. This amazing appliance can cook all sorts of food with less or no oil and the texture is the same as the fried food.

The Air Fryer is a small countertop electric appliance to simulate fried foods without using oil. The powerful fan heats up at high speed to create a crispy layer due to the browning reaction. There are wide range of air fryer these days and their reputation is well established. Well, a little air-cooled machine makes food crisp while taking too many calories off the scale. You can still get the same taste and texture of fried foods with a hot fryer, but the oil only needs a teaspoon with real heat. You can have your crispy addiction without any guilt.

Fundamentals of Air Fryer

In the simplest form, the Air Fryer is essentially a small convection stove. They heat small baskets hot and cold very quickly. The air fry mechanism works with a fan that circulates heat around the cooking basket at high speed.

What is Air Fryer?

The Air Fryer is similar to an oven in which it is baked and roasted, but the difference is that the air fryer mainly uses air to replace the hot oil and uses convection similar to the sun's hot air to heat the food, the hot air forms a rapid circulating heat flow in the closed pot to make the food cooked, which makes the food crispy inside in a few seconds, especially less fatty than fried food. The Air Fryer generally heats up quickly and cooks food quickly and evenly, thanks to a combination of electrical equipment and the size of the pan.

Cleaning is the important part of the air fryer system. Air Fryer baskets are generally washed well in the dishwasher. From frozen chicken wings and homemade fries to grilled vegetables and fresh cookies, there are all kinds of tasty food you can air fry in the Air Fryer.

The best dishes on an Air Fryer are usually deep-fried, but you can also use them for baking vegetables, meat, and cookies.

Following are some of the amazing foods you can cook in the Air Fryer:

Frozen Food

The Air Fryer is a star when it comes to making frozen foods for their fried flavors. Frozen fries, mozzarella sticks, and chicken nuggets are just a few of the Air Fryer snacks you can make.

Homemade Food

If you want to make appetizers from scratch, Air fryer is a great choice for homemade and side dishes. Try Air Fryer Sweet Potato Fries, Air Fryer Pickles, or Relena's Air Fryer Papas. Don't forget that favorite air fryer appetizer.

Poultry, Fish, and Meat

Make delicious, tender, and juicy fried chicken. Try Air Fryer chicken recipes like the Air Fryer Nashville Hot Chicken. For healthier options, Air Fryer Keto Meatballs is a fantastic choice. As far as fish and seafood, you will love the Air-Fryer Crumb-Topped Fish.

Roasted Vegetables

The Air Fryer is particularly suitable for cooking vegetables because it is a small oven. You can make air fryer herbs and lemon cauliflower and fried garlic - Brussels sprouts with rosemary.

Baked Food

The Air Fryer is perfect for dessert, with cookies or apple fritters. You can make Peppermint Air Fryer lava cakes for the winter holidays or Mini Nutella Air Fryer donut holes for a hearty treat all year round. However, you can't do anything with liquid batter.

Benefits of Using Air Fryer

When used properly, air fryers offer many wonderful benefits:

Promote Weight Loss

There is high risk of obesity with more fried food you eat. This is because fried foods seem to have a lot of fat and calories. Switching from fried foods to air-fried foods and cutting down on unhealthy fats can promote weight loss.

Reduce the Risk of Toxic Formation

Frying foods in oil can produce dangerous substances such as acrylamide. These compounds are formed in some foods during hot cooking such as deep frying. Acrylamide has been linked to the development of certain cancers, including endometrial lymphoma, ovarian cancer, lymphoma, breast cancer, and lymphoma. You can reduce the risk of diseases by switching to an Air Fryer.

Reduces Disease Risk

Cooking in oil and eating fried foods regularly can be linked to many health issues. Replacing deep frying with air frying helps you to reduce the risk of health problems.

Budget-friendly

Oils, especially good oils which are safe for high temperatures, can be added during the rapid passage. But with Air Frying, you can enjoy delicious desserts at the investment of your dreams, using very little funds.

Time-saving

Homemade food has many benefits, but free time doesn't always allow it. Fortunately, the Air Fryer is a faster way to cook, thanks to its fast blower, which reduces preheating and saves cooking time for a wide range of foods.

Low Calorie-Controlled Meals

If you want to shed weight healthily while enjoying the taste of yummy fried foods, the Air Fryer is your diet companion. It makes delicious meals with 70-80% less calories than the fried items.

Safe Cooking

Frying requires a lot of hot oil. If you think, this is not safe, the Air Fryer will be the good choice. The Air Fryer, on the other hand, eliminates the risk of splashing hot oil. You can cook food in Air Fryer even when kids and pets are running around you without worrying of oil splashing.

Perfect Post-Cooking Environment

Unlike cooking in a traditional oven, the Air Fryer does not heat the whole house. Moreover, even in the Air Fryer, the smell of fried food does not fill the house.

Step-By-Step Air Frying

The top of the Air Fryer is equipped with a hot coil and a fan that blows hot air. When you put the food in the basket and turn on the power, the heat will circulate the food. This rapid cycle makes food crisp. It looks like tempura, but without the oil. Here's how to use an Air Fryer:

Place Food in the Air Fryer Basket/Pan

Depending on the size of your Air Fryer, the basket can hold from 2 to 10 quarts. Generally, it is recommended to add 1-2 teaspoons of oil to make the food delicious and crispy.

Adjust Time and Temperature

The Air Fryer cooking time and temperature are typically 5 to 25 minutes at 350 ° F-400 ° F, depending on the food to be cooked.

Air Fry the Food

Sometimes it is necessary to turn food or turn it halfway through cooking to ensure the food is evenly crisp. It is important to clean your Air Fryer after cooking.

Cooking Time and Temperature for Various Recipes

Meat and Poultry

You can cook all kinds of poultry and meats in an Air Fryer and get the best ever results. The air frying time depends on the thickness of the meat and the recipe to cook.

TYPE OF MEAT	COOKING TEMPERATURE	COOKING TIME
Bacon	350°F/ 177°C	8-12 minutes
Chicken (Whole)	350°F/177°C	45-65 minutes
Chicken Breasts (Bone-in)	375°F /190°C	25-35 minutes
Chicken Breasts (Bone-less)	350°F /177°C	15-20 minutes
Chicken Tenders	250°F /177°C	8-12 minutes
Chicken Thighs (Bone-in)	400°F /204°C	15-22 minutes
Chicken Thighs (Bone-less)	375°F /190°C	16-21 minutes
Chicken Wings	375°F /190°C	18-28 minutes
Lamb (Leg)	380°F /199°C	17-30 minutes
Lamb (Rack)	250°F /177°C	10-17 minutes
Strip Steak	400°F /204°C	8-14 minutes
Pork Chops	250°F /177°C	10-15 minutes
Pork Tenderloin	375°F /190°C	15-25 minutes
Ribeye/T-Bone	400°F /204°C	15-25 minutes

Seafood

To obtain a fine and crispy fish, do not overfill the basket of your deep fryer. When preparing small dishes such as shrimp and squid, it is recommended that you shake the basket every few minutes for even cooking from all angles.

TYPE OF SEAFOOD	COOKING TEMPERATURE	COOKING TIME
Salmon	375°F/ 190°C	8-13 minutes
Tilapia (Other White Fish)	400°F/204°C	8-12 minutes
Shrimps	350°F /177°C	5-8 minutes
Calamari	400°F /204°C	4-8 minutes
Scallops	400°F /204°C	5-7 minutes

Vegetables

Cooking vegetables in an Air Fryer will give roast texture same like roasting, but crispier on the outside. After preparing the vegetables, it is a good idea to lightly oil the vegetables before air frying them. Naturally, vegetables ripen quickly, but rough, hard roots take a little longer.

VEGETABLES	COOKING TEMPERATURE	COOKING TIME
Asparagus	400°F /204°C	6-10 minutes
Beets (Slices)	350°F /177°C	15-25 minutes
Beet (Whole)	400°F /204°C	30-40 minutes
Bell Pepper (Slices)	350°F /177°C	7-10 minutes
Bok Choy	250°F /177°C	5-6 minutes
Broccoli	400°F /204°C	5-9 minutes
Brussels Sprouts (Sliced)	375°F /190°C	9-16 minutes
Butternut Squash, Chopped	400°F /204°C	15-20 minutes
Carrots (Baby or chopped)	400°F /204°C	10-15 minutes
Cauliflower (Whole)	350°F /177°C	15-20 minutes
Cauliflower (Chopped)	400°F /204°C	10-15 minutes
Corn on the Cob	400°F /204°C	8-10 minutes
Eggplant (Cubed or sliced)	400°F /204°C	15-18 minutes
Green Beans	400°F /204°C	8-10 minutes
Kale Leaves	375°F /190°C	4-5 minutes
Mushrooms (Button)	375°F /190°C	8-13 minutes
Mushrooms (Portobello)	350°F /177°C	8-13 minutes
Okra	350°F /177°C	12-14 minutes
Onions (Sliced)	400°F /204°C	8-10 minutes
Parsnips (Chopped or Halves)	375°F /190°C	10-16 minutes
Peppers (Small, Shishito)	400°F /204°C	4-6 minutes
Potatoes (Whole)	400°F /204°C	30-45 minutes
Potatoes (Chopped)	375°F /190°C	15-30 minutes
Sweet Potatoes (Whole)	400°F /204°C	8-15 minutes
Sweet Potatoes (Chopped)	375°F /190°C	30-35 minutes
Tomatoes (Cherry)	350°F /177°C	5-8 minutes
Tomatoes (Halves)	350°F /177°C	6-12 minutes
Zucchini (Chopped)	350°F /177°C	8-12 minutes
Zucchini (Noodles)	400°F /204°C	10-12 minutes

Prepared Frozen Foods
You can cook prepared food with perfection.

PREPARED FROZEN FOOD	COOKING TEMPERATURE	COOKING TIME
Chicken Tenders (Pre-cooked and breaded)	375°F /190°C	14-18 minutes
Dumplings/Pot-stickers	400°F /204°C	6-10 minutes
Egg Rolls	350°F /177°C	8-14 minutes
Fish Sticks	350°F /177°C	8-12 minutes
French Fries	400°F /204°C	14-17 minutes
Hash Browns	400°F /204°C	6-9 minutes
Mini Pizzas	325°F /163°C	8-15 minutes
Mozzarella Sticks	375°F /190°C	7-10 minutes
Onion Rings	400°F /204°C	8-10 minutes
Tarter Tots	400°F /204°C	10-15 minutes

Straight from The Store

There is a vast range of air fryers and you can buy them as per requirement. Here is some of the air fryer which is best with their performance and the cooked food texture. They are all budget-friendly and you can never regret having one of them.
Here enlist best air fryers you can get straight from the store;
- Best Air Fryer: Ninja Air Fryer
- Value Air Fryer: Chefman TurboFry
- Air Fryer for a Family of Four people: Instant Pot Vortex Plus
- Air Fryer with Rotisserie: Power XL Air Fryer
- Digital Air Fryer: Cosori Air Fryer
- Large-Capacity Air Fryer: GoWise 7-Quart Electric Air Fryer
- Compact Air Fryer: Philips Compact Air Fryer
- Air Fryer for One Person: Dash Compact Air Fryer

Cleaning and Caring for Your Air Fryer

Cleaning your utensils is always encouraged after every cooking, the same is with the Air Fryer. For the long run and cleanliness always clean your Air Fryer.
There are a few rules you might need to keep for the Air Fryer:
1. Materials such as metallic objects, wire brushes, or hard sponges may cause damage. Do not use them to remove debris from the air fryer basket.
2. When cleaning the Air Fryer, do not immerse it in water. Because it is an electric machine that will be damaged.
3. Baskets, pots, and pans should be cleaned at all times using the Air Fryer. It is better to use soap and lukewarm water to clean it.
4. The interior should be cleaned quickly using a cloth dampened with a little soap. After washing, dry all parts of the Air Fryer.
For the deep cleaning, follow the below instructions:
1. Remove electrical appliances and allow them to cool. Do not clean the hot machine.
2. Remove the pans and baskets from the Air Fryer and wash them with hot water and soap.
3. If the parts are greasy, soak them in hot water for 10 minutes and then brush them with a non-abrasive sponge.
4. Use a non-abrasive sponge and dish detergent to clean the inside. Wipe it off with a clean cloth.
5. Wash the exterior of the appliance with a damp cloth and soapy water. Wipe it off with a clean cloth.
6. Dry all cleaning items. Once dry, the Air Fryer can be assembled.

Fish Tacos

Prep time: 10 minutes | Cook time: 15 minutes | Serves: 2

4 big tortillas
1 red bell pepper, chopped
1 yellow onion, chopped
1 cup corn
4 boneless white fish fillets,

½ cup salsa
A handful mixed romaine lettuce
4 tbsp. parmesan, grated

Place the fish fillets in your "Air Fryer Basket" and Air Fry them at 350 degrees F for 6 minutes. Meanwhile, heat up a suitable over medium-high heat Add onion, bell pepper, and corn, stir for 1-2 minutes. Spread the tortillas on a working surface. Divide fish fillets, salsa, mixed vegies and mixed greens and parmesan on each tortilla. Roll your tortillas, place them in the air fryer and Air Fry at 350 degrees F for 6 minutes more. Divide fish tacos on plates. Serve and enjoy.
Nutritional information: Calories: 217; Fat: 9.2g; Total Carbs 1.7g; Net Carbs 1.2g; Protein: 29.8g; Fiber: 0.4g; Sugar: 0.3g

Potatoes with Bacon

Prep time: 10 minutes | Cook time: 20 minutes | Serves: 2

4 potatoes, peeled and cut into medium cubes
6 garlic cloves, minced
4 bacon slices, chopped
2 rosemary springs, chopped

1 tbsp. olive oil
Salt and black pepper to the taste
2 eggs, whisked

In your "Air Fryer Basket", mix up the oil, potatoes, garlic, bacon, rosemary, salt, pepper and eggs. Cook the potatoes at 400 degrees F for 20 minutes on Air Fry mode. When cooked, divide everything on plates and serve for breakfast. Enjoy!
Nutritional information: Calories: 164; Fat: 7.9g; Total Carbs 2g; Net Carbs 2g; Protein: 19.2g; Fiber: 0.1g; Sugar: 0g

Zucchini Mix

Prep time: 10 minutes | Cook time: 35 minutes | Serves: 2

1 lb. zucchini, sliced
1 tbsp. parsley, chopped
1 yellow squash, halved, deseeded, and chopped

1 tbsp. olive oil
Black pepper, to taste
Salt, to taste

Mix up all of the recipe ingredients in a large bowl. Transfer the mixture into the "Air Fryer Basket" and Air Fry at 400 degrees F for 35 minutes. Serve and enjoy.
Nutritional information: Calories 249 Fat 3 g; Total Carbs 4 g; Sugar 2 g; Net Carbs 5g; Protein 1.5 g; Fiber: 0 g

Chicken Vegetable Omelet

Prep time: 10 minutes | Cook time: 12 minutes | Serves: 2

1 tsp. butter
1 small yellow onion, chopped

½ jalapeño pepper, seeded and chopped

3 eggs
Salt and ground black pepper, as required

¼ cup cooked chicken, shredded

In a frying pan, melt the butter over medium heat; add the onion and cook for 4-5 minutes; add the jalapeño pepper and cook for 1 minute. Remove the pan from the heat and then set aside to cool slightly. Meanwhile, in a suitable bowl, add the eggs, salt, and black pepper and beat well. Mix up the onion mixture and chicken until well-combined. Place the chicken mixture into a small baking pan. Arrange pan over the "Wire Rack" and insert in the air fryer. Air Fry the food at 355 degrees F for 6 minutes. Cut the omelet into 2 portions and serve hot.
Nutritional information: Calories 153; Fat 9.1 g; Net Carbs 3.4 g; Fiber 6 g; Total Carbs 4 g; Fiber: 0.9 g; Protein 13.8 g

Mushroom Salad

Prep time: 10 minutes | Cook time: 15 minutes | Serves: 2

10 mushrooms, halved
1 tbsp. fresh parsley, chopped
1 tbsp. olive oil
1 tbsp. mozzarella cheese, grated

1 tbsp. cheddar cheese, grated
1 tbsp. dried mix herbs
Black pepper, to taste
Salt, to taste

Add all the recipe ingredients into the bowl and toss well. Transfer bowl mixture into the air fryer baking dish. Place this dish in the air fryer and cook the food at 380 degrees F on Air Fry mode for 15 minutes. Serve and enjoy.
Nutritional information: Calories 90 Fat 7 g; Total Carbs 2 g; Sugar 1 g; Net Carbs 6g; Protein 5 g; Fiber: 7 g

Scrambled Eggs

Prep time: 5 minutes | Cook time:10 minutes | Serves: 2

4 large eggs.
½ cup shredded sharp Cheddar

cheese.
2 tbsps. unsalted butter; melted.

Crack eggs into 2-cup round baking dish and whisk. Place the dish into the Air Fryer Basket. Adjust the temperature to 400 degrees F and set the timer for 10 minutes. After 5 minutes of cooking time, stir the eggs and add the butter and cheese. Let cook 3 more minutes and stir again. Allow eggs to finish cooking an additional 2 minutes or remove if they are to your desired liking. Use a fork to fluff. Serve warm.
Nutritional information: Calories: 228; Fat: 14.2g; Total Carbs 3.6g; Net Carbs 2g; Protein: 22.6g; Fiber: 1.1g; Sugar: 1.7g

Morning Frittata

Prep time: 5 minutes | Cook time: 15 minutes | Serves: 6

1 fennel bulb; shredded
6 eggs; whisked
2 tsp. cilantro; chopped.
1 tsp. sweet paprika

Cooking spray
Black pepper, to taste
Salt, to taste

In a suitable bowl, and mix all the recipe ingredients except the cooking spray and stir well. Grease a baking pan with the

cooking spray, then pour the frittata mix and spread well Arrange this pan to the Air Fryer and cook at 370 degrees F on Air Fry mode for15 minutes. When cooked, divide the food between plates and serve them for breakfast.
Nutritional information: Calories: 201; Fat: 9.9g; Total Carbs 3g; Net Carbs 2g; Protein: 24.6g; Fiber: 0.7g; Sugar: 1.4g

Strawberries Coconut Oatmeal

Prep time: 5 minutes | Cook time: 15 minutes | Serves: 4

½ cup coconut; shredded	¼ tsp. vanilla extract
¼ cup strawberries	2 tsp. stevia
2 cups coconut milk	Cooking spray

Grease the "Air Fryer Basket" with the cooking spray, then add all of the recipe ingredients inside and toss Cook the mixture at 365 degrees F on Air Fry mode for 15 minutes. When cooked, divide into bowls and serve for breakfast.
Nutritional information: Calories: 198; Fat: 9g; Total Carbs 2.2g; Net Carbs 2g; Protein: 26g; Fiber: 0.2g; Sugar: 0.1g

Asparagus Arugula Salad

Prep time: 5 minutes | Cook time: 10 minutes | Serves: 4

1 cup baby arugula	A pinch of salt and black
1 bunch asparagus; trimmed	pepper
1 tbsp. balsamic vinegar	Cooking spray
1 tbsp. cheddar cheese; grated	

Put the asparagus in your "Air Fryer Basket", grease the asparagus with some cooking spray, season with black pepper and salt and Air Fry at 360 degrees F for 10 minutes. In a bowl, mix the asparagus with the arugula and the vinegar, divide between plates after tossing well and serve hot with cheese sprinkled on top
Nutritional information: Calories: 283; Fat: 16.5g; Total Carbs 7g; Net Carbs 3g; Protein: 27.4g; Fiber: 1.8g; Sugar: 2g

Raspberries Bowls

Prep time: 5 minutes | Cook time: 12 minutes | Serves: 2

1 cup raspberries	2 tbsp. lemon juice
2 tbsp. butter	1 tsp. cinnamon powder

In the Air Fryer Basket, mix all the recipe ingredients and then cover. Cook the mixture at 350 degrees F on Air Fry mode for 12 minutes. When cooked, divide into bowls and serve for breakfast
Nutritional information: Calories 208 Fat 6g; Fiber: 9g; Total Carbs 14g; Net Carbs 2g; Protein: 3g; Sugar: 1g; fiber 2g

Squash Fritters

Prep time: 15 minutes | Cook time: 8 minutes | Serves: 4

2 cups cooked spaghetti squash	2 tbsp. unsalted butter;
2 stalks green onion, sliced	softened.
1 large egg	½ tsp. garlic powder.
¼ cup blanched ground almond flour.	1 tsp. dried parsley.

Remove excess moisture from the squash with a cheesecloth or kitchen towel. Mix all the recipe ingredients in a large bowl. Form into 4 patties from this mixture. Cut a piece of parchment

to fit your Air Fryer Basket. Place each patty on the parchment and place into the "Air Fryer Basket" Air Fry the patties at 400 degrees F for 8 minutes, flipping halfway through. Serve warm.
Nutritional information: Calories 131 Protein 3.8g; Fiber: 2.0g; Fat 10.1g; Total Carbs 7.1g; Sugar 1g; fiber 2g

Mushrooms Spread

Prep time:5 minutes | Cook time: 20 minutes | Serves: 4

¼ cup mozzarella; shredded	A pinch of salt and black
½ cup coconut cream	pepper
1 cup white mushrooms	Cooking spray

Put the mushrooms in your "Air Fryer Basket", grease with some cooking spray. Cook the mushrooms in the air fryer at 370 degrees F on Air Fry mode for 20 minutes. Transfer to a blender, add the remaining ingredients and pulse well, divide into bowls and serve as a spread.
Nutritional information: Calories 202 Fat 12g; Fiber: 2g; Total Carbs 5g; Net Carbs 6g; Protein: 7g; Sugar 1g; fiber 2g

Tuna Onions Salad

Prep time: 5 minutes | Cook time: 15 minutes | Serves: 4

14 oz. canned tuna, drained and flaked	1 tbsp. olive oil
2 spring onions; chopped.	A pinch of salt and black pepper
1 cup arugula	

At 360 degrees F, preheat your air fryer. In a bowl, mix up all of the recipe ingredients except the oil and the arugula. Grease the cooking pan that fits your air fryer with oil. Pour the tuna mix onto the cooking pan and then cook at 360 degrees F on Air Fry mode for 15 minutes In a salad bowl, combine the arugula with the tuna mix, toss and serve.
Nutritional information: Calories 212 Fat 8g; Fiber: 3g; Total Carbs 5g; Net Carbs 8g; Protein: 8g; Sugar 1g; fiber 2g

Tomatoes Chard Salad

Prep time: 5 minutes | Cook time: 15 minutes | Serves: 4

4 eggs, whisked	1 tsp. olive oil
3 oz. Swiss chard; chopped.	Salt and black pepper to taste.
1 cup tomatoes; cubed	

In a bowl, mix the eggs with the rest of the ingredients except the oil. Grease a suitable cooking pan with the oil, pour the swish chard mix and Air Fry at 360 degrees F for 15 minutes. Divide between plates and serve.
Nutritional information: Calories 202 Fat 14g; Fiber: 3g; Total Carbs 5g; Net Carbs 2g; Protein: 12g; Sugar 1g; fiber 2g

Egg Cheese Roll Ups

Prep time: 10 minutes | Cook time: 25 minutes | Serves: 4

12 slices sugar-free bacon.	1 cup shredded sharp Cheddar
½ medium green bell pepper; seeded and chopped	cheese.
6 large eggs.	½ cup mild salsa, for dipping
¼ cup chopped onion	2 tbsps. unsalted butter.

In your skillet, melt the butter over medium heat. Toss in onion and pepper to and sauté for 3 minutes until the onions

are translucent. Beat eggs in a small bowl and pour over the vegies in the skillet, then scramble the eggs for 5 minutes. On work surface, place 3 slices of bacon side by side, overlapping about ¼-inch. Place ¼ cup scrambled eggs in a heap on the side closest to you and sprinkle ¼ cup cheese on top of the eggs. Roll the bacon strips around the eggs and secure it with a toothpick. Place each eggs roll into the "Air Fryer Basket" Select Air Fry mode, adjust the cooking temperature to 350 degrees F and set the timer for 15 minutes. Flip the rolls halfway through. Bacon will be brown and crispy when completely cooked. Serve immediately with salsa for dipping.
Nutritional information: Calories 460 Protein 28.2g; Fiber: 0.8g; Fat 31.7g; Total Carbs 6.1g; Sugar 1g; fiber 2g

Ham Egg Cups

Prep time: 5 minutes | Cook time: 12 minutes | Serves: 2

4 large eggs.	¼ cup diced green bell pepper.
4 (1-oz.) slices deli ham	2 tbsp. diced red bell pepper.
½ cup shredded medium	2 tbsp. diced white onion.
Cheddar cheese.	2 tbsp. full-fat sour cream.

Place a slice of ham at the bottom of 4 suitable baking ramekins. In a large bowl, crack the eggs and then whisk with sour cream; add the red pepper, green pepper, onion and stir well. Pour the prepared egg mixture into ham-lined baking ramekins. Top with Cheddar. Place cups into the Air Fryer Basket. Select Air Fry mode, adjust the temperature to 320 degrees F and set the timer for 12 minutes or cook the food until the tops are browned. Serve warm.
Nutritional information: Calories 382 Protein 29.4g; Fiber: 1.4g; Fat 23.6g; Total Carbs 6.0g; Sugar 1g; fiber 2g

Olives Kale Salad

Prep time:5 minutes | Cook time: 20 minutes | Serves: 4

4 eggs; whisked	2 tbsp. cheddar; grated
1 cup kale; chopped.	Cooking spray
½ cup black olives, pitted and sliced	A pinch of salt and black pepper

In a bowl, mix the eggs with the rest of the ingredients except the cooking spray. Take a pan that fits in your air fryer and grease it with the cooking spray, spread the olives mixture. Put this pan into the air fryer and Air Fry the food at 360 degrees F for 20 minutes. Serve hot.
Nutritional information: Calories 220 Fat 13g; Fiber: 4g; Total Carbs 6g; Net Carbs 6g; Protein 12g; Sugar 1g; fiber 2g

Stuffed Poblanos

Prep time: 10 minutes | Cook time: 20 minutes | Serves: 4

½ lb. spicy ground pork breakfast sausage	softened
4 large poblano peppers	¼ cup canned diced tomatoes and green chilies, drained
4 large eggs	8 tbsp. shredded pepper jack cheese
½ cup full-fat sour cream.	
4 oz. full-fat cream cheese,	

In a suitable skillet, crumble and brown the ground sausage over medium heat. Remove sausage and drain the fat from the pan. Crack eggs into the pan, scramble and cook until no longer runny. Place cooked sausage in a large bowl and fold in cream cheese. Mix in diced tomatoes and chilies. Gently fold in eggs Cut a 4"–5" slit in the top of each poblano, removing the seeds and white membrane with a small knife. Separate the filling into 4 and spoon carefully into each pepper. Top each with 2 tablespoons of pepper jack cheese. Place the peppers into the Air Fryer Basket. Select Air Fry mode, adjust the temperature to 350 degrees F and set the timer for 15 minutes. Serve immediately with the sour cream on the top.
Nutritional information: Calories 489 Protein 22.8g; Fiber: 3.8g; Fat 35.6g; Total Carbs 12.6g; Sugar 1g; fiber 2g

Raspberries Cinnamon Oatmeal

Prep time: 5 minutes | Cook time:15 minutes | Serves: 4

1 ½ cups coconut; shredded	2 tsp. stevia
½ cups raspberries	½ tsp. cinnamon powder
2 cups almond milk	Cooking spray
¼ tsp. nutmeg, ground	

Grease the "Air Fryer Basket" with some cooking spray and then mix up all of the recipe ingredients inside, cover and Air Fry at 360 degrees F for 15 minutes. Divide into bowls and serve.
Nutritional information: Calories 172 Fat 5g; Fiber: 2g; Total Carbs 4g; Net Carbs 6g; Protein 6g; Sugar 1g; fiber 2g

Scotch Eggs

Prep time: 15 minutes | Cook time: 15 minutes | Serves: 4

1-lb. ground breakfast sausage	1 egg
3 tbsp. flour	1 tbsp. water
4 hard-boiled eggs, peeled	¾ cup panko bread crumbs

In a suitable bowl, mix the sausage and 1 tablespoon of flour. Form the prepared sausage mixture into 4 equal parts. Place a hard-boiled egg in the center, then wrap the sausage around the egg, sealing completely. Repeat with remaining sausage parts and hard-boiled eggs. In a suitable bowl, whisk the egg and water until smooth. Add the remaining flour and bread crumbs into separate bowls large enough to dredge the sausage-wrapped eggs. Dredge the sausage-wrapped eggs in the flour, then in the whisked egg, and finally coat in the bread crumbs. Arrange them in the Air Fryer Basket. Cook the food at 375 degrees F on Air Fry mode for 20 minutes. Flip them halfway through, or until the sausage is cooked to desired doneness. Remove from the basket and serve on a plate.
Nutritional information: Calories 509; Fat 16g; Total Carbs 8g; Net Carbs 6g; Protein 24g; Sugar 16g; Fiber 8g

Simple Strawberry Toast

Prep time: 8 minutes | Cook time: 10 minutes | Serves: 4

4 slices bread, ½-inch thick	1 tsp. sugar
1 cup sliced strawberries	Cooking spray

Place the bread slices on a clean plate. Arrange the bread slices (sprayed side down) in the Air Fryer Basket. Evenly spread the strawberries onto them and then sprinkle with sugar. Cook the food at 375 degrees F on Air Fry mode for 8 minutes, or until the tops are covered with a beautiful glaze. Remove from the basket and serve on a plate.
Nutritional information: Calories 375; Fat 22g; Total Carbs 2g; Net Carbs 8g; Protein 14g; Sugar 5g; Fiber 0g

Quiche Cups

Prep time: 11 minutes | Cook time: 15 minutes | Serves: 10

¼ lb. all-natural ground pork	sausage

3 eggs
¾ cup milk
4 oz. sharp Cheddar cheese,
grated
Cooking spray

On a clean work surface, slice the pork sausage into 2-ounce portions. Shape each portion into a ball and gently flatten it with your palm. Lay the patties in the "Air Fryer Basket" and cook them at 375 degrees F on Air Fry mode for 6 minutes. Flip the patties halfway through. When cooked, Remove the patties from the basket and transfer them to a large dish lined with paper towels. Crumble them into small pieces with a fork. Set aside. Line 10 paper liner in each muffin cups and then lightly grease the muffin cups with some cooking spray. Arrange the muffin cups to the muffin pan. Divide crumbled sausage equally among the ten muffin cups and sprinkle the tops with the cheese. Arrange the muffin pan to the Air Fryer Basket. Cook the food at 375 degrees F for 8 minutes on Air Fry mode, until the tops are golden and a toothpick inserted in the middle comes out clean. Remove from the basket and let cool for 5 minutes before serving.
Nutritional information: Calories 497; Fat 25g; Total Carbs 1g; Net Carbs 1g; Protein 28g; Sugar 5g; Fiber 4g

Ham Omelet

Prep time: 10 minutes | Cook time: 20 minutes | Serves: 6

¼ cup ham, diced
¼ cup green or red bell pepper, cored and chopped
¼ cup onion, chopped
1 tsp. butter
4 large eggs
2 tbsps. milk
⅛ tsp. salt
¾ cup sharp Cheddar cheese, grated

In a suitable bowl, whisk the eggs, milk, and salt until smooth and creamy. Add the ham, bell pepper, onion, and butter into a 6×6×2-inch baking pan. Arrange the pan to the Air Fryer Basket. Cook the food at 375 degrees F for 6 minutes on Air Fry mode. Flip the food halfway through, or until the vegetables are soft; gently pour the milk mixture over the ham and vegetables in the pan. Resume cooking the food in your air fryer for 13 minutes more under the same mode. Top it with the cheese and Air Fry for 1 minute more, or until the cheese is bubbly and melted. Remove from the basket and cool for 5 minutes before serving.
Nutritional information: Calories 367; Fat 14g; Total Carbs 13g; Net Carbs 8g; Protein 18g; Sugar 2g; Fiber 2g

Canadian Bacon English Muffin

Prep time: 5 minutes | Cook time: 8 minutes | Serves: 4

4 English muffins
8 slices Canadian bacon
4 slices cheese
Cooking spray

Cut each English muffin in half on a clean work surface. To assemble a sandwich, layer 2 slices of bacon and 1 cheese slice on the bottom of each muffin and put the other half of the bread on top. Repeat with the remaining biscuits, bacon, and cheese slices. Arrange the prepared sandwiches in the "Air Fryer Basket" and spritz with some cooking spray. Cook the sandwiches at 375 degrees F for 8 minutes on Air Fry mode, flipping halfway through. Let them cool for 3 minutes before serving.
Nutritional information: Calories: 225; Fat: 10g; Total Carbs 5.2g; Net Carbs 1.2g; Protein: 26.5g; Fiber: 1.3g; Sugar: 0.9g

Asparagus Egg Strata

Prep time: 15 minutes | Cook time: 20 minutes | Serves: 4

6 asparagus spears, cut into 2-inch pieces
½ cup grated Havarti or Swiss cheese

4 eggs
2 slices whole-wheat bread, cut into ½-inch cubes
3 tbsps. whole milk
2 tbsps. flat-leaf parsley, chopped
1 tbsp. water
Cooking spray

Place a 6×6×2-inch baking pan into the Air Fryer Basket. Add 1 tablespoon of water, and asparagus spears in the baking pan. Cook the asparagus spears at 325 degrees F on Air Fry mode for 3 to 5 minutes. Remove the asparagus spears from the baking pan. Drain and dry them thoroughly. Place the asparagus spears and bread cubes in the pan, then spray with some cooking spray. Set aside. Add the cheese, parsley, salt, and pepper. Air Fry the food at 350 degrees F for 11 to 14 minutes. Remove the strata from the pan. Let cool for 5 minutes before serving.
Nutritional information: Calories: 241; Fat: 12.5g; Total Carbs 4.7g; Net Carbs 2g; Protein: 24.6g; Fiber: 1.1g; Sugar: 1.8g

Shrimp Rice Frittata

Prep time: 15 minutes | Cook time: 18 minutes | Serves: 4

½ cup chopped shrimp, cooked
½ cup baby spinach
½ cup of rice, cooked
4 eggs
½ cup grated Monterey Jack
cheese
½ tsp. dried basil
Pinch salt
Cooking spray

Spritz a 6×6×2-inch baking pan with some cooking spray. Mix the cooked shrimp, rice, and spinach in the pan until combine well. Transfer the pan to the Air Fryer Basket. Air Fry them at 325 degrees F for 14 to 18 minutes. Remove from the pan and cool for 3 minutes before cutting into wedges to serve.
Nutritional information: Calories: 235; Fat: 10.4g; Total Carbs 6g; Net Carbs 2g; Protein: 27.9g; Fiber: 1.3g; Sugar: 1.5g

Monkey Bread with Cinnamon

Prep time: 5 minutes | Cook time: 10 minutes | Serves: 4

1 can (8-oz.) refrigerated biscuits
3 tbsps. brown sugar
¼ cup white sugar
½ tsp. cinnamon
⅛ tsp. nutmeg
3 tbsps. unsalted butter, melted

Divide each biscuit into quarters on a clean work surface. In a suitable mixing bowl, thoroughly mix up the brown and white sugar, nutmeg, and cinnamon. Pour the melted butter into another suitable bowl. Dip each biscuit in the melted butter, then in the sugar mixture to coat thoroughly. Arrange the coated biscuits in a 6×6×2-inch baking pan and then transfer the pan to the Air Fryer Basket. Air Fry the food in batches at 350 degrees F for 6 to 9 minutes. Transfer to a serving dish and cool for 5 minutes before serving.
Nutritional information: Calories: 243; Fat: 14.3g; Total Carbs 7g; Net Carbs 3g; Protein: 23.4g; Fiber: 2.1g; Sugar: 3.3g

Pesto Gnocchi

Prep time: 15 minutes | Cook time: 16 minutes | Serves: 4

1 jar (8-oz.) pesto
⅓ cup Parmesan cheese, grated
1 package (16-oz.) shelf-stable gnocchi
1 onion, chopped
3 cloves garlic, sliced
1 tbsp. olive oil

Mix the oil, onion, garlic, and gnocchi in a 6×6×2-inch baking pan. Place the prepared pan into the Air Fryer Basket. Air Fry the food at 400 degrees F for 16 minutes. Stir once halfway through cooking. When done, transfer the gnocchi to a serving dish. Sprinkle with the Parmesan cheese and pesto. Stir well and serve warm.

Nutritional information: Calories: 229; Fat: 5.6g; Total Carbs 4.7g; Net Carbs 2g; Protein: 38.4g; Fiber: 0.8g; Sugar: 1.6g

Ham Cup

Prep time: 10 minutes | Cook time: 15 minutes | Serves: 18

5 whole eggs	1 ½ cups Swiss cheese
2 ¼ oz. Ham	¼ tsp. Salt
1 cup milk	¼ cup green onion
⅛ tsp. Pepper	½ tsp. Thyme

At 350 degrees F, preheat your air fryer. Beat Eggs into a suitable bowl. Add thyme onion, salt, Swiss cheese pepper, milk to the beaten eggs. Prepare your baking forms for muffins and place ham slices in each baking form. Cover the ham with egg mixture. Transfer the forms to air fryer and cook for 15 minutes at 350 degrees F on Bake mode.

Nutritional information: Calories 80 Fat 5 g; Net Carbs 5g; Protein 7 g; Total Carbs 0 g; Sugar 2g; Fiber: 2 g

Seasoned Cheese Sticks

Prep time: 22 minutes | Cook time: 7 minutes | Serves: 8

6 cheese sticks, snake-sized	¼ cup flour, whole wheat
¼ cup parmesan cheese, grated	¼ tbsp. rosemary, grounded
2 eggs	1 tbsp. garlic powder
1 tbsp. Italian seasoning	

Take cheese sticks and set aside. Take a shallow bowl and beat eggs into it. Mix cheese, flour, and seasonings in another bowl. Roll the cheese sticks in the eggs and then in the batter. Now do the process again till the sticks as well coated. Place them in the Air Fryer Basket. Air Fry them for 6-7 minutes at 370 degrees F. When done, serve and enjoy.

Nutritional information: Calories 50 Net Carbs 6g; Protein 3 g; Total Carbs 3 g; Fat 2 g; Sugar 2g; Fiber: 1.8 g

Broccoli Quiche

Prep time: 20 minutes | Cook time: 30 minutes | Serves: 2

4 eggs	¼ cup feta cheese, crumbled
1 cup whole milk	1 cup grated cheddar cheese
2 medium broccolis, cut into florets	Black pepper and salt, to taste
2 medium tomatoes, diced	1 tsp. Chopped parsley
4 medium carrots, diced	1 tsp. Dried thyme

Put the broccoli and carrots in a food steamer and cook until soft, about 10 minutes. In a suitable bowl, crack in the eggs, add the parsley, salt, pepper, and thyme. Using a whisk, beat the eggs while adding the milk gradually until a pale mixture is attained. Once the broccoli and carrots are ready, strain them through a sieve and then set aside. In a 3 x 3 cm quiche dish, add the broccoli and carrots. Put the tomatoes, then the feta and cheddar cheese on top. Pour the prepared egg mixture over the layering and top with the remaining cheddar cheese. Place the dish in the air fryer and Air Fry the food at 350 degrees F for 20 minutes.

Nutritional information: Calories 316 Fat 23.8 g; Net Carbs 6g; Protein 9.9 g; Total Carbs 5 g; Sugar 2g; Fiber: 1 g

Onion Omelet

Prep time: 5 minutes | Cook time: 10 minutes | Serves: 2

2 eggs	2 tbsp. grated cheddar cheese

1 tsp. soy sauce	¼ tsp. pepper
½ onion, sliced	1 tbsp. olive oil

Whisk the eggs along with the pepper and soy sauce. Add the oil, prepared egg mixture and the onion to a suitable cooking pan. Air Fry the food at 350 degrees F for 8 to 10 minutes. Top with the grated cheddar cheese and enjoy.

Nutritional information: Calories 347 Fat 23.2 g; Net Carbs 3g; Protein 13.6 g; Total Carbs 6 g; Sugar 2g; Fiber: 1.2 g

Shirred Eggs

Prep time: 6 minutes | Cook time: 14 minutes | Serves: 2

2 tsp. butter, for greasing	¼ tsp. paprika
4 eggs, divided	¾ tsp. salt
2 tbsp. heavy cream	¼ tsp. pepper
4 slices ham	2 tsps. chopped chives
3 tbsp. parmesan cheese	

Grease a pie pan with the butter. Place the ham slices on the pan. Whisk one egg along with the salt, heavy cream, and pepper in a suitable bowl. Pour the prepared mixture over the ham slices. Crack the other eggs over the ham. Sprinkle with parmesan cheese. Air Fry the food at 360 degrees F for 14 minutes. Season with paprika, garnish with chives and serve with low carb bread.

Nutritional information: Calories 279; Fat 20 g; Net Carbs 2g; Protein 20.8 g; Total Carbs 1.8 g; Sugar 2g; Fiber: 0.2 g

Cheddar Hash Brown

Prep time: 30 minutes | Cook time: 20 minutes | Serves: 6

1½ lbs. hash browns	1 cup cheddar cheese; shredded
6 bacon slices; chopped.	1 cup almond milk
8 oz. cream cheese; softened	A drizzle of olive oil
1 yellow onion; chopped.	Salt and black pepper to taste
6 eggs	
6 spring onions; chopped.	

At 350 degrees F, preheat your Air Fryer. In a heatproof bowl, mix all other ingredients except the spring onions. Transfer the bowl to the air fryer basket and cook the food at 350 degrees F for 20 minutes on Air Fry mode. Divide between plates, sprinkle the spring onions on top and serve.

Nutritional information: Calories: 202; Fat: 8.9g; Total Carbs 6.6g; Net Carbs 2g; Protein: 22.5g; Fiber: 0.6g; Sugar: 3.2g

Creamy Bread

Prep time: 20 minutes | Cook time: 55 minutes | Serves: 12

1 cup milk	2 tbsps. milk powder
¾ cup whipping cream	1 tsp. salt
1 large egg	¼ cup fine sugar
4½ cups bread flour	3 tsps. dry yeast
½ cup all-purpose flour	

In the baking pan of a bread machine, place all the recipe ingredients in the order recommended by the manufacturer. Place the baking pan in bread machine and close with the lid. Select the Dough cycle and press Start button. Once the cycle is completed, remove the paddles from bread machine but keep the dough inside for 45-50 minutes to proof. Set the cooking temperature of air fryer to 375 degrees F. Grease 2 loaf pans. Remove the dough from pan and place onto a lightly floured surface. Divide the dough into 4 equal-sized balls and then, roll each into a rectangle. Tightly, roll each rectangle like a Swiss roll. Place two rolls into each prepared loaf pan. Set aside for

1 hour. Arrange the loaf pans into the Air Fryer Basket. Air Fry the food at 375 degrees F for 50-55 minutes or until a toothpick inserted in the center comes out clean. Remove the pans from air fryer and place onto a wire rack for 10-15 minutes. Then, remove the bread rolls from pans and place onto a wire rack until they are completely cool before slicing. Cut each roll into desired size slices and serve.

Nutritional information: Calories 215g; Total Carbs 36.9g; Net Carbs 8g; Protein 6.5g; Fat 3.1g; Sugar 5.2g; Fiber 18g

Sunflower Bread

Prep time: 15 minutes | Cook time: 18 minutes | Serves: 4

⅔ cup whole-wheat flour	½ sachet instant yeast
⅔ cup plain flour	1 tsp. salt
⅓ cup sunflower seeds	⅔-1 cup lukewarm water

In a suitable bowl, mix up the flours, sunflower seeds, yeast, and salt. Slowly, add in the water, stirring continuously until a soft dough ball forms. Move the dough onto a lightly floured surface and knead for 5 minutes using your hands. Make a ball from the dough and place into a bowl. With a plastic wrap, cover the bowl and place at a warm place for 30 minutes. Set the cooking temperature of air fryer to 390 degrees F. Grease a suitable cake pan. Coat the top of dough with water and place into the prepared cake pan. Arrange the cake pan into an Air Fryer Basket. Air Fry the food at 390 degrees F for 18 minutes or until a toothpick inserted in the center comes out clean. Remove from air fryer and place the pan onto a wire rack for 10-15 minutes. Carefully, take out the bread from pan and put onto a wire rack until it is completely cool before slicing. Cut the bread into desired size slices and serve.

Nutritional information: Calories 177g; Total Carbs 33g; Net Carbs 6g; Protein 5.5g; Fat 2.4g; Sugar 0.2g; Fiber 58g

Banana Cinnamon Bread

Prep time: 10 minutes | Cook time: 20 minutes | Serves: 8

1 ⅓ cups flour	1 tsp. salt
⅔ cup sugar	½ cup milk
1 tsp. baking soda	½ cup olive oil
1 tsp. baking powder	3 bananas, peeled and sliced
1 tsp. ground cinnamon	

Take a suitable bowl of a stand mixer and mix well all of the ingredients. Grease a loaf pan. Place the prepared mixture into the prepared pan. Arrange the loaf pan into an Air Fryer Basket. Air Fry the food at 330 degrees F for 20 minutes or until a toothpick inserted in the center comes out clean. Remove from air fryer and place the pan onto a wire rack for 10-15 minutes. Carefully, take out the bread from pan and put onto a wire rack until it is completely cool before slicing. Cut the bread into desired size slices and serve.

Nutritional information: Calories 295g; Total Carbs 44g; Net Carbs 5g; Protein 3.1g; Fat 13.3g; Sugar 22.8g; Fiber 5g

Walnut Banana Bread

Prep time: 15 minutes | Cook time: 25 minutes | Serves: 10

1½ cups self-rising flour	2 medium eggs
¼ tsp. bicarbonate of soda	3½ oz. walnuts, chopped
5 tbsp. plus 1 tsp. butter	2 cups bananas, peeled and
⅔ cup plus ½ tbsp. caster sugar	mashed

In a suitable bowl, mix the flour and bicarbonate of soda. In another bowl, add the butter, and sugar. Beat until pale and fluffy. Put the eggs, one at a time along with a little flour and mix them well. Stir in the remaining flour and walnuts. Now, add the bananas and mix well. Grease a loaf pan. Place the prepared mixture evenly into the prepared pan. Arrange the loaf pan into an Air Fryer Basket. Air Fry the food for 10 minutes on 355 degrees F, then cook for 15 minutes more at 340 degrees F. Once done, remove from air fryer and place the pan onto a wire rack for 10-15 minutes. Carefully, take out the bread from pan and put onto a wire rack until it is completely cool before slicing. Cut the bread into desired size slices and serve.

Nutritional information: Calories 337g; Total Carbs 44.5g; Net Carbs 6g; Protein 7.3g; Fat 16g; Sugar 21.6g; Fiber 1g

Walnut Zucchini Bread

Prep time: 15 minutes | Cook time: 20 minutes | Serves: 16

3 cups all-purpose flour	1 cup vegetable oil
1 tsp. baking powder	3 eggs
1 tsp. baking soda	3 tsps. vanilla extract
1 tbsp. ground cinnamon	2 cups zucchini, grated
1 tsp. salt	1 cup walnuts, chopped
2¼ cups white sugar	

Take a suitable bowl and mix the flour, baking powder, baking soda, cinnamon, and salt. In another large bowl, add the sugar, oil, eggs, and vanilla extract. Beat well. Then, add in the flour mixture and stir well. Gently, fold in the zucchini and walnuts. Grease and flour 2 suitable loaf pans. Place the prepared mixture evenly into the prepared pans. Arrange the loaf pans into an Air Fryer Basket. Air Fry the food at 320 degrees F for 20 minutes or until a toothpick inserted in the center comes out clean. Remove the pans from Air Fryer and place onto a wire rack for 10-15 minutes. Carefully, take out the bread from pans and put onto a wire rack until it is completely cool before slicing. Cut the breads into desired size slices and serve.

Nutritional information: Calories 377g; Total Carbs 47.9g; Net Carbs 2g; Protein 5.5g; Fat 19.3g; Sugar 28.7g; Fiber 4g

Zucchini Apple Bread

Prep time: 15 minutes | Cook time: 30 minutes | Serves: 8

For Bread:	1 tsp. vanilla extract
1 cup all-purpose flour	½ cup zucchini, shredded
¾ tsp. baking powder	½ cup apple, cored and
¼ tsp. baking soda	shredded
1¼ tsp. ground cinnamon	5 tbsp. walnuts, chopped
¼ tsp. salt	For Topping:
⅓ cup vegetable oil	1 tbsp. walnuts, chopped
⅓ cup sugar	2 tsp. brown sugar
1 egg	¼ tsp. ground cinnamon

In a suitable bowl, mix the flour, baking powder, baking soda, cinnamon, and salt. In another large bowl, mix well the oil, sugar, egg, and vanilla extract; add in the flour mixture and mix well. Gently, fold in the zucchini, apple and walnuts. To make the topping, in a suitable bowl, add all the topping ingredients and whisk them well. Grease and flour an 8 x 4-inch loaf pan). Place the bread mixture evenly into the prepared pan and sprinkle with the topping mixture. Arrange the loaf pan into an Air Fryer basket. Air Fry the mixture at 325 degrees F for 30 minutes or until a toothpick inserted in the center comes out clean. Remove from air fryer and place the pan onto a wire rack for 10-15 minutes. Carefully, take out the bread from pan and put onto a wire rack until it is completely cool before slicing. Cut the bread into desired size slices and serve.

Nutritional information: Calories 207g; Total Carbs 24.4g; Net Carbs 2g; Protein 3.9g; Fat 13.3g; Sugar 10.9g; Fiber 4g

Spiced Pumpkin Bread

Prep time: 15 minutes | Cook time: 25 minutes | Serves: 4

¼ cup coconut flour	¼ cup canned pumpkin
2 tbsps. stevia blend	2 large eggs
1 tsp. baking powder	2 tbsps. unsweetened almond
¾ tsp. pumpkin pie spice	milk
¼ tsp. ground cinnamon	1 tsp. vanilla extract
⅛ tsp. salt	

In a suitable bowl, mix the flour, stevia, baking powder, spices, and salt. In another large bowl, add the pumpkin, eggs, almond milk, and vanilla extract. Beat well. Then, add in the flour mixture and mix well Line a cake pan with a greased baking paper. Place the prepared mixture evenly into the prepared pan. Arrange the pan into an air fryer basket. Air Fry the mixture at 350 degrees F for 25 minutes or until a toothpick inserted in the center comes out clean. Remove the pans from air fryer and place onto a wire rack for 5 minutes. Carefully, take out the bread from pan and put onto a wire rack to cool for 5-10 minutes before slicing. Cut the bread into desired size slices and serve.

Nutritional information: Calories 67g; Total Carbs 9g; Net Carbs 4g; Protein 3.5g; Fat 2.8g; Sugar 6.9g; Fiber 1g

Chocolate Bread

Prep time: 15 minutes | Cook time: 30 minutes | Serves: 8

¾ cup all-purpose flour	1 egg
¼ cup cocoa powder	⅓ cup unsweetened applesauce
¼ cup sugar	¼ cup plain Greek yogurt
½ tsp. baking soda	½ tsp. vanilla extract
½ tsp. baking powder	⅓ cup creamy peanut butter
⅛ tsp. salt	⅓ cup mini chocolate chips

In a suitable bowl, mix the flour, cocoa powder, sugar, baking soda, baking powder, and salt. In another bowl, add the egg, applesauce, yogurt, and vanilla extract. Beat well. Then, add in the flour mixture and mix well. Add the peanut butter and mix until smooth. Gently, fold in the chocolate chips. Grease a loaf pan. Place the prepared mixture evenly into the prepared pan. Arrange the loaf pan into an Air Fryer Basket. Air Fry the mixture at 350 degrees F for 30 minutes or until a toothpick inserted in the center comes out clean. Remove from Air Fryer and place the pan onto a wire rack for 10-15 minutes. Carefully, take out the bread from pan and put onto a wire rack until it is completely cool before slicing. Cut the bread into desired size slices and serve.

Nutritional information: Calories 191g; Total Carbs 24.9g; Net Carbs 5g; Protein 6.1g; Fat 8.6g; Sugar 12.6g; Fiber 1g

Beef Cabbage Wrap

Prep time: 10 minutes | Cook time: 15 minutes | Serves: 2

½ cup ground beef	¼ tsp. onion powder
½ jalapeno pepper, chopped	1 tsp. dried cilantro
¼ tsp. ground black pepper	½ tsp. ground cumin
½ tsp. salt	2 oz. avocado, chopped
1 tsp. keto tomato sauce	2 big cabbage leaves, steamed
1 tsp. olive oil	2 tbsps. water
¼ tsp. minced garlic	

In the mixing bowl, mix up ground beef, salt, ground black pepper, tomato sauce, olive oil, minced garlic, onion powder, dried cilantro, water, and ground cumin. Then add jalapeno and stir gently. Transfer the ground beef mixture in the Air Fryer Basket. Cook the meat mixture at 360 degrees F for 15 minutes on Air Fry mode. Stir it with the help of the spatula after 8 minutes of cooking. Then place the prepared mixture over the cabbage leaves. Top the ground beef with chopped avocado and roll into the burritos.

Nutritional information: Calories 230g; Total Carbs 15.9g; Net Carbs 2g; Protein 10.4; Fat 15.9g; Sugar 2g; Fiber 9.3g

Sausage Sticks

Prep time: 15 minutes | Cook time: 8 minutes | Serves: 3

6 small pork sausages	2 eggs, beaten
½ cup almond flour	1 tbsp. mascarpone
½ cup Mozzarella cheese, shredded	Cooking spray

Pierce the hot dogs with wooden coffee sticks to get the sausages on the sticks. Then in the bowl, mix up almond flour, Mozzarella cheese, and mascarpone. Microwave the prepared mixture for 15 seconds until melted. Then stir the egg in the cheese mixture and whisk it until smooth. Coat every sausage stick in the cheese mixture. Spray your "Air Fryer Basket" with some cooking spray. Place the sausage sticks in the Air Fryer Basket and cook them at 375 degrees F for 4 minutes per side or until they are light brown. Serve.

Nutritional information: Calories 375g; Total Carbs 5.1g; Net Carbs 2g; Protein 16.3; Fat 32.2g; Sugar 2g; Fiber 0.5

Avocado Cabbage Salad

Prep time: 5 minutes | Cook time: 15 minutes | Serves: 4

2 cups red cabbage, shredded	and sliced
A drizzle of olive oil	Salt and black pepper to the
1 red bell pepper, sliced	taste
small avocado, peeled, pitted	

Grease a suitable cooking pan with the oil. Add all the recipe ingredients, toss, cover and Air Fry them at 400 degrees F for 15 minutes in the air fryer. Divide into bowls and serve cold for breakfast.

Nutritional information: Calories 209g; Total Carbs 4g; Net Carbs 2g; Protein 9; Fat 8g; Sugar 2g; Fiber 2g

Mascarpone Eggs

Prep time: 8 minutes | Cook time: 5 minutes | Serves: 6

7 eggs, beaten	½ tsp. salt
¼ cup mascarpone	1 tsp. avocado oil
1 tsp. ground paprika	

Put eggs in a heatproof bowl and add mascarpone, salt, and ground paprika. With the help of the fork whisk the ingredients until homogenous. Then preheat the air fryer to 395 degrees F. Brush the "Air Fryer Basket" with avocado oil. Transfer the bowl to the Air Fryer Basket. Cook the omelet at 395 degrees F for 5 minutes on Air Fry mode. When done, serve and enjoy.

Nutritional information: Calories 93g; Total Carbs 1g; Net Carbs 2g; Protein 7.7; Fat 6.6g; Sugar 2g; Fiber 0.2g

Lemon Almond Cookies

Prep time: 10 minutes | Cook time: 8 minutes | Serves: 4

4 tbsps. coconut flour	1 tsp. lemon juice
½ tsp. baking powder	¼ tsp. vanilla extract

¼ tsp. lemon zest, grated
2 eggs, beaten
¼ cup of organic almond milk
1 tsp. avocado oil
¼ tsp. Himalayan pink salt

In the big bowl, mix up all the recipe ingredients from the list above. Knead the soft dough and cut it into 4 pieces. At 400 degrees F, preheat your Air Fryer. Then layer the "Air Fryer Basket" with baking paper. Roll the dough pieces in the balls and press them gently to get the shape of flat cookies. Place the cookies in the air fryer and cook them at 400 degrees F on Air Fry mode for 8 minutes. When done, serve and enjoy.
Nutritional information: Calories 74g; Total Carbs 5.6g; Net Carbs 2g; Protein 4.4; Fat 3.8g; Sugar 2g; Fiber 3.1g

Cauliflower Ham Quiche

Prep time: 10 minutes | Cook time: 15 minutes | Serves: 4

5 eggs, beaten
½ cup heavy cream
1 tsp. ground nutmeg
¼ tsp. ground cardamom
¼ tsp. salt
1 tsp. ground black pepper
1 tsp. butter, softened
¼ cup spring onions, chopped
¼ cup cauliflower florets
5 oz. ham, chopped
3 oz. Provolone cheese, grated

Pour the beaten eggs in the bowl. Add heavy cream, ground nutmeg, ground cardamom, ground black pepper, and salt. After this, pour the liquid in a suitable air fryer round pan. Add butter, onion, cauliflower florets, ham, and cheese to the pan. Gently stir the quiche liquid. Place it in the air fryer and cook the quiche for 15 minutes at 385 degrees F on Air Fry mode.
Nutritional information: Calories 280g; Total Carbs 4.4g; Net Carbs 2g; Protein 18.9; Fat 20.9g; Sugar 2g; Fiber 1.1 g

Avocado Onions Frittata

Prep time: 5 minutes | Cook time: 20 minutes | Serves: 4

4 Eggs, whisked
1 tbsp. olive oil
avocado, pitted, peeled and cubed
2 spring onions, chopped
Salt and black pepper to the taste
1 oz. parmesan cheese, grated
½ cup coconut cream

In a suitable bowl, mix the eggs with the rest of the ingredients except the oil and whisk well. Grease a baking pan that fits the air fryer with the oil, pour the avocado mix, spread. Put this pan in the air fryer and Air Fry the food at 360 degrees F for 20 minutes. Divide between plates and serve for breakfast.
Nutritional information: Calories 271; Total Carbs 5g; Net Carbs 2g; Protein 11; Fat 14g; Sugar 2g; Fiber 3g

Healthy Avocado Salad

Prep time: 10 minutes | Cook time: 3 minutes | Serves: 4

1 avocado, peeled, pitted and roughly sliced
½ tsp. minced garlic
¼ tsp. chili flakes
½ tsp. olive oil
1 tbsp. lime juice
¼ tsp. salt
1 tsp. cilantro, chopped
1 cup baby spinach
1 cup cherry tomatoes halved
Cooking spray

At 400 degrees F, preheat your Air Fryer. Grease your "Air Fryer Basket" with some cooking spray. In a suitable cooking pan, combine all the recipe ingredients and then transfer the pan to the basket. Air Fry the food at 400 degrees F for 3 minutes. When done, divide the food into bowls and serve.
Nutritional information: Calories 142g; Total Carbs 4.9g; Net

Carbs 2g; Protein 8.8; Fat 10.2g; Sugar 2g; Fiber 2.7 g

Mozzarella Swirls

Prep time: 15 minutes | Cook time: 12 minutes | Serves: 6

2 tbsp. almond flour
1 tbsp. coconut flour
½ cup Mozzarella cheese, shredded
1 tsp. Truvia
2 tbsps. butter, softened
¼ tsp. baking powder
1 egg, beaten
Cooking spray

In the bowl, mix up almond flour, coconut flour, Mozzarella cheese, Truvia, butter, baking powder, and egg. Knead the soft and non-sticky dough. Roll up the cheese dough and cut it into 6 pieces. Make the swirl from every dough piece. Grease your "Air Fryer Basket" with some cooking spray. Place the cheese swirls in the air fryer and cook them at 355 degrees F for 12 minutes or until they are light brown. Repeat the same step with remaining uncooked dough. Serve the cheese Danish warm.
Nutritional information: Calories 115g; Total Carbs 3.9g; Net Carbs 2g; Protein 4; Fat 10g; Sugar 2g; Fiber 2

Tomatoes Casserole

Prep time: 5 minutes | Cook time: 15 minutes | Serves: 4

4 eggs, whisked
1 tsp. olive oil
3 oz. Swiss chard, chopped
1 cup tomatoes, cubed
Salt and black pepper to the taste

In a suitable bowl, mix the eggs with the rest of the ingredients except the oil and whisk well. Grease a suitable cooking pan with the oil, pour the swish chard mix and then transfer the pan to the air fryer. Air Fry the food at 360 degrees F for 15 minutes. Divide between plates and serve for breakfast.
Nutritional information: Calories 202g; Total Carbs 5g; Net Carbs 2g; Protein 12g; Fat 14g; Sugar 2g; Fiber 3 g

Creamy Ham Muffins

Prep time: 15 minutes | Cook time: 12 minutes | Serves: 4

4 slices of ham
¼ tsp. baking powder
4 tbsp. coconut flour
4 tsp. heavy cream
1 egg, beaten
1 tsp. chives, chopped
1 tsp. olive oil
½ tsp. white pepper

At 365 degrees F, preheat your Air Fryer. Meanwhile, mix up baking powder, coconut flour, heavy cream, egg, chives, and white pepper. Stir the ingredients until getting a smooth mixture. Chop the ham and add it in the muffin liquid. Brush the air fryer muffin molds with olive oil. Then pour the muffin batter in the molds. Place the rack in the "Air Fryer Basket" and place the molds on it. Cook the muffins for 12 minutes at 365 degrees F on Air Fry mode. Cool the muffins to the room temperature and remove them from the molds.
Nutritional information: Calories 125g; Total Carbs 6.1g; Net Carbs 2g; Protein 7.7; Fat 7.8g; Sugar 2g; Fiber 3.5g

Salmon Spinach Scramble

Prep time: 5 minutes | Cook time: 20 minutes | Serves: 4

A drizzle of olive oil
1 spring onion, chopped
1 cup smoked salmon, skinless,
boneless and flaked
4 eggs, whisked
A pinch of black pepper and

salt

¼ cup baby spinach

4 tbsp. parmesan, grated

In a suitable bowl, mix the eggs with the rest of the ingredients except the oil and whisk well. Grease the suitable cooking pan with the oil, pour the eggs and salmon mix and Air Fry at 360 degrees F for 20 minutes. Divide between plates and serve for breakfast.

Nutritional information: Calories 230g; Total Carbs 5g; Net Carbs 2g; Protein 12g; Fat 12g; Sugar 2g; Fiber 3 g

Creamy Peppers Cheese Casserole

Prep time: 15 minutes | Cook time: 5 minutes | Serves: 2

2 medium green peppers
1 chili pepper, chopped
4 oz. chicken, shredded

1 tbsp. cream cheese
½ cup mozzarella, shredded
¼ tsp. chili powder

Remove the seeds from the bell peppers. In the bowl, mix up chili pepper, shredded chicken, cream cheese, and shredded Mozzarella. Add chili powder and stir the prepared mixture until homogenous. After this, fill the bell peppers with chicken mixture and wrap in the foil. Put the peppers in your air fryer and Air Fry them at 375 degrees F for 5 minutes.

Nutritional information: Calories 137g; Total Carbs 3.5g; Net Carbs 2g; Protein 19.4; Fat 4.9g; Sugar 2g; Fiber 1.2 g

Air Fried Mushrooms with Coconut Cream

Prep time: 5 minutes | Cook time: 20 minutes | Serves: 4

3 cup white mushrooms
¼ cup mozzarella, shredded
½ cup coconut cream

A pinch of salt and black pepper
Cooking spray

Put the mushrooms in the "Air Fryer Basket". Grease them with some cooking spray and Air Fry them at 370 degrees F for 20 minutes. Transfer them to a blender, add the remaining ingredients, pulse well, divide into bowls and serve as a spread.

Nutritional information: Calories 202g; Total Carbs 5g; Net Carbs 2g; Protein 7; Fat 12g; Sugar 2g; Fiber 2g

Tuna Arugula Salad

Prep time: 5 minutes | Cook time: 15 minutes | Serves: 4

½ lb. smoked tuna, flaked
1 cup arugula, chopped
1 tbsp. olive oil

A pinch of salt and black pepper

In a suitable bowl, mix up all the recipe ingredients except the oil and the arugula. Grease a suitable cooking pan with the olive oil. Pour the tuna mix, stir well, and Air Fry the mixture at 360 degrees F for 15 minutes. In a suitable salad bowl, mix the arugula with the tuna mix, toss and then serve for breakfast.

Nutritional information: Calories 212g; Total Carbs 5g; Net Carbs 2g; Protein 8; Fat 8g; Sugar 2g; Fiber 3 g

Simple Tomato Cheese Sandwich

Prep time: 8-10 minutes | Cook time: 6 minutes | Serves: 2

8 tomato slices
4 bread slices
2 Swiss cheese slices

Black pepper and salt as needed
4 teaspoons margarine

On a flat kitchen surface, plug your air fryer and turn it on. Preheat your air fryer for about 4-5 minutes to 355 degrees F. Gently coat an air frying basket with cooking oil or spray. In the basket, place one cheese slice over one bread slice. Then add 2 tomato slices on top. Sprinkle with salt and pepper. Top with another bread slice. Insert the basket inside the air fryer. Let it cook for about 5 minutes. Remove the basket; spread 2 teaspoons of margarine on both sides of each sandwich. Cook for about one more minute. Serve warm!

Nutritional information: Calories: 116; Fat: 8g; Total Carbs: 6.5g; Net Carbs: 1g; Fiber: 0.6g; Sugars: 1.4g; Protein: 4.8g

Cheddar Bacon Frittata

Prep time: 8-10 minutes | Cook time: 15 minutes | Serves: 2

¼ cup green bell pepper, seeded and chopped
1 tablespoon olive oil
¼ cup spinach, chopped
2 bacon slices, chopped

4-6 cherry tomatoes, make halves
3 large eggs
¼ cup cheddar cheese, shredded

On a flat kitchen surface, plug your air fryer and turn it on. Preheat your air fryer for about 4-5 minutes to 360 degrees F. Gently coat your air frying basket with cooking oil or spray. In a medium sized bowl, mix the tomatoes, bell pepper, and bacon thoroughly. Place into the basket. Transfer the basket in the air fryer. Let it cook for the next 8 minutes. Mix thoroughly the spinach, cheese, and eggs in a medium sized bowl. Remove the basket; Mix them together and cook for 8 more minutes. Serve warm!

Nutritional information: Calories: 377; Fat: 27.6g; Total Carbs: 11g; Net Carbs: 6.7g; Fiber: 3.2g; Sugars: 7.9g; Protein: 22.4g

Sausage and Potato Frittata

Prep time: 8-10 minutes | Cook time: 10 minutes | Serves: 2

½ cup frozen corn
1 large potato, boiled, peeled and cubed
3 jumbo eggs
1 tablespoon olive oil
½ of chorizo sausage, sliced

2 tablespoons feta cheese, crumbled
1 tablespoon fresh parsley, chopped
Pepper and salt as needed

On a flat kitchen surface, plug your air fryer and turn it on. Preheat your air fryer for about 4-5 minutes to 355 degrees F. Gently coat your air frying basket with cooking oil or spray. Place the potato, sausage, and corn in the air fryer and cook till golden brown for 5-6 minutes. Whisk in salt, pepper, and eggs in a medium sized bowl. Toss the sausage mixture with the egg mixture. Sprinkle with parsley and cheese. Continue cooking for 5 minutes. Remove from the air fryer and serve warm.

Nutritional information: Calories: 366; Fat: 17.1g; Total Carbs: 40.5g; Net Carbs: 0g; Fiber: 5.2g; Sugars: 3.6g; Protein: 15.3g

Coconut Veggie and Eggs Bake

Prep time: 5 minutes | Cook time: 30 minutes | Serves: 6

Cooking spray
2 cups green and red bell pepper, chopped
2 spring onions, chopped
1 teaspoon thyme, chopped

Salt and black pepper to the taste
1 cup coconut cream
4 eggs, whisked
1 cup cheddar cheese, grated

Place all the ingredients except the cooking spray and cheese in a mixing bowl and mix up to combine. Using the cooking spray to grease a suitable pan. Pour the eggs mixture and bell peppers evenly on your pan. Sprinkle the top with the cheese. Transfer the pan inside your air fryer and close the air fryer. Cook at 350 degrees F for 30 minutes. When cooked, transfer onto plates and serve for breakfast.

Nutritional information: Calories: 212; Fat: 18.7g; Total Carbs: 3g; Net Carbs: 1g; Fiber: 1.1g; Sugars: 1.8g; Protein: 9.4g

Yummy Bagel Breakfast

Prep time: 8-10 minutes | Cook time: 6 minutes | Serves: 5-6

2 bagels, make halves	4 teaspoons butter

On a flat kitchen surface, plug your air fryer and turn it on. Preheat your air fryer for about 4-5 minutes to 370 degrees F. Gently coat your air frying basket with cooking oil or spray. Place the bagels to the basket. Transfer the basket in the air fryer. Let it cook for the next 3 minutes. Remove the basket; spread the butter over the bagels and cook for 3 more minutes. Serve warm!

Nutritional information: Calories: 112; Fat: 3.1g; Total Carbs: 17g; Net Carbs: 8g; Fiber: 0.8g; Sugars: 1.8g; Protein: 3.5g

Kale and Eggplant Omelet

Prep time: 10 minutes | Cook time: 20 minutes | Serves: 4

1 eggplant, cubed	Cooking spray
4 eggs, whisked	½ cup kale, chopped
2 teaspoons cilantro, chopped	2 tablespoons cheddar, grated
Salt and black pepper to the taste	2 tablespoons fresh basil, chopped
½ teaspoon Italian seasoning	

Place all the ingredients except the cooking spray in a bowl. Using the cooking spray, coat a suitable pan. Pour in the eggs mix and spread to cook evenly. Put the pan inside the air fryer and cook at 370 degrees F for 20 minutes. When cooked, serve on plates. Enjoy your breakfast!

Nutritional information: Calories: 105; Fat: 5.2g; Total Carbs: 8.1g; Net Carbs: 1g; Fiber: 4.2g; Sugars: 3.9g; Protein: 7.8g

Coconut Muffins with Cinnamon

Prep time: 10 minutes | Cook time: 10 minutes | Serves: 2

⅓ cup almond flour	1 tablespoon coconut oil, softened
2 tablespoons Erythritol	
¼ teaspoon baking powder	1 teaspoon ground cinnamon
1 teaspoon apple cider vinegar	Cooking spray
1 tablespoon coconut milk	

Place Erythritol, ground cinnamon, baking powder, and almond flour in a mixing bowl. Mix up. Pour in coconut oil, coconut milk, and apple cider vinegar. Stir the mixture until well combines. Using cooking spray, grease the muffin molds. Scoop the muffin batter in the muffin molds. Using a spatula to spray every muffin. Before cooking, heat the air fryer to 365 degrees F. Transfer the rack inside your air fryer. Place the muffins onto the rack and cook them for 10 minutes at 365 degrees F. When cooked, transfer to another rack to cool. Remove from the molds and serve.

Nutritional information: Calories: 108; Fat: 10.8g; Total Carbs: 2g; Net Carbs: 0.5g; Fiber: 1.3g; Sugars: 0.3g; Protein: 1.2g

Yogurt Eggs with Chives

Prep time: 5 minutes | Cook time: 20 minutes | Serves: 4

Cooking spray	4 eggs, whisked
Salt and black pepper to the taste	1 tablespoon chives, chopped
	1 tablespoon cilantro, chopped
1 ½ cups Greek yogurt	

Mix the Greek yogurt, eggs, chives, salt, and black pepper in a bowl, and whisk well. Using the cooking spray, grease a suitable pan that fits the air fryer. Pour in the egg mixture evenly on the pan. Transfer the pan to the air fryer and cook inside at 360 degrees F for 20 minutes. When cooked, divide the omelet and serve on plates. Enjoy your breakfast!

Nutritional information: Calories: 101; Fat: 5.4g; Total Carbs: 2g; Net Carbs: 0.5g; Fiber: 0g; Sugars: 2.4g; Protein: 10.6g

Scrambled Eggs with Spinach

Prep time: 5 minutes | Cook time: 20 minutes | Serves: 4

1 tablespoon olive oil	3 cups baby spinach
½ teaspoon smoked paprika	Salt and black pepper to the taste
12 eggs, whisked	

Mix together smoked paprika, eggs, spinach, salt, and pepper in a bowl until whisk well. Grease a suitable pan that fits in your air fryer. Transfer inside the air fryer and preheat your air fryer to 360 degrees F. When it has preheated, mix the spinach mix and eggs in the pan. Close the air fryer and cook for 20 minutes. Serve on plates.

Nutritional information: Calories: 225; Fat: 16.7g; Total Carbs: 2g; Net Carbs: 0.5g; Fiber: 0.6g; Sugars: 1.1g; Protein: 17.3g

Creamy Broccoli Omelet

Prep time: 10 minutes | Cook time: 14 minutes | Serves: 4

4 eggs, beaten	¼ teaspoon salt
1 tablespoon cream cheese	¼ cup heavy cream
½ teaspoon chili flakes	¼ teaspoon white pepper
½ cup broccoli florets, chopped	Cooking spray

In a large bowl, place the beaten eggs, salt, white pepper, and chili flakes. With a hand whisker, stir together until the salt is dissolved. Place the heavy cream and cream cheese in the bowl and again stir until homogenous. Then add the broccoli florets. Before cooking, heat your air fryer to 375 degrees F. Using cooking spray, spray the air fryer basket from inside. Pour in the egg liquid and cook in the air fryer for 14 minutes.

Nutritional information: Calories: 102; Fat: 8.1g; Total Carbs: 1.5g; Net Carbs: 1g; Fiber: 0.3g; Sugars: 0.6g; Protein: 6.2g

Mozzarella Chicken and Pork Muffins

Prep time: 10 minutes | Cook time: 10 minutes | Serves: 6

1 cup ground chicken	½ teaspoon white pepper
1 cup ground pork	1 tablespoon ghee, melted
½ cup Mozzarella, shredded	1 teaspoon dried dill
1 teaspoon dried oregano	2 tablespoons almond flour
½ teaspoon salt	1 egg, beaten
1 teaspoon ground paprika	

Mix together ground pork, ground chicken, salt, ground paprika, dried dill, white pepper, egg, dried oregano, and almond flour in a medium bowl until homogenous. Then add half the Mozzarella and using a spoon gently mix up the mixture. Then brush the silicone muffin molds with melted ghee. Place the meat mixture inside the molds, using a spoon to flatten. Sprinkle the top with the remaining Mozzarella. Before cooking, heat your air fryer to 375 degrees F. Place the muffin molds on the rack of your air fryer. Cook in the air fryer for 10 minutes. Serve the muffins at room temperature.
Nutritional information: Calories: 176; Fat: 8.2g; Total Carbs: 1g; Net Carbs: 0g; Fiber: 0.6g; Sugars: 0.1g; Protein: 23.5g

Hot Egg Cups

Prep time: 10 minutes | Cook time: 3 minutes | Serves: 6

6 eggs, beaten
2 jalapenos, sliced
2 ounces' bacon, chopped, cooked

½ teaspoon salt
½ teaspoon chili powder
Cooking spray

Spray cooking spray onto the inside of the silicone egg molds. Mix up sliced jalapeno, bacon, beaten eggs, chili powder, and salt in the mixing bowl. Gently whisk together the liquid and pour into the egg molds. Before cooking, heat your air fryer to 400 degrees F. Place the egg cups inside the air fryer and close the air fryer. Cook in your air fryer for 3 minutes. Then cool the cooked cups for 2-3 minutes. Remove from the silicone molds and serve.
Nutritional information: Calories: 99; Fat: 7.1g; Total Carbs: 0.8g; Net Carbs: 0g; Fiber: 0.2g; Sugars: 0.5g; Protein: 8g

Classical Eggs Ramekins

Prep time: 5 minutes | Cook time: 6 minutes | Serves: 5

5 eggs
1 teaspoon coconut oil, melted

¼ teaspoon ground black pepper

Using coconut oil, grease the ramekins and whisk in eggs. Sprinkle on the top with ground black pepper. Then place in your air fryer and cook at 355 degrees F for 6 minutes.
Nutritional information: Calories: 89; Fat: 6.6g; Total Carbs: 0.5g; Net Carbs: 0g; Fiber: 0g; Sugars: 0.4g; Protein: 6.9g

Creamy Broccoli Florets with Eggs

Prep time: 10 minutes | Cook time: 20 minutes | Serves: 2

3 eggs
2 tablespoons cream
2 tablespoons parmesan cheese or cheddar cheese, grated
salt to taste

black pepper to taste
½ cup broccoli small florets
½ cup bell pepper cut into small pieces

Using cooking spray, grease a baking pan that fits in your air fryer. Place the broccoli florets and bell pepper inside the pan and cook in your air fryer at 360 degrees F for 7 minutes. While preheating, beat the eggs in a bowl. Add cream and stir together. To season, add salt and pepper. When cooked, toss the broccoli florets with the mixture and then pour the egg mixture on the top. Cook again for 10 minutes. Top with cheese and rest for 3 minutes. Enjoy your meal!
Nutritional information: Calories: 202; Fat: 13.3g; Total Carbs: 4g; Net Carbs: 2g; Fiber: 0.4g; Sugars: 2.3g; Protein: 17.7g

Baked Eggs with Mascarpone

Prep time: 10 minutes | Cook time: 3 minutes | Serves: 2

2 eggs
1 teaspoon mascarpone
¼ teaspoon ground nutmeg
¼ teaspoon dried basil
¼ teaspoon dried oregano

¼ teaspoon dried cilantro
¼ teaspoon ground turmeric
¼ teaspoon onion powder
¼ teaspoon salt

In a mixing bowl, whisk in the eggs. Stir with mascarpone until homogenous. Then add all spices and gently mix up the liquid. Pour the liquid into the silicone egg molds. Place on the air fryer basket. Cook in your air fryer at 400 degrees F for 3 minutes.
Nutritional information: Calories: 72; Fat: 4.9g; Total Carbs: 1g; Net Carbs: 0g; Fiber: 0.2g; Sugars: 0.6g; Protein: 5.9g

Mixed Pepper Hash with Mozzarella Cheese

Prep time: 5 minutes | Cook time: 20 minutes | Serves: 4

1 red bell pepper, cut into strips
1 green bell pepper, cut into strips
1 orange bell pepper, cut into strips

4 eggs, whisked
Salt and black pepper to the taste
2 tablespoons mozzarella, shredded
Cooking spray

Mix the all the bell peppers, pepper, salt, and the eggs in a mixing bowl. Toss well to combine. Before cooking, heat your air fryer to 350 degrees F. Gently grease a baking pan that fits in your air fryer with cooking spray. Pour in the egg mixture and spread it well. Top the mixture with Mozzarella and cook in the preheated air fryer for 20 minutes. When cooked, remove from the air fryer and serve hot on plates. Enjoy your breakfast!
Nutritional information: Calories: 112; Fat: 7g; Total Carbs: 3g; Net Carbs: 1g; Fiber: 0.4g; Sugars: 1.8g; Protein: 9.8g

Baked Cauliflower with Paprika

Prep time: 5 minutes | Cook time: 20 minutes | Serves: 4

2 cups cauliflower florets, separated
4 eggs, whisked

1 teaspoon sweet paprika
2 tablespoons butter, melted
A pinch of salt and black pepper

Before cooking, heat your air fryer to 320 degrees F. Gently grease a baking pan that fits in your air fryer with butter. Place cauliflower florets on the pan and add the whisked eggs, salt, pepper, and paprika. Toss well to combine. Cook in your air fryer for 20 minutes. When the cooking time is up, remove from the air fryer and serve on plates. Enjoy your breakfast.
Nutritional information: Calories: 128; Fat: 10.3g; Total Carbs: 3g; Net Carbs: 1g; Fiber: 1.5g; Sugars: 1.6g; Protein: 6.7g

Cinnamon French Toast

Prep time: 12 minutes | Cook time: 9 minutes | Serves: 2

⅓ cup almond flour
1 egg, beaten
¼ teaspoon baking powder
2 teaspoons Erythritol

¼ teaspoon vanilla extract
1 teaspoon cream cheese
¼ teaspoon ground cinnamon
1 teaspoon ghee, melted

Mix up baking powder, ground cinnamon, and almond flour in a mixing bowl. Add in vanilla extract, cream cheese, egg, and

ghee and stir together with a fork until smooth. Place baking paper on the bottom of the mugs. Add in almond flour mixture and use a fork to flatten well. Before cooking, heat your air fryer to 255 degrees F. Transfer the mugs with toasts inside your air fryer basket. Cook in your air fryer for 9 minutes. When cooked, cool for a while. To serve, sprinkle Erythritol on the toasts.
Nutritional information: Calories: 171; Fat: 13.8g; Total Carbs: 4g; Net Carbs: 2g; Fiber: 2.2g; Sugars: 0.3g; Protein: 6.9g

Tomatoes Hash with Cheddar Cheese

Prep time: 5 minutes | Cook time: 25 minutes | Serves: 4

2 tablespoons olive oil	1½ tablespoons chives, chopped
1-pound tomatoes, chopped	Salt and black pepper to the taste
½ pound cheddar, shredded	6 eggs, whisked

Gently grease a baking pan that fits in your air fryer with oil. Before cooking, heat your air fryer with the baking pan to 350 degrees F. Add the whisked eggs, salt, chopped tomatoes, and pepper in the baking pan and whisk to combine well. Top the mixture with the shredded cheddar cheese. Sprinkle over with the chopped chives. Cook in the preheated air fryer at 3650 degrees F for 25 minutes. When cooked, remove from the air fryer. Serve on plates and enjoy your breakfast.
Nutritional information: Calories: 274; Fat: 17.8g; Total Carbs: 6g; Net Carbs: 2.5g; Fiber: 1.5g; Sugars: 3.9g; Protein: 23.3g

Enticing Scotch Eggs

Prep time: 15 minutes | Cook time: 13 minutes | Serves: 4

4 medium eggs, hard-boiled, peeled	1 ounce coconut flakes
9 ounces ground beef	¼ teaspoon curry powder
1 teaspoon garlic powder	1 egg, beaten
¼ teaspoon cayenne pepper	1 tablespoon almond flour
	Cooking spray

Combine garlic powder and ground beef together in a mixing bowl. Then add almond flour, curry powder, and cayenne pepper and stir until homogenous. Wrap the peeled eggs in the beef mixture. Shape them into meatballs. And coat each ball with beaten egg. Sprinkle with coconut flakes. Before cooking, heat your air fryer to 400 degrees F. Using cooking spray, spray the air fryer basket. Then place the scotch eggs inside. Close your air fryer and cook for about 13 minutes. Flip the eggs on another side halfway cooking for 7 minutes.
Nutritional information: Calories: 301; Fat: 17.9g; Total Carbs: 4g; Net Carbs: 2g; Fiber: 1.5g; Sugars: 1.4g; Protein: 30g

Crispy Fish Sticks

Prep time: 15 minutes | Cook time: 10 minutes | Serves: 4

8 ounces cod fillet	¼ teaspoon Pink salt
1 egg, beaten	⅓ cup coconut flakes
¼ cup coconut flour	1 tablespoon mascarpone
¼ teaspoon ground coriander	1 teaspoon heavy cream
¼ teaspoon ground paprika	Cooking spray
¼ teaspoon ground cumin	

Roughly chop the cod fillet. Then transfer into a blender. Place in coconut flour, paprika, cumin, egg, salt, and ground coriander. Then mix the mixture together until smooth. Then place the mixture into a bowl. Place the fish mixture onto lined parchment paper and then shape into flat square. Cut the square into sticks. Whisk mascarpone and heavy cream together in a separate bowl.

Sprinkle the fish sticks with the mascarpone mixture and coat with coconut flakes. Before cooking, heat your air fryer to 400 degrees F. Using cooking spray, spray the air fryer basket. Place the fish sticks evenly inside the air fryer basket. Cook in the preheated air fryer for 10 minutes. Halfway through cooking, flip the fish sticks to the other side. When cooked, remove from the air fryer and serve with your favorite dip.
Nutritional information: Calories: 295; Fat: 5.4g; Total Carbs: 40g; Net Carbs: 21g; Fiber: 3.1g; Sugars: 0.5g; Protein: 22.2g

Baked Eggs

Prep time: 10 minutes | Cook time: 10 minutes | Serves: 3

3 eggs	3 bacon slices
½ teaspoon ground turmeric	1 teaspoon butter, melted
¼ teaspoon salt	

Using the ½ teaspoon of melted butter, grease the silicone muffin molds. Place the bacon slices on the molds, shaped into circles. Before cooking, heat your air fryer to 400 degrees F. Cook the bacon inside the preheated air fryer for 7 minutes. When cooked, with the remaining butter brush the center of the muffins. Then crack in eggs in every bacon circles. To season, sprinkle with ground turmeric and salt. Cook again in your air fryer for 3 minutes or more.
Nutritional information: Calories: 178; Fat: 13.6g; Total Carbs: 0.9g; Net Carbs: 0g; Fiber: 0.1g; Sugars: 0.4g; Protein: 12.6g

Flavorful Cheesy Frittata

Prep time: 10 minutes | Cook time: 20 minutes | Serves: 6

1 cup almond milk	6 spring onions, chopped
Cooking spray	Salt and black pepper to the
9 ounces cream cheese, soft	taste
1 cup cheddar cheese, shredded	6 eggs, whisked

Grease the baking pan with cooking spray. Preheat your air fryer to 350 degrees F. Mix together eggs with the rest ingredients. Pour into the baking pan and cook in your air fryer for 20 minutes. When cooked, remove from the air fryer and serve on plates.
Nutritional information: Calories: 303; Fat: 26g; Total Carbs: 4g; Net Carbs: 2g; Fiber: 0.4g; Sugars: 1.9g; Protein: 13.9g

Herbed Omelet

Prep time: 5 minutes | Cook time: 20 minutes | Serves: 4

10 eggs, whisked	2 tablespoons basil, chopped
½ cup cheddar, shredded	Cooking spray
2 tablespoons parsley, chopped	Salt and black pepper to the
2 tablespoons chives, chopped	taste

Mix all ingredients except the cheese and the cooking spray together in a bowl until whisked well. Before cooking, heat your air fryer to 350 degrees F. Grease the baking pan with cooking spray. Pour the egg mixture inside the pan. Cook in your air fryer for 20 minutes. Serve on plates.
Nutritional information: Calories: 183; Fat: 12g; Total Carbs: 1g; Net Carbs: 0g; Fiber: 0.1g; Sugars: 1g; Protein: 17.4g

Olives and Eggs Medley

Prep time: 5 minutes | Cook time: 20 minutes | Serves: 4

2 cups black olives, pitted and	chopped

4 eggs, whisked
¼ teaspoon sweet paprika
1 tablespoon cilantro, chopped
½ cup cheddar, shredded

A pinch of salt and black
pepper
Cooking spray

Add the olives into the beaten egg in a bowl and mix together all the ingredients except the cooking spray. Preheat your air fryer to 350 degrees F. Grease your baking pan with the cooking spray. Pour the olive-egg mixture evenly in the pan. Transfer the pan inside your air fryer and cook for 20 minutes. Serve the medley on plates. Enjoy your breakfast.

Nutritional information: Calories: 165; Fat: 12.6g; Total Carbs: 4g; Net Carbs: 2g; Fiber: 2.2g; Sugars: 0.4g; Protein: 9.6g

Fried Bacon with Pork Rinds

Prep time: 10 minutes | Cook time: 12 minutes | Serves: 4

10 ounces bacon
3 ounces pork rinds
2 eggs, beaten
½ teaspoon salt

½ teaspoon ground black
pepper
Cooking spray

Before cooking, heat your air fryer to 396 degrees F. Spray the air fryer basket with cooking spray. While the air fryer is preheating, cut the bacon into 4 cubes and season with salt and ground black pepper. Then dip the bacon in the beaten egg and coat in the pork rinds. Transfer to the greased basket. Cook in the air fryer for 12 minutes and flip to the other side halfway through cooking. Cook for one or a few more minutes if necessary until it is light brown. When cooked, transfer from the air fryer and serve.

Nutritional information: Calories: 411; Fat: 29.6g; Total Carbs: 1g; Net Carbs: 0g; Fiber: 0.1g; Sugars: 0.2g; Protein: 34.1g

Cheddar Biscuits with Nutmeg

Prep time: 15 minutes | Cook time: 8 minutes | Serves: 4

½ cup almond flour
¼ cup Cheddar cheese,
shredded
¾ teaspoon salt
1 egg, beaten
1 tablespoon mascarpone

1 tablespoon coconut oil,
melted
¾ teaspoon baking powder
½ teaspoon apple cider vinegar
¼ teaspoon ground nutmeg

Mix the almond flour, baking powder, salt, and ground nutmeg in a big bowl. Place apple cider vinegar, egg, mascarpone, and coconut oil inside the bowl. Add in cheese and make a dough. Knead until soft. Divide into small balls to make the biscuits. Before cooking, heat your air fryer to 400 degrees F. Line your air fryer basket with parchment paper. Transfer the cheese biscuits onto the parchment paper. Cook in your air fryer at 400 degrees F until golden brown, for 8 minutes or more. Halfway cooking, check the biscuits to avoid burning. Serve.

Nutritional information: Calories: 103; Fat: 9g; Total Carbs: 1g; Net Carbs: 0g; Fiber: 0.4g; Sugars: 0.2g; Protein: 4.3g

Simple Eggplant Spread

Prep time: 5 minutes | Cook time: 20 minutes | Serves: 4

3 eggplants
Salt and black pepper, to taste
2 tablespoons chives, chopped

2 tablespoons olive oil
2 teaspoons sweet paprika

In the air fryer basket, place the eggplants. Cook in your air fryer at 380 degrees F for 20 minutes. Then peel the eggplants. Place the peeled eggplants in a blender. Add the remaining ingredients in the blender. When it had pulsed well, remove from the blender and serve in bowls. Enjoy your breakfast.

Nutritional information: Calories: 166; Fat: 7.9g; Total Carbs: 24g; Net Carbs: 13.5g; Fiber: 15g; Sugars: 12.5g; Protein: 4.2g

Brussel Sprouts Hash

Prep time: 5 minutes | Cook time: 20 minutes | Serves: 4

1 tablespoon olive oil
1 pound Brussels sprouts,
shredded
4 eggs, whisked
½ cup coconut cream

Salt and black pepper to the
taste
1 tablespoon chives, chopped
¼ cup cheddar cheese,
shredded

Before cooking, firstly heat your air fryer to 360 degrees F. Grease the baking pan with oil. Evenly arrange the Brussel sprouts on the greased pan. Then add the whisked eggs as well as the rest ingredients. Toss the mixture for a while and transfer the pan into the air fryer. Cook for 20 minutes. When the cooking time is up, transfer from the air fryer and serve on plates.

Nutritional information: Calories: 240; Fat: 17.8g; Total Carbs: 12g; Net Carbs: 7g; Fiber: 4.9g; Sugars: 3.8g; Protein: 11.9g

Mozzarella Eggs with Basil Pesto

Prep time: 5 minutes | Cook time: 20 minutes | Serves: 4

2 tablespoons butter, melted
6 teaspoons basil pesto
1 cup mozzarella cheese,
grated

6 eggs, whisked
1 tablespoon basil, chopped
A pinch of salt and black
pepper

Before cooking, heat your air fryer to 360 degrees F. Mix the basil pesto, mozzarella cheese, the whisked egg, basil, salt, and black pepper together in a bowl. Whisk. Drizzle the baking pan with butter and then add the mixture. Cook in your air fryer at 360 degrees F for 20 minutes. When the cooking time is up, transfer from the air fryer and serve on plates. Enjoy your breakfast.

Nutritional information: Calories: 166; Fat: 13.6g; Total Carbs: 0.8g; Net Carbs: 1g; Fiber: 0g; Sugars: 0.5g; Protein: 10.4g

Paprika Zucchini Spread

Prep time: 5 minutes | Cook time: 15 minutes | Serves: 4

4 zucchinis, roughly chopped
1 tablespoon sweet paprika
Salt and black pepper to the

taste
1 tablespoon butter, melted

Using butter, brush the bottom of a suitable baking pan. Then add the rest ingredients in the baking pan. Cook in your air fryer at 360 degrees F for 15 minutes. Transfer the cooked mixture to a blender and pulse well. Serve into bowls and enjoy your breakfast.

Nutritional information: Calories: 62; Fat: 3.5g; Total Carbs: 7.5g; Net Carbs: 2.5g; Fiber: 2.8g; Sugars: 3.6g; Protein: 2.7g

Creamy Broccoli Casserole

Prep time: 5 minutes | Cook time: 25 minutes | Serves: 4

1 broccoli head, florets

separated and roughly chopped

2 ounces cheddar cheese, grated
4 eggs, whisked
1 cup almond milk

2 teaspoons cilantro, chopped
Salt and black pepper to the taste

Mix milk, chopped cilantro, salt, pepper, and whisked eggs together. Dip the chopped broccoli in the egg mixture and spread in the air fryer pan and sprinkle with the cheddar cheese. Cook in your air fryer at 350 degrees F for 25 minutes. When it has cooked, transfer from the air fryer and serve in plates. Enjoy your breakfast.

Nutritional information: Calories: 266; Fat: 23.5g; Total Carbs: 5g; Net Carbs: 2g; Fiber: 1.9g; Sugars: 2.8g; Protein: 11.1g

Creamy Baked Sausage

Prep time: 15 minutes | Cook time: 23 minutes | Serves: 6

2 jalapeno peppers, sliced
7 ounces ground sausages
1 teaspoon dill seeds
3 ounces Colby Jack Cheese, shredded

4 eggs, beaten
1 tablespoon cream cheese
½ teaspoon salt
1 teaspoon butter, softened
1 teaspoon olive oil

Before cooking, heat your skillet and then pour the olive oil inside the skillet. Place salt and ground sausage in the skillet and cook for 5 to 8 minutes on medium heat. During cooking, stir the mixture from time to time. At the same time, heat your air fryer ahead of time to 400 degrees F. Using softened butter, grease your air fryer basket. Transfer the cooked sausage inside the greased basket and flatten the mixture. Sprinkle the sliced jalapeno pepper on the top of the mixture. Then add shredded cheese. In a separate bowl, beat eggs and mix together with cream cheese. Pour the egg-cheese mixture over the sausage mixture. Sprinkle with dill seeds. Cook in your air fryer at 400 degrees F for 16 minutes. If prefer crunchy crust, cook for a few more minutes.

Nutritional information: Calories: 230; Fat: 18.9g; Total Carbs: 1g; Net Carbs: 0g; Fiber: 0.3g; Sugars: 0.4g; Protein 13.4g

Cheddar Tomato Frittata

Prep time: 5 minutes | Cook time: 20 minutes | Serves: 4

4 eggs, whisked
1 pound cherry tomatoes, halved
1 tablespoon parsley, chopped

Cooking spray
1 tablespoon cheddar, grated
Salt and black pepper to the taste

In the air fryer basket, add the tomatoes. Cook in your air fryer at 360 degrees F for 5 minutes. Grease a baking pan that fits your air fryer. Transfer the cooked tomatoes to the greased baking pan. Mix the whisked eggs with rest ingredients together. Then pour the egg mixture over the cooker tomatoes. Cook again at 360 degrees F for 15 minutes. When cooked, serve immediately. Enjoy your breakfast.

Nutritional information: Calories: 88; Fat: 4.9g; Total Carbs: 4g; Net Carbs: 2g; Fiber: 1.4g; Sugars: 3.3g; Protein: 7g

Simple Cherry Tarts

Prep time: 15 minutes | Cook time: 10 minutes | Serves: 6

For the tarts:
2 refrigerated piecrusts
⅓ cup cherry preserves
1 teaspoon cornstarch
Cooking oil

For the Frosting:
½ cup vanilla yogurt
1 ounce cream cheese
1 teaspoon stevia
Rainbow sprinkles

Place the piecrusts on a flat surface. Make use of a knife or pizza cutter, cut each piecrust into 3 rectangles, for 6 in total. I discard the unused dough left from slicing the edges. In a suitable bowl, combine the preserves and cornstarch. Mix well. Scoop 1 tablespoon of the preserve mixture onto the top ½ of each piece of piecrust. Fold the bottom of each piece up to close the tart. Press along the edges of each tart to seal using the back of a fork. Sprinkle the breakfast tarts with cooking oil and place them in the air fryer. Cook for almost 10 minutes Allow the breakfast tarts to cool fully before removing from the air fryer. To make the frosting: In a suitable bowl, mix the yogurt, cream cheese, and stevia. Mix well. Spread the breakfast tarts with frosting and top with sprinkles, and serve.

Nutritional information: Calories: 96; Fat: 2g; Total Carbs: 17.5g; Net Carbs: 1g; Fiber: 0.4g; Sugars: 10.1g; Protein: 1.8g

Classical French Frittata

Prep time: 10 minutes | Cook time: 18 minutes | Serves: 3

3 eggs
1 tablespoon heavy cream
1 teaspoon Herbs de Provence
1 teaspoon almond butter,

softened
2 ounces Provolone cheese, grated

Before cooking, heat your air fryer to 365 degrees F. In a medium bowl, whisk the eggs and then add the heavy cream. Whisk again with a hand whisker until smooth. Then add herbs de Provence and the grated cheese. Gently stir the egg mixture. Using almond butter, grease the baking pan. Then pour the egg mixture evenly on the baking pan. Cook in the preheated air fryer for 18 minutes. When it has preheated, cool to room temperature and slice and serve.

Nutritional information: Calories: 179; Fat: 14.3g; Total Carbs: 1.9g; Net Carbs: 1g; Fiber: 0.5g; Sugars: 0.7g; Protein: 11.6g

Baked Parmesan Eggs with Kielbasa

Prep time: 10 minutes | Cook time: 8 minutes | Serves: 4

4 eggs
1 tablespoon heavy cream
1 ounce Parmesan, grated

1 teaspoon dried parsley
3 ounces kielbasa, chopped
1 teaspoon coconut oil

Add the coconut oil in a suitable baking pan and melt it in your air fryer at 385 degrees F for about 2 to 3 minutes. At the same time in a mixing bowl, whisk the eggs and add heavy cream and the dried parsley. Whisk them together. Add the chopped kielbasa in the melted coconut oil. Cook at 385 degrees F for 4 minutes. When cooked, add Parmesan and the whisked egg mixture and use a fork to stir them together. Cook for 4 or more minutes, halfway through cooking scramble the mixture.

Nutritional information: Calories: 157; Fat: 12.2g; Total Carbs: 1g; Net Carbs: 0g; Fiber: 0g; Sugars: 0.3g; Protein: 10.7g

Dill Eggs in Wonton

Prep time: 10 minutes | Cook time: 4 minutes | Serves: 4

2 eggs, hard-boiled, peeled
1 tablespoon cream cheese
1 tablespoon fresh dill, chopped
1 teaspoon ground black

pepper
4 wontons wrap
1 egg white, whisked
1 teaspoon sesame oil

Before cooking, heat your air fryer to 395 degrees F. Grease the air fryer basket with sesame oil. Chop the hard-boiled eggs and in a bowl, mix together with dill, ground pepper, and cream cheese. Separate the egg mixture onto wonton wraps and roll them into rolls. Use the whisked egg white to brush the wontons. Arrange the wontons evenly on the greased air fryer basket. Cook in your air fryer at 395 degrees F for 2 minutes from each side or until golden brown flip to the other side.

Nutritional information: Calories: 68; Fat: 4.3g; Total Carbs: 3g; Net Carbs: 1g; Fiber: 0.3g; Sugars: 0.2g; Protein: 4.6g

Avocado Parsley Omelet

Prep time: 5 minutes | Cook time: 15 minutes | Serves: 4

4 eggs, whisked
1 tablespoon parsley, chopped
½ teaspoon cheddar cheese, shredded

1 avocado, peeled, pitted and cubed
Cooking spray

Mix the whisked eggs, chopped parsley, shredded cheddar cheese, and avocado cubes together in a bowl. Grease a suitable baking pan with cooking spray. Pour the egg mixture on the baking pan and spread. Insert the baking pan inside your air fryer and cook at 370 degrees F for 15 minutes. When cooked, serve warm.

Nutritional information: Calories: 167; Fat: 14.3g; Total Carbs: 4g; Net Carbs: 2g; Fiber: 3.4g; Sugars: 0.6g; Protein: 6.6g

Egg Peppers Cups

Prep time: 10 minutes | Cook time: 12 minutes | Serves: 12

6 green bell peppers
12 egg
½ teaspoon ground black

pepper
½ teaspoon chili flakes

Before cooking, heat your air fryer to 395 degrees F. While preheating, cut the green bell peppers into halves and remove the seeds. In the bell pepper halves, whisk the eggs. Sprinkle the top with chili flakes and ground black pepper. Arrange evenly the bell pepper halves onto a suitable baking pan. Cook in the preheated air fryer for 4 minutes. (2 to 3 halves per batch)

Nutritional information: Calories: 164; Fat: 9.1g; Total Carbs: 9g; Net Carbs: 4.3g; Fiber: 1.7g; Sugars: 6.7g; Protein: 12.3g

Spinach Bacon Spread

Prep time: 5 minutes | Cook time: 10 minutes | Serves: 4

2 tablespoons coconut cream
3 cups spinach leaves
2 tablespoons cilantro
2 tablespoons bacon, cooked

and crumbled
Salt and black pepper to the taste

Combine coconut cream, spinach leaves, salt, and black pepper in a suitable baking pan. Transfer the baking pan into your air fryer and cook at 360 degrees F for 10 minutes. When cooked, transfer to a blender and pulse well. To serve, sprinkle the bacon on the top of the mixture.

Nutritional information: Calories: 74; Fat: 5.9g; Total Carbs: 1g; Net Carbs: 0g; Fiber: 0.7g; Sugars: 0.3g; Protein: 4.3g

Tasty Spinach Frittata

Prep time: 5 minutes | Cook time: 20 minutes | Serves: 4

1 tablespoon chives, chopped

1 eggplant, cubed

8 ounces spinach, torn
Cooking spray
6 eggs, whisked

Salt and black pepper to the taste

Mix the chopped chives, cubed eggs, spinach, whisked eggs, salt, and black pepper together in a bowl. Grease a suitable baking pan with the cooking spray. Pour the egg mixture onto the baking pan and spread. Cook in your air fryer at 380 degrees F for 20 minutes. When the cooking time is up, serve on plates. Enjoy your breakfast.

Nutritional information: Calories: 138; Fat: 7.1g; Total Carbs: 9.3g; Net Carbs: 1g; Fiber: 5.3g; Sugars: 4.2g; Protein: 11.1g

Mozzarella Rolls

Prep time: 15 minutes | Cook time: 6 minutes | Serves: 6

6 wonton wrappers
1 tablespoon keto tomato sauce
½ cup Mozzarella, shredded

1 ounce pepperoni, chopped
1 egg, beaten
Cooking spray

Before cooking, heat your air fryer to 400 degrees F. Grease the air fryer basket with cooking spray. Mix the pepperoni, shredded Mozzarella cheese, and tomato sauce in a big bowl until homogenous. Separate the mixture onto wonton wraps. Roll the wraps into sticks. Use the beaten eggs to brush the sticks. Arrange evenly on the air fryer basket and cook in your air fryer for 6 minutes and flip the sticks halfway through cooking.

Nutritional information: Calories: 137; Fat: 3.7g; Total Carbs: 19g; Net Carbs: 6.7g; Fiber: 0.7g; Sugars: 0.4g; Protein: 5.8g

Parmesan Spinach Muffins

Prep time: 5 minutes | Cook time: 15 minutes | Serves: 4

2 eggs, whisked
Cooking spray
1 and ½ cups coconut milk
1 tablespoon baking powder
4 ounces baby spinach,

chopped
2 ounces parmesan cheese, grated
3 ounces almond flour

Grease the muffin molds with cooking spray. Mix the whisked eggs, coconut milk, baking powder, baby spinach, parmesan cheese, and almond flour together in a mixing bowl. Transfer onto the greased molds. Cook in your air fryer at 380 degrees F for 15 minutes. When the cooking time is up, serve on plates. Enjoy your breakfast.

Nutritional information: Calories: 124; Fat: 9g; Total Carbs: 4g; Net Carbs: 2g; Fiber: 1.1g; Sugars: 0.3g; Protein: 9g

Bacon Muffins

Prep time: 15 minutes | Cook time: 15 minutes | Serves: 8

6 large eggs
3 slices of cooked and chopped bacon
½ cup of chopped green and red bell pepper
½ cup of shredded cheddar cheese

¼ cup of shredded mozzarella cheese
¼ cup of chopped fresh spinach
¼ cup of chopped onions
2 tablespoons milk
Black pepper and salt, to taste

Put eggs, milk, black pepper, and salt into a suitable mixing bowl. Whisk it until well combined. Add in chopped bell peppers, spinach, black peppers, onions, ½ of shredded cheeses, and crumbled bacon. Mix it well. First, place the silicone cups in the air fryer, then pour the egg mixture into them and add the remaining cheeses. At 300 degrees F, preheat your Air fryer. Cook the prepared egg muffins for almost 12–15 minutes. Serve

warm and enjoy your Egg Muffins with Bacon!
Nutritional information: Calories: 127; Fat: 9.3g; Total Carbs: 1g; Net Carbs: 0g; Fiber: 0.1g; Sugars: 0.7g; Protein: 9.6g

Hard-Boiled Eggs

Prep time: 8 minutes | Cook time: 16 minutes | Serves: 2

4 eggs   ¼ teaspoon salt

Cook the eggs in your air fryer at 250 degrees F for 16 minutes. When the cooking time is up, cool the eggs in ice water. Then peel the eggs and cut them into halve. Season the egg halves with salt and serve.
Nutritional information: Calories: 126; Fat: 8.8g; Total Carbs: 0.7g; Net Carbs: 0g; Fiber: 0g; Sugars: 0.7g; Protein: 11.1g

Creamy Eggs and Leeks

Prep time: 5 minutes | Cook time: 7 minutes | Serves: 2

2 leeks, chopped   ½ cup Mozzarella cheese,
4 eggs, whisked   shredded
¼ cup Cheddar cheese,   1 teaspoon avocado oil
shredded

Before cooking, heat your air fryer to 400 degrees F. Using avocado oil, grease your air fryer basket. Combine the whisked eggs with the remaining ingredients. Cook in your air fryer for 7 minutes. When the cooking time is up, remove from the air fryer and serve warm.
Nutritional information: Calories: 260; Fat: 15.3g; Total Carbs: 13g; Net Carbs: 7g; Fiber: 1.7g; Sugars: 4.2g; Protein: 18g

Cheddar Peppers

Prep time: 5 minutes | Cook time: 20 minutes | Serves: 4

½ cup cheddar cheese,   ¼ cup coconut cream
shredded   1 cup red bell peppers,
2 tablespoons chives, chopped   chopped
A pinch of salt and black   Cooking spray
pepper

Grease a suitable baking pan with cooking spray. Mix shredded cheddar cheese, chopped chives, salt, black pepper, coconut cream, and the chopped red bell peppers in a medium bowl. Pour the mixture in the greased pan. Cook in your air fryer at 360 degrees F for 20 minutes. When the cooking time is up, serve warm on plates.
Nutritional information: Calories: 101; Fat: 8.4g; Total Carbs: 3.4g; Net Carbs: 1g; Fiber: 0.8g; Sugars: 2.1g; Protein: 4.2g

Bacon Wrapped Eggs

Prep time: 15 minutes | Cook time: 5 minutes | Serves: 2

2 eggs, hard-boiled, peeled   ½ teaspoon avocado oil
4 bacon slices   1 teaspoon mustard

Before cooking, heat your air fryer to 400 degrees F. Using avocado oil, grease your air fryer basket. Then line the bacon slices inside. Cook the bacon slices 2 minutes per side. When cooked, cool to room temperature and wrap the eggs with bacon slices, two bacon slices for one egg. Then secure the eggs with toothpicks. Transfer onto the air fryer basket and cook in your

air fryer at 400 degrees F for 1 minute.
Nutritional information: Calories: 278; Fat: 20.9g; Total Carbs: 1g; Net Carbs: 0g; Fiber: 0.3g; Sugars: 0.5g; Protein: 20g

Mozzarella Chives Omelet

Prep time: 5 minutes | Cook time: 20 minutes | Serves: 4

6 eggs, whisked   1 cup mozzarella, shredded
1 cup chives, chopped   Salt and black pepper to the
Cooking spray   taste

Grease a suitable baking pan with cooking spray. Mix the whisked eggs, chopped chives, shredded mozzarella, salt, and black pepper in a medium bowl. Pour the egg mixture onto the greased pan and spread. Cook in your air fryer at 350 degrees F for 20 minutes. When cooked, serve on plates.
Nutritional information: Calories: 119; Fat: 8g; Total Carbs: 1g; Net Carbs: 0g; Fiber: 0.3g; Sugars: 0.7g; Protein: 10.7g

Chicken Casserole with Almonds

Prep time: 5 minutes | Cook time: 25 minutes | Serves: 4

¼ cup almonds, chopped   ½ teaspoon oregano, dried
½ cup almond milk   Cooking spray
4 eggs, whisked   Salt and black pepper to the
1 cup chicken meat, cooked   taste
and shredded

Grease a suitable baking pan with the cooking spray. Mix the whisked eggs together with the rest ingredients in a medium bowl. Pour the mixture onto the baking pan and spread Cook in your air fryer at 350 degrees F for 25 minutes. When cooked, serve warm on plates.
Nutritional information: Calories: 233; Fat: 17.1g; Total Carbs: 3g; Net Carbs: 1g; Fiber: 1.5g; Sugars: 1.6g; Protein: 17.6g

Cheddar Broccoli Quiche

Prep time: 15 minutes | Cook time: 10 minutes | Serves: 2

8 small broccoli florets   2 tablespoons of cheddar,
2 eggs   grated
½ cup of heavy cream   Black pepper and salt, to taste

At 325 degrees F, preheat your air fryer. Grease 2 5-inch ceramic dishes with oil or cooking spray. Put eggs, salt, heavy cream, and black pepper into a suitable mixing bowl. Whisk it well then put broccoli florets on the dish's bottom and pour the egg mixture over them. Cook it at 325 degrees F for almost 10 minutes. Serve warm.
Nutritional information: Calories: 303; Fat: 17.2g; Total Carbs: 25g; Net Carbs: 16g; Fiber: 9.5g; Sugars: 6.6g; Protein: 18.1g

Cheese Taquitos with Cilantro

Prep time: 15 minutes | Cook time: 10 minutes | Serves: 3

3 white corn tortillas   3 cheese sticks
3 teaspoons of roasted green   1 tablespoon of cilantro
chilies   1 teaspoon of olive oil
1 teaspoon of crumbled cheese

At 400 degrees F, preheat your air fryer. Lightly grease corn tortillas with olive oil on per side. Cut a small pocket at the center of cheese sticks and put chilies in the pockets. Put the stuffed cheese on the tortillas and roll them up. Put them in the preheated air fryer, seam side down. Cook it at 400 degrees F for 7–10 minutes. Top with cilantro and crumbled cheese. Serve warm and enjoy your Cheesy Taquitos!

Nutritional information: Calories: 209; Fat: 10.5g; Total Carbs: 22g; Net Carbs: 10g; Fiber: 2.5g; Sugars: 0.2g; Protein: 5.6g

Grilled Butter Sandwich

Prep time: 15 minutes | Cook time: 10 minutes | Serves: 1

2 slices of bread
3 slices of any cheese

1 tablespoon of melted butter

At 350 degrees F, preheat your air fryer. Spread the melted butter over 1 side of each piece of bread. Put the cheese slices on the bread and make a sandwich. Put it in the air fryer and fry at 350 degrees F for almost 10 minutes almost. Serve warm and enjoy your Grilled Butter Sandwich! Sandwich Fillings: Spread some pesto inside the sandwich and use just mozzarella cheese. Put cooked bacon and use only cheddar cheese. Add some fresh spinach with Swiss cheese inside the sandwich.

Nutritional information: Calories: 488; Fat: 40g; Total Carbs: 10.2g; Net Carbs: 0g; Fiber: 0.4g; Sugars: 1.2g; Protein: 22.4g

Cheddar Frittata

Prep time: 15 minutes | Cook time: 20 minutes | Serves: 2

4 eggs
½ cup of cooked and chopped sausage
½ cup of shredded cheddar cheese

1 chopped green onion
2 tablespoons of chopped red bell pepper
1 pinch of cayenne powder

At 350 degrees F, preheat your air fryer. Lightly grease a suitable 6-inch cake pan with some oil or cooking spray. Whisk eggs in a suitable bowl. Add the sausage, bell pepper, onion, cheese, and cayenne powder, and stir until well combined. Transfer the prepared egg mixture into the cake pan and cook in the preheated air fryer almost 20 minutes. Serve with any fresh vegetables and greens. Enjoy your Frittata!

Nutritional information: Calories: 291; Fat: 19.4g; Total Carbs: 10.7g; Net Carbs: 1g; Fiber: 1.8g; Sugars: 7g; Protein: 20.1g

Mozzarella Soufflé with Ham

Prep time: 15 minutes | Cook time: 8 minutes | Serves: 4

6 eggs
⅓ cup of milk
½ cup of shredded mozzarella cheese
1 tablespoon of freshly

chopped parsley
½ cup of chopped ham
1 teaspoon of salt
1 teaspoon of black pepper
½ teaspoon of garlic powder

Grease 4 ramekins with a nonstick cooking spray. At 350 degrees F, preheat your air fryer. Using a suitable bowl, add and stir all the recipe ingredients until it mixes properly. Pour the egg mixture into the greased ramekins and place it inside your air fryer. Cook it inside your air fryer for 8 minutes. Then carefully remove the soufflé from your air fryer and allow it to cool off. Serve and enjoy!

Nutritional information: Calories: 145; Fat: 9.1g; Total Carbs: 2g; Net Carbs: 0.5g; Fiber: 0.4g; Sugars: 1.5g; Protein: 12.9g

Banana-Pecan French Toast

Prep time: 15 minutes | Cook time: 10 minutes | Serves: 8

8 slices of whole-grain bread
¾ cup of any milk you like
1 sliced banana
1 cup of rolled oats

1 cup of pecan, chopped
2 tablespoons of ground flax seeds
1 teaspoon of cinnamon

At 350 degrees F, preheat your air fryer. Mix nuts, cinnamon, oats, and flax seeds into a food processor and pulse until crumbly. Pour milk into a deep and wide bowl. Soak 1–2 pieces of bread for almost 15-30 seconds per side. Transfer the soaked bread pieces to the oats mixture and cover with it from per side. Set the prepared soak bread slices into the air fryer basket in 1 layer. Cook them at 350 degrees F for 3 minutes, flip, and continue cooking for 3 more minutes. Repeat the same steps with the remaining bread slices. Serve with maple syrup and banana slices. Enjoy your Banana-Nut French Toast!

Nutritional information: Calories: 206; Fat: 5.2g; Total Carbs: 31g; Net Carbs: 15g; Fiber: 5.5g; Sugars: 6.1g; Protein: 8.5g

Cheddar Mushroom Taquitos

Prep time: 15 minutes | Cook time: 20 minutes | Serves: 8

8 whole-wheat tortillas
2–3 king oyster mushrooms
1 cup of shredded cheddar cheese
1 tablespoon of lime juice
⅛ cup of olive oil
¼ tablespoon of chili powder

1 teaspoon of ground cumin
1 teaspoon of paprika
½ teaspoon of dried oregano
½ teaspoon of garlic powder
¼ teaspoon of salt
¼ teaspoon of black pepper
¼ teaspoon of onion powder

Clean oyster mushrooms before using. Cut them lengthwise into ⅛-inch-thick slices. Mix chili, cumin, paprika, oregano, garlic, salt, black pepper, and onion powder in a suitable mixing bowl. Add lime juice with oil and mix. Place sliced mushroom into the bowl and rub with spices. At 350 degrees F, preheat your air fryer. Air fry the mushroom in the air fryer for 7–10 minutes almost. Divide the cooked mushrooms between all the tortillas. Add shredded cheese and make a thin roll from each stuffed tortilla. Spray all rolled tortillas with some oil and Air fry for almost 10 minutes. Serve.

Nutritional information: Calories: 150; Fat: 8.8g; Total Carbs: 13g; Net Carbs: 7g; Fiber: 2.1g; Sugars: 0.8g; Protein: 5.1g

Sausage Hash Brown Casserole

Prep time: 15 minutes | Cook time: 20 minutes | Serves: 6

4 eggs
1 pound of ground sausage
1 pound of hash browns
1 diced yellow bell pepper

1 diced green bell pepper
1 diced red bell pepper
¼ cup of diced onion
Black pepper and salt, to taste

At 355 degrees F, preheat your air fryer. Grease a suitable cake pan with some oil or cooking spray. First, place hash browns on the bottom of the cake pan, then spread the uncooked sausage, sprinkle black pepper and salt. Cover it with onions and black peppers. Cook in the preheated air fryer at about 355 degrees F for almost 10 minutes. Meanwhile, whisk eggs with seasonings in a suitable mixing bowl. Pour the prepared egg mixture on top of the casserole and continue cooking for almost 10 more minutes. Serve warm.

Nutritional information: Calories: 507; Fat: 33.9g; Total Carbs: 28g; Net Carbs: 11.5g; Fiber: 2.8g; Sugars: 2.6g; Protein: 20.9g

Strawberry and Peach Toast

Prep time: 15 minutes | Cook time: 2 minutes | Serves: 4

2-4 slices bread
Strawberries, as needed
1 peach, corned and sliced
1 teaspoon sugar

Cooking spray
¼ cup cream cheese
1 teaspoon cinnamon

Prepare all the recipe ingredients from the list. Spray the bread with olive oil on per side. Place in the preheated air fryer basket and Cook at almost 375 degrees F for 1 minute on each side. Slice strawberries and peaches and prepare the rest of the ingredients. Spread toast thickly of cream cheese, garnish with strawberries and peach, sprinkle with almonds and cinnamon mixture if you like. Serve with smoothies, coffee or tea.
Nutritional information: Calories: 97; Fat: 5.6g; Total Carbs: 10.1g; Net Carbs: 0g; Fiber: 1.2g; Sugars: 5.1g; Protein: 2.2g

Mushroom Frittata with Mozzarella Cheese

Prep time: 15 minutes | Cook time: 10 minutes | Serves: 4

5 eggs
3 mushrooms, sliced
1 bell pepper
green onions for taste
2 tablespoons butter, melted

1 cup mozzarella cheese, shredded
1 tablespoon black pepper
arugula for serve
1 tablespoon salt

Prepare all the recipe ingredients from the list. Wash and slice vegetables. And beat the eggs. Grate the cheese. Toss mushrooms, black peppers and green onions with melted butter and add into the air fryer basket. Cook at almost 350 degrees F for 5 min. Shake basket twice. Meanwhile, in a suitable bowl, whisk together eggs, black pepper, salt and grated mozzarella. Pour egg mixture over vegetables. Place the dish in the preheated air fryer and cook at almost 350 degrees F for 5 minutes or until eggs are set. Serve with arugula.
Nutritional information: Calories: 167; Fat: 12.7g; Total Carbs: 4.7g; Net Carbs: 1g; Fiber: 1.1g; Sugars: 2.3g; Protein: 10g

Simple Cheddar-Omelet

Prep time: 15 minutes | Cook time: 10 minutes | Serves: 2

4 eggs
4 tablespoons cheddar, grated cheese

½ green onions, sliced
¼ tablespoon black pepper
1 tablespoon olive oil

Prepare all the recipe ingredients from the list. Whisk the eggs along with the black pepper. Preheat the air fryer at about 350 degrees. Sprinkle the air fryer basket with olive oil and add the egg mixture and the green onions. Air fry for 8 to 10 min. Top with the cheddar, grated cheese. Serve and Enjoy.
Nutritional information: Calories: 214; Fat: 16.8g; Total Carbs: 1g; Net Carbs: 0g; Fiber: 0.3g; Sugars: 0.9g; Protein: 14.7g

Crispy Parmesan Asparagus

Prep time: 15 minutes | Cook time: 10 minutes | Serves: 4

1 pound asparagus spears
2 tablespoons butter
½ cup Parmesan cheese, grated

Salt/Black pepper
1 teaspoon lemon zest

Prepare all the recipe ingredients. Peel the asparagus, wash and dry. Season the asparagus spears with black pepper and salt and brush with butter. Arrange them in a deep air fryer basket and cook for about 8 to 10 minutes at 370 degrees F. Shake a couple of times while cooking. Serve with parmesan and lemon zest.
Nutritional information: Calories: 85; Fat: 6.7g; Total Carbs: 4.5g; Net Carbs: 0.5g; Fiber: 2.4g; Sugars: 2.1g; Protein: 3.7g

Mozzarella Vegetable Frittata

Prep time: 15 minutes | Cook time: 20 minutes | Serves: 2

1 small onion, diced
2 cloves of garlic
⅓pack 4 ounces spinach
3 eggs, beaten

3 ounces' mozzarella cheese
1 tablespoon olive oil
Salt/Black pepper

At 370 degrees F, preheat your air fryer. In a baking pan, heat the oil for about 1 minute. Add diced onions and garlic into the pan and cook for 2-3 minutes. Add spinach and cook for about 3-5 minute to about ½ Air fry. In the suitable bowl, whisk the beaten eggs, season with black pepper and salt. Pour the mixture into a baking pan. Place that pan into the preheated air fryer and air fry for 6 to 8 minutes or until cooked. Sprinkle with cheese 2 minutes until tender. Serve and enjoy.
Nutritional information: Calories: 282; Fat: 20.4g; Total Carbs: 6g; Net Carbs: 2.5g; Fiber: 0.9g; Sugars: 2.5g; Protein: 19.3g

Flavorful Scrambled Eggs with Chorizo

Prep time: 15 minutes | Cook time: 13 minutes | Serves: 2

1 dash of Spanish paprika
1 dash of oregano
3 large eggs, beaten

1 tablespoon olive oil
½ zucchini, sliced
½ chorizo sausage, sliced

Prepare all the recipe ingredients. At 350 degrees F, preheat your air fryer. Fry the zucchini in olive oil, season with salt and cook for 2-3 minutes. Add chorizo to the zucchini and cook for another 5-6 minutes. Fill with the egg mixture and send it back to the air fryer for 5 minutes, take out the basket and stir for every minute until tender. Serve and Enjoy.
Nutritional information: Calories: 186; Fat: 15.5g; Total Carbs: 2g; Net Carbs: 0.5g; Fiber: 0.6g; Sugars: 1.4g; Protein: 10.7g

Garlic Chicken Strips

Prep time: 15 minutes | Cook time: 11 minutes | Serves: 4

1 teaspoon garlic powder
1 pound chicken fillet

½ teaspoon salt
½ teaspoon black pepper

Prepare all the recipe ingredients. Cut the chicken fillet into strips. Sprinkle the chicken fillets with salt, black pepper and garlic. At 365 degrees F, preheat your air fryer. Place the butter in the air fryer tray and add the chicken strips. Cook the chicken strips for 6-min. Turn the chicken strips to the other side and cook them for almost an additional 5 minutes. Serve warm
Nutritional information: Calories: 218; Fat: 8.4g; Total Carbs: 0.7g; Net Carbs: 1g; Fiber: 0.1g; Sugars: 0.2g; Protein: 33g

Scrambled Eggs with Mushrooms

Prep time: 15 minutes | Cook time: 11 minutes | Serves: 4

4 eggs

4 strips of bacon

2 mushrooms
black pepper, to taste

salt, to taste

Slice the mushrooms, season with salt, black pepper and sprinkle with oil. Fry in an air fryer at about 360 degrees F, shaking halfway. Fry the bacon strips for 5-6 minutes, shaking halfway. Now we are preparing the scramble. Beat the eggs, mix well, add black pepper and salt to taste. Sprinkle the bottom of the air fryer or a cooking dish with olive oil. Cook the scramble at 360 degrees F for 5 minutes, stirring every minute. Serve and enjoy.
Nutritional information: Calories: 165; Fat: 13.4g; Total Carbs: 0.6g; Net Carbs: 0g; Fiber: 0.1g; Sugars: 0.5g; Protein: 9.8g

Whisked Egg in Bell Pepper

Prep time: 15 minutes | Cook time: 13 minutes | Serves: 2

4 eggs
1 bell pepper, halved and remove seeds
4 small tomatoes finely slice.
oregano

black pepper
garlic powder
olive oil
Salt

Cut and peel the black peppers. Put a mixture of vegetables and seasonings in each half. Whisk 1 egg into each ½ of the black pepper. Place bell pepper halves into the air fryer basket and cook at almost 390 degrees F for 13 minutes. Serve and enjoy.
Nutritional information: Calories: 178; Fat: 9.3g; Total Carbs: 12g; Net Carbs: 7g; Fiber: 3g; Sugars: 8.5g; Protein: 13.3g

Baked Pancakes with Caramelized Apples

Prep time: 15 minutes | Cook time: 4 minutes | Serves: 2

1 tablespoon milk
1 cup flour
1 ½ tablespoons of sugar
1 egg

½ teaspoon salt
½ teaspoon baking soda
1 tablespoon olive oil or another

Mix all dry ingredients. And mix all the liquid ingredients separately. Add rest of the liquid ingredients to dry ingredients and mix well with a whisk. At 370 degrees F, preheat your air fryer. Grease its air fryer basket or special dish with a little olive oil. Cook in portions for 2 minutes on each side. To make the caramelized Apples: peel the apples, cut into cubes and place in the pan. Sprinkle with sugar and cinnamon, cook until the apples are golden and soft.
Nutritional information: Calories: 357; Fat: 10g; Total Carbs: 57g; Net Carbs: 3g; Fiber: 1.7g; Sugars: 9.7g; Protein: 9.5g

Tasty English Breakfast

Prep time: 15 minutes | Cook time: 20 minutes | Serves: 8

8 sausages
8 bacon slices
4 eggs

1 16-ounce can have baked beans
8 slices of toast

Spread the sausages and bacon slices in your air fryer and air fry for almost 10 minutes at a 320 degrees Fahrenheit. Add the baked beans to a ramekin, then place another ramekin and add the eggs and whisk. Increase the temperature to 290 degrees Fahrenheit. Place it in your air fryer and cook it for 10 minutes more. Serve and enjoy!
Nutritional information: Calories: 285; Fat: 15g; Total Carbs: 19g; Net Carbs: 6.7g; Fiber: 3.6g; Sugars: 4.1g; Protein: 17.9g

Garlic Ham Sandwich with Cheese

Prep time: 15 minutes | Cook time: 20 minutes | Serves: 2

4 toast bread
2-4 slices ham
4 slices Pepper Jack Cheese
2 tablespoons spicy mustard

2 tablespoons melted butter
1 tablespoon garlic powder
2 tablespoons parm cheese

Spread spicy mustard on bottom. Top with Pepper Jack Cheese. Top with lots of ham. Melt butter and add garlic. Brush over top of bread and sprinkle on parm cheese. Cook at almost 350 degrees F for 20 minutes or until golden brown. Serve.
Nutritional information: Calories: 520; Fat: 34g; Total Carbs: 26g; Net Carbs: 13g; Fiber: 5g; Sugars: 2.9g; Protein: 26.9g

Mayonnaise Sausage

Prep time: 15 minutes | Cook time: 10 minutes | Serves: 5

10 breakfast sausages
2 tablespoons mayonnaise
1 teaspoon smoked paprika
1 teaspoon fresh chopped

garlic
1 teaspoon lemon juice
dry garlic + black pepper to taste

At 350 degrees F, preheat your air fryer. Spread the breakfast sausage links in a single layer in the preheated air fryer basket. Air fry them of 8-10 minutes and flip once cooked half way through. Serve.
Nutritional information: Calories: 113; Fat: 9.4g; Total Carbs: 1.9g; Net Carbs: 1g; Fiber: 0.2g; Sugars: 0.5g; Protein: 5.2g

Italian Frittata with Feta Cheese

Prep time: 15 minutes | Cook time: 10 minutes | Serves: 6

6 eggs
⅓ cup of milk
4 ounces of chopped Italian sausage
3 cups of stemmed and roughly chopped kale
1 red deseeded and chopped bell pepper

½ cup of a grated feta cheese
1 chopped zucchini
1 tablespoon of freshly chopped basil
1 teaspoon of garlic powder
1 teaspoon of onion powder
1 teaspoon of salt
1 teaspoon of black pepper

At 360 degrees F, preheat your air fryer. Grease its air fryer basket with a nonstick cooking spray. Add the Italian sausage to its basket and cook it inside your air fryer for 5 minutes. While doing that, stir in the remaining ingredients until it mixes properly. Add the prepared egg mixture to the pan and allow it to cook inside your air fryer for 5 minutes. Serve and enjoy!
Nutritional information: Calories: 192; Fat: 12.7g; Total Carbs: 7g; Net Carbs: 3g; Fiber: 1g; Sugars: 2.3g; Protein: 13g

Breakfast Egg and Sausage Burrito

Prep time: 15 minutes | Cook time: 15 minutes | Serves: 6

6 eggs
Salt
Black pepper
Cooking oil
½ cup chopped red bell pepper
½ cup chopped green bell pepper

8 ounces ground chicken sausage
½ cup salsa
6 medium 8-inch flour tortillas
½ cup shredded Cheddar cheese

At 400 degrees F, preheat your air fryer and grease its air fryer basket. In a suitable bowl, whisk the eggs. Add black pepper and salt to taste. Sauté ground beef with veggies, oil and eggs in a skillet for 10 minutes. Divide this filling on top of the tortillas and add salsa and cheese on top. Roll the tortillas and place the burritos in the greased air fryer basket. Air fry them for 5 minutes then serve.

Nutritional information: Calories: 162; Fat: 8.2g; Total Carbs: 13g; Net Carbs: 7g; Fiber: 2g; Sugars: 1.8g; Protein: 9.7g

Vanilla French Toast Sticks

Prep time: 15 minutes | Cook time: 10 minutes | Serves: 6

4 slices Texas toast	1 teaspoon ground cinnamon
1 tablespoon butter	¼ cup milk
1 egg	1 teaspoon vanilla extract
1 teaspoon stevia	Cooking oil

Cut the bread into sticks and keep them aside. Beat the rest of the recipe ingredients in a suitable wide bowl. At 400 degrees F, preheat your air fryer. Dip the bread sticks in the prepared egg mixture and place in the air fryer. Air fry the bread sticks for 10 minutes. Serve.

Nutritional information: Calories: 102; Fat: 3.5g; Total Carbs: 13g; Net Carbs: 7g; Fiber: 0.9g; Sugars: 2g; Protein: 3.3g

Breakfast Muffins with Bacon and Cheese

Prep time: 15 minutes | Cook time: 15 minutes | Serves: 4

1 ½ cup of all-purpose flour	slices
2 teaspoons of baking powder	1 thinly chopped onion
½ cup of milk	½ cup of shredded cheddar
2 eggs	cheese
1 tablespoon of freshly chopped parsley	½ teaspoon of onion powder
4 cooked and chopped bacon	1 teaspoon of salt
	1 teaspoon of black pepper

At 360 degrees F, preheat your air fryer. Using a suitable bowl, add and stir all the recipe ingredients until it mixes properly. Then grease the muffin cups with a nonstick cooking spray or line it with a parchment paper. Pour the batter proportionally into each muffin cup. Place it inside your air fryer and air fry it for almost 15 minutes. Thereafter, carefully remove it from your air fryer and allow it to chill. Serve and enjoy!

Nutritional information: Calories: 290; Fat: 8g; Total Carbs: 42g; Net Carbs: 18g; Fiber: 2.1g; Sugars: 3g; Protein: 12.6g

Home-Made Potatoes with Paprika

Prep time: 15 minutes | Cook time: 25 minutes | Serves: 4

3 large russet potatoes	Black pepper
1 tablespoon canola oil	1 cup chopped onion
1 tablespoon extra-virgin olive oil	1 cup chopped red bell pepper
1 teaspoon paprika	1 cup chopped green bell pepper
Salt	

Cut the potatoes into ½-inch cubes. Place the potatoes in a suitable bowl of cold water and allow them to soak for at least 30 minutes, preferably an hour. Dry out the potatoes and wipe thoroughly with paper towels. Return them to the empty bowl. Add the canola and olive oils, paprika, and black pepper and salt to flavor. Toss to fully coat the potatoes. Transfer the potatoes to the air fryer. Cook for 20 minutes, shaking the air fryer basket every 5 minutes a total of 4 times. Put the onion and red and

green bell peppers to the air fryer basket. Fry for an additional 3 to 4 minutes, or until the potatoes are cooked through and the black peppers are soft. Cool before serving.

Nutritional information: Calories: 275; Fat: 7.5g; Total Carbs: 48g; Net Carbs: 30g; Fiber: 7.9g; Sugars: 6g; Protein: 5.4g

Air-Fried Chicken Wings and Waffles

Prep time: 15 minutes | Cook time: 20 minutes | Serves: 4

8 whole chicken wings	½ cup all-purpose flour
1 teaspoon garlic powder	Cooking oil
Chicken seasoning or rub	8 frozen waffles
Black pepper	Maple syrup

At 400 degrees F, preheat your air fryer. In a suitable bowl, spice the chicken with the garlic powder and chicken seasoning and black pepper to flavor. Put the chicken to a sealable plastic bag and add the flour. Shake to thoroughly coat the chicken. Grease its air fryer basket with cooking oil. Place chicken in the greased air fryer basket and air fry for 20 minutes while tossing occasionally. Transfer the air fried chicken to a plate and add frozen waffles to the air fryer and cook for almost 6 minutes. Serve the air fried chicken with waffles.

Nutritional information: Calories: 423; Fat: 14.4g; Total Carbs: 64g; Net Carbs: 35g; Fiber: 10.5g; Sugars: 10.2g; Protein: 11.9g

Cheddar Tater Tot with Sausage

Prep time: 15 minutes | Cook time: 20 minutes | Serves: 4

4 eggs	12 ounces ground chicken
1 cup milk	sausage
1 teaspoon onion powder	1-pound frozen tater tots
Salt	¾ cup shredded Cheddar
Black pepper	cheese
Cooking oil	

Beat the eggs with onion powder, milk, and black pepper and salt in a bowl. Grease a suitable skillet with cooking oil and place it over medium-high heat. Toss in the ground sausage and sauté for 4 minutes until brown. Grease a suitable barrel pan with cooking oil. Spread the tater tots in the prepared barrel pan. Air fry for 6 minutes almost. Then add the egg and cooked sausage mixture, cook for 6 minutes more. Sprinkle the cheese over the tater tot. Cook for 2 to 3 minutes more. Cool before serving.

Nutritional information: Calories: 181; Fat: 12.7g; Total Carbs: 4g; Net Carbs: 2g; Fiber: 0g; Sugars: 3.4g; Protein: 12.9g

Tasty Hash Browns with Radish

Prep time: 15 minutes | Cook time: 13 minutes | Serves: 4

1 pound radishes, washed and cut off roots	½ teaspoon garlic powder
1 tablespoon olive oil	1 medium onion
½ teaspoon paprika	¼ teaspoon black pepper
½ teaspoon onion powder	¾ teaspoon salt

Slice onion and radishes using a mandolin slicer. Add sliced onion and radishes in a suitable mixing bowl and toss with olive oil. Transfer onion and radish slices in air fryer basket and cook at almost 360 degrees F for 8 minutes. Shake basket twice. Return onion and radish slices in a suitable mixing bowl and toss with seasonings. Again, cook onion and radish slices in air fryer basket for 5 minutes at 400 degrees F. Shake the basket halfway through. Serve and enjoy.

Nutritional information: Calories: 62; Fat: 3.7g; Total Carbs: 7.1g; Net Carbs: 1g; Fiber: 2.6g; Sugars: 3.5g; Protein: 1.2g

Egg-Cilantro Cups

Prep time: 15 minutes | Cook time: 14 minutes | Serves: 4

4 eggs
1 tablespoon cilantro, chopped
4 tablespoon half and half
1 cup cheddar cheese, shredded

1 cup vegetables, diced
Black pepper
Salt

Sprinkle 4 ramekins with cooking spray and set aside. In a suitable mixing bowl, whisk eggs with cilantro, half and half, vegetables, ½ cup cheese, black pepper, and salt. Pour egg mixture into the 4 ramekins. Place the prepared ramekins in air fryer basket and cook at almost 300 degrees F for 12 minutes. Top with remaining ½ cup cheese and cook for 2 minutes more at 400 degrees F. Serve and enjoy.

Nutritional information: Calories: 211; Fat: 15.5g; Total Carbs: 4g; Net Carbs: 2g; Fiber: 1g; Sugars: 1.2g; Protein: 13.7g

Spinach Frittata with Mozzarella

Prep time: 15 minutes | Cook time: 8 minutes | Serves: 1

3 eggs
1 cup spinach, chopped
1 small onion, minced
2 tablespoon mozzarella

cheese, grated
Black pepper
Salt

At 350 degrees F, preheat your air fryer. Spray air fryer basket with cooking spray. In a suitable bowl, whisk eggs with remaining ingredients until well combined. Pour the prepared egg mixture into the pan and place pan in the preheated air fryer basket. Cook frittata for 8 minutes or until set. Serve and enjoy.

Nutritional information: Calories: 384; Fat: 23.3g; Total Carbs: 10.7g; Net Carbs: 0g; Fiber: 2.2g; Sugars: 4.1g; Protein: 34.3g

Mushroom Frittata

Prep time: 15 minutes | Cook time: 6 minutes | Serves: 2

3 eggs, lightly beaten
2 tablespoon cheddar cheese, shredded
2 tablespoons heavy cream
2 mushrooms, sliced

¼ small onion, chopped
¼ bell pepper, diced
Black pepper
Salt

In a suitable bowl, whisk eggs with cream, vegetables, black pepper, and salt. At 400 degrees F, preheat your air fryer. Pour egg mixture into the air fryer pan. Place pan in air fryer basket and cook for 5 minutes. Add shredded cheese on top of the frittata and cook for 1 minute more. Serve and enjoy.

Nutritional information: Calories: 187; Fat: 14.6g; Total Carbs: 3g; Net Carbs: 1g; Fiber: 0.6g; Sugars: 2g; Protein: 11.2g

Zucchini Muffins with Cinnamon

Prep time: 15 minutes | Cook time: 20 minutes | Serves: 8

6 eggs
4 drops stevia
¼ cup Swerve
⅓ cup coconut oil, melted

1 cup zucchini, grated
¾ cup coconut flour
¼ teaspoon ground nutmeg
1 teaspoon ground cinnamon

½ teaspoon baking soda

At 325 degrees F, preheat your air fryer. Add all the recipe ingredients except zucchini in a suitable bowl and mix well. Add zucchini and stir well. Pour batter into the silicone muffin molds and place into the air fryer basket. Cook muffins for 20 minutes. Serve and enjoy.

Nutritional information: Calories: 111; Fat: 5.5g; Total Carbs: 8g; Net Carbs: 3.5g; Fiber: 4.7g; Sugars: 0.8g; Protein: 7.2g

Creamy Soufflés

Prep time: 15 minutes | Cook time: 20 minutes | Serves: 8

6 large eggs, separated
¾ cup heavy cream
¼ teaspoon cayenne pepper
½ teaspoon xanthan gum
½ teaspoon black pepper

¼ teaspoon cream of tartar
2 tablespoons chives, chopped
2 cups cheddar cheese, shredded
1 teaspoon salt

At 325 degrees F, preheat your air fryer. Spray eight ramekins with cooking spray. Set aside. In a suitable bowl, whisk together almond flour, cayenne pepper, black pepper, salt, and xanthan gum. Slowly add heavy cream and mix to combine. Whisk in egg yolks, chives, and cheese until well combined. In a suitable bowl, add egg whites and cream of tartar and beat until stiff peaks form. Fold egg white mixture into the dry almond flour mixture until combined. Pour mixture into the prepared ramekins. Divide ramekins in batches. Place the first batch of ramekins into the air fryer basket. Cook soufflé for 20 minutes. Serve and enjoy.

Nutritional information: Calories: 207; Fat: 17.3g; Total Carbs: 1g; Net Carbs: 0g; Fiber: 0.1g; Sugars: 0.5g; Protein: 12g

Egg Soufflé with Mushroom and Broccoli

Prep time: 15 minutes | Cook time: 20 minutes | Serves: 4

4 large eggs
1 teaspoon onion powder
1 teaspoon garlic powder

1 teaspoon red pepper, crushed
½ cup broccoli florets, chopped
½ cup mushrooms, chopped

Sprinkle 4 ramekins with cooking spray and set aside. In a suitable bowl, whisk eggs with onion powder, garlic powder, and red pepper. Add mushrooms and broccoli and stir well. Pour egg mixture into the prepared ramekins and place ramekins into the air fryer basket. Cook at almost 350 degrees F for almost 15 minutes. Make sure soufflé is cooked if soufflé is not cooked then cook for 5 minutes more. Serve and enjoy.

Nutritional information: Calories: 91; Fat: 5.1g; Total Carbs: 4.7g; Net Carbs: 1g; Fiber: 0.9g; Sugars: 2.6g; Protein: 7.4g

Mushroom and Asparagus Frittata

Prep time: 15 minutes | Cook time: 10 minutes | Serves: 4

6 eggs
3 mushrooms, sliced
10 asparagus, chopped
¼ cup half and half
2 teaspoons butter, melted

1 cup mozzarella cheese, shredded
1 teaspoon black pepper
1 teaspoon salt

Toss mushrooms and asparagus with melted butter and add into the air fryer basket. Cook mushrooms and asparagus at 350 degrees F for 5 minutes. Shake basket twice. Meanwhile, in a suitable bowl, whisk together eggs, half and half, black pepper, and salt. Transfer cook mushrooms and asparagus into the air

fryer basket. Pour egg mixture over mushrooms and asparagus. Place dish in the preheated air fryer and cook at almost 350 degrees F for 5 minutes or until eggs are set. Slice and serve.
Nutritional information: Calories: 162; Fat: 11.6g; Total Carbs: 3g; Net Carbs: 1g; Fiber: 1g; Sugars: 1.5g; Protein: 12.1g

Zoodles with Cheese

Prep time: 15 minutes | Cook time: 45 minutes | Serves: 3

1 egg
½ cup parmesan cheese, grated
½ cup feta cheese, crumbled
1 tablespoon thyme
1 garlic clove, chopped
1 onion, chopped
2 medium zucchinis, trimmed
and spiralized
2 tablespoons olive oil
1 cup mozzarella cheese, grated
½ teaspoon black pepper
½ teaspoon salt

At 350 degrees F, preheat your air fryer. Add spiralized zucchini and salt in a colander and set aside for almost 10 minutes. Wash zucchini noodles and pat dry with a paper towel. Set a suitable pan with oil over medium heat. Add garlic and onion and sauté for 3-4 minutes Stir in zucchini noodles and cook for 4-5 minutes or until softened. Add zucchini mixture into the air fryer basket. Stir in egg, thyme, cheeses. Mix well and season. Place pan in the preheated air fryer and cook for 30-35 minutes. Serve and enjoy.
Nutritional information: Calories: 248; Fat: 19.1g; Total Carbs: 10.3g; Net Carbs: 0g; Fiber: 2.6g; Sugars: 5g; Protein: 11.7g 20g

Scramble Casserole with Cheddar

Prep time: 15 minutes | Cook time: 15 minutes | Serves: 4

6 slices bacon
6 eggs
Salt
Black pepper
Cooking oil
½ cup chopped red bell pepper
½ cup chopped green bell pepper
½ cup chopped onion
¾ cup shredded Cheddar cheese

At 400 degrees F, preheat your air fryer. In a suitable pan, over medium-high heat, cook the bacon, 5 to 7 minutes, flipping too evenly crisp. Dry out on paper towels, crumble, and set aside. In a suitable bowl, whisk the eggs. Add black pepper and salt to taste. Grease a suitable barrel pan with cooking oil. Add the beaten eggs, crumbled bacon, red bell pepper, green bell pepper, and onion to the pan. Place this pan in the air fryer. Cook for 6 minutes more. Drizzle the cheese over the casserole. Cook for an additional 2 minutes. Cool before serving.
Nutritional information: Calories: 345; Fat: 25.5g; Total Carbs: 3g; Net Carbs: 1g; Fiber: 0.5g; Sugars: 2g; Protein 24.5g

Coconut Muffins with Jalapeno

Prep time: 15 minutes | Cook time: 15 minutes | Serves: 8

5 eggs
⅓ cup coconut oil, melted
2 teaspoons baking powder
3 tablespoons erythritol
3 tablespoons jalapenos, sliced
¼ cup unsweetened coconut milk
⅔ cup coconut flour
¾ teaspoon salt

At 325 degrees F, preheat your air fryer. In a suitable bowl, mix together coconut flour, baking powder, erythritol, and salt. Add eggs, jalapenos, coconut milk, and coconut oil until well combined. Pour batter into the silicone muffin molds and place into the air fryer basket. Cook muffins for almost 15 minutes.

Serve and enjoy.
Nutritional information: Calories: 134; Fat: 12.2g; Total Carbs: 3g; Net Carbs: 1g; Fiber: 1.6g; Sugars: 0.3g; Protein: 4g

Mushroom Frittata with Parmesan

Prep time: 15 minutes | Cook time: 13 minutes | Serves: 1

1 cup egg whites
1 cup spinach, chopped
2 mushrooms, sliced
2 tablespoon parmesan cheese, grated
Salt

Sauté mushrooms in a greased skillet for 3 minutes almost. Add spinach and cook for 1-2 minutes. Transfer mushroom spinach mixture into a suitable pan. Beat 1 cup of egg whites with a pinch of salt in a suitable mixing bowl until frothy. Pour prepared egg white mixture into the spinach and mushroom mixture and sprinkle with parmesan cheese. Place this pan in air fryer basket and cook frittata at 350 degrees F for 8 minutes Slice and serve.
Nutritional information: Calories: 321; Fat: 12.6g; Total Carbs: 6g; Net Carbs: 2.5g; Fiber: 1g; Sugars: 2.5g; Protein: 46.5g

Strawberry Tarts

Prep time: 15 minutes | Cook time: 10 minutes | Serves: 6

2 refrigerated piecrusts
½ cup strawberry preserves
1 teaspoon cornstarch
Cooking oil spray
½ cup low-fat vanilla yogurt
1-ounce cream cheese, at room
temperature
3 tablespoons confectioners' sugar
Rainbow sprinkles, for decorating

Place the piecrusts on a flat surface. Cut each piecrust into 3 rectangles using a knife or pizza cutter, for 6 in total. In a suitable bowl, mix cornstarch and the preserves. Mix well. Scoop 1 tablespoon of the strawberry filling onto the top ½ of each piece of piecrust. Fold the bottom of each piece to enclose the filling inside. Press along the edges of each tart to seal using the back of a fork. At 350 degrees F, preheat your air fryer. Once your air fryer is preheated, spray the crisper plate with cooking oil. Work in batches, spray the breakfast tarts with cooking oil and place them into the basket in a single layer. Set the air fryer's temperature to 375 degrees F, and set the time to 10 minutes. Repeat the same steps with remaining ingredients. In a suitable bowl, stir together the cream cheese, yogurt, and confectioners' sugar. Top the breakfast tarts with the frosting and garnish with sprinkles.
Nutritional information: Calories: 166; Fat: 2.2g; Total Carbs: 34.1g; Net Carbs: 1g; Fiber: 1g; Sugars: 14.4g; Protein: 2.3g

Breakfast Cobbler with Blueberries

Prep time: 15 minutes | Cook time: 15 minutes | Serves: 4

⅓ cup whole-wheat pastry flour
¾ teaspoon baking powder
Dash salt
½ cup milk
2 tablespoons pure maple
syrup
½ teaspoon vanilla extract
Cooking oil spray
½ cup fresh blueberries
¼ cup Granola, or plain store-bought granola

In a suitable bowl, whisk the flour, baking powder, and salt. Add maple syrup, the milk, and vanilla and gently whisk. Spray a suitable 6-by-2-inch round baking pan with cooking oil and pour the prepared batter into the pan. Top evenly with the blueberries and granola. At 350 degrees F, preheat your air fryer and cook for almost 15 minutes. Garnish and serve.

Nutritional information: Calories: 111; Fat: 4.6g; Total Carbs: 27g; Net Carbs: 19g; Fiber: 2.1g; Sugars: 12.3g; Protein: 4.5g

Breakfast Granola with Cinnamon

Prep time: 15 minutes | Cook time: 40 minutes | Serves: 2.

1 cup rolled oats	oil
3 tablespoons pure maple syrup	¼ teaspoon salt
1 tablespoon sugar	¼ teaspoon ground cinnamon
1 tablespoon neutral-flavored	¼ teaspoon vanilla extract

In a suitable bowl, stir together the oats, maple syrup, sugar, oil, salt, cinnamon, and vanilla until thoroughly combined. Transfer the granola to a 6-by-2-inch round baking pan. Once your air fryer unit is preheated, place the pan into the basket. At 250 degrees F, preheat your Air fryer and cook for almost 40 minutes. Serve.

Nutritional information: Calories: 258; Fat: 2.7g; Total Carbs: 54g; Net Carbs: 31g; Fiber: 4.3g; Sugars: 24.4g; Protein: 5.4g

Sweet Berry Muffins

Prep time: 15 minutes | Cook time: 17 minutes | Serves: 8

1⅓ cups 1 tablespoon all-purpose flour	2 teaspoons baking powder
¼ cup granulated sugar	2 eggs
2 tablespoons light brown sugar	⅔ cup whole milk
	⅓ cup safflower oil
	1 cup mixed fresh berries

In a suitable bowl, stir together 1⅓ cups of flour, the granulated sugar, brown sugar, and baking powder until mixed well. In a suitable bowl, whisk the eggs, milk, and oil until combined. Add the prepared egg mixture to the dry ingredients just until combined. In another suitable bowl, toss the mixed berries with the left over 1 tablespoon of flour until coated. Gently stir the berries into the batter. Fold together the 16 foil muffin cups to make 8 cups. Once your air fryer unit is preheated, place 4 cups into the basket and fill each three-quarter full with the batter. At 315 degrees F, preheat your air fryer and cook for 17 minutes. Repeat the cooking steps for the rest cups. Serve.

Nutritional information: Calories: 198; Fat: 10.9g; Total Carbs: 22g; Net Carbs: 10g; Fiber: 0.7g; Sugars: 10.2g; Protein: 3.5g

Awesome Everything Bagels

Prep time: 15 minutes | Cook time: 10 minutes | Serves: 2

½ cup self-rising flour	4 teaspoons everything bagel spice mix
½ cup plain Greek yogurt	
1 egg	Cooking oil spray
1 tablespoon water	1 tablespoon butter, melted

In a suitable bowl, using a wooden spoon, stir together the flour and yogurt until a tacky dough forms. Transfer the dough to a lightly floured work surface and roll the dough into a ball. Cut the prepared dough into 2 pieces and roll each piece into a log. Form each log into a bagel shape, pinching the ends together. In a suitable bowl, whisk the egg and water. Brush the egg wash on the bagels. Add 2 teaspoons of the spice mix on each bagel and gently press it into the dough. Once your air fryer unit is preheated, spray the crisper plate with cooking spray. Drizzle with the bagels with the butter and place them into the basket. At

330 degrees F, preheat your air fryer and cook for 10 minutes. When the cooking is complete, the bagels should be lightly golden on the outside. Serve warm.

Nutritional information: Calories 224; Fat: 8.5g; Total Carbs: 25g; Net Carbs: 16g; Fiber: 0.8g; Sugars: 1.5g; Protein: 10.6g

Feta Stuffed Peppers with Broccoli

Prep time: 15 minutes | Cook time: 40 minutes | Serves: 2

4 eggs	1 teaspoon dried thyme
½ cup cheddar cheese, grated	¼ cup feta cheese, crumbled
2 bell peppers cut in ½ and remove seeds	½ cup broccoli, cooked
	¼ teaspoon black pepper
½ teaspoon garlic powder	½ teaspoon salt

At 325 degrees F, preheat your air fryer. Stuff feta and broccoli into the bell peppers halved. Beat egg in a suitable bowl with seasoning and pour egg mixture into the black pepper halved over feta and broccoli. Place bell pepper halved into the air fryer basket and cook for 35-40 minutes. Top with cheddar, grated cheese and cook until cheese melted. Serve and enjoy.

Nutritional information: Calories: 339; Fat: 22.5g; Total Carbs: 13g; Net Carbs: 7g; Fiber: 2.5g; Sugars: 8.2g; Protein: 22.8g

Easy Egg Soufflé

Prep time: 15 minutes | Cook time: 8 minutes | Serves: 2

2 eggs	¼ teaspoon black pepper
¼ teaspoon chili black pepper	1 tablespoon parsley, chopped
2 tablespoons heavy cream	Salt

In a suitable bowl, whisk eggs with remaining gradients. Spray 2 ramekins with cooking spray. Pour egg mixture into the prepared ramekins and place into the air fryer basket. Cook soufflé at 390 degrees F for 8 minutes Serve and enjoy.

Nutritional information: Calories: 116; Fat: 10g; Total Carbs: 1g; Net Carbs: 0g; Fiber: 0.1g; Sugars: 0.4g; Protein 5.9g

Spinach Egg Muffins

Prep time: 15 minutes | Cook time: 21 minutes | Serves: 12

9 eggs	½ teaspoon oregano
½ cup onion, sliced	1 ½ cups spinach
1 tablespoon olive oil	¾ cup bell peppers, chopped
8 ounces ground sausage	Black pepper
¼ cup coconut milk	Salt

At 325 degrees F, preheat your air fryer. Sauté ground sausage in a pan over medium heat for 5 minutes Stir in olive oil, bell pepper, oregano, and onion and sauté until onion is translucent. Add fresh or frozen spinach to the pan and cook for 30 seconds then keep it aside. In a suitable mixing bowl, whisk together eggs, coconut milk, black pepper, and salt. Add sausage-vegetable mixture into the egg mixture and mix well. Pour the prepared mixture into the muffin molds and place into the air fryer basket. Cook muffins for almost 15 minutes Serve and enjoy.

Nutritional information: Calories: 138; Fat: 11g; Total Carbs: 1.7g; Net Carbs: 1g; Fiber: 0.4g; Sugars: 1g; Protein: 8.2g

Snacks and Appetizers Recipes

Cabbage Crackers

Prep time: 10 minutes | Cook time: 30 minutes | Serves: 6

1 large cabbage head, tear cabbage leaves into pieces
2 tbsps. olive oil

¼ cup parmesan cheese, grated
Pepper
Salt

Add all the recipe ingredients into the large mixing bowl and toss well. Spray "Air Fryer Basket" with some cooking spray. Divide cabbage in batches. Add one cabbage batch in "Air Fryer Basket" and Air Fry for 25-30 minutes at 250 degrees F. Cook another batch with the same steps. Serve and enjoy.
Nutritional information: Calories 96; Fat 5.1 g; Total Carbs 12.1 g; Net Carbs 3g; Sugar 6.7 g; Protein 3 g; Fiber 1 g

Broccoli Tots

Prep time: 10 minutes | Cook time: 15 minutes | Serves: 4

1 lb. broccoli, chopped
½ cup almond flour
¼ cup ground flaxseed

½ tsp. garlic powder
1 tsp. salt

Add broccoli into the microwave-safe bowl and microwave for 3 minutes. Transfer steamed broccoli into the food processor and process until it looks like rice. Transfer broccoli to a large mixing bowl. Add the remaining ingredients into the bowl and mix well. Spray the "Air Fryer Basket" with some cooking spray. Make small tots from broccoli mixture and place into the Air Fryer Basket. Cook broccoli tots for 12 minutes at 375 degrees F. Serve and enjoy.
Nutritional information: Calories 161; Fat 9.2 g; Total Carbs 12.8 g; Net Carbs 3g; Sugar 2.1 g; Protein 7.5 g; Fiber 0 g

Crispy Kale Chips

Prep time: 5 minutes | Cook time: 5 minutes | Serves: 2

1 bunch of kale, remove stem and cut into pieces
½ tsp. garlic powder

1 tsp. olive oil
½ tsp. salt

Add all the recipe ingredients into the large bowl and toss well. Transfer the kale mixture into the "Air Fryer Basket" and Air Fry for 3 minutes at 370 degrees F. When the time is up, shake the basket well and Air Fry for 2 minutes more. Serve and enjoy.
Nutritional information: Calories 37; Fat 1 g; Total Carbs 6 g; Sugar 1 g; Net Carbs 5g; Protein 3 g; Fiber 0 g

Juicy Beef Meatballs

Prep time: 10 minutes | Cook time: 14 minutes | Serves: 5

1 lb. ground beef
1 tsp. garlic powder
1 egg, lightly beaten

½ onion, diced
¼ tsp. pepper
1 tsp. salt

Spray "Air Fryer Basket" with some cooking spray. Add all the recipe ingredients into the bowl and mix well. Make small balls from meat mixture and place into the Air Fryer Basket. Cook meatballs for 14 minutes at 390 degrees F on Air Fry mode. Shake the basket 3-4 times while cooking. Serve and enjoy.
Nutritional information: Calories 259; Fat 18 g; Total Carbs 3 g; Sugar 0.5 g; Net Carbs 8g; Protein 17 g; Fiber 95 g

Bacon Poppers

Prep time: 10 minutes | Cook time: 8 minutes | Serves: 10

10 jalapeno peppers, cut in half and remove seeds

⅓ cup cream cheese, softened
5 bacon strips, cut in half

Stuff cream cheese into each jalapeno half. Wrap each jalapeno half with half bacon strip and place in the Air Fryer Basket. Air Fry the food at 370 degrees F for 6-8 minutes. Serve and enjoy.
Nutritional information: Calories 83; Fat 7.4 g; Total Carbs 1.3 g; Sugar 0.5 g; Net Carbs 2g; Protein 2.8 g; Fiber 9 g

BBQ Chicken Wings

Prep time: 10 minutes | Cook time: 15 minutes | Serves: 4

1 lb. chicken wings
½ cup BBQ sauce, sugar-free

¼ tsp. garlic powder
Pepper

Season chicken wings with garlic powder and pepper and place into the Air Fryer Basket. Cook chicken wings for 15 minutes at 400 degrees F on Air Fry mode. Shake basket 3-4 times while cooking. Transfer cooked chicken wings in a large mixing bowl. Pour BBQ sauce over chicken wings and toss to coat. Serve and enjoy.
Nutritional information: Calories 263; Fat 8.5 g; Total Carbs 11.5 g; Sugar 8 g; Net Carbs 6g; Protein 32 g; Fiber 100 g

Vegetable Kabobs

Prep time: 10 minutes | Cook time: 10 minutes | Serves: 4

½ onion
1 zucchini
1 eggplant

2 bell peppers
Black pepper, to taste
Salt, to taste

Cut all vegetables into 1-inch pieces. Thread vegetables onto the soaked wooden skewers and season with pepper and salt. Place the skewers into the "Air Fryer Basket" and Air Fry them for 10 minutes at 390 degrees F. Turn the skewers halfway through cooking. Serve and enjoy.
Nutritional information: Calories 61; Fat 0.5 g; Total Carbs 14 g; Sugar 8 g; Net Carbs 5g; Protein 2 g; Fiber 0 g

Shrimp Kabobs

Prep time: 10 minutes | Cook time: 8 minutes | Serves: 2

1 cup shrimp
1 lime juice
1 garlic clove, minced

¼ tsp. pepper
⅛ tsp. salt

At 350 degrees F, preheat your Air Fryer. Add shrimp, lime

juice, garlic, pepper, and salt into the bowl and toss well. Thread shrimp onto the soaked wooden skewers and place into the Air Fryer Basket. Air Fry the food at 350 degrees F for 8 minutes, flipping halfway through. Serve and enjoy.

Nutritional information: Calories 75; Fat 1 g; Total Carbs 4 g; Sugar 0.5 g; Net Carbs 4g; Protein 13 g; Fiber 1 g

Mild Shishito Peppers

Prep time: 5 minutes | Cook time: 5 minutes | Serves: 2

20 shishito Peppers	Salt
1 tbsp. olive oil	

Add shishito peppers into the bowl and toss with olive oil. Add shishito peppers into the "Air Fryer Basket" and Air Fry them at 390 degrees F for 5 minutes. Shake the basket halfway through. Season shishito peppers with salt. Serve and enjoy.

Nutritional information: Calories 20; Fat 1 g; Total Carbs 5 g; Sugar 2 g; Net Carbs 6g; Protein 1 g; Fiber 0 g

Tofu Steaks

Prep time: 10 minutes | Cook time: 35 minutes | Serves: 4

1 package tofu, press and remove excess liquid	3 garlic cloves, minced
¼ tsp. dried thyme	¼ cup olive oil
¼ cup lemon juice	Black pepper, to taste
2 tbsp. lemon zest	Salt, to taste

Cut the tofu into 8 pieces. In a suitable bowl, mix olive oil, thyme, lemon juice, lemon zest, garlic, pepper, and salt. Add tofu into the bowl and coat well and place in the refrigerator for overnight. Spray "Air Fryer Basket" with some cooking spray. Place marinated tofu into the "Air Fryer Basket" and Air Fry at 350 degrees F for 30-35 minutes. Turn the tofu halfway through cooking. Serve and enjoy.

Nutritional information: Calories 195; Fat 16 g; Total Carbs 5 g; Sugar 1 g; Net Carbs 2g; Protein 7 g; Fiber 0 g

Lemon Tofu

Prep time: 10 minutes | Cook time: 15 minutes | Serves: 4

1 lb. tofu, drained and pressed	2 tbsps. erythritol
1 tbsp. arrowroot powder	½ cup water
1 tbsp. tamari	⅓ cup lemon juice
For sauce:	1 tsp. lemon zest
2 tsps. arrowroot powder	

Cut the tofu into cubes. Add tofu and tamari into the zip-lock bag and shake well. Add 1 tablespoon of arrowroot into the bag and shake well to coat the tofu. Set aside for 15 minutes. While marinating, in a suitable bowl, mix all sauce ingredients and then set aside for later use. Spray "Air Fryer Basket" with some cooking spray. Add tofu cubes into the "Air Fryer Basket" and Air Fry them at 390 degrees F for 10 minutes. Shake the basket halfway through for evenly cooking. Add cooked tofu and sauce mixture into the skillet and cook over medium-high heat for 3-5 minutes. Serve and enjoy.

Nutritional information: Calories 112; Fat 3 g; Total Carbs 13 g; Sugar 8 g; Net Carbs 8g; Protein 8 g; Fiber 0 g

Air Fried Cheese Sticks

Prep time: 10 minutes | Cook time: 8 minutes | Serves: 4 minutes

6 mozzarella cheese sticks	¼ tsp. garlic powder

1 tsp. Italian seasoning	1 large egg, lightly beaten
⅓ cup almond flour	¼ tsp. sea salt
½ cup parmesan cheese, grated	

In a suitable bowl, whisk the egg. In a shallow bowl, mix almond flour, parmesan cheese, Italian seasoning, garlic powder, and salt. Dip the mozzarella cheese stick in egg then coat with almond flour mixture and place on a plate. Refrigerate the coated sticks for1 hour. Spray "Air Fryer Basket" with some cooking spray. Place prepared mozzarella cheese sticks into the "Air Fryer Basket" and Air Fry at 375 degrees F for 8 minutes. Serve and enjoy.

Nutritional information: Calories 245; Fat 18 g; Total Carbs 3 g; Sugar 2 g; Net Carbs 6g; Protein 19 g; Fiber 0 g

Broccoli Nuggets

Prep time: 10 minutes | Cook time: 15 minutes | Serves: 4

¼ cup almond flour	1 cup cheddar cheese, shredded
2 cups broccoli florets, cooked until soft	2 egg whites
	⅛ tsp. salt

Spray "Air Fryer Basket" with some cooking spray. Add cooked broccoli into the bowl and using masher mash broccoli into the small pieces. Add remaining ingredients to the bowl and mix well to combine. Make small nuggets from broccoli mixture and place into the air fryer basket. Cook broccoli nuggets at 325 degrees F for 15 minutes on Air Fry mode. Turn the broccoli nuggets halfway through cooking. Serve and enjoy.

Nutritional information: Calories 175; Fat 13 g; Total Carbs 5 g; Sugar 1 g; Net Carbs 6g; Protein 12 g; Fiber 3 g

Chicken Jalapeno Poppers

Prep time: 10 minutes | Cook time: 20 minutes | Serves: 12

½ cup chicken, cooked and shredded	shredded
	¼ tsp. garlic powder
6 jalapenos, halved and seed removed	4 oz. cream cheese
	¼ tsp. dried oregano
¼ cup green onion, sliced	¼ tsp. dried basil
¼ cup Monterey jack cheese,	¼ tsp. salt

Spray "Air Fryer Basket" with some cooking spray. Mix all the recipe ingredients in a suitable bowl except jalapenos. Spoon 1 tablespoon of mixture into each jalapeno halved and place into the Air Fryer Basket. Air Fry the jalapeno for 20 minutes at 370 degrees F. Serve and enjoy.

Nutritional information: Calories 105; Fat 8.5 g; Total Carbs 1.5 g; Sugar 0.7 g; Net Carbs 6g; Protein 6.3 g; Fiber 5 g

Artichoke Dip

Prep time: 10 minutes | Cook time: 24 minutes | Serves: 6

15 oz. artichoke hearts, drained	1 cup cheddar cheese, shredded
1 tsp. Worcestershire sauce	1 tbsp. onion, minced
3 cups arugula, chopped	½ cup mayonnaise

At 325 degrees F, preheat your Air Fryer. Add all the recipe ingredients into the blender and blend until smooth. Pour artichoke mixture into a suitable baking dish and then place the dish into the Air Fryer Basket. Air Fry dip at 325 degrees F for 24 minutes. Serve with vegetables and enjoy.

Nutritional information: Calories 190; Fat 13 g; Total Carbs 13 g; Sugar 2.5 g; Net Carbs 5g; Protein 7.5 g; Fiber 5 g

Crab Mushrooms

Prep time: 10 minutes | Cook time: 8 minutes | Serves: 16

16 mushrooms, clean and chop stems
¼ tsp. chili powder
¼ tsp. onion powder
¼ cup mozzarella cheese, shredded
2 oz. crab meat, chopped
8 oz. cream cheese, softened
2 tsps. garlic, minced
¼ tsp. pepper

In a suitable mixing bowl, add the stems, chili powder, onion powder, pepper, cheese, crabmeat, cream cheese, and garlic, mix them well. Stuff mushrooms with bowl mixture and then place them into the Air Fryer Basket. Air Fry the stuffed mushrooms at 370 degrees F for 8 minutes. Serve and enjoy.
Nutritional information: Calories 59; Fat 5.1 g; Total Carbs 1.2 g; Sugar 0.4 g; Net Carbs 6g; Protein 2.2 g; Fiber 8 g

Chicken Dip

Prep time: 10 minutes | Cook time: 20 minutes | Serves: 6

2 cups chicken, cooked and shredded
¾ cup sour cream
¼ tsp. onion powder
8 oz. cream cheese, softened
3 tbsp. hot sauce
¼ tsp. garlic powder

At 325 degrees F, preheat your Air Fryer. Add all the recipe ingredients in a suitable bowl and mix well. Transfer mixture in a suitable baking dish and then place the dish in the Air Fryer Basket. Cook chicken dip at 325 degrees F for 20 minutes. Serve and enjoy.
Nutritional information: Calories 245; Fat 17 g; Total Carbs 1.5 g; Sugar 0.2 g; Net Carbs 2g; Protein 16 g; Fiber 5 g

Smoked Almonds

Prep time: 5 minutes | Cook time: 6 minutes | Serves: 6

1 cup almonds
¼ tsp. cumin
1 tsp. chili powder
¼ tsp. smoked paprika
2 tsp. olive oil

Add almonds into the bowl; add the remaining ingredients and toss to coat the almonds well. Transfer the almonds into the "Air Fryer Basket" and Air Fry them at 320 degrees F for 6 minutes. Shake the basket halfway through for evenly cooking. Serve and enjoy.
Nutritional information: Calories 107; Fat 9.6 g; Total Carbs 3.7 g; Sugar 0.7 g; Net Carbs 5g; Protein 3.4 g; Fiber 0 g

Parmesan Zucchini Bites

Prep time: 10 minutes | Cook time: 10 minutes | Serves: 6

1 egg, lightly beaten
4 zucchinis, grated and squeeze out all liquid
1 cup shredded coconut
1 tsp. Italian seasoning
½ cup parmesan cheese, grated

Add all the recipe ingredients into the bowl and mix well. Spray "Air Fryer Basket" with some cooking spray. Make small balls from zucchini mixture and place into the "Air Fryer Basket" and Air Fry the balls at 400 degrees F for 10 minutes. Serve and enjoy.
Nutritional information: Calories 88; Fat 6.2 g; Total Carbs 6.6 g; Sugar 3.2 g; Net Carbs 4g; Protein 3.7 g; Fiber 2g

Broccoli Pop-corn

Prep time: 10 minutes | Cook time: 6 minutes | Serves: 4

2 cups broccoli florets
2 cups coconut flour
¼ cup butter, melted
4 eggs yolks
Pepper
Salt

In a suitable bowl, whisk egg yolk with melted butter, pepper, and salt. Add coconut flour and stir to combine. Spray "Air Fryer Basket" with some cooking spray. Coat each broccoli floret with egg mixture and place them into the "Air Fryer Basket" and Air Fry them at 400 degrees F for 6 minutes. Serve and enjoy.
Nutritional information: Calories 147; Fat 12 g; Total Carbs 7 g; Sugar 2 g; Net Carbs 6g; Protein 2 g; Fiber 3g

Rosemary Beans

Prep time: 10 minutes | Cook time: 5 minutes | Serves: 2

1 cup green beans, chopped
2 garlic cloves, minced
2 tbsps. rosemary, chopped
1 tbsp. butter, melted
½ tsp. salt

Add all the recipe ingredients into the bowl and toss well. Transfer green beans into the "Air Fryer Basket" and Air Fry them at 390 degrees F for 5 minutes. Serve and enjoy.
Nutritional information: Calories 83; Fat 6.4 g; Total Carbs 7 g; Sugar 0.8 g; Net Carbs 6g; Protein 1.4 g; Fiber 1g

Cheesy Brussels Sprouts

Prep time: 10 minutes | Cook time: 5 minutes | Serves: 2

1 cup Brussels sprouts, halved
¼ cup mozzarella cheese, shredded
1 tbsp. olive oil
¼ tsp. salt

Toss the halved Brussels sprouts with oil and season with salt. Transfer Brussels sprouts into the "Air Fryer Basket" and top them with shredded cheese. Air Fry the food at 375 degrees F for 5 minutes. When done, serve and enjoy.
Nutritional information: Calories 89; Fat 7.8 g; Total Carbs 4.1 g; Sugar 1 g; Net Carbs 8g; Protein 2.5 g; Fiber 2g

Mushrooms with Sauce

Prep time: 10 minutes | Cook time: 20 minutes | Serves: 5

1 ½ lbs. mushrooms
1 ½ tbsp. olive oil
1 ½ tbsp. vermouth
2 tbsps. fresh lemon juice
¼ tsp. cayenne pepper
½ tsp. turmeric
½ tbsp. Tahini
¼ tsp. pepper
1 tsp. kosher salt

In a suitable bowl, toss mushrooms with oil, turmeric, cayenne pepper, pepper, and salt. Transfer mushrooms into the "Air Fryer Basket" and Air Fry the mushrooms at 350 degrees F for 20 minutes. Shake the basket halfway through cooking. Meanwhile, in a suitable bowl, mix tahini, lemon juice, and vermouth. Serve cooked mushrooms with tahini sauce.
Nutritional information: Calories 80; Fat 5.5 g; Total Carbs 5.2 g; Sugar 2.5 g; Net Carbs 2g; Protein 4.6 g; Fiber 0g

Cheese Artichoke Dip

Prep time: 10 minutes | Cook time: 17 minutes | Serves: 10

½ cup mozzarella cheese, shredded
3 cups arugula leaves, chopped
½ cup mayonnaise
7 oz. brie cheese
⅓ tsp. dried basil

2 garlic cloves, minced
⅓ cup sour cream
⅓ can artichoke hearts, drained and chopped
⅓ tsp. pepper
1 tsp. sea salt

Add all the recipe ingredients except mozzarella cheese into the suitable baking dish and mix well. Spread the mozzarella cheese on top and then place the dish in the Air Fryer Basket. Air Fry the food at 325 degrees F for 17 minutes. Serve and enjoy.
Nutritional information: Calories 66; Fat 4 g; Total Carbs 6.6 g; Sugar 2.8 g; Net Carbs 5g; Protein 2.7 g; Fiber 1g

Thai Chicken Wings

Prep time: 10 minutes | Cook time: 16 minutes | Serves: 6

½ lb. chicken wings
1 tsp. paprika
⅓ cup Thai chili sauce
2 tsps. garlic powder

2 tsps. ginger powder
2 ½ tbsp. dry sherry
Black pepper, to taste
Salt, to taste

Toss chicken wings with dry sherry, paprika, garlic powder, ginger, powder, pepper, and salt. Add chicken wings into the "Air Fryer Basket" and Air Fry them at 365 degrees F for 16 minutes. Serve the chicken wings with Thai chili sauce and enjoy.
Nutritional information: Calories 120; Fat 2.9 g; Total Carbs 6 g; Sugar 3.9 g; Net Carbs 6g; Protein 11.2 g; Fiber 4 g

Cajun Spiced Kale Chips

Prep time: 10 minutes | Cook time: 5 minutes | Serves: 4

3 kale heads, cut into pieces
2 tbsps. Worcestershire sauce
2 tbsps. sesame oil

1 ½ tsp. Cajun spice mix
Black pepper, to taste
Salt, to taste

Add all the recipe ingredients into the large bowl and toss well. Transfer the kale pieces into the "Air Fryer Basket" and Air Fry them at 195 degrees F for 4-5 minutes. Serve and enjoy.
Nutritional information: Calories 106; Fat 7.1 g; Total Carbs 8.3 g; Sugar 1.7 g; Net Carbs 4g; Protein 2.2 g; Fiber 0 g

Crusted Onion Rings

Prep time: 10 minutes | Cook time: 10 minutes | Serves: 3

1 egg, lightly beaten
1 onion, cut into slices
¾ cup pork rind, crushed
1 cup coconut milk

1 tbsp. baking powder
1 ½ cups almond flour
Pepper
Salt

In a suitable bowl, mix almond flour, baking powder, salt and pepper. In another suitable bowl, whisk the egg with milk. Pour egg mixture into the almond flour mixture and stir to combine. In a shallow dish, add crushed pork rinds. Spray "Air Fryer Basket" with some cooking spray. Dip onion ring in egg batter and coat with pork rind and place into the Air Fryer Basket. Cook onion rings for 10 minutes at 360 degrees F on Air Fry mode. Serve and enjoy.
Nutritional information: Calories 350; Fat 31 g; Total Carbs 13 g; Sugar 4 g; Net Carbs 6g; Protein 10 g; Fiber 6 g

Asparagus Pork Fries

Prep time: 10 minutes | Cook time: 10 minutes | Serves: 5

1 lb. asparagus spears
1 cup pork rinds, crushed
¼ cup almond flour
2 eggs, lightly beaten

½ cup parmesan cheese, grated
Black pepper, to taste
Salt, to taste

In a suitable bowl, mix up the parmesan cheese, almond flour, pepper, and salt. In a shallow bowl, whisk eggs. Add crushed pork rind into the shallow dish. Spray "Air Fryer Basket" with some cooking spray. First coat asparagus with parmesan mixture then into the eggs and finally coat with crushed pork rind. Place coated asparagus into the "Air Fryer Basket" and Air Fry the food at 380 degrees F for 10 minutes. Serve and enjoy.
Nutritional information: Calories 102; Fat 6.1 g; Total Carbs 5 g; Sugar 1.9 g; Net Carbs 2g; Protein 8.1 g; Fiber 71 g

Cheesy Mushrooms

Prep time: 10 minutes | Cook time: 5 minutes | Serves: 6

9 oz. mushrooms, cut stems
1 tsp. dried parsley
1 tsp. dried dill

6 oz. cheddar cheese, shredded
1 tbsp. butter
½ tsp. salt

Chop mushrooms stem and place into the bowl. Add the parsley, dill, cheese, butter, and salt into the bowl and mix well. Stuff bowl mixture into the mushroom caps and place into the Air Fryer Basket. Air Fry the mushrooms at 400 degrees F for 5 minutes. Serve and enjoy.
Nutritional information: Calories 141; Fat 11.5 g; Total Carbs 1.9 g; Sugar 0.9 g; Net Carbs 6g; Protein 8.5 g; Fiber 35 g

Toasted Nuts

Prep time: 10 minutes | Cook time: 9 minutes | Serves: 4

½ cup macadamia nuts
½ cup pecans
1 tbsp. olive oil

¼ cup walnuts
¼ cup hazelnuts
1 tsp. salt

Add all nuts into the "Air Fryer Basket" and Air Fry them at 320 degrees F for 8 minutes. Shake the basket halfway through. When the time is up, drizzle the nuts with olive oil and season with salt and toss well. Cook the nuts for 1 minute more. Serve and enjoy.
Nutritional information: Calories 240; Fat 24.9 g; Total Carbs 4.1 g; Sugar 1.1 g; Net Carbs 4g; Protein 4.1 g; Fiber 0 g

Radish Chips

Prep time: 10 minutes | Cook time: 15 minutes | Serves: 12

1 lb. radish, wash and slice into chips
2 tbsps. olive oil

¼ tsp. pepper
1 tsp. salt

Add all the recipe ingredients into the large bowl and toss well. Add radish slices into the "Air Fryer Basket" and Air Fry them at 375 degrees F for 15 minutes. Shake basket 2-3 times while cooking. Serve and enjoy.
Nutritional information: Calories 26; Fat 2.4 g; Total Carbs 1.3 g; Sugar 0.7 g; Net Carbs 6g; Protein 0.3 g; Fiber 0 g

Turnip Slices

Prep time: 10 minutes | Cook time: 10 minutes | Serves: 8

1 lb. turnip, peel and cut into slices	shredded
1 tbsp. olive oil	1 tsp. garlic powder
3 oz. parmesan cheese,	1 tsp. salt

Add all the recipe ingredients into the mixing bowl and toss to coat. Transfer turnip slices into the "Air Fryer Basket" and Air Fry them at 360 degrees F for 10 minutes. Serve and enjoy.
Nutritional information: Calories 66; Fat 4.1 g; Total Carbs 4.3 g; Sugar 2.2 g; Net Carbs 6g; Protein 4 g; Fiber 8 g

Pepper Kale Chips

Prep time: 10 minutes | Cook time: 8 minutes | Serves: 14

1 lb. kale, wash, dry and cut into pieces	1 tsp. chili pepper
2 tsp. olive oil	1 tsp. salt

At 370 degrees F, preheat your Air Fryer. Add kale pieces into the air fryer basket. Drizzle kale with oil. Sprinkle chili pepper and salt over the kale and toss well. Air Fry the kale piece at 370 degrees F for 5 minutes; when the time is up, shake the basket well and Air Fry the kale pieces for 3 minutes more. Serve and enjoy.
Nutritional information: Calories 22; Fat 0.7 g; Total Carbs 3.4 g; Sugar 0 g; Net Carbs 5g; Protein 1 g; Fiber 0 g

Cucumber Chips

Prep time: 10 minutes | Cook time: 11 minutes | Serves: 12

1 lb. cucumber	1 tbsp. paprika
½ tsp. garlic powder	1 tsp. salt

Wash cucumber and slice thinly using a mandolin slicer. Add cucumber slices into the "Air Fryer Basket" and sprinkle with garlic powder, paprika, and salt. Toss well and then Air Fry the food at 370 degrees F for 11 minutes. Shake halfway through. Serve and enjoy.
Nutritional information: Calories 8; Fat 0.1 g; Total Carbs 1.8 g; Sugar 0.7 g; Net Carbs 2g; Protein 0.4 g; Fiber 0 g

Kohlrabi Chips

Prep time: 10 minutes | Cook time: 20 minutes | Serves: 10

1 lb. kohlrabi, peel and slice thinly	1 tbsp. olive oil
1 tsp. paprika	1 tsp. salt

Add all the recipe ingredients into the bowl and toss to coat. Transfer the coated kohlrabi into the "Air Fryer Basket" and Air Fry at 320 degrees F for 20 minutes. Toss halfway through. Serve and enjoy.
Nutritional information: Calories 13; Fat 1.4 g; Total Carbs 0.1 g; Sugar 0 g; Net Carbs 6g; Protein 0 g; Fiber 0 g

Daikon Chips

Prep time: 10 minutes | Cook time: 16 minutes | Serves: 6

15 oz. Daikon, slice into chips	½ tsp. pepper
1 tbsp. olive oil	1 tsp. salt
1 tsp. chili powder	

At 375 degrees F, preheat your Air Fryer. Add all the recipe ingredients into the bowl and toss well. Transfer daikon chips into the "Air Fryer Basket" and Air Fry them at 375 degrees F for 16 minutes. Toss the chips halfway through. Serve and enjoy.
Nutritional information: Calories 36; Fat 2.4 g; Total Carbs 3.2 g; Sugar 1.5 g; Net Carbs 6g; Protein 1.5 g; Fiber 0 g

Kale Dip

Prep time: 10 minutes | Cook time: 12 minutes | Serves: 6

1 lb. kale, wash and chopped	6 oz. parmesan cheese, shredded
1 cup heavy cream	¼ tsp. pepper
1 onion, diced	1 tsp. salt
1 tsp. butter	

Add all the recipe ingredients into the suitable baking dish and stir well. Place dish in the air fryer and Air Fry the food at 250 degrees F for 12 minutes. Serve and enjoy.
Nutritional information: Calories 211; Fat 14.1 g; Total Carbs 11.2 g; Sugar 0.8 g; Net Carbs 4g; Protein 12 g; Fiber 49 g

Crab Dip

Prep time: 10 minutes | Cook time: 16 minutes | Serves: 8

2 cups crab meat	½ lemon juice
1 cup mozzarella cheese, shredded	2 tsps. coconut amino
½ tsp. garlic powder	2 tsps. mayonnaise
¼ cup pimentos, drained and diced	8 oz. cream cheese, softened
¼ tsp. stevia	1 tbsp. green onion
	¼ tsp. pepper
	Salt

At 325 degrees F, preheat your Air Fryer. Add all the recipe ingredients except half mozzarella cheese into the large bowl and mix well. Transfer bowl mixture into the suitable baking dish and sprinkle with the remaining mozzarella cheese. Place the mixture into your air fryer and Air Fry at 325 degrees F for 16 minutes. Serve and enjoy.
Nutritional information: Calories 141; Fat 11.5 g; Total Carbs 4.9 g; Sugar 1.7 g; Net Carbs 6g; Protein 4.9 g; Fiber 38 g

Jalapeno Dip

Prep time: 10 minutes | Cook time: 16 minutes | Serves: 6

1 ½ cup Monterey jack cheese, grated	⅓ cup mayonnaise
1 ½ cup cheddar cheese, shredded	8 oz. cream cheese, softened
2 jalapeno pepper, minced	8 bacon slices, cooked and crumbled
1 tsp. garlic powder	Black pepper, to taste
⅓ cup sour cream	Salt, to taste

At 325 degrees F, preheat your Air Fryer. Add all the recipe ingredients into the bowl and mix until combined. Transfer the bowl mixture into the air fryer baking dish and then place the dish in the air fryer. Air Fry the food at 325 degrees F for 16 minutes. Serve and enjoy.
Nutritional information: Calories 569; Fat 48.7 g; Total Carbs 6.2 g; Sugar 1.5 g; Net Carbs 5g; Protein 26.8 g; Fiber 133 g

Garlic Mushrooms

Prep time: 10 minutes | Cook time: 20 minutes | Serves: 8

2 lbs. mushrooms, sliced	¼ cup coconut amino

2 garlic cloves, minced   3 tbsps. olive oil

Mix all the recipe ingredients in a suitable mixing bowl. Place the bowl in refrigerator to refrigerate the mixture for 2 hours. Transfer the marinated mushrooms into the "Air Fryer Basket" and Air Fry them at 350 degrees F for 20 minutes. Toss halfway through. Serve and enjoy.
Nutritional information: Calories 78; Fat 5.6 g; Total Carbs 5.5 g; Sugar 2 g; Net Carbs 6g; Protein 3.6 g; Fiber 0 g

Spicy Dip

Prep time: 5 minutes | Cook time: 5 minutes | Serves: 6

12 oz. hot peppers, chopped   Black pepper, to taste
1 ½ cups apple cider vinegar   Salt, to taste

Add all the recipe ingredients into the air fryer baking dish and stir well. Place the dish in the air fryer and Air Fry the food at 380 degrees F for 5 minutes. When cooked, transfer the pepper mixture into the blender and blend until smooth. Serve with the food you like.
Nutritional information: Calories 35; Fat 0.3 g; Total Carbs 5.6 g; Sugar 3.3 g; Net Carbs 2g; Protein 1.1 g; Fiber 0 g

Onion Dip

Prep time: 10 minutes | Cook time: 30 minutes | Serves: 8

2 lbs. onion, chopped   Black pepper, to taste
½ tsp. baking soda   Salt, to taste
6 tbsp. butter, softened

Melt butter in a suitable pan over medium heat. Add onion and baking soda and sauté for 5 minutes. Transfer the onion mixture into the air fryer baking dish. Place the dish in the air fryer and then Air Fry the food at 370 degrees F for 25 minutes. Serve and enjoy.
Nutritional information: Calories 122; Fat 8.8 g; Total Carbs 10.6 g; Sugar 4.8 g; Net Carbs 6g; Protein 1.3 g; Fiber 23 g

Carrot Dip

Prep time: 10 minutes | Cook time: 15 minutes | Serving: 6

2 cups carrots, grated   1 tbsp. chives, chopped
¼ tsp. cayenne pepper   Black pepper, to taste
4 tbsp. butter, melted   Salt, to taste

Add all the recipe ingredients into the air fryer baking dish and stir well. Place the dish in the air fryer and Air Fry the mixture at 380 degrees F for 15 minutes. Transfer cook carrot mixture into the blender and blend until smooth. Serve with the food you like.
Nutritional information: Calories 83; Fat 7.7 g; Total Carbs 3.7 g; Sugar 1.8 g; Net Carbs 5g; Protein 0.4 g; Fiber 20 g

Stuffed Mushrooms

Prep time: 10 minutes | Cook time: 10 minutes | Serving: 12

24 oz. mushrooms, cut stems   ½ bell pepper, diced
½ cup sour cream   ½ onion, diced
1 cup cheddar cheese, shredded   2 bacon slices, diced
1 small carrot, diced

Chop mushroom stems finely. Spray suitable pan with some

cooking spray and heat over medium heat. Add chopped mushrooms, bacon, carrot, onion, and bell pepper into the pan and cook until tender. Remove pan from heat. Add cheese and sour cream into the cooked vegetables and stir well. Stuff vegetable mixture into the mushroom cap and place them into the Air Fryer Basket. Cook the stuffed mushrooms at 350 degrees F for 8 minutes. Serve and enjoy.
Nutritional information: Calories 93; Fat 6.6 g; Total Carbs 3.7 g; Sugar 1.7 g; Net Carbs 4g; Protein 5.7 g; Fiber 8 g

Sesame Okra

Prep time: 10 minutes | Cook time: 4 minutes | Serving: 4

11 oz. okra, wash and chop   1 tbsp. sesame oil
1 egg, lightly beaten   ¼ tsp. pepper
1 tsp. sesame seeds   ½ tsp. salt

In a suitable bowl, whisk the egg with pepper, and salt. Add okra into the whisked egg Sprinkle with sesame seeds. Stir okra well. Spray the "Air Fryer Basket" with some cooking spray. Place okra pieces into the "Air Fryer Basket" and Air Fry them at 400 degrees F for 4 minutes. Serve and enjoy.
Nutritional information: Calories 82; Total Carbs 6.2 g; Net Carbs 6g; Protein 3 g; Fat 5 g; Sugar 1.2 g; Fiber 1 g

Caraway Bread

Prep time: 15 minutes | Cook time: 30 minutes | Serves: 10

3 cups whole-wheat flour   ¼ cup chilled butter, cubed
1 tbsp. sugar   into small pieces
2 tsps. caraway seeds   1 large egg, beaten
1 tsp. baking soda   1½ cups buttermilk
1 tsp. sea salt

In a suitable bowl, mix the flour, sugar, caraway seeds, baking soda and salt and mix well. With a pastry cutter, add in the butter flour until coarse crumbs like mixture is formed. Make a small-well in the center of the dry flour mixture. In the well, add the egg, followed by the buttermilk and with a spatula, mix well. With floured hand, shape the dough into a ball. Place the prepared dough onto a floured surface and lightly need it. Shape the dough into a 6-inch ball. With a serrated knife, score an X on the top of the dough. Arrange the dough in lightly greased the "Air Fryer Basket" and insert in the air fryer. Cook the food at 350 degrees F for 30 minutes on Air Crisp mode. Carefully, invert the bread onto wire rack to cool completely before slicing. Cut the bread into desired-sized slices and serve.
Nutritional information: Calories 205; Total Carbs 31.8 g; Net Carbs 6g; Protein 5.9 g; Fat 5 g; Sugar 1.2 g; Fiber 4 g

Baguette Bread

Prep time: 15 minutes | Cook time: 20 minutes | Serves: 8

¾ cup warm water   ½ cup whole-wheat flour
¾ tsp. quick yeast   ½ cup oat flour
½ tsp. demerara sugar   1¼ tsp. salt
1 cup bread flour

In a suitable bowl, add the warm water, yeast and sugar. Add the bread flour and salt and mix until a stiff dough form. Put the dough onto a floured surface and with your hands, knead until smooth and elastic. Now, shape the dough into a ball. Place the dough into a slightly oiled bowl and turn to coat well. With a plastic wrap, cover the bowl and place in a warm place for 1 hour or until doubled in size. With your hands, punch down the dough and form into a long slender loaf. Place the loaf onto a lightly greased baking pan and set aside in warm place, uncovered, for 30 minutes Cook the loaf at 450 degrees F for 20 minutes on Bake mode. Carefully, invert the bread onto wire rack to cool completely before slicing. Cut the bread into desired-sized slices and serve.

Nutritional information: Calories 114; Total Carbs 22.8 g; Net Carbs 6g; Protein 3.8 g; Fat 5 g; Sugar 1.2 g; Fiber 4 g

Yogurt Bread

Prep time: 20 minutes | Cook time: 40 minutes | Serves: 10

1½ cups warm water, divided	3 cups all-purpose flour
1½ tsp. active dry yeast	1 cup plain Greek yogurt
1 tsp. sugar	2 tsps. kosher salt

Add ½ cup of the warm water, yeast and sugar in a stand mixer's bowl, fitted with the dough hook attachment and mix well. Set aside for 5 minutes Add the flour, yogurt, and salt and mix on medium-low speed until the dough comes together. Then, mix on medium speed for 5 minutes Place the dough into a bowl. With a plastic wrap, cover the bowl and place in a warm place for 2-3 hours or until doubled in size. Transfer the dough onto a lightly floured surface and shape into a smooth ball. Place the dough onto a greased baking paper-lined rack. With a kitchen towel, cover the dough and let rest for 15 minutes With a very sharp knife, cut a 4x½-inch deep cut down the center of the dough. Cook the food at 325 degrees F for 40 minutes on Roast mode. Carefully, invert the bread onto wire rack to cool completely before slicing. Cut the bread into desired-sized slices and serve.

Nutritional information: Calories 157; Total Carbs 31 g; Net Carbs 2g; Protein 5.5 g; Fat 5 g; Sugar 1.2 g; Fiber 1 g

Sweet Date Bread

Prep time: 15 minutes | Cook time: 22 minutes | Serves: 10

2½ cup dates, pitted and chopped	½ cup brown sugar
¼ cup butter	1 tsp. baking powder
1 cup hot water	1 tsp. baking soda
1½ cups flour	½ tsp. salt
	1 egg

In a suitable bowl, add the dates, butter and top with the hot water. Set aside for 5 minutes In another bowl, mix the flour, brown sugar, baking powder, baking soda, and salt. In the same bowl of dates, mix well the flour mixture, and egg Grease a baking pan. Place the prepared mixture into the prepared pan. Cook the mixture at 340 degrees F for 22 minutes on Air Crisp mode. Arrange the pan in "Air Fryer Basket" and insert in the air fryer. Carefully, invert the bread onto wire rack to cool completely before slicing. Cut the bread into desired-sized slices and serve.

Nutritional information: Calories 269; Total Carbs 55.1 g; Net Carbs 3g; Protein 3.6 g; Fat 5 g; Sugar 1.2 g; Fiber 41 g

Date Walnut Bread

Prep time: 15 minutes | Cook time: 35 minutes | Serves: 5

1 cup dates, pitted and sliced	½ tsp. baking powder
¾ cup walnuts, chopped	½ tsp. baking soda
1 tbsp. instant coffee powder	½ cup condensed milk
1 tbsp. hot water	½ cup butter, softened
1¼ cups plain flour	½ tsp. vanilla essence
¼ tsp. salt	

In a suitable bowl, add the dates, butter and top with the hot water. Set aside for 30 minutes Dry out well and set aside. In

a suitable bowl, add the coffee powder and hot water and mix well. In another suitable bowl, mix the flour, baking powder, baking soda and salt. In the third bowl, add the condensed milk and butter and beat until smooth. Add the flour mixture, coffee mixture and vanilla essence and mix well. Fold in dates and ½ cup of walnut. Line a baking pan with a lightly greased baking paper. Place the prepared mixture into the prepared pan and sprinkle with the remaining walnuts. Arrange the pan in "Air Fryer Basket" and insert in the air fryer. Cook the mixture at 320 degrees F for 35 minutes on Air Crisp mode. Carefully, invert the bread onto wire rack to cool completely before slicing. Cut the bread into desired-sized slices and serve.

Nutritional information: Calories 593; Total Carbs 69.4 g; Net Carbs 5g; Protein 11.2 g; Fat 32.6 g; Sugar 1.2 g; Fiber 1 g

Banana Bread

Prep time: 15 minutes | Cook time: 30 minutes | Serves: 4

1 egg	2 tbsps. canola oil
1 ripe banana, peeled and mashed	2 tbsps. brown sugar
	¾ cup plain flour
¼ cup milk	½ tsp. baking soda

Line a very small baking pan with a greased baking paper. In a suitable bowl, add the egg and banana and beat well. Add the milk, oil and sugar and beat well. Add the dry flour and baking soda and mix until combined. Place the prepared mixture into prepared pan. Arrange the pan in "Air Fryer Basket" and insert in the air fryer. Cook the mixture at 320 degrees F for 30 minutes almost on Air Crisp mode. Carefully, invert the bread onto wire rack to cool completely before slicing. Cut the bread into desired-sized slices and serve.

Nutritional information: Calories 214; Fat 8.7 g; Total Carbs 29.9 g; Net Carbs 3g; Protein 4.6 g; Fat 5 g; Sugar 1.2 g; Fiber 4 g

Banana Almonds Bread

Prep time: 15 minutes | Cook time: 25 minutes | Serves: 10

1½ cups self-rising flour	2 medium eggs
¼ tsp. bicarbonate of soda	3½ oz. almonds, chopped
5 tbsp. plus 1 tsp. butter	2 cups bananas, peeled and mashed
⅔ cup plus ½ tbsp. caster sugar	

In a suitable bowl, mix the flour and bicarbonate of soda. In another bowl, add the butter, and sugar and beat until pale and fluffy. Add the eggs, one at a time along with a little flour and mix well. Stir in the remaining flour and almonds. Add the bananas and mix well. Grease a loaf pan. Place the prepared mixture into the prepared pan. Arrange the pan in "Air Fryer Basket" and insert in the air fryer. Cook the mixture at 355 degrees F on Air Crisp mode for 10 minutes in Air Crisp mode. When the time is up, set the cooking temperature at 340 degrees F and resume cooking the mixture for 15 minutes. Carefully, invert the bread onto wire rack to cool completely before slicing. Cut the bread into desired-sized slices and serve.

Nutritional information: Calories 270; Fat 12.8 g; Total Carbs 35.5 g; Net Carbs 3g; Protein 5.8 g; Sugar 1.2 g; Fiber 1g

Banana Raisin Bread

Prep time: 15 minutes | Cook time: 40 minutes | Serves: 6

1½ cups cake flour	½ cup vegetable oil
1 tsp. baking soda	2 eggs
½ tsp. ground cinnamon	½ cup sugar
Salt, to taste	½ tsp. vanilla extract

3 medium bananas, peeled and
mashed

½ cup raisins, chopped

In a suitable bowl, mix the flour, baking soda, cinnamon, and salt. In another bowl, beat well eggs and oil. Add the sugar, vanilla extract, and bananas and beat well. Add the dry flour mixture and stir well. Place the prepared mixture into a lightly greased baking pan and sprinkle with raisins. With a piece of foil, cover the pan loosely. Cook the mixture at 285 degrees F for 30 minutes on Bake mode. Arrange the pan in "Air Fryer Basket" and insert in the air fryer. After 30 minutes of cooking, adjust the cooking temperature to 285 degrees F and resume cooking the mixture for 10 minutes more. Carefully, invert the bread onto wire rack to cool completely before slicing. Cut the bread into desired-sized slices and serve.

Nutritional information: Calories 448; Fat 20.2 g; Total Carbs 63.9 g; Net Carbs 3g; Protein 6.1g; Sugar 1.2 g; Fiber 1g

Cinnamon Banana Bread

Prep time: 15 minutes | Cook time: 28 minutes | Serves: 5

1 medium ripe banana, peeled and mashed
1 large egg
1 tbsp. canola oil
1 tbsp. plain Greek yogurt
¼ tsp. pure vanilla extract

½ cup all-purpose flour
¼ cup granulated white sugar
¼ tsp. ground cinnamon
¼ tsp. baking soda
⅛ tsp. sea salt

In a suitable bowl, add the mashed banana, egg, oil, yogurt and vanilla and beat well. Add the sugar, flour, baking soda, cinnamon and salt and mix well. Place the prepared mixture into a lightly greased mini loaf pan. Arrange the pan in "Air Fryer Basket" and insert in the air fryer. Bake the mixture at 350 degrees F for 28 minutes. When done, place the pan onto the wire rack to cool for about 10 minutes. Carefully, invert the bread onto wire rack to cool completely before slicing. Cut the bread into desired-sized slices and serve.

Nutritional information: Calories 145; Fat 4 g; Total Carbs 25 g; Net Carbs 4g; Protein 3 g; Sugar 1.2 g; Fiber 1g

Sour Cream Banana Bread

Prep time: 15 minutes | Cook time: 37 minutes | Serves: 8

¾ cup all-purpose flour
¼ tsp. baking soda
¼ tsp. salt
2 ripe bananas, peeled and mashed

½ cup granulated sugar
¼ cup sour cream
¼ cup vegetable oil
1 large egg
½ tsp. pure vanilla extract

In a suitable bowl, mix the flour, baking soda and salt. In another bowl, add the bananas, egg, sugar, sour cream, oil and vanilla and beat well. Add the flour mixture and mix well. Place the prepared mixture into a lightly greased pan. Cook the mixture at 310 degrees F on Air Crisp mode for 37 minutes almost. When done, place the pan onto the wire rack to cool for about 10 minutes. Carefully, invert the bread onto wire rack to cool completely before slicing. Cut the bread into desired-sized slices and serve.

Nutritional information: Calories 201; Fat 9.2g; Total Carbs 28.6g; Net Carbs 5g; Protein 2.6g; Sugar 1.2 g; Fiber 1g

Peanut Butter Banana Bread

Prep time: 15 minutes | Cook time: 40 minutes | Serves: 6

1 cup plus 1 tbsp. all-purpose flour

¼ tsp. baking soda
1 tsp. baking powder

¼ tsp. salt
1 large egg
⅓ cup granulated sugar
¼ cup canola oil
2 tbsps. creamy peanut butter
2 tbsps. sour cream

1 tsp. vanilla extract
2 medium ripe bananas, peeled and mashed
¾ cup walnuts, roughly chopped

In a suitable bowl and mix the flour, baking powder, baking soda, and salt together. In another suitable bowl, add the egg, sugar, oil, peanut butter, sour cream, and vanilla extract and beat well. Add the bananas and beat well. Add the flour mixture and mix well. Gently, fold in the walnuts. Place the prepared mixture into a lightly greased pan. Arrange the pan in "Air Fryer Basket" and insert in the air fryer. Cook the mixture at 330 degrees F for 40 minutes on Air Crisp mode. When done, place the pan onto the wire rack to cool for about 10 minutes. Carefully, invert the bread onto wire rack to cool completely before slicing. Cut the bread into desired-sized slices and serve.

Nutritional information: Calories 384; Fat 23 g; Total Carbs 39.3 g; Net Carbs 8g; Protein 8.9 g; Sugar 1.2 g; Fiber 1g

Chocolate Banana Bread

Prep time: 15 minutes | Cook time: 20 minutes | Serves: 8

2 cups flour
½ tsp. baking soda
½ tsp. baking powder
½ tsp. salt
¾ cup sugar
⅓ cup butter, softened

3 eggs
1 tbsp. vanilla extract
1 cup milk
½ cup bananas, peeled and mashed
1 cup chocolate chips

In a suitable bowl, mix the baking soda, flour, baking powder, and salt. In another large bowl, add the butter, and sugar and beat until light and fluffy. Add the eggs, and vanilla extract and whisk well. Add the flour mixture and mix well. Add the milk, and mashed bananas and mix well. Gently, fold in the chocolate chips. Place the prepared mixture into a lightly greased loaf pan. Arrange the pan in "Air Fryer Basket" and insert in the air fryer. Cook the mixture at 360 degrees F for 20 minutes on Air Crisp mode. Place the hot pan onto a wire rack to cool for 10 minutes. Carefully, invert the bread onto wire rack to cool completely before slicing. Cut the bread into desired-sized slices and serve.

Nutritional information: Calories 416; Fat 16.5 g; Total Carbs 59.2 g; Net Carbs 6g; Protein 8.1g; Sugar 1.2 g; Fiber 1g

Pineapple Sticky Ribs

Prep time: 10 minutes | Cook time: 27 minutes | Serves: 4

2 lbs. cut spareribs
7 oz. salad dressing
1 (5-oz) can pineapple juice

2 cups water
Garlic salt to taste
Salt and black pepper

Rub the ribs with black pepper and salt, and place them in a saucepan. Pour water and cook the ribs for 12 minutes on high heat. Dry out the ribs and arrange them in the air fryer; sprinkle with garlic salt. Cook the food for 15minutes at 390 degrees F on Air Fry mode. Prepare the sauce by combining the salad dressing and the pineapple juice. Serve the ribs drizzled with the sauce.

Nutritional information: Calories 316; Fat 3.1 g; Total Carbs 1.9 g; Net Carbs 2g; Protein 5 g; Sugar 1.2 g; Fiber 1g

Egg Roll with Prawns

Prep time: 10 minutes | Cook time: 20 minutes | Serves: 4

2 tbsps. vegetable oil
1-inch piece fresh ginger,

grated
1 tbsp. minced garlic

1 carrot, cut into strips
¼ cup chicken broth
2 tbsps. reduced-sodium soy sauce
1 tbsp. sugar

1 cup shredded Napa cabbage
1 tbsp. sesame oil
8 cooked prawns, minced
1 egg
8 egg roll wrappers

In a skillet, heat vegetable oil over high heat, and cook ginger and garlic for 40 seconds, until fragrant. Stir in carrot and Air Fry for 2 minutes almost. Pour in chicken broth, soy sauce, and sugar and bring to a boil. Add cabbage and let simmer until softened, for 4 minutes. Remove the hot skillet from the heat and stir in sesame oil. Let cool for 15 minutes. Strain cabbage mixture, and fold in minced prawns. Whisk an egg in a suitable bowl. Fill each egg roll wrapper with prawn mixture, arranging the prepared mixture just below the center. Fold the top and bottom part of the wrapper over the filling and tuck under. Fold in both sides and tightly roll up. Use the whisked egg to seal the wrapper. Repeat until all egg rolls are ready. Place the rolls into a greased Air Fryer Basket, grease them with oil and Air Fry for 12 minutes at 370 degrees F, turning once halfway through.
Nutritional information: Calories 215; Fat 7.9 g; Total Carbs 6.7 g; Net Carbs 6g; Protein 8g; Sugar 1.2 g; Fiber 1g

Sesame Chicken Wings

Prep time: 10 minutes | Cook time: 40 minutes | Serves: 4

1-lb. chicken wings
1 cup soy sauce, divided
½ cup brown sugar
½ cup apple cider vinegar
2 tbsps. fresh ginger, minced

2 tbsps. fresh garlic, minced
1 tsp. ground black pepper
2 tbsps. cornstarch
2 tbsps. cold water
1 tsp. sesame seeds

In a suitable bowl, add chicken wings, and pour in half cup soy sauce. Refrigerate the coated chicken wings for 20 minutes; dry them out and pat them dry. Arrange the wings to the baking pan in the air fryer basket and Air Fry them for 30 minutes at 380 degrees F, turning once halfway through. Make sure you check them towards the end to avoid overcooking. In a skillet, add the sugar, half cup soy sauce, vinegar, ginger, garlic, and black pepper, cook them for about 4 to 6 minutes over medium heat until sauce has reduced slightly. Dissolve 2 tablespoons of cornstarch in cold water, in a suitable bowl, and stir in the slurry into the sauce, until it thickens, for 2 minutes almost. Pour the sauce over wings and sprinkle with sesame seeds.
Nutritional information: Calories 413; Fat 8.3 g; Total Carbs 7 g; Net Carbs 6g; Protein 8.3 g; Sugar 1.2 g; Fiber 1g

Chicken Nuggets with Parmesan Cheese

Prep time: 5 minutes | Cook time: 20 minutes | Serves: 4

1 lb. chicken breast, boneless, skinless, cubed
½ tsp. ground black pepper
¼ tsp. kosher salt
¼ tsp. seasoned salt

2 tbsps. olive oil
5 tbsps. plain breadcrumbs
2 tbsps. panko breadcrumbs
2 tbsps. grated Parmesan cheese

At 380 degrees F, preheat your Air Fryer and grease. Grease a suitable cooking pan. Season the chicken with pepper, kosher salt, and seasoned salt; set aside. In a suitable bowl, pour olive oil. In a separate bowl, add crumb, and Parmesan cheese. Place the chicken pieces in the oil to coat, then dip into breadcrumb mixture, and transfer to the prepare cooking pan. Work in batches if needed. Lightly spray chicken with some cooking spray. Cook the chicken pieces at 380 degrees F on Air Fry mode for 10 minutes, flipping once halfway through. Cook until golden and no pinker on the inside. When done, serve and enjoy.
Nutritional information: Calories 312; Fat 8.9 g; Total Carbs 7

g; Net Carbs 4g; Protein 10 g; Sugar 1.2 g; Fiber 1g

Butternut Squash with Thyme

Prep time: 5 minutes | Cook time: 15 minutes | Serves: 4

2 cups butternut squash, peeled, cubed
1 tbsp. olive oil
¼ tsp. salt

¼ tsp. black pepper
¼ tsp. dried thyme
1 tbsp. chopped fresh parsley

In a suitable bowl, add squash, oil, salt, pepper, and thyme, and toss until squash is well-coated. Place squash in the air fryer and Air Fry for 14 minutes at 360 degrees F. When ready, sprinkle with freshly chopped parsley and serve chilled.
Nutritional information: Calories 219; Fat 4.3 g; Total Carbs 9.4 g; Net Carbs 6g; Protein 7.8 g; Sugar 1.2 g; Fiber 1g

Mouthwatering Squash Bites

Prep time: 8-10 minutes | Cook time: 20 minutes | Serves: 5-6

1 ½ pounds winter squash, peeled and make chunks
¼ cup dark brown sugar
2 tablespoons sage, chopped
Zest of 1 small-sized lemon

2 tablespoons coconut oil, melted
A coarse pinch salt
A pinch pepper
⅛ teaspoon allspice, ground

Prepare your clean air fryer. Preheat the air fryer for 4 to 5 minutes at 350 degrees F. Oil or spray the air-frying basket lightly. In addition to the squash, mix the other ingredients thoroughly in a medium-size bowl. Let the squash chunks be covered with the mixture. Arrange the chunks to the air-frying basket and place the basket to the air fryer. Cook the food for 10 minutes. When the time is up, increase temperature to 400 degrees F and cook for 8 more minutes. Once done, serve warm!
Nutritional information: Calories: 110; Fat: 4.7g; Total Carbs: 18g; Net Carbs: 9.5g; Fiber: 2g; Sugars: 5.9g; Protein: 1g

Mayo Tortellini

Prep time: 10 minutes | Cook time: 10 minutes | Serves: 4-5

½ cup flour
½ teaspoon dried oregano
1 ½ cups breadcrumbs
¾ cup mayonnaise

2 tablespoons mustard
1 egg
2 tablespoons olive oil
2 cups cheese tortellini, frozen

Prepare your clean air fryer. Preheat the air fryer for 4 to 5 minutes at 355 degrees F. Let the flour and oregano be combined in a bowl, and the breadcrumbs and olive oil be combined in another bowl. Mix the mustard and mayonnaise in a bowl of medium size, and set aside. Thoroughly whisk the egg in another same-sized bowl. Add the tortellini to the egg mixture, then into the flour, then into the egg again. At last, add the breadcrumbs to coat well. Arrange the basket in the air fryer with the prepared tortellini in it. Cook for 10 minutes until turn golden. When done, serve with the mayonnaise.
Nutritional information: Calories: 558; Fat: 24.6g; Total Carbs: 70.8g; Net Carbs: 0g; Fiber: 2.5g; Sugars: 4.7g; Protein: 14.6g

Squash Chips with Sauce

Prep time: 15 minutes | Cook time: 25 minutes | Serves: 4

½ cup seasoned breadcrumbs
½ cup Parmesan cheese, grated

Sea salt and ground black pepper, to taste

¼-teaspoon oregano
2 yellow squash, cut into slices
½ tablespoon grapeseed oil
Sauce:
½ cup Greek-style yogurt

1 tablespoon fresh cilantro, chopped
1 garlic clove, minced
Freshly ground black pepper, to your liking

Thoroughly combine the seasoned breadcrumbs, Parmesan, salt, black pepper, and oregano in a prepared shallow bowl. Dip the yellow squash slices in the prepared batter and press to make it adhere. Place the squash slices in the basket of your air fryer and brush them with grapeseed oil. Cook at 400 degrees F for 12 minutes. Shake the basket periodically to ensure even cooking. Work in batches. Meanwhile, whisk the sauce ingredients; place in your refrigerator until ready to serve. Enjoy!
Nutritional information: Calories: 117; Fat: 7.1g; Total Carbs: 8g; Net Carbs: 3.5g; Fiber: 1.3g; Sugars: 4.5g; Protein: 5g

Air Fried Shrimp & Bacon

Prep time: 10 minutes | Cook time: 10 minutes | Serves: 4-6

16 ounces sliced bacon
20 ounces peeled shrimp,

deveined

Prepare your clean air fryer. Preheat the air fryer for 4 to 5 minutes at 390 degrees F. Make the shrimps under the bacon regularly. Put them in the refrigerator and cool for 15 to 20 minutes. After that, take out the shrimps and place them in the air-frying basket. Let the shrimps be cooked for 6 minutes in the air fryer. When the time is up, serve and enjoy!
Nutritional information: Calories: 482; Fat: 35.3g; Total Carbs: 4.5g; Net Carbs: 0.5g; Fiber: 0.1g; Sugars: 0g; Protein: 34.4g

Sprouts Wraps Appetizer

Prep time: 5 minutes | Cook time: 20 minutes | Serves: 12

12 bacon strips
12 Brussels sprouts

A drizzle of olive oil

Use a bacon strip to wrap each Brussels. Brush the wraps with olive oil before arranging them to the air fryer basket.
Cook the wraps for 20 minutes at 30 degrees F. When done, serve as an appetizer.
Nutritional information: Calories: 108; Fat: 9.1g; Total Carbs: 1g; Net Carbs: 0g; Fiber: 0.7g; Sugars: 0.4g; Protein: 4.7g

Bacon Pickle Spear Rolls

Prep time: 5 minutes | Cook time: 20 minutes | Serves: 4

4 dill pickle spears, sliced in half

8 bacon slices, halved
1 cup avocado mayonnaise

Use a bacon slice to wrap a pickle spear. Arrange the wraps in the basket of air fryer and cook them for 20 minutes at 400 degrees F. After dividing into bowls and serve as a snack with the mayonnaise.
Nutritional information: Calories: 213; Fat: 16g; Total Carbs: 2g; Net Carbs: 0.5g; Fiber: 0.8g; Sugars: 0.7g; Protein: 14.3g

Zucchini Chips with Cheese

Prep time: 10 minutes | Cook time: 13 minutes | Serves: 8

2 zucchinis, thinly sliced
4 tablespoons almond flour

2 oz. Parmesan
2 eggs, beaten

½ teaspoon white pepper

Cooking spray

Prepare your clean air fryer and preheat it to 355 degrees F. Thoroughly mix up almond flour, Parmesan and white pepper in a large bowl. After that, dip the zucchini slices in the egg and coat in the almond flour mixture. Place the prepared zucchini slices in the preheated air fryer and cook them for 10 minutes. Flip the vegetables on another side and cook them for 3 minutes more or until crispy. When the time is up, serve and enjoy.
Nutritional information: Calories: 114; Fat: 7.1g; Total Carbs: 4.9g; Net Carbs: 1g; Fiber: 1.5g; Sugars: 1.9g; Protein: 9.3g

Chicken Bites with Coconut

Prep time: 5 minutes | Cook time: 20 minutes | Serves: 4

2 teaspoons garlic powder
2 eggs
Salt and black pepper to the taste

¾ cup coconut flakes
Cooking spray
1 pound chicken breasts, skinless, boneless and cubed

In a bowl, put the coconut in and mix the eggs with garlic powder, salt and pepper in a second one. Dredge the chicken cubes in eggs and then in coconut. Arrange all the prepared chicken cubes to the basket. Grease with cooking spray and cook them at 370 degrees F for 20 minutes. When cooked, place the chicken bites on a platter and serve as an appetizer.
Nutritional information: Calories: 306; Fat: 15.8g; Total Carbs: 3.5g; Net Carbs: 0.5g; Fiber: 1.5g; Sugars: 1.4g; Protein: 36.3g

Delicious Mushroom Pizzas

Prep time: 10 minutes | Cook time: 7 minutes | Serves: 6

6 cremini mushroom caps
3 oz. Parmesan, grated
1 tablespoon olive oil

½ tomato, chopped
½ teaspoon dried basil
1 teaspoon ricotta cheese

Oil the mushroom caps and arrange them in the air fryer. Sprinkle the mushroom caps with olive oil and put in the air fryer basket in one layer. Cook them for 3 minutes at 400 degrees F. After this, mix up the ricotta cheese and tomato. Fill the mushroom caps with tomato mixture. Then top them with parmesan and sprinkle with dried basil. Cook the mushroom pizzas for 4 minutes at 400 degrees F. When done, serve and enjoy.
Nutritional information: Calories: 132; Fat: 8.2g; Total Carbs: 5g; Net Carbs: 2g; Fiber: 0.1g; Sugars: 1.7g; Protein: 10.1g

Bacon with Chocolate Coating

Prep time: 5 minutes | Cook time: 10 minutes | Serves: 4

4 bacon slices, halved
1 cup dark chocolate, melted A

pinch of pink salt

Make each bacon slice be coated some chocolate and then sprinkle pink salt over them. Arrange them in the cooking tray of your air fryer. Cook at 350 degrees F for 10 minutes. When cooked, serve as a snack.
Nutritional information: Calories: 327; Fat: 20.4g; Total Carbs: 25g; Net Carbs: 16g; Fiber: 1.4g; Sugars: 21.6g; Protein: 10.3g

Bacon Smokies with Tomato Sauce

Prep time: 15 minutes | Cook time: 10 minutes | Serves: 10

12 oz. pork and beef smokies

3 oz. bacon, sliced

1 teaspoon keto tomato sauce
1 teaspoon Erythritol

1 teaspoon avocado oil
½ teaspoon cayenne pepper

Use the cayenne pepper and tomato sauce to sprinkle the smokies, then repeat the step with the Erythritol and olive oil. After that, wrap every smokie in the bacon and use the toothpick to secure each roll. Arrange the bacon smokies in the air fryer and cook for 10 minutes at 400 degrees F. During cooking, to avoid over cooking, shake them gently. When done, serve and enjoy.
Nutritional information: Calories: 287; Fat: 24g; Total Carbs: 2g; Net Carbs: 0.5g; Fiber: 0g; Sugars: 2.4g; Protein: 14g

Simple Pizza Bites

Prep time: 15 minutes | Cook time: 3 minutes | Serves:10

10 Mozzarella cheese slices   10 pepperoni slices

Line the air fryer pan with baking paper and put Mozzarella cheese slices in it. Cook them for 3 minutes at 400 degrees F or until melted. Once cooked, remove the cheese from the air fryer and cool them to room temperature. Put the pepperoni slices on the cheese and fold the cheese in the shape of turnovers. Enjoy!
Nutritional information: Calories: 107; Fat: 7.4g; Total Carbs: 1g; Net Carbs: 0g; Fiber: 0g; Sugars: 0g; Protein: 9.3g

Crispy Paprika Chips

Prep time: 2 minutes | Cook time: 5 minutes | Serves: 4

8 ounces' cheddar cheese, shredded

1 teaspoon sweet paprika

Divide the cheese in small heaps in a suitable pan. After sprinkling the paprika on top, arrange the cheeses to the air fryer and cook at 400 degrees F for 5 minutes. Cool the chips down before serving them.
Nutritional information: Calories: 139; Fat: 11.3g; Total Carbs: 0.7g; Net Carbs: 1g; Fiber: 0.2g; Sugars: 0.2g; Protein: 8.6g

Mexican Beef Muffins with Tomato Sauce

Prep time: 10 minutes | Cook time: 15 minutes | Serves:4

1 cup ground beef
1 teaspoon taco seasonings
2 oz. Mexican blend cheese,

shredded
1 teaspoon tomato sauce
Cooking spray

Thoroughly mix up ground beef and taco seasonings in a mixing bowl. Spray the muffin molds with cooking spray. Transfer the ground beef mixture in the muffin molds. Place the cheese and tomato sauce on the top. Transfer the muffin molds in the prepared air fryer and cook them for 15 minutes at 375 degrees F. When cooked, serve and enjoy.
Nutritional information: Calories: 202; Fat: 10.1g; Total Carbs: 0.7g; Net Carbs: 0g; Fiber: 0g; Sugars: 0.7g; Protein: 25.5g

Delectable Chaffles

Prep time: 10 minutes | Cook time: 25 minutes | Serves:4

4 eggs, beaten
2 oz. bacon, chopped, cooked
1 cucumber, pickled, grated

2 oz. Cheddar cheese, shredded
¼ teaspoon salt
½ teaspoon ground black

pepper   Cooking spray

The chaffle batter should be cooked. Spray the air fryer pan with cooking spray. Mix up eggs, bacon, pickled cucumber, cheese, salt, and ground black pepper in a mixing bowl. Whisk the mixture gently. Pour ¼ part of the liquid on the pan. Arrange the pan to the air fryer and cook the chaffle for 6 minutes at 400 degrees F. When cooked, transfer the cooked chaffle in the plate. Repeat the same steps with the remaining chaffle batter and you should get 4 chaffles. Enjoy.
Nutritional information: Calories: 209; Fat: 15.1g; Total Carbs: 3g; Net Carbs: 1g; Fiber: 0.5g; Sugars: 1.7g; Protein: 14.8g

Coconut Granola with Almond

Prep time: 10 minutes | Cook time: 12 minutes | Serves:4

1 teaspoon monk fruit
1 teaspoon almond butter
1 teaspoon coconut oil
2 tablespoons almonds, chopped
1 teaspoon pumpkin puree
½ teaspoon pumpkin pie spices

2 tablespoons coconut flakes
2 tablespoons pumpkin seeds, crushed
1 teaspoon hemp seeds
1 teaspoon flax seeds
Cooking spray

Mix up almond butter and coconut oil in a big bowl and then microwave the mixture until melted. Continue to mix up the pumpkin spices, pumpkin seeds, monk fruit, coconut flakes, hemp seeds and flax seeds in another suitable bowl. Add the pumpkin puree and melted coconut oil, then stir the mixture until homogenous. Arrange the pumpkin mixture on the baking paper and make the shape of square, then cut the square on the serving bars and transfer in the air fryer. Cook them for 12 minutes at 350 degrees F. Once done, serve and enjoy.
Nutritional information: Calories: 88; Fat: 7.9g; Total Carbs: 3g; Net Carbs: 1g; Fiber: 1.4g; Sugars: 0.6g; Protein: 2.8g

Olives Fritters with Zucchinis

Prep time: 5 minutes | Cook time: 12 minutes | Serves: 6

Cooking spray
½ cup parsley, chopped
1 egg
½ cup almond flour

Salt and black pepper to the taste 3 spring onions, chopped
½ cup Kalamata olives, pitted and minced 3 zucchinis, grated

In addition to the cooking spray, thoroughly mix up the other ingredients in a bowl and then shape medium fritters. Grease the fritters with cooking spray after placing them in the basket of your air fryer. Cook for 12 minutes at 380 degrees F, flipping halfway through. Serve them as an appetizer.
Nutritional information: Calories: 59; Fat: 4.6g; Total Carbs: 2g; Net Carbs: 0.5g; Fiber: 1.2g; Sugars: 0.1g; Protein: 2.5g

Delicious Zucchini Crackers

Prep time: 15 minutes | Cook time: 20 minutes | Serves:12

1 cup zucchini, grated
2 tablespoons flax meal
1 teaspoon salt
3 tablespoons almond flour
¼ teaspoon baking powder

¼ teaspoon chili flakes
1 tablespoon xanthan gum
1 tablespoon butter, softened
1 egg, beaten
Cooking spray

Squeeze the zucchini to remove the vegetable juice and transfer to a large bowl. Thoroughly mix up the flax meal, salt, almond flour, baking powder, chili flakes and xanthan gum. Add butter and egg. Knead the non- sticky dough. Place the mixture on the baking paper and cover with another baking paper. Roll up the dough into the flat square. After this, remove the baking paper from the dough surface. Cut it on medium size crackers. Line the air fryer basket with baking paper and put the crackers inside it. Spray them with cooking spray. Cook them for 20 minutes at 355 degrees F When the time is up, serve and enjoy.

Nutritional information: Calories: 62; Fat: 5.1g; Total Carbs: 2g; Net Carbs: 0.5g; Fiber: 1.2g; Sugars: 0.2g; Protein: 2.3g

Garlic Mushroom Bites

Prep time: 5 minutes | Cook time: 12 minutes | Serves: 6

Salt and black pepper to the taste	1 tablespoons basil, minced
1 ¼ cups coconut flour	½ pound mushrooms, minced
2 garlic clove, minced	1 egg, whisked

In addition to the cooking spray, thoroughly mix up other ingredients and shape medium balls out of this mix. Arrange the balls in the basket of your air fryer and grease them with cooking spray. Air fry at 350 degrees F for 6 minutes on each side. Serve as an appetizer.

Nutritional information: Calories: 90; Fat: 2.8g; Total Carbs: 12.5g; Net Carbs: 6g; Fiber: 6.6g; Sugars: 1.1g; Protein: 5.3g

Easy-to-Make Cheese Rounds

Prep time: 10 minutes | Cook time: 6 minutes | Serves:4

1 cup Cheddar cheese,	shredded

Preheat the air fryer to 400F. Line the air fryer basket with baking paper. Sprinkle the cheese on the baking paper in the shape of small rounds. Cook them for 6 minutes or until the cheese is melted and starts to be crispy. When the time is up, serve and enjoy!

Nutritional information: Calories: 114; Fat: 9.4g; Total Carbs: 0.4g; Net Carbs: 1g; Fiber: 0g; Sugars: 0.2g; Protein: 7g

Cheese Sticks with Coconut

Prep time: 10 minutes | Cook time: 4 minutes | Serves:4

1 egg, beaten	6 oz. Provolone cheese
4 tablespoons coconut flakes	Cooking spray
1 teaspoon ground paprika	

Cut the cheese into sticks. Dip every cheese stick in the beaten egg. After this, mix up coconut flakes and ground paprika. Coat the cheese sticks in the coconut mixture. Preheat the air fryer to 400F. Put the cheese sticks in the air fryer and spray them with cooking spray. Cook the meal for 2 minutes from each side. Cool them well before serving.

Nutritional information: Calories: 184; Fat: 14.2g; Total Carbs: 2g; Net Carbs: 0.5g; Fiber: 0.7g; Sugars: 0.7g; Protein: 12.5g

Avocado Balls

Prep time: 5 minutes | Cook time: 5 minutes | Serves: 4

1 avocado, peeled, pitted and mashed	1 tablespoon lime juice
¼ cup ghee, melted	2 tablespoons cilantro
garlic cloves, minced 2 spring onions, minced	A pinch of salt and black pepper
1 chili pepper, chopped	4 bacon slices, cooked and crumbled cooking spray

In addition to the cooking spray, mix the other ingredients well in a bowl and shape medium balls out of this mix. Grease the balls with cooking spray after placing them in the basket of your air fryer. Cook the balls at 370 degrees F for 5 minutes. Serve as a snack.

Nutritional information: Calories: 319; Fat: 30.5g; Total Carbs: 5g; Net Carbs: 2g; Fiber: 3.5g; Sugars: 0.3g; Protein: 8.1g

Fresh Shrimp Balls

Prep time: 5 minutes | Cook time: 15 minutes | Serves: 4

1 pound shrimp, peeled, deveined and minced	shredded
1 egg, whisked	½ cup coconut flour
3 tablespoons coconut,	1 tablespoon avocado oil
	1 tablespoon cilantro, chopped

In a bowl, mix all the ingredients well and shape medium balls out of this mix. Arrange the balls in your lined air fryer's basket. Cook the balls at 350 degrees F for 15 minutes. When done, you can serve as an appetizer.

Nutritional information: Calories: 228; Fat: 6.2g; Total Carbs: 12g; Net Carbs: 7g; Fiber: 6.5g; Sugars: 0.3g; Protein: 29.4g

Salmon Bites with Coconut

Prep time: 5 minutes | Cook time: 10 minutes | Serves: 12

2 avocados, peeled, pitted and mashed	2 tablespoons coconut cream
4 ounces smoked salmon, skinless, boneless and chopped	1 teaspoon avocado oil
	1 teaspoon dill, chopped
	A pinch of salt and black pepper

Mix all the ingredients well in a clean bowl. Shape medium balls out of this mix. Place the balls in the basket of your air fryer. Cook at 350 degrees F for 10 minutes. Serve as an appetizer.

Nutritional information: Calories: 171; Fat: 15.1g; Total Carbs: 6g; Net Carbs: 2.5g; Fiber: 4.6g; Sugars: 0.5g; Protein: 4.9g

Turmeric Chicken Cubes with Coriander

Prep time: 10 minutes | Cook time: 12 minutes | Serves: 6

8 oz. chicken fillet	½ teaspoon ground paprika
½ teaspoon ground black pepper	3 egg whites, whisked
½ teaspoon ground turmeric	4 tablespoons almond flour
¼ teaspoon ground coriander	Cooking spray

Mix up ground black pepper, turmeric, coriander, and paprika well in a shallow bowl. Chop the chicken fillet on the small cubes. Sprinkle them with spice mixture. Stir well and add egg white. Mix up the chicken and egg whites well. After that, coat every chicken cube with the almond flour. Preheat the air fryer to 375F. Arrange the chicken cubes to the basket of your air fryer and gently spray with cooking spray. Cook the chicken cubes for 7 minutes at 375 degrees F, then shake the chicken popcorn well and cook it for 5 minutes more. Once cooked, serve and enjoy!

Nutritional information: Calories: 110; Fat: 5.1g; Total Carbs: 1g; Net Carbs: 0g; Fiber: 0.7g; Sugars: 0.2g; Protein: 13.8g

Eggplant Chips

Prep time: 10 minutes | Cook time: 25 minutes | Serves:4

1 eggplant, sliced	1 teaspoon garlic powder

1 tablespoon olive oil

Mix the garlic powder and olive oil well. Brush every eggplant slice with a garlic powder mixture. Place the eggplant slices in the cooking pan of your air fryer. Cook them for 15 minutes at 400 degrees F. When the time is up, flip the eggplant slices and cook the other side for 10 minutes. Serve and enjoy!
Nutritional information: Calories: 61; Fat: 3.7g; Total Carbs: 7g; Net Carbs: 3g; Fiber: 4.1g; Sugars: 3.6g; Protein: 1.2g

Beef Meatballs with Chives

Prep time: 5 minutes | Cook time: 20 minutes | Serves: 6

1 pound beef meat, ground	pepper
1 teaspoon onion powder	2 tablespoons chives, chopped
1 teaspoon garlic powder	Cooking spray
A pinch of salt and black	

In addition to the cooking spray, mix the other ingredients well in a bowl and shape medium meatballs out of this mix. Place the balls in the basket of your air fryer and oil them. Cook for 20 minutes at 360 degrees F. When done, serve as an appetizer.
Nutritional information: Calories: 167; Fat: 6.5g; Total Carbs: 0.7g; Net Carbs: 0g; Fiber: 0.1g; Sugars: 0.3g; Protein: 24.9g

Pickles with Egg Wash

Prep time: 10 minutes | Cook time: 8 minutes | Serves:4

2 pickles, sliced	1 egg, beaten
1 tablespoon dried dill	2 tablespoons flax meal

Coat the sliced pickles with the egg, then sprinkle with the dried ill and flax meal. Arrange the pickles to the basket of your air fryer and cook for 8 minutes at 400 degrees F.
Nutritional information: Calories: 110; Fat: 5.1g; Total Carbs: 1.5g; Net Carbs: 1g; Fiber: 0.7g; Sugars: 0.2g; Protein: 13.8g

Simple Apple Chips

Prep time: 10 minutes | Cook time: 8 minutes | Serves: 3

3 medium apples, washed, cored, and thinly sliced	juice
Non-stick cooking spray	1 teaspoon cinnamon
½ cup freshly squeezed lemon	2 tablespoons avocado oil

Coat the apple slices with lemon juice and avocado oil lightly. Arrange the apple slices to the air fryer and cook for 8 minutes at 200 degrees F, turning once or twice during cooking to ensure even cooking. Cooking in batches is suggested. When done, take the apple slices out and serve, sprinkle with cinnamon and store them in an airtight container. Enjoy!
Nutritional information: Calories: 140; Fat: 1.9g; Total Carbs: 32g; Net Carbs: 12g; Fiber: 6.4g; Sugars: 24.1g; Protein: 1.1g

Squash Chips with Parmesan

Prep time: 10 minutes | Cook time: 12 minutes | Serves 3

¾ pound butternut squash, cut into thin rounds	pepper, to taste
½ cup Parmesan cheese, grated	1 teaspoon butter
Sea salt and ground black	½ cup ketchup
	1 teaspoon Sriracha sauce

Stir the butternut squash with butter, Parmesan cheese, salt

and black pepper. Transfer the butternut squash rounds to the cooking basket of your air fryer. Cook the butternut squash for 12 minutes at 400 degrees F. When cooking, shake the basket periodically to ensure even cooking. Work with batches. Whisk the ketchup and siracha While the Parmesan squash chips are baking, set it aside. When done, serve the Parmesan squash chips with Sriracha ketchup and enjoy!
Nutritional information: Calories: 116; Fat: 2.5g; Total Carbs: 23g; Net Carbs: 11g; Fiber: 2.4g; Sugars: 11.6g; Protein: 3.3g

Coated Cauliflower

Prep time: 10 minutes | Cook time: 30 minutes | Serves: 2

½ lemon, juiced	½ teaspoon curry powder
1 head cauliflower	Sea salt to taste
½-tablespoon olive oil	Ground black pepper to taste

Cut out the leaves and core of the cauliflower and wash it. Chop the processed cauliflower into equally-sized florets. Mix together the fresh lemon juice and curry powder in a suitable bowl, then add in the cauliflower florets. After sprinkling in the pepper and salt, mix again and coat the florets well. Oil the cooking pan in your air fryer and then arrange the florets to it. Cook the food for 20 minutes at 390 degrees F. Serve warm,
Nutritional information: Calories: 66; Fat: 3.8g; Total Carbs: 7g; Net Carbs: 3g; Fiber: 3.6g; Sugars: 3.2g; Protein: 2.8g

Spicy Cocktail Wieners

Prep time: 10 minutes | Cook time: 15 minutes | Serves: 4

1 lb. pork cocktail sausages	¼- ½ teaspoon balsamic vinegar
For the Sauce:	
¼ cup mayonnaise	1 garlic clove, finely minced
¼ cup cream cheese	¼ teaspoon chili powder
1 whole grain mustard	

Pork the sausages a few times with a fork, them place them on the cooking pan of your air fryer. Cook the sausages at 390 degrees F for 15 minutes; After 8 minutes of cooking, turn the sausages over and resume cooking. Check for doneness and take the sausages out of the machine. At the same time, thoroughly combine all the ingredients for the sauce. Serve with warm sausages and enjoy!
Nutritional information: Calories: 149; Fat: 12.8g; Total Carbs: 5.5g; Net Carbs: 1g; Fiber: 0.2g; Sugars: 1.1g; Protein: 3.6g

Parmesan Cauliflower Dip

Prep time: 15 minutes | Cook time: 45 minutes | Serves: 10

1 cauliflower head, cut into florets	1 teaspoon Worcestershire sauce
1 ½ cups parmesan cheese, shredded	½ cup sour cream
2 tablespoons green onions, chopped	¾ cup mayonnaise
2 garlic clove	8 ounces cream cheese, softened
	2 tablespoons olive oil

Toss cauliflower florets with olive oil. Add cauliflower florets into the air fryer basket and cook at almost 390 degrees F for 20-25 minutes. Add cooked cauliflower, 1 cup of parmesan cheese, green onion, garlic, Worcestershire sauce, sour cream, mayonnaise, and cream cheese into the food processor and process until smooth. Transfer cauliflower mixture into the 7-inch dish and top with remaining parmesan cheese. Place dish in air fryer basket and Cook at almost 360 degrees F for almost 10-15

minutes. Serve and enjoy.
Nutritional information: Calories: 194; Fat: 17.1g; Total Carbs: 7.2g; Net Carbs: 1g; Fiber: 0.7g; Sugars: 2g; Protein: 4.2g

Parmesan Steak Nuggets

Prep time: 15 minutes | Cook time: 18 minutes | Serves: 4

1 pound beef steak, cut into chunks	½ cup pork rind, crushed
1 large egg, lightly beaten	½ cup parmesan cheese, grated
	½ teaspoon salt

Add egg in a suitable bowl. In a suitable bowl, mix pork rind, cheese, and salt. Dip each steak chunk in egg then coat with pork rind mixture and place on a plate. Place in refrigerator for 30 minutes. Grease its air fryer basket with cooking spray. At 400 degrees F, preheat your air fryer. Place steak nuggets in air fryer basket and cook for almost 15-18 minutes or until cooked. Serve and enjoy.
Nutritional information: Calories: 306; Fat: 13.4g; Total Carbs: 0.9g; Net Carbs: 1g; Fiber: 0g; Sugars: 0.1g; Protein: 43.9g

Potato Pastries

Prep time: 15 minutes | Cook time: 37 minutes | Serves: 8

2 large potatoes, peeled	1 tablespoon fresh ginger, minced
1 tablespoon olive oil	½ cup green peas, shelled
½ cup carrot, peeled and chopped	Salt and ground black pepper, as needed
½ cup onion, chopped	3 puff pastry sheets
2 garlic cloves, minced	

Boil water in a suitable pan, then put the potatoes and cook for about 15-20 minutes When cooked, drain the potatoes well and mash the potatoes. Heat the oil over medium heat in a skillet, then add the carrot, onion, ginger, garlic and sauté for about 4-5 minutes. Drain all the fat: from the skillet. Stir in the mashed potatoes, peas, salt and black pepper. Continue to cook for about 1-2 minutes. Remove the potato mixture from heat and set aside to cool completely. After placing the puff pastry onto a smooth surface, cut each puff pastry sheet into four pieces and then cut each piece in a round shape. Add about 2 tablespoons of veggie filling over each pastry round. Use your wet finger to moisten the edges. To seal the filling, fold each pastry round in half. Firmly press the edges with a fork. Set the temperature of Air Fryer to 390 degrees F. Arrange the pastries in the basket of your air fryer and air fry for about 5 minutes at 390 minutes. Work in 2 batches. Serve.
Nutritional information: Calories: 192; Fat: 8.7g; Total Carbs: 25.8g; Net Carbs: 11g; Fiber: 3.4g; Sugars: 2.4g; Protein: 3.6g

Delectable Fish Nuggets

Prep time: 10 minutes | Cook time: 10 minutes | Serves: 4

1 cup all-purpose flour	strips
2 eggs	Pinch of salt
¾ cup breadcrumbs	1 tablespoon olive oil
1 lb. cod, cut into 1x2½-inch	

Preheat the Air fryer to 380 degrees F and grease an Air fryer basket. In a shallow dish, place the dish, and whisk the eggs in another dish. In the third shallow dish, mix up the breadcrumbs, salt and oil. Let the fish strips be coated evenly in flour and dip in the egg. Roll into the breadcrumbs evenly and arrange the nuggets in the basket of your air fryer. Cook for about 10 minutes at 380 degrees F. When the time is up, dish out to serve

warm.
Nutritional information: Calories: 344; Fat: 4.6g; Total Carbs: 38.6g; Net Carbs: 9g; Fiber: 1.8g; Sugars: 1.5g; Protein: 34.6g

Zucchini with Parmesan Cheese

Prep time: 10 minutes | Cook time: 30 minutes | Serves: 6

6 medium zucchini, cut into sticks	½-teaspoon garlic powder
6 tablespoons Parmesan cheese, grated	1 cup bread crumbs
4 egg whites, beaten	Pepper to taste
	Salt to taste

Pre-heat the Air Fryer to 400°F. Mix up the beaten egg whites with some salt and pepper in a suitable bowl. In another bowl, add the bread crumbs, garlic powder, and Parmesan cheese and combine well. Before rolling in the bread crumbs, dredge each zucchini stick in the egg whites. Place the coated zucchini in the basket of your air fryer and for 20 minutes at 400 degrees F.
Nutritional information: Calories: 130; Fat: 2.3g; Total Carbs: 20g; Net Carbs: 11g; Fiber: 3g; Sugars: 4.7g; Protein 8.7g

Crispy Cauliflower Florets

Prep time: 8 minutes | Cook time: 20 minutes | Serves: 2

3 cups cauliflower florets	Sea salt and cracked black pepper, to taste
½ teaspoon sesame oil	½ teaspoon paprika
½ teaspoon onion powder	
½ teaspoon garlic powder	

Start by preheating your Air Fryer to 400 degrees F. Toss the cauliflower with the remaining ingredients well until coat completely. Arrange the coated cauliflower to the basket of the air fryer and cook for 12 minutes at 400 degrees F, shaking the cooking basket halfway through the cooking time. They will crisp up as they cool, Bon appétit!
Nutritional information: Calories: 66; Fat: 2.4g; Total Carbs: 9g; Net Carbs: 4.3g; Fiber: 4g; Sugars: 4.4g; Protein: 3.3g

Roasted Nut Mixture

Prep time: 10 minutes | Cook time: 20 minutes| Serves: 6

½ cup walnuts	1 packet stevia
½ cup pecans	½-tablespoon ground cinnamon
½ cup almonds	A pinch of cayenne pepper
1 egg white	

Mix up all of the ingredients in a bowl. Arrange the nuts to the basket in the preheated air fryer (you can lay a piece of baking paper). Cook the nuts for about 20 minutes at 320 degrees F, stirring once halfway through. Once done, transfer the hot nuts in a glass or steel bowl and serve.
Nutritional information: Calories: 121; Fat: 11g; Total Carbs: 3.4g; Net Carbs: 1g; Fiber: 2.1g; Sugars: 0.5g; Protein: 4.6g

Air-fried Sweet Potato Bites

Prep time: 8 minutes | Cook time: 15 minutes | Serves: 2

2 sweet potatoes, diced into 1-inch cubes	1 tablespoon olive oil
½ teaspoon red chili flakes	1½ tablespoon honey
1½ teaspoon cinnamon	½ cup fresh parsley, chopped

Heat your Air Fryer at 350°F ahead of time. In a bowl, stir all of the ingredients well and then coat the sweet potato cubes entirely. Put the sweet potato mixture into the basket. Cook for 15 minutes at 350 degrees F. When the time is up, serve and enjoy.

Nutritional information: Calories: 277; Fat: 7.4g; Total Carbs: 52.4g; Net Carbs: 13g; Fiber: 7.3g; Sugars: 9.5g; Protein: 2.8g

Cinnamon Almonds

Prep time: 5 minutes | Cook time: 10 minutes | Serves: 4

½ tsp ground cinnamon	1 egg white
½ tsp smoked paprika	Sea salt to taste
1 cup almonds	

In a bowl, beat the egg white and stir with the cinnamon, paprika and almonds well. Spread the almonds on the oiled cooking basket. Cook at 310 degrees F for 12 minutes, flipping once or twice. When cooked, sprinkle with sea salt and serve.

Nutritional information: Calories: 143; Fat: 11.9g; Total Carbs: 5.5g; Net Carbs: 1g; Fiber: 3.2g; Sugars: 1.1g; Protein: 6g

Cauliflower Bites

Prep time: 5 minutes | Cook time: 15 minutes | Serves: 4

1 tbsp. Italian seasoning	1 egg, beaten
1 cup flour	1 head cauliflower, cut into
1 cup milk	florets

After mixing the flour, milk, egg, and Italian seasoning well, coat the cauliflower with the mixture and drain the excess liquid. Spray the florets with cooking spray and cook them in your air fryer at 390 degrees F for 7 minutes. After that, shake and cook for 5 minutes more. Cool down before serving.

Nutritional information: Calories: 187; Fat: 3.8g; Total Carbs: 30.8g; Net Carbs: 5g; Fiber: 2.5g; Sugars: 4.8g; Protein: 7.9g

Roasted Coconut Carrots with Chili Powder

Prep time: 5 minutes | Cook time: 10 minutes | Serves: 4

1 tbsp. coconut oil, melted	Salt and black pepper to taste
1 lb. horse carrots, sliced	½ tsp chili powder

Mix the carrots with coconut oil, chili powder, salt, and pepper well in a suitable bowl. Arrange the coated carrots to the cooking basket and cook at 400 degrees F for 7 minutes. After that, shake the basket and cook for 5 minutes more or until golden brown. When done, serve and enjoy.

Nutritional information: Calories: 31; Fat: 3.5g; Total Carbs: 0.4g; Net Carbs: 0g; Fiber: 0.2g; Sugars: 0.1g; Protein: 0.1g

Stuffed Mushrooms with Bacon

Prep time: 15 minutes | Cook time: 15 minutes | Serves: 24

24 mushrooms, caps and stems diced	1 cup cheddar cheese, shredded
1 ½ tablespoon mozzarella cheese, shredded	2 bacon slices, diced
	1 small onion, diced
½ cup sour cream	½ onion, diced
	½ bell pepper, chopped

Add bacon, carrot, diced mushrooms stems, onion, and bell pepper to pan and heat over medium heat. Cook this vegetable mixture until softened, for about 5 minutes. Add sour cream and cheddar cheese and cook until cheese is melted, about 2 minutes. At 350 degrees F, preheat your air fryer. Divide the vegetable cheese mixture into the mushroom caps and place them in the air fryer basket. Sprinkle mozzarella cheese on top. Cook mushrooms for almost 8 minutes or until cheese is melted. Serve and enjoy.

Nutritional information: Calories: 49; Fat: 3.6g; Total Carbs: 1.4g; Net Carbs: 0g; Fiber: 0.3g; Sugars: 0.6g; Protein: 3g

Cauliflower Wings with Buffalo Sauce

Prep time: 15 minutes | Cook time: 14 minutes | Serves: 4

1 cauliflower head, cut into florets	½ cup buffalo sauce
	Black pepper
1 tablespoon butter, melted	Salt

Grease its air fryer basket with cooking spray. In a suitable bowl, mix together buffalo sauce, butter, black pepper, and salt. Add cauliflower florets into the air fryer basket and cook at almost 400 degrees F for 7 minutes. Transfer cauliflower florets into the buffalo sauce mixture and toss well. Again, add cauliflower florets into the air fryer basket and cook for 7 minutes more at 400 degrees F. Serve and enjoy.

Nutritional information: Calories: 44; Fat: 3g; Total Carbs: 3.8g; Net Carbs: 1g; Fiber: 1.8g; Sugars: 1.6g; Protein: 1.3g

Crispy Bacon Strips

Prep time: 15 minutes | Cook time: 10 minutes | Serves: 4

4 bacon strips, cut into small pieces	½ cup pork rinds, crushed
	¼ cup hot sauce

Add bacon pieces in a suitable bowl. Add hot sauce and toss well. Add crushed pork rinds and toss until bacon pieces are well coated. Transfer bacon pieces in air fryer basket and cook at almost 350 degrees F for almost 10 minutes. Serve and enjoy.

Nutritional information: Calories: 182; Fat: 14.1g; Total Carbs: 0.3g; Net Carbs: 0g; Fiber: 0g; Sugars: 0.2g; Protein: 13.1g

Enticing Jalapeno Poppers

Prep time: 15 minutes | Cook time: 13 minutes | Serves: 5

5 jalapeno peppers, slice in ½ and deseeded	¼ teaspoon chili powder
	½ teaspoon garlic, minced
2 tablespoons salsa	Black pepper
4 ounces goat cheese, crumbled	Salt

In a suitable bowl, mix together cheese, salsa, chili powder, garlic, black pepper, and salt. Spoon cheese mixture into each jalapeno halves and place in air fryer basket. Cook jalapeno poppers at 350 degrees F for 13 minutes. Serve and enjoy.

Nutritional information: Calories: 111; Fat: 8.3g; Total Carbs: 2.1g; Net Carbs: 0g; Fiber: 0.7g; Sugars: 1.2g; Protein: 7.3g

Roasted Almonds with Paprika

Prep time: 15 minutes | Cook time: 8 minutes | Serves: 8

2 cups almonds	1 teaspoon paprika
¼ teaspoon black pepper	1 tablespoon garlic powder

1 tablespoon soy sauce

Add black pepper, paprika, garlic powder, and soy sauce in a suitable bowl and stir well. Add almonds and stir to coat. Grease its air fryer basket with cooking spray. Add almonds in air fryer basket and cook for 6-8 minutes at 320 degrees F. Serve and enjoy.

Nutritional information: Calories: 143; Fat: 11.9g; Total Carbs: 6.2g; Net Carbs: 1g; Fiber: 3.2g; Sugars: 1.3g; Protein: 5.4g

Mayonnaise Crab Dip

Prep time: 15 minutes | Cook time: 7 minutes | Serves: 4

1 cup crabmeat	½ cup green onion, sliced
2 tablespoons parsley, chopped	2 cups cheese, grated
2 tablespoons fresh lemon juice	¼ cup mayonnaise
2 tablespoons hot sauce	¼ teaspoon black pepper
	½ teaspoon salt

In a 6-inch dish, mix together crabmeat, hot sauce, cheese, mayo, black pepper, and salt. Place dish in air fryer basket and cook dip at 400 degrees F for 7 minutes. Remove dish from the air fryer. Drizzle dip with lemon juice and garnish with parsley. Serve and enjoy.

Nutritional information: Calories: 313; Fat: 23.9g; Total Carbs: 8.8g; Net Carbs: 1g; Fiber: 0.6g; Sugars: 3.1g; Protein: 16.2g

Garlic Spinach Dip

Prep time: 15 minutes | Cook time: 20 minutes | Serves: 8

8 ounces cream cheese, softened	1 cup mayonnaise
¼ teaspoon garlic powder	1 cup parmesan cheese, grated
½ cup onion, minced	1 cup frozen spinach, thawed and squeeze out all liquid
⅓ cup water chestnuts, drained and chopped	½ teaspoon black pepper

Grease its air fryer basket with cooking spray. Add all the recipe ingredients into the bowl and mix until well combined. Transfer bowl mixture into the prepared baking dish and place dish in air fryer basket. Cook at almost 300 degrees F for 35-40 minutes. After 20 minutes of cooking stir dip. Serve and enjoy.

Nutritional information: Calories: 245; Fat: 20.5g; Total Carbs: 12g; Net Carbs: 7g; Fiber: 0.3g; Sugars: 2.3g; Protein: 4g

Italian Dip with Cheese

Prep time: 15 minutes | Cook time: 12 minutes | Serves: 8

8 ounces cream cheese, softened	½ cup roasted red peppers
1 cup mozzarella cheese, shredded	⅓ cup basil pesto
	¼ cup parmesan cheese, grated

Add parmesan cheese and cream cheese into the food processor and process until smooth. Transfer cheese mixture into the air fryer basket and spread evenly. Pour basil pesto on top of cheese layer. Sprinkle roasted black pepper on top of basil pesto layer. Sprinkle mozzarella cheese on top of black pepper layer and place dish in air fryer basket. Cook dip at 250 degrees F for 12 minutes. Serve and enjoy.

Nutritional information: Calories: 157; Fat: 13.6g; Total Carbs: 2.1g; Net Carbs: 1g; Fiber: 0.2g; Sugars: 0.6g; Protein: 7.8g

Cajun Sweet Potato Tots

Prep time: 15 minutes | Cook time: 31 minutes | Serves:

2 sweet potatoes, peeled	Salt
½ teaspoon Cajun seasoning	

Add water in large pot and bring to boil. Add sweet potatoes in pot and boil for almost 15 minutes. Drain well. Grated boil sweet potatoes into a suitable bowl using a grated. Add Cajun seasoning and salt in grated sweet potatoes and mix until well combined. Grease its air fryer basket with cooking spray. Make small tot of sweet potato mixture and place in air fryer basket. Cook at almost 400 degrees F for 8 minutes. Turn tots to another side and cook for 8 minutes more. Serve and enjoy.

Nutritional information: Calories: 177; Fat: 0.3g; Total Carbs: 41.8g; Net Carbs: 11g; Fiber: 6.2g; Sugars: 0.8g; Protein: 2.3g

Zucchini Slices with Parsley

Prep time: 15 minutes | Cook time: 15 minutes | Serves: 4

2 zucchinis, sliced	2 tablespoons almond flour
1 tablespoon olive oil	1 tablespoon parsley, chopped
4 tablespoon parmesan cheese, grated	Black pepper
	Salt

At 350 degrees F, preheat your air fryer. In a suitable bowl, mix together cheese, parsley, oil, almond flour, black pepper, and salt. Top zucchini pieces with cheese mixture and place in the air fryer basket. Cook zucchini for almost 15 minutes at 350 degrees F. Serve and enjoy.

Nutritional information: Calories: 178; Fat: 13g; Total Carbs: 5.8g; Net Carbs: 1g; Fiber: 1.9g; Sugars: 1.7g; Protein: 11.7g

Simple Curried Sweet Potato Fries

Prep time: 15 minutes | Cook time: 20 minutes | Serves: 3

2 small sweet potatoes, peel and cut into fry shape	½ teaspoon curry powder
¼ teaspoon coriander	2 tablespoons olive oil
	¼ teaspoon salt

Add all the recipe ingredients into the suitable mixing bowl and toss well. Grease its air fryer basket with cooking spray. Transfer sweet potato fries in the air fryer basket. Cook for 20 minutes at 370 degrees F. Shake halfway through. Serve and enjoy.

Nutritional information: Calories: 199; Fat: 9.6g; Total Carbs: 28.1g; Net Carbs: 13g; Fiber: 4.2g; Sugars: 0.5g; Protein: 1.6g

Flavorful Kale Chips

Prep time: 15 minutes | Cook time: 5 minutes | Serves: 4

4 cups kale, stemmed	2 teaspoons ranch seasoning
1 tablespoon nutritional yeast flakes	2 tablespoons olive oil
	¼ teaspoon salt

Add all the recipe ingredients into the suitable mixing bowl and toss well. Grease its air fryer basket with cooking spray. Add kale in air fryer basket and cook for 4-5 minutes at 370 degrees F. Serve and enjoy.

Nutritional information: Calories: 102; Fat: 7.1g; Total Carbs: 8g; Net Carbs: 3.5g; Fiber: 1.6g; Sugars: 0g; Protein: 3.2g

Crunchy Zucchini Fries with Parmesan

Prep time: 15 minutes | Cook time: 10 minutes | Serves: 4

2 medium zucchinis, cut into fry shape
½ teaspoon garlic powder
1 teaspoon Italian seasoning
½ cup parmesan cheese, grated
½ cup almond flour
1 egg, lightly beaten
Black pepper
Salt

Add egg in a suitable bowl and whisk well. In a shallow bowl, mix together almond flour, spices, parmesan cheese, black pepper, and salt. Grease its air fryer basket with cooking spray. Dip those zucchini fries in egg then coat with almond flour mixture and place in the air fryer basket. Cook zucchini fries for almost 10 minutes at 400 degrees F. Serve and enjoy.
Nutritional information: Calories: 68; Fat: 4g; Total Carbs: 4g; Net Carbs: 2g; Fiber: 1.5g; Sugars: 2g; Protein: 4.5g

Crispy Eggplant with Paprika

Prep time: 15 minutes | Cook time: 20 minutes | Serves: 4

1 eggplant, cut into 1-inch pieces
½ teaspoon Italian seasoning
1 teaspoon paprika
½ teaspoon red pepper
1 teaspoon garlic powder
2 tablespoons olive oil

Add all the recipe ingredients into the suitable mixing bowl and toss well. Transfer eggplant mixture into the air fryer basket. Cook at almost 375 degrees F for 20 minutes. Shake basket halfway through. Serve and enjoy.
Nutritional information: Calories: 99; Fat: 7.5g; Total Carbs: 8g; Net Carbs: 3.5g; Fiber: 4.5g; Sugars: 4.5g; Protein: 1.5g

Barbecue Chicken Wings

Prep time: 15 minutes | Cook time: 12 minutes | Serves: 6

For the Sauce:
1 tablespoon yellow mustard
1 tablespoon apple cider vinegar
1 tablespoon olive oil
¼ cup unsulfured blackstrap molasses
¼ cup ketchup
2 tablespoons sugar
1 garlic clove, minced
Salt and black pepper, to taste
⅛ teaspoon ground allspice
¼ cup water
For the Wings
2 pounds chicken wings
¼ teaspoon celery salt
¼ cup habanero hot sauce
Chopped fresh parsley, or garnish

Put all the recipe ingredients for the sauce in a pan over a medium-to-high heat and bring the mixture to a boil. Lower its heat and allow to simmer and thicken. In the meantime, at 400 degrees F, preheat your air fryer. Place the chicken wings in the air fryer and cook for 6 minutes. Turn the wings and cook for another 6 minutes on the other side. Sprinkle some celery salt over them. Serve the chicken wings with the prepared sauce.
Nutritional information: Calories: 335; Fat: 13.7g; Total Carbs: 6g; Net Carbs: 2.5g; Fiber: 0.2g; Sugars: 6.3g; Protein: 44.1g

Crispy Black Pepperoni Chips

Prep time: 15 minutes | Cook time: 8 minutes | Serves: 6

6 ounces black pepperoni   slices

Place 1 batch of black pepperoni slices in the air fryer basket.

Cook for 8 minutes at 360 degrees F. Cook remaining black pepperoni slices using same steps. Serve and enjoy.
Nutritional information: Calories: 282; Fat: 17.7g; Total Carbs: 5g; Net Carbs: 2g; Fiber: 0.2g; Sugars: 1.6g; Protein: 25.3g

Stuffed Jalapeno Poppers

Prep time: 15 minutes | Cook time: 5 minutes | Serves: 5

10 Fresh jalapeno peppers, cut in ½ and remove seeds
2 bacon slices, cooked and crumbled
¼ cup cheddar cheese, shredded
6 ounces cream cheese, softened

In a suitable bowl, combine together bacon, cream cheese, and cheddar cheese. Stuff each jalapeno ½ with bacon cheese mixture. Grease its air fryer basket with cooking spray. Place stuffed jalapeno halved in air fryer basket and cook at almost 370 degrees F for 5 minutes. Serve and enjoy.
Nutritional information: Calories: 195; Fat: 17.3g; Total Carbs: 3g; Net Carbs: 1g; Fiber: 1.1g; Sugars: 1g; Protein: 7.2g

Garlicky Radish Chips

Prep time: 15 minutes | Cook time: 10 minutes | Serves: 1

2 cups water
1 pound radishes
½ teaspoon garlic powder
¼ teaspoon onion powder
2 tablespoons coconut oil, melted

Boil the water over the stove. Slice off the radish's tops and bottoms and, using a mandolin, shave into thin slices of equal size. Put the radish chips in the pot of boiling water and allow to cook for 5 minutes, ensuring they become translucent. Take care when removing from the water and place them on a paper towel to dry. Add the radish chips, garlic powder, onion powder, and melted coconut oil into a bowl and toss to coat. Cook at almost 320 degrees F for 5 minutes. Serve.
Nutritional information: Calories: 314; Fat: 27.7g; Total Carbs: 16g; Net Carbs: 7g; Fiber: 7.4g; Sugars: 9g; Protein: 3.4g

Mayonnaise Zucchini Sticks

Prep time: 15 minutes | Cook time: 12 minutes | Serves: 2

1 zucchini, slice into strips
2 tablespoons mayonnaise
¼ cup tortilla chips, crushed
¼ cup Romano cheese, shredded
Sea black pepper and salt, to taste
1 tablespoon garlic powder
½ teaspoon red pepper flakes

Coat the zucchini with mayonnaise. Mix the crushed tortilla chips, cheese and spices in a shallow dish. Then, coat the zucchini sticks with the cheese/chips mixture. Cook these sticks in the preheated air fryer at about 400 degrees F for 12 minutes. Work in batches until the sticks are crispy and golden brown. Serve
Nutritional information: Calories: 164; Fat: 10.1g; Total Carbs: 12g; Net Carbs: 7g; Fiber: 1.8g; Sugars: 3.9g; Protein 7.9g

BBQ Cocktail Sausage

Prep time: 15 minutes | Cook time: 15 minutes | Serves: 6

1 pound beef cocktail wieners
10 ounces barbecue sauce, no
sugar added

At 380 degrees F, preheat your air fryer. Prick holes into your sausages using a fork and transfer them to the baking pan. Cook for 13 minutes. Spoon the barbecue sauce into the pan and cook an additional 2 minutes. Serve with toothpicks.

Nutritional information: Calories: 254; Fat: 13.5g; Total Carbs: 22.1g; Net Carbs: 9g; Fiber: 0.3g; Sugars: 14g; Protein: 6.7g

Parmesan Zucchini Chips

Prep time: 15 minutes | Cook time: 25 minutes | Serves: 2

3 medium zucchini, sliced	grated
1 teaspoon parsley, chopped	Black pepper to taste
3 tablespoon parmesan cheese,	Salt to taste

At 425 degrees F, preheat your air fryer. Put the sliced zucchini on a sheet of baking paper and spritz with cooking spray. Combine the cheese, black pepper, parsley, and salt. Use this mixture to sprinkle over the zucchini. Transfer to the preheated air fryer and cook for 25 minutes. Serve.

Nutritional information: Calories: 182; Fat: 9.5g; Total Carbs: 11g; Net Carbs: 6.7g; Fiber: 3.3g; Sugars: 5.1g; Protein: 17.1g

Grilled Tomatoes with Herbs

Prep time: 15 minutes | Cook time: 20 minutes | Serves: 2

2 tomatoes, medium to large	Black pepper to taste
Herbs of your choice, to taste	High quality cooking spray

Wash and dry the tomatoes, before chopping them in half. Lightly spritz them all over with cooking spray. Season each ½ with oregano, basil, parsley, rosemary, thyme, sage, etc. as desired and black pepper. Put the halves in the tray of your air fryer. Cook for 20 minutes at 320 degrees F. Serve.

Nutritional information: Calories: 22; Fat: 0.3g; Total Carbs: 4.8g; Net Carbs: 1g; Fiber: 1.5g; Sugars: 3.2g; Protein: 1.1g

Deviled Eggs with Ricotta

Prep time: 15 minutes | Cook time: 17 minutes | Serves: 4

2 eggs	¼ teaspoon chili powder
½ teaspoon harissa	1 teaspoon ricotta cheese
½ teaspoon chili flakes	½ teaspoon dried thyme

At 250 degrees F, preheat your air fryer. Place 2 eggs in the air fryer basket and cook them for almost 17 minutes. Then cool and peel the eggs. Cut the peeled eggs into halves and remove the egg yolks. Stir the egg yolks with the help of the fork until they are smooth. After this, add chili flakes, harissa, chili powder, ricotta cheese, and dried thyme. Stir the mass until smooth. Fill the egg whites with hot egg yolk mixture. Serve.

Nutritional information: Calories: 36; Fat: 2.4g; Total Carbs: 0.7g; Net Carbs: 0g; Fiber: 0.1g; Sugars: 0.4g; Protein: 3g

Garlicky Eggplant Chips

Prep time: 15 minutes | Cook time: 13 minutes | Serves: 4

2 eggplants, peeled and thinly sliced	½ cup water
Salt	1 teaspoon garlic powder
½ cup tapioca starch	½ teaspoon dried dill weed
¼ cup canola oil	½ teaspoon black pepper, to taste

Season and rub the eggplant slices with salt and leave for ½ an hour. Run them under cold water to rinse off any excess salt. In a suitable bowl, coat the eggplant slices with all of the other ingredients. Cook at almost 390 degrees F for 13 minutes. Serve.

Nutritional information: Calories: 260; Fat: 14.2g; Total Carbs: 33.7g; Net Carbs: 13g; Fiber: 10g; Sugars: 9g; Protein: 2.9g

Crispy Vegetable Nuggets

Prep time: 15 minutes | Cook time: 10 minutes | Serves: 4

1 zucchini, chopped roughly	1 egg
½ of carrot, chopped roughly	1 cup panko breadcrumbs
1 cup all-purpose flour	1 tablespoon garlic powder
½ tablespoon mustard powder	
1 tablespoon onion powder	Black pepper and salt, to taste

At 380 degrees F, preheat your air fryer and grease its air fryer basket. Put zucchini, carrot, mustard powder, garlic powder, onion powder, black pepper and salt in a food processor and pulse until combined. Place the dry flour in a shallow dish and whisk the eggs with milk in a second dish. Place breadcrumbs in a third shallow dish. Coat the vegetable nuggets evenly in flour and dip in the egg mixture. Roll into the breadcrumbs evenly and arrange the nuggets in an air fryer basket. Cook for about 10 minutes and dish out to serve warm.

Nutritional information: Calories: 178; Fat: 2.1g; Total Carbs: 23.5g; Net Carbs: 10g; Fiber: 2.6g; Sugars: 2.7g; Protein: 6.6g

Garlicky Cucumber Chips

Prep time: 15 minutes | Cook time: 11 minutes | Serves: 12

1 pound cucumber	1 tablespoon paprika
½ teaspoon garlic powder	1 teaspoon salt

Wash cucumber and slice thinly using a mandolin slicer. At 370 degrees F, preheat your air fryer. Add cucumber slices into the air fryer basket and sprinkle with garlic powder, paprika, and salt. Toss well and cook for 11 minutes. Shake halfway through. Serve and enjoy.

Nutritional information: Calories: 8; Fat: 0.1g; Total Carbs: 1.8g; Net Carbs: 0g; Fiber: 0.4g; Sugars: 0.7g; Protein: 0.4g

Cauliflower Popcorn with Turmeric

Prep time: 15 minutes | Cook time: 11 minutes | Serves: 4

1 cup cauliflower florets	2 tablespoons almond flour
1 teaspoon ground turmeric	1 teaspoon salt
2 eggs, beaten	Cooking spray

Cut the cauliflower into small pieces and sprinkle with ground turmeric and salt. Then dip the vegetables in the eggs and coat in the almond flour. At 400 degrees F, preheat your air fryer. Place the cauliflower popcorn in the air fryer in 1 layer and cook for 7 minutes. Give a good shake to the vegetables and cook them for almost 4 minutes more. Serve.

Nutritional information: Calories: 124; Fat: 8.9g; Total Carbs: 4.9g; Net Carbs: 1g; Fiber: 2.3g; Sugars: 0.8g; Protein: 6.3g

Parmesan Cabbage Chips

Prep time: 15 minutes | Cook time: 30 minutes | Serves: 6

1 large cabbage head, tear	cabbage leaves into pieces

2 tablespoons olive oil
¼ cup parmesan cheese, grated

Black pepper
Salt

At 250 degrees F, preheat your air fryer. Add all the recipe ingredients into the suitable mixing bowl and toss well. Grease its air fryer basket with cooking spray. Divide cabbage in batches. Add 1 cabbage chips batch in air fryer basket and cook for 25-30 minutes at 250 degrees F or until chips are crispy and lightly golden brown. Serve and enjoy.
Nutritional information: Calories: 96; Fat: 5.1g; Total Carbs: 12.1g; Net Carbs: 6g; Fiber: 5.2g; Sugars: 6.7g; Protein: 3g

Garlic Sesame Broccoli

Prep time: 15 minutes | Cook time: 20 minutes | Serves: 4

1 large head broccoli
½ lemon, juiced
3 garlic cloves, minced
1 tablespoon coconut oil

1 tablespoon white sesame seeds
2 teaspoons Maggi sauce or other seasonings to taste

Wash and dry the broccoli. Chop it up into small florets. Place the minced garlic in your air fryer basket, along with the coconut oil, lemon juice and Maggi sauce. Heat for 2 minutes at 320 degrees F and give it a stir. Put the garlic and broccoli in the basket and cook for another 13 minutes. Top the broccoli with the white sesame seeds and resume cooking for 5 more minutes, ensuring the seeds become nice and toasty.
Nutritional information: Calories: 58; Fat: 5g; Total Carbs: 2.8g; Net Carbs: 1g; Fiber: 0.7g; Sugars: 0.4g; Protein: 1.3g

Crispy Mustard Fried Leek

Prep time: 15 minutes | Cook time: 10 minutes | Serves: 4

1 large-sized leek, cut into
½-inch wide rings
Black pepper and salt, to taste
1 teaspoon mustard
1 cup milk

1 egg
½ cup almond flour
½ teaspoon baking powder
½ cup pork rinds, crushed

Toss your leeks with black pepper and salt. In a suitable mixing bowl, whisk the mustard, milk and egg until frothy and pale. Now, combine almond flour and baking powder in another mixing bowl. In the third bowl, place the pork rinds. Coat the leek slices with the almond meal mixture. Dredge the floured leek slices into the milk/egg mixture, coating well. Finally, roll them over the pork rinds. Air-fry for approximately 10 minutes at 370 degrees F. Serve!
Nutritional information: Calories: 95; Fat: 4.9g; Total Carbs: 7g; Net Carbs: 3g; Fiber: 0.9g; Sugars: 3.8g; Protein: 5.8g

Spring Rolls

Prep time: 15 minutes | Cook time: 10 minutes | Serves: 6

2 tablespoons vegetable oil, divided
1¾ ounces fresh mushrooms, sliced
1-ounce canned water chestnuts, sliced
1 teaspoon fresh ginger, finely grated
1 ounce bean sprouts

1 carrot, peeled and cut into matchsticks
2 scallions green part, chopped
1 tablespoon soy sauce
1 teaspoon Chinese five-spice powder
3½ ounces cooked shrimps
12 spring roll wrappers
1 egg, beaten

Take a skillet, heat 1 tablespoon of oil over medium heat and sauté the mushrooms, water chestnuts, and ginger for about 2-3 minutes. Add in the beans sprouts, carrot, scallion, soy sauce, and five-spice powder. Sauté for about 1 minute. Add the shrimps and remove from heat. Set aside to cool. Divide the veggie mixture evenly between spring rolls. Roll the wrappers around the filling and seal with beaten egg. Coat each roll with the remaining oil. At 390 degrees F, preheat your air fryer. Grease its air fryer basket. Place rolls into the prepared air fryer basket in a single layer in 2 batches. Air fry for about 5 minutes. Serve.
Nutritional information: Calories: 275; Fat: 6.6g; Total Carbs: 41.1g; Net Carbs: 15g; Fiber: 1.6g; Sugars: 0.9g; Protein: 12g

Awesome Lemony Green Beans

Prep time: 15 minutes | Cook time: 12 minutes | Serves: 4

1 lemon, juiced
1-pound green beans, washed and destemmed
¼ teaspoon extra virgin olive

oil
Salt to taste
Black pepper to taste

At 400 degrees F, preheat your air fryer. Put the green beans in your air fryer basket and drizzle the lemon juice over them. Sprinkle on the black pepper and salt. Pour in the oil, and toss to coat the green beans well. Cook for almost 10-12 minutes and serve warm.
Nutritional information: Calories: 38; Fat: 0.4g; Total Carbs: 8g; Net Carbs: 3.5g; Fiber: 3.9g; Sugars: 1.6g; Protein: 2.1g

Apple Pastries with Cinnamon

Prep time: 15 minutes | Cook time: 10 minutes | Serves: 8

½ of apple, peeled, cored and chopped
1 teaspoon fresh orange zest, finely grated

½ tablespoon white sugar
½ teaspoon ground cinnamon
7.05 oz. prepared frozen puff pastry

In a suitable bowl, mix together all the recipe ingredients except puff pastry. Cut the pastry in 16 squares. Using a teaspoon, place apple mixture in the center of each square. Fold each square into a triangle and slightly press the edges with your wet fingers. Then, using a fork, firmly press the edges. At 390 degrees F, preheat your air fryer. Add the pastries into an air fryer basket in a single layer in 2 batches. Air fry for about 10 minutes. Enjoy!
Nutritional information: Calories: 150; Fat: 9.6g; Total Carbs: 14.3g; Net Carbs: 9g; Fiber: 0.8g; Sugars: 2.4g; Protein: 1.9g

Buttered Bacon

Prep time: 15 minutes | Cook time: 10 minutes | Serves: 5

½ cup butter

3 ounces bacon, chopped

At 400 degrees F, preheat your air fryer and put the bacon inside. Cook it for 8 minutes. Stir the bacon every 2 minutes. Meanwhile, soften the butter in the air fryer and put it in the butter mold. Add cooked bacon and churn the butter. Refrigerate the butter for 30 minutes. Serve.
Nutritional information: Calories: 255; Fat: 25.5g; Total Carbs: 0.3g; Net Carbs: 0g; Fiber: 0g; Sugars: 0g; Protein: 6.5g

Crusted Prawns

Prep time: 15 minutes | Cook time: 8 minutes | Serves: 4

1 egg
½ pound nacho chips, crushed

18 prawns, peeled and deveined

In a shallow dish, crack the egg, and beat well. Put the crushed nacho chips in another dish. Now, dip the prawn into beaten egg and then, coat with the nacho chips. At 355 degrees F, preheat your air fryer. Place the prepared prawns in the air fryer basket in a single layer. Air fry for about 8 minutes. Serve hot.

Nutritional information: Calories: 425; Fat: 17.6g; Total Carbs: 36.6g; Net Carbs: 9g; Fiber: 2.6g; Sugars: 2.2g; Protein: 28.6g

Ranch Kale Chips

Prep time: 15 minutes | Cook time: 5 minutes | Serves: 4

4 cups kale, stemmed	2 teaspoons ranch seasoning
1 tablespoon nutritional yeast flakes	2 tablespoons olive oil
	¼ teaspoon salt

Add all the recipe ingredients into the suitable mixing bowl and toss well. Grease its air fryer basket with cooking spray. Add kale in air fryer basket and cook for 4 to 5 minutes at 370 degrees F. Shake halfway through. Serve and enjoy.

Nutritional information: Calories: 102; Fat: 7.1g; Total Carbs: 8g; Net Carbs: 3.5g; Fiber: 1.6g; Sugars: 0g; Protein: 3.2g

Spicy Chickpeas with Paprika

Prep time: 15 minutes | Cook time: 10 minutes | Serves: 4

1 15-ounces can chickpeas, rinsed and drained	½ teaspoon cayenne pepper
1 tablespoon olive oil	½ teaspoon smoked paprika
½ teaspoon ground cumin	Salt, to taste

At 390 degrees F, preheat your air fryer. In a suitable bowl, add all the recipe ingredients and toss to coat well. Add the chickpeas in an air fryer basket in 2 batches. Air fry for about 8-10 minutes. Serve.

Nutritional information: Calories: 214; Fat: 6.7g; Total Carbs: 30.7g; Net Carbs: 10g; Fiber: 8.9g; Sugars: 5.4g; Protein: 9.8g

Panko Crusted Chicken Tenders

Prep time: 15 minutes | Cook time: 10 minutes | Serves: 4

12 ounces chicken breasts, cut into tenders	⅛ cup flour
1 egg white	½ cup panko bread crumbs
	Black pepper and salt, to taste

At 350 degrees F, preheat your air fryer. and grease its air fryer basket. Season the chicken tenders with some black pepper and salt. Coat the chicken tenders with flour, then dip in egg whites and then dredge in the panko bread crumbs. Arrange the prepared tender in the air fryer basket and cook for about 10 minutes. Dish out in a platter and serve warm.

Nutritional information: Calories: 233; Fat: 7.1g; Total Carbs: 12g; Net Carbs: 7g; Fiber: 0.7g; Sugars: 0.9g; Protein: 27.7g

Honey-Glazed Chicken Drumettes

Prep time: 15 minutes | Cook time: 28 minutes | Serves: 6

1 ½ pounds chicken drumettes	1 tablespoon sesame oil
Salt and black pepper, to taste	¼ cup soy sauce
2 tablespoons fresh chives, roughly chopped	½ cup water
Teriyaki Sauce:	¼ cup honey
	½ teaspoon Five-spice powder

2 tablespoons rice wine vinegar	2 garlic cloves, crushed
½ teaspoon fresh ginger, grated	1 tablespoon corn starch
	3 tablespoons of water

At 380 degrees F, preheat your air fryer. Rub the cleaned chicken drumettes with some black pepper and salt. Cook in the preheated air fryer almost 15 minutes. Turn them and continue cooking for 7 minutes. Meanwhile, mix soy sauce, sesame oil, honey, five-spice powder, water, ginger, vinegar, and garlic in a pan over medium heat. Cook for 5 minutes, with occasional stirring. Add the cornstarch slurry, reduce the heat, and let it simmer until the glaze thickens. After that, brush the glaze all over the chicken drumettes. Air-fry for 6 minutes more. Serve with the remaining glaze on top and garnished with fresh chives. Serve

Nutritional information: Calories: 220; Fat: 8.3g; Total Carbs: 14.4g; Net Carbs: 5g; Fiber: 0.2g; Sugars: 11.8g; Protein: 22.8g

Air Fried Pumpkin Seeds

Prep time: 15 minutes | Cook time: 40 minutes | Serves: 4

1 ½ cups pumpkin seeds	1 ½ teaspoon salt
1 teaspoon smoked paprika	Olive oil

Run the pumpkin seeds under some cold water. Over a medium heat, boil 2 quarts of salted water in a pot. Add in the pumpkin seeds and cook in the water for 8 to 10 minutes. Dump the contents of the pot into a sieve to drain the seeds. Place them son paper towels and allow them to dry for at least 20 minutes. At 350 degrees F, preheat your Air Fryer. In a suitable bowl, coat the pumpkin seeds with olive oil, smoked paprika and salt. Put them in the fryer's basket and air fry for at least 30 minutes until slightly browned and crispy. Shake the air fryer basket a few times during the cooking time. Allow the seeds to cool. Serve with a salad or keep in an airtight container for snacking.

Nutritional information: Calories: 282; Fat: 23.8g; Total Carbs: 9.5g; Net Carbs: 5g; Fiber: 2.2g Sugars 0.6g; Protein: 12.8g

Avocado Wedges with Almond

Prep time: 15 minutes | Cook time: 8 minutes | Serves: 4

4 avocados, peeled, pitted and cut into wedges	A pinch of black pepper and salt
1 egg, whisked	Cooking spray
1 and ½ cups almond meal	

Put the egg in a suitable bowl, and the almond meal in another. Season avocado wedges with black pepper and salt, coat them in egg and then in meal almond. Arrange the avocado bites in your air fryer's basket, grease them with cooking spray and Cook at almost 400 degrees F for 8 minutes. Serve as a snack right away.

Nutritional information: Calories: 468; Fat: 43.7g; Total Carbs: 18g; Net Carbs: 9.5g; Fiber: 14.2g; Sugars: 1.1g; Protein: 6.7g

Ranch Broccoli with Cheddar

Prep time: 15 minutes | Cook time: 35 minutes | Serves: 6

4 cups broccoli florets	¼ cup heavy whipping cream
¼ cup ranch dressing	Kosher black pepper and salt to taste
½ cup sharp cheddar cheese, shredded	

At 375 degrees F preheat your air fryer. In a suitable bowl, combine all of the recipe ingredients until the broccoli is well-

covered. In a casserole dish, spread out the broccoli mixture. Air fry for 30 minutes. Take out of your fryer and mix. If the florets are not tender, Air fry for another 5 minutes until tender. Serve!
Nutritional information: Calories: 79; Fat: 5.2g; Total Carbs: 4g; Net Carbs: 2g; Fiber: 1.6g; Sugars: 1.4g; Protein: 4.3g

Roasted Buttery Cashews

Prep time: 15 minutes | Cook time: 4 minutes | Serves: 8

2 cups raw cashew nuts
1 teaspoon butter, melted

Salt and freshly black pepper, as needed

At 355 degrees F, preheat your air fryer. In a suitable bowl, mix together all the recipe ingredients. Place the cashews nuts in an air fryer basket in a single layer. You can lay a piece of grease-proof baking paper. Air fry for about 4 minutes, shaking once halfway through. Serve.
Nutritional information: Calories: 201; Fat: 16.4g; Total Carbs: 11g; Net Carbs: 6.7g; Fiber: 1g; Sugars: 1.7g; Protein: 5.3g

Homemade Chicken Drumsticks

Prep time: 10 minutes | Cook time: 20 minutes | Serves: 5

For the Sauce:
1 tablespoon Worcestershire sauce
1 tablespoon red wine vinegar
1 tablespoon olive oil
1 ½ cup ketchup
1 tablespoon mustard
1 tablespoon brown sugar
1 tablespoon honey

½ teaspoon granulated garlic
Salt and pepper, to taste
⅛ teaspoon ground allspice
¼ cup water
For the Chicken Drumsticks:
2 lb. chicken drumsticks
⅓ teaspoon Kosher salt
⅓ cup fresh parsley, finely chopped

Sauté all the sauce ingredients in a sauté pan over medium-high heat and let them simmer a few minutes. Reduce the heat and cook until thickens. In your air fryer, cook the chicken drumsticks at 390 degrees F for 15 minutes. When cooked, season them with Kosher salt. Serve warm with the prepared sauce and top with finely chopped parsley. Bon appétit!
Nutritional information: Calories: 437; Fat: 14.1g; Total Carbs: 25g; Net Carbs: 16g; Fiber: 0.7g; Sugars: 22.5g; Protein: 51.9g

Zucchini Fritters with Olives

Prep time: 15 minutes | Cook time: 12 minutes | Serves: 6

Cooking spray
½ cup parsley, chopped
1 egg
½ cup almond flour
Black pepper and salt to the

taste
3 spring onions, chopped
½ cup Kalamata olives, pitted and minced
3 zucchinis, grated

In a suitable bowl, mix all the recipe ingredients except the cooking spray, stir well and shape medium fritters out of this mixture. Place the fritters in your air fryer basket, grease them

with cooking spray and cook at almost 380 degrees F for 6 minutes on each side. Serve them as an appetizer.
Nutritional information: Calories: 57; Fat: 3.3g; Total Carbs: 5g; Net Carbs: 2g; Fiber: 2.1g; Sugars: 2g; Protein 3g

Corn with Coriander and Parmesan Cheese

Prep time: 10 minutes | Cook time: 15 minutes | Serves: 2

2 ears corn, husked and cleaned
1 tablespoon melted butter
1 tablespoon fresh coriander,

finely chopped
2 tablespoons Parmesan cheese, finely chopped

Butter the corn and then arrange the corn in the air fryer. Cook for 14 minutes at 400 degrees F. When done, serve warm and top with the Parmesan cheese and fresh coriander. Bon appétit!
Nutritional information: Calories: 363; Fat: 19.6g; Total Carbs: 31g; Net Carbs: 15g; Fiber: 4.2g; Sugars: 5g; Protein: 23.1g

Mini Sausages with Dijon Dip

Prep time: 10 minutes | Cook time: 20 minutes | Serves: 2

½ lb. cocktail sausages
For the Dijon Dip:
4 tablespoons mayonnaise
2 tablespoons Dijon mustard

1 ½ tablespoon honey
1 teaspoon lemon juice
¼ teaspoon pepper

Pork the sausages a few times with a fork. Arrange the sausages to the basket of your air fryer and cook for 17 minutes at 390 degrees F. Shake the basket halfway through the cooking time. While cooking, mix all the ingredients for the Dijon dip in a bowl. With the mustard dip on the side, enjoy the warm sausages!
Nutritional information: Calories: 374; Fat: 27.5g; Total Carbs: 23g; Net Carbs: 11g; Fiber: 0.6g; Sugars: 16g; Protein: 11g

Garlic Cauliflower Appetizer

Prep time: 10 minutes | Cook time: 20 minutes | Serves: 2

5 cups cauliflower florets
½ teaspoon Kosher salt
½ teaspoon paprika

½ teaspoon garlic powder
2 tablespoons avocado oil

Prepare a large bowl, add the Kosher salt, avocado oil, paprika, garlic powder, and cauliflower florets. Coat well. Arrange the coated cauliflower to the basket of your air fryer and cook at 390 degrees F for 18 minutes, shaking the basket halfway through. Cooking in batches is suggested. When done, serve immediately. Bon appétit!
Nutritional information: Calories: 85; Fat: 2.1g; Total Carbs: 14g; Net Carbs: 9.5g; Fiber: 7.1g; Sugars: 6.3g; Protein: 5.3g

Vegetables and Sides Recipes

Carrots with Honey Glaze

Prep time: 5 minutes | Cook time: 10 minutes | Serves: 1

1 tbsp. of olive oil
3 cups of chopped into ½-inch pieces' carrots

salt and black pepper, to taste
2 tbsps. of honey
1 tbsp. of brown sugar

At 390 degrees F, preheat your air fryer. Using a bowl, add and toss the carrot pieces, olive oil, honey, brown sugar, salt, and the black pepper until it is properly covered. Place it inside your air fryer and add the seasoned glazed carrots. Cook it for 12 minutes at 390 degrees F, shaking the basket halfway through. Serve and enjoy!
Nutritional information: Calories 90, Fat 3.5g, Fiber: 2g; Total Carbs 13g, Protein 1g; Sugar 1.2 g; Fiber 1g

Buffalo Cauliflower Bites

Prep time: 5 minutes | Cook time: 20 minutes | Serves: 4

1 large chopped into florets cauliflower head
3 beaten eggs

⅔ cup of cornstarch
2 tbsp. of melted butter
¼ cup of hot sauce

Preheat your air fryer to 360 degrees F. In a large mixing bowl, add and mix the eggs and the cornstarch a properly. Add the cauliflower, gently toss it until it is properly covered with the batter, shake it off in case of any excess batter and set it aside. Grease your "Air Fryer Basket" with a nonstick cooking spray and add the cauliflower bites which will require you to work in batches. Cook the cauliflower bites at 360 degrees F on Air Fry mode for 15 to 20 minutes or until it has a golden-brown color and a crispy texture, while still shaking occasionally. Then, using a small mixing bowl, add and mix the melted butter and hot sauce properly. Once the cauliflower bites are done, remove it from your air fryer and place it into a large bowl. Drizzle the buffalo sauce over the cauliflower bites and toss it until it is properly covered. Serve and enjoy!
Nutritional information: Calories 240, Fat 5.5g, Fiber: 6.3g, Protein 8.8g; Total Carbs 37g; Sugar 1.2 g; Fiber 1g

Air-Fried Eggplant

Prep time: 5 minutes | Cook time: 20 minutes | Serves: 4

2 thinly sliced or chopped into chunks eggplants
1 tsp. of salt

1 tsp. of black pepper
1 cup of rice flour
1 cup of white wine

In a bowl, add the rice flour, white wine and mix properly until it gets smooth. Add the salt, black pepper and stir again. Dredge the eggplant slices or chunks into the batter and remove any excess batter. At 390 degrees F, preheat your Air Fryer. Grease your "Air Fryer Basket" with a nonstick cooking spray. Add the eggplant slices or chunks into your air fryer and cook them at 390 degrees F on Air Fry mode for 15 to 20 minutes or until it has a golden brown and crispy texture, while still shaking it occasionally. Carefully remove it from your air fryer and allow it to cool off.
Serve and enjoy!

Nutritional information: Calories 380; Total Carbs 51g, Net Carb 2g; Fat 15g, Protein 13g; Sugar 1g; Fiber: 6.1g

Cauliflower Hash

Prep time: 10 minutes | Cook time: 15 minutes | Serves: 6

1-lb. cauliflower
2 eggs
1 tsp. salt

½ tsp. ground paprika
4-oz. turkey fillet, chopped

Wash the cauliflower, chop, and set aside. In a bowl, crack the eggs and whisk well; add the salt and ground paprika and stir well. Place the chopped turkey in the "Air Fryer Basket" and cook them for 4 minutes at 365 degrees F on Air Fry mode, stirring halfway through. After this, add the chopped cauliflower and stir the prepared mixture. Air Fry the turkey/cauliflower mixture for 6 minutes more at 370 degrees F, stirring it halfway through. Then pour in the whisked egg mixture and stir it carefully. Air Fry the cauliflower hash for 5 minutes more at 365 degrees F. When the cauliflower hash is done, let it cool and transfer to serving bowls. Serve and enjoy.
Nutritional information: Calories 143; Total Carbs 4.5g; Net Carbs 2g; Protein 10.4; Fat 9.5g; Sugar 2g; Fiber 2

Asparagus with Almonds

Prep time: 10 minutes | Cook time: 5 minutes | Serves: 2

9 oz. asparagus
1 tsp. almond flour
1 tbsp. almond flakes

¼ tsp. salt
1 tsp. olive oil

Combine the almond flour and almond flakes; stir the prepared mixture well. Sprinkle the asparagus with the olive oil and salt. Shake it gently and coat in the almond flour mixture. Place the asparagus in the "Air Fryer Basket" and Air Fry them at 400 degrees F for 5 minutes, stirring halfway through. Then cool a little and serve.
Nutritional information: Calories 143; Total Carbs 8.6g; Net Carbs 2g; Protein 6.4; Fat 11g; Sugar 2g; Fiber 4.6

Zucchini Cubes

Prep time: 7 minutes | Cook time: 8 minutes | Serves: 2

1 zucchini
½ tsp. ground black pepper
1 tsp. oregano

2 tbsp. chicken stock
½ tsp. coconut oil

Chop the zucchini into cubes. Combine the ground black pepper, and oregano; stir the prepared mixture. Sprinkle the zucchini cubes with the spice mixture and stir well. After this, sprinkle the vegetables with the chicken stock. Place the coconut oil in the "Air Fryer Basket" and heat it to 360 degrees F for 20 seconds. Then add the zucchini cubes and Air Fry the vegetables for 8 minutes at 390 degrees F, stirring halfway through. Transfer to serving plates and enjoy!
Nutritional information: Calories 30; Total Carbs 4.3g; Net Carbs 2g; Protein 1.4; Fat 1.5g; Sugar 2g; Fiber 1.6g

Sweet Potato Onion Mix

Prep time: 10 minutes | Cook time: 15 minutes | Serves: 4

2 sweet potatoes, peeled
1 red onion, peeled
1 white onion, peeled

1 tsp. olive oil
¼ cup almond milk

Chop the sweet potatoes and the onions into cubes. Sprinkle the sweet potatoes with olive oil. Place the peeled and diced sweet potatoes in the "Air Fryer Basket" and Air Fry them for 5 minutes at 400 degrees F. When the time is up, stir the sweet potatoes and add the chopped onions; pour in the almond milk and stir gently. Air Fry the mix for 10 minutes more at 400 degrees F. When the mix is cooked, let it cool a little and serve.
Nutritional information: Calories 56; Total Carbs 3.5g; Net Carbs 2g; Protein 0.6; Fat 4.8g; Sugar 2g; Fiber 0.9g

Spicy Eggplant

Prep time: 10 minutes | Cook time: 20 minutes | Serves: 2

12 oz. eggplants
½ tsp. cayenne pepper
½ tsp. ground black pepper

½ tsp. cilantro
½ tsp. ground paprika

Rinse the eggplants and slice them into cubes. Sprinkle the eggplant cubes with the cayenne pepper and ground black pepper. Add the cilantro and ground paprika. Stir the prepared mixture well and let it rest for 10 minutes. After this, sprinkle the eggplants with olive oil and place in the air fryer basket. Cook the eggplants for 20 minutes at 380 degrees F on Air Fry mode, stirring halfway through. When the eggplant cubes are done, serve them right away!
Nutritional information: Calories 67; Total Carbs 10.9g; Net Carbs 2g; Protein 1.9; Fat 2.8g; Sugar 2g; Fiber 6.5g

Roasted Garlic Head

Prep time: 5 minutes | Cook time: 10 minutes | Serves: 4

1-lb. garlic head
1 tbsp. olive oil

1 tsp. thyme

Cut the ends of the garlic head and place it in the Air Fryer Basket. Then sprinkle the garlic head with the olive oil and thyme. Air Fry the garlic head for 10 minutes at 400 degrees F. When the garlic head is cooked, it should be soft and aromatic. Serve immediately.
Nutritional information: Calories 200; Total Carbs 37.7g; Net Carbs 2g; Protein 7.2; Fat 4.1g; Sugar 2g; Fiber 2.5g

Wrapped Asparagus

Prep time: 10 minutes | Cook time: 5 minutes | Serves: 4

12 oz. asparagus
½ tsp. ground black pepper

3-oz. turkey fillet, sliced
¼ tsp. chili flakes

Sprinkle the asparagus with the ground black pepper and chili flakes. Stir carefully. Wrap the asparagus in the sliced turkey fillet and place in the Air Fryer Basket. Cook the asparagus at 400 degrees F for 5 minutes, turning halfway through cooking. Let the wrapped asparagus cool for 2 minutes before serving.
Nutritional information: Calories 133; Total Carbs 3.8g; Net Carbs 2g; Protein 9.8; Fat 9g; Sugar 2g; Fiber 1.9g

Baked Yams

Prep time: 10 minutes | Cook time: 8 minutes | Serves: 2

2 yams
1 tbsp. fresh dill

1 tsp. coconut oil
½ tsp. minced garlic

Wash the yams carefully and cut them into halves. Sprinkle the yam halves with the coconut oil and then rub with the minced garlic. Place the yams in the "Air Fryer Basket" and Air Fry for 8 minutes at 400 degrees F. After this, mash the yams gently with a fork and then sprinkle with the fresh dill. Serve the yams immediately.
Nutritional information: Calories 25; Total Carbs 1.2g; Net Carbs 2g; Protein 0.4; Fat 2.3g; Sugar 2g; Fiber 0.2g

Honey Onions

Prep time: 10 minutes | Cook time: 20 minutes | Serves: 2

2 large white onions
1 tbsp. raw honey

1 tsp. water
1 tbsp. paprika

Peel the onions and using a knife, make cuts in the shape of a cross. Then combine the raw honey and water; stir. Add the paprika and stir the prepared mixture until smooth. Place the onions in the "Air Fryer Basket" and sprinkle them with the honey mixture. Cook the onions for 16 minutes at 380 degrees F on Air Fry mode. When the onions are cooked, they should be soft. Transfer the cooked onions to serving plates and serve.
Nutritional information: Calories 102; Total Carbs 24.6g; Net Carbs 2g; Protein 2.2; Fat 0.6g; Sugar 2g; Fiber 4.5g

Roasted Garlic Slices

Prep time: 10 minutes | Cook time: 8 minutes | Serves: 4

1 tsp. coconut oil
½ tsp. dried cilantro

¼ tsp. cayenne pepper
12 oz. garlic cloves, peeled

Sprinkle the garlic cloves with the cayenne pepper and dried cilantro. Mix up the garlic and the spices, and then transfer to the Air Fryer Basket. Add the coconut oil and Air Fry the garlic mixture for 8 minutes at 400 degrees F, stirring halfway through. When the garlic cloves are done, transfer them to serving plates and serve.
Nutritional information: Calories 137; Total Carbs 28.2g; Net Carbs 2g; Protein 5.4; Fat 1.6g; Sugar 2g; Fiber 1.8g

Air Fried Artichokes

Prep time: 10 minutes | Cook time: 13 minutes | Serves: 4

1-lb. artichokes
1 tbsp. coconut oil
1 tbsp. water

½ tsp. minced garlic
¼ tsp. cayenne pepper

Trim the ends of the artichokes, sprinkle them with the water, and rub them with the minced garlic. Sprinkle with the cayenne pepper and the coconut oil. After this, wrap the artichokes in foil and place in the Air Fryer Basket. Air Fry the artichokes for 10 minutes at 370 degrees F. When the time is up, remove the artichokes from the foil and Air Fry them for 3 minutes more at 400 degrees F. Transfer the cooked artichokes to serving plates and allow to cool a little. Serve!
Nutritional information: Calories 83; Total Carbs 12.1g; Net Carbs 2g; Protein 3.7; Fat 3.6g; Sugar 2g; Fiber 6.2g

Roasted Mushrooms

Prep time: 10 minutes | Cook time: 5 minutes | Serves: 2

12 oz. mushroom hats
¼ cup fresh dill, chopped
¼ tsp. onion, chopped

1 tsp. olive oil
¼ tsp. turmeric

Combine the chopped dill and onion in a suitable bowl. Add the turmeric and stir the prepared mixture. After this, add the olive oil and mix until homogenous. Then fill the mushroom hats with the dill mixture and place them in the Air Fryer Basket. Cook the mushrooms for 5 minutes at 400 degrees F on Air Fry mode. When the vegetables are cooked, let them cool to room temperature before serving.
Nutritional information: Calories 73; Total Carbs 9.2g; Net Carbs 2g; Protein 6.6; Fat 3.1g; Sugar 2g; Fiber 2.6g

Mashed Yams

Prep time: 10 minutes | Cook time: 10 minutes | Serves: 5

1 lb. yams
1 tsp. olive oil
1 tbsp. almond milk

¾ tsp. salt
1 tsp. dried parsley

Peel the yams and chop. Place the chopped yams in the "Air Fryer Basket" and sprinkle with the salt and dried parsley. Add the olive oil and stir the prepared mixture. Cook the yams at 400 degrees F for 10 minutes on Air Fry mode, stirring twice during cooking. When the yams are done, blend them well with a hand blender until smooth. Add the almond milk and stir carefully. Serve, and enjoy!
Nutritional information: Calories 120; Total Carbs 25.1g; Net Carbs 2g; Protein 1.4; Fat 1.8g; Sugar 2g; Fiber 3.6g

Shredded Cabbage

Prep time: 15 minutes | Cook time: 15 minutes | Serves: 4

15 oz. cabbage
¼ tsp. salt

¼ cup chicken stock
½ tsp. paprika

Shred the cabbage and sprinkle it with the salt and paprika. Stir the cabbage and let it sit for 10 minutes. Then transfer the cabbage to the "Air Fryer Basket" and add the chicken stock. Air Fry the food for 15 minutes at 250 degrees F, stirring halfway through. When the cabbage is soft, it is done. Serve immediately.
Nutritional information: Calories 132; Fat 2.1g; Total Carbs 32.1 g; Net Carbs 2g; Protein 1.78g; Sugar 2g; Fiber 2.5g

Fried Leeks

Prep time: 5 minutes | Cook time: 10 minutes | Serves: 4

4 leeks; ends cut off and halved
1 tbsp. butter; melted

1 tbsp. lemon juice
Salt and black pepper to the taste

Coat the leeks with melted butter, flavor with black pepper and salt, put in your air fryer and Air Fry at 350 degrees F for 7 minutes. When cooked, arrange on a platter, drizzle lemon juice all over and serve.
Nutritional information: Calories 100; Fat 4; Fiber: 2g; Total Carbs 6g; Net Carbs 2g; Protein 2 g; Sugar 2g; Fiber 2.5g

Brussels Sprouts Tomatoes Mix

Prep time: 5 minutes | Cook time: 10 minutes | Serves: 4

1 lb. Brussels sprouts; trimmed
6 cherry tomatoes; halved
¼ cup green onions; chopped.

1 tbsp. olive oil
Salt and black pepper to the taste

Season Brussels sprouts with black pepper and salt, put them in your air fryer and Air Fry them at 350 degrees F for 10 minutes Transfer them to a bowl, add salt, pepper, cherry tomatoes, green onions and olive oil, toss well and serve.
Nutritional information: Calories 121; Fat 4; Fiber: 4g; Total Carbs 11g; Net Carbs 2g; Protein 4 g; Sugar 2g; Fiber 2.5g

Radish Hash

Prep time: 5 minutes | Cook time: 7 minutes | Serves: 4

½ tsp. onion powder
⅓ cup parmesan; grated
4 eggs

1 lb. radishes; sliced
Salt and black pepper to the taste

In a bowl, mix the radishes with salt, pepper, onion, eggs and parmesan. Transfer radishes to a suitable pan and Air Fry them at 350 degrees F for 7 minutes Divide hash on plates and serve.
Nutritional information: Calories 80; Fat 5; Fiber: 2g; Total Carbs 5g; Net Carbs 2g; Protein 7 g; Sugar 2g; Fiber 2.5g

Broccoli Salad

Prep time: 5 minutes | Cook time: 10 minutes | Serves: 4

1 broccoli head; florets separated
1 tbsp. Chinese rice wine vinegar
1 tbsp. peanut oil

6 garlic cloves; minced
Salt and black pepper to the taste

In a bowl; mix broccoli with salt, pepper and half of the oil, toss. Transfer the food to your air fryer and Air Fry them at 350 degrees F for 8 minutes, shaking the fryer halfway When cooked, transfer broccoli to a salad bowl, add the rest of the peanut oil, garlic and rice vinegar, toss really well and serve.
Nutritional information: Calories 121; Fat 3; Fiber: 4g; Total Carbs 4g; Net Carbs 2g; Protein 4 g; Sugar 2g; Fiber 2.5g

Chili Broccoli

Prep time: 5 minutes | Cook time: 15 minutes | Serves: 4

1-lb. broccoli florets
2 tbsps. olive oil
2 tbsps. chili sauce

Juice of 1 lime
A pinch of salt and black pepper

Mix all of the recipe ingredients in a suitable bowl, and toss well. Put the broccoli florets in your "Air Fryer Basket" and Air Fry them at 400 degrees F for 15 minutes. Divide between plates and serve.
Nutritional information: Calories 173g; Total Carbs 6g; Net Carbs 2g; Protein 8g; Fat 6g; Sugar 2g; Fiber 2g

Broccoli and Asparagus

Prep time: 5 minutes | Cook time: 15 minutes | Serves: 4

1 broccoli head, florets separated

½ lb. asparagus, trimmed
Juice of 1 lime

Salt and black pepper to the taste

2 tbsps. olive oil
3 tbsps. parmesan, grated

In a suitable bowl, combine the asparagus with the broccoli and all the other ingredients except the parmesan, toss well. Transfer the food to your "Air Fryer Basket" and Air Fry them at 400 degrees F for 15 minutes. Divide between plates, sprinkle the parmesan on top and serve.

Nutritional information: Calories 172g; Total Carbs 4g; Net Carbs 2g; Protein 9 Fat 5g; Sugar 2g; Fiber 2g

Broccoli Mix

Prep time: 5 minutes | Cook time: 15 minutes | Serves: 4

1-lb. broccoli florets
A pinch of salt and black pepper

1 tsp. sweet paprika
½ tbsp. butter, melted

In a suitable bowl, combine the broccoli with the rest of the ingredients, and toss well. Put the broccoli in your "Air Fryer Basket", Air Fry the food at 350 degrees F for 15 minutes, When cooked, divide between plates and serve.

Nutritional information: Calories 130g; Total Carbs 4g; Net Carbs 2g; Protein 8g; Fat 3g; Sugar 2g; Fiber 3g

Balsamic Kale

Prep time: 2 minutes | Cook time: 12 minutes | Serves: 6

2 tbsps. olive oil
3 garlic cloves, minced
2 and ½ lbs. kale leaves

Salt and black pepper to the taste
2 tbsps. balsamic vinegar

In a pan that fits the air fryer, combine all the recipe ingredients and toss. Put this pan in your air fryer and Air Fry the food at 300 degrees F for 12 minutes. Divide between plates and serve.

Nutritional information: Calories 122g; Total Carbs 4g; Net Carbs 2g; Protein 5; Fat 4g; Sugar 2g; Fiber 3g

Kale Olives Salad

Prep time: 5 minutes | Cook time: 15 minutes | Serves: 4

1 an ½ lbs. kale, torn
2 tbsp. olive oil
Salt and black pepper to the taste

1 tbsp. hot paprika
2 tbsp. black olives, pitted and sliced

In a pan that fits the air fryer, combine all the recipe ingredients and toss well. Put this pan in your air fryer, Air Fry the food at 370 degrees F for 15 minutes. When cooked, divide between plates and serve.

Nutritional information: Calories 154g; Total Carbs 4g; Net Carbs 2g; Protein 6; Fat 3g; Sugar 2g; Fiber 2 g

Kale Mushrooms Mix

Prep time: 5 minutes | Cook time: 15 minutes | Serves: 4

1 lb. brown mushrooms, sliced
1-lb. kale, torn
Salt and black pepper to the

taste
2 tbsps. olive oil
14 oz. coconut milk

In a pot that fits your air fryer, mix the kale with the rest of the ingredients and toss. Put this pan in the fryer, Air Fry the food at 380 degrees F for 15 minutes. When cooked, divide between plates and serve.

Nutritional information: Calories 162g; Total Carbs 3g; Net Carbs 2g; Protein 5; Fat 4g; Sugar 2g; Fiber 1g

Oregano Kale

Prep time: 5 minutes | Cook time: 10 minutes | Serves: 4

1-lb. kale, torn
1 tbsp. olive oil

A pinch of salt and black pepper
2 tbsps. oregano, chopped

In a pan that fits the air fryer, combine all the recipe ingredients and toss well. Put this pan in the air fryer and Air Fry the food at 380 degrees F for 10 minutes. Divide between plates and serve.

Nutritional information: Calories 140g; Total Carbs 3g; Net Carbs 2g; Protein 5; Fat 3; Fiber 2 g; Sugar 2g; Fiber 2.5g

Olives Avocado Mix

Prep time: 5 minutes | Cook time: 15 minutes | Serves: 4

2 cups Kalamata olives, pitted
2 small avocados, pitted, peeled and sliced

¼ cup cherry tomatoes, halved
Juice of 1 lime
1 tbsp. coconut oil, melted

In a pan that fits the air fryer, combine the olives with the other ingredients and toss well. Put this pan in your air fryer and Air Fry the food at 370 degrees F for 15 minutes. Divide the mix between plates and serve.

Nutritional information: Calories 153g; Total Carbs 4g; Net Carbs 2g; Protein 6; Fat 3g; Sugar 2g; Fiber 3g

Olives, Green Beans and Bacon

Prep time: 5 minutes | Cook time: 15 minutes | Serves: 4

½ lb. green beans, trimmed and halved
1 cup black olives, pitted and halved

¼ cup bacon, cooked and crumbled
1 tbsp. olive oil
¼ cup tomato sauce

In a pan that fits the air fryer, combine all the recipe ingredients and toss well. Put this pan in the air fryer and Air Fry the food at 380 degrees F for 15 minutes. Divide between plates and serve.

Nutritional information: Calories 160g; Total Carbs 5g; Net Carbs 2g; Protein 4; Fat 4g; Sugar 2g; Fiber 3g

Cajun Peppers

Prep time: 4 minutes | Cook time: 12 minutes | Serves: 4

1 tbsp. olive oil
½ lb. mixed bell peppers, sliced

1 cup black olives, pitted and halved
½ tbsp. Cajun seasoning

In a pan that fits the air fryer, combine all the recipe ingredients. Put this pan it in your air fryer and Air Fry the food at 390 degrees F for 12 minutes. Divide the mix between plates and serve.

Nutritional information: Calories 151g; Total Carbs 4g; Net Carbs 2g; Protein 5; Fat 3g; Sugar 2g; Fiber 2g

Sweet Potato Fries

Prep time: 10 minutes | Cook time: 12-15 minutes | Serves: 4

3 large sweet potatoes, peeled
1 tbsp. olive oil

A pinch tsp. sea salt

Cut the sweet potatoes in quarters, cutting them lengthwise to make fries. Combine the uncooked fries with a tbsp. of sea salt and olive oil. Make sure all of your fries are coated well. Place your sweet potato pieces in the Air Fryer Basket, cook them at 390 degrees F on Air Fry mode for 12 minutes. Air Fry the food for 2 to 3 minutes more if you want it to be crispier. Add more salt to taste, and serve when cooled.
Nutritional information: Calories 150; Fat 6g; Total Carbs 8; Net Carb 2g; Protein 9; Fat 3g; Sugar 2g; Fiber 2g

Crisp Cabbage

Prep time: 5 minutes | Cook time: 10 minutes | Serves: 2

½ head white cabbage, chopped & washed
1 tbsp. coconut oil, melted
¼ tsp. cayenne pepper
¼ tsp. chili powder
¼ tsp. garlic powder

At 390 degrees F, preheat your Air Fryer. Mix your cabbage, spices and coconut oil together in a suitable bowl, making sure your cabbage is coated well. Place it in the air fryer basket and Air Fry the food at 390 degrees F for 10 minutes. When done, serve and enjoy.
Nutritional information: Calories 100; Fat 2g; Total Carbs 3; Net Carb 2g; Protein 5; Fat 3g; Sugar 2g; Fiber 2g

Garlic Potatoes

Prep time: 10 minutes | Cook time: 40 minutes | Serves: 4

3 baking potatoes, large
2 tbsp. olive oil
2 tbsp. garlic, minced
1 tbsp. salt
½ tbsp. onion powder

At 390 degrees F, preheat your Air Fryer. Create holes in your potatoes, and then sprinkle it with oil and salt. Mix the garlic and onion powder together, and then evenly rub the potatoes with the mixture. Put the potatoes into the Air Fryer Basket, and then cook them at 390 degrees F for 35 to 40 minutes on Bake mode. When done, serve and enjoy.
Nutritional information: Calories 160 Fat 6g; Total Carbs 9; Net Carb 2g; Protein 9; Fat 3g; Sugar 2g; Fiber 2

Green Bean Casserole

Prep time: 5minutes | Cook time: 34 minutes | Serves: 4

1 lb. green beans, diced
1 can (10.5 oz.) cream of mushroom soup
¾ cup milk
1½ cups crispy fried onions
¼ tsp. black pepper
⅛ tsp. kosher salt

Add the green beans to the preheated air fryer and Air Fry them at 400 degrees F for 14 minutes. Mix cream of mushroom soup, half of the crispy fried onions, green beans, milk, black pepper, and salt until fully incorporated, then place in the casserole dish. Place casserole dish in your preheated air fryer and cook the food at 400 degrees F for 20 minutes on Bake mode. Place the remaining crispy fried onions on top of the casserole after 14 minutes of cooking time. Serve immediately.
Nutritional information: Calories 926; Total Carbs 70.3g; Net Carbs 2g; Protein 13g; Fat 3g; Sugar 2g; Fiber 2

Spiced Cauliflower with Nuts

Prep time: 5minutes | Cook time: 20 minutes | Serves: 3-4

2 lbs. cauliflower, cut into   florets

2 tbsps. vegetable oil
2 tsps. curry powder
2 tsps. crushed red chili flakes
2 tsps. kosher salt
½ cup raisins
¼ cup macadamia nuts, chopped

Combine cauliflower, vegetable oil, curry powder, red chili flakes, and salt in a suitable bowl. Mix well. At 400 degrees F, preheat your Air Fryer. Layer the "Air Fryer Basket" with baking paper and spread the cauliflower evenly on top. Insert the "Air Fryer Basket" in your preheated air fryer and cook the food at 400 degrees F for 20 minutes on Broil mode. Remove the cauliflower when done, mix in raisins and macadamia nuts, then serve.
Nutritional information: Calories 258; Total Carbs 28.1g; Net Carbs 2g; Protein 5.8g; Fat 3g; Sugar 2g; Fiber 2

Baked Grape Tomatoes

Prep time: 5minutes | Cook time: 30 minutes | Serves: 3-4

12 oz. grape tomatoes
3 sprigs thyme
2 tbsps. olive oil
3 cloves garlic, minced
¼ tsp. oregano
¼ tsp. red pepper flakes
¼ tsp. kosher salt
¼ tsp. cracked black pepper

At 400 degrees F, preheat your Air Fryer. Mix all the recipe ingredients in a suitable bowl, then set aside. Layer the "Air Fryer Basket" with baking paper, then spread the tomatoes evenly on top. Insert the "Air Fryer Basket" at in your preheated air fryer and cook the food at 370 degrees F on Bake mode for 30 minutes Remove tomatoes when done, then serve.
Nutritional information: Calories 89; Total Carbs 4.7g; Net Carbs 2g; Protein 1g; Fat 3g; Sugar 2g; Fiber 2

Zucchini Pizzas

Prep time: 5minutes | Cook time: 25 minutes | Serves: 2-3

1 large zucchini squash, cut into ¼-inch thick slices
Shredded mozzarella cheese,
for topping
Mini pepperonis, for topping

Layer the baking pan with baking paper and place zucchini slices on top. Top each zucchini slice with mozzarella cheese and mini pepperonis. Set aside. Place the prepared baking pan in your preheated air fryer and cook the food at 375 degrees F on Bake mode for 25 minutes. Remove when done and allow to cool for 5 minutes, then serve.
Nutritional information: Calories 72; Total Carbs 0.3g; Net Carbs 2g; Protein 4.3g; Fat 3g; Sugar 2g; Fiber 2g

Chinese Green Beans

Prep time: 5minutes | Cook time: 20 minutes | Serves: 3-4

12 oz. green beans
1 tbsp. vegetable oil
2 tsps. Xiao Xing wine
2 tsps. soy sauce
½ tsp. kosher salt
3 garlic cloves, minced
3 tbsps. peanuts, chopped

Mix all the recipe ingredients except peanuts in a suitable bowl, then set aside. Layer the "Air Fryer Basket" with baking paper, then spread the green bean mixture evenly on top. Place this basket in the air fryer and cook the green bean mixture at 400 degrees F for 20 minutes on Broil mode. Remove when done, top with chopped peanuts, then serve.
Nutritional information: Calories 109; Total Carbs 8.1g; Net Carbs 2g; Protein 3.6g; Fat 3g; Sugar 2g; Fiber 2g

Spinach Cheddar Quiches

Prep time: 5minutes | Cook time: 25 minutes | Serves: 6

2 (9-inch) premade pie crusts	¼ cup frozen spinach, drained
2 eggs	½ tsp. salt
¼ cup heavy cream	A pinch of black pepper
¼ cup whole milk	A pinch of garlic powder
½ cup sharp cheddar cheese, shredded	A pinch of onion powder
	A pinch of nutmeg

Cut pie crust into 6 circles with 3-inch diameters. Place the circles into the muffin pan. Poke some small holes in the pie crusts with a fork. Set aside. Whisk the remaining ingredients together in a suitable bowl well. Pour the prepared egg mixture evenly between the pie crusts; place in the air fryer. Cook the food at 375 degrees F for 25 minutes on Bake mode. Remove when done, then serve.
Nutritional information: Calories 117; Total Carbs 4.1g; Net Carbs 2g; Protein 5g; Fat 3g; Sugar 2g; Fiber 2g

Tomato Spinach Frittatas

Prep time: 5minutes | Cook time: 15 minutes | Serves: 6

4 eggs	2 tbsp. heavy cream
¼ cup Parmesan cheese, shredded	¾ tsp. salt
½ cup mozzarella cheese, grated	¼ tsp. black pepper
¾ cup baby spinach, chopped	9 grape tomatoes, halved
	Cooking spray

Stir together heavy cream, eggs, mozzarella, Parmesan, spinach, salt, and pepper. Grease a suitable muffin cups with some cooking spray. Pour the prepared egg mixture evenly between the muffin cups. Add 3 tomato halves to each muffin cup then place them in the air fryer. Cook the food at 350 degrees F for 15 minutes on Bake mode. Remove the frittatas when done and serve.
Nutritional information: Calories 107; Total Carbs 7.8g; Net Carbs 2g; Protein 6.2g; Fat 3g; Sugar 2g; Fiber 2 g

Potato Wedges

Prep time: 8minutes | Cook time: 30 minutes | Serves: 4

3 medium russet potatoes, cut into wedges	½ tsp. ancho chili powder
2 tsps. olive oil	½ tsp. garlic powder
1 tsp. dried rosemary	¼ tsp. black pepper, freshly cracked
½ tsp. ground Mexican chili pepper	A pinch of salt

At 350 degrees F, preheat your Air Fryer. Coat the potato wedges in olive oil, then add the remaining ingredients and mix thoroughly. Place the wedges into the Air Fryer Basket and cook them at 350 degrees F on Air Fry mode for 30 minutes. Remove wedges when done, then serve with your sauce of choice.
Nutritional information: Calories 138; Total Carbs 26g; Net Carbs 2g; Protein 3g; Fat 3g; Sugar 2g; Fiber 2g

Baked Sweet Potato

Prep time: 5minutes | Cook time: 60 minutes | Serves: 3

2 large sweet potatoes	2 tbsp. chives, chopped
1 cup plain whole-milk yogurt	¼ tsp. kosher salt
2 tbsp. honey	

At 350 degrees F, preheat your Air Fryer. Place sweet potatoes in your preheated air fryer and Air Fry them at 350 degrees F for 60 minutes. Mix yogurt, honey, chives, and kosher salt in a suitable bowl and refrigerate until the sweet potatoes are fully baked. Remove sweet potatoes when done and let cool for 5 minutes. Make an incision in the middle of the potatoes and serve with a dollop of chive yogurt sauce.
Nutritional information: Calories 264; Total Carbs 38g; Net Carbs 2g; Protein 10g; Fat 3g; Sugar 2g; Fiber 2g

Parmesan Brussel Sprouts

Prep time: 10minutes | Cook time: 20 minutes | Serves: 4

10 Brussel sprouts halved	½ tbsp. Parmesan cheese, grated
3 tbsps. olive oil, divided	3 cups of water
¼ tsp. kosher salt	
3 cloves garlic, minced	

Mix 2 tablespoons of olive oil with salt, garlic, and Parmesan in a suitable bowl. Boil Brussel sprouts in 3 cups of water for 5 minutes, then set aside. At 400 degrees F, preheat your Air Fryer. Place Brussel sprouts into the Air Fryer Basket and brush with the remaining olive oil. Cook the Brussel sprouts for 15 minutes at 400 degrees F on Air Fry mode. Brush Parmesan mixture on each Brussel sprout half when there are 7 minutes of cook time left. Remove when done and serve immediately.
Nutritional information: Calories 127; Total Carbs 5g; Net Carbs 2g; Protein 2g; Fat 3g; Sugar 2g; Fiber 2g

Air Fried Corn Ears

Prep time: 5minutes | Cook time: 18 minutes | Serves: 3

3 whole ears of corn, without husks	2 tbsp. butter
	¼ tsp. salt

At 400 degrees F, preheat your Air Fryer. Place ears of corn in the "Air Fryer Basket" and cook them at 400 degrees F for 18 minutes on Air Fry mode. Remove when done, brush butter and sprinkle salt on each ear of corn, and serve immediately.
Nutritional information: Calories 209; Total Carbs 27g; Net Carbs 2g; Protein 5g; Fat 3g; Sugar 2g; Fiber 2g

Air Fried Eggplant

Prep time: 10minutes | Cook time: 20 minutes | Serves: 4

1 eggplant, cut lengthwise into ½-inch thick slices	½ tsp. salt
2 tbsps. olive oil	1 tsp. garlic powder
3 tbsps. balsamic vinegar	½ tsp. ground black pepper

Whisk olive oil, balsamic vinegar, salt, garlic powder, and black pepper until fully combined. At 400 degrees F, preheat your Air Fryer. Brush balsamic mix on both sides of the eggplant slices then places into the Air Fryer Basket. Cook the eggplant slices at 400 degrees F for 20 minutes on Air Fry mode. Remove when done and serve immediately.
Nutritional information: Calories 99; Total Carbs 8g; Net Carbs 2g; Protein 1g; Fat 7g; Sugar 2g; Fiber 2g

Parmesan Asparagus

Prep time: 5minutes | Cook time: 10 minutes | Serves: 4

1 lb. fresh asparagus	2 tsp. olive oil

¼ tsp. kosher salt
A pinch of black pepper

3 tbsps. Parmesan cheese, grated

Hold the ends of an asparagus spear and bend until it snaps to remove the woody end. Cut the ends of the rest of the asparagus in line with the snapped asparagus. Layer the "Air Fryer Basket" with baking paper. Place the asparagus on top and drizzle with olive oil. Drizzle kosher salt and black pepper and cook the food at 400 degrees F for 10 minutes on Air Fry mode. After 5 minutes of cooking, sprinkle the asparagus with Parmesan cheese. Remove the asparagus when done, then serve.
Nutritional information: Calories 102; Total Carbs 5g; Net Carbs 2g; Protein 7g; Fat 6g; Sugar 2g; Fiber 2g

Pesto Pinwheels

Prep time: 5minutes | Cook time: 15 minutes | Serves: 3

⅓ cup fresh basil
3 cloves garlic
3 tbsps. pine nuts
⅓ tbsp. Parmesan cheese, grated
⅓ tbsp. olive oil

Salt & pepper, to taste
½ sheet store-bought puff pastry
½ cup mozzarella cheese, shredded

Combine pine nuts, garlic, basil, and Parmesan cheese in a food processor. Pulse the ingredients until chopped. Drizzle in olive oil while blending. Season the prepared pesto with black pepper and salt to taste. Spread the pesto on the sheet of puff pastry, then sprinkle with mozzarella cheese. Roll the puff pastry lengthwise and pinch edge to seal. Cut into ½-inch-thick slices. At 375 degrees F, preheat your Air Fryer. Line a suitable baking pan with baking paper and set the pinwheels on top. Place the baking pan in your preheated air fryer and cook the food for 15 minutes on Bake mode. Remove when done and serve.
Nutritional information: Calories 105; Total Carbs 3g; Net Carbs 2g; Protein 3g; Fat 9g; Sugar 2g; Fiber 2g

Vegetarian Quesadillas

Prep time: 10minutes | Cook time: 12 minutes | Serves: 2

2 tbsps. vegetable oil
¼ onion, diced
½ cup canned whole corn kernels, strained
½ cup canned black beans, strained
⅛ tsp. kosher salt

⅛ tsp. black pepper
1 tsp. taco seasoning
¼ lime, juiced
2 medium-sized flour tortillas
½ cup queso Chihuahua or mozzarella cheese, grated

At 400 degrees F, preheat your Air Fryer. Place vegetable oil, onion, corn, and black beans in a skillet over medium heat. Sauté for 5 minutes. Add salt, taco seasoning, pepper, and lime juice to the skillet and cook for 3 minutes. Select Bake function, adjust the cooking time to 400 degrees F and set the cooking time to 4 minutes. Place the bean mix on 1 of the tortillas, leaving a 1-inch border. Sprinkle cheese on top of the bean mix, then place the remaining tortilla on top. Place quesadilla on the "Air Fryer Basket" then inserts "Air Fryer Basket" in your preheated air fryer and cook. Cut quesadillas into 4 pieces and serve with guacamole, sour cream, or your favorite salsa.
Nutritional information: Calories 437; Total Carbs 55g; Net Carbs 2g; Protein 16g; Fat 17g; Sugar 2g; Fiber 2g

Tangy Corn

Prep time: 10minutes | Cook time: 26 minutes | Serves: 3

3 whole ears of corn, without   husks

2 tbsp. butter
¼ tsp. salt
½ tsp. chili powder

¼ tsp. black pepper
1 lime, juiced and divided
1 tbsp. grated Parmesan

At 400 degrees F, preheat your Air fryer. Place ears of corn in your preheated air fryer and cook them on Roast mode for 18 minutes. Cool corn for 5 minutes and cut kernels into a bowl. Heat a suitable skillet over medium heat and add butter, letting it melt. Add salt, Chile powder, black pepper, and half the lime juice to the corn and cook for 3 minutes. Sprinkle Parmesan and remaining lime juice on top of the corn and serve immediately
Nutritional information: Calories 251; Total Carbs 31g; Net Carbs 2g; Protein 7g; Fat 11g; Sugar 2g; Fiber 2g

Zucchini Patties

Prep time: 15 minutes | Cook time: 10 minutes | Serves: 4

2 zucchinis, trimmed, grated
1 egg yolk
½ tsp. salt
1 tsp. ground turmeric

½ tsp. ground paprika
1 tsp. cream cheese
3 tbsps. flax meal
1 tsp. sesame oil

Squeeze the juice from the zucchinis and put them in the big bowl. Add egg yolk, salt, ground turmeric, ground paprika, flax meal, and cream cheese. Stir the prepared mixture well with the help of the spoon. Then make medium size patties from the zucchini mixture. At 385 degrees F, preheat your Air Fryer. Brush the "Air Fryer Basket" with sesame oil and put the patties inside. Air Fry them for 5 minutes per side.
Nutritional information: Calories 67; Total Carbs 5.5g; Net Carbs 2g; Protein 3.1; Fat 5g; Sugar 2g; Fiber 2g

Asparagus with a Sauce

Prep time: 4 minutes | Cook time: 10 minutes | Serves: 4

1 lb. asparagus, trimmed
2 tbsp. olive oil
A pinch of salt and black pepper
1 tsp. garlic powder
1 tsp. oregano, dried

1 cup Greek yogurt
cup basil, chopped
½ cup parsley, chopped
¼ cup chives, chopped
¼ cup lemon juice
garlic cloves, minced

In a suitable bowl, mix the asparagus with the oil, salt, pepper, oregano and garlic powder, and toss. Put the asparagus in the "Air Fryer Basket" and Air Fry them at 400 degrees F for 10 minutes. Meanwhile, in a blender, mix the yogurt with basil, chives, parsley, lemon juice and garlic cloves and pulse well. Divide the asparagus between plates, drizzle the sauce all over and serve.
Nutritional information: Calories 194g; Total Carbs 4g; Net Carbs 2g; Protein 8; Fat 6g; Sugar 2g; Fiber 2g

Cheesy Patties

Prep time: 20 minutes | Cook time: 6 minutes | Serves: 2

1 ½ cup fresh spinach, chopped
3 oz. provolone cheese, shredded
1 egg, beaten

¼ cup almond flour
½ tsp. salt
Cooking spray

Put the chopped spinach in the blender and blend it until you get a smooth mixture. After this, transfer the grinded spinach in the big bowl. Add shredded provolone cheese, beaten egg, almond flour, and salt. Stir the spinach mixture with the help of the spoon until it is homogenous. Then make the patties from the spinach mixture. At 400 degrees F, preheat your Air Fryer.

Grease your "Air Fryer Basket" with some cooking spray from inside and put the spinach patties. Air Fry them for 6 minutes, flipping halfway through. The patties should be light brown when done. Serve and enjoy.

Nutritional information: Calories 206g; Total Carbs 2.7g; Net Carbs 2g; Protein 15; Fat 15.4g; Sugar 2g; Fiber 0.9

Asparagus and Tomatoes

Prep time: 5 minutes | Cook time: 10 minutes | Serves: 4

1 lb. asparagus, trimmed
2 cups cherry tomatoes, halved
¼ cup parmesan, grated
½ cup balsamic vinegar
2 tbsps. olive oil
A pinch of salt and black pepper

In a suitable bowl, mix the asparagus with the rest of the ingredients except the parmesan, and toss. Put the asparagus and tomatoes in your "Air Fryer Basket" and Air Fry them at 400 degrees F for 10 minutes Divide between plates and serve with the parmesan sprinkled on top.

Nutritional information: Calories 173; Fat 4g; Sugar 2g; Fiber 2g; Total Carbs 4g; Net Carbs 2g; Protein 8; Fat 3g; Sugar 2g; Fiber 2g

Mozzarella Green Beans

Prep time: 10 minutes | Cook time: 6 minutes | Serves: 4

1 cup green beans, trimmed
2 oz. Mozzarella, shredded
1 tsp. butter
½ tsp. chili flakes
¼ cup beef broth

Sprinkle the green beans with chili flakes and put them in the suitable cooking pan. Add beef broth and butter. Then top the vegetables with shredded Mozzarella. At 400 degrees F, preheat your Air Fryer. Put this pan with green beans in the air fryer and Air Fry the meal for 6 minutes. When done, serve and enjoy.

Nutritional information: Calories 80g; Total Carbs 5.8g; Net Carbs 2g; Protein 6.3; Fat 3.7g; Sugar 2g; Fiber 1.9

Cheddar Asparagus

Prep time: 5 minutes | Cook time: 10 minutes | Serves: 4

2 lbs. asparagus, trimmed
2 tbsps. olive oil
1 cup cheddar cheese, shredded
4 garlic cloves, minced
4 bacon slices, cooked and crumbled

In a suitable bowl, mix the asparagus with the other ingredients except the bacon, toss and put in your "Air Fryer Basket". Air Fry the food at 400 degrees F for 10 minutes Divide between plates, sprinkle the bacon on top and serve.

Nutritional information: Calories 172g; Total Carbs 5g; Net Carbs 2g; Protein 8; Fat 3g; Sugar 2g; Fiber 2g

Sesame Fennel

Prep time: 10 minutes | Cook time: 15 minutes | Serves: 2

8 oz. fennel bulb, halved
1 tsp. sesame oil
½ tsp. salt
1 tsp. white pepper

Then sprinkle the fennel bulb with salt, white pepper, and sesame oil. At 370 degrees F, preheat your Air Fryer. Put the fennel bulb halves in the air fryer and Air Fry them for 15

minutes.

Nutritional information: Calories 58g; Total Carbs 9g; Net Carbs 2g; Protein 1.5; Fat 2.5g; Sugar 2g; Fiber 3.8g

Mustard Garlic Asparagus

Prep time: 5 minutes | Cook time: 12 minutes | Serves: 4

1 lb. asparagus, trimmed
2 tbsps. olive oil
¼ cup mustard
3 garlic cloves, minced
½ cup parmesan, grated

In a suitable bowl, mix the asparagus with the oil, garlic and mustard and toss really well. Put the asparagus spears in your "Air Fryer Basket" and Air Fry them at 400 degrees F for 12 minutes. Divide between plates, sprinkle the parmesan on top and serve.

Nutritional information: Calories 162g; Total Carbs 6g; Net Carbs 2g; Protein 9; Fat 3g; Sugar 2g; Fiber 2g

Mozzarella Asparagus Mix

Prep time: 5 minutes | Cook time: 10 minutes | Serves: 4

1 lb. asparagus, trimmed
2 tbsp. olive oil
A pinch of salt and black pepper
2 cups mozzarella, shredded
½ cup balsamic vinegar
2 cups cherry tomatoes, halved

In a suitable pan, mix the asparagus with the rest of the ingredients except the mozzarella and toss. Put this pan in the air fryer and Air Fry the food at 400 degrees F for 10 minutes. Divide between plates and serve.

Nutritional information: Calories 200; Fat 6g; Sugar 2g; Fiber 2g; Total Carbs 3g; Net Carbs 2g; Protein 6; Fat 3g; Sugar 2g; Fiber 2g

Thyme Radish Mix

Prep time: 10 minutes | Cook time: 5 minutes | Serves: 3

2 cups radish, trimmed
½ tsp. onion powder
½ tsp. salt
½ tsp. thyme
½ tsp. ground black pepper
½ tsp. ground paprika
1 tsp. ghee

Chop the radish roughly and mix it up with onion powder, salt, thyme, ground black pepper, ad paprika. After this, preheat your Air Fryer to 375 degrees F. Put the roughly chopped radish in the air fryer and Air Fry the food for 2 minutes. Then add ghee, shake well and cook the vegetables for 3 minutes more. When cooked, serve and enjoy.

Nutritional information: Calories 29; Total Carbs 3.5g; Net Carbs 2g; Protein 0.7; Fat 1.6g; Sugar 2g; Fiber 1.5g

Paprika Asparagus

Prep time: 5 minutes | Cook time: 10 minutes | Serves: 4

1 lb. asparagus, trimmed 3 tbsp. olive oil
A pinch of salt and black
pepper
1 tbsp. sweet paprika

In a suitable bowl, mix the asparagus with the rest of the ingredients and toss. Put the asparagus in your "Air Fryer Basket". Air Fry the food at 400 degrees F for 10 minutes. Divide between plates and serve.

Nutritional information: Calories 200; Total Carbs 4g; Net

Carbs 2g; Protein 6; Fat 5g; Sugar 2g; Fiber 2g

Pancetta Okra

Prep time: 10 minutes | Cook time: 10 minutes | Serves: 4

1-lb. okra, trimmed
3 oz. pancetta, sliced
½ tsp. ground nutmeg

½ tsp. salt
1 tsp. sunflower oil

Sprinkle okra with ground nutmeg and salt. Then put the vegetables in the air fryer and sprinkle with sunflower. Chop pancetta roughly. Top the okra with pancetta and Air Fry the meal for 10 minutes at 360 degrees F in the air fryer. When done, serve and enjoy.
Nutritional information: Calories 172g; Total Carbs 8.9g; Net Carbs 2g; Protein 10.1; Fat 10.4g; Sugar 2g; Fiber 3.7g

Lemon Asparagus

Prep time: 5 minutes | Cook time: 12 minutes | Serves: 4

1 lb. asparagus, trimmed
A pinch of salt and black pepper
2 tbsps. olive oil

3 garlic cloves, minced
3 tbsps. parmesan, grated
Juice of 1 lemon

In a suitable bowl, mix the asparagus with the rest of the ingredients and toss. Put the asparagus in your "Air Fryer Basket" and Air Fry the food at 390 degrees F for 12 minutes. Divide between plates and serve.
Nutritional information: Calories 175g; Total Carbs 4g; Net Carbs 2g; Protein 8; Fat 5g; Sugar 2g; Fiber 2g

Feta Peppers

Prep time: 15 minutes | Cook time: 10 minutes | Serves: 4

5 oz. Feta, crumbled
8 oz. banana pepper, trimmed
1 tsp. sesame oil
1 garlic clove, minced

½ tsp. fresh dill, chopped
1 tsp. lemon juice
½ tsp. lime zest, grated

Clean the seeds from the peppers and cut them into halves. Then sprinkle the peppers with sesame oil and put in the air fryer. Cook them for 10 minutes at 385 degrees F. Flip the peppers on another side after 5 minutes of cooking. Meanwhile, mix up minced garlic, fresh dill, lemon juice, and lime zest. Put the cooked banana peppers on the plate and sprinkle with lemon juice mixture. Then top the vegetables with crumbled feta.
Nutritional information: Calories 107g; Total Carbs 2.2g; Net Carbs 2g; Protein 5.2; Fat 8.7g; Sugar 2g; Fiber 0.2g

Spicy Kale

Prep time: 5 minutes | Cook time: 10 minutes | Serves: 4

1 lb. kale, torn
1 tbsp. olive oil
1 tsp. hot paprika

A pinch of salt and black pepper
2 tbsps. oregano, chopped

In a pan that fits the air fryer, combine all the recipe ingredients and toss. Put this pan in the air fryer and Air Fry the food at 380 degrees F for 10 minutes. Divide between plates and serve.
Nutritional information: Calories 140; Total Carbs 3g; Net Carbs 2g; Protein 5g; Fat 3g; Sugar 2g; Fiber 2g

Awesome Mushroom Tots

Prep time: 15 minutes | Cook time: 6 minutes | Serves: 2

1 cup white mushrooms, grinded
1 teaspoon onion powder
1 egg yolk
3 teaspoons flax meal

½ teaspoon ground black pepper
1 teaspoon avocado oil
1 tablespoon coconut flour

Add the onion powder, flax meal, ground black pepper, coconut flour, and grinded white mushrooms in a mixing bowl. Mix until smooth and homogenous. Then make the mushroom tots from the mixture. Before cooking, heat your air fryer to 400 degrees F. Grease the air fryer basket with coconut oil. Arrange evenly the mushroom tots on the air fryer basket. Cook in your air fryer for 3 minutes. Then flip the tots to the other side and continue cooking for 2to 3 minutes or until they are lightly brown.
Nutritional information: Calories: 88; Fat: 4.7g; Total Carbs: 8g; Net Carbs: 3.5g; Fiber: 4.7g; Sugars: 1.1g; Protein: 4.4g

Pungent Mushroom Pizza

Prep time: 8-10 minutes | Cook time: 8 minutes | Serves: 3-4

3 tablespoons olive oil
3 cleaned portabella mushroom caps, scooped
3 tablespoons tomato sauce
12 slices pepperoni

3 tablespoons mozzarella, shredded
1 pinch salt
1 pinch dried Italian seasonings

On a flat kitchen surface, plug your air fryer and turn it on. Preheat your air fryer to 330 degrees F for 4 to 5 minutes. Gently coat your air fryer basket with cooking oil or spray. Toss the mushrooms with olive oil. Season the inner side with Italian seasoning and salt. Sprinkle the top with tomato sauce and cheese. Arrange evenly the mushrooms onto the grease air fryer basket. Cook in your air fryer at 330 degrees F for 2 minutes. When the cooking time is up, add the pepperoni slices and continue cooking for 4 to 5 minutes. To serve, sprinkle the top with red pepper flakes and more cheese as you like.
Nutritional information: Calories: 242; Fat: 21.6g; Total Carbs: 2g; Net Carbs: 0.5g; Fiber: 0.2g; Sugars: 0.5g; Protein: 10.6g

Enticing Cauliflower Tots

Prep time: 15 minutes | Cook time: 8 minutes | Serves: 4

1 teaspoon cream cheese
5 ounces Monterey Jack cheese, shredded
1 cup cauliflower, chopped,

boiled
¼ teaspoon garlic powder
1 teaspoon sunflower oil

In a blender, add the boiled cauliflower, garlic powder, shredded Monterey Jack cheese, and cream cheese and mix until smooth. Then make the cauliflower tots and cool them in the refrigerator for 10 minutes. Before cooking, heat your air fryer to 365 degrees F. Transfer the broccoli tots inside the air fryer basket. Sprinkle sunflower oil on the top and cook in your air fryer for 8 minutes. Flip to the other side halfway through cooking.
Nutritional information: Calories: 152; Fat: 12.2g; Total Carbs: 1g; Net Carbs: 0g; Fiber: 0.7g; Sugars: 0.8g; Protein: 9.3g

Zucchini and Potato Polenta

Prep time: 10-15 minutes | Cook time: 40 minutes | Serves: 5-6

½ pound zucchini, cut into

bite-sized chunks

½ pound potatoes, make bite-sized chunks
½ teaspoon ground black pepper
½ teaspoon dried dill weed
1 tablespoon olive oil
1 cup onions, chopped

2 cloves garlic, finely minced
1 teaspoon paprika
½ teaspoon salt
14 ounces pre-cooked polenta tube, make slices
¼ cup cheddar cheese, shaved

On a flat kitchen surface, plug your air fryer and turn it on. Before cooking, heat your air fryer to 400 degrees F for 4 to 5 minutes. In the air fryer basket, mix together the veggies, paprika, salt, olive oil, dill, and pepper until well-combined. Cook in your air fryer for 6 minutes. Shake for a while and continue cooking for 6 minutes or more. Then add polenta and some cooking oil. Cook for 20 to 25 minutes. Flip the polenta and continue cooking for 10 more minutes. To serve, cut the polenta into slices and top with the roasted vegetables and cheese.

Nutritional information: Calories: 123; Fat: 6.1g; Total Carbs: 14g; Net Carbs: 9.5g; Fiber: 2.9g; Sugars: 3g; Protein: 4g

Mushroom Risotto Croquettes

Prep time: 10-15 minutes | Cook time: 15 minutes | Serves: 4

2 garlic cloves, peeled and minced
½ cup mushrooms, chopped
6 ounces cooked rice
1 tablespoon rice bran oil
1 onion, chopped
Sea salt as needed
¼ teaspoon ground black

pepper
1 tablespoon Colby cheese, grated
1 egg, beaten
1 cup breadcrumbs
½ teaspoon dried dill weed
1 teaspoon paprika

Add oil, onion, and garlic in a medium sized saucepan. Heat the pan over medium heat for a few minutes until turn soft. Then add the mushrooms in the pan. Cook until the liquid thickens. Cool down the mixture. Add and combine salt, black pepper, dill, paprika, and the cooked rice together. Then mix with cheese. Divide the mixture into risotto balls. Dip in the beaten eggs and coat the balls with breadcrumbs. On a flat kitchen surface, plug your air fryer and turn it on. Preheat your air fryer to 390 degrees F for 4 to 5 minutes. Gently grease your air fryer basket with cooking oil or spray. Arrange the balls evenly on the basket. Then cook in your air fryer for 7 minutes. If needed, cook 2 more minutes. When cooked, remove from the air fryer and serve warm with marinara sauce.

Nutritional information: Calories: 332; Fat: 6.9g; Total Carbs: 57g; Net Carbs: 3g; Fiber: 2.7g; Sugars: 3.2g; Protein: 9.2g

Mushroom Mozzarella Risotto

Prep time: 5 minutes | Cook time: 20 minutes | Serves: 4

1 pound white mushrooms, sliced
¼ cup mozzarella, shredded
1 cauliflower head, florets separated and riced
1 cup chicken stock

1 tablespoon thyme, chopped
1 teaspoon Italian seasoning
A pinch of salt and black pepper
2 tablespoons olive oil

Grease a suitable baking pan with oil and then heat to medium heat. Add the cauliflower rice and mushrooms. Toss and cook for a few minutes. Add the shredded mozzarella, chicken stock, Italian seasoning, salt, and black pepper in the pan. Cook in your air fryer at 360 degrees F for 20 minutes. To serve, sprinkle the chopped thyme on the top.

Nutritional information: Calories: 114; Fat: 8.2g; Total Carbs: 8g; Net Carbs: 3.5g; Fiber: 3.1g; Sugars: 3.8g; Protein: 5.6g

Roasted Pepper Salad with Pine Nuts

Prep time: 10 minutes | Cook time: 25 minutes | Serves: 4

2 yellow bell peppers
2 red bell peppers
2 green bell peppers
1 Serrano pepper
4 tbsps. olive oil
2 tbsps. cider vinegar
2 garlic cloves, peeled and pressed

1 tsp. cayenne pepper
Sea salt, to taste
½ tsp. mixed peppercorns, freshly crushed
½ cup pine nuts
¼ cup loosely packed fresh Italian parsley leaves, roughly chopped

Before cooking, heat your air fryer to 400 degrees F. Using cooking oil, lightly brush the air fryer basket. Then transfer the peppers in the air fryer basket and roast in your air fryer for 5 minutes. Turn the peppers and roast the other side for another 5 minutes. Flip again and roast until it is soft and charred on the surface. Peel the peppers and cool them to room temperature. Whisk vinegar, olive oil, garlic, salt, crushed peppercorns, and cayenne pepper together. Then dress the salad and set it aside. Then add the pine nuts inside the air fryer basket. Roast them in your air fryer at 360 degrees F for 4 minutes. Toss the nuts well. Roast again in the air fryer for 3 to 4 minutes. Sprinkle the toasted nuts over the peppers. Garnish with parsley. Enjoy your meal.

Nutritional information: Calories: 270; Fat: 25.9g; Total Carbs: 10.5g; Net Carbs: 0g; Fiber: 2.6g; Sugars: 5.4g; Protein: 3.6g

Buttery Mozzarella Eggplants

Prep time: 5 minutes | Cook time: 15 minutes | Serves: 4

2 tablespoons olive oil
2 eggplants, roughly cubed
8 ounces mozzarella cheese, shredded

3 spring onions, chopped
Juice of 1 lime
2 tablespoons butter, melted
4 eggs, whisked

Heat oil and butter in a suitable cooking pan over medium-high heat. Add eggplants and spring onion in the pan and stir. Cook in your air fryer at 380 degrees F for 5 minutes. Then add lime juice and the eggs in the cooking pan. Cook at 380 degrees F for 10 minutes. Serve on plates as a side dish.

Nutritional information: Calories: 406; Fat: 27.6g; Total Carbs: 19g; Net Carbs: 6.7g; Fiber: 10g; Sugars: 8.8g; Protein: 24.5g

Spicy Bean Meal

Prep time: 8-10 minutes | Cook time: 8 minutes | Serves: 4

½ teaspoon black pepper
1 teaspoon sea salt flakes
½ cup all-purpose flour
1 teaspoon smoky chipotle

powder
2 eggs, beaten
10 ounces wax beans
½ cup saltines, crushed

Mix the black pepper, salt, flour, and chipotle powder in a medium sized bowl. Then whisk in eggs. In another bowl, add the crushed saltines. Coat the beans with the flour mixture, then dip in the whisked eggs. Coat the beans with the crushed saltines. Spray the beans with non-stick cooking spray. On a flat kitchen surface, plug your air fryer and turn it on. Before cooking, heat your air fryer to 360 degrees F for 4 to 5 minutes. Place the mixture into the air fryer basket. Cook in your air fryer for 4 minutes. Then shake for a while and continue cooking for 3 minutes or more. Serve warm.

Nutritional information: Calories: 125; Fat: 3g; Total Carbs:

18g; Net Carbs: 9.5g; Fiber: 1.9g; Sugars: 1.4g; Protein: 5.6g

Spinach Salad with Mustard

Prep time: 5 minutes | Cook time: 10 minutes | Serves: 4

1 pound baby spinach
Salt and black pepper to the taste
1 tablespoon mustard

Cooking spray
¼ cup apple cider vinegar
1 tablespoon chives, chopped

Spray a suitable baking pan with cooking spray. In the pan, combine all the ingredients together. Cook in your air fryer at 350 degrees F for 10 minutes. Serve on plates as a side dish.
Nutritional information: Calories: 44; Fat: 1.4g; Total Carbs: 5g; Net Carbs: 2g; Fiber: 2.9g; Sugars: 0.7g; Protein: 4g

Cheddar Mushroom Cakes

Prep time: 10 minutes | Cook time: 8 minutes | Serves: 4

9 ounces mushrooms, finely chopped
¼ cup coconut flour
1 teaspoon salt
1 egg, beaten
3 ounces Cheddar cheese,

shredded
1 teaspoon dried parsley
½ teaspoon ground black pepper
1 teaspoon sesame oil
1 ounce spring onion, chopped

Mix the coconut flour, salt, dried parsley, minced onion, ground black pepper, egg, and the chopped mushrooms until smooth. Then add Cheddar cheese. Use a fork to stir. Before cooking, heat your air fryer to 385 degrees F. Line baking paper over the air fryer pan. Use a spoon to make medium-size patties from the mixture. Then arrange evenly on the pan. Sprinkle the patties with sesame oil and cook in your air fryer for 4 minutes from each side.
Nutritional information: Calories: 188; Fat: 11g; Total Carbs: 13g; Net Carbs: 7g; Fiber: 6.9g; Sugars: 1.5g; Protein: 10.8g

Cheddar Tomatillos with Lettuce

Prep time: 10 minutes | Cook time: 4 minutes | Serves: 4

2 tomatillos
¼ cup coconut flour
2 eggs, beaten
¼ teaspoon ground nutmeg

¼ teaspoon chili flakes
1 ounce Cheddar cheese, shredded
4 lettuce leaves

Cut the tomatillos into slices. Mix ground nutmeg, chili flakes, and beaten eggs in a bowl. Brush the tomatillo slices with the egg mixture. Then coat with coconut flour. Repeat above steps with the rest slices. Before cooking, heat your air fryer to 400 degrees F. Place the coated tomatillo slices in the air fryer basket in a single layer. Cook in your air fryer for 2 minutes from each side. When cooked, add the lettuce leaves on the top of the tomatillos. To serve, sprinkle with shredded cheese.
Nutritional information: Calories: 127; Fat: 6.3g; Total Carbs: 11.5g; Net Carbs: 5g; Fiber: 6.4g; Sugars: 0.3g; Protein: 6.7g

Cauliflower Bake with Basil Pesto

Prep time: 5 minutes | Cook time: 20 minutes | Serves: 6

1 cup heavy whipping cream
2 tablespoons basil pesto
Salt and black pepper to the taste

Juice of ½ lemon
1 pound cauliflower, florets separated
4 ounces cherry tomatoes,

halved
3 tablespoons ghee, melted

7 ounces cheddar cheese, grated

Drizzle a suitable baking pan with ghee. Gently toss together the lemon juice, pesto, cream, and the cauliflower in the pan. Add the tomatoes and cover the top with cheese. Cook in your air fryer at 380 degrees F for 20 minutes. Serve on plates as a side dish.
Nutritional information: Calories: 281; Fat: 24.9g; Total Carbs: 5g; Net Carbs: 2g; Fiber: 2.1g; Sugars: 2.5g; Protein: 10.4g

Turmeric Tofu Cubes

Prep time: 10 minutes | Cook time: 9 minutes | Serves: 2

6 ounces tofu, cubed
1 teaspoon avocado oil
1 teaspoon apple cider vinegar
1 garlic clove, diced

¼ teaspoon ground turmeric
¼ teaspoon ground paprika
½ teaspoon dried cilantro
¼ teaspoon lemon zest, grated

Before cooking, firstly heat your air fryer to 400 degrees F. Mix together apple cider vinegar, ground turmeric, diced garlic, paprika, avocado oil, lime zest, and cilantro in a bowl. Coat the tofu cubes with the oil mixture. Transfer the tofu cubes in the air fryer basket and cook in your air fryer for 9 minutes. During cooking shake the basket from time to time.
Nutritional information: Calories: 67; Fat: 3.9g; Total Carbs: 2g; Net Carbs: 0.5g; Fiber: 1.1g; Sugars: 0.6g; Protein: 7.2g

Fried Brussel Sprouts

Prep time: 5 minutes | Cook time: 20 minutes | Serves: 4

1 pound Brussels sprouts, trimmed and halved
Salt and black pepper to the taste

2 tablespoons ghee, melted
½ cup coconut cream
2 tablespoons garlic, minced
1 tablespoon chives, chopped

Grease the air fryer basket with the melted ghee. Mix the Brussels sprouts with the remaining ingredients in the air fryer basket. Cook in your air fryer at 370 degrees F for 20 minutes. Serve on plates as a side dish.
Nutritional information: Calories: 181; Fat: 13.9g; Total Carbs: 13g; Net Carbs: 7g; Fiber: 5g; Sugars: 3.5g; Protein: 4.9g

Sweet and Spicy Tofu

Prep time: 15 minutes | Cook time: 23 minutes | Serves: 3

For Tofu:
1 (14-ounce) block firm tofu, pressed and cubed
½ cup arrowroot flour
½ teaspoon sesame oil
For Sauce:
4 tablespoons low-sodium soy sauce

1½ tablespoons rice vinegar
1½ tablespoons chili sauce
1 tablespoon agave nectar
2 large garlic cloves, minced
1 teaspoon fresh ginger, peeled and grated
2 scallions (green part), chopped

Mix arrowroot flour, sesame oil, and tofu together in a bowl. Before cooking, heat your air fryer to 360 degrees F. Gently grease an air fryer basket. Place the tofu evenly on the air fryer basket in a layer. Cook in your air fryer for 20 minutes. Halfway through cooking, shake the air fryer basket once. To make the sauce, add soy sauce, rice vinegar, chili sauce, agave nectar, garlic, and ginger in a bowl. Beat the mixture to combine well. When the tofu has cooked, remove from the air fryer and transfer to a skillet. Add the sauce and heat the skillet over medium heat. Cook for about 3 minutes. Stir the meal from time

to time. Add the scallions to garnish and serve hot.
Nutritional information: Calories: 146; Fat: 6.5g; Total Carbs: 7g; Net Carbs: 3g; Fiber: 1.9g; Sugars: 2.7g; Protein: 13.4g

Open-faced Sandwich

Prep time: 10 minutes | Cook time: 25 minutes | Serves: 4

1 can chickpeas, drained and rinsed	2 ripe avocados, mashed
1 medium-sized head of cauliflower, cut into florets	2 tbsps. lemon juice
	4 flatbreads, toasted
1 tbsp. extra-virgin olive oil	salt and pepper to taste

Before cooking, heat your air fryer to 425 degrees F. Combine chickpea, olive oil, lemon juice, and the cauliflower together in a mixing bowl. Transfer the mixture inside the air fryer basket. Cook in your air fryer for 25 minutes. When cooked, spread the mixture on half of the flatbread and then add avocado mash. To season, add more salt and pepper as you like. Serve the meal with hot sauce.
Nutritional information: Calories: 470; Fat: 26.3g; Total Carbs: 50.1g; Net Carbs: 0g; Fiber: 20.7g; Sugars: 10.9g; Protein: 15.7g

Mozzarella Broccoli and Cauliflower

Prep time: 5 minutes | Cook time: 20 minutes | Serves: 4

15 ounces broccoli florets	2 ounces butter, melted
10 ounces cauliflower florets	2 tablespoons mustard
1 leek, chopped	1 cup sour cream
2 spring onions, chopped	5 ounces mozzarella cheese, shredded
Salt and black pepper to the taste	

Spread butter on a suitable baking pan that fits in your air fryer. Add cauliflower, broccoli florets, chopped leek, chopped spring onions, salt, black pepper, mustard, and sour cream in the baking pan. Toss together. Then drizzle the mozzarella on the top. Cook in your air fryer at 380 degrees F for 20 minutes. Serve on plates as a side dish.
Nutritional information: Calories: 421; Fat: 31.9g; Total Carbs: 20.2g; Net Carbs: 0g; Fiber: 6g; Sugars: 5g; Protein: 18.2g

Spiced Cauliflower Medley

Prep time: 5 minutes | Cook time: 15 minutes | Serves: 4

1 pound cauliflower florets, roughly grated	3 tablespoons butter, melted
	Salt and black pepper to the taste
3 eggs, whisked	1 tablespoon sweet paprika

Heat a pan over high heat and melt the butter in the pan. Then add the cauliflower in the pan and cook until brown for 5 minutes. Add salt, the whisked eggs, paprika, and pepper. Toss well. Cook in your air fryer at 400 degrees F for 10 minutes. Serve on plates.
Nutritional information: Calories: 157; Fat: 12.3g; Total Carbs: 7g; Net Carbs: 3g; Fiber: 3.5g; Sugars: 3.2g; Protein: 6.8g

Roasted Spiced Broccoli with Masala

Prep time: 5 minutes | Cook time: 15 minutes | Serves: 2

¼ teaspoon chat masala	¼ teaspoon turmeric powder

½ teaspoon salt	2 cups broccoli florets
1 tablespoon chickpea flour	2 tablespoons yogurt

In a bowl, add chat masala, turmeric powder, salt, chickpea flour, broccoli florets, and yogurt and combine together. Transfer the mixture inside the air fryer baking pan. Cook in your air fryer at 330 degrees F for 15 minutes. Halfway through cooking, shake the baking pan.
Nutritional information: Calories: 66; Fat: 0.9g; Total Carbs: 11g; Net Carbs: 6.7g; Fiber: 3.5g; Sugars: 3.3g; Protein: 4.7g

Baked Mozzarella Portobello Pasta

Prep time: 10 minutes | Cook time: 30 minutes | Serves: 4

1 cup milk	mushrooms, thinly sliced
1 cup shredded mozzarella cheese	2 tablespoons all-purpose flour
	2 tablespoons soy sauce
1 large clove garlic, minced	4 ounces penne pasta, cooked
1 tablespoon vegetable oil	according to manufacturer's
¼ cup margarine	Directions for Cooking
¼ teaspoon dried basil	5 ounces frozen chopped
¼-pound Portobello	spinach, thawed

Using oil, gently grease a baking pan that fits in your air fryer. Insert in your air fryer and preheat your air fryer to 360 degrees F for about 2 minutes. Add mushroom in the preheated baking pan and cook for 1 minute. When cooked, transfer to a plate. Melt margarine in the baking pan for 1 minutes. Add garlic, flour, and basil and stir. Cook for another 2 minutes. Pour half of the milk and stir slowly. Cook for 2 minutes. Then add the remaining milk and stir again. Cook for 3 minutes. Mix in half of the cheese. Then add soy sauce, mushrooms, pasta, and spinach and mix together. Top the remaining cheese over the meal. Cook in your air fryer at 390 degrees F for 15 minutes or until lightly browned. When cooked, remove from the air fryer and serve warm. Enjoy!
Nutritional information: Calories: 310; Fat: 18.1g; Total Carbs: 26g; Net Carbs: 13g; Fiber: 2g; Sugars: 3.1g; Protein: 12.3g

Chinese Cabbage with Bacon

Prep time: 5 minutes | Cook time: 12 minutes | Serves: 2

8 ounces Chinese cabbage, roughly chopped	1 tablespoon sunflower oil
	½ teaspoon onion powder
2 ounces bacon, chopped	½ teaspoon salt

In your air fryer, add the chopped bacon and cook at 400 degrees F for 10 minutes. During cooking, stir from time to time. Sprinkle the cooked bacon with salt and onion powder. Then add Chinese cabbage and shake to mix well. Cook for 2 minutes. Before serving, add sunflower oil and stir. Serve on plates.
Nutritional information: Calories: 232; Fat: 19.1g; Total Carbs: 3g; Net Carbs: 1g; Fiber: 1.2g; Sugars: 1.6g; Protein: 12.3g

Zucchinis and Arugula Salad

Prep time: 5 minutes | Cook time: 20 minutes | Serves: 4

1-pound zucchinis, sliced	4 ounces arugula leaves
1 tablespoon olive oil	¼ cup chives, chopped
Salt and white pepper to the taste	1 cup walnuts, chopped

Combine the chopped chives, zucchini, olive oil, salt, and white pepper in the air fryer basket. Toss well. Cook in your air fryer at 360 degrees F for 20 minutes. Place the cooked veggies in a salad bowl and toss with the walnuts and arugula. Serve as a

side salad.
Nutritional information: Calories: 249; Fat: 22.4g; Total Carbs: 8g; Net Carbs: 3.5g; Fiber: 3.9g; Sugars: 2.9g; Protein: 9.7g

Tasty Lemon Tempeh

Prep time: 8 minutes | Cook time: 12 minutes | Serves: 4

1 teaspoon lemon juice	¼ teaspoon ground coriander
1 tablespoon sunflower oil	6 ounces tempeh, chopped

In a small bowl, add lemon juice, ground coriander, and sunflower oil and mix to combine. Sprinkle the tempeh with the mixture. Before cooking, heat your air fryer to 325 degrees F. Cook in your air fryer at 325 degrees F for 12 minutes. Flip the tempeh every 2 minutes during cooking.
Nutritional information: Calories: 113; Fat: 8.1g; Total Carbs: 4g; Net Carbs: 2g; Fiber: 0g; Sugars: 0g; Protein: 7.9g

Mozzarella Eggplant Gratin

Prep time: 10 minutes | Cook time: 30 minutes | Serves: 2

¼ cup chopped red pepper	1 teaspoon capers
¼ cup chopped green pepper	¼ teaspoon dried basil
¼ cup chopped onion	¼ teaspoon dried marjoram
⅓ cup chopped tomatoes	Salt and pepper to taste
1 clove garlic, minced	Cooking spray
1 tablespoon sliced pimiento-stuffed olives	¼ cup grated mozzarella cheese
	1 tablespoon breadcrumbs

Before cooking, heat your air fryer to 300 degrees F. Add the green pepper, red pepper, eggplant, onion, olives, garlic, capers, basil marjoram, salt, tomatoes, and pepper in a large bowl. Using olive oil cooking spray, lightly grease a suitable baking dish. Evenly line the eggplant mixture into the baking dish. Then flatten the mixture. Add the mozzarella cheese on the top and spread over with breadcrumbs. Cook in your air fryer for 20 minutes.
Nutritional information: Calories: 47; Fat: 1.3g; Total Carbs: 7g; Net Carbs: 3g; Fiber: 1.3g; Sugars: 2.7g; Protein: 2.3g

Coconut Brussels Sprouts

Prep time: 10 minutes | Cook time: 15 minutes | Serves: 4

8 ounces Brussels sprouts	2 egg whites
2 tablespoons almonds, grinded	½ teaspoon salt
1 teaspoon coconut flakes	½ teaspoon white pepper
	Cooking spray

In a bowl, whisk the egg white. Season with white pepper and salt. Cut the Brussels sprouts into halves and place in the halves the egg white mixture. Shake the vegetables and coat the vegetables with coconut flakes and grinded almonds. Before cooking, heat your air fryer to 380 degrees F. Transfer the Brussels sprouts in the air fryer basket. Cook in your air fryer at 380 degrees F for 15 minutes. After cooking for 8 minutes, shake the basket.
Nutritional information: Calories: 52; Fat: 1.9g; Total Carbs: 6g; Net Carbs: 2.5g; Fiber: 2.6g; Sugars: 1.5g; Protein: 4.4g

Lemon Fennel with Sunflower Seeds

Prep time: 5 minutes | Cook time: 15 minutes | Serves: 4

1 pound fennel, cut into small	wedges

A pinch of salt and black pepper
3 tablespoons olive oil
Salt and black pepper to the

taste
Juice of ½ lemon
2 tablespoons sunflower seeds

Mix fennel wedges, salt, black pepper, olive oil, and lemon in a suitable baking pan. Cook the mixture in your air fryer at 400 degrees F for 15 minutes. When cooked, sprinkle on top with the sunflower seeds. Serve on plates as a side dish.
Nutritional information: Calories: 134; Fat: 11.5g; Total Carbs: 8g; Net Carbs: 3.5g; Fiber: 3.7g; Sugars: 0g; Protein: 1.7g

Creamy Cauliflower Mash

Prep time: 5 minutes | Cook time: 20 minutes | Serves: 4

2 pounds cauliflower florets	Juice of ½ lemon
1 teaspoon olive oil	Zest of ½ lemon, grated
2 ounces parmesan, grated	Salt and black pepper to the
4 ounces butter, soft	taste

Before cooking, heat your air fryer with the air fryer basket to 380 degrees F. Add the cauliflower in the preheated air fryer basket and add oil to rub well. Cook in your air fryer for 20 minutes. When cooked, remove the cauliflower to a bowl. Mash well and place the remaining ingredients in the bowl. Stir well. Serve on plates as a side dish.
Nutritional information: Calories: 316; Fat: 27.4g; Total Carbs: 12g; Net Carbs: 7g; Fiber: 5.7g; Sugars: 5.5g; Protein: 9.3g

Garlic Brussel Sprouts with Celery

Prep time: 15 minutes | Cook time: 13 minutes | Serves: 6

1 pound Brussels sprouts	1 tablespoon butter, melted
1 teaspoon minced garlic	1 teaspoon cayenne pepper
2 ounces celery stalks, minced	¼ teaspoon salt

Roughly chop the Brussels sprouts with celery, cayenne pepper, butter, salt, and minced garlic. Shake the mixture and marinate for 10 minutes. Before cooking, heat the air fryer to 385 degrees F. Cook the marinated Brussels sprouts in your air fryer for 13 minutes. During cooking, shake the basket from time to time.
Nutritional information: Calories: 53; Fat: 2.3g; Total Carbs: 7.5g; Net Carbs: 2.5g; Fiber: 3.1g; Sugars: 1.8g; Protein: 2.7g

Flavorful Radish Salad

Prep time: 8-10 minutes | Cook time: 30 minutes | Serves: 4

1 ½ pounds radishes, trimmed and halved	1 teaspoon olive oil
2 tablespoons olive oil	1 tablespoon balsamic vinegar
Pepper and salt, as needed	½ pound mozzarella, sliced
For the Salad:	1 teaspoon honey
	Pepper and salt, as needed

Mix thoroughly the salt, black pepper, oil, and the radishes in medium sized bowl. On a flat kitchen surface, plug your air fryer and turn it on. Before cooking, heat your air fryer to 350 degrees F for 4 to 5 minutes. Place the mixture onto the air fryer basket. Cook in your air fryer for 3 minutes. In another medium sized bowl, mix thoroughly the cheese and fried radish. Mix the remaining ingredients in a small bowl. Drizzle over the salad to serve.
Nutritional information: Calories: 103; Fat: 7.8g; Total Carbs: 7g; Net Carbs: 3g; Fiber: 2.7g; Sugars: 4.6g; Protein: 2.2g

Lemony Cabbage Slaw

Prep time: 5 minutes | Cook time: 20 minutes | Serves: 4

1 green cabbage head, shredded
Juice of ½ lemon
A pinch of salt and black pepper
½ cup coconut cream
½ teaspoon fennel seeds
1 tablespoon mustard

Combine all the ingredients in a suitable baking pan. Cook in your air fryer at 350 degrees F for 20 minutes. Serve on plates as a side dish.
Nutritional information: Calories: 128; Fat: 8.2g; Total Carbs: 13g; Net Carbs: 7g; Fiber: 5.6g; Sugars: 6.9g; Protein: 3.7g

Creamy Cilantro Peppers Mix

Prep time: 5 minutes | Cook time: 20 minutes | Serves: 4

8 ounces mini bell peppers, halved
1 tablespoon olive oil
1 tablespoon cilantro, chopped
8 ounces cream cheese, soft
1 cup cheddar cheese, shredded
Salt and black pepper to the taste

Brush the olive oil gently over a suitable baking dish. Arrange the bell pepper evenly inside the air fryer basket. Mix all the ingredients in a mixing bowl. Then spread the mixture over the bell pepper. Cook in your air fryer at 370 degrees F for 20 minutes. Serve on plate as a side dish.
Nutritional information: Calories: 358; Fat: 32.6g; Total Carbs: 5g; Net Carbs: 2g; Fiber: 0.7g; Sugars: 2.3g; Protein: 12g

Creamy Cauliflower Puree

Prep time: 10 minutes | Cook time: 8 minutes | Serves: 2

1 ½ cup cauliflower, chopped
1 tablespoon butter, melted
½ teaspoon salt
1 tablespoon fresh parsley,
chopped
¼ cup heavy cream
Cooking spray

Spray the air fryer basket with cooking spray. Place the cauliflower in the air fryer basket. Cook in your air fryer at 400 degrees F for 8 minutes. Stir the cauliflower every 4 minutes. Heat the heavy cream until it is hot. Then pour in a blender, add parsley, butter, salt, and cauliflower. Blend until it is smooth.
Nutritional information: Calories: 122; Fat: 11.4g; Total Carbs: 4.5g; Net Carbs: 0.5g; Fiber: 1.9g; Sugars: 1.8g; Protein: 1.9g

Lemon Cabbage with Cilantro

Prep time: 4 minutes | Cook time: 25 minutes | Serves: 4

1 green cabbage head, shredded and cut into large wedges
2 tablespoons olive oil
1 tablespoon cilantro, chopped
1 tablespoon lemon juice
A pinch of salt and black pepper

Before cooking, heat your air fryer to 370 degrees F. In the air fryer basket, mix all the ingredients. Cook in your air fryer for 25 minutes. Serve on plates as a side dish.
Nutritional information: Calories: 106; Fat: 7.2g; Total Carbs: 10.5g; Net Carbs: 0g; Fiber: 4.5g; Sugars: 5.8g; Protein: 2.3g

Rutabaga Fries

Prep time: 5 minutes | Cook time: 20 minutes | Serves: 4

15 ounces rutabaga, cut into   fries

4 tablespoons olive oil
½ teaspoon chili powder
A pinch of salt and black pepper

Mix all the ingredients in a bowl. Transfer into your air fryer basket. Cook in your air fryer at 400 degrees F for 20 minutes. Serve on plates as a side dish.
Nutritional information: Calories: 159; Fat: 14.3g; Total Carbs: 8g; Net Carbs: 3.5g; Fiber: 2.8g; Sugars: 6g; Protein: 1.3g

Mozzarella Spinach Mash

Prep time: 10 minutes | Cook time: 13 minutes | Serves: 4

3 cups spinach, chopped
½ cup Mozzarella, shredded
4 bacon slices, chopped
1 teaspoon butter
1 cup heavy cream
½ teaspoon salt
½ jalapeno pepper, chopped

In the air fryer basket, place the chopped bacon slices. Cook in your air fryer at 400 degrees F for 8 minutes. During cooking, stir the bacon with a spatula from time to time. In the air fryer casserole mold, add the cooked bacon. Add spinach, heavy cream, salt, and jalapeno pepper, Mozzarella, and butter. Gently stir the mixture. Cook the mash at 400 degrees F for 5 minutes. Using a spoon, carefully stir the spinach mash.
Nutritional information: Calories: 230; Fat: 20.7g; Total Carbs: 2g; Net Carbs: 0.5g; Fiber: 0.6g; Sugars: 0.2g; Protein: 9.3g

Stuffed Peppers

Prep time: 5 minutes | Cook time: 16 minutes | Serves: 1

1 bell pepper
½ tablespoon diced onion
½ diced tomato, plus one tomato slice
¼ teaspoon smoked paprika
Salt and pepper, to taste
1 teaspoon olive oil
¼ teaspoon dried basil

Before cooking, heat your air fryer to 350 degrees F. The bell pepper should be cored and cleaned for stuffing. Using half of the olive oil to brush the pepper on the outside. Combine together the diced onion, the diced tomato, smoked paprika, salt, and pepper in a small bowl. Then stuff the cored pepper with the mixture and add the tomato slice on the top. Using the remaining olive oil, brush the tomato slice. Sprinkle the stuffed pepper with basil. Cook in your air fryer for 10 minutes or until thoroughly cooked.
Nutritional information: Calories: 87; Fat: 5.1g; Total Carbs: 11g; Net Carbs: 6.7g; Fiber: 2.3g; Sugars: 7.1g; Protein: 1.6g

Garlic Provolone Asparagus

Prep time: 10 minutes | Cook time: 5 minutes | Serves: 3

9 ounces Asparagus
¼ teaspoon chili powder
¼ teaspoon garlic powder
1 teaspoon olive oil
4 Provolone cheese slices

Sprinkle the trimmed asparagus with garlic powder and chili powder. Before cooking, heat your air fryer to 400 degrees F. Transfer the asparagus in the air fryer basket. Sprinkle with olive oil. Cook the asparagus in your air fryer for 3 minutes. Sprinkle the Provolone cheese on the top and continue cooking for 3 or more minutes.
Nutritional information: Calories: 163; Fat: 11.6g; Total Carbs: 4g; Net Carbs: 2g; Fiber: 1.9g; Sugars: 1.9g; Protein: 11.5g

Parsley Cabbage

Prep time: 5 minutes | Cook time: 20 minutes | Serves: 4

2 ounces butter, melted
1 green cabbage head, shredded 1 and ½ cups heavy cream

¼ cup parsley, chopped
1 tablespoon sweet paprika
1 teaspoon lemon zest, grated

Heat butter on a suitable cooking pan. Then add cabbage and cook for 5 minutes. Place the remaining ingredients in the pan. Toss well and transfer the pan into your air fryer. Cook in your air fryer at 380 degrees F for 5 minutes. Serve on plates as a side dish.
Nutritional information: Calories: 153; Fat: 11.9g; Total Carbs: 11g; Net Carbs: 6.7g; Fiber: 5.3g; Sugars: 6g; Protein: 2.8g

Cheese Broccoli with Basil

Prep time: 10 minutes | Cook time: 7 minutes | Serves: 4

1 cup broccoli, chopped, boiled
1 teaspoon nut oil
1 teaspoon salt
1 teaspoon dried basil

½ cup Cheddar cheese, shredded
½ cup of coconut milk
½ teaspoon butter, softened

In the air fryer basket, place the broccoli, nut oil, dried dill, and salt. Stir together the mixture and then pour in the coconut milk. Drizzle butter and Cheddar cheese on the top of the meal. Before cooking, heat your air fryer to 400 degrees F. Cook the mixture inside the preheated air fryer for 7 minutes.
Nutritional information: Calories: 148; Fat: 13.5g; Total Carbs: 3g; Net Carbs: 1g; Fiber: 1.3g; Sugars: 1.5g; Protein: 4.9g

Turmeric Cauliflower Patties

Prep time: 15 minutes | Cook time: 10 minutes | Serves: 2

¼ cup cauliflower, shredded
1 egg yolk
½ teaspoon ground turmeric
¼ teaspoon onion powder
¼ teaspoon salt
2 ounces Cheddar cheese,

shredded
¼ teaspoon baking powder
1 teaspoon heavy cream
1 tablespoon coconut flakes
Cooking spray

Squeeze the shredded cauliflower and put it in the bowl. Add egg yolk, ground turmeric, baking powder, onion powder, heavy cream, salt, and coconut flakes. Then melt Cheddar cheese and add it in the cauliflower mixture. Stir the ingredients until you get the smooth mass. After this, make the medium size cauliflower patties. At 365 degrees F, preheat your air fryer. Grease its air fryer basket with cooking spray and put the patties inside. Cook them for almost 5 minutes from each side. Serve warm.
Nutritional information: Calories: 165; Fat: 13.5g; Total Carbs: 2g; Net Carbs: 0.5g; Fiber: 0.7g; Sugars: 0.8g; Protein: 8.9g

Brussel Sprouts and Mushrooms

Prep time: 5 minutes | Cook time: 20 minutes | Serves: 4

1 pound Brussels sprouts, halved
1 tablespoon olive oil
8 ounces brown mushrooms, halved

8 ounces cherry tomatoes, halved
½ teaspoon rosemary, dried
A pinch of salt and black pepper
Juice of 1 lime

Mix Brussels sprouts, olive oil, mushrooms, cherry tomatoes, rosemary, salt, and pepper in the air fryer basket. Cook in your air fryer at 380 degrees F for 20 minutes. Serve on plates as a side dish.
Nutritional information: Calories: 105; Fat: 4.1g; Total Carbs: 15g; Net Carbs: 5.6g; Fiber: 5.3g; Sugars: 4.9g; Protein: 5.8g

Turmeric Cauliflower with Cilantro

Prep time: 10 minutes | Cook time: 8 minutes | Serves: 4

1 pound cauliflower head
1 tablespoon ground turmeric
1 tablespoon coconut oil

½ teaspoon dried cilantro
¼ teaspoon salt

Before cooking, heat your air fryer to 400 degrees F. Cut the cauliflower into 4 steaks. Rub together with salt, dried cilantro, ground turmeric, and the cauliflower steak. Sprinkle the mixture with coconut oil. Transfer the mixture inside the air fryer basket and cook in your air fryer for 4 minutes from each side.
Nutritional information: Calories: 105; Fat: 4.1g; Total Carbs: 15g; Net Carbs: 5.6g; Fiber: 5.3g; Sugars: 4.9g; Protein: 5.8g

Green Beans with Parsley

Prep time: 5 minutes | Cook time: 20 minutes | Serves: 4

10 ounces green beans, trimmed
A pinch of salt and black pepper
3 ounces butter, melted

1 cup coconut cream
Zest of ½ lemon, grated
¼ cup parsley, chopped
2 garlic cloves, minced

Add salt, black pepper, butter, coconut cream, lemon zest, parsley, and garlic cloves in a bowl. Whisk them together. Place the green beans in a suitable pan. Then add the butter mixture over the green beans. Cook in your air fryer at 370 degrees F for 20 minutes. Serve on plates as a side dish.
Nutritional information: Calories: 316; Fat: 31.7g; Total Carbs: 9g; Net Carbs: 4.3g; Fiber: 3.9g; Sugars: 3.1g; Protein: 3.1g

Herbed Mushroom Pilau

Prep time: 8 minutes | Cook time: 25 minutes | Serves: 4

1 ½ cups cauliflower rice
3 cups vegetable broth
2 tbsps. olive oil
1 lb. fresh porcini mushrooms, sliced
2 tablespoons olive oil

2 garlic cloves
1 onion, chopped
¼ cup dry vermouth
1 tsp. dried thyme
½ tsp. dried tarragon
1 tsp. sweet Hungarian paprika

Lightly grease a suitable baking dish. Mix all the ingredients in the dish until well combined. Before cooking, heat your air fryer to 370 degrees F. Place the baking dish in your air fryer. Cook for 20 minutes. Check periodically to make sure it is evenly cooked. Serve your meal in bowls. Enjoy!
Nutritional information: Calories: 73; Fat: 1.9g; Total Carbs: 7g; Net Carbs: 3g; Fiber: 1.1g; Sugars: 3.6g; Protein: 6.2g

Tomato Rolls

Prep time: 5 minutes | Cook time: 15 minutes | Serves: 5

10 egg roll wrappers
1 tomato, diced

¼ tsp pepper
½ tsp salt

In a medium bowl, add the diced tomato, salt, and pepper. Use a fork to mash until smooth. It is also fine to leave chunks for the filling. Then divide them onto the egg wrappers. With your wet finger, brush along the edges to seal the rolls well. Line a suitable baking sheet with baking paper. Arrange the rolls evenly on the baking sheet. Cook in your air fryer at 350 degrees F for 5 minutes. Serve the rolls with sweet chili dipping. Enjoy!
Nutritional information: Calories: 189; Fat: 0.2g Total Carbs: 37.6g; Net Carbs: 4.2 g Fiber1.3g; Sugars: 0.3g; Protein 6.4g

Mozzarella Cabbage Wedges

Prep time: 5 minutes | Cook time: 25 minutes | Serves: 4

2 cups Parmesan cheese, chopped
4 tablespoons melted butter

Salt and pepper to taste
½ cup blue cheese sauce

Before cooking, heat your air fryer to 380 degrees F. Coat the cabbage wedges with melted butter, then with the Mozzarella. In the air fryer basket, place the coated cabbage. Cook in your air fryer at 380 degrees F for 20 minutes. Serve the wedges with blue cheese sauce.
Nutritional information: Calories: 376; Fat: 17.5g; Total Carbs: 0.8g; Net Carbs: 0g; Fiber: 0g; Sugars: 0.3g; Protein: 4.9g

Provolone Zucchini Balls

Prep time: 10 minutes | Cook time: 12 minutes | Serves: 4

¼ teaspoon salt
¼ teaspoon ground cumin
1 zucchini, grated
2 ounces Provolone cheese, grated

¼ teaspoon chili flakes
1 egg, beaten
¼ cup coconut flour
1 teaspoon sunflower oil

Mix ground cumin, zucchini, Provolone cheese, egg, chili flakes, and salt together. Use a spoon to make small balls from the mixture. Line baking paper over the air fryer basket. Brush the bottom of the baking paper with sunflower oil. Cook in your air fryer at 375 degrees F for 12 minutes. To avoid burning, shake the balls every 2 minutes.
Nutritional information: Calories: 114; Fat: 6.9g; Total Carbs: 7g; Net Carbs: 3g; Fiber: 3.6g; Sugars: 1g; Protein: 6.6g

Tasty Spiced Tofu

Cook time: 13 minutes | Serves: 3

1 (14-ounce) block extra-firm tofu, pressed and cut into ¾-inch cubes
3 teaspoons. cornstarch
1½ tablespoons avocado oil

1½ teaspoons paprika
1 teaspoon onion powder
1 teaspoon garlic powder
Salt and black pepper, to taste

Before cooking, heat your air fryer to 390 degrees F. Using cooking spray or the avocado oil, grease the air fryer basket. In a bowl, add cornstarch, spices, and tofu and mix together. Toss to coat the tofu well. Then evenly arrange the coated tofu inside the greased basket. Cook in your air fryer for 13 minutes, tossing the tofu twice in between. When cooked, dish out the meal and serve hot on plates.
Nutritional information: Calories: 273; Fat: 7.3g; Total Carbs: 45g; Net Carbs: 24g; Fiber: 3.8g; Sugars: 1.5g; Protein: 8.1g

Maple Glazed Parsnips

Cook time: 44 minutes | Serves: 6

2 pounds parsnips, peeled and   cut into 1-inch chunks

1 tablespoon butter, melted
2 tablespoons maple syrup
1 tablespoon dried parsley

flakes, crushed
¼ teaspoon red pepper flakes, crushed

Before cooking, heat your air fryer to 355 degrees F. Using cooking spray, spray the air fryer basket. In a bowl, add butter and parsnips and toss well to coat. Then evenly arrange the parsnips on the air fryer basket. Cook in your air fryer for about 40 minutes. In a large bowl, mix the remaining ingredients. Transfer the mixture inside the air fryer basket. Cook for about 4 minutes or more. When cooked, remove from the air fryer and serve warm.
Nutritional information: Calories: 148; Fat: 2.4g; Total Carbs: 31g; Net Carbs: 15g; Fiber: 7.5g; Sugars: 11.3g; Protein: 1.9g

Lemon Broccoli

Cook time: 20 minutes | Serves: 3

1 tablespoon butter
2 teaspoons vegetable bouillon granules
1 large head broccoli, cut into bite-sized pieces
1 tablespoon fresh lemon juice

3 garlic cloves, sliced
½ teaspoon fresh lemon zest, finely grated
½ teaspoon red pepper flakes, crushed

Before cooking, heat your air fryer to 355 degrees F. Using cooking spray, lightly grease a suitable baking pan. In the baking pan, add bouillon granules, lemon juice, and butter. Cook in your air fryer for 1½ minutes. Then add garlic and stir. Cook for about 30 seconds and add lemon zest, red pepper flakes, and broccoli. Cook for about 18 minutes. When cooked, remove from the air fryer and serve hot in a bowl.
Nutritional information: Calories: 51; Fat: 4.1g; Total Carbs: 3g; Net Carbs: 1g; Fiber: 1g; Sugars: 0.7g; Protein: 1.2g

Mozzarella Veggie Tacos

Cook time: 30 minutes | Serves: 3

1 cup kidney beans, drained
1 cup black beans, drained
½ cup tomato puree
1 fresh jalapeño chili, chopped
1 cup fresh cilantro, chopped
1 cup corn kernels

½ teaspoon ground cumin
½ teaspoon cayenne pepper
Salt and black pepper
1 cup grated mozzarella cheese
Guacamole to serve

Add kidney beans, black beans, tomato puree, jalapeno chili, the chopped cilantro, corn, ground cumin, cayenne pepper, salt, and pepper in a mixing bowl. Stir together. Spoon the mixture onto the half of the taco. Sprinkle the top with the mozzarella cheese and fold. Spray the air fryer basket with cooking spray. Ladle the tacos inside the air fryer basket. Then cook in your air fryer at 360 degrees F for 14 minutes. When cooked, remove from the air fryer and serve hot with guacamole.
Nutritional information: Calories: 517; Fat: 4.1g; Total Carbs: 92g; Net Carbs: 35g; Fiber: 21.6g; Sugars: 6.4g; Protein: 33g

Italian Eggplant and Tomato Bites

Prep time: 10 minutes | Cook time: 10 minutes | Serves: 5

2 medium eggplants, trimmed
1 tomato
1 teaspoon Italian seasonings

1 teaspoon avocado oil
3 ounces Parmesan, sliced

Cut the eggplants into 5 slices and thinly slice the tomato into 5 slices. Transfer the eggplant slices in the air fryer basket in a single layer. Cook in your air fryer at 400 degrees F for 3 minutes from each side. Then top the eggplants with tomato slices. Season with avocado oil and Italian seasonings. Sprinkle

on top with Parmesan. Cook in your air fryer at 400 degrees F for 4 minutes.
Nutritional information: Calories: 116; Fat 4.5g; Total Carbs 20.99g; Net Carbs:5.39g Fiber 6.9g; Sugars 8.7g; Protein 7.7g

Creamy Spinach with Nutmeg

Prep time: 15 minutes | Cook time: 15 minutes| Serves: 2

10 ounces frozen spinach, thawed	1 teaspoon black pepper
¼ cup parmesan cheese, shredded	4 ounces cream cheese, diced
½ teaspoon ground nutmeg	2 teaspoons garlic, minced
	1 small onion, chopped
	1 teaspoon salt

Spray 6-inch pan with cooking spray and set aside. In a suitable bowl, mix together spinach, cream cheese, garlic, onion, nutmeg, black pepper, and salt. Pour spinach mixture into the prepared pan. Place dish in air fryer basket and air fry at 350 degrees F for almost 10 minutes. Open air fryer basket and sprinkle parmesan cheese on top of spinach mixture and air fry at 400 degrees F for 5 minutes more. Serve and enjoy.
Nutritional information: Calories: 217; Fat: 16.3g; Total Carbs: 6g; Net Carbs: 2.5g; Fiber: 2.2g; Sugars: 1.2g; Protein: 13.5g

Parmesan Zucchini Gratin

Cook time: 15 minutes | Serves: 2

5 ounces parmesan cheese, shredded	1 tablespoon dried parsley
1 tablespoon coconut flour	2 zucchinis
	1 teaspoon butter, melted

In a bowl, add the coconut flour and parmesan cheese together. To season, add parsley. Cut the zucchinis lengthwise in half and slice the halves into four slices. Before cooking, heat your air fryer to 400 degrees F. Then coat the zucchinis with the melted butter and dip in the parmesan-flour mixture to thoroughly coat the zucchini slices. Cook in your air fryer for 13 minutes.
Nutritional information: Calories: 292; Fat: 17.8g; Total Carbs: 11g; Net Carbs: 6.7g; Fiber: 3.7g; Sugars: 3.4g; Protein: 25.7g

Crispy Pickles with Parmesan

Prep time: 15 minutes | Cook time: 6 minutes | Serves: 4

16 dill pickles, sliced	3 tablespoon parmesan cheese, grated
1 egg, lightly beaten	½ cup pork rind, crushed
½ cup almond flour	

Take 3 bowls. Mix together pork rinds and cheese in the first bowl. In a second bowl, add the egg. In the third bowl, spread the almond flour for coating. Coat each pickle slice with almond flour then dip in egg and finally coat with pork and cheese mixture. Grease its air fryer basket with cooking spray. Place coated pickles in the air fryer basket. Cook pickles for 6 minutes at 370 degrees F. Serve and enjoy.
Nutritional information: Calories: 206; Fat: 13.4g; Total Carbs: 9g; Net Carbs: 4.3g; Fiber: 4.6g; Sugars: 2.8g; Protein: 13.1g

Garlic Broccoli with Sriracha

Prep time: 15 minutes | Cook time: 20 minutes | Serves: 4

1 pound broccoli, cut into florets	1 tablespoon garlic, minced
1 teaspoon rice vinegar	5 drops liquid stevia
2 teaspoons sriracha	1 ½ tablespoons sesame oil
2 tablespoons soy sauce	Salt

In a suitable bowl, toss together broccoli, garlic, oil, and salt. Spread broccoli in air fryer basket and cook for almost 15-20 minutes at 400 degrees F. Meanwhile, in a microwave-safe bowl, mix together soy sauce, vinegar, liquid stevia, and sriracha and microwave for almost 10 seconds. Transfer broccoli to a bowl and toss well with soy mixture to coat. Serve and enjoy.
Nutritional information: Calories: 94; Fat: 5.5g; Total Carbs: 9g; Net Carbs: 4.3g; Fiber: 3.1g; Sugars: 2.1g; Protein: 3.8g

Stuffed Peppers with Cottage

Cook time: 20 minutes | Serves: 2

1 red bell pepper, top and seeds removed	Salt and pepper, to taste
1 yellow bell pepper, top and seeds removed	1 cup Cottage cheese
	4 tablespoons mayonnaise
	2 pickles, chopped

Lightly grease an air fryer basket. Before cooking, heat your air fryer to 400 degrees F. Arrange evenly the peppers inside the air fryer basket. Then cook in your air fryer for 15 minutes. To season, add salt and pepper. Combine the mayonnaise, chopped pickles, and the cream cheese in a mixing bowl. Fill the pepper with the cheese mixture. Serve immediately.
Nutritional information: Calories: 243; Fat: 12.3g; Total Carbs: 17g; Net Carbs: 8g; Fiber: 1.6g; Sugars: 5.9g; Protein: 16.6g

Italian-Style Rice and Peas

Cook time: 20 minutes | Serves: 4

2 cups brown rice	1 cup brown mushrooms, sliced
4 cups water	2 garlic cloves, minced
½ cup frozen green peas	1 small-sized onion, chopped
3 tbsps. soy sauce	1 tbsp. fresh parsley, chopped
1 tbsp. olive oil	

In a pot, add the brown rice and water and heat over high heat. Bring it to boil and then reduce heat to simmer. Cook for 35 minutes. Cool the rice completely and transfer to a lightly greased baking pan. Add all the rest of the ingredients in the baking pan and stir together until well combined. Cook in your air fryer at 360 degrees F for 18 to 22 minutes. When cooked, remove from the air fryer and serve warm.
Nutritional information: Calories: 396; Fat: 6.2g; Total Carbs: 76g; Net Carbs: 32g; Fiber: 4.3g; Sugars: 1.4g; Protein: 8.7g

Crispy Spiced Asparagus

Cook time: 15 minutes | Serves: 5

¼ cup almond flour	2 large eggs, beaten
½ teaspoon garlic powder	2 tablespoons parsley, chopped
½ teaspoon smoked paprika	Salt and pepper to taste
10 medium asparagus, trimmed	

Before cooking, heat your air fryer to 350 degrees F for about 5 minutes. Combine garlic powder, smoked paprika, almond flour, and parsley in a mixing bowl. To season, add salt and pepper. Dredge the asparagus in the beaten eggs and then coat the asparagus with almond flour mixture. Cook in your air fryer at 350 degrees F for 15 minutes.
Nutritional information: Calories: 118; Fat: 5g; Total Carbs: 12g; Net Carbs: 7g; Fiber: 6.4g; Sugars: 5.3g; Protein: 9.8g

Crispy 'n Healthy Avocado Fingers

Cook time: 10 minutes | Serves: 4

½ cup panko breadcrumbs	and sliced
½ teaspoon salt	liquid from 1 can white beans
1 pitted Haas avocado, peeled	or aquafaba

Before cooking, heat your air fryer to 350 degrees F. Toss the salt and breadcrumbs in a shallow bowl until they are combined well. Firstly, dredge the avocado slices in the aquafaba, then coat with the breadcrumb mixture. Arrange the avocado slices inside the air fryer basket. Then cook in your air fryer for 10 minutes. Halfway through cooking shake the basket.

Nutritional information: Calories: 138; Fat: 10g; Total Carbs: 11g; Net Carbs: 6.7g; Fiber: 4.4g; Sugars: 0.5g; Protein: 2g

Crispy Tofu with Soy Sauce

Prep time: 15 minutes | Cook time: 35 minutes | Serves: 4

1 block firm tofu, pressed and diced	2 teaspoon sesame oil
1 tablespoon arrowroot flour	1 teaspoon vinegar
	2 tablespoon soy sauce

In a suitable bowl, toss tofu with oil, vinegar, and soy sauce and let sit for almost 15 minutes. Toss marinated tofu with arrowroot flour. Grease its air fryer basket with cooking spray. Add tofu in air fryer basket and cook for 20 minutes at 370 degrees F. Shake basket halfway through. Serve and enjoy.

Nutritional information: Calories: 42; Fat: 3.2g; Total Carbs: 1g; Net Carbs: 0g; Fiber: 0.3g; Sugars: 0.3g; Protein: 2.4g

Roasted Bell Peppers

Prep time: 15 minutes | Cook time: 8 minutes | Serves: 3

3 ½ cups bell peppers, cut into chunks	Black pepper
	Salt

Grease its air fryer basket with cooking spray. Add bell peppers into the air fryer basket and cook at almost 360 degrees F for 8 minutes. Season bell peppers with black pepper and salt. Serve and enjoy.

Nutritional information: Calories: 44; Fat: 0.4g; Total Carbs: 10.5g; Net Carbs: 0g; Fiber: 1.9g; Sugars: 7g; Protein: 1.4g

Balsamic Brussels Sprouts

Prep time: 15 minutes | Cook time: 10 minutes | Serves: 6

2 cups Brussels sprouts, sliced	1 tablespoon olive oil
1 tablespoon balsamic vinegar	¼ teaspoon salt

Add all the recipe ingredients into the suitable bowl and toss well. Grease its air fryer basket with cooking spray. Transfer Brussels sprouts mixture into the air fryer basket. Cook Brussels sprouts at 400 degrees F for almost 10 minutes. Shake basket halfway through. Serve and enjoy.

Nutritional information: Calories: 33; Fat: 2.4g; Total Carbs: 2g; Net Carbs: 0.5g; Fiber: 1.1g; Sugars: 0.6g; Protein: 1g

Tamari Green Beans

Prep time: 15 minutes | Cook time: 10 minutes | Serves: 2

8 ounces green beans, trimmed	1 tablespoon tamari
1 teaspoon sesame oil	

Add all the recipe ingredients into the suitable mixing bowl and toss well. Grease its air fryer basket with cooking spray. Transfer green beans in air fryer basket and cook at almost 400 degrees F for almost 10 minutes. Toss halfway through. Serve and enjoy.

Nutritional information: Calories: 61; Fat: 2.4g; Total Carbs: 8g; Net Carbs: 3.5g; Fiber: 3.9g; Sugars: 1.7g; Protein: 3g

Spiced Okra

Prep time: 15 minutes | Cook time: 20 minutes | Serves: 2

½ pound okra, ends trimmed and sliced	½ teaspoon ground coriander
1 teaspoon olive oil	½ teaspoon ground cumin
½ teaspoon mango powder	⅛ teaspoon black pepper
½ teaspoon chili powder	¼ teaspoon salt

At 350 degrees F, preheat your air fryer. Add all the recipe ingredients into the suitable bowl and toss well. Grease its air fryer basket with cooking spray. Transfer okra mixture into the air fryer basket and cook for almost 10 minutes. Shake basket halfway through. Toss okra well and cook for 2 minutes more. Serve and enjoy.

Nutritional information: Calories: 70; Fat: 2.8g; Total Carbs: 9g; Net Carbs: 4.3g; Fiber: 3.9g; Sugars: 1.7g; Protein: 2.4g

Garlicky Roasted Eggplant

Prep time: 15 minutes | Cook time: 12 minutes | Serves: 2

1 eggplant, washed and cubed	¼ teaspoon oregano
½ teaspoon garlic powder	1 tablespoon olive oil
¼ teaspoon marjoram	

Grease its air fryer basket with cooking spray. Add all the recipe ingredients into the mixing bowl and toss well. Transfer eggplant mixture into the air fryer basket and cook at almost 390 degrees F for 6 minutes. Toss well and cook for 6 minutes more. Serve and enjoy.

Nutritional information: Calories: 120; Fat: 7.5g; Total Carbs: 14g; Net Carbs: 9.5g; Fiber: 8.3g; Sugars: 7.1g; Protein: 2.4g

Roasted Butternut Squash with Cranberries

Prep time: 15 minutes | Cook time: 35 minutes | Serves: 6

4 cups butternut squash, diced	1 tablespoon olive oil
¼ cup dried cranberries	8 ounces mushrooms, quartered
3 garlic cloves, minced	
1 tablespoon soy sauce	1 cup green onions, sliced
1 tablespoon balsamic vinegar	

In a suitable mixing bowl, mix together squash, mushrooms, and green onion and set aside. In a suitable bowl, whisk together oil, garlic, vinegar, and soy sauce. Pour oil mixture over squash and toss to coat. Grease its air fryer basket with cooking spray. Add squash mixture into the air fryer basket and cook for 30-35 minutes at 400 degrees F. Shake after every 5 minutes. Toss with cranberries and serve hot.

Nutritional information: Calories: 82; Fat: 2.6g; Total Carbs: 14.5g; Net Carbs: 7g; Fiber: 2.9g; Sugars: 3.3g; Protein: 2.7g

Turmeric Eggplant Slices

Prep time: 15 minutes | Cook time: 10 minutes | Serves: 2

1 eggplant, sliced	½ teaspoon curry powder
1 garlic clove, minced	⅛ teaspoon turmeric
1 tablespoon olive oil	Salt

At 300 degrees F, preheat your air fryer. Add all the recipe ingredients into the suitable mixing bowl and toss to coat. Transfer eggplant slices into the air fryer basket. Cook eggplant slices for almost 10 minutes or until lightly brown. Shake basket halfway through. Serve and enjoy.

Nutritional information: Calories: 122; Fat: 7.5g; Total Carbs: 14g; Net Carbs: 9.5g; Fiber: 8.3g; Sugars: 6.9g; Protein: 2.4g

Garlicky Cabbage Wedges

Prep time: 15 minutes | Cook time: 14 minutes | Serves: 6

1 small cabbage head, cut into wedges
3 tablespoons olive oil
¼ teaspoon red chili flakes
½ teaspoon fennel seeds
1 teaspoon garlic powder
1 teaspoon onion powder
Black pepper
Salt

Grease its air fryer basket with cooking spray. In a suitable bowl, mix together garlic powder, red chili flakes, fennel seeds, onion powder, black pepper, and salt. Coat cabbage wedges with oil and rub with garlic powder mixture. Place cabbage wedges into the air fryer basket and cook at almost 400 degrees F for 8 minutes. Turn cabbage wedges to another side and cook for 6 minutes more. Serve and enjoy.

Nutritional information: Calories: 66; Fat: 7g; Total Carbs: 1g; Net Carbs: 0g; Fiber: 0.4g; Sugars: 0.6g; Protein: 0.3g

Sweet Corn Fritters with Avocado

Prep time: 15 minutes | Cook time: 8 minutes | Serves: 3

2 cups sweet corn kernels
1 small-sized onion, chopped
1 garlic clove, minced
2 eggs, whisked
1 teaspoon baking powder
2 tablespoons fresh cilantro,
chopped
Salt and black pepper, to taste
1 avocado, peeled, pitted and diced
2 tablespoons sweet chili sauce

In a suitable mixing bowl, thoroughly combine the corn, onion, garlic, eggs, baking powder, cilantro, salt, and black pepper. Shape the corn mixture into 6 patties and transfer them to the lightly greased air fryer basket. Cook in the preheated air fry at 370 degrees for 8 minutes; turn them over and cook for 7 minutes longer. Serve the fritters with the avocado and chili sauce.

Nutritional information: Calories: 291; Fat: 17g; Total Carbs: 31g; Net Carbs: 15g; Fiber: 6.7g; Sugars: 7.9g; Protein: 7.9g

Air Fried Bell peppers with Onion

Prep time: 15 minutes | Cook time: 15 minutes | Serves: 3

6 bell pepper, sliced
1 tablespoon Italian seasoning
1 tablespoon olive oil
1 onion, sliced

Add all the recipe ingredients into the suitable mixing bowl and toss well. At 320 degrees F, preheat your air fryer. Transfer bell pepper and onion mixture into the air fryer basket and cook for almost 15 minutes. Toss well and cook for almost 10 minutes more. Serve and enjoy.

Nutritional information: Calories: 145; Fat: 6.7g; Total Carbs: 21g; Net Carbs: 9g; Fiber: 4g; Sugars: 14g; Protein 2.8g

Coconut Broccoli with Cheddar

Prep time: 15 minutes | Cook time: 30 minutes | Serves: 4

3 tablespoons ghee, melted
15 ounces coconut cream
2 eggs, whisked
2 cups cheddar, grated

1 cup parmesan, grated
1 tablespoon mustard
1 pound broccoli florets
A pinch of black pepper and salt
1 tablespoon parsley, chopped

Grease a baking pan that fits the air fryer with the ghee and arrange the broccoli on the bottom. Add the cream, mustard, salt, black pepper and the eggs and toss. Sprinkle the cheese on top, put the pan in the preheated air fryer and cook at almost 380 degrees F for 30 minutes. Divide between plates and serve.

Nutritional information: Calories: 347; Fat: 23.6g; Total Carbs: 12g; Net Carbs: 7g; Fiber: 3.4g; Sugars: 2.6g; Protein: 23.4g

Garlic Cauliflower & Broccoli

Prep time: 15 minutes | Cook time: 12 minutes | Serves: 6

3 cups cauliflower florets
3 cups broccoli florets
¼ teaspoon paprika
½ teaspoon garlic powder
2 tablespoons olive oil
⅛ teaspoon black pepper
¼ teaspoon salt

At 400 degrees F, preheat your Air fryer. Add broccoli in microwave-safe bowl and microwave for 3 minutes. Drain well. Add broccoli in a suitable mixing bowl. Add remaining ingredients and toss well. Transfer broccoli and cauliflower mixture into the air fryer basket and cook for 12 minutes. Toss halfway through. Serve and serve.

Nutritional information: Calories: 69; Fat: 4.9g; Total Carbs: 5g; Net Carbs: 2g; Fiber: 2.5g; Sugars: 2g; Protein: 2.3g

Yellow Squash Chips with Parmesan

Prep time: 15 minutes | Cook time: 10 minutes | Serves: 4

½ cup flour
Black pepper and salt to taste
2 eggs
1 tablespoon soy sauce
¾ cup panko breadcrumbs
1 tablespoon dried dill
¼ cup Parmesan cheese, grated
Greek yogurt dressing, for serving

At 380 degrees F, preheat your Air fryer. Grease its air fryer basket with cooking spray. In a suitable bowl, mix the flour, dill, salt, and black pepper. In another bowl, beat the eggs with soy sauce. In a third, pour the panko breadcrumbs and Parmesan cheese. Dip the squash rounds in the flour, then in the eggs, and then coat with the breadcrumbs. Place in the air fryer basket. Cook for almost 10 minutes, flipping once halfway through. Serve with Greek yogurt dressing.

Nutritional information: Calories: 137; Fat: 4.3g; Total Carbs: 17g; Net Carbs: 8g; Fiber: 0.7g; Sugars: 0.3g; Protein: 7.6g

Garlicky Vegetable Rainbow Fritters

Prep time: 15 minutes | Cook time: 12 minutes | Serves: 2

1 zucchini, grated and squeezed
1 cup corn kernels
½ cup canned green peas
4 tablespoons all-purpose flour
2 tablespoons fresh shallots,
minced
1 teaspoon fresh garlic, minced
1 tablespoon peanut oil
Salt and black pepper, to taste
1 teaspoon cayenne pepper

In a suitable mixing bowl, thoroughly combine all the recipe ingredients until everything is well incorporated. Shape the mixture into patties. Grease its air fryer basket with cooking spray. Cook in the preheated air fryer at about 365 degrees F for 6 minutes almost. Flip and cook for a 6 minutes more. Serve immediately and enjoy!

Nutritional information: Calories: 240; Fat: 8.3g; Total Carbs: 37g; Net Carbs: 19g; Fiber: 5.7g; Sugars: 6.4g; Protein: 7.7g

Garlicky Mushrooms with Parsley

Prep time: 15 minutes | Cook time: 12 minutes | Serves: 2

8 ounces mushrooms, sliced	1 tablespoon olive oil
1 tablespoon parsley, chopped	Black pepper
1 teaspoon soy sauce	Salt
½ teaspoon garlic powder	

Add all the recipe ingredients into the mixing bowl and toss well. Transfer mushrooms in air fryer basket and cook at almost 380 degrees F for almost 10-12 minutes. Shake basket halfway through. Serve and enjoy.

Nutritional information: Calories: 89; Fat: 7.4g; Total Carbs: 4g; Net Carbs: 2g; Fiber: 1.3g; Sugars: 2.2g; Protein: 3.9g

Stuffed Bell Peppers with Mayonnaise

Prep time: 15 minutes | Cook time: 15 minutes | Serves: 2

2 red bell peppers, tops and seeds removed	Black pepper and salt, to taste
2 yellow bell peppers, tops and seeds removed	1 cup cream cheese
	4 tablespoons mayonnaise
	2 pickles, chopped

Arrange the black peppers in the lightly greased cooking basket. Cook in the preheated air fryer at about 400 degrees F for almost 15 minutes, turning them over halfway through the cooking time. Season with black pepper and salt. Then, in a suitable mixing bowl, combine the cream cheese with the mayonnaise and chopped pickles. Stuff the black pepper with the cream cheese mixture and serve. Enjoy!

Nutritional information: Calories: 294; Fat: 25.5g; Total Carbs: 13g; Net Carbs: 7g; Fiber: 2.2g; Sugars: 5.8g; Protein: 5.7g

Herbed Potatoes with Tomato Sauce

Prep time: 15 minutes | Cook time: 16 minutes | Serves: 4

2 pounds potatoes; cubed	½ teaspoon oregano; dried
4 garlic cloves; minced	½ teaspoon parsley; dried
1 yellow onion; chopped.	2 tablespoons basil; chopped
1 cup tomato sauce	2 tablespoons olive oil

Heat up a pan that fits your air fryer with the oil over medium heat, add onion; stir and cook for 1-2 minutes. Add garlic, potatoes, parsley, tomato sauce and oregano; stir, introduce in your air fryer and cook at almost 370 degrees F and cook for 16 minutes. Add basil, toss everything, divide among plates and serve.

Nutritional information: Calories: 225; Fat: 7.3g; Total Carbs: 37g; Net Carbs: 19g; Fiber: 5g; Sugars: 6.6g; Protein: 4.8g

Buffalo Crusted Cauliflower

Prep time: 15 minutes | Cook time: 18 minutes | Serves: 4

3 tablespoons buffalo hot sauce	1 cup panko breadcrumbs
1 egg white	½ teaspoon salt

¼ teaspoon freshly black pepper	florets
½ head of cauliflower, cut into	Cooking spray

In a suitable bowl, add butter, hot sauce, and egg white. Mix breadcrumbs with black pepper and salt, in a separate bowl. Toss the florets in the hot sauce mixture until well-coated. Toss the coated cauliflower in crumbs until coated, then transfer the coated florets to the air fryer. Spray with cooking spray. Cook for 18 minutes at 340 degrees F. Cook in batches if needed. Serve.

Nutritional information: Calories: 94; Fat: 0.5g; Total Carbs: 19g; Net Carbs: 6.7g; Fiber: 2.9g; Sugars: 3.2g; Protein: 3.6g

Fava Beans and Bacon Medley

Prep time: 15 minutes | Cook time: 15 minutes | Serves: 4

3 pounds fava beans, shelled	crumbled
1 teaspoon olive oil	½ cup white wine
Black pepper and salt to taste	1 tablespoon parsley, chopped
4 ounces bacon, cooked and	

Place all of the recipe ingredients into a pan that fits your air fryer and mix well. Put the pan in the preheated air fryer and cook at almost 380 degrees F for almost 15 minutes. Serve.

Nutritional information: Calories: 32; Fat: 13.5g; Total Carbs: 25g; Net Carbs: 16g; Fiber: 7.9g; Sugars: 0.2g; Protein: 19.9g

Broccoli with Paprika

Prep time: 15 minutes | Cook time: 15 minutes | Serves: 4

1 broccoli head, florets separated	½ cup keto tomato sauce
	1 tablespoon sweet paprika
Black pepper and salt to the taste	¼ cup scallions, chopped
	1 tablespoon olive oil

In a pan that fits the air fryer, combine the broccoli with the rest of the ingredients, toss, put the pan in the air fryer and cook at almost 380 degrees F for almost 15 minutes. Divide between plates and serve.

Nutritional information: Calories: 52; Fat: 3.9g; Total Carbs: 4g; Net Carbs: 2g; Fiber: 1.9g; Sugars: 2g; Protein: 1.4g

Parmesan Risotto

Prep time: 15 minutes | Cook time: 20 minutes | Serves: 6

2 tablespoons butter, melted	1 cup parmesan, grated
1 pound cauliflower, riced	3 tablespoons. sun-dried
2 garlic cloves, minced	tomatoes
½ cup chicken stock	½ teaspoon nutmeg, ground
1 cup heavy cream	

Add the cauliflower and rest of the recipe ingredients to air fryer basket. Air fryer at almost 360 degrees F for 20 minutes almost. Serve.

Nutritional information: Calories: 150; Fat: 13.2g; Total Carbs: 5g; Net Carbs: 2g; Fiber: 2g; Sugars: 2.3g; Protein: 3.9g

Awesome Chicken Taquitos

Prep time: 15 minutes | Cook time: 12 minutes | Serves: 4

1 cup shredded mozzarella cheese	¼ cup Greek yogurt
	Salt and black pepper
¼ cup salsa	8 flour tortillas

In a suitable bowl, mix chicken, cheese, salsa, sour cream, salt, and black pepper. Spray 1 side of the tortilla with cooking spray. Lay 2 tablespoon of the chicken mixture at the center of the non-oiled side the tortillas. Roll tightly around the mixture. Arrange taquitos on your air fryer basket. Cook for almost 12 minutes at 380 degrees F. Serve.

Nutritional information: Calories: 138; Fat: 2.9g; Total Carbs: 23g; Net Carbs: 11g; Fiber: 3.3g; Sugars: 1.4g; Protein 6.2g

Roasted Zucchinis with Thyme

Prep time: 15 minutes | Cook time: 12 minutes | Serves: 8

12 ounces zucchini, cubed	2 eggs, beaten
⅓ cup spring onions, chopped	3 tablespoons coconut milk
1 teaspoon fresh thyme	1 teaspoon olive oil

At 400 degrees F, preheat your air fryer. In the air fryer basket, mix the zucchinis with spring onions and the other ingredients and cook for 12 minutes. Divide between plates and serve.

Nutritional information: Calories: 42; Fat: 3.1g; Total Carbs: 2g; Net Carbs: 0.5g; Fiber: 0.8g; Sugars: 1.1g; Protein: 2.1g

Breadcrumb Crusted Agnolotti

Prep time: 15 minutes | Cook time: 14 minutes | Serves: 6

1 cup flour	2 cups breadcrumbs
Black pepper and salt	Cooking spray
4 eggs, beaten	

Mix flour with black pepper and salt. Dip pasta into the flour, then into the egg, and finally in the breadcrumbs. Spray with oil and arrange in the preheated air fryer in an even layer. Set its temperature to 400 degrees F and cook for 14 minutes, turning once halfway through cooking. Cook until nice and golden. Serve with goat cheese.

Nutritional information: Calories: 260; Fat: 5g; Total Carbs: 42g; Net Carbs: 18g; Fiber: 2.2g; Sugars: 2.5g; Protein: 10.7g

Roasted Broccoli and Sesame Seeds

Prep time: 15 minutes | Cook time: 10 minutes | Serves: 2

1 pound broccoli florets	Salt and black pepper, to taste
2 tablespoons sesame oil	½ teaspoon cumin powder
½ teaspoon shallot powder	¼ teaspoon paprika
½ teaspoon porcini powder	2 tablespoons sesame seeds
1 teaspoon garlic powder	

At 400 degrees F, preheat your air fryer. Blanch the broccoli florets in boiling water until al dente, about 3 to 4 minutes. Drain well and transfer to the lightly greased air fryer basket. Add the sesame oil, shallot powder, porcini powder, garlic powder, salt, black pepper, cumin powder, paprika, and sesame seeds. Cook for almost 6 minutes, tossing halfway through the cooking time. Serve

Nutritional information: Calories: 257; Fat: 19g; Total Carbs: 18g; Net Carbs: 9.5g; Fiber: 7.3g; Sugars: 4.3g; Protein: 8.3g

Balsamic Sautéed Greens

Prep time: 15 minutes | Cook time: 15 minutes | Serves: 4

1 pound collard greens	A pinch of black pepper and
¼ cup cherry tomatoes, halved	salt
1 tablespoon balsamic vinegar	2 tablespoons chicken stock

In a suitable pan that fits your air fryer, mix the collard greens with the other ingredients, toss gently, introduce in the preheated air fryer and cook at almost 360 degrees F for almost 15 minutes. Serve.

Nutritional information: Calories: 34; Fat: 0.8g; Total Carbs: 6g; Net Carbs: 2.5g; Fiber: 3.9g; Sugars: 0.3g; Protein 2.6g

Fried Pickles with Mayo Sauce

Prep time: 15 minutes | Cook time: 10 minutes | Serves: 2

1 egg, whisked	Mayo Sauce:
2 tablespoons buttermilk	¼ cup mayonnaise
½ cup fresh breadcrumbs	½ tablespoon mustard
¼ cup Romano cheese, grated	½ teaspoon molasses
½ teaspoon onion powder	1 tablespoon ketchup
½ teaspoon garlic powder	¼ teaspoon black pepper
1 ½ cups dill pickle chips	

In a suitable shallow bowl, whisk the egg with buttermilk. In another bowl, mix the breadcrumbs, cheese, onion powder, and garlic powder. Dredge the pickle chips in the egg mixture, then, in the breadcrumb/cheese mixture. Cook in the preheated air fryer at about 400 degrees F for 5 minutes; shake the basket and cook for 5 minutes more. Meanwhile, mix all the sauce ingredients until well combined. Serve the fried pickles with the mayo sauce for dipping.

Nutritional information: Calories: 303; Fat: 15.4g; Total Carbs: 32g; Net Carbs: 12g; Fiber: 1.8g; Sugars: 7.7g; Protein: 9.3g

Garlic Asparagus with Provolone

Prep time: 15 minutes | Cook time: 6 minutes | Serves: 3

9 ounces Asparagus	1 teaspoon olive oil
¼ teaspoon chili powder	4 Provolone cheese slices
¼ teaspoon garlic powder	

Trim the asparagus and sprinkle with chili powder and garlic powder. At 400 degrees F, preheat your air fryer. Spread the asparagus in the air fryer basket and sprinkle with olive oil. Cook the vegetables for 3 minutes. Then top the asparagus with Provolone cheese and cook for 3 minutes more. Serve.

Nutritional information: Calories: 163; Fat: 11.6g; Total Carbs: 4g; Net Carbs: 2g; Fiber: 1.9g; Sugars: 1.9g; Protein 11.5g

Bacon and Cabbage

Prep time: 15 minutes | Cook time: 12 minutes | Serves: 2

8 ounces Chinese cabbage, roughly chopped	1 tablespoon sunflower oil
2 ounces bacon, chopped	½ teaspoon onion powder
	½ teaspoon salt

Cook the bacon at 400 degrees F for almost 10 minutes. Stir it from time to time. Then sprinkle it with onion powder and salt. Add Chinese cabbage and shake the mixture well. Cook it for 2 minutes. Then add sunflower oil, stir the meal and place in the serving plates. Serve.

Nutritional information: Calories: 232; Fat: 19.1g; Total Carbs: 3g; Net Carbs: 1g; Fiber: 1.2g; Sugars: 1.6g; Protein: 12.3g

Turmeric Roasted Broccoli

Prep time: 15 minutes | Cook time: 15 minutes | Serves: 2

2 cups broccoli florets	2 tablespoons yogurt

1 tablespoon chickpea flour ½ teaspoon salt
¼ teaspoon turmeric powder ¼ teaspoon chaat masala

Place all the recipe ingredients in a suitable bowl and toss to combine. Place the baking dish accessory into the air fryer and place the food into the dish. Close the air fryer and cook for almost 15 minutes at 350 degrees F. Halfway through the cooking time, give the baking dish a good shake.
Nutritional information: Calories: 66; Fat: 0.9g; Total Carbs: 11g; Net Carbs: 6.7g; Fiber: 3.5g; Sugars: 3.3g; Protein: 4.7g

Indian Veggie Balls

Prep time: 15 minutes | Cook time: 33 minutes | Serves: 8

Veggie Balls: ½ teaspoon cumin seeds
1-pound potatoes, peeled and 2 garlic cloves, roughly
diced chopped
½ pound cauliflower, broken 1 onion, chopped
into small florets 1 Kashmiri chili black pepper,
2 tablespoons olive oil seeded and minced
2 garlic cloves, minced 1 1-inch piece ginger, chopped
1 tablespoon Garam masala 1 teaspoon paprika
1 cup chickpea flour 1 teaspoon turmeric powder
Salt and black pepper, to taste 2 ripe tomatoes, pureed
Sauce: ½ cup vegetable broth
1 tablespoon sesame oil ¼ cup full fat coconut milk

At 400 degrees F, preheat your air fryer. Place the potato and cauliflower in a lightly greased cooking basket. Cook for almost 15 minutes, shaking the basket halfway through the cooking time. Mash the cauliflower and potatoes in a suitable mixing bowl. Add the remaining ingredients for the veggie balls and stir to combine well. Use the vegetable mixture to make small balls and arrange them in the cooking basket. Cook in the preheated air fryer at about 360 degrees F for almost 15 minutes or until thoroughly cooked and crispy. Repeat the process until you run out of ingredients. Heat the sesame oil in a suitable saucepan over medium heat and add the cumin seeds. Sauté for a minute then add the garlic, onions, chili black pepper, and ginger. Sauté for almost 2 to 3 minutes. Add the paprika, turmeric powder, tomatoes, and broth; let it simmer, covered, for 4 to 5 minutes, with occasional stirring. Add the coconut milk. Heat off; add the veggie balls and gently stir to combine. Serve!
Nutritional information: Calories: 199; Fat: 7.2g; Total Carbs: 28g; Net Carbs: 11.5g; Fiber: 7.2g; Sugars: 5.5g; Protein: 7.2g

Balsamic Greens and Green Beans Medley

Prep time: 15 minutes | Cook time: 12 minutes | Serves: 4

1 bunch mustard greens, trimmed 3 garlic cloves, minced
1-pound green beans, halved Black pepper and salt to the
2 tablespoons olive oil taste
¼ cup keto tomato sauce 1 tablespoon balsamic vinegar

In a suitable pan that fits your air fryer, mix the mustard greens with the rest of the ingredients, toss, put the pan in the air fryer and cook at almost 350 degrees F for 12 minutes. Divide everything between plates and serve.
Nutritional information: Calories: 103; Fat: 7.2g; Total Carbs: 9g; Net Carbs: 4.3g; Fiber: 4.4g; Sugars: 1.9g; Protein: 2.6g

Tasty Cauliflower Croquettes

Prep time: 15 minutes | Cook time: 20 minutes | Serves: 4

1 pound cauliflower florets 2 eggs

1 tablespoon olive oil ½ cup parmesan cheese, grated
2 tablespoons scallions, Salt and black pepper, to taste
chopped ¼ teaspoon dried dill weed
1 garlic clove, minced 1 teaspoon paprika
1 cup Colby cheese, shredded

Blanch the cauliflower in salted boiling water about 3 to 4 minutes until al dente. Drain well and pulse in a food processor. Add the remaining ingredients; mix to combine well. Shape the cauliflower mixture into bite-sized tots. At 375 degrees F, preheat your air fryer. Grease its air fryer basket with cooking spray. Cook in the preheated air fryer for almost 16 minutes, shaking halfway through the cooking time. Serve with your favorite sauce for dipping. Serve!
Nutritional information: Calories: 205; Fat: 15g; Total Carbs: 7g; Net Carbs: 3g; Fiber: 3.2g; Sugars: 3.2g; Protein: 11.9g

Garlic Sautéed Artichokes

Prep time: 15 minutes | Cook time: 15 minutes | Serves: 4

10 ounces artichoke hearts, ¼ cup veggie stock
halved 2 teaspoons lime juice
3 garlic cloves Black pepper and salt to the
2 cups baby spinach taste

In a suitable pan that fits your air fryer, mix all the recipe ingredients, toss, introduce in the fryer and cook at almost 370 degrees F for almost 15 minutes almost. Divide between plates and serve as a side dish.
Nutritional information: Calories: 80; Fat: 0.4g; Total Carbs: 17.5g; Net Carbs: 2.5g; Fiber: 8.4g; Sugars: 1.6g; Protein 5.8g

Cayenne Chicken Wing Dip

Prep time: 15 minutes | Cook time: 20 minutes | Serves: 4

1 teaspoon cayenne pepper 3 ounces gorgonzola cheese,
Salt to taste crumbled
2 tablespoon grapeseed oil ½ lemon, juiced
2 teaspoon chili flakes ½ teaspoon garlic powder
1 cup heavy cream

At 380 degrees F, preheat your air fryer. Coat the chicken with cayenne pepper, salt, and oil. Place in the basket and cook for 20 minutes. In a suitable bowl, mix heavy cream, gorgonzola cheese, lemon juice, and garlic powder. Serve with chicken wings.
Nutritional information: Calories: 240; Fat: 24g; Total Carbs: 2g; Net Carbs: 0.5g; Fiber: 0.8g; Sugars: 0.2g; Protein: 5.4g

Potato-Nut Casserole Dish

Prep time: 15 minutes | Cook time: 30 minutes | Serves: 4

3 pounds sweet potatoes; ½ cup walnuts; soaked, drained
scrubbed and ground
¼ cup milk ¼ cup sugar
2 tablespoons white flour 1 teaspoon cinnamon powder
¼ teaspoon allspice; ground 5 tablespoons butter
½ teaspoon nutmeg; ground ¼ cup pecans; soaked, drained
Salt to the taste and ground
For the topping: ¼ cup coconut; shredded
½ cup almond flour 1 tablespoon chia seeds

Place potatoes in your air fryer basket, prick them with a fork and cook at almost 360 degrees F, for 30 minutes. Meanwhile; in a bowl, mix almond flour with pecans, walnuts, ¼ cup coconut, ¼ cup sugar, chia seeds, 1 teaspoon cinnamon and the butter and stir everything. Transfer potatoes to a cutting board, cool them, peel and place them in a baking dish that fits your air fryer. Add milk, flour, salt, nutmeg and allspice and stir Add crumble mix you've made earlier on top; place dish in your air fryer's basket and Cook at almost 400 degrees F, for almost 8 minutes. Divide among plates and serve as a side dish.

Nutritional information: Calories: 458; Fat: 14.8g; Total Carbs: 46g; Net Carbs: 21g; Fiber: 10.6g; Sugars: 31.5g; Protein: 6.3g

Air Fried Brussels Sprouts

Prep time: 15 minutes | Cook time: 20 minutes | Serves: 4

1 pound Brussels sprouts, trimmed and halved	2 tablespoons ghee, melted
Black pepper and salt to the taste	½ cup coconut cream
	2 tablespoons. garlic, minced
	1 tablespoon chives, chopped

In your air fryer, mix the sprouts with the rest of the ingredients except the chives, toss well, introduce in the preheated air fryer and cook them at 370 degrees F for 20 minutes. Divide the Brussels sprouts between plates, sprinkle the chives on top and serve as a side dish.

Nutritional information: Calories: 131; Fat: 6.9g; Total Carbs: 16g; Net Carbs: 7g; Fiber: 4.6g; Sugars: 2.6g; Protein: 5g

Beans and Sweet Potato Boats

Prep time: 15 minutes | Cook time: 20 minutes | Serves: 4

2 tablespoons olive oil	¼ cup mozzarella cheese, grated
1 shallot, chopped	
1 cup canned mixed beans	Black pepper and salt to taste

At 400 degrees F, preheat your air fryer. Grease a suitable baking dish with the olive oil. Set aside. Scoop out the flesh from potatoes, so shells are formed. Chop the potato flesh and put it in a suitable bowl. Add in shallot, mixed beans, salt, and black pepper and mix to combine. Fill the hollow potato shells with the mixture and top with the cheese. Arrange on the baking dish. Place this baking dish the preheated air fryer and cook for 20 minutes. Serve.

Nutritional information: Calories: 142; Fat: 8.1g; Total Carbs: 11g; Net Carbs: 6.7g; Fiber: 3g; Sugars: 0g; Protein: 5.1g

Swiss Vegetable Casserole

Prep time: 15 minutes | Cook time: 33 minutes | Serves: 6

1 tablespoon olive oil	tots
1 shallot, sliced	6 eggs
2 garlic cloves, minced	1 cup milk
1 red bell pepper, seeded and sliced	Salt and black pepper, to your liking
1 yellow bell pepper, seeded and sliced	1 cup Swiss cheese, shredded
1 ½ cups kale	4 tablespoons seasoned breadcrumbs
1 28-ounce bag frozen tater	

Sauté the shallot, garlic, and black peppers with oil in a skillet for 2 to 3 minutes. Add the kale and cook until wilted. Arrange the tater tots evenly over the bottom of a lightly greased casserole dish. Spread the sautéed mixture over the top. In a suitable mixing bowl, thoroughly combine the eggs, milk, salt, black pepper, and shredded cheese. Pour the mixture into the casserole dish. Lastly, top with the seasoned breadcrumbs. Air fry at 330 degrees F for 30 minutes or until top is golden brown. Serve!

Nutritional information: Calories: 181; Fat: 12.6g; Total

Carbs: 5g; Net Carbs: 2g; Fiber: 0.3g; Sugars: 3.4g; Protein: 12g

Mint Lemon Squash

Prep time: 15 minutes | Cook time: 25 minutes | Serves: 4

4 summer squash, cut into wedges	½ cup mint, chopped
¼ cup olive oil	1 cup mozzarella, shredded
¼ cup lemon juice	Black pepper and salt to the taste

In a suitable pan that fits your air fryer, mix the squash with the rest of the ingredients, toss, introduce the pan in the preheated air fryer and cook at almost 370 degrees F for 25 minutes. Serve.

Nutritional information: Calories: 161; Fat: 14.4g; Total Carbs: 6.5g; Net Carbs: 1g; Fiber: 2.1g; Sugars: 4.8g; Protein: 3.8g

Buttered Kale Mix

Prep time: 15 minutes | Cook time: 12 minutes | Serves: 2

3 tablespoons butter, melted	½ cup yellow onion, chopped
2 cups kale leaves	2 teaspoons turmeric powder
Black pepper and salt to taste	

Place all the recipe ingredients in a pan that fits your air fryer and mix well. Put the pan in the air fryer and cook at almost 250 degrees F for 12 minutes. Divide between plates and serve.

Nutritional information: Calories: 205; Fat: 17.5g; Total Carbs: 11g; Net Carbs: 6.7g; Fiber: 2.1g; Sugars: 1.3g; Protein: 2.7g

Cheese Cauliflower Tots

Prep time: 15 minutes | Cook time: 12 minutes | Serves: 8

1 large head cauliflower	shredded
½ cup parmesan cheese, grated	1 teaspoon seasoned salt
1 cup mozzarella cheese,	1 egg

Set a suitable steamer basket over a pot of boiling water, ensuring the water is not high enough to enter the basket. Cut up the cauliflower into florets and transfer to the steamer basket. Cover the pot with a lid and leave to steam for seven minutes, making sure the cauliflower softens. Place the florets on a cheesecloth and leave to cool. Remove as much moisture as possible. This is crucial as it ensures the cauliflower will harden. In a suitable bowl, break up the cauliflower with a fork. Add the parmesan, mozzarella, seasoned salt, and egg, incorporating the cauliflower well with all of the other ingredients. Using your hand, mold about 2 tablespoons of the mixture into tots and repeat until you have used up all of the mixture. Put each tot into your air fryer basket. They may need to be cooked in multiple batches. Cook at almost 320 degrees F for twelve minutes, turning them halfway through. Ensure they are brown in color before serving.

Nutritional information: Calories: 133; Fat: 5.6g; Total Carbs: 12g; Net Carbs: 7g; Fiber: 5.3g; Sugars: 5.1g; Protein: 12g

Mashed Chives and Celery

Prep time: 15 minutes | Cook time: 20 minutes | Serves: 4

14 ounces celery stalks	taste
1 cup cauliflower florets	2 garlic cloves, minced
Black pepper and salt to the	⅓ cup heavy cream

4 ounces butter, melted
1 tablespoon chives, chopped

Zest of 1 lemon, grated

Mix all the recipe ingredients except the chives and the cream in a suitable pan. Introduce this pan to the air fryer and air fryer at almost 360 degrees F for 20 minutes. Mash the mix, add the rest of the ingredients, whisk well. Serve.
Nutritional information: Calories: 262; Fat: 26.9g; Total Carbs: 5g; Net Carbs: 2g; Fiber: 2.3g; Sugars: 2g; Protein: 1.8g

Balsamic Tomatoes with Garlic

Prep time: 15 minutes | Cook time: 15 minutes | Serves: 4

1 tablespoon olive oil
1 pound cherry tomatoes, halved
1 tablespoon dill, chopped

6 garlic cloves, minced
1 tablespoon balsamic vinegar
Black pepper and salt to the taste

In a pan that fits the air fryer, combine all the recipe ingredients, toss gently. Put the pan in your preheated air fryer and air fryer at almost 380 degrees F for almost 15 minutes. Divide between plates and serve.
Nutritional information: Calories: 60; Fat: 3.8g; Total Carbs: 6g; Net Carbs: 2.5g; Fiber: 1.6g; Sugars: 3.1g; Protein: 1.5g

Herbed Potatoes Medley

Prep time: 15 minutes | Cook time: 30 minutes | Serves: 4

3 large potatoes, peeled and diced
1 teaspoon parsley, chopped
1 teaspoon chives, chopped

1 teaspoon oregano, chopped
1 tablespoon garlic, minced
Black pepper and salt to taste
2 tablespoons olive oil

Mix all of the recipe ingredients in your air fryer, and stir well. Cook at almost 370 degrees F for 30 minutes. Serve.
Nutritional information: Calories: 255; Fat: 7.3g; Total Carbs: 44g; Net Carbs: 21g; Fiber: 6.9g; Sugars: 3.2g; Protein: 4.8g

Tasty Sweet Potato Wedges

Prep time: 15 minutes | Cook time: 25 minutes | Serves: 2

1 tablespoon olive oil
¼ teaspoon salt
½ teaspoon chili powder
½ teaspoon garlic powder

½ teaspoon smoked paprika
½ teaspoon dried thyme
A pinch cayenne pepper

In a suitable bowl, mix olive oil, salt, chili and garlic powder, smoked paprika, thyme, and cayenne. Toss in the potato wedges. Arrange the wedges on the air fryer, and cook for 25 minutes at 380 degrees F, flipping once.
Nutritional information: Calories: 67; Fat: 7.2g; Total Carbs: 1g; Net Carbs: 0g; Fiber: 0.6g; Sugars: 0.3g; Protein: 0.3g

Easy Melty Stuffed Mushrooms

Prep time: 15 minutes | Cook time: 10 minutes | Serves: 2

Black pepper and salt to taste
10 button mushroom caps
2 cups mozzarella cheese, chopped

2 cups cheddar cheese, chopped
3 tablespoon mixture of Italian herbs

At 340 degrees F, preheat your Air fryer. in a suitable bowl, mix oil, salt, black pepper, and herbs to form a marinade. Add the

10 button mushrooms to the marinade and toss to coat well. in a separate bowl, mix both kinds of cheese. Stuff mushrooms with the cheese mixture. Place in air fryer basket and cook for almost 10 minutes.
Nutritional information: Calories: 277; Fat: 21.4g; Total Carbs: 2g; Net Carbs: 0.5g; Fiber: 0.5g; Sugars: 1.1g; Protein 19.5g

Kale and Brussels Sprouts

Prep time: 15 minutes | Cook time: 15 minutes | Serves: 8

1 pound Brussels sprouts, trimmed
2 cups kale, torn
1 tablespoon olive oil

Black pepper and salt to the taste
3 ounces. mozzarella, shredded

In a pan that fits the air fryer, combine all the recipe ingredients except the mozzarella and toss. Put the pan in the preheated Air Fryer and Cook at almost 380 degrees F for almost 15 minutes. Divide between plates, sprinkle the cheese on top and serve.
Nutritional information: Calories: 155; Fat: 7.6g; Total Carbs: 14g; Net Carbs: 9.5g; Fiber: 4.8g; Sugars: 2.5g; Protein: 10.9g

Horseradish Turkey Burgers

Prep time: 15 minutes | Cook time: 18 minutes | Serves: 4

½ cup breadcrumbs
¼ cup grated Parmesan cheese
1 egg, beaten
1 tablespoon minced garlic
1 tablespoon olive oil

1 teaspoon horseradish sauce
4 tablespoons Greek yogurt
4 buns, halved
4 tomato slices

At 380 degrees F, preheat your air fryer. Grease its air fryer basket with cooking spray. In a suitable bowl, combine ground turkey, breadcrumbs, Parmesan cheese, egg, garlic, salt, and black pepper and mix well. Form into balls and flatten to make patties. Brush olive oil and insert in the air fryer basket. Cook for 18 minutes, flipping once. Mix the yogurt with horseradish sauce. Assemble burgers with the yogurt mixture, patties, and tomato slices and serve.
Nutritional information: Calories: 389; Fat: 12.4g; Total Carbs: 40.7g; Net Carbs: 0g; Fiber: 1.7g; Sugars: 12.1g; Protein: 28.3g

Cheese Spinach

Prep time: 15 minutes | Cook time: 16 minutes | Serves: 6

1 pound fresh spinach
6 ounces gouda cheese, shredded
8 ounces cream cheese

1 teaspoon garlic powder
1 tablespoon onion, minced
Black pepper
Salt

At 370 degrees F, preheat your air fryer. Grease its air fryer basket with cooking spray and set aside. Spray a large pan with cooking spray and heat over medium heat. Add spinach to the same pan and cook until wilted. Add cream cheese, garlic powder, and onion and stir until cheese is melted. Remove pan from heat and add Gouda cheese and season with black pepper and salt. Transfer spinach mixture to the prepared baking dish and place into the air fryer. Cook for 16 minutes. Serve and enjoy.
Nutritional information: Calories: 252; Fat: 21.3g; Total Carbs: 4g; Net Carbs: 2g; Fiber: 1.8g; Sugars: 1.2g; Protein: 12.2g

Buttered Smoked Tempeh

Prep time: 15 minutes | Cook time: 6 minutes | Serves: 2

1 cup tempeh	½ teaspoon garlic powder
1 teaspoon apple cider vinegar	1 teaspoon liquid smoke
1 teaspoon sesame oil	1 teaspoon butter, melted

In the shallow bowl, mix up melted butter, liquid smoke, garlic powder, sesame oil, and apple cider vinegar. Cut the tempeh into halves and brush with apple cider vinegar mixture from per side. After this, at 400 degrees F, preheat your air fryer. Put the tempeh in the preheated air fryer and cook it for 3 minutes from each side or until it is light brown. Transfer the cooked tempeh to the serving plate. Serve.

Nutritional information: Calories: 200; Fat: 13.2g; Total Carbs: 8g; Net Carbs: 3.5g; Fiber: 0.1g; Sugars: 0.2g; Protein: 15.5g

Radishes and Green Onions Mix

Prep time: 15 minutes | Cook time: 15 minutes | Serves: 4

20 radishes, halved	taste
1 tablespoon olive oil	3 teaspoons black sesame
3 green onions, chopped	seeds
Black pepper and salt to the	2 tablespoons olive oil

In a suitable bowl, mix all the recipe ingredients and toss well. Put the radishes in your air fryer basket, Cook at almost 400 degrees F for almost 15 minutes. Serve.

Nutritional information: Calories: 50; Fat: 4.7g; Total Carbs: 2g; Net Carbs: 0.5g; Fiber: 0.9g; Sugars: 0.7g; Protein: 0.8g

Air-Fried Asparagus

Prep time: 15 minutes | Cook time: 6 minutes | Serves: 4

12 ounces asparagus, trimmed	½ cup coconut flour
2 eggs, beaten	1 teaspoon olive oil
¼ cup Swiss cheese, shredded	1 teaspoon salt

In the mixing bowl, mix up Swiss cheese, coconut flour, and salt. Then dip the asparagus in the beaten eggs and coat in the coconut flour mixture. Repeat the same steps 1 more time and transfer the coated asparagus in the air fryer basket. Cook the vegetables for 6 minutes at 395 degrees F. Serve.

Nutritional information: Calories: 144; Fat: 6.8g; Total Carbs: 13g; Net Carbs: 7g; Fiber: 7.8g; Sugars: 1.9g; Protein: 8.5g

Apple Brussel Sprout Salad

Prep time: 15 minutes | Cook time: 15 minutes | Serves: 4

1 pound Brussels sprouts	Dressing:
1 apple, cored and diced	¼ cup olive oil
½ cup mozzarella cheese, crumbled	2 tablespoons champagne vinegar
½ cup pomegranate seeds	1 teaspoon Dijon mustard
1 small-sized red onion, chopped	1 teaspoon honey
4 eggs, hardboiled and sliced	Salt and black pepper, to taste

At 380 degrees F, preheat your air fryer. Add the Brussels sprouts to the cooking basket. Spritz with cooking spray and cook for almost 15 minutes. Toss the Brussels sprouts with the apple, cheese, pomegranate seeds, and red onion. Mix all the recipe ingredients for the dressing and toss to combine well. Serve topped with the hard-boiled eggs. Serve

Nutritional information: Calories: 279; Fat: 18.1g; Total Carbs: 23g; Net Carbs: 11g; Fiber: 5.8g; Sugars: 11.6g; Protein: 10.7g

Garlic Kale Mash

Prep time: 15 minutes | Cook time: 20 minutes | Serves: 4

1 cauliflower head, florets separated	2 scallions, chopped
	A pinch of black pepper and salt
4 teaspoons butter, melted	
4 garlic cloves, minced	⅓ cup coconut cream
3 cups kale, chopped	1 tablespoon parsley, chopped

In a pan that fits the air fryer, combine the cauliflower with the butter, garlic, scallions, salt, black pepper and the cream, toss, introduce the pan in the machine and cook at almost 380 degrees F for 20 minutes. Mash the mix well, add the remaining ingredients, whisk, divide between plates and serve.

Nutritional information: Calories: 112; Fat: 8.6g; Total Carbs: 8g; Net Carbs: 3.5g; Fiber: 1.5g; Sugars: 0.9g; Protein: 2.4g

Tasty Air Fried Mushrooms

Prep time: 15 minutes | Cook time: 8 minutes | Serves: 1

12 button mushrooms, cleaned	Black pepper
1 teaspoon olive oil	Salt
¼ teaspoon garlic salt	

Add all the recipe ingredients into the bowl and toss well. Grease its air fryer basket with cooking spray. Transfer mushrooms into the air fryer basket and Cook at almost 380 degrees F for 8 minutes. Toss halfway through. Serve and enjoy.

Nutritional information: Calories: 89; Fat: 5.3g; Total Carbs: 7g; Net Carbs: 3g; Fiber: 2.2g; Sugars: 3.9g; Protein: 6.9g

Coconut Green Beans

Prep time: 15 minutes | Cook time: 7 minutes | Serves: 2

8 ounces green beans	¼ cup coconut flakes
1 egg, beaten	½ teaspoon black pepper
1 teaspoon cream cheese	½ teaspoon salt
¼ cup almond flour	1 teaspoon sesame oil

In the mixing bowl mix up cream cheese, egg, and black pepper. Add salt in the separated bowl mix up coconut flakes and almond flour. At 400 degrees F, preheat your air fryer. Dip the cut green beans in the egg mixture and then coat in the coconut flakes mixture. Repeat the step 1 more time and transfer the vegetables in the air fryer. Sprinkle them with sesame oil and cook for 5 minutes. Shake the vegetables after 2 minutes of cooking. Serve.

Nutritional information: Calories: 107; Fat: 7.6g; Total Carbs: 6g; Net Carbs: 2.5g; Fiber: 3.2g; Sugars: 1.2g; Protein: 4.2g

Fish and Seafood Recipes

Hot Sauce Crab Dip

Prep time: 10 minutes | Cook time: 7 minutes | Serving: 2

½ cup crabmeat, cooked
½ tsp. pepper
1 tbsp. hot sauce
¼ cup scallions
1 cup cheese, grated

1 tbsp. mayonnaise
1 tbsp. parsley, chopped
1 tbsp. lemon juice
¼ tsp. salt

In an air fryer baking dish, mix crabmeat, hot sauce, scallions, cheese, mayonnaise, pepper, and salt. Place dish into the "Air Fryer Basket" and Air Fry the food at 400 degrees F for 7 minutes. Add parsley and lemon juice. Stir well. Serve and enjoy.
Nutritional information: Calories 295; Fat 21 g; Total Carbs 4 g; Net Carbs 2g; Sugar 1.3 g; Protein 20 g; Fiber 9 g

Fish Packets

Prep time: 10 minutes | Cook time: 15 minutes | Serving: 2

2 cod fish fillets
½ tsp. dried tarragon
½ cup bell peppers, sliced
¼ cup celery, cut into julienne
½ cup carrots, cut into julienne

1 tbsp. olive oil
1 tbsp. lemon juice
2 pats butter, melted
Pepper
Salt

In a suitable bowl, mix the butter, lemon juice, tarragon, and salt. Add vegetables and toss well. Set aside. Take 2 parchments paper pieces to fold vegetables and fish. Spray fish with some cooking spray and season with pepper and salt. Place a fish fillet on each baking paper piece and top with vegetables. Fold baking paper around the fish and vegetables. Place vegie fish packets into the "Air Fryer Basket" and Air Fry them at 350 degrees F for 15 minutes. Serve and enjoy.
Nutritional information: Calories 281; Fat 8 g; Total Carbs 6 g; Net Carbs 2g; Sugar 3 g; Protein 41 g; Fiber 1g

Air Fried Scallops

Prep time: 10 minutes | Cook time: 10 minutes | Serving: 2

8 sea scallops
1 tbsp. tomato paste
¾ cup heavy whipping cream
12 oz. frozen spinach, thawed and drained

1 tsp. garlic, minced
1 tbsp. fresh basil, chopped
½ tsp. pepper
½ tsp. salt

Spray "Air Fryer Basket" with some cooking spray. Add spinach in the pan. Spray scallops with some cooking spray and season with pepper and salt. Place scallops on top of spinach. In a suitable bowl, mix garlic, basil, tomato paste, whipping cream, pepper, and salt and pour over scallops and spinach. Place pan into the air fryer and Air Fry the food at 350 degrees F for 10 minutes. Serve and enjoy.
Nutritional information: Calories 311; Fat 18.3 g; Total Carbs 12 g; Net Carbs 2g; Sugar 1 g; Protein 26 g; Fiber 1 g

Spicy Prawns

Prep time: 10 minutes | Cook time: 8 minutes | Serving: 2

6 prawns
¼ tsp. pepper
½ tsp. chili powder

1 tsp. chili flakes
¼ tsp. salt

At 350 degrees F, preheat your Air Fryer. In a suitable bowl, mix spices add prawns. Spray "Air Fryer Basket" with some cooking spray. Transfer prawns into the "Air Fryer Basket" and Air Fry them for 8 minutes. Serve and enjoy.
Nutritional information: Calories 80; Fat 1.2 g; Total Carbs 1 g; Net Carbs 2g; Sugar 0.1 g; Protein 15.2 g; Fiber 1 g

Salmon Fillets

Prep time: 10 minutes | Cook time: 7 minutes | Serving: 2

2 salmon fillets
2 tsps. olive oil
2 tsps. paprika

Pepper
Salt

Rub salmon fillet with oil, paprika, pepper, and salt. Place prepared salmon fillets in the "Air Fryer Basket" and Air Fry them at 390 degrees F for 7 minutes. Serve and enjoy.
Nutritional information: Calories 280; Fat 15 g; Total Carbs 1.2 g; Net Carbs 2g; Sugar 0.2 g; Protein 35 g; Fiber 75 g

Air Fried Prawns

Prep time: 10 minutes | Cook time: 6 minutes | Serving: 4

12 king prawns
1 tbsp. vinegar
1 tbsp. ketchup
3 tbsps. mayonnaise

½ tsp. pepper
1 tsp. chili powder
1 tsp. red chili flakes
½ tsp. sea salt

At 350 degrees F, preheat your Air Fryer. Spray "Air Fryer Basket" with some cooking spray. Add prawns, chili flakes, chili powder, pepper, and salt to the bowl and toss well. Transfer the prawns to the "Air Fryer Basket" and Air Fry them for 6 minutes. In a suitable bowl, mix mayonnaise, ketchup, and vinegar. Serve with mayo mixture and enjoy.
Nutritional information: Calories 130; Fat 5 g; Total Carbs 5 g; Net Carbs 2g; Sugar 1 g; Protein 15 g; Fiber 0 g

Spicy Shrimp

Prep time: 10 minutes | Cook time: 6 minutes | Serving: 2

½ lb. shrimp, peeled and deveined
½ tsp. old bay seasoning
1 tsp. cayenne pepper

1 tbsp. olive oil
¼ tsp. paprika
⅛ tsp. salt

At 390 degrees F, preheat your Air Fryer. Add all the recipe ingredients into the bowl and toss well. Transfer shrimps into the "Air Fryer Basket" and Air Fry them for 6 minutes. Serve and

enjoy.
Nutritional information: Calories 195; Fat 9 g; Total Carbs 2 g; Net Carbs 2g; Sugar 0.1 g; Protein 26 g; Fiber 0 g

Lemon Butter Salmon

Prep time: 10 minutes | Cook time: 11 minutes | Serving: 2

2 salmon fillets	2 tbsps. fresh lemon juice
½ tsp. olive oil	¼ cup white wine
2 tsps. garlic, minced	Pepper
2 tbsps. butter	Salt

At 350 degrees F, preheat your Air Fryer. Spray the "Air Fryer Basket" with some cooking spray. Season salmon with pepper and salt and place into the "Air Fryer Basket" and Air Fry for 6 minutes. Meanwhile, in a saucepan, add the remaining ingredients and heat over low heat for 4-5 minutes. Place cooked salmon on serving dish then pour prepared sauce over salmon. Serve and enjoy.
Nutritional information: Calories 379; Fat 23 g; Total Carbs 2 g; Net Carbs 2g; Sugar 0.5 g; Protein 35 g; Fiber 0 g

Crab Patties

Prep time: 10 minutes | Cook time: 10 minutes | Serving: 4

1 egg	1 cup almond flour
12 oz. crabmeat	1 tsp. old bay seasoning
2 green onions, chopped	1 tsp. red pepper flakes
¼ cup mayonnaise	1 tbsp. fresh lemon juice

At 400 degrees F, preheat your Air Fryer. Spray the "Air Fryer Basket" with some cooking spray. Add ½ cup of almond flour into the mixing bowl. Add the remaining ingredients and mix well. Make patties from mixture and coat with remaining almond flour and place into the Air Fryer Basket. Cook the patties for 10 minutes, flipping them halfway through. Serve and enjoy.
Nutritional information: Calories 184 Fat 11 g; Total Carbs 5 g; Net Carbs 2g; Sugar 1 g; Protein 12 g; Fiber 0 g

Air Fried Catfish

Prep time: 10 minutes | Cook time: 20 minutes | Serving: 4

4 catfish fillets	¼ cup fish seasoning
1 tbsp. olive oil	1 tbsp. fresh parsley, chopped

At 400 degrees F, preheat your Air Fryer. Spray "Air Fryer Basket" with some cooking spray. Seasoned fish with seasoning and place into the Air Fryer Basket. Drizzle fish fillets with oil and Air Fry them for 20 minutes, turning the fillets halfway through. Garnish with parsley and serve.
Nutritional information: Calories 245 Fat 15 g; Total Carbs 0.1 g; Net Carbs 2g; Sugar 0 g; Protein 24 g; Fiber 0 g

Bacon-Wrapped Shrimp

Prep time: 10 minutes | Cook time: 7 minutes | Serving: 4

16 shrimp, deveined	16 bacon slices
¼ tsp. pepper	

At 390 degrees F, preheat your Air Fryer. Spray "Air Fryer Basket" with some cooking spray. Wrap each shrimp with one bacon slice and then place them into the "Air Fryer Basket". Air

Fry for 5 minutes. Turn shrimp to another side and Air Fry for 2 minutes more. Season shrimp with pepper. Serve and enjoy.
Nutritional information: Calories 515 Fat 33 g; Total Carbs 2 g; Net Carbs 2g; Sugar 0 g; Protein 45 g; Fiber 0 g

Almond Shrimp

Prep time: 10 minutes | Cook time: 5 minutes | Serving: 4

16 oz. shrimp, peeled	½ cup unsweetened shredded
½ cup almond flour	coconut
2 egg whites	½ tsp. salt
¼ tsp. cayenne pepper	

At 400 degrees F, preheat your Air Fryer. Spray "Air Fryer Basket" with some cooking spray. Whisk egg whites in a shallow dish. In a suitable bowl, mix the shredded coconut, almond flour, and cayenne pepper. Dip shrimps into the prepared egg mixture and then coat them with coconut mixture. Place coated shrimp into the "Air Fryer Basket" and Air Fry for 5 minutes. Serve and enjoy.
Nutritional information: Calories 200 Fat 7 g; Total Carbs 4 g; Net Carbs 2g; Sugar 1 g; Protein 28 g; Fiber 0 g

Cajun Cheese Shrimp

Prep time: 10 minutes | Cook time: 5 minutes | Serving: 4

1 lb. shrimp	1 tbsp. Cajun seasoning
½ cup almond flour	2 tbsps. parmesan cheese
1 tsp. olive oil	2 garlic cloves, minced

Add all the recipe ingredients into the bowl and toss well. Spray "Air Fryer Basket" with some cooking spray. Transfer shrimp mixture into the "Air Fryer Basket" and Air Fry the food at 390 degrees F for 5 minutes. Shake the basket halfway through. Serve and enjoy.
Nutritional information: Calories 175 Fat 5 g; Total Carbs 3 g; Net Carbs 2g; Sugar 0.2 g; Protein 27 g; Fiber 0 g

Creamy Shrimp

Prep time: 10 minutes | Cook time: 8 minutes | Serving: 4

1 lb. shrimp, peeled	½ tsp. paprika
1 tbsp. garlic, minced	1 tsp. sriracha
1 tbsp. tomato ketchup	½ tsp. salt
3 tbsp. mayonnaise	

In a suitable bowl, mix mayonnaise, paprika, sriracha, garlic, ketchup, and salt. Add shrimp and stir well. Add shrimp mixture into the air fryer baking dish and place in the air fryer. Air Fry the food at 325 degrees F for 8 minutes, stirring halfway through cooking. Serve and enjoy.
Nutritional information: Calories 185 Fat 5 g; Total Carbs 6 g; Net Carbs 2g; Sugar 1 g; Protein 25 g; Fiber 0 g

Chili Shrimp

Prep time: 10 minutes | Cook time: 5 minutes | Serving: 4

1 lb. shrimp, peeled and deveined	1 red chili pepper, sliced
	½ tsp. garlic powder
1 tbsp. olive oil	Pepper
1 lemon, sliced	Salt

At 400 degrees F, preheat your Air Fryer. Spray "Air Fryer

Basket" with some cooking spray. Add all the recipe ingredients into the bowl and toss well. Add the coated shrimps into the "Air Fryer Basket" and Air Fry them for 5 minutes. Shake the basket twice during cooking. Serve and enjoy.
Nutritional information: Calories 170 Fat 5 g; Total Carbs 3 g; Net Carbs 2g; Sugar 0.5 g; Protein 25 g; Fiber 0 g

Thai Shrimp

Prep time: 10 minutes | Cook time: 10 minutes | Serving: 4

1 lb. shrimp, peeled and deveined	2 tbsps. Thai chili sauce
1 tsp. sesame seeds, toasted	1 tbsp. arrowroot powder
2 garlic cloves, minced	1 tbsp. green onion, sliced
2 tbsps. soy sauce	⅛ tsp. ginger, minced

Spray "Air Fryer Basket" with some cooking spray. Toss shrimp with arrowroot powder and place into the Air Fryer Basket. Cook shrimp at 350 degrees F for 10 minutes, shaking the basket halfway through. Meanwhile, in a suitable bowl, mix soy sauce, ginger, garlic, and chili sauce. Add shrimp to the bowl and toss well. Garnish with green onions and sesame seeds. Serve and enjoy.
Nutritional information: Calories 155 Fat 2 g; Total Carbs 6 g; Net Carbs 2g; Sugar 2 g; Protein 25 g; Fiber 0 g

Lemon Cajun Cod

Prep time: 5 minutes | Cook time: 12 minutes | Serves: 2

2 (8-oz.) cod fillets, cut to fit into the "Air Fryer Basket"	½ tsp. freshly ground black pepper
1 tbsp. Cajun seasoning	2 tbsps. unsalted butter, melted
½ tsp. lemon pepper	1 lemon, cut into 4 wedges
1 tsp. salt	

In a small mixing bowl, combine the Cajun seasoning, lemon pepper, salt, and pepper. Rub the seasoning mix onto the fish. Place the cod into the greased Air Fryer Basket. Brush the top of each fillet with melted butter. Set the cooking temperature of your air fryer to 360 degrees F. Set the timer and Air Fry for 6 minutes. After 6 minutes, open up your air fryer drawer and flip the fish. Brush the top of each fillet with more melted butter. Reset the timer and Air Fry the fillets for 6 minutes more. Squeeze fresh lemon juice over the fillets.
Nutritional information: Calories 283; Fat 14g; Total Carbs 0g; Net Carb: 0g; Sugar 0g; Protein 40g; Fiber 6g

Steamed Salmon with Sauce

Prep time: 5 minutes | Cook time: 10 minutes | Serves: 2

1 cup water	½ cup plain Greek yogurt
2 (6 oz.) fresh salmon	½ cup sour cream
2 tsps. vegetable oil	2 tbsps. chopped dill
A pinch of salt for each fish	Salt to taste

Pour the water into the bottom of the air fryer and start heating to 285 degrees F. Drizzle oil over the salmons and spread it. Salt the fish to taste. Now pop them into the fryer and Air Fry them at 285 degrees F for 10 minutes. In the meantime, mix the yogurt, cream, dill and a bit of salt to make the sauce. When done, serve the salmons with the sauce and garnish with sprigs of dill.
Nutritional information: Calories 322; Fat 22 g; Total Carbs 5 g; Net Carbs 2g; Sugar 1 g; Protein 20 g; Fiber 0 g

Savory Breaded Shrimp

Prep time: 5 minutes | Cook time: 20 minutes | Serves: 2

½ lb. of fresh shrimp, peeled from their shells and rinsed	½ tsp. of turmeric powder
2 raw eggs	½ tsp. of red chili powder
½ cup of breadcrumbs	½ tsp. of cumin powder
½ white onion, peeled and rinsed and chopped	½ tsp. of black pepper powder
1 tsp. of ginger-garlic paste	½ tsp. of dry mango powder
	Pinch of salt

Cover the Air Fryer Basket with a lining of tin foil, leaving the edges uncovered to allow air to circulate through the basket. At 350 degrees F, preheat your Air Fryer. In a large mixing bowl, beat the eggs until fluffy and until the yolks and whites are fully combined. Dunk all the shrimp in the prepared egg mixture, fully submerging. In a separate mixing bowl, combine the bread crumbs with all the dry ingredients until evenly blended. One by one, coat the egg-covered shrimp in the mixed dry ingredients so that fully covered, and place on the foil-lined air-fryer basket. Set the air-fryer timer to 20 minutes. Halfway through the Cook Time, shake the handle of the air-fryer so that the breaded shrimp jostles inside and fry-coverage is even. After 20 minutes, when the fryer shuts off, the shrimp will be perfectly cooked and their breaded crust golden-brown and delicious! Using tongs, remove from the air fryer and set on a serving dish to cool.
Nutritional information: Calories: 190; Fat: 9.5g; Total Carbs 0.6g; Net Carbs 2g; Protein: 24g; Fiber: 0.3g; Sugar: 0.2g

Indian Fish Fingers

Prep time: 35 minutes | Cook time: 15 minutes | Serves: 4

½lb. fish fillet	Generous pinch of black pepper
1 tbsp. chopped fresh mint	Salt to taste
⅓ cup bread crumbs	¾ tbsp. lemon juice
1 tsp. ginger garlic paste	¾ tsp. garam masala powder
1 hot green chili chopped	⅓ tsp. rosemary
½ tsp. paprika	1 egg

Remove any skin on the fish, wash and then pat the fish fillet dry. Cut the fish fillet into fingers. In a suitable bowl, mix all the recipe ingredients except for fish, mint, and bread crumbs. Bury the fingers in the prepared mixture and refrigerate for 30 minutes. Remove from the bowl from the fridge and mix in mint leaves. In a separate bowl beat the egg, pour bread crumbs into a third bowl. Dip the fingers in the egg bowl then toss them in the bread crumbs bowl. Air Fry the food at 360 degrees for 15 minutes, tossing the fingers halfway through. When done, serve and enjoy.
Nutritional information: Calories: 246; Fat: 8.5g; Total Carbs 3.7g; Net Carbs 2g; Protein: 36.6g; Fiber: 1g; Sugar: 1.9g

Spicy Shrimp Kebab

Prep time: 25 minutes | Cook time: 20 minutes | Serves: 4

½ lbs. jumbo shrimp, cleaned, shelled and deveined	½ tsp. dried oregano
1-lb. cherry tomatoes	½ tsp. dried basil
1 tbsp. butter, melted	1 tsp. dried parsley flakes
1 tbsp. sriracha sauce	½ tsp. marjoram
Salt and black pepper, to taste	½ tsp. mustard seeds

Toss all the recipe ingredients in a suitable mixing bowl until the shrimp and tomatoes are covered on all sides. Soak the wooden skewers in water for 15 minutes. Thread the jumbo shrimp and cherry tomatoes onto skewers. Air Fry the skewers at 400 degrees F for 5 minutes, working with batches. When cooked, serve and enjoy.

Nutritional information: Calories 247 Fat 8.4g; Total Carbs 6g; Net Carbs 2g; Protein 36.4 Sugars: 3.5g; Fiber: 1.8 g

Fish Fillets with Tarragon

Prep time: 25 minutes | Cook time: 20 minutes | Serves: 4

2 eggs, beaten
½ tsp. tarragon
4 fish fillets, halved
2 tbsps. dry white wine

⅓ cup parmesan cheese, grated
1 tsp. seasoned salt
⅓ tsp. mixed peppercorns
½ tsp. fennel seed

Add the parmesan cheese, salt, peppercorns, fennel seeds, and tarragon to your food processor; blitz for 20 seconds. Drizzle fish fillets with dry white wine. Dump the egg into a shallow dish. Now, coat the fish fillets with the beaten egg on all sides. Then, coat them with the seasoned cracker mix. Air Fry the coated fillets at 345 degrees F for 17 minutes. When done, serve and enjoy.

Nutritional information: Calories: 209; Fat: 5g; Total Carbs 0g; Net Carbs 1.2g; Protein: 39.8g; Fiber: 0g; Sugar: 0g

Smoked White Fish

Prep time: 20 minutes | Cook time: 15 minutes | Serves: 4

½ tbsp. yogurt
⅓ cup spring garlic, chopped
Fresh chopped chives, for garnish
3 eggs, beaten
½ tsp. dried dill weed
1 tsp. dried rosemary
⅓ cup scallions, chopped

⅓ cup smoked whitefish, chopped
1 ½ tbsps. crème fraiche
1 tsp. kosher salt
1 tsp. dried marjoram
⅓ tsp. ground black pepper, or more to taste
Cooking spray

Firstly, spritz 4 oven-safe ramekins with some cooking spray. Then, divide smoked whitefish, spring garlic, and scallions among greased ramekins. Crack one egg into each ramekin; add the crème, yogurt, and all seasonings. Air Fry the food for about 13 minutes at 355 degrees F. Taste for doneness and eat warm garnished with fresh chives.

Nutritional information: Calories: 215; Fat: 5.1g; Total Carbs 1g; Net Carbs 2g; Protein: 40g; Fiber: 0.3g; Sugar: 0.2g

Paprika Baked Tilapia

Prep time: 20 minutes | Cook time: 15 minutes | Serves: 6

1 cup parmesan cheese, grated
1 tsp. paprika
1 tsp. dried dill weed
2 lbs. tilapia fillets

⅓ cup mayonnaise
½ tbsp. lime juice
Salt and ground black pepper, to taste

Mix the mayonnaise, parmesan, paprika, salt, black pepper, and dill weed until everything is combined. Then, drizzle tilapia fillets with the lime juice. Cover each fish fillet with parmesan/mayo mixture; roll them in parmesan/paprika mixture. Cook the food at 335 degrees F for 10 minutes on Bake mode. Serve and eat warm.

Nutritional information: Calories: 242; Fat: 8.5g; Total Carbs 0.4g; Net Carbs 2g; Protein: 39.9g; Fiber: 0.1g; Sugar: 0.2g

Tangy Cod Fillets

Prep time: 20 minutes | Cook time: 10 minutes | Serves: 2

½ tbsp. sesame oil

½ heaping tsp. dried parsley

flakes
⅓ tsp. fresh lemon zest, grated
2 medium-sized cod fillets
1 tsp. sea salt flakes
A pinch of black pepper and

salt
⅓ tsp. ground black pepper, or more to savor
½ tbsp. fresh lemon juice

At 375 degrees F, preheat your Air Fryer. Season each cod fillet with sea salt flakes, black pepper, and dried parsley flakes. Now, drizzle them with sesame oil. Place the seasoned cod fillets in a single layer at the bottom of the Air Fryer Basket. Air Fry the cod fillets for approximately 10 minutes. While the fillets are cooking, prepare the sauce by mixing the other ingredients. Serve cod fillets on 4 individual plates garnished with the creamy citrus sauce.

Nutritional information: Calories: 212; Fat: 8.1g; Total Carbs 0.5g; Net Carbs 2g; Protein: 33.3g; Fiber: 0.3g; Sugar: 0.1g

Fish and Cauliflower Cakes

Prep time: 2 hours 20 minutes | Cook time: 15 minutes | Serves: 4

½-lb. cauliflower florets
½ tsp. English mustard
2 tbsp. butter, room temperature
½ tbsp. cilantro, minced

2 tbsp. sour cream
2 ½ cups cooked white fish
Salt and freshly cracked black pepper, to savor

Boil the cauliflower until tender. Then, purée the cauliflower in your blender. Transfer to a mixing dish. Now, stir in the fish, cilantro, salt, and black pepper. Add the sour cream, English mustard, and butter; mix until everything's well incorporated. Using your hands, shape into patties. Place in the refrigerator for 2 hours. Air Fry the food for 13 minutes at 395 degrees F. Serve with some extra English mustard.

Nutritional information: Calories: 313; Fat: 14.5g; Total Carbs 2.4g; Net Carbs 3g; Protein: 40.6g; Fiber: 0.7g; Sugar: 0.5g

Marinated Scallops with Butter and Beer

Prep time: 1 hour 10 minutes | Cook time: 10 minutes | Serves: 4

2 lbs. sea scallops
½ cup beer
4 tbsps. butter

2 sprigs rosemary, only leaves
salt and black pepper, to taste

In a ceramic dish, mix the sea scallops with beer; let it marinate for 1 hour. Meanwhile, preheat your air fryer to 400 degrees F. Melt the butter and add the rosemary leaves. Stir for a few minutes. Discard the marinade and transfer the sea scallops to the Air Fryer Basket. Season with salt and black pepper. Air Fry the scallops in your preheated air fryer for 7 minutes, shaking the basket halfway through.

Nutritional information: Calories: 330; Fat: 17.5g; Total Carbs 0g; Net Carbs 1.2g; Protein: 29.9g; Fiber: 0g; Sugar: 0g

Cheesy Fish Gratin

Prep time: 30 minutes | Cook time: 20 minutes | Serves: 4

1 tbsp. avocado oil
1-lb. hake fillets
1 tsp. garlic powder
Sea salt and white pepper, to taste
1 tbsp. shallots, chopped
1 bell pepper, seeded and

chopped
½ cup cottage cheese
½ cup sour cream
1 egg, well whisked
1 tsp. yellow mustard
1 tbsp. lime juice
½ cup Swiss cheese, shredded

Brush the bottom and sides of a casserole dish with avocado oil. Add the hake fillets to the casserole dish and sprinkle with garlic powder, salt, and pepper. Add the chopped shallots and bell peppers. In a suitable mixing bowl, combine the cottage cheese, sour cream, egg, mustard, and lime juice. Pour the prepared mixture over fish and spread evenly. Air Fry the food at 370 degrees F for 10 minutes. When the time is up, top with the Swiss cheese and cook an additional 7 minutes. Let it rest for 10 minutes before slicing and serving.

Nutritional information: Calories: 343; Fat: 8.4g; Total Carbs 0.8g; Net Carbs 2g; Protein: 56g; Fiber: 0.4g; Sugar: 0.2g

Fijian Coconut Fish

Prep time: 20 minutes | Cook time: 15 minutes | Serves: 2

1 cup coconut milk	½ tsp. ginger powder
1 tbsp. lime juice	½ Thai bird's eye chili, seeded
1 tbsp. shoyu sauce	and chopped
Salt and white pepper, to taste	1-lb. tilapia
1 tsp. turmeric powder	2 tbsps. olive oil

In a suitable mixing bowl, combine the coconut milk with the lime juice, shoyu sauce, salt, pepper, turmeric, ginger, and chili pepper. Add tilapia and let it marinate for 1 hour. Brush the "Air Fryer Basket" with olive oil. Discard the marinade and place the tilapia fillets in the Air Fryer Basket. Air Fry the tilapia in air fryer at 400 degrees F for 6 minutes. Turn them over and Air Fry for 6 minutes more. Work in batches. Serve with some extra lime wedges if desired.

Nutritional information: Calories: 356; Fat: 18g; Total Carbs 0.5g; Net Carbs 2g; Protein: 45.1g; Fiber: 0.1g; Sugar: 0g

Sole Fish and Cauliflower Fritters

Prep time: 30 minutes | Cook time: 25 minutes | Serves: 2

½ lb. sole fillets	½ tsp. scotch bonnet pepper,
½ lb. mashed cauliflower	minced
1 egg, well beaten	1 tbsp. olive oil
½ cup red onion, chopped	1 tbsp. coconut aminos
2 garlic cloves, minced	½ tsp. paprika
1 tbsp. fresh parsley, chopped	Salt and white pepper, to taste
1 bell pepper, chopped	

At 395 degrees F, preheat your Air Fryer. Air Fry the sole fillets in your preheated air fryer for 10 minutes, flipping them halfway through. In a suitable mixing bowl, mash the sole fillets into flakes. Stir in the remaining ingredients. Shape the fish mixture into patties. Cook the patties in air fryer at 390 degrees F for 14 minutes on Bake mode, flipping them halfway through. When done, serve and enjoy.

Nutritional information: Calories: 281; Fat: 17.1g; Total Carbs 3.6g; Net Carbs 1.2g; Protein: 27.8g; Fiber: 0.3g; Sugar: 0.2g

Garlic Shrimp

Prep time: 10 minutes | Cook time: 15 minutes | Serves: 2

1 lb. of peeled raw shrimp	Chili flakes, to taste
¼ tsp. of garlic powder	Minced cilantro, for garnishing
Olive oil, to coat	Lemon wedges, for serving
Pinch of salt, black pepper	

At 400 degrees F, preheat your Air Fryer. Add the shrimp, garlic powder, oil, pepper, and salt to a mixing bowl. Mix it until all shrimp are coated. Transfer the shrimps in your preheated "Air Fryer Basket" in a single layer. Air Fry the shrimps at 400 degrees F for 10–14 minutes, stirring and flipping occasionally.

Top with minced cilantro and chili flakes, serve warm with lemon wedges. Enjoy your Garlic Shrimp!

Nutritional information: Calories: 280g; Total Carbs 0.3 g; Net Carb 2g; Fat 16 g; Protein 36 g; Sugar 0.1 g; Fiber 2 g

Tender Salmon

Prep time: 10 minutes | Cook time: 10-12 minutes | Serves: 4

4 salmon fillets	1 tsp. of minced garlic
4 tsps. of soy sauce	⅛ tsp. of black pepper
3 tbsps. of maple syrup	

Add soy sauce, maple syrup, black pepper, and garlic to a bowl. Mix it well. Put the cleaned salmon fillets in a Ziploc bag and pour in the prepared marinade. Leave it for 10–30 minutes for good flavor. At 350 degrees F, preheat your Air Fryer. Spray some oil inside the Air Fryer Basket. Transfer the marinated fillets into the "Air Fryer Basket" in a single layer. Air Fry the fillets at 350 degrees F for 8–10 minutes if you like medium-rare. Air Fry the fillets for 10–12 minutes, if you prefer well done. The internal temperature for medium-rare should be 120–125 degrees F, and for well-done will be 140 degrees F. Serve warm and enjoy!

Nutritional information: Calories 222g; Total Carbs 10 g; Net Carbs 2g; Fat 7 g; Protein 25 g; Sugar 9 g; Fiber 3 g

Parmesan White Fish

Prep time: 10 minutes | Cook time: 20 minutes | Serves: 2

2 filets of white fish	1 tbsp. of olive oil
½ cup of grated Parmesan cheese	Pinch of black pepper and salt, to taste
½ tsp. of smoked paprika	Lemon wedges, for serving
½ tsp. of onion powder	Chopped parsley, for
½ tsp. of garlic powder	garnishing

At 380 degrees F, preheat your Air Fryer. Grease the fish filets with oil. Season both sides with pepper, garlic powder, paprika, onion powder, salt, and pepper. Coat both sides generously with grated cheese. Cover the "Air Fryer Basket" with the perforated baking paper. Lightly spray it with oil. Put the coated fillets in your preheated air fryer and Air Fry them for 6–12 minutes. Serve with lemon wedges and top with the chopped parsley. Enjoy!

Nutritional information: Calories 338g; Total Carbs 2 g; Net Carbs 2g; Fat 17 g; Protein 44 g; Sugar 1 g; Fiber: 7 g

Crab Cakes

Prep time: 10 minutes | Cook time: 15 minutes | Serves: 4

8 oz. of lump crab meat	3 tbsps. of mayonnaise
3 chopped green onions	2 tsps. of Old Bay seasoning
1 chopped red bell pepper	1 tsp. of lemon juice
3 tbsps. of bread crumbs	Lemon wedges, for serving

At 370 degrees F, preheat your Air Fryer. Cover the inside of the "Air Fryer Basket" with the perforated baking paper. Mix the crab meat, onions, bread crumbs, lemon juice, seasonings, pepper, and mayonnaise in a suitable bowl well. Gently form same-sized patties. Transfer the formed patties in your preheated "Air Fryer Basket" in a single layer. Air Fry the patties at 370 degrees F for 8–10 minutes until the crust is golden-brown. Serve with your favorite sauce and lemon wedges.

Nutritional information: Calories 158g; Total Carbs 8 g; Net Carbs 2g; Fat 9 g; Protein 12 g; Sugar 2 g; Fiber 1g

Tuna Steaks

Prep time: 10 minutes | Cook time: 6 minutes | Serves: 2

2 yellowfin tuna steaks	1 tsp. of sesame or olive oil
¼ cup of soy sauce	1 tsp. of grated ginger
½ tsp. of rice vinegar	Lime wedges and avocado-cucumber salsa, for serving
2 tsps. of honey	

Mix soy sauce, ginger, honey, vinegar, and oil in a large mixing bowl. Put the tuna steaks in the bowl. Keep covered for 20–30 minutes in the fridge. At 380 degrees F, preheat your Air Fryer. Cover the inside of "Air Fryer Basket" with the perforated baking paper. Put the marinated tuna steaks in the "Air Fryer Basket". Air Fry the marinated tuna steaks at 380 degrees F for 4 minutes. Let it rest for 1–2 minutes before serving. Serve with your favorite salsa and lime wedges. Enjoy!

Nutritional information: Calories 422g; Total Carbs 8 g; Net Carbs 2g; Fat 23 g; Protein 44 g; Sugar 6 g; Fiber: 1 g

Tuna Patties

Prep time: 70 minutes | Cook time: 15 minutes | Serves: 3

2 (7-oz.) cans of albacore tuna fish in the water (drained)	Parmesan cheese
2 whisked eggs	1 tsp. of minced garlic
½ cup of chopped onions	1 tsp. of sriracha
¼ cup of chopped fresh parsley	1 tbsp. of lime juice
1 stack of celery	1 tbsp. of butter
½ chopped red bell pepper	1 tbsp. of olive oil
1 cup of panko crumbs	¼ tsp. of salt
¼ cup 3 tbsp. of grated	½ tsp. of oregano
	Pinch of black pepper, to taste

Add butter and oil in a skillet over medium-high heat. Add in the bell pepper, garlic, and onions. Sauté for 5–7 minutes. Drain the tuna cans and transfer them into a suitable bowl. Squeeze it with lime juice. Transfer the cooked vegetables into the bowl. Add in parsley, celery, oregano, sriracha, pepper, salt, half cup of panko crumbs, and 3 tbsp. of cheese. Mix it well. Add in the whisked eggs, mix, and form 6 same-sized patties. If your patties are falling apart, add extra panko crumbs. Keep it in a refrigerator for 20–60 minutes. Mix in a separate bowl a half cup of panko crumbs with ¼ cup of grated cheese. Remove patties from the refrigerator and coat them with this mixture. Spray tops with some oil. At 390 degrees F, preheat your Air Fryer. Cover the inside of "Air Fryer Basket" with the perforated baking paper. Put patties in the air fryer in a single layer. Avoid touching each other. Air Fry the patties at 390 degrees F for 4 minutes. Gently flip it, spray with oil, and Air Fry for 4 minutes more. Serve warm and enjoy your Tuna Patties!

Nutritional information: Calories 387 g; Total Carbs 21 g; Net Carbs 2g; Fat 17 g; Protein 38 g; Sugar 4 g; Fiber: 6 g

Crispy Fish Tacos

Prep time: 10 minutes | Cook time: 40 minutes | Serves: 5

1 lb. of the firm and white fish	1 tsp. of black pepper
3 eggs	1 tsp. of red chili flakes (optional)
2 cups of sour cream	
¾ cup of AP flour	1 tsp. of lemon pepper (optional)
1 package of corn tortillas	
1 cup of panko bread crumbs	For Toppings
1–2 limes	Lettuce leaves
1 tsp. of cumin	Salsa
1 tsp. of onion powder	Avocado
1 tsp. of garlic powder	Tomatoes
1 tsp. of salt	Radishes

cabbage,   hot sauce

Thaw the fish fillets and dry them with a paper towel. Cut into 2–3 pieces depending on the size of the fillets. Season both sides with pepper and salt. Add AP flour in one bowl. Whisk 3 eggs in a separate bowl. Mix the panko bread crumbs, lemon pepper, cumin, red chili flakes, onion powder, garlic powder, ½ teaspoon of black pepper and salt in a third bowl. Dip the fish piece into the flour, then into the whisked eggs, and finally into the bread crumb mixture, lightly pressing it. Put the coated fillet on a big plate. Repeat the same with the remaining part of the fish. At 370 degrees F, preheat your Air Fryer. Spray some oil inside the Air Fryer Basket. Transfer the coated fillets into your preheated basket; avoid them touching. Air Fry the coated fillets at 370 degrees F for 6 minutes. When the time is up, gently flip the fillets and Air Fry for 6 minutes more. When cooked, remove and set aside. Repeat this step until all pieces of fish are cooked. To cook the lime crema: Add the sour cream in a suitable bowl. Add in zest and juice from 2 limes. Season with a pinch of salt and whisk it with a fork. To serve: Warm tortillas in a microwave or on the pan. Put the crispy fish in the middle. Top with the prepared lime crema and add vegetables or hot sauce you like. Serve warm and enjoy!

Nutritional information: Calories 534g; Total Carbs 69 g; Net Carbs 2g; Fat 18 g; Protein 27 g; Sugar 3 g; Fiber: 2 g

Bang Bang Shrimp

Prep time: 10 minutes | Cook time: 30 minutes | Serves: 4

1 lb. of peeled jumbo shrimp	¼ cup of sweet chili sauce
1 cup of mayonnaise	½ tsp. of sriracha
1 cup of bread crumbs	Chopped fresh parsley, for garnishing
¾ cup of corn starch	
½ cup of buttermilk	

At 400 degrees F, preheat your Air Fryer. Spray some oil inside the air fryer basket. Add mayonnaise, sweet chili sauce, and sriracha in a suitable bowl. Mix it well until combined. Take 6–8 shrimps at a time, generously coat in cornstarch. Then dip in buttermilk and finally roll them in bread crumbs until fully covered. Transfer the coated shrimps in the Air Fryer Basket; avoid them touching. Air Fry the shrimps at 400 degrees F for 5 minutes, spray tops with some oil, flip them, and Air Fry for extra 5 minutes. Remove and set aside. Repeat the last 2 steps with the rest of the shrimp. Put all cooked shrimp in a medium mixing bowl, pour in the mayonnaise-chili sauce, and toss until the shrimp are fully covered. Top with fresh parsley, serve warm, and enjoy your Bang Bang Shrimp!

Nutritional information: Calories 744 g; Total Carbs 51 g; Net Carbs 2g; Fat 46 g; Protein 28 g; Sugar 12 g; Fiber: 3g

Shrimp Tempura

Prep time: 10 minutes | Cook time: 30 minutes | Serves: 6

2 lbs. of peeled raw shrimp	1 cup of all-purpose flour
2 eggs	2 tbsps. of olive oil
2 ½ cups of panko bread crumbs	2 tsps. of water

At 350 degrees F, preheat your Air Fryer. Spray some oil inside the Air Fryer Basket. Whisk eggs with 2 teaspoons of water in a suitable bowl. Put flour in a separate bowl. Add bread crumbs in a third bowl. Coat the shrimp with the flour, then dip into the prepared egg mixture, and finally roll in the bread crumbs until fully covered. Spread the coated shrimps in the "Air Fryer Basket" in a single layer; avoid them touching. Air Fry the shrimps at 350 degrees F for 4 minutes; when the time is up, spray their tops with some oil, flip them, and Air Fry them

for extra 4 minutes. Repeat the last 2 steps until all shrimp are cooked. Serve warm with any sauce you like.
Nutritional information: Calories 387g; Total Carbs 34 g; Net Carbs 2g; Fat 10 g; Protein 38 g; Sugar 2 g; Fiber: 4 g

Salmon Patties

Prep time: 10 minutes. Cook time: 15 minutes | Serves: 2

2 (7.5-oz) cans of unsalted pink salmon
½ cup of panko bread crumbs
1 large egg
2 tbsps. of mayonnaise

2 tbsps. of chopped fresh dill
Pinch of black pepper and salt
2 tsps. of mustard
Lime wedges, for serving

At 400 degrees F, preheat your Air Fryer. Spray some oil inside the Air Fryer Basket. Drain water from the salmon, remove skin and large bones, put it in a suitable bowl. Add in bread crumbs, mayonnaise, egg, mustard, pepper, and dill. Mix it well until combined. Form 4 same-sized patties. Put the patties in the "Air Fryer Basket" in a single layer; avoid them touching. Air Fry the patties at 400 degrees F for 6 minutes; when the time is up, gently flip them, and Air Fry them for 6 minutes until browned. Serve warm with lemon wedges and enjoy!
Nutritional information: Calories 517g; Total Carbs 14.7 g; Net Carbs 1g; Protein 51 g; Fat 26.7 g; Sugar 0.6 g; Fiber 3g

Enjoyable White Fish

Prep time: 15 minutes | Cook time: 12 minutes | Serves: 2

12 oz. white fish fillets
½ tbsp. onion powder
½ tbsp. lemon pepper seasoning

½ tbsp. garlic powder
1 tbsp. olive oil
pepper
salt

Spray the "Air Fryer Basket" with some cooking spray. At 360 degrees F, preheat your Air Fryer. Coat fish fillets with olive oil and season with onion powder, lemon pepper seasoning, garlic powder, pepper, and salt. Place fish fillets in "Air Fryer Basket" and Air Fry them for 10-12 minutes. Enjoy.
Nutritional information: Calories 387g; Total Carbs 34 g; Net Carbs 2g; Fat 10 g; Protein 38 g; Sugar 2 g; Fiber: 4 g

Shrimp and Celery Salad

Prep time: 10 minutes | Cook time: 5 minutes | Serves: 4

3 oz. chevre cheese
1 tsp. avocado oil
½ tsp. dried oregano
8 oz. shrimps, peeled

1 tsp. butter, melted
½ tsp. salt
½ tsp. chili flakes
4 oz. celery stalk, chopped

Sprinkle the shrimps with dried oregano and melted butter and put in the air fryer. Air Fry the seafood at 400 degrees F for 5 minutes. Meanwhile, crumble the chevre cheese. Put the chopped celery stalk in the salad bowl. Add crumbled chevre, chili flakes, salt, and avocado oil. Mix up the salad well and top it with cooked shrimps.
Nutritional information: Calories 158g; Total Carbs 4.2g; Net Carbs 2g; Protein 17.7; Fat 7.5g; Sugar 2g; Fiber 0.6

Basil and Paprika Cod

Prep time: 5 minutes | Cook time: 15 minutes | Serves: 4

4 cod fillets, boneless

1 tsp. red pepper flakes

½ tsp. hot paprika
2 tbsps. olive oil
1 tsp. basil, dried

Salt and black pepper to the taste

In a suitable bowl, mix the cod with all the other ingredients and toss. Put the fish in your "Air Fryer Basket" and Air Fry them at 380 degrees F for 15 minutes. Divide the cod between plates and serve.
Nutritional information: Calories 194g; Total Carbs 4g; Net Carbs 2g; Protein 12; Fat 7g; Sugar 2g; Fiber 2g

Cajun Shrimps

Prep time: 10 minutes | Cook time: 6 minutes | Serves: 4

8 oz. shrimps, peeled
1 tsp. Cajun spices
1 tsp. cream cheese

1 egg, beaten
½ tsp. salt
1 tsp. avocado oil

Sprinkle the shrimps with Cajun spices and salt. In the mixing bowl mix up cream cheese and egg, Dip every shrimp in the prepared egg mixture. At 400 degrees F, preheat your Air Fryer. Place the shrimps in the air fryer and sprinkle with avocado oil. Air Fry the popcorn shrimps at 400 degrees F for 6 minutes, shaking the basket halfway through cooking. When cooked, serve and enjoy.
Nutritional information: Calories 88g; Total Carbs 1g; Net Carbs 2g; Protein 14.4; Fat 2.5g; Sugar 2g; Fiber 0.1g

Balsamic Cod

Prep time: 5 minutes | Cook time: 15 minutes | Serves: 4

4 cod fillets, boneless
Salt and black pepper to the taste
1 cup parmesan

4 tbsps. balsamic vinegar
A drizzle of olive oil
3 spring onions, chopped

Season fish with salt, pepper, grease with the oil, and coat it in parmesan. Put the fillets in your "Air Fryer Basket" and Air Fry them at 370 degrees F for 14 minutes. Meanwhile, in a suitable bowl, mix the spring onions with salt, pepper and the vinegar and whisk. Divide the cod between plates, drizzle the spring onions mix all over and serve with a side salad.
Nutritional information: Calories 220g; Total Carbs 5g; Net Carbs 2g; Protein 13; Fat 12g; Sugar 2g; Fiber 2g

Wrapped Scallops

Prep time: 15 minutes | Cook time: 7 minutes | Serves: 4

1 tsp. ground coriander
½ tsp. ground paprika
¼ tsp. salt

16 oz. scallops
4 oz. bacon, sliced
1 tsp. sesame oil

Sprinkle the scallops with ground coriander, ground paprika, and salt. Then wrap the scallops in the bacon slices and secure with toothpicks. Sprinkle the scallops with sesame oil. At 400 degrees F, preheat your Air Fryer. Put the scallops in the "Air Fryer Basket" and Air Fry them for 7 minutes.
Nutritional information: Calories 264g; Total Carbs 3.2g; Net Carbs 2g; Protein 29.6; Fat 13.9g; Sugar 2g; Fiber 0.1g

Thyme Catfish

Prep time: 10 minutes | Cook time: 12 minutes | Serves: 4

20 oz. catfish fillet (4 oz. each   fillet)

2 eggs, beaten
1 tsp. dried thyme
½ tsp. salt
1 tsp. apple cider vinegar

1 tsp. avocado oil
¼ tsp. cayenne pepper
⅓ cup coconut flour

Sprinkle the catfish fillets with dried thyme, salt, apple cider vinegar, cayenne pepper, and coconut flour. Then sprinkle the fish fillets with avocado oil. At 385 degrees F, preheat your Air Fryer. Put the catfish fillets in the "Air Fryer Basket" and cook them for 8 minutes at 385 degrees F on Air Fry mode. When the time is up, flip the fillets and Air Fry them for 4 minutes more. When done, serve and enjoy.
Nutritional information: Calories 198; Fiber 4.2g; Total Carbs 6.5g; Net Carbs 2g; Protein 18.3; Fat 10.7g; Sugar 2g

Garlic Shrimp Mix

Prep time: 10 minutes | Cook time: 5 minutes | Serves: 3

1-lb. shrimps, peeled
½ tsp. garlic powder
¼ tsp. minced garlic
1 tsp. ground cumin

¼ tsp. lemon zest, grated
½ tbsp. avocado oil
½ tsp. dried parsley

In the mixing bowl, mix up shrimps, garlic powder, minced garlic, ground cumin, lemon zest, and dried parsley; add avocado oil and mix up the shrimps well. At 400 degrees F, preheat your Air Fryer. Put the shrimps in your preheated "Air Fryer Basket" and Air Fry them for 5 minutes. When done, serve and enjoy.
Nutritional information: Calories 187; Total Carbs 3.2g; Net Carbs 2g; Protein 34.7 Fat 3g; Sugar 2g; Fiber 0.2g;

Salmon and Creamy Chives Sauce

Prep time: 5 minutes | Cook time: 20 minutes | Serves: 4

4 salmon fillets, boneless
½ cup heavy cream
1 tbsp. chives, chopped
1 tsp. lemon juice
A pinch of salt and black

pepper
1 tsp. dill, chopped
2 garlic cloves, minced
¼ cup ghee, melted

In a suitable bowl, mix all the recipe ingredients except the salmon and whisk well. Arrange the coated salmon fillets in a pan that fits the air fryer, drizzle the sauce all over, transfer the pan in the air fryer and Air Fry the fillets at 360 degrees F for 20 minutes. Divide everything between plates and serve.
Nutritional information: Calories 220; Total Carbs 5g; Net Carbs 2g; Protein 12 Fat 14g; Sugar 2g; Fiber 2g

Tilapia and Tomato Salsa

Prep time: 5 minutes | Cook time: 15 minutes | Serves: 4

4 tilapia fillets, boneless
1 tbsp. olive oil
A pinch of salt and black pepper
12 oz. tomatoes, chopped

2 tbsps. green onions, chopped
2 tbsps. sweet red pepper, chopped
1 tbsp. balsamic vinegar

Arrange the tilapia in a baking pan that fits the air fryer and season with black pepper and salt. In a suitable bowl, combine all the other ingredients, toss and spread over the fish. Place the pan in the fryer and Air Fry the fillets at 350 degrees F for 15 minutes. Divide the mix between plates and serve.
Nutritional information: Calories 221; Total Carbs 5g; Net Carbs 2g; Protein 14; Fat 12g; Sugar 2g; Fiber 2g

Crusted Turmeric Salmon

Prep time: 15 minutes | Cook time: 8 minutes | Serves: 4

12 oz. salmon fillet
¼ cup pistachios, grinded
1 tsp. cream cheese
½ tsp. ground nutmeg
2 tbsps. coconut flour

½ tsp. ground turmeric
¼ tsp. sage
½ tsp. salt
1 tbsp. heavy cream
Cooking spray

Cut the salmon fillet on 4 servings. In the mixing bowl mix up cream cheese, ground turmeric, sage, salt, and heavy cream. Then in the separated bowl mix up coconut flour and pistachios. Dip the salmon fillets in the cream cheese mixture and then coat in the pistachio mixture. At 380 degrees F, preheat your Air Fryer. Place the coated salmon fillets in the air fryer basket and grease them with the cooking spray. Cook the fish for 8 minutes at 380 degrees F on Air Fry mode. When done, serve and enjoy.
Nutritional information: Calories 168; Total Carbs 3.7g; Net Carbs 2g; Protein 18.2; Fat 9.5g; Sugar 2g; Fiber 2g

Catfish with Spring Onions and Avocado

Prep time: 5 minutes | Cook time: 15 minutes | Serves: 4

2 tsps. oregano, dried
2 tsps. cumin, ground
2 tsps. sweet paprika
A pinch of salt and black pepper
4 catfish fillets

avocado, peeled and cubed
½ cup spring onions, chopped
2 tbsps. cilantro, chopped
2 tsps. olive oil
tbsp. lemon juice

In a suitable bowl, mix all the recipe ingredients except the fish and toss. Arrange this in a baking pan that fits the air fryer, top with the fish, introduce the pan in the air fryer and Air Fry the food at 360 degrees F for 15 minutes, flipping the fish halfway. Divide between plates and serve.
Nutritional information: Calories 280; Total Carbs 5g; Net Carbs 2g; Protein 14; Fat 14g; Sugar 2g; Fiber 3g

Paprika Tilapia

Prep time: 5 minutes | Cook time: 20 minutes | Serves: 4

4 tilapia fillets, boneless
3 tbsp. ghee, melted
A pinch of salt and black pepper
2 tbsps. capers

1 tsp. garlic powder
½ tsp. smoked paprika
½ tsp. oregano, dried
2 tbsp. lemon juice

In a suitable bowl, mix all the recipe ingredients except the fish and toss. Arrange the fish in a pan that fits the air fryer, pour the capers mix all over. Put this pan in the air fryer and Air Fry the fillets at 360 degrees F for 20 minutes, shaking the basket halfway through. Divide between plates and serve hot.
Nutritional information: Calories 224; Total Carbs 2g; Net Carbs 2g; Protein 18; Fat 10g; Sugar 2g; Fiber 0g

Shrimp Skewers

Prep time: 10 minutes | Cook time: 5 minutes | Serves: 5

4-lbs. shrimps, peeled
2 tbsps. fresh cilantro, chopped
2 tbsps. apple cider vinegar

1 tsp. ground coriander
1 tbsp. avocado oil
Cooking spray

In the shallow bowl mix up avocado oil, ground coriander, apple cider vinegar, and fresh cilantro. Then put the shrimps in the big

bowl and sprinkle with avocado oil mixture. Mix them well and leave for 10 minutes to marinate. After this, string the shrimps on the skewers. At 400 degrees F, preheat your Air Fryer. Arrange the shrimp skewers in the Air Fryer Basket and Air Fry them for 5 minutes.
Nutritional information: Calories 223; Total Carbs 5.5g; Net Carbs 2g; Protein 17.4; Fat 14.9g; Sugar 2g; Fiber 3.1g

Lime Cod

Prep time: 5 minutes | Cook time: 14 minutes | Serves: 4

4 cod fillets, boneless	taste
1 tbsp. olive oil	2 tsps. sweet paprika
Salt and black pepper to the	Juice of 1 lime

In a suitable bowl, mix all the recipe ingredients, transfer the cod fillets to your "Air Fryer Basket" and Air Fry them at 350 degrees F for 7 minutes on each side. Divide the fish between plates and serve with a side salad.
Nutritional information: Calories 240; Total Carbs 4g; Net Carbs 2g; Protein 16; Fat 14g; Sugar 2g; Fiber 2g

Chili Haddock

Prep time: 10 minutes | Cook time: 8 minutes | Serves: 4

12 oz. haddock fillet	½ tsp. salt
1 egg, beaten	1 tbsp. flax meal
1 tsp. cream cheese	Cooking spray
1 tsp. chili flakes	

Cut the haddock on 4 pieces and sprinkle with chili flakes and salt. After this, in the small bowl mix up egg and cream cheese. Dip the haddock pieces in the prepared egg mixture and generously sprinkle with flax meal. At 400 degrees F, preheat your Air Fryer. Put the prepared haddock pieces in the air fryer in one layer and Air Fry them for 4 minutes from each side or until they are golden brown.
Nutritional information: Calories 122g; Total Carbs 0.6g; Net Carbs 2g; Protein 22.5; Fat 2.8g; Sugar 2g; Fiber 0.5g

Butter Crab Muffins

Prep time: 15 minutes | Cook time: 20 minutes | Serves: 2

5 oz. crab meat, chopped	½ tsp. apple cider vinegar
2 eggs, beaten	½ tsp. ground paprika
2 tbsp. almond flour	1 tbsp. butter, softened
¼ tsp. baking powder	Cooking spray

Grind the chopped crab meat and put it in the bowl. Add eggs, almond flour, baking powder, apple cider vinegar, ground paprika, and butter. Stir the prepared mixture until homogenous. At 365 degrees F, preheat your Air Fryer Grease the muffin molds with some cooking spray. Pour the crab meat batter in the muffin molds and place them in your preheated air fryer. Air Fry the crab muffins for 20 minutes or until they are light brown. Cool the cooked muffins to the room temperature and remove from the muffin mold.
Nutritional information: Calories 340; Total Carbs 8.2g; Net Carbs 2g; Protein 20.5; Fat 25.5g; Sugar 2g; Fiber 3.2g

Tilapia and Kale

Prep time: 5 minutes | Cook time: 20 minutes | Serves: 4

4 tilapia fillets, boneless	taste
Salt and black pepper to the	2 garlic cloves, minced
1 tsp. fennel seeds	1 bunch kale, chopped
½ tsp. red pepper flakes, crushed	Tablespoons olive oil

In a suitable air fryer, combine all the recipe ingredients. Put this pan in the fryer and Air Fry the fillets at 360 degrees F for 20 minutes. Divide everything between plates and serve.
Nutritional information: Calories 240; Total Carbs 4g; Net Carbs 2g; Protein 12; Fat 12g; Sugar 2g; Fiber 2g

Mackerel with Spring Onions and Peppers

Prep time: 15 minutes | Cook time: 20 minutes | Serves: 5

1-lb. mackerel, trimmed	1 tbsp. avocado oil
1 tbsp. ground paprika	1 tsp. apple cider vinegar
1 green bell pepper	½ tsp. salt
½ cup spring onions, chopped	

Wash the mackerel if needed and sprinkle with ground paprika. Chop the green bell pepper. Then fill the mackerel with bell pepper and spring onion. After this, sprinkle the fish with avocado oil, apple cider vinegar, and salt. At 375 degrees F, preheat your Air Fryer. Place the mackerel in the "Air Fryer Basket" and Air Fry the food for 20 minutes. When done, serve and enjoy.
Nutritional information: Calories 258; Total Carbs 3.8g; Net Carbs 2g; Protein 22.2; Fat 16.8g; Sugar 2g; Fiber 1.2g

Ginger Salmon

Prep time: 5 minutes | Cook time: 12 minutes | Serves: 4

2 tbsps. lime juice	4 tsp. olive oil
1 lb. salmon fillets, boneless, cubed	1 tbsp. coconut aminos
1 tbsp. ginger, grated	1 tbsp. sesame seeds, toasted
	1 tbsp. chives, chopped

In a pan that fits the air fryer, combine all the recipe ingredients and toss well. Place the pan in the air fryer and Air Fry the food at 360 degrees F for 12 minutes. Divide into bowls and serve.
Nutritional information: Calories 206; Total Carbs 4g; Net Carbs 2g; Protein 13; Fat 8g; Sugar 2g; Fiber 1g

Wonderful Parmesan Almond Salmon

Prep time: 15 minutes | Cook time:12 minutes | Serves: 4

2 salmon fillets	1 tbsp. olive oil
¼ cup parmesan cheese, grated	1 tbsp. lemon rind
½ cup almond flour	

At 370 degrees F, preheat your Air Fryer. Spray an Air Fryer baking dish with some cooking spray. Place the salmon fillets on a baking dish. Mix ground almond flour with parmesan cheese, oil, and lemon rind. Stir well. Spoon mixture over the salmon and press gently. Place in the Air Fryer and Air Fry the coated salmon fillets for 12 minutes. Enjoy.
Nutritional information: Calories 391; Total Carbs 36.2; Net Carbs 0.5g; Protein 15.7.5g; Fat 22.4g; fibers: 3g; Sugars: 6g

Halibut Soy Treat with Rice

Prep time: 15-20 minutes | Cook time: 12 minutes | Serves: 4

16-ounce Halibut steak	To make the marinade:

⅔ cup soy sauce
½ cup cooking vine
¼ cup sugar
2 tablespoons lime juice
¼ cup orange juice

¼ teaspoon red pepper flakes, crushed
¼ teaspoon ginger ground
1 clove garlic (smashed)

Add the marinade ingredients in a medium-size saucepan. Heat the pan over medium heat for a few minutes. Cool down completely. To marinate, in a zip-lock bag, combine the steak and marinade. Seal and refrigerate for 30-40 minutes. Coat the air-frying basket gently with cooking oil or spray. Place the steak in the basket of your air fryer and cook for 12 minutes at 355 degrees F. When done, serve warm with cooked rice!
Nutritional information: Calories: 396; Fat: 6.8g; Total Carbs: 17g; Net Carbs: 8g; Fiber: 0.4g; Sugars: 14.5g; Protein: 63.3g

Salmon with Sweet Potato

Prep time: 10 minutes | Cook time: 40 minutes | Serves: 4

For the Fillets:
2 tablespoons capers
1 teaspoon celery salt
4 (6 ounces) skin-on salmon fillets
1 tablespoon extra-virgin olive oil
1 teaspoon smoked cayenne pepper

¼ teaspoon black pepper
A pinch of dry mustard
A pinch of ground mace
For the Potatoes:
4 sweet potatoes, peeled and make wedges
1 tablespoon sesame oil
Kosher salt and pepper, as needed

Oil the salmon on all sides, season as needed. Place the salmon in the basket that has been coated with cooking oil or spray. Arrange the basket to the air fryer and cook at 360 degrees F for 5 minutes. When the time is up, set aside and clean the basket. In the basket, add the sweet potatoes, oil, salt and pepper. Toss and cook for 30 minutes at 380 degrees F, flipping halfway through. Serve warm with salmon fillets!
Nutritional information: Calories: 600; Fat: 12.8g; Total Carbs: 28g; Net Carbs: 11.5g; Fiber: 4.2g; Sugars: 0.5g; Protein: 93.6g

Tilapia Fillets with Mayonnaise

Prep time: 5 minutes | Cook time: 12 minutes | Serves: 4

1 tablespoon olive oil, extra-virgin
4 tilapia fillets
Celery salt, as needed
Freshly cracked pink peppercorns, as needed

For the Sauce:
½ cup crème fraiche
¼ cup Cottage cheese
2 tablespoons mayonnaise
1 tablespoon capers, finely chopped

Thoroughly mix up the olive oil, celery salt, and cracked peppercorns in a medium-sized bowl, then let the fillets be coated with the mixture. Coat the air-frying basket with the cooking oil and spray. Arrange the fillets to the basket and cook for 12 minutes at 360 degrees F. To make a sauce, in a bowl of medium size, thoroughly mix the remaining ingredients to make a sauce. When the time is up, serve warm with the sauce!
Nutritional information: Calories: 194; Fat: 8.5g; Total Carbs: 2g; Net Carbs: 0.5g; Fiber: 0.1g; Sugars: 0.5g; Protein: 29.2g

Glazed Fillets

Prep time: 8-10 minutes | Cook time: 15 minutes | Serves: 4

4 flounder fillets
1 ½ tablespoons dark sesame oil
2 tablespoons sake

Sea salt and cracked mixed peppercorns, as needed
¼ cup soy sauce

1 teaspoon brown sugar
1 tablespoon grated lemon rind

2 garlic cloves, minced
Fresh chopped chives, to serve

To marinate, prepare a large deep dish, add the ingredients except for chives and stir a little. Cover and refrigerate for 2-3 hours. Add the fish to the basket that has been coated with the cooking oil or spray. Arrange it to the air fryer and cook at 360 degrees F for 12 minutes, flipping halfway through. Pour the remaining marinade into a saucepan; simmer over medium-low heat until it has thickened. Serve the fish with the marinade and chives on top!
Nutritional information: Calories: 208; Fat: 7.1g; Total Carbs: 2g; Net Carbs: 0.5g; Fiber: 0.3g; Sugars: 1.1g; Protein 31.8g

Fish Mania with Mustard

Prep time: 10-15 minutes | Cook time: 10 minutes | Serves: 4-5

1 cup soft bread crumbs
1 teaspoon whole-grain mustard
2 cans canned fish
2 celery stalks, chopped

1 egg, whisked
½ teaspoon sea salt
¼ teaspoon black peppercorns, cracked
1 teaspoon paprika

Thoroughly mix the fish, breadcrumbs, celery and other ingredients in a large bowl. Make four cakes shapes from the mixture and refrigerate for 45-50 minutes. Place the cakes in the basket that has been coated with cooking oil or spray. Arrange it to air fryer and cook for 5 minutes at 360 degrees F. After 5 minutes, flip the cakes gently and cook for another 4 minutes Serve over mashed potatoes.
Nutritional information: Calories: 152; Fat: 4g; Total Carbs: 5g; Net Carbs: 2g; Fiber: 0.6g; Sugars: 0.6g; Protein: 22.5g

Tuna Steak with Niçoise Salad

Prep time: 10 minutes | Cook time: 15 minutes | Serves: 4

1 pound tuna steak
Sea salt and ground black pepper, to taste
½ teaspoon red pepper flakes, crushed
¼ teaspoon dried dill weed
½ teaspoon garlic paste
1 pound green beans, trimmed
2 handfuls baby spinach
2 handfuls iceberg lettuce, torn into pieces

½ red onion, sliced
1 cucumber, sliced
2 tablespoons lemon juice
1 tablespoon olive oil
1 teaspoon Dijon mustard
1 tablespoon balsamic vinegar
1 tablespoon roasted almonds, coarsely chopped
1 tablespoon fresh parsley, coarsely chopped

Pat the tuna steak dry. Combine the salt, black pepper, red pepper, dill, garlic paste and toss with the tuna steak well. Spritz the coated tuna steak with a nonstick cooking spray. Cook the tuna steak at 400 degrees F for 10 minutes, flipping halfway through. When the time is up, remove the tuna steak and add the green beans. Spritz green beans with a nonstick cooking spray. Cook at 400 degrees F for 5 minutes, shaking once or twice for evenly cooking. Cut your tuna into thin strips and transfer to a salad bowl; add in the green beans. Add in the onion, cucumber, baby spinach and iceberg lettuce. Whisk the lemon juice, olive oil, mustard and vinegar. Dress the salad and garnish with roasted almonds and fresh parsley. Bon appétit!
Nutritional information: Calories: 307; Fat: 11.8g; Total Carbs: 13g; Net Carbs: 7g; Fiber: 5.2g; Sugars: 3.8g; Protein: 37.5g

Tasty Coconut Prawns

Prep time: 8-10 minutes | Cook time: 10 minutes | Serves: 4-5

1 medium-sized egg, whisked   ⅓ cup beer

½ cup all-purpose flour
12 prawns, cleaned and deveined
Salt and ground black pepper as needed
½ teaspoon cumin powder
1 teaspoon lemon juice
1 teaspoon baking powder
1 tablespoon curry powder
½ teaspoon fresh ginger, grated
1 cup flaked coconut

Thoroughly mix the prawns with salt, pepper, cumin powder, and lemon juice in a medium-size bowl. Prepare another medium-size bowl, thoroughly whisk the egg. Mix the beer, ¼ cup of flour, baking powder, curry, and the ginger well. In another mixing bowl, place the remaining flour. Add the coconut into a third bowl. Dip the prawns in the flour, then dip them in the beer mix. Lastly, roll them over flaked coconut. Arrange them to the basket which has been coated with cooking oil or spray of your air fryer. Cook them for 5 minutes at 360 degrees F. When the time is up, turn and continue cooking for 4 minutes. Serve warm!

Nutritional information: Calories: 239; Fat: 9.4g; Total Carbs: 18g; Net Carbs: 9.5g; Fiber: 2.8g; Sugars: 1.5g; Protein: 19.1g

Pasta Shrimp

Prep time: 10 minutes | Cook time: 5 minutes | Serves: 4

½ teaspoon hot paprika
2 garlic cloves, peeled and minced
1 teaspoon onion powder
½ teaspoon salt
1 teaspoon lemon-pepper seasoning
18 shrimps, shelled and
deveined
2 tablespoons extra-virgin olive oil
¼ teaspoon cumin powder
2 tablespoons squeezed lemon juice
½ cup parsley, coarsely chopped

Thoroughly mix the ingredients in a medium-size bowl, then cover it with a foil and refrigerate for 30-45 minutes. Place the shrimps in the basket that has been coated with cooking oil or spray. Arrange the basket to the air fryer and cook at 400 degrees F for 5 minutes or until turn pink. Serve warm with cooked pasta or just shrimps!

Nutritional information: Calories: 187; Fat: 8.8g; Total Carbs: 3g; Net Carbs: 1g; Fiber: 0.5g; Sugars: 0.3g; Protein: 23g

Creamy Savory Salmon

Prep time: 10-15 minutes | Cook time: 25 minutes | Serves: 4

For salmon:
2 teaspoons olive oil
24-ounce (4 pieces) salmon
1 pinch salt
For the sauce:
½ cup sour cream
½ cup non-fat: Greek yogurt
1 pinch salt
2 tablespoons dill, finely chopped

Make the salmon pieces of 6 ounces each, brush the pieces with olive oil and then top them with salt. Place the pieces in the basket that has been coated with cooking oil or spray. Arrange the basket to the air fryer and cook at 270 degrees F for 20-25 minutes. In a bowl of medium size, thoroughly mix the sauce ingredients. When the pieces have finished, serve warm with the sauce!

Nutritional information: Calories: 327; Fat: 18.9g; Total Carbs: 4g; Net Carbs: 2g; Fiber: 0.3g; Sugars: 1.9g; Protein: 35.7g

Typical Cod Nuggets

Prep time: 10-15 minutes | Cook time: 10 minutes | Serves: 4

16-ounce cod
To make the breading:
1 cup all-purpose flour
2 tablespoons olive oil
2 eggs, beaten
1 pinch salt
¾ cup panko breadcrumbs, finely processed

Thoroughly mix the oil, salt and crumbs in a medium-size bowl. Take the cod, make pieces from it of about 2.5 inches by 1 inch. In a bowl of medium size, thoroughly mix the salt, oil and crumbs. Side by side place three bowls; add the flour in the first bowl, crumb mixture in the second and eggs in the third. One by one dip the fish in the flour mix and then in the egg mix. Lastly coat with the crumb mixture completely. Place the fish pieces in the basket that has been coated with cooking oil or spray. Arrange the basket to the air fryer and cook at 390 degrees F for 10 minutes or until turn pink. Serve the crispy fish!

Nutritional information: Calories: 377; Fat: 10.9g; Total Carbs: 35g; Net Carbs: 20g; Fiber: 2.3g; Sugars: 0.6g; Protein: 33.4g

Delicious Fillets with Avocado Sauce

Cook time: 20 minutes | Serves: 2

2 cod fish fillets
1 egg
Sea salt, to taste
1 teaspoon olive oil
½ avocado, peeled, pitted, and mashed
½ tablespoon mayonnaise
1 tablespoon sour cream
½-teaspoon yellow mustard
½ teaspoon lemon juice
1 garlic clove, minced
¼-teaspoon black pepper
¼-teaspoon salt
¼-teaspoon hot pepper sauce

Coat the basket of your air fryer with cooking oil. Use a kitchen towel to pat dry the fish fillets. In a shallow bowl, beat the egg, add in the salt and olive oil. Coat the fillets with the egg mixture thoroughly. Place the fillets in the basket and then arrange it to the air fryer. Cook the fillets at 360 degrees F for 12 minutes or until turn pink. Meanwhile, in another clean bowl, make the avocado sauce by mixing the remaining ingredients in a bowl. Place in your refrigerator until ready to serve. Serve the fish fillets with chilled avocado sauce on the side. Bon appétit!

Nutritional information: Calories: 389; Fat: 19.7g; Total Carbs: 7g; Net Carbs: 3g; Fiber: 3.5g; Sugars: 1g; Protein: 45.3g

Chip-Crusted Tilapia with Parmesan Cheese

Prep time: 10 minutes | Cook time: 10 minutes | Serves: 3

1 ½ pounds tilapia, slice into 4 portions
Sea salt and ground black pepper, to taste
½ teaspoon cayenne pepper
1 teaspoon granulated garlic
¼ cup almond flour
¼ cup parmesan cheese, preferably freshly grated
1 egg, beaten
2 tablespoons buttermilk
1 cup tortilla chips, crushed

Season the tilapia with cayenne pepper, salt and black pepper generously and orderly. On a bread station, add the granulated garlic, almond flour and parmesan cheese to a rimmed plate. In another bowl, add the egg, buttermilk and mix well. In the third bowl, place the crushed tortilla chips. Coat the tilapia pieces with the flour mixture and egg mixture in order and then roll them in the crushed chips, press to adhere well. Cook the tilapia pieces in your air fryer at 400 degrees F for 10 minutes, flipping halfway through. Serve with chips if desired. Bon appétit!

Nutritional information: Calories: 217; Fat: 4g; Total Carbs: 0.9g; Net Carbs: 0g; Fiber: 0.2g; Sugars: 0.6g; Protein: 44.6g

Flounder Fillets with Coconut Aminos

Cook time: 12 minutes | Serves: 2

2 flounder fillets, boneless
2 garlic cloves, minced

2 teaspoons coconut aminos	pepper
2 tablespoons lemon juice	½-teaspoon stevia
A pinch of salt and black	1 tablespoon olive oil

Mix up all the ingredients in the cooking pan of your air fryer. Arrange the pan to the air fryer and cook for 12 minutes at 390 degrees F. Divide into bowls and serve.

Nutritional information: Calories: 155; Fat 2g; Total Carbs 1.2g; Net Carbs: 0.8g; Fiber 0.1g; Sugars: 0.2g; Protein: 30.9g

Bean Burritos with Cheddar Cheese

Cook time: 15 minutes | Serves: 4

4 tortillas	¼-teaspoon chili powder
1 can beans	¼-teaspoon garlic powder
1 cup cheddar cheese, grated	Salt and pepper to taste
¼-teaspoon paprika	

Heat the Air Fryer to 350°F ahead of time. Mix up the paprika, chili powder, garlic powder, salt and pepper in a suitable bowl. Before adding the spice mixture and cheddar cheese, fill each tortilla with an equal portion of beans. Roll the tortilla wraps into burritos. Use the parchment paper to cover the base of a baking dish. Arrange the burritos to the baking dish and place the dish in the air fryer. Cook the burritos for about 5 minutes at 350 degrees F. When cooked, serve hot.

Nutritional information: Calories: 168; Fat: 10.1g; Total Carbs: 11.5g; Net Carbs: 5g; Fiber: 1.7g; Sugars: 0.4g; Protein: 8.5g

Red Snapper with Hot Chili Paste

Cook time: 15 minutes | Serves: 4

4 red snapper fillets, boneless	1 tablespoon coconut aminos
A pinch of salt and black	1 tablespoon lime juice
pepper	1 tablespoon hot chili paste
2 garlic cloves, minced	1 tablespoon olive oil

In addition to the fish, mix up the other ingredients in a bowl and stir well. Use the mixture to rub the fish, then place the fish in the basket of your air fryer. Cook for 15 minutes at 380 degrees F. Serve with a side salad.

Nutritional information: Calories: 262; Fat: 7.1g; Total Carbs: 2g; Net Carbs: 0.5g; Fiber: 0g; Sugars: 1g; Protein: 45.1g

Tasty Juicy Salmon

Cook time: 13 minutes | Serves: 2

2 salmon fillets	Salt and black pepper, to taste
4 asparagus stalks	¼ cup white sauce
¼ cup champagne	1½ teaspoon olive oil

Heat the air fryer ahead of time. In a bowl, mix all the ingredients and divide this mixture evenly over 2 foil papers. Arrange the foil papers in the basket of your air fryer and cook for about 13 minutes at 355 degrees F. Dish out in a platter and serve hot.

Nutritional information: Calories: 319; Fat: 16.7g; Total Carbs: 4g; Net Carbs: 2g; Fiber: 0.7g; Sugars: 2g; Protein: 36.4g

Lemon Salmon Fillet

Cook time: 15 minutes | Serves: 1

1 salmon fillet	¼-teaspoon sugar
½ teaspoon Cajun seasoning	2 lemon wedges, for serving
½ lemon, juiced	

Heat the Air Fryer to 350°F ahead of time. Combine the lemon juice and sugar, then coat the salmon with the sugar mixture. Coat the salmon with the Cajun seasoning. Place a sheet of parchment paper on the base of your air fryer. Arrange the salmon to the air fryer and cook for 7 minutes.

Nutritional information: Calories: 239; Fat: 11g; Total Carbs: 1g; Net Carbs: 0g; Fiber: 0g; Sugars: 1g; Protein: 34.6g

Flavored Salmon Grill with Oregano & Cumin

Cook time: 15 minutes | Serves: 4

1 ½ lbs. skinless salmon fillet (preferably wild), cut into 1" pieces	2 lemons, very thinly sliced into rounds
1 teaspoon ground cumin	1 tablespoon chopped fresh oregano
1 teaspoon kosher salt	1 tablespoon olive oil
¼-teaspoon crushed red pepper flakes	1 teaspoon sesame seeds

Prepare a small bowl, mix well oregano, sesame seeds, cumin, salt, and pepper flakes. Thread salmon and folded lemon slices in a skewer. Brush the salmon with oil and sprinkle with spice. Arrange the skewers to the air fryer and cook for 5 minutes at 360 degrees F. When the time is up, serve and enjoy.

Nutritional information: Calories: 240; Fat: 16.1g; Total Carbs: 1g; Net Carbs: 0g; Fiber: 0.7g; Sugars: 0.1g; Protein: 22.4g

Thai Coconut Fish

Cook time: 20 minutes | Serves: 2

1 cup coconut milk	½-teaspoon ginger powder
1 tablespoon lime juice	½ Thai Bird's Eye chili, seeded
1 tablespoon Shoyu sauce	and finely chopped
Salt and white pepper, to taste	1 lb. tilapia
1 teaspoon turmeric powder	1 tablespoon olive oil

Prepare a mixing bowl, thoroughly combine the coconut milk with the lime juice, Shoyu sauce, salt, pepper, turmeric, ginger, and chili pepper. Coat the tilapia with the mixture and let it marinate for 1 hour. Brush the basket of your air fryer with olive oil. Take the tilapia fillets out of the marinade and place them in the basket. Cook the tilapia fillets in the preheated Air Fryer at 400 degrees F for 12 minutes, flipping halfway through. Working in batches is suggested. Serve with some extra lime wedges if desired. Enjoy!

Nutritional information: Calories: 474; Fat: 30.8g; Total Carbs: 9.5g; Net Carbs: 5g; Fiber: 3g; Sugars: 4.4g; Protein: 45.2g

Sea Bream Fillet with Tomato Sauce

Cook time: 8 minutes | Serves: 4

1 tablespoon keto tomato sauce	pepper
1 tablespoon avocado oil	½-teaspoon salt
1 teaspoon ground black	12 oz. sea bream fillet

Cut the sea bream fillet on 4 servings. After that, mix up tomato sauce, avocado oil, salt, and ground black pepper in a mixing bowl. Rub the fish fillets with tomato mixture on both sides. Line the air fryer basket with foil. Put the sea bream fillets on the foil and cook them for 8 minutes at 390 degrees F.

Nutritional information: Calories: 499; Fat: 23.3g; Total Carbs: 47g; Net Carbs: 22g; Fiber: 3g; Sugars: 3.9g; Protein: 23.9g

Shrimp with Parsley

Cook time: 12 minutes | Serves: 4

1 lb. shrimp, peeled and deveined
1 teaspoon cumin, ground
1 tablespoon parsley, chopped
1 tablespoon olive oil
A pinch of salt and black pepper
4 garlic cloves, minced
1 tablespoon lime juice

Mix all of the ingredients in a pan that fits your air fryer, toss well. Arrange the pan to the air fryer and cook at 370 degrees F for 12 minutes, flipping halfway through. Divide into bowls and serve.
Nutritional information: Calories: 172; Fat: 5.6g; Total Carbs: 3g; Net Carbs: 1g; Fiber: 0.2g; Sugars: 0.1g; Protein: 26.1g

Pollock Fillets with Rosemary & Oregano

Cook time: 15 minutes | Serves: 3

1 tablespoon olive oil
1 red onion, sliced
2 cloves garlic, chopped
1 Florina pepper, deveined and minced
3 Pollock fillets, skinless
2 ripe tomatoes, diced
12 Kalamata olives, pitted and chopped
1 tablespoon capers
1 teaspoon oregano
1 teaspoon rosemary
Sea salt, to taste
½ cup white wine

Start by preheating your Air Fryer to 360 degrees F. Heat the oil in a baking pan. Once hot, sauté the onion, garlic, and pepper for 2 to 3 minutes or until fragrant. Add the fish fillets to the baking pan, then top with the tomatoes, olives, and capers. After sprinkling with the oregano, rosemary and salt, pour in white wine and transfer to the pan. Cook for 10 minutes at 395 degrees F. Taste for seasoning and serve on individual plates, garnished with some extra Mediterranean herbs if desired. Enjoy!
Nutritional information: Calories: 229; Fat: 7.9g; Total Carbs: 10.2g; Net Carbs: 0g; Fiber: 2.8g; Sugars: 4.1g; Protein: 23.6g

Crusty Catfish with Parmesan Cheese

Cook time: 50 minutes | Serves: 2

½ lb. catfish
½ cup bran cereal
¼ cup Parmesan cheese, grated
Sea salt and ground black pepper, to taste
1 teaspoon smoked paprika
½ teaspoon garlic powder
¼-teaspoon ground bay leaf
1 egg
½ tablespoon butter, melted
4 sweet potatoes, cut French fries

Use the kitchen towel to pat the catfish dry. In a shallow bowl, combine the bran cereal with the Parmesan cheese and all spices in a shallow bowl. In another shallow bowl, whisk the egg. Coat the fish evenly and completely with the egg mixture, then dredge in the bran cereal mixture, turning a couple of times to coat evenly. Arrange the catfish to the basket that has been sprayed and cook at 390 degrees F for 10 minutes; turn them over and cook for 4 minutes more. After that, drizzle the melted butter all over the sweet potatoes; cook them at 380 degrees F for 30 minutes, shaking occasionally. Serve over the warm fish fillets. Bon appétit!
Nutritional information: Calories: 755; Fat: 25g; Total Carbs: 106g; Net Carbs: 43g; Fiber: 18.6g; Sugars: 5.1g; Protein: 31.4g

Healthy Hot Salmon

Cook time: 25 minutes | Serves: 2

1 teaspoon olive oil
Juice of 1 lime

1 teaspoon chili flakes
Salt and black pepper
1 lb. salmon fillets
1 teaspoon olive oil
1 tablespoon soy sauce

Mix up the oil, lime juice, flakes, salt and black pepper in a bowl, then rub the fillets with the mixture. Lay the florets into your air fryer and drizzle with oil. Arrange the fillets around or on top and cook at 340 degrees F for 10 minutes. Drizzle the florets with soy sauce to serve!
Nutritional information: Calories: 325; Fat: 16.3g; Total Carbs: 0.7g; Net Carbs: 0g; Fiber: 0.1g; Sugars: 0.2g; Protein: 44.5g

Beer Squid

Cook time: 20 minutes | Serves: 3

1 cup beer
1 lb. squid, cleaned and cut into rings
1 cup all-purpose flour
2 eggs
½ cup cornstarch
Sea salt, to taste
½-teaspoon ground black pepper
1 tablespoon Old Bay seasoning

Preheat your Air Fryer to 390 degrees F. Add the beer and squid in a glass bowl, cover and let it sit in your refrigerator for 1 hour. Rinse the squid before patting it dry. In a shallow bowl, add the flour in a shallow bowl; in another bowl, whisk the eggs. Lastly, in a third shallow bowl, add the cornstarch and seasonings. Dredge the calamari in the flour. Dip them into the egg mixture and coat them with the cornstarch on all sided. Arrange them in the cooking basket. Spritz with cooking oil and cook for 9 to 12 minutes, depending on the desired level of doneness. Work in batches. Serve warm with your favorite dipping sauce. Enjoy!
Nutritional information: Calories: 449; Fat: 5.4g; Total Carbs: 59g; Net Carbs: 26g; Fiber: 1.4g; Sugars: 0.3g; Protein 32g

Rosemary Salmon

Cook time: 15 minutes | Serves: 4

½-teaspoon dried rosemary
½-teaspoon dried thyme
½-teaspoon dried basil
½-teaspoon ground coriander
½-teaspoon ground cumin
½-teaspoon ground paprika
½-teaspoon salt
1 pound salmon
1 tablespoon olive oil

Mixed up the dried rosemary, thyme, basil, coriander, cumin, paprika, and salt in a suitable bowl. Rub the salmon with the spice mixture gently and sprinkle it with the olive oil. Preheat the air fryer to 375F. Put the prepared salmon on the cooking pan with the baking paper under it. Cook the fish at 375 degrees F for 15 minutes, or until you get the light crunchy crust. Once done, serve and enjoy.
Nutritional information: Calories: 153; Fat: 7.1g; Total Carbs: 0.4g; Net Carbs: 0g; Fiber: 0.2g; Sugars: 0g; Protein: 22.1g

Cajun Fish Cakes

Cook time: 30 minutes | Serves: 4

2 catfish fillets
1 cup all-purpose flour
1 ounce butter
1 teaspoon baking powder
1 teaspoon baking soda
½ cup buttermilk
1 teaspoon Cajun seasoning
1 cup Swiss cheese, shredded

Boil a pot of water, the put in the fish fillets and boil for 5 minutes or until it is opaque. When done, flake the fish into small pieces. In a bowl, mix up the other ingredients, then add the fish and mix them well. Form 12 fish patties from the mixture. Place the patties to the cooking pan and arrange the pan to your air fryer. Cook at 380 degrees F for 15 minutes. Working in batches is suggested. Enjoy!

Nutritional information: Calories: 389; Fat: 19.9g; Total Carbs: 27g; Net Carbs: 19g; Fiber: 0.9g; Sugars: 1.9g; Protein: 24g

Spicy Salmon and Fennel Salad

Prep time: 10 minutes | Cook time: 20 minutes | Serves: 3

1 pound salmon	1 tablespoon lime juice
1 fennel, quartered	1 tablespoon extra-virgin olive
1 teaspoon olive oil	oil
Sea salt and ground black	1 tomato, sliced
pepper, to taste	1 cucumber, sliced
½ teaspoon paprika	1 tablespoon sesame seeds,
1 tablespoon balsamic vinegar	lightly toasted

Combine the olive oil, salt, black pepper and paprika well, then stir the salmon and fennel with the spice mixture. Cook the salmon at 380 degrees F for 12 minutes, shaking the basket once or twice for even cooking. After cutting the salmon into bite-sized strips, transfer them to a nice salad bowl. In the same bowl, add in the fennel, balsamic vinegar, lime juice, 1 tablespoon of extra-virgin olive oil, tomato and cucumber, then combine well. Serve garnished with lightly toasted sesame seeds. Enjoy!

Nutritional information: Calories: 260; Fat: 12.6g; Total Carbs: 7.5g; Net Carbs: 2.5g; Fiber: 2.1g; Sugars: 2.3g; Protein: 31.1g

Chunky Fish with Mustard

Cook time: 10 minutes | Serves: 4

2 cans canned fish	mustard
2 celery stalks, trimmed and	½-teaspoon sea salt
finely chopped	¼-teaspoon freshly cracked
1 egg, whisked	black peppercorns
1 cup bread crumbs	½ teaspoon paprika
1 teaspoon whole-grain	

Add all of the ingredients one by one and combine well. Form four equal-sized cakes from the mixture, then leave to chill in the refrigerator for 50 minutes. Spray all sides of each cake after putting them on the cooking pan of your air fryer. Arrange the pan to the air fryer and grill at 360 degrees F for 5 minutes. After 5 minutes, turn the cakes over and resume cooking for an additional 3 minutes. Serve with mashed potatoes if desired.

Nutritional information: Calories: 150; Fat: 3.9g; Total Carbs: 4g; Net Carbs: 2g; Fiber: 0.4g; Sugars: 0.6g; Protein: 22.4g

Crumbed Fish Fillets with Parmesan Cheese

Cook time: 25 minutes | Serves: 4

2 eggs, beaten	⅓ cup Parmesan cheese, grated
½-teaspoon tarragon	1 teaspoon seasoned salt
4 fish fillets, halved	⅓-teaspoon mixed peppercorns
½ tablespoon dry white wine	½-teaspoon fennel seed

Add the Parmesan cheese, salt, peppercorns, fennel seeds, and tarragon to your food processor; blitz for about 20 seconds. Drizzle dry white wine on the top of these fish fillets. In a shallow dish, dump the egg. Now, coat the fish fillets with the beaten egg on all sides, then coat them with the seasoned cracker mix. Air-fry at 345 degrees F for about 17 minutes. Bon appétit!

Nutritional information: Calories: 254; Fat: 13.9g; Total Carbs: 16g; Net Carbs: 7g; Fiber: 0.6g; Sugars: 0.2g; Protein: 16.9g

Buttered Shrimp Fry

Cook time: 15 minutes | Serves: 4

1 tablespoon chopped chives	1 tablespoon minced garlic
or 1-teaspoon dried chives	21-25 count defrosted shrimp
1 tablespoon lemon juice	1 tablespoon chicken stock (or
1 tablespoon minced basil	white wine)
leaves plus more for sprinkling	1 teaspoon red pepper flakes
or 1-teaspoon dried basil	1 tablespoon butter

Lightly spray the baking pan of your air fryer. Melt butter for 2 minutes at 330 degrees F. After stirring in red pepper flakes and garlic, cook for 3 minutes. Add remaining ingredients in pan and toss well to coat. Cook for 5 minutes at 330 degrees F. Stir and let it stand for another 5 minutes. When done, serve and enjoy.

Nutritional information: Calories: 168; Fat: 5g; Total Carbs: 2g; Net Carbs: 0.5g; Fiber: 0.2g; Sugars: 0.2g; Protein: 26.6g

Trimmed Mackerel with Spring Onions

Cook time: 20 minutes | Serves: 5

1 pound mackerel, trimmed	1 tablespoon avocado oil
1 tablespoon ground paprika	1 teaspoon apple cider vinegar
1 green bell pepper	½-teaspoon salt
½ cup spring onions, chopped	

Sprinkle the clean mackerel with ground paprika. Chop the green bell pepper. Fill the mackerel with bell pepper and spring onion. After this, sprinkle the fish with avocado oil, salt and apple cider vinegar. Preheat the air fryer to 375 degrees F. Place the mackerel in the basket and arrange the basket to the air fryer. Cook the mackerel for 20 minutes at 375 degrees F. When cooked, serve and enjoy.

Nutritional information: Calories: 256; Fat: 16.8g; Total Carbs: 3.5g; Net Carbs: 0.5g; Fiber: 1.2g; Sugars: 1.6g; Protein: 22.3g

Salmon Burgers

Cook time: 15 minutes | Serves: 4

1 lb. salmon	1 teaspoon rice wine
1 egg	1 ½-tablespoon soy sauce
1 garlic clove, minced	A pinch of salt
2 green onions, minced	1 teaspoon gochutgaru (Korean
1 cup parmesan cheese	red chili pepper flakes)
Sauce:	

Start by preheating your Air Fryer to 380 degrees F. Spritz the Air Fryer basket with cooking oil. Oil the basket of your air fryer. Mix up the salmon with egg, garlic, green onions, and Parmesan cheese in a bowl. Knead it with your hands until everything comes together nicely. Shape the mixture into equally sized patties. Transfer your patties to the basket and arrange the basket to the air fryer. Cook the fish patties for 10 minutes, flipping halfway through. Meanwhile, make the sauce by whisking all ingredients. With the sauce on the side, serve and enjoy the warm fish patties.

Nutritional information: Calories: 197; Fat: 9.6g; Total Carbs: 2g; Net Carbs: 0.5g; Fiber: 0.3g; Sugars: 0.7g; Protein: 26.2g

Clams with Spring Onions

Cook time: 20 minutes | Serves: 4

15 small clams	Juice of 1 lime
1 tablespoon spring onions,	10 oz. coconut cream
chopped	1 tablespoon cilantro, chopped

1 teaspoon olive oil

Heat up a pan that fits your air fryer with the oil over medium heat, add the spring onions and sauté for 2 minutes. Add lime juice, coconut cream and the cilantro, stir and cook for 2 minutes more. Add the clams, toss, introduce in the fryer and cook at 390 degrees F for 15 minutes. Divide into bowls and serve hot.
Nutritional information: Calories: 193; Fat: 18.2g; Total Carbs: 8g; Net Carbs: 3.5g; Fiber: 1.8g; Sugars: 3.8g; Protein: 1.9g

Cajun Lemon Branzino

Cook time: 8 minutes | Serves: 4

1 pound branzino, trimmed, washed	1 tablespoon sesame oil
	1 tablespoon lemon juice
1 teaspoon Cajun seasoning	1 teaspoon salt

Carefully coat the branzino with salt and Cajun seasoning. Sprinkle the fish with the lemon juice and sesame oil. Preheat the air fryer to 380 degrees F. Place the fish in the air fryer and cook it for 8 minutes at 380 degrees F. When done, serve and enjoy.
Nutritional information: Calories: 196; Fat: 7.2g; Total Carbs: 0.1g; Net Carbs: 0g; Fiber: 0g; Sugars: 0.1g; Protein: 31.5g

Garlic Scallops with Parsley

Cook time: 10 minutes | Serves: 4

1 cup bread crumbs	3 pinches ground nutmeg
¼ cup chopped parsley	1½ tablespoons olive oil
16 sea scallops, rinsed and drained	5 cloves garlic, minced
	2 tablespoons butter, melted
2 shallots, chopped	salt and pepper to taste

Coat the baking pan that fits your air fryer with cooking spray lightly. Mix in melted butter, shallots, garlic and scallops, then season with nutmeg, salt and pepper. Whisk the olive oil and bread crumbs well in a small bowl, then sprinkle over the processed scallops. Cook the scallops at 390 degrees for 10 minutes or until the tops are lightly browned. Sprinkle the parsley, serve and enjoy.
Nutritional information: Calories: 276; Fat: 8.9g; Total Carbs: 23g; Net Carbs: 11g; Fiber: 1.5g; Sugars: 1.8g; Protein: 24.1g

Spicy Jumbo Shrimps

Cook time: 6 minutes | Serves: 4

¼-teaspoon cayenne pepper	1 tablespoon coconut oil
¼-teaspoon red chili flakes	1 teaspoon cilantro
1 teaspoon cumin	1 teaspoon onion powder
1 teaspoon oregano	1 teaspoon smoked paprika
1 teaspoon salt	20 jumbo shrimps, peeled and deveined
1 teaspoon thyme	

In addition to the shrimps, combine the other ingredients well and then coat the shrimps. Place the shrimps on the cooking pan and arrange the pan to your air fryer. Cook for 6 minutes at 390 degrees F. When done, serve and enjoy.
Nutritional information: Calories: 237; Fat: 3.7g; Total Carbs: 1.5g; Net Carbs: 0g; Fiber: 0.6g; Sugars: 5.3g; Protein: 50.3g

Catfish Fillets with Tortilla Chips

Cook time: 30 minutes | Serves: 4

2 catfish fillets [catfish]	1 cup tortilla chips
1 medium egg, beaten	1 lemon, juiced and peeled
1 cup bread crumbs	1 teaspoon parsley

Salt and pepper to taste

Slice the catfish fillets neatly and then drizzle lightly with the lemon juice. Mix up the bread crumbs with the lemon rind, parsley, tortillas, salt and pepper in a bowl, then pour into your food processor and pulse. Distributes the fillets evenly on the base of the cooking tray. Cover the fish fillets well with the prepared mixture. Arrange the tray to your air fryer and cook the fillets at 350 degrees F for 15 minutes. When done, serve with chips and a refreshing drink.
Nutritional information: Calories: 160; Fat: 7.6g; Total Carbs: 7g; Net Carbs: 3g; Fiber: 0.6g; Sugars: 0.5g; Protein: 14.8g

Homemade Lobster Tails Ever

Prep time: 10 minutes | Cook time: 7 minutes | Serves: 2

2 (6-ounce) lobster tails	1 teaspoon deli mustard
1 teaspoon fresh cilantro, minced	Sea salt and ground black pepper, to taste
½ teaspoon dried rosemary	1 teaspoon olive oil
½ teaspoon garlic, pressed	

In addition to the lobster tails, combine the remaining ingredients well and coat the lobster tails well on all sides. Cook the lobster tails at 370 degrees F for 7 minutes, flipping halfway through. Serve warm and enjoy!
Nutritional information: Calories: 174; Fat: 3.8g; Total Carbs: 0.4g; Net Carbs: 0g; Fiber: 0.1g; Sugars: 0g; Protein: 32.4g

Garlic Tilapia Fillets

Cook time: 10 minutes | Serves: 5

1 tablespoon all-purpose flour	oil
Sea salt and white pepper, to taste	½ cup cornmeal
1 teaspoon garlic paste	5 tilapia fillets, slice into halves
1 tablespoon extra-virgin olive	

Prepare a Ziploc bag and mix up the flour, salt, white pepper, garlic paste, olive oil, and cornmeal. Add the fish fillets and coat them well with the spice mixture. Oil the basket of your air fryer with cooking spray and then put the coated fillets in it. Arrange the basket to the air fryer and cook at 400 degrees F for 10 minutes. After 10 minutes, flip the fillets and cook for more 6 minutes. Working in batches is suggested. When done, serve with lemon wedges if desired. Enjoy!
Nutritional information: Calories: 197; Fat: 5.5g; Total Carbs: 10.8g; Net Carbs: 0g; Fiber: 0.9g; Sugars: 0.1g; Protein: 28.3g

Old Bay Cod Fish Fillets

Prep time: 10 minutes | Cook time: 12 minutes | Serves: 2

2 cod fish fillets	2 tablespoons coconut milk, unsweetened
1 teaspoon butter, melted	
1 teaspoon Old Bay seasoning	⅓ cup coconut flour, unsweetened
1 egg, beaten	

Prepare a Ziploc bag, add the cod fish fillets, butter and Old Bay seasoning, shake to coat the fillets well on all sides. Whisk the egg and coconut milk until frothy in a shallow bowl. In another bowl, place the coconut flour. Coat the fish fillets with the egg mixture and coconut flour in order, pressing to adhere. Cook the fish fillets at 390 degrees F for 12 minutes, or until the fillets flake easily when tested with a fork. Flip halfway through. Bon appétit!
Nutritional information: Calories: 352; Fat: 11.2g; Total Carbs: 14g; Net Carbs: 9.5g; Fiber: 8.3g; Sugars: 0.7g; Protein: 46.9g

Salmon Bowl with Lime Drizzle

Prep time: 10 minutes | Cook time: 10 minutes | Serves: 3

1 pound salmon steak
2 teaspoons sesame oil
Sea salt and Sichuan pepper, to taste
½ teaspoon coriander seeds

1 lime, juiced
2 tablespoons reduced-sodium soy sauce
1 teaspoon honey

Drizzle the salmon which has been patted dry in advance with 1 teaspoon of sesame oil. After seasoning the salmon with coriander seeds, salt and pepper, transfer the salmon to the basket of your air fryer. Cook the salmon at 400 degrees F for 10 minutes, flipping halfway through. At the same time, in a small saucepan, warm the remaining ingredients to make the lime drizzle. Cut the fish into bite-sized strips, drizzle with the sauce. Serve and enjoy!

Nutritional information: Calories: 240; Fat: 12.4g; Total Carbs: 2g; Net Carbs: 0.5g; Fiber: 0.1g; Sugars: 2.1g; Protein 30g

Typical Crab Cakes with Lemon Wedges

Prep time: 10 minutes | Cook time: 10 minutes | Serves: 3

1 egg, beaten
2 tablespoons milk
2 crustless bread slices
1 pound lump crabmeat
2 tablespoons scallions, chopped

1 garlic clove, minced
1 teaspoon deli mustard
1 teaspoon Sriracha sauce
Sea salt and ground black pepper, to taste
4 lemon wedges, for serving

Beat the egg and milk until white and frothy, then add the bread in and let it soak for a few minutes. In addition to the lemon wedges, stir in the remaining ingredients. Form 4 equal-size patties, place the patties in the cooking basket of your air fryer and then spray them with a non-stick cooking spray. Arrange the basket to the air fryer and cook the patties at 400 degrees F for 10 minutes, flipping halfway through. Serve warm, garnished with lemon wedges. Bon appétit!

Nutritional information: Calories: 239; Fat: 5.1g; Total Carbs: 12g; Net Carbs: 7g; Fiber: 1.1g; Sugars: 1.6g; Protein: 35g

Ginger-Garlic Swordfish

Prep time: 10 minutes | Cook time: 10 minutes | Serves: 3

1 pound swordfish steak
1 teaspoon ginger-garlic paste
Sea salt and ground black pepper, to taste

¼ teaspoon cayenne pepper
¼ teaspoon dried dill weed
½ pound mushrooms

Mix up the ginger-garlic paste; season with salt, black pepper, cayenne pepper and dried dill, then rub the swordfish steak with the mixture. Spritz the fish with a nonstick cooking spray and transfer to the Air Fryer cooking basket. Cook at 400 degrees F for 5 minutes. Now, add the mushrooms to the cooking basket and continue to cook for 5 minutes longer until tender and fragrant. Eat warm.

Nutritional information: Calories: 262; Fat: 9g; Total Carbs: 3g; Net Carbs: 1g; Fiber: 0.8g; Sugars: 1.3g; Protein: 40.9g

Herbed and Garlic Salmon Fillets

Prep time: 10 minutes | Cook time: 12 minutes | Serves: 3

1 pound salmon fillets

Sea salt and ground black

pepper, to taste
1 tablespoon olive oil
1 sprig thyme

2 sprigs rosemary
2 cloves garlic, minced
1 lemon, sliced

Season the salmon fillets that have been patted dry with salt and pepper. Drizzle the salmon fillets with olive oil and place them in the cooking basket of your air fryer. Cook the salmon fillets at 380 degrees F for 12 minutes. After 7 minutes of cooking time, turn them over, top with thyme, rosemary and garlic and continue to cook for 5 minutes more. Serve topped with lemon slices and enjoy!

Nutritional information: Calories: 243; Fat: 14g; Total Carbs: 0.7g; Net Carbs: 0g; Fiber: 0g; Sugars: 0g; Protein: 29.5g

Grouper with Miso-Honey Sauce

Prep time: 10 minutes | Cook time: 10 minutes | Serves: 2

¾ pound grouper fillets
Salt and white pepper, to taste
1 tablespoon sesame oil
1 teaspoon water
1 teaspoon deli mustard or

Dijon mustard
¼ cup white miso
1 tablespoon mirin
1 tablespoon honey
1 tablespoon Shoyu sauce

Sprinkle salt and white pepper on the grouper fillets, then drizzle them with a nonstick cooking oil. Arrange the fillets to the air fryer and cook them at 400 degrees F for 10 minutes, flipping halfway through. Meanwhile, whisk the other ingredients to make the sauce. Serve the warm fish with the miso-honey sauce on the side. Bon appétit!

Nutritional information: Calories: 375; Fat: 11.2g; Total Carbs: 21g; Net Carbs: 9g; Fiber: 2g; Sugars: 12.8g; Protein: 46.4g

Simple Fish Sticks

Prep time: 10 minutes | Cook time: 10 minutes | Serves: 2

½ pound fish sticks, frozen
½ pound Vidalia onions, halved
1 teaspoon sesame oil
Sea salt and ground black pepper, to taste
½ teaspoon red pepper flakes

4 tablespoons mayonnaise
4 tablespoons Greek-style yogurt
¼ teaspoon mustard seeds
1 teaspoon chipotle chili in adobo, minced

Drizzle the fish sticks and Vidalia onions with sesame oil. Toss the fish sticks with red pepper flakes, salt and black pepper. Transfer the fish sticks to the cooking basket and arrange the basket to the air fryer. Cook the fish sticks and onions at 400 degrees F for 10 minutes, shaking the basket halfway through. Mix up the mayonnaise, Greek-style yogurt, mustard seeds and chipotle chili at the same time. Garnish the warm sticks with Vidalia onions and the sauce on the side. Bon appétit!

Nutritional information: Calories: 402; Fat: 28g; Total Carbs: 22g; Net Carbs: 10g; Fiber: 1.6g; Sugars: 14.4g; Protein: 13.2g

Flavor Moroccan Harissa Shrimp

Prep time: 10 minutes | Cook time: 10 minutes | Serves: 3

1-pound breaded shrimp, frozen
1 teaspoon extra-virgin olive oil
Sea salt and ground black

pepper, to taste
1 teaspoon coriander seeds
1 teaspoon caraway seeds
1 teaspoon crushed red pepper
1 teaspoon fresh garlic, minced

Arrange the breaded shrimp tossed with olive oil to the cooking basket and then arrange the basket to the air fryer. Cook the shrimp at 400 degrees F for 5 minutes. After 5 minutes, shake the basket and cook an additional 4 minutes. During cooking, mix the remaining ingredients until well combined. Taste and adjust seasonings. Toss the warm shrimp with the harissa sauce and serve immediately. Enjoy!

Nutritional information: Calories: 438; Fat: 24.7g; Total Carbs: 37g; Net Carbs: 19g; Fiber: 0.5g; Sugars: 0.1g; Protein: 17.7g

Cajun Shrimp with Veggie

Prep time: 15 minutes | Cook time: 20 minutes | Serves: 4

50 small shrimp	1 bag of frozen mix vegetables
1 tablespoon Cajun seasoning	1 tablespoon olive oil

Line air fryer basket with aluminum foil. Add all the recipe ingredients into the suitable mixing bowl and toss well. Transfer shrimp and vegetable mixture into the air fryer basket and cook at almost 350 degrees F for almost 10 minutes. Toss well and cook for almost 10 minutes more. Serve and enjoy.

Nutritional information: Calories: 357; Fat: 8.2g; Total Carbs: 4g; Net Carbs: 2g; Fiber: 0g; Sugars: 0g; Protein: 62.7g

Flavor Calamari with Mediterranean Sauce

Prep time: 10 minutes | Cook time: 4 minutes | Serves: 4

½ pound calamari tubes cut into rings, cleaned	¼ teaspoon cayenne pepper
Sea salt and ground black pepper, to season	½ cup breadcrumbs
½ cup almond flour	¼ cup mayonnaise
½ cup all-purpose flour	¼ cup Greek-style yogurt
4 tablespoons parmesan cheese, grated	1 clove garlic, minced
½ cup ale beer	1 tablespoon fresh lemon juice
	1 teaspoon fresh parsley, chopped
	1 teaspoon fresh dill, chopped

Sprinkle salt and black pepper on the calamari. In a bowl, mix the flour, cheese and beer until well combined. In another bowl, mix cayenne pepper and breadcrumbs Coat the calamari pieces with the flour mixture and then roll them onto the breadcrumb mixture, pressing to coat on all sides. Lightly oil the cooking basket and transfer the calamari pieces in it. Cook the calamari pieces at 400 degrees F for 4 minutes, shaking the basket halfway through. Meanwhile, thoroughly mix the remaining ingredients well. Serve warm calamari with the sauce for dipping. Enjoy!

Nutritional information: Calories: 446; Fat: 21g; Total Carbs: 34g; Net Carbs: 18g; Fiber: 2.6g; Sugars: 2.6g; Protein: 24.9g

Garlic Butter Scallops with Lemon Zest

Prep time: 10 minutes | Cook time: 8 minutes | Serves: 2

½ pound scallops	¼ teaspoon dried basil
Coarse sea salt and ground black pepper, to taste	2 tablespoons butter pieces, cold
¼ teaspoon cayenne pepper	1 teaspoon garlic, minced
¼ teaspoon dried oregano	1 teaspoon lemon zest

Sprinkle the salt, black pepper, cayenne pepper, oregano and basil on the scallops. Spray the scallops with a nonstick cooking oil and transfer them to the cooking basket of your air fryer. Cook the scallops at 400 degrees F for 6 to 7 minutes, shaking the basket halfway through the cooking time. At the same time,

in a small saucepan, melt the butter over medium-high heat. Once hot, add in the garlic and continue to sauté for about 1 minute, until fragrant. Add in lemon zest, taste and adjust the seasonings. Spoon the garlic butter over the warm scallops and serve.

Nutritional information: Calories: 104; Fat: 0.9g; Total Carbs: 3g; Net Carbs: 1g; Fiber: 0.2g; Sugars: 0.1g; Protein: 19.2g

Pancetta-Wrapped Scallops with Pancetta Slices

Prep time: 10 minutes | Cook time: 10 minutes | Serves: 3

1 pound sea scallops	½ teaspoon dried dill
1 tablespoon deli mustard	Sea salt and ground black pepper, to taste
2 tablespoons soy sauce	4 ounces' pancetta slices
¼ teaspoon shallot powder	
¼ teaspoon garlic powder	

Transfer the sea scallops that have patted dry in advance to a mixing bowl, the add the deli mustard, soy sauce, shallot powder, garlic powder, dill, salt, black pepper and toss well. Use a bacon slice to wrap one scallop, when finished, transfer the scallop wraps to the cooking basket. Cook the scallop wraps in your Air Fryer at 400 degrees F for 7 minutes. After 4 minutes of cooking time, turn them over and cook an additional 3 minutes. Serve with hot sauce for dipping if desired. Bon appétit!

Nutritional information: Calories: 145; Fat: 1.2g; Total Carbs: 4g; Net Carbs: 2g; Fiber: 0.1g; Sugars: 0.2g; Protein: 26.1g

Tasty Anchovies and Cheese Wontons

Prep time: 10 minutes | Cook time: 10 minutes | Serves: 4

½ pound anchovies	1 tablespoon Shoyu sauce
½ cup cheddar cheese, grated	Himalayan salt and ground black pepper, to taste
1 cup fresh spinach	½ pound wonton wrappers
2 tablespoons scallions, minced	1 teaspoon sesame oil
1 teaspoon garlic, minced	

Mix the mashed anchovies with the cheese, spinach, scallions, garlic and Shoyu sauce, then season with salt and black pepper. Fill the wontons with 1 tablespoon of the filling mixture and fold into triangle shape, then brush the side with a bit of oil and water to seal the edges. Cook the wontons at 390 degrees F for 10 minutes, flipping halfway through for even cooking. When done, serve with the seasoned anchovies and enjoy!

Nutritional information: Calories: 355; Fat: 12.2g; Total Carbs: 33g; Net Carbs: 12g; Fiber: 1.3g; Sugars: 0.2g; Protein: 25.8g

Baked Sardines

Prep time: 10 minutes | Cook time: 40 minutes | Serves: 3

1-pound fresh sardines	mix
Sea salt and ground black pepper, to taste	2 cloves garlic, minced
1 teaspoon Italian seasoning	3 tablespoons olive oil
	½ lemon, freshly squeezed

Toss salt, black pepper, Italian seasoning mix and the sardines well. Cook the sardines in your air fryer at 325 degrees F for 35 to 40 minutes or until skin is crispy. To make the sauce, whisk the remaining ingredients Serve warm sardines with the sauce on the side. Bon appétit!

Nutritional information: Calories: 437; Fat: 31.3g; Total

Carbs: 0.7g; Net Carbs: 0g; Fiber: 0g; Sugars: 0g; Protein: 37.4g

Haddock Cakes

Prep time: 10 minutes | Cook time: 10 minutes | Serves: 3

1 pound haddock	minced
1 egg	Sea salt and ground black
2 tablespoons milk	pepper, to taste
1 bell pepper, deveined and	½ teaspoon cumin seeds
finely chopped	¼ teaspoon celery seeds
2 stalks fresh scallions, minced	½ cup breadcrumbs
½ teaspoon fresh garlic,	1 teaspoon olive oil

In addition to the breadcrumbs and olive oil, thoroughly combine the other ingredients. Form 3 patties from the mixture and coat them with breadcrumbs, pressing to adhere. Place the patties on the cooking basket and then drizzle the olive oil on them. Arrange the basket to the air fryer and cook at 400 degrees F for 10 minutes, flipping halfway through. Bon appétit!
Nutritional information: Calories: 241; Fat: 5.4g; Total Carbs: 17g; Net Carbs: 8g; Fiber: 1.7g; Sugars: 3.9g; Protein: 29.5g

Greek Sardines with Sauce

Prep time: 10 minutes | Cook time: 55 minutes | Serves: 2

4 sardines, cleaned	minced
¼ cup all-purpose flour	¼ cup sweet white wine
Sea salt and ground black	1 tablespoon fresh coriander,
pepper, to taste	minced
4 tablespoons extra-virgin	¼ cup baby capers, drained
olive oil	1 tomato, crushed
½ red onion, chopped	¼ teaspoon chili paper flakes
½ teaspoon fresh garlic,	

Coat your sardines with all-purpose flour on all sides. Drizzle salt and black pepper on the sardines and then transfer them to the cooking basket. Arrange the basket to the air fryer and cook the sardines at 325 degrees F for 35 to 40 minutes or until the skin is crispy. While cooking the sardines, heat the olive oil in a frying pan over a moderate flame, then sauté the onion and garlic for 4 to 5 minutes or until tender and aromatic. Add the remaining ingredients and stir well, cover and let the mixture simmer for about 15 minutes or until thickened and reduced. When simmered, spoon the sauce over the warm sardines. Serve warm and enjoy!
Nutritional information: Calories: 496; Fat: 13.2g; Total Carbs: 61g; Net Carbs: 25g; Fiber: 10.4g; Sugars: 10.8g; Protein: 25.6g

Delicious Grouper Filets

Prep time: 10 minutes | Cook time: 10 minutes | Serves: 3

1 pound grouper filets	¼ teaspoon oregano
¼ teaspoon shallot powder	½ teaspoon marjoram
¼ teaspoon porcini powder	½ teaspoon sage
1 teaspoon fresh garlic, minced	1 tablespoon butter, melted
½ teaspoon cayenne pepper	Sea salt and black pepper, to
½ teaspoon hot paprika	taste

Use the kitchen towels to pat dry the grouper filets. Mix up the remaining ingredients until well incorporated, then rub the grouper filets on all sides with the mixture. Cook the grouper filets in the preheated Air Fryer at 400 degrees F for 10 minutes, flipping halfway through. Serve over hot rice if desired. Bon appétit!
Nutritional information: Calories: 355; Fat: 7.4g; Total Carbs: 0.7g; Net Carbs: 0g; Fiber: 0.2g; Sugars: 0.1g; Protein: 67.1g

Easy Air Fried Salmon

Prep time: 15 minutes | Cook time: 10 minutes | Serves: 2

2 salmon fillets, skinless and	Black pepper
boneless	Salt
1 teaspoon olive oil	

Coat boneless salmon fillets with olive oil and season with black pepper and salt. Place salmon fillets in air fryer basket and Cook at almost 360 degrees F for 8-10 minutes. Serve and enjoy.
Nutritional information: Calories: 255; Fat: 13.3g; Total Carbs: 0g; Net Carbs: 0g; Fiber: 0g; Sugars: 0g; Protein: 34.5g

Lemon Jumbo Scallops

Prep time: 10 minutes | Cook time: 11 minutes | Serves: 4

8 jumbo scallops	minced
1 teaspoon sesame oil	1 teaspoon garlic, minced
Sea salt and red pepper flakes,	1 tablespoon oyster sauce
to season	1 tablespoon soy sauce
1 tablespoon coconut oil	¼ cup coconut milk
1 Thai chili, deveined and	2 tablespoons fresh lime juice

Mix up the 1 teaspoon of sesame oil, salt, red pepper and the jumbo scallops that have been patted dry in advance. Cook the jumbo scallops in your Air Fryer at 400 degrees F for 4 minutes. After that, turn them over and cook an additional 3 minutes. While cooking the scallops, in a frying pan, heat the coconut oil over medium-high heat. Once hot, add the Thai chili, garlic and cook for 1 minute or so until just tender and fragrant. Add in the oyster sauce, soy sauce and coconut milk and continue to simmer, partially covered, for 5 minutes longer. Lastly, add fresh lime juice and stir to combine well. Add the warm scallops to the sauce and serve immediately.
Nutritional information: Calories: 337; Fat: 18.1g; Total Carbs: 11.5g; Net Carbs: 5g; Fiber: 0.4g; Sugars: 6.6g; Protein: 20.6g

Southwestern Prawns with Asparagus

Prep time: 10 minutes | Cook time: 5 minutes | Serves: 3

1-pound prawns, deveined	crushed
½ pound asparagus spears, cut	Salt, to taste
into 1-inch chinks	1 ripe avocado
1 teaspoon butter, melted	1 lemon, sliced
¼ teaspoon oregano	½ cup chunky-style salsa
½ teaspoon mixed peppercorns,	

Toss your prawns and asparagus with melted butter, oregano, salt and mixed peppercorns. Cook the prawns and asparagus at 400 degrees F for 5 minutes, shaking the basket halfway through the cooking time. Divide the prawns and asparagus between serving plates and garnish with avocado and lemon slices. Serve with the salsa on the side. Bon appétit!
Nutritional information: Calories: 343; Fat: 17g; Total Carbs: 11g; Net Carbs: 6.7g; Fiber: 6.1g; Sugars: 1.8g; Protein: 37.4g

Spicy Halibut Steak

Prep time: 10 minutes | Cook time: 10 minutes | Serves: 3

1 pound halibut steak	pepper, to taste
1 teaspoon olive oil	7 ounces Cremini mushrooms
Sea salt and ground black	1 teaspoon butter, melted

¼ teaspoon onion powder
¼ teaspoon garlic powder
½ teaspoon rosemary

½ teaspoon basil
½ teaspoon oregano

Combine the halibut steak with olive oil, salt and black pepper and toss well. Transfer the halibut steak to the cooking basket and arrange the basket to the air fryer. Cook the halibut steak at 400 degrees F for 5 minutes, then, turn the halibut steak, put the Cremini mushrooms on the top and cook for an additional 5 minutes or until the mushrooms are fragrant. Once done, serve and enjoy.

Nutritional information: Calories: 343; Fat: 17g; Total Carbs: 11g; Net Carbs: 6.7g; Fiber: 6.1g; Sugars: 1.8g; Protein: 37.4g

Flounder Filets with Parmesan Cheese

Prep time: 10 minutes | Cook time: 10 minutes | Serves: 3

1 pound flounder filets
1 teaspoon garlic, minced
2 tablespoons soy sauce
1 teaspoon Dijon mustard
¼ cup malt vinegar
1 teaspoon granulated sugar

Salt and black pepper, to taste
½ cup plain flour
1 egg
2 tablespoons milk
½ cup parmesan cheese, grated

In a suitable bowl, combine the flounder filets with garlic, soy sauce, mustard, vinegar and sugar. Marinate the flounder filets by refrigerating it for at least 1 hour. When marinated, take the flounder filets out of the marinade and season with salt and pepper. In a shallow bowl, place the plain flour. In another bowl, beat the egg and add milk until pale and well combined, then in the third bowl, place the Parmesan cheese. Coat the flounder filet with the flour, egg mixture and Parmesan in order, pressing to adhere. Coat the remaining flounder filets with the same steps. Cook the flounder filets in the preheated Air Fryer at 400 degrees F for 10 minutes, flipping halfway through. When done, serve and enjoy.

Nutritional information: Calories: 374; Fat: 6.9g; Total Carbs: 19g; Net Carbs: 6.7g; Fiber: 0.7g; Sugars: 2.2g; Protein: 57.3g

Sea Bass with Greek-Style Sauce

Prep time: 10 minutes | Cook time: 11 minutes | Serves: 2

½ pound sea bass
1 garlic clove, halved
Sea salt and ground black pepper, to taste
½ teaspoon rigani (Greek oregano)
½ teaspoon dried dill weed
¼ teaspoon ground bay leaf

¼ teaspoon ground cumin
½ teaspoon shallot powder
Greek sauce:
½ Greek yogurt
1 teaspoon olive oil
½ teaspoon Tzatziki spice mix
1 teaspoon lime juice

Use kitchen towels to pat dry the sea bass. Use garlic halves to rub the sea bass. Toss the sea bass well with rigani, dill, ground bay leaf, ground cumin, shallot powder, salt and black pepper. Cook the sea bass in your Air Fryer at 400 degrees F for 5 minutes. After that, turn the filets over and cook on the other side for 5 to 6 minutes. To make the Greek-style sauce, simply blend the remaining ingredients. Serve the warm fish dolloped with Greek-style sauce and enjoy!

Nutritional information: Calories: 187; Fat: 6g; Total Carbs: 2g; Net Carbs: 0.5g; Fiber: 0.1g; Sugars: 2g; Protein 29.1g

Dijon Crab Cakes

Prep time: 15 minutes | Cook time: 40 minutes | Serves: 4

8 ounces crab meat

2 tablespoons butter, melted

2 teaspoons Dijon mustard
1 tablespoon mayonnaise
1 egg, lightly beaten
½ teaspoon old bay seasoning
1 green onion, sliced

2 tablespoons parsley, chopped
¼ cup almond flour
¼ teaspoon black pepper
½ teaspoon salt

Add all the recipe ingredients except butter in a suitable mixing bowl and mix until well combined. Make 4 equal shapes of patties from mixture and place on parchment lined plate. Place plate in the fridge for 30 minutes. Grease its air fryer basket with cooking spray. Brush melted butter on per side of crab patties. Place crab patties in air fryer basket and cook for almost 10 minutes at 350 degrees F. Turn patties halfway through. Serve and enjoy.

Nutritional information: Calories: 178; Fat: 12.6g; Total Carbs: 4g; Net Carbs: 2g; Fiber: 1g; Sugars: 0.5g; Protein: 10.3g

Roasted Prawns with Firecracker Sauce

Prep time: 15 minutes | Cook time: 10 minutes | Serves: 4

Black pepper and salt to taste
1 egg
½ cup flour
¼ cup sesame seeds
¾ cup seasoned breadcrumbs

Firecracker sauce
⅓ cup sour cream
2 tablespoons buffalo sauce
¼ cup spicy ketchup
1 green onion, chopped

At 390 degrees F, preheat your air fryer. Grease its air fryer basket with cooking spray. Beat the eggs in a suitable bowl with salt. In a separate bowl, mix seasoned breadcrumbs with sesame seeds. In a third bowl, pour the flour mixed with black pepper. Dip prawns in the flour and then in the eggs, and finally in the breadcrumb mixture. Spray with cooking spray and add to the cooking basket. Cook for almost 10 minutes, flipping halfway through. Meanwhile, mix well all the sauce ingredients, except for the green onion in a suitable bowl. Serve the prawns with firecracker sauce.

Nutritional information: Calories: 208; Fat: 8.4g; Total Carbs: 27g; Net Carbs: 19g; Fiber: 2.3g; Sugars: 0.2g; Protein: 6.9g

Tomato Shrimp Kebab

Prep time: 15 minutes | Cook time: 20 minutes | Serves: 4

1 ½ pounds jumbo shrimp, cleaned, shelled and deveined
1 pound cherry tomatoes
2 tablespoons butter, melted
1 tablespoon Sriracha sauce
Salt and black pepper, to taste

½ teaspoon dried oregano
½ teaspoon dried basil
1 teaspoon dried parsley flakes
½ teaspoon marjoram
½ teaspoon mustard seeds

Toss all the recipe ingredients in a suitable mixing bowl until the shrimp and tomatoes are covered on all sides. Soak the wooden skewers in water for almost 15 minutes. Thread the jumbo shrimp and cherry tomatoes onto skewers. Cook in the preheated air fryer at about 400 degrees F for 5 minutes, working with batches. Serve.

Nutritional information: Calories: 196; Fat: 6.1g; Total Carbs: 4g; Net Carbs: 2g; Fiber: 1.6g; Sugars: 6.1g; Protein 31.6g

Garlicky Tuna Patties

Prep time: 15 minutes | Cook time: 10 minutes | Serves: 2

2 cans tuna
½ lemon juice
½ teaspoon onion powder

1 teaspoon garlic powder
½ teaspoon dried dill
1 ½ tablespoons mayonnaise

1 ½ tablespoons almond flour   ¼ teaspoon salt
¼ teaspoon black pepper

At 400 degrees F, preheat your air fryer. Add all the recipe ingredients in a suitable mixing bowl and mix until well combined. Grease its air fryer basket with cooking spray. Make 4 patties from mixture and place in the air fryer basket. Cook patties for almost 10 minutes at 400 degrees F if you want crispier patties then cook for 3 minutes more. Serve and enjoy.
Nutritional information: Calories: 371; Fat: 16.9g; Total Carbs: 2g; Net Carbs: 0.5g; Fiber: 0.8g; Sugars: 0.6g; Protein: 48.7g

Cajun Fish Sticks

Prep time: 15 minutes | Cook time: 10 minutes | Serves: 4

1-pound white fish, cut into pieces
¾ teaspoon Cajun seasoning
1 ½ cups pork rind, crushed
2 tablespoons water
2 tablespoons Dijon mustard
¼ cup mayonnaise
Black pepper
Salt

Grease its air fryer basket with cooking spray. In a suitable bowl, whisk water, mayonnaise, and mustard. In a shallow bowl, mix black pepper, pork rind, Cajun seasoning, and salt. Dip fish pieces in mayo mixture and coat well with pork rind mixture them set in the air fryer basket evenly. Cook at almost 400 degrees F for 5 minutes. Flip the fish sticks and continue cooking for 5 minutes more. Serve and enjoy.
Nutritional information: Calories: 427; Fat: 38.3g; Total Carbs: 3g; Net Carbs: 1g; Fiber: 0.3g; Sugars: 1g; Protein: 18g

Awesome Parmesan Shrimp

Prep time: 15 minutes | Cook time: 10 minutes | Serves: 6

2 pounds cooked shrimp, peeled and deveined
2 tablespoons olive oil
½ teaspoon onion powder
1 teaspoon basil
½ teaspoon oregano
⅔ cup parmesan cheese, grated
3 garlic cloves, minced
¼ teaspoon black pepper

In a suitable mixing bowl, combine together garlic, oil, onion powder, oregano, black pepper, and cheese. Add shrimp in a suitable bowl and toss until well coated. Grease its air fryer basket with cooking spray. Add shrimp into the air fryer basket and cook at almost 350 degrees F for 8-10 minutes. Serve and enjoy.
Nutritional information: Calories: 253; Fat: 9.3g; Total Carbs: 3g; Net Carbs: 1g; Fiber: 0.1g; Sugars: 0.1g; Protein: 37.6g

Yummy White Fish

Prep time: 15 minutes | Cook time: 12 minutes | Serves: 2

12 ounces white fish fillets
½ teaspoon onion powder
½ teaspoon lemon pepper seasoning
½ teaspoon garlic powder
1 tablespoon olive oil
Black pepper
Salt

Grease its air fryer basket with cooking spray. At 360 degrees F, preheat your air fryer. Coat fish fillets with olive oil and season with onion powder, lemon pepper seasoning, garlic powder, black pepper, and salt. Place fish fillets in air fryer basket and cook for almost 10-12 minutes. Serve and enjoy.
Nutritional information: Calories: 358; Fat: 19.8g; Total Carbs: 1g; Net Carbs: 0g; Fiber: 0.2g; Sugars: 0.4g; Protein: 41.9g

Lemon Salmon Fillets

Prep time: 15 minutes | Cook time: 15 minutes | Serves: 2

2 salmon fillets
½ teaspoon garlic powder
¼ cup plain yogurt
1 teaspoon fresh lemon juice
1 tablespoon fresh dill,
chopped
1 lemon, sliced
Black pepper
Salt

Place lemon slices into the air fryer basket. Season salmon with black pepper and salt and place on top of lemon slices into the air fryer basket. Cook salmon at 330 degrees F for almost 15 minutes. Meanwhile, in a suitable bowl, mix together yogurt, garlic powder, lemon juice, dill, black pepper, and salt. Place the prepared salmon on serving plate and top with yogurt mixture. Serve and enjoy.
Nutritional information: Calories: 264; Fat: 11.5g; Total Carbs: 3g; Net Carbs: 1g; Fiber: 0.3g; Sugars: 2.4g; Protein: 36.7g

Healthy Cardamom Salmon

Prep time: 15 minutes | Cook time: 12 minutes | Serves: 2

2 salmon fillets
1 tablespoon olive oil
¼ teaspoon ground cardamom
½ teaspoon paprika
Salt

At 350 degrees F, preheat your air fryer. Coat salmon fillets with paprika, cardamom, olive oil, and salt and place into the air fryer basket. Cook salmon for almost 10-12 minutes. Turn halfway through. Serve and enjoy.
Nutritional information: Calories: 298; Fat: 18.1g; Total Carbs: 0.5g; Net Carbs: 0g; Fiber: 0.3g; Sugars: 0.1g; Protein: 34.6g

Buttery Shrimp Scampi

Prep time: 15 minutes | Cook time: 10 minutes | Serves: 4

1 pound shrimp, peeled and deveined
10 garlic cloves, peeled
2 tablespoons olive oil
1 fresh lemon, cut into wedges
¼ cup parmesan cheese, grated
2 tablespoons butter, melted

At 370 degrees F, preheat your air fryer. Mix together shrimp, lemon wedges, olive oil, and garlic cloves in a suitable bowl. Pour shrimp mixture into the air fryer basket and place into the air fryer and cook for almost 10 minutes. Drizzle melted butter and parmesan cheese. Serve and enjoy.
Nutritional information: Calories: 262; Fat: 15.1g; Total Carbs: 4g; Net Carbs: 2g; Fiber: 0.2g; Sugars: 0.1g; Protein: 26.9g

Lemon Salmon with Chili

Prep time: 15 minutes | Cook time: 17 minutes | Serves: 4

2 pounds salmon fillet, skinless and boneless
2 lemon juice
1 orange juice
1 tablespoon olive oil
1 bunch fresh dill
1 chili, sliced
Black pepper
Salt

At 325 degrees F, preheat your air fryer. Place salmon fillets in its air fryer basket. Drizzle with olive oil, lemon juice, and orange juice. Sprinkle chili slices over salmon and season with

black pepper and salt. Place pan in the preheated air fryer and cook for almost 15-17 minutes. Garnish with dill and serve.
Nutritional information: Calories: 345; Fat: 17.7g; Total Carbs: 2g; Net Carbs: 0.5g; Fiber: 0.1g; Sugars: 2.3g; Protein: 44.3g

Mayonnaise Salmon with Spinach

Prep time: 15 minutes | Cook time: 19 minutes | Serves: 4

25 ounces salmon fillet
1 tablespoon green pesto
1 cup mayonnaise
½ ounce olive oil
1 pound fresh spinach

2 ounces parmesan cheese, grated
Black pepper
Salt

At 370 degrees F, preheat your air fryer. Grease its air fryer basket with cooking spray. Season salmon fillet with black pepper and salt and place into the air fryer basket. In a suitable bowl, mix together mayonnaise, parmesan cheese, and pesto and spread over the salmon fillet. Cook salmon for 14-16 minutes. Meanwhile, in a pan, sauté spinach with olive oil until spinach is wilted, about 2-3 minutes. Season with black pepper and salt. Transfer spinach in serving plate and top with cooked salmon. Serve and enjoy.
Nutritional information: Calories: 563; Fat: 37.3g; Total Carbs: 18g; Net Carbs: 9.5g; Fiber: 2.5g; Sugars: 4.2g; Protein: 42.7g

Parmesan Salmon with Walnuts

Prep time: 15 minutes | Cook time: 12 minutes | Serves: 4

4 salmon fillets
¼ cup parmesan cheese, grated
½ cup walnuts

1 teaspoon olive oil
1 tablespoon lemon rind

At 370 degrees F, preheat your air fryer. Grease its air fryer basket with cooking spray. Place salmon on a suitable baking dish. Add walnuts into the food processor and process until finely ground. Mix ground walnuts with parmesan cheese, oil, and lemon rind. Stir well. Spoon walnut mixture over the salmon and press gently. Place the coated salmon the preheated air fryer and cook for 12 minutes. serve and enjoy.
Nutritional information: Calories: 343; Fat: 21.4g; Total Carbs: 1g; Net Carbs: 0g; Fiber: 1.2g; Sugars: 0.3g; Protein: 38.3g

Basil Parmesan Salmon

Prep time: 15 minutes | Cook time: 16 minutes | Serves: 2

2 salmon fillets
¼ cup parmesan cheese, grated
For pesto:
¼ cup pine nuts
¼ cup olive oil
1 ½ cups fresh basil leaves

2 garlic cloves, peeled and chopped
¼ cup parmesan cheese, grated
½ teaspoon black pepper
½ teaspoon salt

Add all pesto recipes ingredients to the blender and blend until smooth. At 370 degrees F, preheat your air fryer. Grease its air fryer basket with cooking spray. Place salmon fillet into the air fryer basket and spread 2 tablespoons of the pesto on each salmon fillet. Sprinkle grated cheese on top of the pesto. Cook salmon for 16 minutes. Serve and enjoy.
Nutritional information: Calories: 587; Fat: 48.7g; Total Carbs: 4g; Net Carbs: 2g; Fiber: 1.1g; Sugars: 0.7g; Protein: 38.8g

Garlic Shrimp with Paprika

Prep time: 15 minutes | Cook time: 8 minutes | Serves: 2

12 ounces shrimp, peeled and deveined
1 lemon sliced
¼ teaspoon garlic powder

¼ teaspoon paprika
1 teaspoon lemon pepper
1 lemon juice
1 tablespoon olive oil

In a suitable bowl, mix together oil, lemon juice, garlic powder, paprika, and lemon pepper. Add shrimp to the bowl and toss well to coat. Grease its air fryer basket with cooking spray. Transfer shrimp into the air fryer basket and cook at almost 400 degrees F for 8 minutes. Garnish with lemon slices and serve.
Nutritional information: Calories: 267; Fat: 9.9g; Total Carbs: 3g; Net Carbs: 1g; Fiber: 0.4g; Sugars: 0.1g; Protein: 39g

Mayonnaise Breaded Shrimp

Prep time: 15 minutes | Cook time: 10 minutes | Serves: 4

¼ cup all-purpose flour
1 cup panko breadcrumbs
1 pound shrimp, peeled and deveined

½ cup mayonnaise
¼ cup sweet chili sauce
1 tablespoon Sriracha sauce

At 400 degrees F, preheat your air fryer and grease its air fryer basket. Spread flour in a shallow bowl and mix the mayonnaise, chili sauce, and Sriracha sauce in another bowl. Place the breadcrumbs in a third bowl. Coat each shrimp with the flour, dip into mayonnaise mixture and finally, dredge in the breadcrumbs. Arrange ½ of the coated shrimps into the air fryer basket and cook for about 10 minutes. Dish out the coated shrimps onto serving plates and repeat with the remaining mixture.
Nutritional information: Calories: 378; Fat: 21.8g; Total Carbs: 15g; Net Carbs: 5.6g; Fiber: 0.2g; Sugars: 2.9g; Protein: 26.9g

Garlic Cod Fish

Prep time: 15 minutes | Cook time: 10 minutes | Serves: 2

2 cod fish fillets
1 tablespoon garlic, chopped

2 teaspoons swerve
2 tablespoons miso

Add all the recipe ingredients to the zip-lock bag. Shake well place in the refrigerator for overnight. Place marinated fish fillets into the air fryer basket and cook at almost 350 degrees F for almost 10 minutes. Serve and enjoy.
Nutritional information: Calories: 229; Fat: 2.6g; Total Carbs: 5g; Net Carbs: 2g; Fiber: 1g; Sugars: 1.1g; Protein: 43.4g

Old Bay Tilapia Fillets

Prep time: 15 minutes | Cook time: 7 minutes | Serves: 2

2 tilapia fillets
1 teaspoon old bay seasoning
½ teaspoon butter

¼ teaspoon lemon pepper
Black pepper
Salt

Grease its air fryer basket with cooking spray. Place prepared fish fillets into the air fryer basket and season with lemon pepper, old bay seasoning, black pepper, and salt. Spray fish fillets with cooking spray and cook at almost 400 degrees F for 7 minutes. Serve and enjoy.
Nutritional information: Calories: 381; Fat: 5g; Total Carbs: 0.2g; Net Carbs: 0g; Fiber: 0.1g; Sugars: 0g; Protein: 84.1g

Pesto Fish Finger Sandwich

Prep time: 15 minutes | Cook time: 15 minutes | Serves: 4

4 finger fish fillets	2 ounces breadcrumbs
2 tablespoons flour	4 tablespoons pesto sauce
10 capers	4 lettuce leaves
4 bread rolls	Black pepper and salt, to taste

At 370 degrees F, preheat your air fryer. Season the finger fish fillets with black pepper and salt, and coat them with the dry flour first; then dip in the breadcrumbs. Arrange the fillets onto a baking mat and cook in the air fryer for almost 10 to 15 minutes. Cut the bread rolls in half. Place a lettuce leaf on top of the bottom halves; put the fillets over. Spread a tablespoon of pesto sauce on top of each fillet, and top with the remaining halves. Serve.

Nutritional information: Calories: 295; Fat: 10.9g; Total Carbs: 38g; Net Carbs: 23.5g; Fiber: 3g; Sugars: 5g; Protein: 11.2g

Lemon Foil Salmon

Prep time: 15 minutes | Cook time: 12 minutes | Serves: 2

2 x 4-oz. skinless salmon fillets	½ teaspoon garlic powder
2 tablespoons unsalted butter, melted	1 medium lemon
	½ teaspoon dried dill

Take a sheet of aluminum foil and cut into 2 squares measuring roughly 5" x 5". Lay each of the salmon fillets at the center of each piece. Brush both fillets with a tablespoon of bullet and season with a quarter-teaspoon of garlic powder. Halve the lemon and grate the skin of 1 ½ over the fish. Cut 4 half-slices of lemon, using 2 to top each fillet. Season each fillet with a quarter-teaspoon of dill. Fold the tops and sides of the aluminum foil over the fish to create a kind of packet. Place each 1 in the air fryer. Cook for 12 minutes at 400 degrees F. The salmon is ready when it flakes easily. Serve hot.

Nutritional information: Calories: 377; Fat: 23.5g; Total Carbs: 0.7g; Net Carbs: 0g; Fiber: 0.1g; Sugars: 0.2g; Protein: 41.3g

Crumbs Crusted Shrimp

Prep time: 15 minutes | Cook time: 8 minutes | Serves: 8

2 pounds shrimp, peeled and deveined	1 cup flour
4 egg whites	½ teaspoon cayenne pepper
2 tablespoons olive oil	1 cup bread crumbs
	Black pepper and salt to taste

Combine together the flour, black pepper, and salt in a shallow bowl. In a separate bowl, mix the egg whites using a whisk. In a third bowl, combine the bread crumbs, cayenne pepper, and salt. At 400 degrees F, preheat your air fryer. Cover the shrimp with the flour mixture before dipping it in the egg white and lastly rolling in the bread crumbs. Put the coated shrimp in the fryer's basket and top with a light drizzle of olive oil. Air fry the shrimp at almost 400 degrees F for 8 minutes, in multiple batches if necessary.

Nutritional information: Calories: 284; Fat: 6.3g; Total Carbs: 23g; Net Carbs: 11g; Fiber: 1.1g; Sugars: 1g; Protein: 31.1g

Parmesan Tilapia with Parsley

Prep time: 15 minutes | Cook time: 10 minutes | Serves: 4

1 pound tilapia fillets	¾ cup parmesan cheese, grated
1 tablespoon parsley, chopped	1 tablespoon olive oil
2 teaspoons paprika	Black pepper and salt to taste

At 400 degrees F, preheat your air fryer. In a shallow dish, combine together the paprika, grated cheese, black pepper, salt and parsley. Pour a little olive oil over the tilapia fillets. Cover the fillets with the paprika and cheese mixture. Lay the fillets on a sheet of aluminum foil and transfer to the Air Fryer basket. Air fry for almost 10 minutes. Serve hot.

Nutritional information: Calories: 144; Fat: 5.8g; Total Carbs: 0.8g; Net Carbs: 0g; Fiber: 0.4g; Sugars: 0.1g; Protein: 23g

Lime Trout with Parsley

Prep time: 15 minutes | Cook time: 12 minutes | Serves: 4

4 trout fillets, boneless	Juice of 1 lime
4 tablespoons butter, melted	1 tablespoon chives, chopped
Black pepper and salt to the taste	1 tablespoon parsley, chopped

Mix the fish fillets with the melted butter, black pepper and salt, rub gently, put the fish in your air fryer basket and cook at almost 390 degrees F for 6 minutes per side. Divide between plates and serve with lime juice drizzled on top and with parsley and chives sprinkled at the end.

Nutritional information: Calories: 220; Fat: 16.8g; Total Carbs: 0.1g; Net Carbs: 0g; Fiber: 0.1g; Sugars: 0g; Protein: 16.7g

Parsley Saltine Fillets

Prep time: 15 minutes | Cook time: 12 minutes | Serves: 4

1 cup crushed saltines	1 egg, well whisked
¼ cup extra-virgin olive oil	4 white fish fillets
1 teaspoon garlic powder	Salt and black pepper to taste
½ teaspoon shallot powder	Fresh Italian parsley to serve

In a shallow bowl, combine the crushed saltines and olive oil. In a separate bowl, mix together the garlic powder, shallot powder, and the beaten egg. Sprinkle a good amount of black pepper and salt over the fish, before dipping each fillet into the egg mixture. Coat the fillets with the crumb mixture. Air fry the fish at 370 degrees F for almost 10 - 12 minutes. Serve with fresh parsley.

Nutritional information: Calories: 439; Fat: 26.6g; Total Carbs: 8g; Net Carbs: 3.5g; Fiber: 0.4g; Sugars: 0.3g; Protein: 40.2g

Crispy Cod Sticks

Prep time: 15 minutes | Cook time: 12 minutes | Serves: 5

1-pound cod	2 large eggs, beaten
3 tablespoons milk	½ teaspoon black pepper
1 cup meal	¼ teaspoon salt
2 cups bread crumbs	

Combine together the milk and eggs in a suitable bowl. In a shallow dish, stir together bread crumbs, black pepper, and salt. Pour the meal into a second shallow dish. Coat the cod sticks with the meal before dipping each 1 in the egg and rolling in bread crumbs. Put the prepared fish sticks in the air fryer basket. Cook at almost 350 degrees F for 12 minutes, shaking the basket halfway through cooking. Serve.

Nutritional information: Calories: 388; Fat: 5.7g; Total Carbs: 50.5g; Net Carbs: 0g; Fiber: 2.6g; Sugars: 3.3g; Protein: 31.5g

Tasty Creole Crab

Prep time: 15 minutes | Cook time: 6 minutes | Serves: 6

1 teaspoon Creole seasonings	1 teaspoon dried dill
4 tablespoons almond flour	1 teaspoon ghee
¼ teaspoon baking powder	13 ounces crab meat, chopped
1 teaspoon apple cider vinegar	1 egg, beaten
¼ teaspoon onion powder	Cooking spray

In the mixing bowl, mix up crab meat, egg, dried dill, ghee, onion powder, apple cider vinegar, baking powder, and Creole seasonings. Then add almond flour and stir the mixture with the help of the fork until it is homogenous. Make the small balls hushpuppies. At 390 degrees F, preheat your air fryer. Put the hushpuppies in the preheated air fryer basket and spray with cooking spray. Cook them for almost 3 minutes. Then flip them on another side and cook for 3 minutes more or until the hushpuppies are golden brown.

Nutritional information: Calories: 101; Fat: 4.8g; Total Carbs: 2g; Net Carbs: 0.5g; Fiber: 0.5g; Sugars: 0.1g; Protein 9.6g

Glazed Salmon with Soy Sauce

Prep time: 15 minutes | Cook time: 14 minutes | Serves: 2

1 teaspoon water	⅓ cup honey
2 3½-ounce salmon fillets	3 teaspoons rice wine vinegar
⅓ cup soy sauce	

At 355 degrees F, preheat your air fryer. and grease an air fryer grill pan. Mix all the recipe ingredients in a suitable bowl except salmon. Reserve ½ of the mixture in a suitable bowl and coat the salmon in remaining mixture. Refrigerate, covered for about 2 hours and place the salmon in the air fryer basket. Cook for about 13 minutes, flipping once in between and coat with reserved marinade. Place the leftover salmon marinade in a small pan and cook for about 1 minute. Serve salmon with marinade sauce and enjoy.

Nutritional information: Calories: 527; Fat: 15.3g; Total Carbs: 49g; Net Carbs: 21g; Fiber: 0.5g; Sugars: 47.1g; Protein: 51g

Garlic Lobster with Herbs

Prep time: 15 minutes | Cook time: 10 minutes | Serves: 3

1 teaspoon garlic, minced	Black pepper and salt to taste
1 tablespoon butter	½ tablespoon lemon Juice

Add all the recipe ingredients to a food processor, except shrimp, and blend well. Clean the skin of the lobster and cover with the marinade. At 380 degrees F, preheat your air fryer. Place the lobster in your air fryer basket and cook for almost 10 minutes. Serve with fresh herbs and enjoy!

Nutritional information: Calories: 36; Fat: 3.9g; Total Carbs: 0.4g; Net Carbs: 0g; Fiber: 0g; Sugars: 0.1g; Protein: 0.1g

Ginger Mushroom Flounder

Prep time: 15 minutes | Cook time: 15 minutes | Serves: 4

4 flounder fillets, boneless	grated
2 tablespoons coconut aminos	2 teaspoons olive oil
A pinch of black pepper and salt	2 green onions, chopped
1 and ½ teaspoons. ginger,	2 cups mushrooms, sliced

Heat a suitable pan that fits your air fryer with the oil over medium-high heat, add the mushrooms and all the other ingredients except the fish, toss and sauté for 5 minutes. Add the fish, toss gently, introduce the pan in the air fryer and cook at almost 390 degrees F for almost 10 minutes. Serve.

Nutritional information: Calories: 178; Fat: 4.4g; Total Carbs: 1g; Net Carbs: 0g; Fiber: 0.6g; Sugars: 0.8g; Protein: 31.9g

Fish Tacos with Mango Salsa

Prep time: 15 minutes | Cook time: 10 minutes | Serves: 4

½ cup mango salsa	diced
1 cup corn kernels	4 large burrito-size tortillas
1 cup mixed greens	4 pieces fish fillets
1 red bell pepper, seeded and diced	Juice from ½ lemon
1 yellow onion, peeled and	Black pepper and salt to taste

At 330 degrees F, preheat your air fryer. Season the fish with lemon juice, black pepper and salt. Place seasoned fish on the double layer rack. Cook for almost 10 minutes. Assemble the taco wraps by laying the tortillas on a flat surface and add fish fillet together with the onions, black pepper, corn kernels, and mixed greens. This makes 4 tortilla wraps Serve with mango salsa.

Nutritional information: Calories: 417; Fat: 15.2g; Total Carbs: 52g; Net Carbs: 18g; Fiber: 5.1g; Sugars: 5g; Protein: 19.4g

Coconut Catfish Bites

Prep time: 15 minutes | Cook time: 10 minutes | Serves: 4

¼ cup coconut flakes	3 eggs, beaten
3 tablespoons coconut flour	10 ounces catfish fillet
1 teaspoon salt	Cooking spray

Cut the catfish fillet on the small-piece nuggets and sprinkle with salt. After this, dip the catfish pieces in the egg and coat in the coconut flour. Then dip the fish pieces in the egg again and coat in the coconut flakes. At 385 degrees F, preheat your air fryer. Place the catfish nuggets in the air fryer basket and cook them for almost 6 minutes. Then flip the nuggets on another side and cook them for almost 4 minutes more.

Nutritional information: Calories: 183; Fat: 10.9g; Total Carbs: 4g; Net Carbs: 2g; Fiber: 2.7g; Sugars: 0.6g; Protein 16.1g

Spiced Catfish Fillets

Prep time: 15 minutes | Cook time: 7 minutes | Serves: 4

1 lb. catfish fillets	1 teaspoon dried basil
1 tablespoon olive oil	1 tablespoon Jamaican allspice, ground
1 teaspoon paprika	½ lemon, juiced
1 teaspoon garlic powder	

At 390 degrees F, preheat your air fryer. Grease its air fryer basket with cooking spray. In a suitable bowl, mix paprika, garlic powder, and Jamaican allspice seasoning. Rub the catfish fillets with the spice mixture. Transfer to the cooking basket and drizzle the olive oil. Cook for 7 minutes, slide out the air fryer basket and turn the fillets; cook further for 6 minutes. Serve sprinkled with lemon juice.

Nutritional information: Calories: 233; Fat: 15.2g; Total Carbs: 7g; Net Carbs: 3g; Fiber: 0.9g; Sugars: 0.2g; Protein: 16g

Flavorful White Fish

Prep time: 15 minutes | Cook time: 12 minutes | Serves: 2

12 ounces white fish fillets
½ teaspoon onion powder
½ teaspoon lemon pepper seasoning

½ teaspoon garlic powder
1 tablespoon olive oil
Black pepper, to taste
Salt, to taste

Grease its air fryer basket with cooking spray. At 360 degrees F, preheat your air fryer. Coat fish fillets with olive oil and season with onion powder, lemon pepper seasoning, garlic powder, black pepper, and salt. Place fish fillets in air fryer basket and cook for almost 10-12 minutes. Serve and enjoy.
Nutritional information: Calories: 358; Fat: 19.8g; Total Carbs: 1g; Net Carbs: 0g; Fiber: 0.2g; Sugars: 0.4g; Protein 41.9g

Hearty Lemon Salmon

Prep time: 15 minutes | Cook time: 12 minutes | Serves: 2

2 salmon steaks
Coarse salt, to taste
1 tablespoon sesame oil
Zest of 1 lemon
¼ teaspoon black pepper

1 tablespoon fresh lemon juice
1 teaspoon garlic, minced
½ teaspoon smoked cayenne pepper
½ teaspoon dried dill

At 380 degrees F, preheat your air fryer. Pat dry the salmon steaks with a kitchen towel. In a ceramic dish, combine the remaining ingredients until everything is well whisked. Add the salmon steaks to the ceramic dish and let them sit in the refrigerator for 1 hour. Now, place the salmon steaks in the cooking basket. Reserve the marinade. Cook for 12 minutes, flipping halfway through the cooking time. Meanwhile, cook the marinade in a small sauté pan over a moderate flame. Cook until the sauce has thickened. Pour the prepared spicy sauce over the steaks and serve.
Nutritional information: Calories: 301; Fat: 17.9g; Total Carbs: 0.9g; Net Carbs: 0g; Fiber: 0.2g; Sugars: 0.2g; Protein: 34.8g

Oregano Pollock with Capers

Prep time: 15 minutes | Cook time: 13 minutes | Serves: 3

2 tablespoons olive oil
1 red onion, sliced
2 garlic cloves, chopped
1 Florina pepper, deveined and minced
3 Pollock fillets, skinless
2 ripe tomatoes, diced

12 Kalamata olives, pitted and chopped
2 tablespoons capers
1 teaspoon oregano
1 teaspoon rosemary
Salt, to taste
½ cup white wine

At 360 degrees F, preheat your air fryer. Heat the oil in a suitable baking pan. Once hot, sauté the onion, garlic, and black pepper for 2 to 3 minutes or until fragrant. Add the fish fillets to the baking pan. Top with the tomatoes, olives, and capers. Sprinkle with the oregano, rosemary, and salt. Pour in white wine and transfer to the cooking basket. Turn the temperature to 395 degrees F and air fry for almost 10 minutes. Enjoy!
Nutritional information: Calories: 186; Fat: 3.2g; Total Carbs: 9g; Net Carbs: 4.3g; Fiber: 2.9g; Sugars: 4.1g; Protein: 23.5g

Sweet and Sour Glazed Salmon

Prep time: 15 minutes | Cook time: 12 minutes | Serves: 2

2 salmon fillets, boneless

1 tablespoon honey

½ cup blackberries
1 tablespoon olive oil

Juice of ½ lemon
Black pepper and salt to taste

In a blender, mix the blackberries with the honey, oil, lemon juice, salt, and black pepper; pulse well. Spread the blackberry mixture over the salmon, and then place the fish in your air fryer basket. Cook at almost 380 degrees F for 12 minutes, flipping the fish halfway. Serve hot, and enjoy!
Nutritional information: Calories: 343; Fat: 18.2g; Total Carbs: 12g; Net Carbs: 7g; Fiber: 1.9g; Sugars: 10.4g; Protein: 35.1g

Parmesan Cod with Onion

Prep time: 15 minutes | Cook time: 14 minutes | Serves: 4

4 cod fillets, boneless
Black pepper and salt to the taste
1 cup parmesan

4 tablespoons balsamic vinegar
A drizzle of olive oil
3 spring onions, chopped

Season fish with salt, black pepper, grease with the oil, and coat it in parmesan. Put the fillets in your air fryer basket and cook at almost 370 degrees F for 14 minutes. Meanwhile, in a suitable bowl, mix the spring onions with salt, black pepper and the vinegar and whisk. Divide the cod between plates, drizzle the spring onions mix all over and serve with a side salad.
Nutritional information: Calories: 119; Fat: 2.5g; Total Carbs: 1g; Net Carbs: 0g; Fiber: 0.3g; Sugars: 0.3g; Protein: 22.5g

Herbed Catfish

Prep time: 15 minutes | Cook time: 12 minutes | Serves: 4

20 ounces catfish fillet, 4 ounces each fillet
2 eggs, beaten
1 teaspoon dried thyme
½ teaspoon salt

1 teaspoon apple cider vinegar
1 teaspoon avocado oil
¼ teaspoon cayenne pepper
⅓ cup coconut flour

Sprinkle the catfish fillets with dried thyme, salt, apple cider vinegar, cayenne pepper, and coconut flour. Then sprinkle the fish fillets with avocado oil. At 385 degrees F, preheat your air fryer. Put the catfish fillets in the air fryer basket and cook them for almost 8 minutes. Then flip the fish on another side and cook for 4 minutes more.
Nutritional information: Calories: 226; Fat: 13.1g; Total Carbs: 0.5g; Net Carbs: 0g; Fiber: 0.2g; Sugars: 0.2g; Protein: 24.9g

Crusted Shrimp with Coconut

Prep time: 15 minutes | Cook time: 15 minutes | Serves: 4

1 pound shrimp
1 cup panko breadcrumbs
1 cup shredded coconut

2 eggs
⅓ cup all-purpose flour

At 360 degrees F, preheat your air fryer. Peel and devein the shrimp. Whisk the seasonings with the flour as desired. In another dish, whisk the eggs, and in the third container, combine the breadcrumbs and coconut. Dip the cleaned shrimp into the flour, egg wash, and finish it off with the coconut mixture. Lightly spray the basket of the fryer and set the timer for almost 10-15 minutes. Air-fry until it's a golden brown before serving.
Nutritional information: Calories: 292; Fat: 11g; Total Carbs: 16g; Net Carbs: 7g; Fiber: 2.6g; Sugars: 1.6g; Protein: 30.9g

Old Bay Shrimp

Prep time: 15 minutes | Cook time: 5 minutes | Serves: 6

1 ¼-pound/16-20 tiger shrimp
1 tablespoon olive oil
½ teaspoon old Bay seasoning
¼ teaspoon smoked paprika
¼ teaspoon black pepper

At 390 degrees F, preheat your air fryer. Cover the shrimp using the oil and spices. Spread the spiced shrimp in the air fryer basket and set the timer for 5 minutes. Serve with your favorite side dish.
Nutritional information: Calories: 121; Fat: 3.5g; Total Carbs: 1g; Net Carbs: 0g; Fiber: 0.1g; Sugars: 0g; Protein: 22.1g

Breaded Cod Nuggets

Prep time: 15 minutes | Cook time: 20 minutes | Serves: 4

1 pound cod fillet
3 eggs
4 tablespoons olive oil
1 cup almond flour
1 cup breadcrumbs

Warm the air fryer at about 390 degrees Fahrenheit. Slice the cod into nuggets. Prepare 3 bowls. Whisk the eggs in one. Combine the salt, oil, and breadcrumbs in another. Sift the almond flour into the third one. Cover each of the nuggets with the flour, dip in the eggs, and the breadcrumbs. Arrange the nuggets in the basket and set the timer for 20 minutes. Serve the fish with your favorite dips or sides.
Nutritional information: Calories: 532; Fat: 33g; Total Carbs: 25g; Net Carbs: 16g; Fiber: 4.2g; Sugars: 1.9g; Protein: 33.8g

Dilled Salmon

Prep time: 15 minutes | Cook time: 10 minutes | Serves: 4

1 tablespoon chopped dill
1 tablespoon olive oil
3 tablespoons sour cream
1.76 oz. plain yogurt
6 pieces salmon

At 285 degrees F, preheat your air fryer. Shake the salt over the salmon and add them to the fryer basket with the olive oil to air-fry for almost 10 minutes. Whisk the yogurt, salt, and dill. Serve the salmon with the sauce with your favorite sides.
Nutritional information: Calories: 413; Fat: 22.1g; Total Carbs: 1g; Net Carbs: 0g; Fiber: 0.1g; Sugars: 0.9g; Protein: 53g

Lemon Breaded Fish

Prep time: 15 minutes | Cook time: 12 minutes | Serves: 4

½ cup breadcrumbs
4 tablespoons vegetable oil
1 egg
4 fish fillets
1 lemon

Heat the air fryer to reach 355 degrees Fahrenheit. Whisk the oil and breadcrumbs until crumbly. Dip the prepared fish into the egg, then the crumb mixture. Arrange the fish in the cooker and air-fry for 12 minutes. Garnish using the lemon.
Nutritional information: Calories: 405; Fat: 26.6g; Total Carbs: 26g; Net Carbs: 13g; Fiber: 1.5g; Sugars: 1.3g; Protein: 16.7g

Crispy Fried Catfish

Prep time: 15 minutes | Cook time: 13 minutes | Serves: 4

1 tablespoon olive oil
¼ cup seasoned fish fry
4 catfish fillets

At 400 degrees F, preheat your air fryer. Rinse the catfish and pat dry using a paper towel. Dump the seasoning into a sizeable zipper-type bag. Add the fish and shake to cover each fillet. Spray with a spritz of cooking oil spray and add to the basket. Set the timer for almost 10 minutes. Flip, and reset the timer for ten additional minutes. Turn the fish once more and cook for 2-3 minutes. Once it reaches the desired crispiness, transfer to a plate, and serve.
Nutritional information: Calories: 246; Fat: 15.6g; Total Carbs: 0g; Net Carbs: 0g; Fiber: 0g; Sugars: 0g; Protein: 24.9g

Roasted Sardines

Prep time: 15 minutes | Cook time: 14 minutes | Serves: 2

5 sardines
Herbs de Provence

At 380 degrees F, preheat your air fryer. Spray the basket and place your sardines in the basket of your air fryer. Set the timer for 14 minutes. After 7 minutes, remember to turn the sardines so that they are roasted on per side. Serve.
Nutritional information: Calories: 125; Fat: 6.9g; Total Carbs: 0g; Net Carbs: 0g; Fiber: 0g; Sugars: 0g; Protein: 14.8g

Creamy Tuna with Zucchinis

Prep time: 15 minutes | Cook time: 20 minutes | Serves: 4

4 medium zucchinis
120g of tuna in oil canned drained
30g grated cheese
1 teaspoon pine nuts
Salt, black pepper to taste

Cut the zucchini in ½ laterally and empty it with a small spoon set aside the pulp that will be used for filling; place them in the basket. In a food processor, put the zucchini pulp, drained tuna, pine nuts and grated cheese. Mix until you get a homogeneous and dense mixture. Fill the zucchini. Set the air fryer to 360 degrees F. Air fry for almost 20 minutes depending on the size of the zucchini. Let cool before serving.
Nutritional information: Calories: 126; Fat: 5.8g; Total Carbs: 6g; Net Carbs: 2.5g; Fiber: 2.2g; Sugars: 3.5g; Protein: 13.1g

Ginger Salmon Fillet

Prep time: 15 minutes | Cook time: 22 minutes | Serves: 4

2 salmon fillets
60g cane sugar
4 tablespoons soy sauce
50g sesame seeds
Unlimited Ginger

Preheat the air fryer at about 360 degrees F for 5 minutes. Put the sugar and soy sauce in the basket. Cook everything for 5 minutes. In the meantime, wash the fish well, pass it through sesame to cover it completely and place it inside the tank and add the fresh ginger. Cook for 12 minutes. Turn the fish over and finish cooking for another 8 minutes.
Nutritional information: Calories: 258; Fat: 11.7g; Total Carbs: 19g; Net Carbs: 6.7g; Fiber: 1.6g; Sugars: 14.6g; Protein: 20.5g

Fried Breaded Prawns

Prep time: 15 minutes | Cook time: 8 minutes | Serves: 6

12 prawns
2 eggs
Flour to taste

Breadcrumbs
1 teaspoon oil

Remove the head of the prawns and shell carefully. Pass the prawns first in the flour, then in the beaten egg and then in the breadcrumbs. At 350 degrees F, preheat your air fryer. Add the prawns and cook for 4 minutes. If the prawns are large, it will be necessary to cook 6 at a time. Turn the prawns and cook for another 4 minutes. They should be served with a yogurt or mayonnaise sauce.

Nutritional information: Calories: 151; Fat: 3.9g; Total Carbs: 13g; Net Carbs: 7g; Fiber: 0.8g; Sugars: 1.2g; Protein: 14.3g

Air Fried Mussels with Parsley

Prep time: 15 minutes | Cook time: 12 minutes | Serves: 5

1 ⅔ pound mussels
1 garlic clove
1 teaspoon oil

Black pepper to taste
Parsley Taste

Clean and scrape the mold cover and remove the byssus. Pour the oil, clean the mussels and the crushed garlic in the air fryer basket. At 425 degrees F, preheat your air fryer and air fry for 12 minutes. Towards the end of cooking, add black pepper and chopped parsley. Finally, distribute the mussel juice well at the bottom of the basket, stirring the basket.

Nutritional information: Calories: 139; Fat: 4.3g; Total Carbs: 5g; Net Carbs: 2g; Fiber: 0g; Sugars: 0g; Protein: 18g

Caper Monkfish

Prep time: 15 minutes | Cook time: 40 minutes | Serves: 4

1 monkfish
10 cherry tomatoes

50 g cailletier olives
5 capers

Spread aluminum foil inside the air fryer basket and place the monkfish clean and skinless. Add chopped tomatoes, olives, capers, oil, and salt. At 380 degrees F, preheat your Air Fryer. Cook the monkfish for about 40 minutes.

Nutritional information: Calories: 240; Fat: 14g; Total Carbs: 12.5g; Net Carbs: 5g; Fiber: 4g; Sugars: 8.1g; Protein: 18.7g

Spiced Shrimp with Zucchini

Prep time: 15 minutes | Cook time: 25 minutes | Serves: 4

2 zucchinis
30 shrimp
7 cherry tomatoes

Black pepper and salt to taste
1 garlic clove

Pour the oil in the air fryer, add the garlic clove and diced zucchini. Cook for almost 15 minutes at 300 degrees F. Add the shrimp and the pieces of tomato, salt, and spices. Cook for another 5 to 10 minutes or until the shrimp water evaporates.

Nutritional information: Calories: 252; Fat: 3.4g; Total Carbs: 14g; Net Carbs: 9.5g; Fiber: 3.7g; Sugars: 7.4g; Protein: 40.7g

Flavorful Salmon with Pistachio

Prep time: 15 minutes | Cook time: 25 minutes | Serves: 4

600 g salmon fillet
50g pistachios

Salt to taste

Put the parchment paper on the bottom of the air fryer basket and place the salmon fillet in it. Cut the pistachios in thick pieces; grease the top of the fish, salt and cover everything with the pistachios. At 360 degrees F, preheat your air fryer and air fry for 25 minutes. Serve warm.

Nutritional information: Calories: 265; Fat: 15.1g; Total Carbs: 3g; Net Carbs: 1g; Fiber: 1.3g; Sugars: 0.8g; Protein: 31.6g

Poultry Mains Recipes

Turkey Breasts

Prep time: 5 minutes | Cook time: 1 hour | Serves: 4

3 lbs. boneless turkey breast
¼ cup mayonnaise
2 tsps. poultry seasoning

black pepper and salt to taste
½ tsp. garlic powder

At 360 degrees F, preheat your Air Fryer. Season the turkey with mayonnaise, seasoning, salt, garlic powder, and black pepper. Cook the mayo turkey breasts in the air fryer for 1 hour at 360 degrees F on Air Fry mode, turning the turkey breasts every 15 minutes. The turkey breasts are done when they reach 165 degrees F.
Nutritional information: Calories 558 g; Total Carbs 1g; Fat 18g; Protein 98g; Fat 22.4g; fibers: 3g; Sugars: 6g

BBQ Chicken Breasts

Prep time: 5 minutes | Cook time: 15 minutes | Serves: 4

4 boneless (about 6 oz.)
chicken breasts,

2 tbsps. BBQ seasoning
Cooking spray

Rub the chicken breasts with BBQ seasoning and marinate them in the refrigerator for 45 minutes. At 400 degrees F, preheat your Air Fryer. Grease the air fryer basket with oil and place in the chicken breasts. Spray oil on top. Air Fry the chicken breasts for 13 to 14 minutes, flipping halfway through cooking. Serve.
Nutritional information: Calories 131 g; Total Carbs 2g; Fat 3g; Protein 24g; Fat 22.4g; fibers: 3g; Sugars: 6g

Honey-Mustard Chicken Breasts

Prep time: 5 minutes | Cook time: 25 minutes | Serves: 6

6 (6-oz, each) boneless,
chicken breasts
2 tbsps. fresh rosemary minced

3 tbsps. honey
1 tbsp. Dijon mustard
black pepper and salt to taste

Combine the mustard, honey, pepper, rosemary and salt in a suitable bowl. Rub the chicken breasts with this mixture. Grease the "Air Fryer Basket" with oil. Air Fry the chicken breasts at 350 degrees F for 20 to 24 minutes or until the chicken reaches 165 degrees F. Serve.
Nutritional information: Calories 236 g; Total Carbs 9.8g; Fat 5g; Protein 38g; Fat 22.4g; fibers: 3g; Sugars: 6g

Chicken Parmesan Wings

Prep time: 5 minutes | Cook time: 15 minutes | Serves: 4

2 lbs. chicken wings. cut into
drumettes, pat dried
½ cup parmesan, plus 6 tbsps.
grated

1 tsp. herbs de Provence
1 tsp. paprika
Salt to taste

Combine the parmesan, herbs, paprika, and salt in a suitable bowl and rub the chicken with this mixture. At 350 degrees F, preheat your Air Fryer. Grease the air fryer basket with some cooking spray. Air Fry the coated chicken wings for 15 minutes, flipping halfway through. Garnish with parmesan and serve.
Nutritional information: Calories 490 g; Total Carbs 1g; Fat 22g; Protein 72g; Fat 22.4g; fibers: 3g; Sugars: 6g

Air Fryer Chicken Wings

Prep time: 5 minutes | Cook time: 35 minutes | Serves: 4

2 lbs. chicken wings
Black pepper and salt to taste

Cooking spray

Flavor the chicken wings with black pepper and salt. Add the seasoned chicken wings to your air fryer basket and Air Fry them at 400 degrees F for 35 minutes. Flip 3 times during cooking for even cooking. Serve.
Nutritional information: Calories 277 g; Total Carbs 1g; Fat 8g; Protein 50g; Fat 22.4g; fibers: 3g; Sugars: 6g

Whole Chicken

Prep time: 5 minutes | Cook time: 45 minutes | Serves: 6

1 (2 ½ lbs.) whole chicken,
washed and pat dried
2 tbsps. dry rub

1 tsp. salt
Cooking spray

At 350 degrees F, preheat your Air Fryer. Rub the dry rub on the chicken. Then rub with salt. Cook it at 350 degrees F for 45 minutes on Air Fry mode. After 30 minutes of cooking time, flip the chicken and finish cooking. Chicken is done when it reaches 165 degrees F. Serve and enjoy.
Nutritional information: Calories 412 g; Total Carbs 1g; Fat 28g; Protein 35g; Fat 22.4g; fibers: 3g; Sugars: 6g

Honey Duck Breasts

Prep time: 5 minutes | Cook time: 25 minutes | Serves: 2

1 smoked duck breast, halved
1 tsp. honey
1 tsp. tomato paste

1 tbsp. mustard
½ tsp. apple vinegar

Mix tomato paste, honey, mustard, and vinegar in a suitable bowl. Whisk well. Add duck breast pieces and coat well. Cook in your air fryer at 370 degrees F for 15 minutes on Air Fry mode. Remove the duck breast from the air fryer and add to the honey mixture, coat well. Cook again at 370 degrees F for 6 minutes more. Serve.
Nutritional information: Calories 274 g; Total Carbs 22g; Fat 11g; Protein 13g; Fat 22.4g; fibers: 3g; Sugars: 6g

Creamy Coconut Chicken

Prep time: 5 minutes | Cook time: 25 minutes | Serves: 4

4 big chicken legs
5 tsps. turmeric powder

2 tbsps. Ginger, smashed
salt and black pepper to taste

4 tbsps. coconut cream

In a suitable bowl, mix salt, pepper, ginger, turmeric and cream. Add chicken pieces, coat and marinate them for 2 hours. Transfer the chicken pieces to your preheated air fryer and Air Fry them at 370 degrees F for 25 minutes. Serve.
Nutritional information: Calories 300 g; Total Carbs 22g; Fat 4g; Protein 20g; Fat 22.4g; fibers: 3g; Sugars: 6g

Buffalo Chicken Tenders

Prep time: 5 minutes | Cook time: 20 minutes | Serves: 4

1 lb. boneless chicken tenders
¼ cup hot sauce
1 ½ oz. pork rinds, ground
1 tsp. chili powder
1 tsp. garlic powder

Put the chicken breasts in a suitable bowl and pour hot sauce over them. Toss to coat. Mix ground pork rinds, chili powder and garlic powder in another bowl. Place each tender in the ground pork rinds, and coat well. With wet hands, press down the pork rinds into the chicken. Place the tenders in a single layer into the air fryer basket. Air Fry the chicken tenders at 375 degrees F for 20 minutes, flipping halfway through. Serve.
Nutritional information: Calories 160 g; Total Carbs 0.6g; Fat 4.4g; Protein 27.3g; Fat 22.4g; fibers: 3g; Sugars: 6g

Teriyaki Wings

Prep time: 5 minutes | Cook time: 25 minutes | Serves: 4

2 lbs. chicken wings
½ cup teriyaki sauce
2 tsp. minced garlic
¼ tsp. ground ginger
2 tsps. baking powder

Except for the baking powder, place all the recipe ingredients in a suitable bowl and marinate for 1 hour in the refrigerator. Place the seasoned wings into the "Air Fryer Basket" and sprinkle with baking powder. Gently rub into wings. Air Fry the chicken wings at 400 degrees F for 25 minutes. Shake the basket 2 or 3-times during cooking. Serve.
Nutritional information: Calories 446 g; Total Carbs 3.1g; Fat 29.8g; Protein 41.8g; Fat 22.4g; fibers: 3g; Sugars: 6g

Lemon Chicken Drumsticks

Prep time: 5 minutes | Cook time: 25 minutes | Serves: 2

2 tsps. baking powder
½ tsp. garlic powder
8 chicken drumsticks
4 tbsps. salted butter melted
1 tbsp. lemon pepper seasoning

Sprinkle garlic powder and baking powder over drumsticks and rub into chicken skin. Place drumsticks into the air fryer basket. Air Fry the chicken drumsticks at 375 degrees F for 25 minutes. Flip the drumsticks once halfway through cooking. Mix seasoning and butter in a suitable bowl. When cooked, add drumsticks to the bowl and toss to coat. Serve.
Nutritional information: Calories 532 g; Total Carbs 1.2g; Fat 32.3g; Protein 48.3g; Fat 22.4g; fibers: 3g; Sugars: 6g

Parmesan Chicken Tenders

Prep time: 5 minutes | Cook time: 10 minutes | Serves: 4

1 lb. chicken tenderloins
3 large egg whites
½ cup Italian-style bread crumbs

¼ cup grated Parmesan cheese

Trim off any white, fat from the chicken tenderloins. In a suitable bowl, whisk the egg whites until frothy. In a separate small mixing bowl, combine the bread crumbs and Parmesan cheese. Mix well. Dip the chicken tenderloins into the prepared egg mixture, then into the Parmesan and bread crumbs. Shake off any excess breading. Place the chicken tenderloins in the greased "Air Fryer Basket" in a single layer. Generously Grease the chicken with olive oil to avoid powdery, uncooked breading. At 370 degrees F, preheat your Air Fryer. Air Fry the chicken tenderloins for 4 minutes. Using tongs, flip the chicken tenders and Air Fry for 4 minutes more. Check that the chicken has reached an internal temperature of 165 degrees F. Add Cook Time if needed. Once the chicken is fully cooked, plate, serve, and enjoy.
Nutritional information: Calories 210; Fat 4g; Net Carbs 1g; Total Carbs 10g; Protein 33g; Fiber: 1g; Sugar 1g

Simple Lemon Chicken Thighs

Prep time: 5 minutes | Cook time: 25 minutes | Serves: 4

Salt and black pepper to taste
2 tbsps. olive oil
2 tbsps. Italian seasoning
2 tbsps. freshly squeezed
lemon juice
1 lb. chicken thighs
1 lemon, sliced

Set the chicken thighs in a medium mixing bowl and season them with the black pepper and salt. Add the olive oil, Italian seasoning, and lemon juice and toss until the chicken thighs are coated with oil. Add the sliced lemons. Place the chicken thighs into the "Air Fryer Basket" in a single layer. At 350 degrees F, preheat your Air Fryer. Air Fry the food for 10 minutes. Using tongs, flip the chicken. Air Fry for 10 minutes more. Add Cook Time if needed. Once the chicken is fully cooked, plate, serve, and enjoy.
Nutritional information: Calories 325g; Total Carbs 1g; Fat 26g; Protein 20g; Fat 22.4g; fibers: 3g; Sugars: 6g

Air Fryer Chicken Breasts

Prep time: 5 minutes | Cook time: 14 minutes | Serves: 4

salt and black pepper to taste
1 tsp. dried parsley
½ tsp. garlic powder
2 tbsps. olive oil, divided
3 boneless, chicken breasts

In a suitable bowl, combine together the garlic powder, salt, pepper, and parsley. Rub each chicken breast with oil and seasonings. Place the prepared chicken breasts in the air fryer basket. At 370 degrees F, preheat your Air Fryer. Air Fry the chicken breasts for 14 minutes, flipping the chicken breasts halfway through and brushing the remaining olive oil and spices onto them. When cooked, the chicken breasts should reach an internal temperature of 165 degrees F. Transfer it to a platter and serve.
Nutritional information: Calories 182g; Total Carbs 0g; Fat 9g; Protein 26g; Fat 22.4g; fibers: 3g; Sugars: 6g

Crispy Air Fryer Butter Chicken

Prep time: 5 minutes | Cook time: 15 minutes | Serves: 4

2 (8-oz.) boneless, chicken breasts
1 sleeve Ritz crackers
4 tbsps. (½ stick) cold unsalted butter, cut into 1-tbsp. slices

Dip the chicken breasts in water. Put the crackers in a Ziploc bag. Using a mallet or your hands, crush the crackers. Place the chicken breasts inside the bag one at a time and coat them with the cracker crumbs. Place the chicken in the greased air fryer basket, or on the greased baking pan set into the air fryer basket. Put 1 to 2 tablespoons of butter onto each piece of chicken. At 370 degrees F, preheat your Air Fryer. Set the timer and Air Fry the chicken breasts for 14 minutes; after 7 minutes of cooking time, flip them and grease them generously with olive oil to avoid uncooked breading. When cooked, the chicken breasts should reach an internal temperature of 165 degrees F. Serve.

Nutritional information: Calories 750; Fat 40g; Total Carbs 38g; Protein 57g; Fat 22.4g; fibers: 3g; Sugars: 6g

Light and Airy Breaded Chicken Breasts

Prep time: 5 minutes | Cook time: 15 minutes | Serves: 2

2 large eggs
1 cup bread crumbs or panko bread crumbs
1 tsp. Italian seasoning

4 to 5 tbsp. vegetable oil
2 boneless, skinless, chicken breasts

At 370 degrees F, preheat your Air Fryer. In a suitable bowl, whisk the eggs until frothy. In a separate small mixing bowl, mix the bread crumbs, Italian seasoning, and oil. Dip the chicken in the prepared egg mixture, then in the bread crumb mixture. Place the chicken directly into the greased air fryer basket, or on the greased baking pan set into the basket. Grease the chicken generously and with olive oil to avoid powdery, uncooked breading. Air Fry the chicken breasts at 370 degrees F for 14 minutes; after 7 minutes of cooking time, flip the chicken breasts and generously spray them with the olive oil. When cooked, the chicken breasts should reach an internal temperature of 165 degrees F. Once the chicken is fully cooked, use tongs to remove it from the air fryer and serve.

Nutritional information: Calories 833; Fat 46g; Total Carbs 40g; Protein 65g; Fat 22.4g; fibers: 3g; Sugars: 6g

Chicken Fillets, Brie & Ham

Prep time: 5 minutes | Cook time: 15 minutes | Serves: 4

2 large chicken fillets
freshly ground black pepper
4 small slices of brie

1 tbsp. freshly chopped chives
4 slices cured ham

Slice the fillets into 4 and make incisions as you would for a hamburger bun. Leave a little "hinge" uncut at the back. Season the inside and pop some brie and chives in there. Close them, and wrap them each in a slice of ham. Brush with oil and pop them into the air fryer basket. At 350 degrees F, preheat your Air Fryer. Roast the food for 15 minutes until they look tasty. Serve and enjoy.

Nutritional information: Calories 850g; Total Carbs 43 g; Net Carbs 5g; Protein 76 g; Fat 22.4g; fibers: 3g; Sugars: 6g

Air Fryer Cornish Hen

Prep time: 5 minutes | Cook time: 30 minutes | Serves: 2

2 tbsp. Montreal chicken seasoning

1 (1½ to 2-lb.) Cornish hen

At 390 degrees F, preheat your Air Fryer. Rub the prepared seasoning over the chicken, coating it thoroughly. Put the chicken in the air fryer basket. Air Fry the chicken at 390 degrees F for 30 minutes, flipping halfway through. Add Cook

Time if needed. When done, the chicken should reach an internal temperature of 165 degrees F. Serve and enjoy.

Nutritional information: Calories 520; Fat 36g; Total Carbs 0g; Protein 45g; Fat 22.4g; fibers: 3g; Sugars: 6g

Air Fried Turkey Wings

Prep time: 5 minutes | Cook time: 26 minutes | Serves: 4

2 lbs. turkey wings
3 tbsps. olive oil or sesame oil

3 to 4 tbsps. chicken rub

Put the turkey wings in a large mixing bowl. Pour the olive oil into the bowl and add the rub. Using your hands, rub the oil mixture over the turkey wings. Place the prepared turkey wings in the air fryer basket. Air Fry the turkey wings at 380 degrees F for 26 minutes, flipping the wings halfway through. Serve and enjoy.

Nutritional information: Calories 521; Fat 34g; Total Carbs 4g; Protein 52g; Fat 22.4g; fibers: 3g; Sugars: 6g

Cheesy Chicken Tenders

Prep time: 10 minutes | Cook time: 30 minutes | Serves: 4

1 large white meat chicken breast
1 cup of breadcrumbs
2 medium-sized eggs

Pinch of black pepper and salt
1 tbsp. of grated or powdered parmesan cheese

Cover the Air Fryer Basket with a layer of tin foil, leaving the edges open to allow air to flow through the basket. At 350 degrees F, preheat your Air Fryer. In a suitable bowl, whisk the eggs until fluffy and until the yolks and whites are fully combined, and set aside. In a separate bowl, mixt he breadcrumbs, parmesan, black pepper and salt. Dip each piece chicken into the bowl with dry ingredients. Then submerge into the bowl with wet ingredients, then dip again into the dry ingredients. Put the coated chicken pieces on the foil covering the Air Fryer Basket, in a single flat layer. Air Fry the chicken pieces at 350 degrees F for 15 minutes. Flip each piece of chicken over to ensure a full all over fry. Reset the air fryer to 320 degrees and resume cooking on Air Fry mode for 15 minutes more. Remove the fried chicken strips using tongs and set on a serving plate. Eat once cool enough to handle, and enjoy.

Nutritional information: Calories 278; Fat 15g; Protein 29g; Sugar 7g; Fat 22.4g; fibers: 3g; Sugars: 6g

Bacon Lovers' Stuffed Chicken

Prep time: 10 minutes | Cook time: 20 minutes | Serves: 4

4 (5-oz.) boneless, chicken breasts, sliced into ¼ inch thick
2 packages Boursin cheese

8 slices thin-cut bacon or beef bacon
Sprig of fresh cilantro, for garnish

Grease the "Air Fryer Basket" with avocado oil. At 400 degrees F, preheat your Air Fryer. Put one of the chicken breasts on a cutting board. Make a 1-inch-wide cut at the top of the breast. Carefully cut into the breast to form a large pocket, leaving a ½-inch border along the sides and bottom. Repeat with the other 3 chicken breasts. Cut the corner of a large Ziploc bag to form a ¾-inch hole. Add Boursin cheese in the bag and pipe the cheese into the pockets in the chicken breasts, dividing the cheese evenly among them. Wrap 2 slices of bacon around each chicken breast and secure the ends with toothpicks. Place the bacon-wrapped chicken in the "Air Fryer Basket" and cook for 18 to 20 minutes, flipping after 10 minutes of cooking time. Garnish

with a sprig of cilantro before serving, if desired.
Nutritional information: Calories 446; Total Carbs 13g; Net Carbs 6g; Protein 36g; Fat 22.4g; fibers: 3g; Sugars: 6g

Air Fryer Turkey Breast

Prep time: 5 minutes | Cook time: 60 minutes | Serves: 6

Pepper and salt
1 oven-ready turkey breast

Turkey seasonings of choice

At 350 degrees F, preheat your Air Fryer. Season the turkey breast with pepper, salt, and other desired seasonings. Place turkey in Air Fryer Basket. Set the cooking temperature to 350 degrees F, and set time to 60 minutes. Cook the food for 60 minutes. The meat should be at 165 degrees when done. Allow to rest 10-15 minutes before slicing. Enjoy.
Nutritional information: Calories 212; Total Carbs 13g; Net Carbs 6g; Protein24g; Sugar 0g; Fat 22.4g; fibers: 3g; Sugars: 6g

Mustard Chicken Tenders

Prep time: 5 minutes | Cook time: 20 minutes | Serves: 4

½ cup coconut flour
1 tbsp. spicy brown mustard

2 beaten eggs
1 lb. of chicken tenders

Season tenders with pepper and salt. Place a thin layer of mustard onto tenders and then dredge in flour and dip in egg. Arrange the food to the Air Fryer Basket in air fryer and cook them at 390 degrees F for 20 minutes on Air Fry mode. When cooked, serve and enjoy.
Nutritional information: Calories 346; Fat 10g; Total Carbs 12g; Net Carbs 4g; Protein 31g; Fat 22.4g; fibers: 3g; Sugars: 6g

Homemade Breaded Nugget in Doritos

Prep time: 10 minutes | Cook time: 15 minutes | Serves: 4

½ lb. boneless, chicken breast
¼ lb. Doritos snack
1 cup of wheat flour

1 egg
Salt, garlic and black pepper to taste.

Cut the chicken breast in the width direction, 1 to 1.5 cm thick, so that it is already shaped like pips. Season with salt, garlic, black pepper to taste and some other seasonings if desired. You can also season with those seasonings or powdered onion soup. Put the Doritos snack in a food processor or blender and beat until everything is crumbled, but don't beat too much, you don't want flour. Now bread, passing the pieces of chicken breast first in the wheat flour, then in the beaten eggs and finally in the Doritos, without leaving the excess flour, eggs or Doritos. Place the food in the "Air Fryer Basket" and Air Fry them for 15 minutes at 400 degrees F, and half the time they brown evenly.
Nutritional information: Calories 42; Total Carbs 1.65g; Fat 1.44g; Net Carbs 2g; Protein 5.29g; Sugar 0.1g; Fiber: 2g

Breaded Chicken without Flour

Prep time: 10 minutes | Cook time: 30 minutes | Serves: 6

1 ⅙ oz. of grated parmesan cheese
1 unit of egg

1 lb. of chicken breast
Salt and black pepper to taste

Cut the chicken breast into 6 fillets and season with a little black

pepper and salt. Beat the egg in a suitable bowl. Pass the chicken breast in the egg and then in the grated cheese, sprinkling the fillets. Transfer the chicken breast slices to the Air Fryer Basket in air fryer and Air Fry them at 400 degrees F for 30 minutes or until golden brown, When cooked, serve warm.
Nutritional information: Calories 114; Total Carbs 13g; Fat 5.9g; Net Carbs 6g; Protein 2.3g; Sugar 3.2g; Fiber: 1g

Coxinha Fit

Prep time: 10 minutes | Cook time: 10-15 minutes | Serves: 4

½ lb. seasoned and minced chicken
1 cup light cottage cheese

1 egg
Condiments to taste
Flaxseed or oatmeal

In a suitable bowl, mix all the ingredients together except flour. Knead well with your hands and mold into coxinha format. If you prefer you can fill it, add chicken or cheese. Repeat the process until all the dough is gone. Pass the drumsticks in the flour and then transfer them to the air fryer. Air Fry them for 10 to 15 minutes at 390 degrees F or until golden. Serve and enjoy!
Nutritional information: Calories 220; Total Carbs 40g; Fat 18g; Net Carbs 6g; Protein 100g; Sugar 5g; Fiber:0g

Rolled Turkey Breast

Prep time: 5 minutes | Cook time: 10 minutes | Serves: 4

1 box of cherry tomatoes

¼ lb. turkey breast, sliced

Wrap the turkey in the tomatoes, close with the help of toothpicks. Air Fry the food in the air fryer for 10 minutes at 390 degrees F. You can increase the filling with ricotta and other preferred light ingredients.
Nutritional information: Calories 172; Total Carbs 3g; Fat 2g; Net Carbs 6g; Protein 34g; Sugar 1g; Fiber: 30g

Chicken in Beer

Prep time: 5 minutes | Cook time: 45 minutes | Serves: 4

2 ¼ lbs. chicken thighs
½ can of beer
4 cloves of garlic

1 large onion
Pepper and salt to taste

Wash the chicken thighs and, if desired, remove the skin to be healthier. Place the clean chicken thighs on an ovenproof plate. In the blender, add the beer, onion, garlic, and add black pepper and salt, mix all together. Cover the chicken thighs with this mixture; it has to stay like swimming in the beer. Cook the chicken thighs at 390 degrees F for 45 minutes under Roast mode. The thighs are done when they have a brown cone on top and the beer has dried a bit.
Nutritional information: Calories 674; Total Carbs 5.47g; Fat 41.94g; Net Carbs 4g; Protein 61.94g; Sugar 1.62g; Fiber: 20g

Chicken Fillet

Prep time: 5 minutes | Cook time: 20 minutes | Serves: 4

4 chicken fillets
salt to taste
1 garlic clove, crushed

thyme, to taste
black pepper, to taste

Add seasoning to fillets, wrapping well for flavor. At 350 degrees F, preheat your Air Fryer. Place the chicken fillets in the air fryer basket and cook them for 20 minutes at 350 degrees F on Air Fry mode. After 15 minutes of cooking time, turn the fillets and raise the temperature to 390 degrees F. Serve!

Nutritional information: Calories 90; Total Carbs1g; Fat 1g; Net Carbs 2g; Protein 17g; Sugar 0g; Fiber: 4g

Chicken with Lemon and Bahian Seasoning

Prep time: 2 hours | Cook time: 20 minutes | Serves: 4

5 pieces of chicken to bird;
2 garlic cloves, crushed;
4 tbsps. of lemon juice;

1 coffee spoon of Bahian spices;
salt and black pepper to taste.

Place the chicken pieces in a covered bowl and add the spices. Add the lemon juice. Cover the container and let the chicken marinate for 2 hours. Place each piece of chicken in the Air Fryer Basket, without overlapping the pieces. Air Fry the chicken pieces at 390 degrees F for 20 minutes, flipping halfway through cooking. Serve!

Nutritional information: Calories 316.2; Total Carbs 4.9g; Fat 15.3g; Net Carbs 6g; Protein 32.8g; Sugar 0g; Fiber: 4g

Chicken Meatballs

Prep time: 5 minutes | Cook time: 15 minutes | Serves: 2

½ lb. chicken breast
1 tbsp. of garlic
1 tbsp. of onion
½ chicken broth

1 tbsp. of oatmeal, whole wheat flour or of your choice
1 pinch of paprika
Salt and black pepper

Place all of the recipe ingredients in a food processor and beat well until well mixed and ground. Make balls from the mixture and place them in the Air Fryer Basket. Cook the food for 15 minutes at 400 degrees F on Air Fry mode. Shake the basket halfway through cooking so that the meatballs loosen and fry evenly. When done, serve and enjoy.

Nutritional information: Calories 45; Total Carbs 1.94g; Fat 1.57g; Net Carbs 6g; Protein 5.43g; Sugar 0.41g; Fiber: 23g

Basic BBQ Chicken

Prep time: 5 minutes | Cook time: 20 minutes | Serves: 4

2 tbsps. Worcestershire Sauce
1 tbsp. honey
¾ cup ketchup

2 tsps. chipotle chili powder
6 chicken drumsticks

At 370 degrees F, preheat your Air Fryer. In a big bowl, mix up the Worcestershire sauce, honey, ketchup and chili powder. Drop in the drumsticks and turn them so they are all coated with the prepared mixture. Grease the Air Fryer Basket with nonstick spray and then place 3 chicken drumsticks in. Air Fry the chicken drumsticks at 370 degrees F for 17 minutes for large drumsticks or 15 minutes for smaller ones, flipping when it reaches half the time. Repeat with the other 3 drumsticks. When done, serve and enjoy.

Nutritional information: Calories 145; Total Carbs 4.5g; Fat 2.6g; Net Carbs 5g; Protein 13g; fibers: 3g; Sugars: 6g

Classic No Frills Turkey Breast

Prep time: 5 minutes | Cook time: 50 minutes | Serves: 4

1 bone in turkey breast (about   8 lbs.)

2 tbsps. olive oil
2 tbsps. sea salt

1 tbsp. black pepper

At 360 degrees F, preheat your Air Fryer. Rub the washed turkey breast with the olive oil both on the skin and on the inside of the cavity. Add sea salt and black pepper on top. Spray the Air Fryer Basket with butter or olive oil flavored nonstick spray. Put the turkey in with the breast side down. Air Fry the turkey breast at 360 degrees F for 40 minutes; after 20 minutes of cooking, turn the food over and spray with the oil. When done, check with thermometer and it should read 165 degrees F. If not, put it back in for a few minutes. Let the breast rest at least 15 minutes before cutting and serving.

Nutritional information: Calories 375; Total Carbs 8.2g; Fat 6.8g; Net Carbs 5g; Protein 15g; fibers: 3g; Sugars: 6g

Faire-Worthy Turkey Legs

Prep time: 5 minutes | Cook time: 30 minutes | Serves: 4

1 turkey leg
1 tsp. garlic powder
1 tsp. olive oil

1 tsp. poultry seasoning
Salt and black pepper to taste

Coat the leg with the olive oil. Just use your hands and rub it in. In a suitable bowl, mix the poultry seasoning, garlic powder, black pepper and salt. Rub it on the turkey leg. Place the turkey leg in the air fryer basket. Air Fry the turkey leg at 350 degrees F for 27 minutes, flipping halfway through. When cooked, the turkey leg should have an internal temperature of 165 degrees F.

Nutritional information: Calories 325; Total Carbs 8.3g; Fat 10g; Net Carbs 6g; Protein 18g; fibers: 3g; Sugars: 6g

Herb Air Fried Chicken Thighs

Prep time: 30 minutes | Cook time: 20 minutes | Serves: 4

2 lbs. deboned chicken thighs
1 tsp. rosemary
1 tsp. thyme

1 tsp. garlic powder
1 large lemon
black and salt

Trim fat from thighs; season with the black pepper and salt all sides. In a suitable bowl, combine the rosemary, thyme, and garlic powder. Sprinkle over the chicken thighs and press the prepared mixture in putting them on a baking pan. Cut the lemon and squeeze the juice over all the chicken thighs. Cover with plastic wrap and put in the refrigerator for 30 minutes. At 360 degrees F, preheat your Air Fryer. Spray the Air Fryer Basket with butter flavored cooking spray. Place the prepared thighs in the Air Fryer Basket, as many will fit in one layer. Air Fry the food at 360 degrees F for 15 minutes, turning after 7 minutes. When cooked, serve and enjoy.

Nutritional information: Calories 534; Fat 27.8g; Total Carbs 2.5 g; Sugar 0.5 g; Net Carbs 6g; Protein 66.2 g; Fiber 2 g

Western Chicken Wings

Prep time: 10 minutes | Cook time: 15 minutes | Serves: 4

2 lbs. chicken wings
1 tsp. Herb de Provence
1 tsp. paprika

½ cup parmesan cheese, grated
Black pepper and salt

Add cheese, paprika, herb de Provence, pepper, and salt into the large mixing bowl. Place the chicken wings into the bowl and toss well to coat. At 350 degrees F, preheat your Air Fryer. Place the chicken wings into the air fryer basket. Spray top of chicken wings with some cooking spray. Air Fry the chicken wings at 350 degrees F for 15 minutes. Turn chicken wings halfway through cooking. Serve and enjoy.

Nutritional information: Calories 473; Fat 19.6g; Total Carbs 0.8 g; Sugar 0.1 g; Net Carbs 6g; Protein 69.7 g; Fiber 1 g

Perfect Chicken Thighs

Prep time: 10 minutes | Cook time: 15 minutes | Serves: 4

4 chicken thighs, bone-in & skinless	2 tsps. paprika
¼ tsp. ground ginger	2 tsps. garlic powder
	black pepper and salt

In a suitable bowl, mix ginger, paprika, garlic powder, pepper, and salt together and rub all over chicken thighs. Spray chicken thighs with some cooking spray. Place the prepared chicken thighs into the "Air Fryer Basket" and Air Fry them at 400 degrees F for 10 minutes. When the time is up, turn chicken thighs and Air Fry for 5 minutes more. Serve and enjoy.

Nutritional information: Calories 286; Fat 11g; Total Carbs 1.8 g; Sugar 0.5 g; Net Carbs 2g; Protein 42.7 g; Fiber 1 g

Perfectly Spiced Chicken Tenders

Prep time: 10 minutes | Cook time: 13 minutes | Serves: 4

6 chicken tenders	1 tsp. paprika
1 tsp. onion powder	1 tsp. kosher salt
1 tsp. garlic powder	

At 380 degrees F, preheat your Air Fryer. In a suitable bowl, mix onion powder, garlic powder, paprika and salt together and rub all over chicken tenders. Spray chicken tenders with some cooking spray. Place the prepared chicken tenders into the "Air Fryer Basket" and Air Fry them at 380 degrees F for 13 minutes. Serve and enjoy.

Nutritional information: Calories 423; Fat 16.4g; Total Carbs 1.5 g; Sugar 0.5 g; Net Carbs 6g; Protein 63.7 g; Fiber 1 g

Pretzel Crusted Chicken with Spicy Mustard Sauce

Prep time: 15 minutes | Cook time: 20 minutes | Serves: 6

2 eggs	1 tbsp. cornstarch
1 ½ lb. chicken breasts, boneless, diced	3 tbsps. Worcestershire sauce
½ cup crushed pretzels	3 tbsps. tomato paste
1 tsp. shallot powder	1 tbsp. apple cider vinegar
1 tsp. paprika	2 tbsps. olive oil
Salt and black pepper, to taste	2 garlic cloves, chopped
½ cup vegetable broth	1 jalapeno pepper, minced
	1 tsp. yellow mustard

At 390 degrees F, preheat your Air Fryer. In a mixing dish, whisk the eggs until frothy; toss the chicken chunks into the whisked eggs and coat well. In another dish, combine the crushed pretzels with shallot powder, paprika, black pepper and salt. Then, lay the chicken chunks in the pretzel mixture; turn it over until well coated. Place the chicken pieces in the Air Fryer Basket. Air Fry the chicken pieces at 390 degrees F for 12 minutes, shaking the basket halfway through. Meanwhile, whisk the vegetable broth with cornstarch, Worcestershire sauce, tomato paste, and apple cider vinegar. Preheat a cast-iron skillet over medium flame. Add the olive oil to heat and sauté the garlic with jalapeno pepper for 30 to 40 seconds, stirring frequently. Add the cornstarch mixture and let it simmer until the sauce has thickened a little. Now, add the air-fried chicken and mustard; let it simmer for 2 minutes more or until heated through. Serve immediately and enjoy!

Nutritional information: Calories 357; Fat 20.3g; Total Carbs 28.1g; Net Carbs 6g; Protein 2.8g; Sugars 1g; Fiber: 4g

Chinese-Style Sticky Turkey Thighs

Prep time: 20 minutes | Cook time: 35 minutes | Serves: 6

1 tbsp. sesame oil	6 tbsps. honey
2 lbs. turkey thighs	1 tbsp. Chinese rice vinegar
1 tsp. Chinese Five-spice powder	2 tbsps. soy sauce
1 tsp. pink Himalayan salt	1 tbsp. sweet chili sauce
¼ tsp. Sichuan pepper	1 tbsp. mustard

Brush the turkey thighs with sesame oil. Season them with spices. Air Fry the turkey thighs at 360 degrees F for 23 minutes, turning over once or twice. Make sure to work in batches to ensure even cooking In the meantime, combine the remaining ingredients in a wok (or similar type pan) that is preheated over medium-high heat. Cook and stir until the sauce reduces by about a third. Add the fried turkey thighs to the wok; gently stir to coat with the sauce. Let the turkey rest for 10 minutes before slicing and serving. Enjoy!

Nutritional information: Calories 279; Fat 19g; Total Carbs 27.7g; Net Carbs 6g; Protein 17.9g; Sugars 1g; Fiber: 4g

Easy Hot Chicken Drumsticks

Prep time: 40 minutes | Cook time: 40 minutes | Serves: 6

6 chicken drumsticks	3 tbsps. tamari sauce
Sauce:	1 tsp. dried thyme
6 oz. hot sauce	½ tsp. dried oregano
3 tbsps. olive oil	

Spray the Air Fryer Basket with the non-stick cooking spray and then arrange the chicken drumsticks to it. Air Fry the chicken drumsticks at 380 degrees F for 35 minutes, flipping them over halfway through. Meanwhile, heat the hot sauce, olive oil, tamari sauce, thyme, and oregano in a pan over medium-low heat; reserve. Drizzle the sauce over the prepared chicken drumsticks; toss to coat well and serve. Bon appétit!

Nutritional information: Calories 280; Fat 2.6g; Total Carbs 24.1g; Net Carbs 6g; Protein 1.4g; Sugars 1g; Fiber: 4g

Crunchy Chicken Tenders with Peanuts

Prep time: 25 minutes | Cook time: 20 minutes | Serves: 4

1 ½ lbs. chicken tenderloins	½ tsp. garlic powder
2 tbsps. peanut oil	1 tsp. red pepper flakes
½ cup tortilla chips, crushed	2 tbsps. peanuts, roasted and roughly chopped
Salt and black pepper, to taste	

At 360 degrees F, preheat your Air Fryer. Brush the chicken tenderloins with peanut oil on all sides. In a suitable mixing bowl, combine the crushed chips, salt, black pepper, garlic powder, and red pepper flakes. Dredge the chicken tenderloin pieces in the breading, shaking off any residual coating. Lay the chicken tenderloins into the Air Fryer Basket. Air Fry the chicken tenderloins at 360 degrees F for 12 to 13 minutes or until it is no longer pink in the center. Work in batches; an instant-read thermometer should read at least 165 degrees F. Serve garnished with roasted peanuts. Bon appétit!

Nutritional information: Calories 343; Fat 10.6g; Total Carbs 36.8g; Net Carbs 6g; Protein 1g; Sugar 2g; Fiber: 4g

Tarragon Turkey Tenderloins with Baby Potatoes

Prep time: 50 minutes | Cook time: 50 minutes | Serves: 6

2 lbs. turkey tenderloins
2 tsps. olive oil
Salt and ground black pepper, to taste
1 tsp. smoked paprika

2 tbsps. dry white wine
1 tbsp. fresh tarragon leaves, chopped
1-lb. baby potatoes, rubbed

Place the turkey tenderloins in a suitable cooking pan. Brush the turkey tenderloins with 1 teaspoon of olive oil. Season them with salt, black pepper, and paprika. Afterwards, add the white wine and tarragon leaves. Air Fry the turkey tenderloins at 350 degrees F for 30 minutes, flipping them over halfway through. Let them rest for 5 to 9 minutes before slicing and serving. After that, spritz the sides and bottom of the "Air Fryer Basket" with the remaining olive oil. Arrange the baby potatoes to the basket. Air Fry the potatoes at 400 degrees F for 15 minutes. When cooked, serve with the turkey and enjoy!
Nutritional information: Calories 317; Fat 14.2g; Total Carbs 45.7g; Net Carbs 6g; Protein 1.1g; Sugars 1g; Fiber: 4g

Mediterranean Chicken Breasts with Roasted Tomatoes

Prep time: 1 hour | Cook time: 35 minutes | Serves: 8

2 tsps. olive oil, melted
3 lbs. chicken breasts, bone-in
½ tsp. black pepper, freshly ground
½ tsp. salt
1 tsp. cayenne pepper

2 tbsps. fresh parsley, minced
1 tsp. fresh basil, minced
1 tsp. fresh rosemary, minced
4 medium-sized Roma tomatoes, halved

At 370 degrees F, preheat your Air Fryer. Brush the "Air Fryer Basket" with 1 teaspoon of olive oil and then arrange the chicken breasts to it. Sprinkle the chicken breasts with all seasonings listed above. Air Fry the chicken breasts at 370 degrees F for 25 minutes or until chicken breasts are slightly browned. Work in batches. Arrange the tomatoes in the "Air Fryer Basket" and brush them with the remaining olive oil. Season with sea salt. Air Fry the tomatoes at 350 degrees F for 10 minutes, shaking halfway through. Serve with chicken breasts. Bon appétit!
Nutritional information: Calories 315; Fat 2.7g; Total Carbs 36g; Net Carbs 8g; Protein 1.7g; Sugars 1g; Fiber: 4g

Thai Red Duck with Candy Onion

Prep time: 25 minutes | Cook time: 25 minutes | Serves: 4

1 ½ lbs. duck breasts, skin removed
1 tsp. kosher salt
½ tsp. cayenne pepper
⅓ tsp. black pepper

½ tsp. smoked paprika
1 tbsp. Thai red curry paste
1 cup candy onions, halved
¼ small pack coriander, chopped

Set the duck breasts between 2 sheets of foil; then, use a rolling pin to bash the duck until they are 1-inch thick. At 395 degrees F, preheat your Air Fryer. Rub the duck breasts with salt, cayenne pepper, black pepper, paprika, and red curry paste. Place the duck breasts in the Air Fryer Basket. Air Fry the duck breasts for 11 to 12 minutes. Top with candy onions and Air Fry for 10 to 11 minutes more. Serve garnished with coriander and enjoy!
Nutritional information: Calories 362; Fat 4g; Total Carbs 42.3g; Net Carbs 2g; Protein 1.3g; Sugars 2g; Fiber: 4g

Rustic Chicken Legs with Turnip Chips

Prep time: 30 minutes | Cook time: 30 minutes | Serves: 3

1-lb. chicken legs
1 tsp. Himalayan salt
1 tsp. paprika

½ tsp. ground black pepper
1 tsp. butter, melted
1 turnip, trimmed and sliced

Season the chicken legs with salt, paprika, and ground black pepper, then arrange them to the Air Fryer Basket. Air Fry the chicken legs at 370 degrees F for 10 minutes. When the time is up, drizzle turnip slices with melted butter and transfer them to the basket with the chicken. Air Fry the turnips and chicken at 380 degrees F for 15 minutes more, flipping them halfway through. As for the chicken, an instant-read thermometer should read at least 165 degrees F. Serve and enjoy!
Nutritional information: Calories 207; Fat 3.4g; Total Carbs 29.5g; Net Carbs 5g; Protein 1.6g; Sugars 1g; Fiber: 4g

Old-Fashioned Chicken Drumettes

Prep time: 30 minutes | Cook time: 22 minutes | Serves: 3

⅓ cup all-purpose flour
½ tsp. ground white pepper
1 tsp. seasoning salt
1 tsp. garlic paste
1 tsp. rosemary

1 whole egg + 1 egg white
6 chicken drumettes
1 heaping tbsp. fresh chives, chopped

At 390 degrees F, preheat your Air Fryer. Mix the flour with white pepper, salt, garlic paste, and rosemary in a small-sized bowl. In another suitable bowl, beat the egg and egg white until frothy. Dip the chicken into the flour mixture, then into the beaten eggs; coat with the flour mixture one more time. Air Fry the chicken drumettes at 390 degrees F for 22 minutes. Garnish with chives and serve warm.
Nutritional information: Calories 347; Fat 11.3g; Total Carbs 41g; Net Carbs 6g; Protein 0.1g; Sugars 1g; fibers 1g

Easy Ritzy Chicken Nuggets

Prep time: 20 minutes | Cook time: 8-9 minutes | Serves: 4

1 ½ lbs. chicken tenderloins, cut into small pieces
½ tsp. garlic salt
½ tsp. cayenne pepper
¼ tsp. black pepper, freshly cracked

4 tbsps. olive oil
⅓ cup saltines (e.g., Ritz crackers), crushed
4 tbsps. Parmesan cheese, freshly grated

At 390 degrees F, preheat your Air Fryer. Season the chicken pieces with garlic salt, cayenne pepper, and black pepper. In a suitable mixing bowl, combine the olive oil with crushed saltines. Dip each chicken piece in the cracker mixture. Finally, roll the chicken pieces over the Parmesan cheese. Air Fry the food for 8 minutes, working in batches. If you want to warm the chicken nuggets, add them to the basket and Air Fry them for 1 minute more. Serve with French fries, if desired.
Nutritional information: Calories 355; Fat; 5.3g; Total Carbs; 36.6g; Net Carbs 6g; Protein; 0.2g; Sugars 1g; fibers 1g

Asian Chicken Filets with Cheese

Prep time: 50 minutes | Cook time: 20 minutes | Serves: 2

4 rashers smoked bacon

2 chicken filets

½ tsp. coarse sea salt
¼ tsp. black pepper, preferably freshly ground
1 tsp. garlic, minced
1 (2-inch) piece ginger, peeled and minced

1 tsp. black mustard seeds
1 tsp. mild curry powder
½ cup coconut milk
⅓ cup tortilla chips, crushed
½ cup Pecorino Romano cheese, grated

At 400 degrees F, preheat your Air Fryer. Add the smoked bacon and cook in your preheated air fryer for 5 to 7 minutes on Air Fry mode. Reserve. In a suitable mixing bowl, place the chicken fillets, salt, black pepper, garlic, ginger, mustard seeds, curry powder, and milk. Let the chicken fillets marinate in your refrigerator about 30 minutes. In another bowl, mix the crushed chips and grated Pecorino Romano cheese. Dredge the chicken fillets through the chips mixture and transfer them to the Air Fryer Basket. Air Fry the chicken fillets at 380 degrees F for 12 minutes, turning them over halfway through. Repeat the same until you have run out of ingredients. Serve with reserved bacon. Enjoy!

Nutritional information: Calories 376; Fat 12.1g; Total Carbs 36.2g; Net Carbs 4g; Protein 3.4g; Sugars 1g; fibers 1g

Paprika Chicken Legs with Brussels Sprouts

Prep time: 30 minutes | Cook time: 35 minutes | Serves: 2

2 chicken legs
½ tsp. paprika
½ tsp. kosher salt

½ tsp. black pepper
1-lb. Brussels sprouts
1 tsp. dill, fresh or dried

At 370 degrees F, preheat your Air Fryer. Now, season your chicken with paprika, salt, and pepper. Transfer the prepared chicken legs to the Air Fryer Basket. Air Fry them for 20 minutes, flipping the chicken legs halfway through. Reserve. Add the Brussels sprouts to the Air Fryer Basket; sprinkle with dill. Air Fry the food at 380 degrees F for 15 minutes, shaking the basket halfway through. Serve with the reserved chicken legs. Bon appétit!

Nutritional information: Calories 355; Fat 5.3g; Total Carbs 36.6g; Net Carbs 6g; Protein 0.2g; Sugars 1g; fibers 1g

Chinese Duck

Prep time: 30 minutes | Cook time: 20 minutes | Serves: 6

2 lbs. duck breast, boneless
2 green onions, chopped
1 tbsp. light soy sauce
1 tsp. Chinese 5-spice powder
1 tsp. Szechuan peppercorns
3 tbsps. Shaoxing rice wine

1 tsp. coarse salt
½ tsp. ground black pepper
Glaze:
¼ cup molasses
3 tbsps. orange juice
1 tbsp. soy sauce

In a ceramic bowl, place the duck breasts, green onions, light soy sauce, Chinese 5-spice powder, Szechuan peppercorns, and Shaoxing rice wine. Marinate the duck breasts for 1 hour in your refrigerator. Discard the marinade and season the duck breasts with black pepper and salt. Transfer them to the Air Fryer Basket. Air Fry the duck breasts at 400 degrees F for 12 to 15 minutes or until they are golden brown. Repeat with the other ingredients. In the meantime, add the reserved marinade to the saucepan that is preheated over medium-high heat. Add the molasses, orange juice, and 1 tablespoon of soy sauce. Bring to a simmer and then, whisk constantly until it gets syrupy. Brush the surface of duck breasts with glaze so they are completely covered. Place duck breasts back in the basket and cook an additional 5 minutes. Enjoy!

Nutritional information: Calories: 201; Fat: 9g; Total Carbs 2.9g; Net Carbs 2g; Protein: 26.1g; Fiber: 0.1g; Sugar: 0.2g

Turkey Bacon with Scrambled Eggs

Prep time: 25 minutes | Cook time: 25 minutes | Serves: 4

½-lb. turkey bacon
4 eggs
⅓ cup milk
2 tbsps. yogurt

½ tsp. sea salt
1 bell pepper, chopped
2 green onions, chopped
½ cup Colby cheese, shredded

Place ½ pound of turkey bacon in the Air Fryer Basket. Air Fry them at 360 degrees F for 9 to 11 minutes. Work in batches. Reserve the fried bacon. In a suitable mixing bowl, whisk the eggs with milk and yogurt. Add salt, bell pepper, and green onions. Brush the sides and bottom of the baking pan with the reserved 1 teaspoon of bacon grease. Pour the prepared egg mixture into the baking pan. Air Fry the mixture at 355 degrees F about 5 minutes. Top with shredded Colby cheese and then Air Fry for 5 to 6 minutes more. Serve the scrambled eggs with the reserved bacon and enjoy!

Nutritional information: Calories: 160; Fat: 7.9g; Total Carbs 2.7g; Net Carbs 3g; Protein: 19.1g; Fiber: 0g; Sugar: 0g

Italian Chicken and Cheese Frittata

Prep time: 25 minutes | Cook time: 25 minutes | Serves: 4

1 (1-lb.) fillet chicken breast
Salt and black pepper, to taste
1 tbsp. olive oil
4 eggs

½ tsp. cayenne pepper
½ cup Mascarpone cream
¼ cup Asiago cheese, grated

Flatten the chicken breast with a meat mallet. Season with black pepper and salt. Heat the olive oil in a suitable frying pan over medium heat. Add the chicken breast and cook for 10 to 12 minutes; when cooked, slice into small strips and reserve. Then, in a suitable mixing bowl, combine the eggs, and cayenne pepper; season with salt to taste. Add the cheese and stir to combine. Add the reserved chicken. Then, pour the prepared mixture into a lightly greased pan. Put this pan into the Air Fryer Basket. Air Fry the food at 355 degrees F for 10 minutes, flipping over halfway through.

Nutritional information: Calories 329; Total Carbs 21.1g; Net Carbs 1g; Protein 2.3g; Fat 3.4g; Sugars 1g; fibers 1g

Parmigiana Chicken

Prep time: 3 minutes | Cook time: 12 minutes | Serves: 4

2 eggs
½ cup Parmesan cheese, grated
1 cup seasoned bread crumbs
1-lb. chicken breast halves

2 sprigs rosemary, chopped
Salt and ground black pepper, to taste

At 380 degrees F, preheat your Air Fryer. Spritz the "Air Fryer Basket" with some cooking spray. Beat the egg in the first bowl and sprinkle with salt and black pepper. Combine the Parmesan and bread crumbs in the second bowl. Dredge the chicken in the first bowl to coat well, then in the second the bowl. Shake the excess off. Air Fry the chicken breasts at 380 degrees F for 12 minutes or until the internal temperature reaches at least 165 degrees F. Flip the chicken halfway through. Transfer the chicken to a plate and serve with rosemary on top.

Nutritional information: Calories 430 Fat 25.0g; Total Carbs 21.5g; Net Carbs 6g; Protein 48.0g Sugars 1g; fibers 1g

Easy Paprika Chicken

Prep time: 7 minutes | Cook time: 18 minutes | Serves: 4

4 chicken breasts
1 tbsp. paprika
¼ tsp. garlic powder
2 tbsps. fresh thyme, chopped

Salt and ground black pepper, to taste
2 tbsps. butter, melted

At 360 degrees F, preheat your Air Fryer. Spritz the "Air Fryer Basket" with some cooking spray. On a clean work surface, rub the chicken breasts with paprika, garlic powder, salt, and black pepper, then brush with butter. Transfer the chicken breasts to the sprayed basket. Air Fry the chicken breasts at 360 degrees F for 18 minutes or until the internal temperature reaches at least 165 degrees F. Flip the chicken with tongs halfway through. Serve the cooked chicken on a plate immediately with thyme on top.

Nutritional information: Calories 368 Fat 14.1g; Total Carbs 2.3g; Net Carbs 6g; Protein 57.9g Sugars 1g; fibers 1g

Spinach and Cheese Stuffed Chicken Breasts

Prep time: 3 minutes | Cook time: 12 minutes | Serves: 4

1 cup spinach, chopped
4 tbsp. cottage cheese
2 chicken breasts

2 tbsp. Italian seasoning
Juice of ½ lime

At 390 degrees F, preheat your Air Fryer. Spritz the "Air Fryer Basket" with some cooking spray. Combine the chopped spinach and cheese in a suitable bowl. Set aside. Butterfly the chicken breasts and flatten with a rolling pin. Sprinkle with Italian seasoning, then wrap the spinach and cheese mixture in the butterflied chicken breasts. Secure with toothpicks. Place the prepared chicken breasts in your "Air Fryer Basket" and spritz with some cooking spray. Air Fry the chicken breasts at 390 degrees F for 12 minutes or until the internal temperature reaches at least 165 degrees F. Flip the chicken halfway through. Remove the chicken from the air fryer basket. Discard the toothpicks and serve drizzled with lemon juice.

Nutritional information: Calories 248 Fat 11.0g; Total Carbs 4.1g; Net Carbs 6g; Protein 31.0g; Sugars 1g; fibers 1g

Texas Thighs

Prep time: 10 minutes | Cook time: 20 minutes | Serves: 8

8 chicken thighs
2 tsps. Texas BBQ Jerky seasoning
2 tbsps. cilantro, chopped

1 tbsp. olive oil
Salt and ground black pepper, to taste

At 380 degrees F, preheat your air fryer. Arrange the chicken thighs in the Air Fryer Basket, then brush with olive oil on all sides. Sprinkle with BBQ seasoning, salt, and black pepper. Air Fry the chicken thighs at 380 degrees F for 20 minutes or until the internal temperature of the thighs reaches at least 165 degrees F. Flip the thighs 3 times during the Cook Time. Serve with cilantro on top.

Nutritional information: Calories 444 Fat 33.8g; Total Carbs 1.0g; Net Carbs 2g; Protein 31.9g; Sugars 1g; fibers 1g

Chicken Wings with Sweet Chili Sauce

Prep time: 6 minutes | Cook time: 14 minutes | Serves: 4

1-lb. chicken wings
1 tsp. garlic powder
1 tbsp. tamarind powder

¼ cup sweet chili sauce
Salt and ground black pepper, to taste

At 390 degrees F, preheat your air fryer. Spritz the air fryer with some cooking spray. Rub the chicken wings with garlic powder, tamarind powder, salt, and black pepper. Place the wings in the basket and Air Fry them at 390 degrees F for 6 minutes, then spread the chili sauce on top and Air Fry for an additional 8 minutes or until the internal temperature of the wings reaches at least 165 degrees F. Remove the wings from the air fryer. Allow to cool for a few minutes and serve.

Nutritional information: Calories 165 Fat 4.1g; Total Carbs 4.5g; Net Carbs 5g; Protein 25.5g; Sugars 1g; fibers 1g

Crunchy Golden Nuggets

Prep time: 5 minutes | Cook time: 10 minutes | Serves: 4

2 chicken breasts, cut into nuggets
4 tbsps. sour cream
½ cup bread crumbs

½ tbsp. garlic powder
½ tsp. cayenne pepper
Salt and ground black pepper, to taste

At 360 degrees F, preheat your air fryer. Spritz the "Air Fryer Basket" with some cooking spray. Put the sour cream in a suitable bowl. Combine the bread crumbs, cayenne pepper, garlic powder, salt, and black pepper on a large plate. Dredge the chicken nuggets in the bowl of sour cream, shake the excess off, then roll the nuggets through the bread crumbs mixture to coat well. Place the prepared nuggets in the "Air Fryer Basket" and Air Fry them at 360 degrees F for 10 minutes or until the chicken nuggets are golden brown and crispy. Flip the nuggets halfway through. Remove the nuggets from the basket and serve warm.

Nutritional information: Calories 324 Fat 15.5g; Total Carbs 11.7g; Net Carbs 5g; Protein 32.7g; Sugars 1g; fibers 1g

Buttered Roasted Whole Chicken

Prep time: 10 minutes | Cook time: 40 minutes | Serves: 4

1 (3-lb. / 1.4-kg) chicken, rinsed and patted dry
1 garlic bulb
1 sprig fresh tarragon

1 lemon, cut into wedges
2 tbsps. butter, melted
Salt and ground black pepper, to taste

At 380 degrees F, preheat your Air Fryer. Spritz the "Air Fryer Basket" with some cooking spray. On a clean work surface, brush the chicken with butter and rub with salt and black pepper. Stuff the chicken with garlic, tarragon, and lemon wedges. Arrange the chicken in the "Air Fryer Basket" and Air Fry the chicken at 380 degrees F for 40 minutes or until an instant-read thermometer inserted in the thickest part of the chicken registers at least 165 degrees F. Remove the chicken from the basket and put on a large platter. Carve the chicken and slice to serve.

Nutritional information: Calories 440 Fat 15.0g; Total Carbs 2.6g; Net Carbs 6g; Protein 69.7g; Sugars 1g; fibers 1g

Cheesy Chicken Thighs with Marinara Sauce

Prep time: 10 minutes | Cook time: 10 minutes | Serves: 4

2 tbsps. grated Parmesan cheese
½ cup Italian bread crumbs
4 chicken thighs

½ cup shredded Monterrey Jack cheese
½ cup marinara sauce
1 tbsp. butter, melted

At 380 degrees F, preheat your Air Fryer. Spritz the suitable cooking pan with some cooking spray. Combine the Parmesan and bread crumbs in a suitable bowl. On a clean work surface, brush the chicken thighs with butter, then dredge the thighs in the Parmesan mixture to coat. Place the chicken thighs in the sprayed pan. Air Fry the chicken thighs at 380 degrees F for 5 minutes. Then spread the Monterrey Jack cheese over and pour the marinara sauce on the thighs, and then Air Fry for 4 more minutes until the thighs are golden brown and the cheese melts. Transfer the thighs onto a plate and serve warm.
Nutritional information: Calories 617 Fat 42.1g; Total Carbs 17.7g; Net Carbs 6g; Protein 39.6g; Sugars 1g; fibers 1g

Chicken in Bacon Wrap

Prep time: 5 minutes | Cook time: 15 minutes | Serves: 4

2 chicken breasts
8 oz. onion and chive cream cheese
6 slices turkey bacon

1 tbsp. fresh parsley, chopped
Juice from ½ lemon
1 tbsp. butter
Salt, to taste

At 390 degrees F, preheat your Air Fryer. Spritz the "Air Fryer Basket" with some cooking spray. On a clean work surface, brush the chicken breasts with cream cheese and butter on both sides. Sprinkle with salt. Wrap each chicken breast with 3 slices of bacon and secure with 1 or 2 toothpicks. Arrange the bacon-wrapped chicken to the Air Fryer Basket and Air Fry them 390 degrees F for 14 minutes. Flip them halfway through the Cook Time. Serve with parsley and lemon juice on top.
Nutritional information: Calories 437 Fat 28.6g; Total Carbs 5.2g; Net Carbs 6g; Protein 39.8g; Sugars 1g; fibers 1g

Chicken Thighs with Honey-Dijon Sauce

Prep time: 5 minutes | Cook time: 20 minutes | Serves: 4

8 bone-in and chicken thighs
Chicken seasoning or rub, to taste
½ cup honey

¼ cup Dijon mustard
2 garlic cloves, minced
Salt and ground black pepper, to taste

At 400 degrees F, preheat your Air Fryer. Rub the chicken thighs with chicken seasoning, salt, and black pepper. Transfer the chicken thighs to the Air Fryer Basket Air Fry the chicken thighs at 400 degrees F for 15 minutes, flipping them halfway through. While cooking, combine the honey, Dijon mustard, and garlic in a saucepan, and cook over medium-high heat for 3 to 4 minutes until the sauce reduced by one third. Keep stirring during the cooking. Baste the thighs with the cooked sauce and serve warm.
Nutritional information: Calories 382 Fat 18.0g; Total Carbs 36.0g; Net Carbs 4g; Protein 21.0g; Sugars 1g; fibers 1g

Lemon and Honey Glazed Game Hen

Prep time: 10 minutes | Cook time: 20 minutes | Serves: 2

1 (2-lb.) Cornish game hen, split in half
¼ tsp. dried thyme
Juice and zest of 1 lemon
¼ cup honey
1½ tsps. chopped fresh thyme

leaves
1 tbsp. olive oil
Salt and ground black pepper, to taste
½ tsp. soy sauce

At 390 degrees F, preheat your Air Fryer. Spritz the "Air Fryer Basket" with some cooking spray. On a clean work surface, brush the game hen halves with olive oil, then sprinkle with dried thyme, salt, and black pepper to season. Air Fry the hen at 390 degrees F for 15 minutes or until the hen is lightly browned, flipping halfway through. While cooking, mix the lemon juice and zest, honey, thyme leaves, soy sauce, and black pepper in a suitable bowl. Baste the game hen with the honey glaze, then Air Fry it for an additional 4 minutes or until the hen is well glazed and a meat thermometer inserted in the hen reads at least 165 degrees F. Remove the game hen from the basket. Allow to cool for a few minutes and slice to serve.
Nutritional information: Calories 724 Fat 22.0g; Total Carbs 37.5g; Net Carbs 6g; Protein 91.3g; Sugars 1g; fibers 1g

Cheesy Spinach Stuffed Chicken Breasts

Prep time: 20 minutes | Cook time: 15 minutes | Serves: 4

1 (10-oz. / 284-g) package frozen spinach, thawed and drained well
1 cup feta cheese, crumbled

4 boneless chicken breasts
Salt and ground black pepper, to taste

At 380 degrees F, preheat your Air Fryer. Spritz the "Air Fryer Basket" with some cooking spray. Make the filling: Chop the spinach and put in a suitable bowl, then add the feta cheese and ½ tsp. of ground black pepper. Stir to mix well. On a clean work surface, using a knife, cut a 1-inch incision into the thicker side of each chicken breast horizontally. Make a 3-inch long pocket from the incision and keep the sides and bottom intact. Stuff the chicken pockets with the filling and secure with 1 or 2 toothpicks. Arrange the stuffed chicken breasts to the sprayed basket. Sprinkle with salt and black pepper and spritz with some cooking spray. Air Fry the food at 380 degrees F for 12 minutes or until the internal temperature of the chicken reads at least 165 degrees F. Flip the chicken halfway through the Cook Time. Discard the toothpicks and allow to cool for 10 minutes before slicing to serve.
Nutritional information: Calories 648 Fat 38.7g; Total Carbs 4.5g; Net Carbs 2g; Protein 68.2g; Sugars 1g; fibers 1g

Turkey and Pepper Sandwich

Prep time: 5 minutes | Cook time: 5 minutes | Serves: 1

2 slices whole grain bread
2 tsps. Dijon mustard
2 oz. cooked turkey breast, thinly sliced

2 slices low-fat Swiss cheese
3 strips roasted red bell pepper
Salt and ground black pepper, to taste

At 330 degrees F, preheat your Air Fry. Spritz the "Air Fryer Basket" with some cooking spray. On a dish, place a slice of bread, then top the bread with 1 tsp. of Dijon mustard, use a knife to smear the mustard evenly. Layer the turkey slices, Swiss cheese slices, and red pepper strips on the bread. Top them with remaining tsp. of Dijon mustard and remaining bread slice. Place the sandwich in the sprayed basket and spritz with some cooking spray. Sprinkle with salt and black pepper. Air Fry the food at 330 degrees F for 5 minutes until the cheese melts and the bread is lightly browned, flipping halfway through cooking. Serve the sandwich immediately.

Nutritional information: Calories 328 Fat 5.0g; Total Carbs 38.0g; Net Carbs 8g; Protein 29.0g; Sugars 1g; fibers 1g

Spicy Turkey Breast

Prep time: 5 minutes | Cook time: 40 minutes | Serves: 4

2-lb. turkey breast	1 tsp. red pepper flakes
2 tsps. taco seasonings	Salt and ground black pepper,
1 tsp. ground cumin	to taste

At 350 degrees F, preheat your Air Fryer. Spritz the "Air Fryer Basket" with some cooking spray. On a clean work surface, rub the turkey breast with taco seasoning, ground cumin, red pepper flakes, salt, and black pepper. Arrange the turkey breast to the sprayed basket and Air Fry them at 350 degrees F for 40 minutes or until the internal temperature of the turkey reads at least 165 degrees F. Flip the turkey breast halfway through the Cook Time. Allow to cool for 15 minutes before slicing to serve.

Nutritional information: Calories 235 Fat 5.6g; Total Carbs 6.6g; Net Carbs 6g; Protein 37.3g; Sugars 1g; fibers 1g

Chicken, Mushroom, and Pepper Kabobs

Prep time: 1 hour 5 minutes | Cook time: 15-20 minutes | Serves: 4

⅓ cup raw honey	3 green or red bell peppers,
2 tbsp. sesame seeds	diced
2 boneless chicken breasts, cut into cubes	⅓ cup soy sauce
6 white mushrooms, cut in halves	Salt and ground black pepper, to taste

Combine the honey, soy sauce, sesame seeds, salt, and black pepper in a suitable bowl. Stir to mix well. Dunk the chicken cubes in this bowl, then wrap the bowl in plastic and refrigerate to marinate for at least an hour. At 390 degrees F, preheat your Air Fryer. Spritz the "Air Fryer Basket" with some cooking spray. Remove the chicken cubes from the marinade, then run the skewers through the chicken cubes, mushrooms, and bell peppers alternatively. Baste the chicken, mushrooms, and bell peppers with the marinade, then arrange them in the sprayed basket. Spritz them with some cooking spray and Air Fry them at 390 degrees F for 15 to 20 minutes or until the mushrooms and bell peppers are tender and the chicken cubes are well browned. Flip them halfway through the Cook Time. Transfer the skewers to a large plate and serve hot.

Nutritional information: Calories 380 Fat 16.0g; Total Carbs 26.1g; Net Carbs 6g; Protein 34.0g; Sugars 1g; fibers 1g

Chicken & Zucchini

Prep time: 30 minutes | Cook time: 20 minutes | Serves: 6

¼ cup olive oil	into cubes
1 tbsp. lemon juice	1 zucchini, sliced
2 tbsps. red wine vinegar	1 red onion, sliced
1 tsp. oregano	1 cup cherry tomatoes, sliced
1 tbsp. garlic, chopped	Black pepper and salt to taste
2 chicken breast fillet, sliced	

In a suitable bowl, mix the olive oil, lemon juice, vinegar, oregano and garlic. Pour half of mixture into another bowl. Toss chicken in half of the prepared mixture. Cover and marinate for 15 minutes. Toss the vegies in the remaining mixture. Season both chicken and vegies with black pepper and salt. Add chicken to the Air Fryer Basket. Spread vegies on top. Air Fry the food at 380 degrees F for 15 to 20 minutes.

Nutritional information: Calories 527; Total Carbs 37.2; Net Carbs 4g; Protein 16g; Fat 34.4g; fibers: 3g; Sugars: 6g

Buffalo Chicken Wings

Prep time: 15 minutes | Cook time: 30 minutes | Serves: 4

2 lbs. chicken wings	½ cup Buffalo sauce
2 tbsps. oil	

Coat the chicken wings with oil. Transfer the wings to the Air Fryer Basket. Air Fry the wings at 390 degrees F for 30 minutes, shaking the basket halfway through. Dip in Buffalo sauce before serving.

Nutritional information: Calories 281; Fat: 17.1g; Total Carbs 3.6g; Net Carbs 1.2g; Protein: 27.8g; Fiber: 0.3g; Sugar: 0.2g

Mustard Chicken

Prep time: 20 minutes | Cook time: 50 minutes | Serves: 4

¼ cup Dijon mustard	1 tbsp. dry oregano
¼ cup cooking oil	2 tsps. dry Italian seasoning
Black pepper and salt to taste	1 tbsp. lemon juice
2 tbsps. honey	6 chicken pieces

Combine all the recipe ingredients except chicken in a suitable bowl. Mix well. Toss the chicken pieces in the prepared mixture. Transfer the chicken pieces to the Air Fryer Basket and cook them at 350 degrees F for 30 minutes on Roast mode. When the time is up, turn the pieces over and cook them 15 to 20 minutes more. When done, serve and enjoy.

Nutritional information: Calories 243; Fat: 8.5g; Total Carbs 8.2g; Net Carbs 2g; Protein: 29g; Fiber: 2.1g; Sugar: 0.4g

Honey & Rosemary Chicken

Prep time: 15 minutes | Cook time: 35 minutes | Serves: 6

1 tsp. paprika	¼ cup honey
Salt to taste	1 tbsp. lemon juice
½ tsp. baking powder	1 tbsp. garlic, minced
2 lb. chicken wings	1 tbsp. rosemary, chopped

Mix the paprika, salt and baking powder in a suitable bowl. Add the chicken wings and rub them with them mixture. Add the chicken wings to the air fryer basket and Air Fry them at 390 degrees F for 30 minutes, flipping the wings halfway through. In a suitable bowl, mix the remaining ingredients. Coat the wings with the sauce and Air Fry them for 5 minutes more.

Nutritional information: Calories 225; Fat: 8.2g; Total Carbs 8g; Net Carbs 2g; Protein: 27.5g; Fiber: 1.3g; Sugar: 2.3g

Flavorful Chicken with Bacon

Prep time: 8-10 minutes | Cook time: 25 minutes | Serves: 4

4 medium-sized skin-on chicken drumsticks	Provence
1 ½ teaspoons herbs de	1 tablespoon rice vinegar
	2 tablespoons olive oil

Salt and pepper as needed
2 garlic cloves, crushed
12 ounces crushed canned tomatoes

1 leek, thinly sliced
2 slices smoked bacon, chopped

Mix thoroughly the herbs de Provence, salt, chicken, and pepper in a medium sized bowl. Then add rice vinegar and olive oil inside and mix to toss well. On a flat kitchen surface, plug your air fryer and turn it on. Before cooking, heat your air fryer to 360 degrees F for about 4 to 5 minutes. Gently coat an air fryer basket with cooking oil or spray. Then add the chicken mixture inside. Insert the basket inside your air fryer and cook for 10 minutes. When cooked, remove the basket from the air fryer and then add the remaining ingredients inside. Stir well. Cook in the air fryer for 15 more minutes. Serve the chicken warm with lemon wedges or steamed rice.

Nutritional information: Calories: 303; Fat: 19.2g; Total Carbs: 6g; Net Carbs: 2.5g; Fiber: 1.4g; Sugars: 0.9g; Protein: 24.2g

Tasty Pasta Chicken

Prep time: 8-10 minutes | Cook time: 15 minutes | Serves: 4

¼ cup green onions, chopped
1 green garlic, minced
4 tablespoons seasoned breadcrumbs
½ teaspoon cumin powder
1 cup chicken meat, ground

1 sweet red pepper, minced
¼ teaspoon mixed peppercorns, ground
1 package penne pasta, cooked
1 tablespoon coriander, minced
½ teaspoon sea salt

Mix thoroughly red pepper, garlic, green onions, and the chicken in a medium sized bowl. Mix in seasonings and the breadcrumbs until well combined. Make small balls out from the mixture. On a flat kitchen surface, plug your air fryer and turn it on. Before cooking, heat your air fryer to 350 degrees F for about 4 to 5 minutes. Gently coat an air fryer basket with cooking oil or spray. Arrange the balls to the greased basket. When cooked, remove the balls from the air fryer and serve warm with cooked pasta as you like.

Nutritional information: Calories: 457; Fat: 6g; Total Carbs: 74g; Net Carbs: 41g; Fiber: 0.7g; Sugars: 1.7g; Protein: 25.4g

Turkey Sausage with Veggies

Prep time: 10 minutes | Cook time: 15 minutes | Serves: 2

4 turkey sausages
½ pound Brussels sprouts, trimmed and halved
1 teaspoon olive oil
Sea salt and ground black

pepper, to taste
½ teaspoon cayenne pepper
½ teaspoon shallot powder
¼ teaspoon dried dill weed

Arrange the turkey sausage in the air fryer basket. Mix the Brussels sprouts, spices, and olive oil together in a mixing dish and toss well. Spread the Brussels sprouts around the sausages. Cook in your air fryer at 380 degrees F for 15 minutes. Halfway through cooking, shake the basket. Enjoy!

Nutritional information: Calories: 159; Fat: 10.2g; Total Carbs: 10.6g; Net Carbs: 0g; Fiber: 4.4g; Sugars: 2.5g; Protein: 9g

Honey Turkey Tenderloin

Prep time: 10-15 minutes | Cook time: 55 minutes | Serves: 4

1 tablespoon honey
¼ cup vermouth
2 tablespoons lemon juice
1 teaspoon marjoram

1 teaspoon oregano, dried
1 turkey tenderloin, quartered
1 tablespoon sesame oil
Sea salt flakes as needed

¾ teaspoon smoked paprika
1 teaspoon crushed sage

leaves, dried
½ teaspoon ground pepper

To marinate, combine honey, vermouth, lemon juice, marjoram, and oregano together in a zip-lock bag. Seal and marinate at room temperature for 3 hours. On a flat kitchen surface, plug your air fryer and turn it on. Before cooking, heat your air fryer to 355 degrees F for 4 to 5 minutes. Gently coat the air fryer basket with cooking oil or spray. Place the turkey tenderloin inside the air fryer basket. Cook in your air fryer for 50 to 55 minutes. When cooked, remove from the air fryer and serve warm.

Nutritional information: Calories: 175; Fat: 5g; Total Carbs: 5g; Net Carbs: 2g; Fiber: 0.5g; Sugars: 4.5g; Protein: 28.3g

Sweet Marinated Chicken Wings

Prep time: 8-10 minutes | Cook time: 12 minutes | Serves: 6-8

16 chicken wings
To make the marinade:
2 tablespoons honey
2 tablespoons light soya sauce
½ teaspoon sea salt

¼ teaspoon black pepper
¼ teaspoon white pepper, ground
2 tablespoons lemon juice

To marinate, combine the marinade ingredients with the chicken wings in the zip-log bag. Then seal and refrigerate for 4 to 6 minutes. On a flat kitchen surface, plug your air fryer and turn it on. Before cooking, heat the air fryer to 355 degrees F for 4 to 5 minutes. Gently coat the air fryer basket with cooking oil or spray. Place the chicken wings inside the air fryer basket. Cook in your air fryer for 5 to 6 minutes. When cooked, remove the air fryer basket from the air fryer and serve warm with lemon wedges as you like.

Nutritional information: Calories: 152; Fat: 5.2g; Total Carbs: 4g; Net Carbs: 2g; Fiber: 0.1g; Sugars: 4.5g; Protein: 20.5g

Peanut Butter Turkey Wings

Prep time: 10-15 minutes | Cook time: 40 minutes | Serves: 4

1 teaspoon garlic powder
¾ teaspoon paprika
2 tablespoons soy sauce
¾ pound turkey wings, make pieces
1 teaspoon ginger powder
1 handful lemongrass, minced

Sea salt flakes and ground black pepper, to savor
1 tablespoon sesame oil
½ cup sweet chili sauce
2 tablespoons rice wine vinegar
¼ cup peanut butter

Bring water to a boil in a saucepan and add the turkey wings and cook for 18 to 20 minutes. In a large mixing dish, place the turkey wings and toss them with garlic powder, paprika, soy sauce, ginger powder, lemongrass, sea salt flakes, ground black pepper, sesame oil, rice wine vinegar, and peanut butter. On a flat kitchen surface, plug your air fryer and turn it on.
Before cooking, heat your air fryer to 350 degrees F for 4 to 5 minutes. Place the turkey mixture inside the air fryer basket. Cook in your air fryer for 20 minutes. When cooked, remove from the air fryer and serve warm with lemon wedges and chili sauce.

Nutritional information: Calories: 233; Fat: 13.5g; Total Carbs: 16g; Net Carbs: 7g; Fiber: 1.3g; Sugars: 13.9g; Protein: 9.1g

Turmeric Chicken Sticks

Prep time: 20-30 minutes | Cook time: 20 minutes | Serves: 4-5

¼ teaspoon turmeric powder
1 lemon juice
2 eggs

1 tablespoon ginger paste
8 medium pieces (make horizontal slits) chicken

drumsticks
1 tablespoon garlic paste
2 tablespoons vinegar
1 teaspoon each chili powder

1 teaspoon corn flour
Breadcrumbs as required
Salt as required
Oil as required to brush

Mix thoroughly the vinegar, chili powder, lemon juice, garlic, drumsticks, ginger paste, salt, and turmeric powder in a medium sized bowl. To marinate, add the bowl mixture in a zip-lock bag. Seal and refrigerate for 4 to 6 hours. On a flat kitchen surface, plug your air fryer and turn it on. Gently coat the air fryer basket with cooking oil or spray. Before cooking, heat your air fryer to 355 degrees F for 4 to 5 minutes. Mix thoroughly a dash of chili powder, eggs, and salt in a medium sized bowl. In a separate bowl, place the breadcrumbs. Dip the chicken sticks in the egg mixture and dredge in the crumb mixture until coat well. Arrange the drumsticks inside the air fryer basket. Cook in your air fryer for 10 to 15 minutes. When cooked, remove from the air fryer and serve warm.
Nutritional information: Calories: 466; Fat: 26.3g; Total Carbs: 2g; Net Carbs: 0.5g; Fiber: 0.3g; Sugars: 0.3g; Protein: 49.1g

Garlic-Basil Turkey Breast

Prep time: 10 minutes | Cook time: 42 minutes | Serves: 4

1 ½ pounds turkey breast
2 tablespoons olive oil
2 cloves garlic, minced
Sea salt and ground black

pepper, to taste
1 teaspoon basil
2 tablespoons lemon zest, grated

Using paper towels pat dry the turkey breast. Toss the turkey breast with salt, pepper, lemon zest, basil, garlic, and olive oil. Before cooking, heat your air fryer to 380 degrees F. Arrange the chicken breast inside the air fryer basket. Cook in your air fryer for 20 minutes. Then flip the turkey breast and cook for 20 to 22 minutes. Enjoy!
Nutritional information: Calories: 241; Fat: 9.9g; Total Carbs: 8g; Net Carbs: 3.5g; Fiber: 1.1g; Sugars: 6.2g; Protein: 29.2g

Chicken and Carrot

Prep time: 10-15 minutes | Cook time: 30-35 minutes | Serves: 4

2 chicken breasts, make bite-sized chunks
1 cup scallions, chopped
1 parsnip, chopped
⅓ cup cornstarch
⅓ cup flour

1 carrot, thinly sliced
For the Sauce:
¼ cup dry white wine
¼ cup soy sauce
¼ cup honey
⅓ cup chicken broth

On a flat kitchen surface, plug your air fryer and turn it on. Before cooking, heat your air fryer to 365 degrees F for about 4 to 5 minutes. Gently coat the air fryer basket with cooking oil or spray. Mix thoroughly the cornstarch, flour, and chicken chunks. Place the chicken to the air fryer basket. Cook in your air fryer for 20 minutes. When cooked, remove from the air fryer and add the veggies. Cook for 7 minutes. To make the sauce, whisk the sauce ingredients in a saucepan over moderate heat. Once done, serve the chicken with the sauce.
Nutritional information: Calories: 339; Fat: 5.6g; Total Carbs: 46g; Net Carbs: 23g; Fiber: 3.2g; Sugars: 20.8g; Protein: 23.8g

Basil Turkey with Chili Mayo

Prep time: 10 minutes | Cook time: 40 minutes | Serves: 4

3 teaspoons olive oil
½ teaspoon marjoram
1 teaspoon basil

½ teaspoon garlic powder
1 teaspoon shallot powder
Coarse salt and ground black

pepper, to taste
2 pounds turkey breast, boneless
Chili mayo:
¼ cup mayonnaise

¼ cup sour cream
1 tablespoon chili sauce
½ teaspoon stone-ground mustard

Before cooking, heat your air fryer to 360 degrees F. Combine thoroughly the spices with olive oil in a mixing bowl. Using the spice mixture, rub the turkey to coat the turkey on all sides. Cook in your air fryer for 40 minutes. Flip the turkey halfway through cooking. When cooked, the internal temperature should be 165 degrees F. To make the chili mayo, mix all the ingredients. Cool in the refrigerator until ready to serve. Slice the turkey breast against the grain skin-side up. Serve the meal with chili mayo. Enjoy your meal.
Nutritional information: Calories: 356; Fat: 15.2g; Total Carbs: 14g; Net Carbs: 9.5g; Fiber: 1.2g; Sugars: 9.1g; Protein: 39.4g

Simple Chicken Burgers

Prep time: 10 minutes | Cook time: 11 minutes | Serves: 4

1 ¼ pounds chicken white meat, ground
½ white onion, finely chopped
1 teaspoon fresh garlic, finely chopped
Sea salt and ground black pepper, to taste
1 teaspoon paprika

½ cup cornmeal
1 ½ cups breadcrumbs
4 burger buns
4 lettuce leaves
2 small pickles, sliced
2 tablespoons ketchup
1 teaspoon yellow mustard

In a mixing dish, combine thoroughly the onion, salt, black pepper, garlic, and chicken. Then make 4 equal patties from the mixture. Mix cornmeal, breadcrumbs, and paprika in a shallow bowl. Dredge the patties in the breadcrumb mixture. Press the patties to coat the both sides. Using a non-stick cooking spray, spritz an air fryer basket. Place the coated patties inside the air fryer basket. Cook the patties in your air fryer at 370 degrees F for 11 minutes or until it reaches the doneness as you desired. When cooked, remove from the air fryer and place on burger buns. Serve with toppings. Enjoy! Place your burgers on burger buns and serve with toppings. Bon appétit!
Nutritional information: Calories: 424; Fat: 17.8g; Total Carbs: 16g; Net Carbs: 7g; Fiber: 1.9g; Sugars: 2.7g; Protein: 48.8g

Parmesan Turkey Meatballs

Prep time: 10 minutes | Cook time: 10 minutes | Serves: 5

1 ½ pounds ground turkey
½ cup parmesan cheese, grated
½ cup tortilla chips, crumbled
1 yellow onion, finely chopped
2 tablespoons Italian parsley, finely chopped

1 egg, beaten
2 cloves garlic, minced
1 tablespoon soy sauce
1 teaspoon Italian seasoning mix
1 teaspoon olive oil

Combine all the ingredients thoroughly. Form 10 equal meatballs from the mixture. Using a non-stick cooking spray, spritz an air fryer basket. Place the meatballs inside the air fryer basket. Cook in your air fryer at 360 degrees F for about 10 minutes or as your desired. Enjoy!
Nutritional information: Calories: 356; Fat: 19.5g; Total Carbs: 7g; Net Carbs: 3g; Fiber: 1.2g; Sugars: 1.2g; Protein: 43.1g

Mayonnaise Chicken Drumettes with Peppers

Prep time: 10 minutes | Cook time: 45 minutes | Serves: 3

½ cup all-purpose four

1 teaspoon kosher salt

1 teaspoon shallot powder
½ teaspoon dried basil
½ teaspoon dried oregano
½ teaspoon smoked paprika
1 tablespoon hot sauce
¼ cup mayonnaise
¼ cup milk
1 pound chicken drumettes
2 bell peppers, sliced

Before cooking, heat your air fryer to 380 degrees F. Mix salt, shallot powder, oregano, smoked paprika, basil, and flour in a shallow bowl. Mix mayonnaise, milk, and hot sauce in another bowl. Coat the chicken drumettes with the flour mixture, then dip in the milk mixture thoroughly. Cook in the preheated air fryer for 28 to 30 minutes. Flip to the other side halfway through cooking. Keep warm and reserve the chicken drumettes. Cook the pepper slices at 400 degrees F for 13 to 15 minutes. Flip once and shake the peppers halfway cooking.
Nutritional information: Calories: 489; Fat: 30.8g; Total Carbs: 15g; Net Carbs: 5.6g; Fiber: 1.5g; Sugars: 5.5g; Protein: 34.9g

Crispy Chicken Nuggets with Turnip

Prep time: 10 minutes | Cook time: 32 minutes | Serves: 3

1 egg
½ teaspoon cayenne pepper
⅓ cup panko crumbs
¼ teaspoon Romano cheese, grated
2 teaspoons canola oil
1 pound chicken breast, cut
into slices
1 medium-sized turnip, trimmed and sliced
½ teaspoon garlic powder
Sea salt and ground black pepper, to taste

Whisk the egg together with the cayenne pepper until frothy in a bowl. Mix the cheese together with the panko crumbs in another shallow until well combined. Dredge the chicken slices firstly in the egg mixture, then in the panko mixture until coast well. Then using the 1 teaspoon of canola oil brush the slices. To season, add salt and pepper. Before cooking, heat your air fryer to 380 degrees F. Cook the chicken slices in the air fryer for 12 minutes. Shake the basket halfway through cooking. When done, the internal temperature of the meat should read 165 degrees F. Remove from the air fryer and reserve. Keep warm. With the remaining canola oil, drizzle over the turnip slices. To season, add salt, pepper, and garlic powder. Cook the slices in your air fryer at 370 degrees F for about 20 minutes. Serve the parsnip slices with chicken nuggets. Enjoy!
Nutritional information: Calories: 229; Fat: 8.9g; Total Carbs: 6g; Net Carbs: 2.5g; Fiber: 0.8g; Sugars: 1.6g; Protein: 29.1g

Classical Buffalo Wings

Prep time: 10 minutes | Cook time: 22 minutes | Serves: 4

1 ½ pounds chicken wings
Coarse salt and ground black pepper, to season
½ teaspoon onion powder
½ teaspoon cayenne pepper
1 teaspoon granulated garlic
4 tablespoons butter, at room
temperature
2 tablespoons hot pepper sauce
1 (1-inch) piece ginger, peeled and grated
2 tablespoons soy sauce
2 tablespoons molasses

Using kitchen towels, dry the chicken wings and then set aside. To season, add pepper, salt, cayenne pepper, granule garlic, and onion powder to toss the chicken wings. Place the seasoned chicken wings evenly in the air fryer basket. Cook in your air fryer at 380 degrees F for 22 minutes until both sides are golden brown. Meanwhile, mix together hot pepper sauce, soy sauce, molasses, butter, and ginger. Pour the sauce mixture over the chicken wings. Serve hot. Enjoy!
Nutritional information: Calories: 464; Fat: 24.2g; Total

Carbs: 9g; Net Carbs: 4.3g; Fiber: 0.3g; Sugars: 6g; Protein: 50.1g

Crusted Chicken Tenders

Prep time: 10 minutes | Cook time: 10 minutes | Serves: 3

1 pound chicken tenders
Sea salt and black pepper, to taste
½ teaspoon shallot powder
½ teaspoon porcini powder
½ teaspoon dried rosemary
⅓ cup tortilla chips, crushed

Before cooking, heat your air fryer to 360 degrees F. Rub salt, shallot powder, dried rosemary, pepper, tortilla chips, and porcini powder over the chicken tenders. Using a nonstick cooking spray, spritz the air fryer basket. Transfer the chicken tenders inside the air fryer basket. Cook in your air fryer for 10 minutes. Flip halfway through cooking. Serve warm with your favorite dipping sauce.
Nutritional information: Calories: 293; Fat: 11.3g; Total Carbs: 1g; Net Carbs: 0g; Fiber: 0.2g; Sugars: 0g; Protein: 43.9g

Awesome Duck with Potato Rösti

Prep time: 10 minutes | Cook time: 15 minutes | Serves: 2

½ pound duck breast, skin-on, boneless
1 clove garlic, halved
Coarse sea salt and ground black pepper, to taste
½ teaspoon marjoram
¼ teaspoon mustard seeds
¼ teaspoon fennel seeds
Potato Rösti:
½ pound potatoes, grated
2 tablespoons butter, melted
1 teaspoon fresh rosemary, chopped
Coarse sea salt and ground black pepper, to taste

Butterfly the duck breast to render the fat: and season with fresh garlic on all sides. To season, add salt, marjoram, mustard seeds, fennel seeds, and pepper. Transfer the duck breast onto the air fryer basket skin-side up. Cook in your air fryer at 400 degrees F for 10 minutes. Flip the duck breast halfway through cooking. When cooked, rest for 5 to 8 minutes before serving. To make the potato rösti, mix all the ingredients in a bowl until well combined. Then make 2 equal patties from the mixture. Cook at 400 degrees F for 15 minutes. When cooked, remove from the air fryer and serve the warm duck breast with potato rösti.
Nutritional information: Calories: 334; Fat: 16.4g; Total Carbs: 19g; Net Carbs: 6.7g; Fiber: 3.2g; Sugars: 1.4g; Protein: 27.3g

Mayonnaise Chicken Drumsticks

Prep time: 10 minutes | Cook time: 20 minutes | Serves: 4

½ teaspoon shallot powder
½ teaspoon garlic powder
½ teaspoon coriander
¼ teaspoon red pepper flakes
Sea salt and ground black pepper, to season
2 chicken drumsticks, skinless
and boneless
¼ cup blue cheese, softened
4 tablespoons mayonnaise
4 tablespoons sour cream
1 teaspoon fresh garlic, pressed
1 teaspoon fresh lime juice

Add coriander, garlic powder, shallot powder, salt, red pepper, and black pepper in a re-sealable bag. Dredge in the chicken drumsticks and shake to coat well. Using a nonstick cooking oil, spritz the chicken drumsticks. Transfer to the air fryer basket. Cook in your air fryer at 370 degrees F for 20 minutes. Flip over halfway through cooking. To make the sauce, whisk all the rest of the ingredients. Refrigerate until ready to serve. Serve the chicken with the sauce. Enjoy!

Nutritional information: Calories: 154; Fat: 11.2g; Total Carbs: 4g; Net Carbs: 2g; Fiber: 0.1g; Sugars: 1.1g; Protein: 8.8g

Dijon Turkey with Gravy

Prep time: 10 minutes | Cook time: 50 minutes | Serves: 4

1 ½ pounds turkey breast	½ teaspoon garlic powder
1 tablespoon Dijon mustard	Gravy:
2 tablespoons butter, at room temperature	2 cups vegetable broth
	¼ cup all-purpose flour
Sea salt and ground black pepper, to taste	Freshly ground black pepper, to taste
1 teaspoon cayenne pepper	

Before cooking, heat your air fryer to 360 degrees F. Rub the turkey breast with butter and Dijon mustard. To season, toss the turkey with black pepper, cayenne pepper, garlic powder, and salt. Transfer the turkey breast inside the air fryer basket. Cook in your air fryer at 360 degrees F for about 50 minutes. Flip halfway through cooking. Transfer the fat: drippings to a sauté pan. Add in 1 cup of broth and ⅛ cup of all-purpose flour. Cook and whisk continuously until smooth. Add in the rest of the ingredients and simmer to thicken the gravy to half.

Nutritional information: Calories: 281; Fat: 9.6g; Total Carbs: 14g; Net Carbs: 9.5g; Fiber: 1.3g; Sugars: 6.5g; Protein: 32.6g

Mayonnaise Taco Chicken

Prep time: 10 minutes | Cook time: 20 minutes | Serves: 3

1 pound chicken legs, skinless, boneless	½ teaspoon cayenne pepper
½ cup mayonnaise	⅓ cup tortilla chips, crushed
½ cup milk	1 teaspoon Taco seasoning blend
⅓ cup all-purpose flour	½ teaspoon dried Mexican oregano
Sea salt and ground black pepper, to season	

Before cooking, heat your air fryer to 385 degrees F. Pat the chicken legs dry and set aside. Combine milk, flour, black pepper, cayenne pepper, salt, and mayonnaise together in a mixing bowl. Mix taco seasoning blend, Mexican oregano, and the crushed tortilla chip in another shallow bowl. Dredge the chicken legs with the mayonnaise mixture. Coat the tortilla chip mixture over the chicken legs. Shake off any excess crumbs. Cook for 20 minutes. Flip halfway through cooking. Serve and enjoy!

Nutritional information: Calories: 530; Fat: 25.6g; Total Carbs: 25g; Net Carbs: 16g; Fiber: 1.1g; Sugars: 4.5g; Protein: 47.4g

Marinated Chicken with Peppercorns

Prep time: 10-15 minutes | Cook time: 15 minutes | Serves: 4

1 ½ cups all-purpose flour	1 pound chicken tenders
Salt, as needed	½ teaspoon cumin powder
½ teaspoon peppercorns, cracked	1 tablespoon sesame oil
1 teaspoon shallot powder	1 ½ teaspoon smoked cayenne pepper
¾ cup of buttermilk	

In a deep marinade dish, add chicken and the buttermilk and stir gently to coat well. Marinate the chicken for 1 hour. Mix thoroughly all seasonings with the flour in a medium sized bowl. Dredge the chicken tenders in the flour mixture and coat well.

Then add in the buttermilk and put in the flour mixture to coat. Using sesame oil, grease the chicken. On a flat kitchen surface, plug your air fryer and turn it on. Before cooking, heat your air fryer to 365 degrees F for about 4 to 5 minutes. Place the tenders in the air fryer basket and insert the basket inside your air fryer. Cook for 15 minutes. During cooking, shake the basket every 5 minutes. When cooked, remove from the air fryer and serve warm.

Nutritional information: Calories: 436; Fat: 12.7g; Total Carbs: 38g; Net Carbs: 23.5g; Fiber: 1.4g; Sugars: 2.3g; Protein: 39.3g

Flavorful Cornstarch Chicken

Prep time: 10 minutes | Cook time: 40-45 minutes | Serves: 3-4

¼ cup soy sauce	1 teaspoon lemon juice
¼ cup honey	1 teaspoon garam masala
¼ cup tomato puree	3 chicken legs
1 tablespoon water	1 tablespoon peanut oil
1 tablespoon cornstarch	Sea salt and ground black pepper as needed
1 teaspoon garlic paste	
½ teaspoon ginger, grated	

Add soy sauce, water, honey, ginger, cornstarch, garlic, and tomato puree in a medium sized saucepan. Cook to thicken until it reduces to half. Then completely cool down the sauce. To marinate, combine the pan mixture, chicken, and other ingredients. Then seal the bag and set aside at room temperature for 30 minutes. On a flat kitchen surface, plug your air fryer and turn it on. Gently coat an air fryer basket with cooking oil or spray. Before cooking, heat your air fryer to 390 degrees F for 4 to 5 minutes. When cooked, remove from the air fryer and Place the chicken marinate inside the air fryer basket. Cook in your air fryer for 20 minutes. When cooked, remove from the air fryer and serve warm with naan (Indian-style bread) or other bread as your like.

Nutritional information: Calories: 318; Fat: 11.2g; Total Carbs: 22g; Net Carbs: 10g; Fiber: 0.5g; Sugars: 18.5g; Protein: 31.8g

Spicy and Crispy Duck

Prep time: 10 minutes | Cook time: 20 minutes | Serves 3

2 tablespoons peanuts, chopped	1 small-sized white onion, sliced
1 tablespoon honey	1 teaspoon garlic, chopped
1 tablespoon olive oil	1 celery stick, diced
1 tablespoon hoisin sauce	1 thumb ginger, sliced
1 pound duck breast	4 baby potatoes, diced

Lightly grease the air fryer basket with cooking oil. In a mixing bowl, combine honey, hoisin sauce, peanuts, and olive oil. Rub the duck breast with mixture and transfer to the air fryer basket. Spread garlic, celery, potatoes, ginger and onion over the duck breast. Cook at 400 degrees F for 20 minutes. Serve the duck breast with Mandarin pancakes.

Nutritional information: Calories: 333; Fat: 13.9g; Total Carbs: 15g; Net Carbs: 5.6g; Fiber: 2g; Sugars: 7.5g; Protein: 36.4g

Creamy Turkey Sausage Cups

Prep time: 10 minutes | Cook time: 11 minutes | Serves 2

1 smoked turkey sausage, chopped	4 tablespoons cheddar cheese, shredded
4 eggs	4 tablespoons fresh scallions, chopped
4 tablespoons cream cheese	

½ teaspoon garlic, minced
¼ teaspoon mustard seeds

¼ teaspoon chili powder
Salt and red pepper, to taste

In the 4 silicone baking cups, add the chopped sausage. Beat the eggs in a mixing bowl until frothy. Then mix together with the rest of the ingredients until well combined. Then divide the egg mixture into the four cups. Cook in your air fryer at 330 degrees F for 10 to 11 minutes. When cooked, remove the cups to a wire rack and cool slightly before unmolding.
Nutritional information: Calories: 441; Fat: 31.7g; Total Carbs: 6g; Net Carbs: 2.5g; Fiber: 0.5g; Sugars: 4.3g; Protein: 33.1g

Lemon Chicken in Oyster Sauce

Prep time: 8-10 minutes | Cook time: 20 minutes | Serves: 4-5

1 tablespoon oyster sauce
1 teaspoon lemon juice
2 ½ tablespoons maple syrup
1 tablespoon tamari soy sauce
1 teaspoon fresh ginger, minced

1 teaspoon garlic puree
Seasoned salt and ground pepper as needed
2 chicken breasts, boneless and skinless

Combine together tamari sauce, oyster sauce, ginger, garlic puree, syrup, and lemon juice in a deep dish. To season, toss the chicken with salt and pepper. To marinate, combine the chicken and the tamari mixture in a zip-lock bag. Seal the bag and cook in the refrigerator for 3 to 4 hours. On a flat kitchen surface, plug your air fryer and turn it on. Before cooking, heat your air fryer to 365 degrees F for 4 to 5 minutes. Gently grease an air fryer basket with cooking oil or spray. Place the marinated chicken in the air fryer basket. Insert the basket inside the air fryer and cook for 7 minutes. Then flip the chicken and cook the other side for 7 minutes. Add the marinade to a saucepan and simmer to thicken to half. When cooked, serve the chicken with warm marinade sauce.
Nutritional information: Calories: 171; Fat: 5.3g; Total Carbs: 9g; Net Carbs: 4.3g; Fiber: 0.1g; Sugars: 7.6g; Protein: 20.8g

Cheddar Chicken Stuffed Mushrooms

Prep time: 10 minutes | Cook time: 9 minutes | Serves: 4

9 medium-sized button mushrooms, cleaned and steams removed
½ pound chicken white meat, ground
2 ounces goat cheese, room temperature
2 ounces cheddar cheese,

grated
1 teaspoon soy sauce
2 tablespoons scallions, finely chopped
1 teaspoon fresh garlic, finely chopped
Sea salt and red pepper, to season

Dry the mushrooms and set aside. Combine chicken, goat cheese, soy sauce, scallions, fresh garlic, sea salt, and red pepper in a mixing bowl. Stir them together until well combine. Then stuff the mushrooms with the mixture. Cook in your air fryer at 370 degrees F for 5 minutes. Sprinkle cheddar cheese on the top and continue cooking for 3 to 4 minutes or until the cheese melts. Enjoy!
Nutritional information: Calories: 293; Fat: 18.9g; Total Carbs: 2g; Net Carbs: 0.5g; Fiber: 0.5g; Sugars: 1.2g; Protein: 28.8g

Turkey Sausage Casserole

Prep time: 10 minutes | Cook time: 12 minutes | Serves: 5

4 tablespoons bacon bits

1 pound turkey sausage,

chopped
½ cup sour cream
1 cup milk
5 eggs

½ teaspoon smoked paprika
Sea salt and ground black pepper, to your liking
1 cup Colby cheese, shredded

Lightly grease a suitable baking dish. Add the bacon bites and chopped sausage in the dish. Combine thoroughly milk, eggs, salt, black pepper, and paprika in a mixing dish. Add the mixture inside the baking dish. Cook in your air fryer at 310 degrees F for about 10 minutes. Sprinkle Colby cheese on the top and continue cooking for 2 minutes or until the cheese is bubbly. Enjoy!
Nutritional information: Calories: 513; Fat: 41.3g; Total Carbs: 3g; Net Carbs: 1g; Fiber: 0.1g; Sugars: 2.3g; Protein: 30.4g

Chicken and Veggies Salad

Prep time: 10 minutes | Cook time: 12 minutes | Serves: 2

½ pound chicken breasts, boneless and skinless
1 cup grape tomatoes, halved
1 Serrano pepper, deveined and chopped
2 bell peppers, deveined and chopped
2 tablespoons olives, pitted and sliced
1 cucumber, sliced
1 red onion, sliced
1 cup arugula

1 cup baby spinach
¼ cup mayonnaise
2 tablespoons Greek-style yogurt
1 teaspoon lime juice
¼ teaspoon oregano
¼ teaspoon basil
¼ teaspoon red pepper flakes, crushed
Sea salt and ground black pepper, to taste

Before cooking, heat your air fryer to 380 degrees F. Using a nonstick cooking oil, spray the chicken breasts. Transfer the chicken breasts inside the air fryer basket. Cook in your air fryer for 12 minutes. When the cooking time is up, cool for a while and cut into strips. In a salad bowl, add the chicken strips and the remaining ingredients. Then place in your refrigerator. When ready, serve and enjoy!
Nutritional information: Calories: 447; Fat: 20g; Total Carbs: 32g; Net Carbs: 12g; Fiber: 5.6g; Sugars: 15.5g; Protein: 37.5g

Chicken in Soy Sauce

Prep time: 10 minutes | Cook time: 50 minutes | Serves: 3

1 pound chicken cutlets
1 teaspoon sesame oil
1 tablespoon lemon juice
1 tablespoon Mirin
1 tablespoon soy sauce

1 teaspoon ginger, peeled and grated
2 garlic cloves, minced
1 teaspoon cornstarch

Before cooking, heat your air fryer to 360 degrees F. Pat the chicken cutlets dry and set aside. Combine the remaining ingredients in a mixing bowl until well incorporated. Brush the chicken cutlets with the oil mixture. Transfer to the refrigerator for 30 to 40 minutes. Cook in your air fryer for 10 minutes. Flip halfway through cooking. Serve the chicken cutlets with shirataki noodles.
Nutritional information: Calories: 321; Fat: 12.8g; Total Carbs: 4g; Net Carbs: 2g; Fiber: 0.2g; Sugars: 1.6g; Protein: 44.3g

Roasted Turkey Thighs and Cauliflower

Prep time: 10 minutes | Cook time: 53 minutes | Serves: 4

1 tablespoon butter, room temperature

2 pounds turkey thighs
½ teaspoon smoked paprika

½ teaspoon dried marjoram
¼ teaspoon dried dill
Sea salt and ground black pepper, to taste
1 pound cauliflower, broken

into small florets
⅓ cup Pecorino Romano cheese, freshly grated
1 teaspoon garlic, minced

Before cooking, heat your air fryer to 360 degrees F. Toss the turkey thighs with butter. To season, rub the turkey thighs with marjoram, smoked paprika, salt, black pepper, and dill. Roast the turkey thighs at 360 degrees F for about 20 minutes. Then flip to cook the other side for 20 minutes. Mix the cauliflower, garlic, and Pecorino Romano, and salt together. Toss well. Cook in your air fryer at 400 degrees F for 12 to 13 minutes. When cooked, serve the turkey with the cauliflower. Enjoy!

Nutritional information: Calories: 192; Fat: 12.2g; Total Carbs: 6g; Net Carbs: 2.5g; Fiber: 3g; Sugars: 2.9g; Protein: 15.1g

Farmhouse Chicken Rolls

Prep time: 10 minutes | Cook time: 14 minutes | Serves: 4

4 slices smoked bacon, chopped
4 slices Monterey-Jack cheese, sliced
1 ½ pounds chicken fillets
1 celery stick, chopped

1 small sized onion, chopped
1 teaspoon hot sauce
Sea salt and ground black pepper, to season
1 lemon, cut into slices

Before cooking, heat your air fryer to 380 degrees F. On the chicken fillets, add 1 bacon slice and 1 cheese slice for each. Then add onion and celery between the fillets. Drizzle hot sauce on the top and add salt and black pepper to season as you like. Then roll up and tie with kitchen twine. Roast in your air fryer for 8 minutes. Flip and cook for 5 to 6 minutes or more. Serve the rolls with lemon slices. Enjoy!

Nutritional information: Calories: 526; Fat: 28.5g; Total Carbs: 1g; Net Carbs: 0g; Fiber: 0g; Sugars: 0g; Protein: 63.3g

Indian-style Chicken with Raita

Prep time: 10 minutes | Cook time: 12 minutes | Serves: 2

2 chicken fillets
Sea salt and ground black pepper, to taste
2 teaspoons garam masala
1 teaspoon ground turmeric
½ cup plain yogurt
1 English cucumber, shredded

and drained
1 tablespoon fresh cilantro, coarsely chopped
½ red onion, chopped
A pinch of grated nutmeg
A pinch of ground cinnamon

Before cooking, heat your air fryer to 380 degrees F. Rub pepper, garam masala, ground turmeric and salt over the chicken fillets until well coated. Cook in your air fryer for 12 minutes. Flip once or twice halfway through cooking. To make additional raita, mix all the rest of the ingredients in a mixing bowl. Serve the chicken with raita sauce.

Nutritional information: Calories: 174; Fat: 5.7g; Total Carbs: 6g; Net Carbs: 2.5g; Fiber: 0.9g; Sugars: 4g; Protein: 22.7g

Chicken Drumettes with Mustard

Prep time: 10 minutes | Cook time: 12 minutes | Serves: 3

¼ cup soy sauce
1 teaspoon brown mustard
1 teaspoon garlic paste
2 tablespoons tomato paste

2 tablespoons sesame oil
1 tablespoon brown sugar
2 tablespoons rice vinegar
1 pound chicken drumettes

Add all the ingredients in a resealable bag and let it marinate for

2 hours. Transfer the chicken drumettes to the air fryer basket and reserve the rest mixture. Cook in your air fryer at 400 degrees F for 12 minutes. Shake the basket once or twice to cook evenly. Meanwhile, in a small saucepan, boil the reserved marinade and reduce heat to low to simmer until the sauce thickens. Pour the sauce over the chicken drumettes. Serve immediately.

Nutritional information: Calories: 486; Fat: 33.1g; Total Carbs: 6g; Net Carbs: 2.5g; Fiber: 0.6g; Sugars: 4.6g; Protein: 35.2g

Cojita Chicken Taquitos

Prep time: 10 minutes | Cook time: 18 minutes | Serves: 3

1 pound chicken breast, boneless
Sea salt and ground black pepper, to taste
½ teaspoon cayenne pepper

½ teaspoon onion powder
½ teaspoon garlic powder
½ teaspoon mustard powder
1 cup Cotija cheese, shredded
6 corn tortillas

Before cooking, heat your air fryer to 380 degrees F. To season, rub the chicken with black pepper, onion powder, mustard power, garlic powder, cayenne paper, and salt. Cook in the preheated air fryer for 12 minutes. Halfway through cooking, flip the chicken to evenly cook the meal. When cooked, remove the chicken from the air fryer and cool. On a cutting board, shred the chicken with two forks. Place the chicken and Cojita cheese on the taquitos. Then roll them up. Bake in your air fryer at 390 degrees F for 5 to 6 minutes. When cooked, remove from your air fryer and serve immediately.

Nutritional information: Calories: 216; Fat: 4.3g; Total Carbs: 16g; Net Carbs: 7g; Fiber: 2.4g; Sugars: 0.5g; Protein: 26.5g

Huli-Huli Turkey Drumsticks

Prep time: 10 minutes | Cook time: 35 minutes | Serves: 2

2 turkey drumsticks
Sea salt and ground black pepper, to season
1 teaspoon paprika
1 teaspoon hot sauce
1 teaspoon garlic paste

1 teaspoon olive oil
½ teaspoon rosemary
½ small pineapple, cut into wedges
1 teaspoon coconut oil, melted
2 stalks scallions, sliced

Before cooking, heat your air fryer to 360 degrees F. Rub the turkey drumsticks with black pepper, salt, garlic paste, hot sauce, paprika, rosemary, and olive oil. Place the seasoned turkey drumsticks inside the air fryer basket. Cook in the preheated air fryer for 25 minutes. Reserve. When the cooking time is up, remove the turkey from the air fryer, add pineapple wedges in the air fryer and brush the wedges with coconut oil. Increase the temperature to 400 degrees F and cook for 8 to 9 minutes. Then garnish the drumsticks with the cooked pineapple wedges and scallions. Serve and enjoy!

Nutritional information: Calories: 183; Fat: 8.9g; Total Carbs: 7g; Net Carbs: 3g; Fiber: 1.5g; Sugars: 4.6g; Protein: 19.8g

Balsamic Turkey in Hoisin Sauce

Cook time: 50 minutes | Serves: 4

2 pounds turkey drumsticks
2 tablespoons balsamic vinegar
2 tablespoons dry white wine
1 tablespoon sesame oil
1 sprig rosemary, chopped
Salt and ground black pepper,

to your liking
2 ½ tablespoons butter, melted
For the Hoisin Sauce:
2 tablespoons hoisin sauce
1 tablespoon mustard

Before cooking, heat your air fryer to 350 degrees F. In a mixing dish, add the turkey drumsticks, vinegar, sesame oil, rosemary, and wine. Marinate the mixture for 3 hours. To season, add salt and pepper in the marinate. Drizzle over with the melted butter. Transfer the turkey drumsticks inside an air fryer basket. Cook in the preheated air fryer at 350 degrees F for 30 to 35 minutes, in batches if possible. During cooking, flip the drumsticks from time to time to ensure even cook. To make the hoisin sauce, mix all the sauce ingredients. When the cooking time is up, drizzle the sauce over the turkey and cook again for 5 minutes. When cooked, let it rest for about 10 minutes. Carve the turkey into your desired size and serve. Enjoy! While the turkey drumsticks are roasting, prepare the Hoisin sauce by mixing the ingredients. After that, drizzle the turkey with the sauce mixture; roast for a further 5 minutes. Let it rest about 10 minutes before carving and serving. Bon appétit!

Nutritional information: Calories: 376; Fat: 27.4g; Total Carbs: 9g; Net Carbs: 4.3g; Fiber: 1.3g; Sugars: 4.9g; Protein: 21.1g

Sriracha Chicken Thighs

Prep time: 10 minutes | Cook time: 12 minutes | Serves: 2

1 pound chicken thighs	pepper, to taste
1 cup buttermilk	1 teaspoon cayenne pepper
½ teaspoon garlic paste	¼ cup corn flour
¼ cup Sriracha sauce	¼ cup all-purpose flour
Sea salt and ground black	

Using kitchen towel, pat the chicken thighs dry. Combine the garlic paste, Sriracha sauce, black pepper, cayenne pepper, and the buttermilk thoroughly. Place the chicken into the mixture and dredge until it is well coated. Refrigerate for 2 hours. In a separate shallow bowl, add the flour and place the chicken thighs in to coat well. Set your air fryer at 395 degrees F and timer for 12 minutes. Cook. Serve and enjoy!

Nutritional information: Calories: 594; Fat: 18.8g; Total Carbs: 29g; Net Carbs: 14.3g; Fiber: 1.7g; Sugars: 6.1g; Protein: 72.4g

Classical Greek Keftedes

Prep time: 10 minutes | Cook time: 10 minutes | Serves: 2

½ pound ground chicken	chopped
1 egg	1 teaspoon olive oil
1 slice stale bread, cubed and soaked in milk	½ teaspoon dried oregano
	½ teaspoon dried basil
1 teaspoon fresh garlic, pressed	⅛ teaspoon grated nutmeg
2 tablespoons Romano cheese, grated	Sea salt and ground black pepper, to taste
1 bell pepper, deveined and	2 pita bread

Combine together the ground chicken, egg, stale bread slice, fresh garlic, Romano cheese, bell pepper, olive oil, oregano, basil, nutmeg, salt, and black pepper thoroughly in a mixing bowl. Stir well. Lightly grease an air fryer basket. Make 6 meatballs from the mixture and arrange the meatballs inside the air fryer basket. Cook the meatballs in your air fryer at 390 degrees F for 10 minutes. During cooking, shake the basket from time to time to cook evenly. When cooked, add the keftedes inside the pita bread. If desired, serve the meal with tomato and tzatziki sauce.

Nutritional information: Calories: 399; Fat: 14.7g; Total Carbs: 30.4g; Net Carbs: 0g; Fiber: 2.2g; Sugars: 3.3g; Protein: 35.1g

Baked Chicken with Parmesan Cheese

Prep time: 10 minutes | Cook time: 12 minutes | Serves: 2

2 chicken fillets	1 teaspoon garlic paste
1 egg, beaten	1 tablespoon fresh cilantro, chopped
2 tablespoons milk	

½ cup seasoned breadcrumbs	4 slices parmesan cheese
4 tablespoons marinara sauce	

Before cooking, heat your air fryer to 380 degrees F. Using a nonstick cooking oil, spritz the air fryer basket. In a shallow bowl, beat the egg, milk, cilantro, and garlic paste. Place the seasoned breadcrumbs in a separate bowl. Dredge the chicken fillet in the egg mixture and then in the seasoned breadcrumbs to coat well the fillet. Press to ensure the fillet is well coated. Set the temperature to 380 degrees F and the timer to 6 minutes. Turn the chicken over halfway cooking. Drizzle the marinara sauce and parmesan cheese over the chicken fillet and cook again in the air fryer for 6 minutes. Serve immediately and enjoy!

Nutritional information: Calories: 312; Fat: 14.6g; Total Carbs: 12g; Net Carbs: 7g; Fiber: 0.9g; Sugars: 1.8g; Protein: 32.7g

Marjoram Chicken Drumsticks

Prep time: 10 minutes | Cook time: 30 minutes | Serves: 3

3 chicken drumsticks	½ teaspoon onion powder
Sea salt and ground black pepper, to season	½ teaspoon garlic powder
	1 teaspoon dried marjoram
½ teaspoon red pepper flakes, crushed	¼ cup cornstarch
	2 tablespoons balsamic vinegar
½ teaspoon shallot powder	2 tablespoons milk

Before cooking, heat your air fryer to 380 degrees F. Using the paper towels, pat the chicken dry. To season, rub the chicken drumsticks with all seasonings. Mix balsamic vinegar, milk, and cornstarch together in a shallow bowl. Dredge the chicken drumsticks in the cornstarch mixture and press the drumsticks to coat thoroughly. Then shake off any excess mixture. Set the temperature to 380 degrees F and timer for 30 minutes. Halfway through cooking, flip the chicken. Serve and enjoy!

Nutritional information: Calories: 130; Fat: 2.9g; Total Carbs: 11g; Net Carbs: 6.7g; Fiber: 0.3g; Sugars: 0.8g; Protein: 13.2g

Tasty Chicken Fajitas

Prep time: 10 minutes | Cook time: 22 minutes | Serves: 3

1 pound chicken breast, skinless and boneless	crushed
	½ teaspoon Mexican oregano
1 teaspoon butter, melted	½ teaspoon garlic powder
Sea salt and ground black pepper, to taste	3 bell peppers, thinly sliced
	1 red onion, sliced
½ teaspoon red pepper flakes,	

Before cooking, heat your air fryer to 380 degrees F. Using the melted butter, brush all sides of the chicken. To season, rub black pepper, salt, oregano, garlic powder, and red pepper. Set the cooking temperature to 380 degrees F and timer for 12 minutes. Cook in your air fryer until golden brown. Flip halfway through cooking. Set the chicken aside to cool for 10 minutes. Then slice into strips and reserve to keep it warm. In the air fryer basket, add peppers and onions. Cook in your air fryer at 400 degrees F for 10 minutes. Taste to adjust the seasonings and add some seasoning as you like. When cooked, place the vegetables on a bowl. Stir to combine well and serve immediately!

Nutritional information: Calories: 240; Fat: 5.5g; Total Carbs: 13g; Net Carbs: 7g; Fiber: 2.6g; Sugars: 7.7g; Protein: 33.8g

Chicken Quesadillas with Ricotta Cheese

Prep time: 10 minutes | Cook time: 10 minutes | Serves: 2

½ pound chicken breasts,	boneless and skinless

Salt to taste
3 eggs
4 ounces Ricotta cheese
2 tablespoons flaxseed meal

1 teaspoon psyllium husk powder
Black pepper, to taste

Before cooking, heat your air fryer to 380 degrees F. Transfer the chicken inside an air fryer basket. Then cook it in the preheated air fryer at 380 degrees F. Flip the chicken halfway through cooking. Add salt to season and cut the chicken into small strips. Whisk the eggs, cheese, psyllium husk powder, black pepper, and flaxseed meal in a mixing bowl. Gently grease a baking pan that fits in your air fryer. Transfer the mixture inside the baking pan. Bake in your air fryer at 380 degrees F for 9 to 10 minutes. Spread the chicken pieces onto the quesadilla. Then pour the cheese mixture on the top and fold the quesadilla in half. Cut into two pieces and serve.

Nutritional information: Calories: 425; Fat: 21.6g; Total Carbs: 5.5g; Net Carbs: 1g; Fiber: 1.9g; Sugars: 0.8g; Protein 48.9g

Chicken Wings with Garlic Butter Sauce

Prep time: 10 minutes | Cook time: 18 minutes | Serves: 3

1 pound chicken wings
Salt and black pepper, to taste
2 tablespoons butter

1 teaspoon garlic paste
1 lemon, cut into slices

Before cooking, heat your air fryer to 380 degrees F. Using a kitchen towel, pat the chicken wings dry and add black pepper and salt to taste. Mix the garlic paste and butter together in a bowl. Dredge the wings thoroughly in the mixture to toss well. Set the cooking temperature to 380 degrees F and timer for 18 minutes. Then cook. Garnish the chicken wings with lemon slices and serve.

Nutritional information: Calories: 357; Fat: 18.9g; Total Carbs: 0.3g; Net Carbs: 0g; Fiber: 0g; Sugars: 0g; Protein: 43.9g

Crunchy Chicken Bites

Prep time: 10 minutes | Cook time: 10 minutes | Serves: 3

1 pound chicken tenders
¼ cup all-purpose flour
½ teaspoon onion powder
½ teaspoon garlic powder
½ teaspoon cayenne pepper

Sea salt and ground black pepper, to taste
½ cup breadcrumbs
1 egg
1 tablespoon olive oil

Using kitchen towels, pat the chicken dry and cut the chicken into bites. Mix the onion powder, cayenne pepper, garlic powder, black pepper, and salt in a shallow bowl. Dip the chicken bites in the mixture and rub to coat the bites well. Add the breadcrumbs into a separate bowl. Beat the egg in a third bowl. Dip the chicken firstly in the whisked egg, and then dredge in the breadcrumbs pressing to coat well. Brush olive oil over the chicken fingers. Cook the chicken bites in the air fryer at 360 degrees F for 8 to 10 minutes. Halfway through cooking, turn the chicken fingers over to cook evenly. As you desired, serve the chicken fingers with your favorite dipping sauce.

Nutritional information: Calories: 461; Fat: 18.4g; Total Carbs: 21g; Net Carbs: 9g; Fiber: 1.2g; Sugars: 1.5g; Protein: 49.2g

Alfredo Chicken with Mushrooms

Prep time: 10 minutes | Cook time: 15 minutes | Serves: 3

1 pound chicken breasts, boneless

1 medium onion, quartered
1 teaspoon butter, melted
½ pound mushrooms, cleaned

12 ounces Alfredo sauce
Salt and black pepper, to taste

Before cooking, heat your air fryer to 380 degrees F. In the air fryer basket, add the onion and chicken and drizzle over with melted butter. Cook for 6 minutes. When the cooking time is up, add mushrooms in the air fryer basket and cook again for 5 to 6 minutes or more. Cut the chicken into strips. Add the chopped mushrooms and onions and stir in the Alfredo sauce. Add pepper and salt as you desired to taste. Serve the chicken with the hot cooked fettuccine. Enjoy!

Nutritional information: Calories: 478; Fat: 20g; Total Carbs: 35g; Net Carbs: 20g; Fiber: 0.9g; Sugars: 1.7g; Protein: 38g

Rosemary Chicken with Sweet Potatoes

Prep time: 10 minutes | Cook time: 35 minutes | Serves: 2

2 chicken legs, bone-in
2 garlic cloves, minced
1 teaspoon sesame oil
Sea salt and ground black

pepper, to taste
2 sprigs rosemary, leaves picked and crushed
½ pound sweet potatoes

Before cooking, heat your air fryer to 380 degrees F. Rub the chicken legs with the garlic cloves. Drizzle the sesame oil over the chicken legs and sweet potatoes. Then sprinkle rosemary and salt over them. Transfer the sweet potatoes and chicken legs inside the air fryer basket. Then set the cooking temperature to 380 degrees F and the timer for 30 minutes. Cook in your air fryer until the sweet potatoes are completely cooked and the internal temperature of the chicken legs is 165 degrees F. When cooked, remove from the air fryer and serve. Enjoy!

Nutritional information: Calories: 424; Fat: 12.9g; Total Carbs: 32g; Net Carbs: 12g; Fiber: 4.7g; Sugars: 0.6g; Protein: 42.4g

Awesome Chicken with Mustard Rosemary Sauce

Cook time: 20 minutes | Serves: 4

½ cup full-fat sour cream
1 teaspoon ground cinnamon
½ teaspoon whole grain mustard
1 ½ tablespoons mayonnaise
1 pound chicken thighs, boneless, skinless, and cut into pieces

1 ½ tablespoons olive oil
2 heaping tablespoons fresh rosemary, minced
½ cup white wine
3 cloves garlic, minced
½ teaspoon smoked paprika
Salt and freshly cracked black pepper, to taste

Toss the chicken thighs with white wine and olive oil in a mixing dish and stir well to coat. Then add the smoked paprika, salt, ground cinnamon, black pepper, and garlic in the bowl. Let it marinade in the refrigerator for 1 to 3 hours. Roast the chicken thighs in your air fryer at 375 degrees F for 18 minutes. Flip the chicken wings halfway through cooking. Cook in batches if possible. For the sauce, mix together the whole grain, mayonnaise, mustard, rosemary, and sour cream. Sprinkle the sauce on the top to serve. Enjoy!

Nutritional information: Calories: 348; Fat: 15.8g; Total Carbs: 9g; Net Carbs: 4.3g; Fiber: 1.2g; Sugars: 2.7g; Protein: 34.2g

Barbecued Chicken Skewers

Cook time: 15 minutes | Serves: 4

4 cloves garlic, chopped

4 scallions, chopped

2 tablespoons sesame seeds, toasted
1 tablespoon fresh ginger, grated

½ cup pineapple juice
½ cup soy sauce
⅓ cup sesame oil
A pinch of black pepper

Skew the tenders with any excess fat: trimmed. In a bowl, mix together the chopped garlic, scallions, sesame seeds, fresh ginger, the pineapple juice, soy sauce, sesame oil, and black pepper. Add the chicken skewers together with the mixture in the bowl and refrigerate for about 4 hours. Before cooking, heat your air fryer to 375 degrees F. Cook in the preheated air fryer for 12 minutes.

Nutritional information: Calories: 234; Fat: 20.6g; Total Carbs: 10.6g; Net Carbs: 0g; Fiber: 1.5g; Sugars: 4.1g; Protein: 3.5g

Grilled Cajun Chicken

Cook time: 20 minutes | Serves: 2

2 medium skinless, boneless chicken breasts
½ teaspoon salt

3 tablespoons Cajun spice
1 tablespoon olive oil

Before cooking, heat your air fryer to 370 degrees F. Rub the chicken breasts with Cajun sauce and salt. Drizzle olive oil over the chicken breast. Transfer the chicken breasts in an air fryer basket. Cook in the preheated air fryer for 7 minutes. When the cooking time is up, flip the both chicken breasts to the other side and cook again for 3 to 4 minutes. When cooked, remove onto a cutting board and slice into your desired size. Serve and enjoy!

Nutritional information: Calories: 200; Fat: 11g; Total Carbs: 0g; Net Carbs: 0g; Fiber: 0g; Sugars: 0g; Protein: 25.2g

Balsamic Chicken Drumsticks

Cook time: 40 minutes | Serves: 2

½ cup balsamic vinegar
½ cup soy sauce
2½ pounds chicken drumsticks
2 cloves of garlic, minced

2 green onions, sliced thinly
2 tbsps. sesame seeds
3 tbsps. honey

To marinate, combine the balsamic vinegar, garlic, honey, and chicken in a zip-lock bag and refrigerate for at least 30 minutes. Before cooking, heat your air fryer to 330 degrees F. Transfer the marinated chicken onto a grill grate that fits in your air fryer. Cook in the preheated air fryer for 30 to 40 degrees F. Flip the chicken every 10 minutes to ensure even cook. While cooking, transfer the remaining marinate sauce in a sauce pan and simmer to thicken. When the cooking time is up, serve the chicken with the sauce. Sprinkle green onions and sesame seeds over the meal to garnish. Enjoy!

Nutritional information: Calories: 439; Fat: 13g; Total Carbs: 7.5g; Net Carbs: 2.5g; Fiber: 1g; Sugars: 1.7g; Protein: 66.8g

Crispy Chicken Nuggets

Cook time: 40 minutes | Serves: 4

2 slices bread crumbs
9 ounces chicken breast, chopped
1 teaspoon garlic, minced
1 teaspoon tomato ketchup

2 medium egg
1 tablespoon olive oil
1 teaspoon. paprika
1 teaspoon parsley
Salt and pepper to taste

To make the batter, combine together the paprika, pepper, salt, oil, and breadcrumbs. Whisk one egg in a separate bowl. Whisk the egg, with ketchup and parsley over the chopped chicken and press to coat well. Make several nuggets from the chicken mixture and dip each in the egg. Then coat the chicken with breadcrumbs. Cook in your air fryer at 390 degrees F for 10 minutes. If desired, serve the chicken nuggets with your favorite

sauce.

Nutritional information: Calories: 273; Fat: 14.6g; Total Carbs: 1.5g; Net Carbs: 0g; Fiber: 0.1g; Sugars: 0.9g; Protein: 32.7g

Marjoram Butter Chicken

Prep time: 30 to 60 minutes | Cook time: 30 minutes | Serves: 2

2 skinless, boneless small chicken breasts
2 tablespoons butter
1 teaspoon sea salt

½ teaspoon red pepper flakes, crushed
2 teaspoon marjoram
¼ teaspoon lemon pepper

Before cooking, heat your air fryer to 390 degrees F. Combine all the ingredients in a bowl and toss together to coat well. Let it marinate for 30 to 60 minutes. Cook in your air fryer for 20 minutes, and flip the chicken halfway through cooking. Use an instant-read thermometer to check the doneness of the chicken. When cooked, serve with jasmine rice.

Nutritional information: Calories: 38; Fat: 19.7g; Total Carbs: 0.8g; Net Carbs: 0g; Fiber: 0.4g; Sugars: 0.1g; Protein: 50.3g

Spiced Duck Legs

Cook time: 30 minutes | Serves: 2

½ tbsp. fresh thyme, chopped
½ tbsp. fresh parsley, chopped
2 duck legs
1 garlic clove, minced

1 tsp. five spice powder
Salt and black pepper, as required

Gently grease an air fryer basket. Before cooking, heat your air fryer to 340 degrees F. In a bowl, combine together herbs, salt, black pepper, garlic, and five spice powder. Rub the garlic mixture over the duck legs. Then transfer to the air fryer basket. Cook in the preheated air fryer at 390 degrees F for 25 minutes. When the cooking time is up, cook for 5 more minutes if needed. Remove from the air fryer and serve hot. Enjoy☐

Nutritional information: Calories: 138; Fat: 4.5g; Total Carbs: 1g; Net Carbs: 0g; Fiber: 0.3g; Sugars: 0g; Protein: 22g

Chicken and Onion Sausages

Cook time: 10 minutes | Serves: 4

1 garlic clove, diced
1 spring onion, chopped
1 cup ground chicken
½ teaspoon salt

½ teaspoon ground black pepper
4 sausage links
1 teaspoon olive oil

Mix together the ground chicken, ground black pepper, onion, and the diced garlic clove in a mixing dish to make the filling. Fill the sausage links with the chicken mixture. Then cut the sausages into halves and make sure the endings of the sausage halves are secured. Before cooking, heat your air fryer to 365 degrees F. Brush olive oil over the sausages. Arrange in the air fryer basket and cook in the preheated air fryer for 10 minutes. Then flip the sausage to ensure even cook. Cook again for 5 minutes or more. Or increase the temperature to 390 degrees F and cook for 8 minutes for a faster result.

Nutritional information: Calories: 130; Fat: 8.3g; Total Carbs: 1g; Net Carbs: 0g; Fiber: 0.2g; Sugars: 0.3g; Protein: 12.2g

Roasted Turkey with Veggies

Cook time: 1 hour 15 minutes | Serves: 4

1 red onion, cut into wedges
1 carrot, trimmed and sliced
1 celery stalk, trimmed and

sliced
1 cup Brussel sprouts, trimmed and halved

1 cup roasted vegetable broth
1 tablespoon. apple cider vinegar
1 teaspoon. maple syrup
2 turkey thighs
½ teaspoon. mixed

peppercorns, freshly cracked
1 teaspoon fine sea salt
1 teaspoon cayenne pepper
1 teaspoon onion powder
½ teaspoon garlic powder
⅓ teaspoon mustard seeds

Arrange the veggies on a baking dish that fits in your air fryer. Pour roasted vegetable broth in the dish. Place the rest of the ingredients in a large-sized bowl. Then set it aside to marinate for about 30 minutes. Then add over the veggies. Roast in your air fryer at 330 degrees F for 40 to 45 minutes. Serve and enjoy!
Nutritional information: Calories: 167; Fat: 3.8g; Total Carbs: 10.3g; Net Carbs: 0g; Fiber: 3.1g; Sugars: 3.8g; Protein: 22g

Garlic Chicken with Bacon

Prep time: 30 minutes | Cook time: 15 minutes | Serves: 2

4 rashers smoked bacon
2 chicken filets
½ teaspoon coarse sea salt
¼ teaspoon black pepper, preferably freshly ground
1 teaspoon garlic, minced
1 (2-inch) piece ginger, peeled

and minced
1 teaspoon. black mustard seeds
1 teaspoon mild curry powder
½ cup coconut milk
½ cup parmesan cheese, grated

Before cooking, heat your air fryer to 400 degrees F. In the air fryer basket, place the smoked bacon. Cook in your air fryer for 5 to 7 minutes. Set aside for later use. Add the salt, chicken fillets, garlic, mustard seed, milk, curry powder, black pepper, and ginger in a mixing dish. Refrigerate for about 30 minutes to make the marinate. Add the grated parmesan cheese in a second separate bowl. Then dip the parmesan bowl and coat well. Place in the air fryer basket. Decrease the air fryer to 380 degrees F and set the timer for 6 minutes. Start to cook. When the cooking time is up, flip and cook again for 6 minutes. Repeat the prepare cooking steps for the remaining ingredients. Serve with the cooked bacon.
Nutritional information: Calories: 543; Fat: 37.7g; Total Carbs: 19g; Net Carbs: 6.7g; Fiber: 3g; Sugars: 2.1g; Protein: 32.6g

Mediterranean Fried Chicken

Cook time: 21 minutes | Serves: 2

2 boneless skinless chicken breast halves (6 ounces each)
3 tablespoons olive oil
6 pitted Greek or ripe olives, sliced

2 tablespoons. capers, drained
½-pint grape tomatoes
¼ teaspoon salt
¼ teaspoon. pepper

Before cooking, heat your air fryer to 390 degrees F. Using the cooking spray, gently grease a baking pan that fits in your air fryer. To season, add salt and pepper, as well as the chicken inside the baking pan and toss well. Brown in the preheated air fryer for 6 minutes, flipping to the other side halfway through cooking. Add olives, oil, capers, and tomatoes in the baking pan and stir to combine. Cook in your air fryer at 330 degrees F for 15 minutes. When cooked, remove from the air fryer and serve.
Nutritional information: Calories: 477; Fat: 33g; Total Carbs: 4g; Net Carbs: 2g; Fiber: 1.5g; Sugars: 2.4g; Protein: 41.4g

Spiced Chicken with Pork Rind

Prep time: 15 minutes | Cook time: 12 minutes | Serves: 6

4 eggs
1 ½ pounds chicken breasts,

diced into small chunks
1 teaspoon paprika

½ teaspoon garlic powder
1 teaspoon onion powder
2 ½ cups pork rind, crushed

¼ cup coconut flour
Black pepper
Salt

In a suitable bowl, mix together coconut flour, black pepper, and salt. In another bowl, whisk eggs until combined.
Take 1 more bowl and mix together pork panko, paprika, garlic powder, and onion powder. Add chicken pieces in a suitable mixing bowl. Sprinkle coconut flour mixture over chicken and toss well. Dip chicken pieces in the prepared egg mixture and coat with pork panko mixture and place on a plate. Grease its air fryer basket with cooking spray. At 400 degrees F, preheat your Air fryer. Add ½ prepared chicken in air fryer basket and cook for almost 10-12 minutes. Shake basket halfway through. Cook remaining ½ using the same method. Serve and enjoy.
Nutritional information: Calories: 314; Fat: 14g; Total Carbs: 4g; Net Carbs: 2g; Fiber: 2.2g; Sugars: 0.5g; Protein: 41.1g

Herbed Cornish Game Hens

Cook time: 16 minutes | Serves: 4

1 teaspoon fresh rosemary, chopped
1 teaspoon fresh thyme, chopped
2 pounds Cornish game hen, backbone removed and halved
½ cup olive oil

¼ teaspoon sugar
¼ teaspoon red pepper flakes, crushed
Salt and black pepper, to taste
1 teaspoon fresh lemon zest, finely grated

Lightly grease an air fryer basket with cooking spray or oil. Before cooking, heat your air fryer to 390 degrees F. In a mixing dish, add the herbs, olive oil, sugar, spices, and lemon zest. Dredge the Cornish game hen in and stir well. Then marinate in the fridge for about 24 hours. Place the marinated Cornish game hen inside the air fryer basket. Cook in your air fryer for about 16 minutes. When cooked, remove from the air fryer and serve hot on plates. Enjoy!
Nutritional information: Calories: 440; Fat: 38.2g; Total Carbs: 0.5g; Net Carbs: 0g; Fiber: 0.2g; Sugars: 0.2g; Protein: 25.4g

Southern Fried Chicken

Cook time: 30 minutes | Serves: 2

2 x 6-oz. boneless skinless chicken breasts
2 tbsp. hot sauce

½ tsp. onion powder
1 tbsp. chili powder
2 oz. pork rinds, finely ground

Cut the chicken breasts in half lengthwise and rub in the hot sauce. Combine the onion powder with the chili powder, then rub into the chicken. Leave to marinate for at least a half hour. Use the ground pork rinds to coat the chicken breasts in the ground pork rinds, covering them thoroughly. Place the chicken in your air fryer. Set the fryer at 350°F and cook the chicken for 13 minutes. Flip the chicken and cook the other side for another 13 minutes or until golden. Test the chicken with a meat thermometer. When fully cooked, it should reach 165°F. Serve hot, with the sides of your choice.
Nutritional information: Calories: 327; Fat: 13.8g; Total Carbs: 5g; Net Carbs: 2g; Fiber: 1.4g; Sugars: 0.7g; Protein: 45.8g

Herbed Chicken and Broccoli

Cook time: 15 minutes | Serves: 6

3 tablespoons dried parsley, crushed
1 tablespoon onion powder
1 tablespoon garlic powder
½ teaspoon red chili powder

½ teaspoon paprika
2 pounds boneless, skinless chicken breasts, sliced
3 cups instant white rice
¾ cup cream soup

3 cups small broccoli florets   3 cups water
⅓ cup butter

In a large mixing dish, add spices and the parsley together. Dredge the chicken slices in the spice mixture until coat well. Line 6 large foil pieces on a flat table. Arrange ½ cup of rice over each foil piece. Then add the, 2 tablespoons of cream soup, ½ cup of broccoli, 1/6 of chicken, ½ cup of water, and 1 tablespoon of butter. Then fold tightly the foil to ensure the rice mixture is sealed. Arrange onto the air fryer basket. Air fry the foil packets in your air fryer at 390 degrees F for about 15 minutes. When the cooking time is up, remove from the air fryer and serve hot on plates.
Nutritional information: Calories: 424; Fat: 22.7g; Total Carbs: 7g; Net Carbs: 3g; Fiber: 0.6g; Sugars: 0.8g; Protein: 45.2g

Cheddar Chicken Fajitas

Cook time: 15 minutes | Serves: 4

4 chicken breasts   seasoning
1 onion, sliced   2 tablespoons olive oil
1 bell pepper, sliced   ¾ cup cheddar cheese,
1 ½ tablespoons fajita   shredded

Before cooking, heat your air fryer to 380 degrees F. Brush oil over the chicken and toss together with seasoning. Place the chicken in a baking dish that fits in your air fryer. Then add the onion and bell peppers on the top. Sprinkle with shredded cheese and cook in the preheated air fryer for 1 to 2 minutes or until the cheese is melted. When cooked, remove from the air fryer and serve. Enjoy!
Nutritional information: Calories: 327; Fat: 13.8g; Total Carbs: 5g; Net Carbs: 2g; Fiber: 1.4g; Sugars: 0.7g; Protein: 45.8g

Simple Chicken Meatballs

Prep time: 15 minutes | Cook time: 10 minutes | Serves: 4

1-pound ground chicken   3 tablespoons fresh parsley,
1 egg, lightly beaten   chopped
½ cup mozzarella cheese,   1 small onion, minced
shredded   Black pepper
1 ½ tablespoon taco seasoning Salt
3 garlic cloves, minced

Add all the recipe ingredients into the suitable mixing bowl and mix until well combined. Make small balls from mixture and place in the air fryer basket. Cook meatballs for almost 10 minutes at 400 degrees F. Serve and enjoy.
Nutritional information: Calories: 253; Fat: 12.2g; Total Carbs: 12.2g; Net Carbs: 3g; Fiber: 1g; Sugar: 0.9g; Protein: 25.8g

Creamy Chicken Breasts with Jalapeno

Cook time: 25 minutes | Serves: 2

2 ounces. full-fat cream   ½ cup sharp cheddar cheese,
cheese, softened   shredded and divided
4 slices sugar-free bacon,   2 (6-ounce) boneless skinless
cooked and crumbled   chicken breasts
¼ cup pickled jalapenos, sliced

Mix bacon, half of the Cheddar cheese, cream cheese, and jalapeno slices together in a mixing dish until well incorporated. Cut a ¾-length slits in the chicken breasts. Be care not to cut all the way down. Six to eight slices will be made in this way,

depending on the chicken breast. Fill the slits with the cheese mixture divided into even sized dollops. Sprinkle the remaining cheddar cheese on the top. In the air fryer basket, place the chicken. Cook in your air fryer at 350 degrees F for 20 minutes or until the internal temperature measures 165 degrees F. When cooked, remove from the air fryer and serve hot. Enjoy now!
Nutritional information: Calories: 424; Fat: 22.7g; Total Carbs: 7g; Net Carbs: 3g; Fiber: 0.6g; Sugars: 0.8g; Protein: 45.2g

Garlic Turkey with Tomato Mix

Cook time: 25 minutes | Serves: 4

1 pound turkey meat, cubed   3 garlic cloves, chopped
and browned   1 and ½ tsps. cumin, ground
A pinch of salt and black   12 ounces veggies stock
pepper   1 cup tomatoes, chopped
1 green bell pepper, chopped

Mix the turkey, salt, black pepper, green bell pepper, garlic cloves, ground cumin, veggies stock, and the chopped tomatoes together in a baking pan that fits in your air fryer. Toss well to season. Cook in your air fryer at 380 degrees F for 25 minutes. When the cooking time is up, remove from the air fryer. Serve hot on plates and enjoy!
Nutritional information: Calories: 351; Fat: 31g; Total Carbs: 4g; Net Carbs: 2g; Fiber: 0.8g; Sugar: 3.7g; Protein: 24g

Roasted Whole Chicken

Prep time: 15 minutes | Cook time: 20 minutes | Serves: 4

3 pounds' whole chicken,   ½ teaspoon onion powder
remove giblets and pat dry   ¼ teaspoon paprika
chicken   ¼ teaspoon black pepper
1 teaspoon Italian seasoning   1 ½ teaspoon salt
½ teaspoon garlic powder

In a suitable bowl, mix together Italian seasoning, garlic powder, onion powder, paprika, black pepper, and salt. Rub spice mixture from inside and outside of the chicken. Place chicken breast side down in air fryer basket. Roast chicken for 30 minutes at 360 degrees F. Turn chicken and roast for 20 minutes more or internal temperature of chicken reaches at 165 degrees F. Serve and enjoy.
Nutritional information: Calories: 400; Fat: 25g; Total Carbs: 2.6g; Net Carbs: 3g; Fiber: 0g; Sugar: 1g; Protein: 27.4g

Chicken Wings with BBQ Sauce

Prep time: 15 minutes | Cook time: 12 minutes | Serves: 4

1 ½ pounds chicken wings   1 tablespoon olive oil
2 tablespoons unsweetened   1 teaspoon garlic powder
BBQ sauce   Black pepper
1 teaspoon paprika   Salt

In a suitable bowl, toss chicken wings with garlic powder, oil, paprika, black pepper, and salt. At 360 degrees F, preheat your Air fryer. Add chicken wings in air fryer basket and cook for 12 minutes. Turn chicken wings to another side and cook for 5 minutes more. Remove chicken wings from air fryer and toss with BBQ sauce. Return chicken wings in air fryer basket and cook for 2 minutes more. Serve and enjoy.
Nutritional information: Calories: 351; Fat: 31g; Total Carbs: 4.3g; Net Carbs: 3g; Fiber: 0.8g; Sugar: 3.7g; Protein: 24g

Flavorful Spiced Chicken Pieces

Prep time: 15 minutes | Cook time: 20 minutes | Serves: 10

5 pounds' chicken, about 10 pieces	1 teaspoon celery salt
1 tablespoon coconut oil	⅓ teaspoon oregano
2 ½ teaspoon white black pepper	½ teaspoon basil
1 teaspoon ground ginger	½ teaspoon thyme
1 ½ teaspoon garlic salt	2 cups pork rinds, crushed
1 tablespoon paprika	1 tablespoon vinegar
1 teaspoon dried mustard	1 cup unsweetened almond milk
1 teaspoon black pepper	½ teaspoon salt

Add chicken in a suitable mixing bowl. Add milk and vinegar over chicken and place in the refrigerator for 2 hours. In a shallow dish, mix together pork rinds, white black pepper, ginger, garlic salt, paprika, mustard, black pepper, celery salt, oregano, basil, thyme, and salt. Coat air fryer basket with coconut oil. Coat each chicken piece with pork rind mixture and place on a plate. Place ½ coated chicken in the air fryer basket. Cook chicken at 360 degrees F for almost 10 minutes then turn chicken and continue cooking for almost 10 minutes more or until internal temperature reaches at 165 F. Cook remaining chicken using the same method. Serve and enjoy.
Nutritional information: Calories: 539; Fat: 17.8g; Total Carbs: 21g; Net Carbs: 3g; Fiber: 1.4g; Sugar: 0.8g; Protein: 38.4g

Delectable Chicken Nuggets

Prep time: 15 minutes | Cook time: 12 minutes | Serves: 4

1-pound chicken breast, skinless, boneless and cut into chunks	4 egg whites
	½ teaspoon ground ginger
6 tablespoons sesame seeds, toasted	¼ cup coconut flour
	1 teaspoon sesame oil
	Pinch of salt

At 400 degrees F, preheat your Air fryer. Toss chicken with oil and salt in a suitable bowl until well coated. Add coconut flour and ginger in a zip-lock bag and shake to mix. Add chicken to the same bag and shake well to coat. In a suitable bowl, add egg whites. Add chicken in egg whites and toss until well coated. Add sesame seeds in a large zip-lock bag. Shake excess egg off from chicken and add chicken in sesame seed bag. Shake bag until chicken well coated with sesame seeds. Grease its air fryer basket with cooking spray. Place chicken in air fryer basket and air fry for 6 minutes. Turn chicken and continue cooking for 6 minutes more. Serve and enjoy.
Nutritional information: Calories: 265; Fat: 11.5g; Total Carbs: 8.6g; Net Carbs: 3g; Fiber: 0g; Sugar: 0g; Protein: 45.6g

Quick & Easy Spice Chicken Wings

Prep time: 15 minutes | Cook time: 30 minutes | Serves: 3

1 ½ pounds chicken wings	½ teaspoon smoked paprika
1 tablespoon baking powder, gluten-free	1 tablespoon olive oil
	½ teaspoon black pepper
½ teaspoon onion powder	¼ teaspoon salt
½ teaspoon garlic powder	

Add chicken wings and oil in a suitable mixing bowl and toss well. Mix together remaining ingredients and sprinkle over chicken wings and toss to coat. Grease its air fryer basket with cooking spray. Evenly spread chicken wings in air fryer basket and cook at almost 400 degrees F for almost 15 minutes. Toss

well. Turn chicken wings to another side and cook for almost 15 minutes more. Serve and enjoy.
Nutritional information: Calories: 200; Fat: 19g; Total Carbs: 7.3g; Net Carbs: 3g; Fiber: 0g; Sugar: 0.6g; Protein: 22g

Quick Air Fried Chicken Breast

Prep time: 15 minutes | Cook time: 22 minutes | Serves: 4

4 chicken breasts, skinless and boneless	½ teaspoon garlic powder
	2 tablespoons olive oil
½ teaspoon dried oregano	⅛ teaspoon black pepper
½ teaspoon dried basil	½ teaspoon salt
½ teaspoon dried thyme	

In a suitable bowl, mix together olive oil, oregano, basil, thyme, garlic powder, black pepper, and salt. Rub herb oil mixture all over chicken breasts. Grease its air fryer basket with cooking spray. Place chicken in air fryer basket and cook at 360 degrees F for almost 10 minutes. Flip the chicken and continue cooking for 8-12 minutes more or until the internal temperature of chicken reaches at 165 degrees F. Serve and enjoy.
Nutritional information: Calories: 316; Fat: 17g; Total Carbs: 4.3g; Net Carbs: 3g; Fiber: 0.9g; Sugar: 2.1g; Protein: 35g

Simple & Delicious Chicken Wings

Prep time: 15 minutes | Cook time: 20 minutes | Serves: 8

1 ½ pounds chicken wings	Black pepper
2 tablespoons olive oil	Salt

Toss chicken wings with oil and place in the air fryer basket. Cook chicken wings at 370 degrees F for almost 15 minutes. Shake basket and cook at 400 degrees F for 5 minutes more. Season cooked chicken wings with black pepper and salt. Serve and enjoy.
Nutritional information: Calories: 192; Fat: 17.7g; Total Carbs: 1.7g; Net Carbs: 3g; Fiber: 0.5g; Sugar: 0.4g; Protein: 24.6g

Turkey Breast with Fresh Herbs

Prep time: 15 minutes | Cook time: 35 minutes | Serves: 4

2 pounds' turkey breast	1 teaspoon fresh thyme, chopped
1 teaspoon fresh sage, chopped	
1 teaspoon fresh rosemary, chopped	Black pepper
	Salt

Grease its air fryer basket with cooking spray. In a suitable bowl, mix together sage, rosemary, and thyme. Season turkey breast with black pepper and salt and herb mixture. Set the seasoned turkey breast in air fryer basket and cook at almost 390 degrees F for 30-35 minutes. Slice and serve.
Nutritional information: Calories: 264; Fat: 17g; Total Carbs: 0.9g; Net Carbs: 3g; Fiber: 0.3g; Sugar: 0g; Protein: 27g

Spice Chicken Pieces

Prep time: 15 minutes | Cook time: 20 minutes | Serves: 6

3 pounds' chicken, cut into eight pieces	1 ½ teaspoons garlic powder
	1 ½ teaspoons dried oregano
¼ teaspoon cayenne	½ tablespoon dried thyme
1 teaspoon paprika	Black pepper
2 teaspoons onion powder	Salt

Season chicken with black pepper and salt. In a suitable bowl, mix together spices and herbs and rub spice mixture over chicken pieces. Spray its air fryer basket with cooking spray. Place prepared chicken in air fryer basket and cook at 350 degrees F for almost 20 minutes, turning halfway through. Serve and enjoy.
Nutritional information: Calories: 449; Fat: 26.1 g; Total Carbs: 37.5g; Net Carbs: 3g; Fiber: 5.4g; Sugar: 27.4g; Protein: 19.2g

Chicken Drumsticks with Pesto

Prep time: 15 minutes | Cook time: 20 minutes | Serves: 2

4 chicken drumsticks	2 tablespoons olive oil
6 garlic cloves	1 tablespoon ginger, sliced
½ jalapeno pepper	½ cup cilantro
2 tablespoons lemon juice	1 teaspoon salt

Add all the recipe ingredients except chicken into the blender and blend until smooth. Pour blended mixture into the suitable bowl. Add chicken and stir well to coat. Place in refrigerator for 2 hours. Grease its air fryer basket with cooking spray. Place marinated chicken into the air fryer basket and cook at almost 390 degrees F for 20 minutes. Turn halfway through. Serve and enjoy.
Nutritional information: Calories: 597; Fat: 17.1 g; Total Carbs: 66.5g; Net Carbs: 3g; Fiber: 9.3g; Sugar: 45g; Protein: 48.6g

Garlic Chicken Popcorn

Prep time: 15 minutes | Cook time: 15 minutes | Serves: 1

1 pound skinless, boneless chicken breast	½ cup flour
1 teaspoon chili flakes	1 tablespoon olive oil cooking spray
1 teaspoon garlic powder	

Pre-heat your fryer at 365 degrees F. Spray with olive oil. Cut the chicken breasts into cubes and place in a suitable bowl. Toss with the chili flakes, garlic powder, and additional seasonings to taste. Add the coconut flour and toss once more. Cook the chicken in the air fryer for ten minutes almost. Flip and cook for a further 5 minutes before serving.
Nutritional information: Calories: 373; Fat: 8.5 g; Total Carbs: 0.8g; Net Carbs: 3g; Fiber: 0.3g; Sugar: 7.6g; Protein: 74.5g

Spicy Asian Chicken Thighs with Soy Sauce

Prep time: 40 minutes | Cook time: 20 minutes | Serves: 4

4 chicken thighs, skin-on, and bone-in	2 tablespoons chili garlic sauce
2 teaspoons ginger, grated	¼ cup olive oil
1 lime juice	⅓ cup soy sauce

In a suitable bowl, whisk together chili garlic sauce, ginger, lime juice, soy sauce oil. Add chicken to the same bowl and coat well with the prepared marinade, cover and place in the refrigerator for almost 30 minutes. Set marinated chicken in your air fryer basket and air fryer at 400 degrees F for 15-20 minutes. Serve and enjoy.
Nutritional information: Calories: 720; Fat: 50.1 g; Total Carbs: 44.5g; Net Carbs: 3g; Fiber: 8.2g; Sugar: 33g; Protein: 25.2g

Chicken & Mushroom Meatballs

Prep time: 15 minutes | Cook time: 18 minutes | Serves: 2

½ pound boneless chicken thighs	½ cup mushrooms
1 teaspoon minced garlic	1 teaspoon extra virgin olive oil
1-¼ cup roasted pecans	

At 375 degrees F, preheat your Air fryer. Cube the chicken thighs. Place them in the food processor along with the garlic, pecans, and other seasonings as desired. Pulse until a smooth consistency is achieved. Chop the mushrooms finely, then add them to the chicken mixture and combine well. Using your hands, shape the mixture into balls and brush them with olive oil. Put the balls into the air fryer and cook for 18 minutes. Serve hot.
Nutritional information: Calories: 512; Fat: 7.1 g; Total Carbs: 28.5g; Net Carbs: 3g; Fiber: 2.1g; Sugar: 13.4g; Protein: 1.2g

Lemon Whole Chicken

Prep time: 15 minutes | Cook time: 28 minutes | Serves: 2

1-pound whole chicken	1 tablespoon soy sauce
1 lemon, juiced	1 ½ tablespoon honey
1 teaspoon lemon zest	

Place all of the recipe ingredients in a suitable bowl and combine well. Refrigerate for 1 hour. Put the marinated and seasoned chicken in the air fryer basket. Air fry at 320 degrees F for almost 18 minutes. Raise the air fryer's heat to 350 degrees F and cook for another 10 minutes or until chicken has turned light brown. Serve.
Nutritional information: Calories: 559; Fat: 23.8 g; Total Carbs: 18.3g; Net Carbs: 3g; Fiber: 0.3g; Sugar: 17.6g; Protein: 65.8g

Italian Seasoned Chicken Breasts with Spinach

Prep time: 15 minutes | Cook time: 12 minutes | Serves: 4

4 tablespoons cottage cheese	Juice of ½ lime
2 boneless, skinless chicken breasts	2 tablespoons Italian seasoning
	2 tablespoons olive oil

At 390 degrees F, preheat your Air fryer. Grease its air fryer basket with cooking spray. Mix the spinach with the cottage cheese in a suitable bowl. Halve the chicken breasts with a knife and flatten them with a meat mallet. Season with Italian seasoning. Divide the spinach/cheese mixture between the 4 chicken pieces. Roll up to form cylinders and use toothpicks to secure them. Brush with olive oil and transfer to the air fryer basket. Cook for 12 minutes, flipping halfway through. Serve with salad.
Nutritional information: Calories: 210; Fat: 5.4 g; Total Carbs: 18.5g; Net Carbs: 3g; Fiber: 2.4g; Sugar: 13.1g; Protein: 23.5g

Spice Chicken with Broccoli

Prep time: 15 minutes | Cook time: 20 minutes | Serves: 4

1-pound chicken breast, boneless, and cut into chunks	2 teaspoons vinegar
2 cups broccoli florets	1 teaspoon sesame oil
2 teaspoons hot sauce	1 tablespoon soy sauce
	1 tablespoon ginger, minced

½ teaspoon garlic powder
1 tablespoon olive oil
½ onion, sliced

Black pepper
Salt

Add all the recipe ingredients into the suitable mixing bowl and toss well. Grease its air fryer basket with cooking spray. Transfer chicken and broccoli mixture into the air fryer basket. Cook at almost 380 degrees F for almost 15-20 minutes. Shake halfway through. Serve and enjoy.
Nutritional information: Calories: 203; Fat: 6.6g; Total Carbs: 8.5g; Net Carbs: 3g; Fiber: 1.4g; Sugar: 1.6g; Protein: 30g

Parmesan Chicken Tenderloins

Prep time: 15 minutes | Cook time: 12 minutes | Serves: 6

1 lime
2 pounds' chicken tenderloins, cut up
½ cup pork rinds, crushed
½ cup Parmesan cheese, grated
1 tablespoon olive oil

Salt and black pepper, to taste
1 teaspoon cayenne pepper
⅓ teaspoon ground cumin
1 teaspoon chili powder
1 egg

Squeeze and rub the lime juice all over the chicken. Spritz the cooking basket with a nonstick cooking spray. In a suitable mixing bowl, thoroughly combine the pork rinds, Parmesan, olive oil, salt, black pepper, cayenne pepper, cumin, and chili powder. In a suitable shallow bowl, whisk the egg until well beaten. Dip the chicken tenders in the egg, then in pork rind mixture. Transfer the coated and breaded chicken to the prepared cooking basket. Cook in the preheated Air Fryer at 380 degrees F for 12 minutes almost. Turn them once cooked halfway through. Serve immediately.
Nutritional information: Calories: 183; Fat: 0.4 g; Total Carbs: 5.6g; Net Carbs: 3g; Fiber: 0.6g; Sugar: 8.4g; Protein: 40.2g

Chicken Breasts and Spinach Salad

Prep time: 15 minutes | Cook time: 12 minutes | Serves: 2

2 chicken breasts; skinless and boneless
2 teaspoons parsley; dried
½ teaspoon onion powder
1 avocado; pitted, peeled and chopped
¼ cup olive oil
1 tablespoon tarragon; chopped.

2 teaspoons sweet paprika
½ cup lemon juice
5 cups baby spinach
8 strawberries; sliced
1 small red onion; sliced
2 tablespoons balsamic vinegar
Black pepper and salt to the taste

Put chicken in a bowl, add lemon juice, parsley, onion powder and paprika and toss. Transfer chicken to your air fryer and cook at 360 degrees F for 12 minutes. In a bowl, mix spinach, onion, strawberries and avocado and toss. In another bowl, mix oil with vinegar, salt, black pepper and tarragon, whisk well, add to the salad and toss. Divide chicken on plates, add spinach salad on the side and serve.
Nutritional information: Calories: 274; Fat: 9.5 g; Total Carbs: 6.3g; Net Carbs: 3g; Fiber: 0.9g; Sugar: 4.6g; Protein: 40.5g

Flavor Chicken with Chopped Peanuts

Prep time: 15 minutes | Cook time: 13 minutes | Serves: 4

1 ½ pounds chicken tenderloins
2 tablespoons peanut oil

½ cup parmesan cheese, grated
Salt and black pepper, to taste

½ teaspoon garlic powder
1 teaspoon red pepper flakes

2 tablespoons peanuts, roasted and roughly chopped

At 360 degrees F, preheat your Air Fryer. Brush the chicken tenderloins with peanut oil on all sides. In a suitable mixing bowl, thoroughly combine grated parmesan cheese, salt, black pepper, garlic powder, and red pepper flakes. Dredge the chicken in the prepared breading, shaking off any residual coating. Lay the chicken tenderloins into the cooking basket. Cook for almost 12 to 13 minutes or until it is no longer pink in the center. Garnish with roasted peanuts. Serve
Nutritional information: Calories: 445; Fat: 28.2 g; Total Carbs: 6.2g; Net Carbs: 3g; Fiber: 2.2g; Sugar: 1.4g; Protein: 43.7g

Chicken Tenderloins with Parmesan Cheese

Prep time: 15 minutes | Cook time: 12 minutes | Serves: 6

1 lime
2 pounds' chicken tenderloins cut up
1 cup cornflakes, crushed
½ cup Parmesan cheese, grated
1 tablespoon olive oil

Salt and black pepper, to taste
1 teaspoon cayenne pepper
⅓ teaspoon ground cumin
1 teaspoon chili powder
1 egg

Squeeze and rub the lime juice all over the chicken. Spritz the cooking basket with a nonstick cooking spray. In a suitable mixing bowl, thoroughly combine the cornflakes, Parmesan, olive oil, salt, black pepper, cayenne pepper, cumin, and chili powder. In a suitable shallow bowl, whisk the egg until well beaten. Dip the chicken tenders in the egg, then in cornflakes mixture. Transfer the coated chicken to the prepared cooking basket. Cook in the preheated Air Fryer at about 380 degrees F for 12 minutes almost. Flip them halfway through the cooking time. Serve immediately.
Nutritional information: Calories: 376; Fat: 34.2 g; Total Carbs: 2.4g; Net Carbs: 3g; Fiber: 0.5g; Sugar: 0.3g; Protein: 16.2g

Turkey Breast with Shallot Sauce

Prep time: 15 minutes | Cook time: 28 minutes | Serves: 4

1 big turkey breast, skinless, boneless and cubed
1 tablespoon olive oil
¼ teaspoon sweet paprika
Black pepper and salt to the

taste
1 cup chicken stock
3 tablespoons butter, melted
4 shallots, chopped

Heat up a pan that fits the air fryer with the olive oil and the butter over medium high heat, add the turkey cubes, and brown for 3 minutes on each side. Add the shallots, stir and sauté for 5 minutes more. Add the paprika, stock, black pepper and salt, toss, put the pan in the air fryer and cook at almost 370 degrees F for 20 minutes. Divide into bowls and serve.
Nutritional information: Calories: 379; Fat: 20.9 g; Total Carbs: 10g; Net Carbs: 3g; Fiber: 2.2g; Sugar: 2.1g; Protein: 37g

Za'atar Chives Chicken with Lemon Zest

Prep time: 15 minutes | Cook time: 18 minutes | Serves: 4

1-pound chicken drumsticks, bone-in
1 tablespoon za'atar

1 teaspoon garlic powder
½ teaspoon lemon zest, grated
1 teaspoon chives, chopped

1 tablespoon avocado oil

In the mixing bowl mix up za'atar, garlic powder, lemon zest, chives, and avocado oil. Then rub the chicken drumsticks with the za'atar mixture. At 375 degrees F, preheat your Air fryer. Put the prepared chicken drumsticks in the air fryer basket and cook for 15 minutes. Then flip the drumsticks on another side and cook them for 3 minutes more. Serve.

Nutritional information: Calories: 319; Fat: 14.7 g; Total Carbs: 30.3g; Net Carbs: 3g; Fiber: 4g; Sugar: 12.3g; Protein: 24g

Chicken Tenders with Italian Seasoning

Prep time: 15 minutes | Cook time: 10 minutes | Serves: 2

2 eggs, lightly beaten
1 ½ pounds chicken tenders
½ teaspoon onion powder
½ teaspoon garlic powder
1 teaspoon paprika
1 teaspoon Italian seasoning
2 tablespoons' ground flax seed
1 cup almond flour
½ teaspoon black pepper
1 teaspoon salt

At 400 degrees F, preheat your Air fryer. Season chicken with black pepper and salt. In a suitable bowl, whisk eggs to combine. In a shallow dish, mix together almond flour, all seasonings, and flaxseed. Dip chicken into the egg then coats with almond flour mixture and place on a plate. Grease its air fryer basket with cooking spray. Place ½ chicken tenders in air fryer basket and cook for almost 10 minutes, turning halfway through. Cook remaining chicken tenders using same steps. Serve and enjoy.

Nutritional information: Calories: 315; Fat: 28g; Total Carbs: 22.3g; Net Carbs: 3g; Fiber: 0.9g; Sugar: 0.6g; Protein: 17g

Cheese Turkey Meatloaf

Prep time: 15 minutes | Cook time: 47 minutes | Serves: 6

2 pounds' turkey mince
½ cup scallions, chopped
2 garlic cloves, finely minced
1 teaspoon dried thyme
½ teaspoon dried basil
¾ cup Colby cheese, shredded
1 tablespoon tamari sauce
Black pepper and salt, to your liking
¼ cup roasted red pepper tomato sauce
¾ tablespoons. olive oil
1 medium-sized egg, well beaten

In a nonstick skillet, that is preheated over a moderate heat, sauté the turkey mince, scallions, garlic, thyme, and basil until just tender and fragrant. Then set your Air Fryer to cook at almost 360 degrees. Combine sautéed mixture with the cheese and tamari sauce; then form the mixture into a loaf shape. Mix the remaining items and pour them over the meatloaf. Cook in the preheated air fryer basket for 45 to 47 minutes. Serve warm.

Nutritional information: Calories: 362; Fat: 22.6 g; Total Carbs: 2.9g; Net Carbs: 3g; Fiber: 1.4g; Sugar: 0.5g; Protein: 37.4g

Turkey Wings with Thai-Style Sauce

Prep time: 15 minutes | Cook time: 40 minutes | Serves: 4

¾ pound turkey wings, cut into pieces
1 teaspoon ginger powder
1 teaspoon garlic powder
¾ teaspoon paprika
2 tablespoons soy sauce
1 handful minced lemongrass
Salt flakes and black pepper to taste
2 tablespoons rice wine

vinegar
¼ cup peanut butter
1 tablespoon sesame oil
½ cup Thai sweet chili sauce

Boil the turkey wings in a suitable saucepan full of water for 20 minutes. Put the turkey wings in a suitable bowl and cover them with the remaining ingredients, minus the Thai sweet chili sauce. Transfer to the Air Fryer and fry for 20 minutes at 350 degrees F, turning once halfway through the cooking time. Ensure they are cooked through before serving with the Thai sweet chili sauce, as well as some lemon wedges if desired.

Nutritional information: Calories: 596; Fat: 10.8 g; Total Carbs: 14.9g; Net Carbs: 3g; Fiber: 1.9g; Sugar: 21.9g; Protein: 112.2g

Homemade Chicken Sliders

Prep time: 15 minutes | Cook time: 30 minutes | Serves: 3

½ cup all-purpose flour
1 teaspoon garlic salt
½ teaspoon black pepper
1 teaspoon celery seeds
½ teaspoon mustard seeds
½ teaspoon dried basil
1 egg
2 chicken breasts, cut in thirds
6 small-sized dinner rolls

In mixing bowl, thoroughly combine the flour and seasonings. In a separate shallow bowl, beat the egg until frothy. Dredge the cleaned chicken through the flour mixture, then into egg; afterwards, roll them over the flour mixture again. Spritz the chicken pieces with a cooking spray on all sides. Transfer them to the cooking basket. Cook in the preheated Air Fryer at 380 degrees F for 15 minutes; turn them over and cook an additional 10 to 12 minutes. Test for doneness and adjust the seasonings. Serve immediately on dinner rolls.

Nutritional information: Calories: 540; Fat: 26.8 g; Total Carbs: 2.6g; Net Carbs: 3g; Fiber: 0.4g; Sugar: 1.2g; Protein: 69.9g

Seasoned Chicken Breast

Prep time: 15 minutes | Cook time: 20 minutes | Serves: 4

1-pound chicken breast, skinless, boneless, and cut into chunks
2 cups broccoli florets
2 teaspoons hot sauce
2 teaspoons vinegar
1 teaspoon sesame oil
1 tablespoon soy sauce
1 tablespoon ginger, minced
½ teaspoon garlic powder
1 tablespoon olive oil
½ onion, sliced
Black pepper
Salt

Add all the recipe ingredients into the suitable mixing bowl and toss well. Grease its air fryer basket with cooking spray. Transfer chicken and broccoli mixture into the air fryer basket. Cook at almost 380 degrees F for almost 15-20 minutes. Shake halfway through. Serve and enjoy.

Nutritional information: Calories: 457; Fat: 10.1 g; Total Carbs: 1.6g; Net Carbs: 3g; Fiber: 0.5g; Sugar: 0.4g; Protein: 14.9g

Duck Breasts with Thai Red Curry Paste

Prep time: 15 minutes | Cook time: 22 minutes | Serves: 6

1 ½ pounds duck breasts, skin removed
1 teaspoon kosher salt
½ teaspoon cayenne pepper
⅓ teaspoon black pepper
½ teaspoon smoked paprika
1 tablespoon Thai red curry paste
1 cup candy onions, halved
¼ small pack coriander,

chopped

Place the duck breasts between 2 foil sheet; then, use a rolling pin to bash the duck until they are 1-inch thick. At 395 degrees F, preheat your Air fryer. Rub the duck breasts with salt, cayenne pepper, black pepper, paprika, and red curry paste. Place the duck breast in the cooking basket. Cook for 11 to 12 minutes. Top with candy onions and cook for another 10 to 11 minutes. Serve garnished with coriander.
Nutritional information: Calories: 273; Fat: 24 g; Total Carbs: 12.8g; Net Carbs: 3g; Fiber: 1g; Sugar: 1.4g; Protein: 20g

Chicken Fillets with Lemon Pepper & Cheddar Cheese

Prep time: 15 minutes | Cook time: 14 minutes | Serves: 2

1 lemon pepper	½ teaspoon dried cilantro
¼ cup Cheddar cheese, shredded	1 teaspoon coconut oil, melted
8 oz. chicken fillets	¼ teaspoon smoked paprika

Cut the lemon pepper into halves and remove the seeds. Then cut the chicken fillet into 2 fillets. Make the horizontal cuts in every chicken fillet. Then sprinkle the chicken fillets with smoked paprika and dried cilantro. After this, fill them with lemon pepper halves and Cheddar cheese. At 385 degrees F, preheat your air fryer. Put the chicken fillets in the preheated Air Fryer and sprinkle with melted coconut oil. Cook the chicken for 14 minutes. Carefully transfer the chicken fillets in the serving plates. Serve.
Nutritional information: Calories: 487; Fat: 15 g; Total Carbs: 0g; Net Carbs: 3g; Fiber: 0g; Sugar: 0g; Protein: 85.4g

Chicken Breast and Sausage Bites

Prep time: 15 minutes | Cook time: 15 minutes | Serves: 4

4 4-ounces skinless, boneless chicken breasts	4 sausages, casing removed

Place the boneless chicken breasts onto a smooth surface and with a meat mallet, pound each into an even thickness. Place 1 sausage over each chicken breast. Roll each breast around the sausage and secure with toothpicks. At 375 degrees F, preheat your Air Fryer. Grease its air fryer basket. Arrange chicken breasts into the prepared Air Fryer basket. Air Fry for about 15 minutes. Remove from Air Fryer and transfer the chicken breasts onto a serving platter. Serve hot.
Nutritional information: Calories: 467; Fat: 18.1 g; Total Carbs: 6.6g; Net Carbs: 3g; Fiber: 0.5g; Sugar: 5.5g; Protein: 66.1g

Tender Chicken with Parmesan Cheese

Prep time: 15 minutes | Cook time: 20 minutes | Serves: 2

1 tablespoon butter, melted	2 tablespoons parmesan cheese
2 chicken breasts	6 tablespoons almond flour

At 350 degrees F, preheat your Air Fryer. Combine the 6 tablespoons of almond flour and parmesan cheese in a plate. Drizzle the chicken breasts with butter. Dredge in the almond flour mixture. Place in the air fryer basket. Cook for 20 minutes at 350 degrees F. When cooked, serve and enjoy.
Nutritional information: Calories: 546; Fat: 40 g; Total Carbs: 3.1g; Net Carbs: 3g; Fiber: 0.2g; Sugar: 0.9g; Protein: 40.4g

Glazed Chicken Tenderloins

Prep time: 15 minutes | Cook time: 15 minutes | Serves: 4

8 chicken tenderloins	1 cup bread crumbs
1 egg, beaten	Black pepper and salt to taste
2 tablespoons olive oil	

At 350 degrees F, preheat your Air Fryer. Combine the bread crumbs, olive oil, black pepper, and salt in a shallow dish. Put the beaten egg in separate dish. Dip the chicken tenderloins into the egg before rolling them in the bread crumbs. Transfer to the Air Fryer basket. Air fry the chicken for 12 minutes. When done, serve and enjoy.
Nutritional information: Calories: 322; Fat: 14 g; Total Carbs: 1.1g; Net Carbs: 3g; Fiber: 0.2g; Sugar: 0.7g; Protein: 45.5g

Classic Mongolian Chicken

Prep time: 15 minutes | Cook time: 15 minutes | Serves: 5

12 oz. chicken wings	2 tablespoons red pepper paste
8 oz. flour	1 tablespoon apple cider vinegar
8 oz. breadcrumbs	2 tablespoons honey
3 beaten eggs	1 tablespoon soy sauce
4 tablespoons canola oil	Sesame seeds, to serve
Black pepper and salt to taste	
2 tablespoons sesame seeds	

Separate the chicken wings into winglets and drummettes. In a suitable bowl, mix salt, oil and black pepper. At 350 degrees F, preheat your Air fryer. Coat the chicken with beaten eggs followed by breadcrumbs and flour. Place the chicken in air fryer's cooking basket. Spray with a bit of oil and cook for almost 15 minutes. Mix red pepper paste, apple cider vinegar, soy sauce, honey and ¼ cup of water in a suitable saucepan and bring to a boil. Transfer the chicken to sauce mixture and toss to coat. Garnish with sesame to serve.
Nutritional information: Calories: 363; Fat: 17.1 g; Total Carbs: 19.8g; Net Carbs: 3g; Fiber: 3.4g; Sugar: 12.9g; Protein: 33.7g

Herbs Chicken Drumsticks with Tamari Sauce

Prep time: 15 minutes | Cook time: 35 minutes | Serves: 6

6 chicken drumsticks	3 tablespoons tamari sauce
Sauce:	1 teaspoon dried thyme
6 oz. hot sauce	½ teaspoon dried oregano
3 tablespoons olive oil	

Spritz the sides and bottom of the cooking basket with a nonstick cooking spray. Cook the chicken drumsticks at 380 degrees F for 35 minutes, flipping them over halfway through. Meanwhile, heat the hot sauce, olive oil, tamari sauce, thyme, and oregano in a pan over medium-low heat; reserve. Drizzle the sauce over the prepared chicken drumsticks; toss to coat well and serve.
Nutritional information: Calories: 297; Fat: 18.4 g; Total Carbs: 11.6g; Net Carbs: 3g; Fiber: 0.6g; Sugar: 10.9g; Protein: 20.5g

Chicken Sausage Meatballs with Cooked Penne

Prep time: 15 minutes | Cook time: 15 minutes | Serves: 4

1 cup chicken meat, ground	1 sweet red pepper, minced

¼ cup green onions, chopped
1 green garlic, minced
4 tablespoon bread crumbs
½ teaspoon cumin powder
1 tablespoon fresh coriander,

minced
½ teaspoon salt
¼ teaspoon mixed black peppercorns, ground
1 package penne pasta, cooked

Pre-heat the Air Fryer at about 350 degrees F. Put the chicken, red pepper, green onions, and garlic into a mixing bowl and stir together to combine. Throw in the seasoned bread crumbs and all of the seasonings. Combine again. Use your hands to mold equal amounts of the mixture into small balls, each 1 roughly the size of a golf ball. Put them in the air fryer and cook for almost 15 minutes. Shake once or twice throughout the cooking time for even results. Serve with cooked penne pasta.
Nutritional information: Calories: 384; Fat: 20.5g; Total Carbs: 5.1g; Net Carbs: 3g; Fiber: 2.1g; Sugar: 0.7g; Protein: 45g

Coated Chicken Wings

Prep time: 15 minutes | Cook time: 6 minutes | Serves: 4

8 chicken wings
2 tablespoons. all-purpose flour
1 teaspoon garlic, chopped finely

1 tablespoon fresh lemon juice
1 tablespoon soy sauce
½ teaspoon dried oregano, crushed
Salt and black pepper, to taste

At 355 degrees F, preheat your Air fryer. and grease its air fryer basket. Mix all the recipe ingredients except wings in a suitable bowl. Coat wings generously with the marinade and refrigerate for about 2 hours. Remove the chicken wings from marinade and sprinkle with flour evenly. Transfer the wings in the preheated Air Fryer tray and cook for about 6 minutes, flipping once in between. Dish out the chicken wings in a platter and serve hot.
Nutritional information: Calories: 328; Fat: 28.7 g; Total Carbs: 7.4g; Net Carbs: 3g; Fiber: 2.8g; Sugar: 0.7g; Protein: 13g

Grilled Chicken with Salsa Verde

Prep time: 15 minutes | Cook time: 40 minutes | Serves: 2

½ red onion, chopped
½ teaspoon chili powder
1 jalapeno thinly sliced
1 jar salsa Verde, divided
1-pound boneless skinless chicken breasts
2 cloves of garlic, minced

2 tablespoons chopped cilantro
2 tablespoons extra virgin olive oil
4 slices Monterey Jack cheese
Juice from ½ lime
Lime wedges for serving

In a Ziploc bag, add ½ of the salsa Verde, olive oil, lime juice, garlic, chili powder and chicken. Let this chicken marinate in the fridge for at least 2 hours. At 390 degrees F, preheat your Air fryer. Set a suitable grill pan accessory in the air fryer basket. Cook the prepared chicken in your air fryer for 40 minutes almost. Flip the chicken every 10 minutes to cook evenly. Serve the chicken with the cheese, jalapeno, red onion, cilantro, and lime wedges.
Nutritional information: Calories: 667; Fat: 18.4 g; Total Carbs: 22.5g; Net Carbs: 3g; Fiber: 3.2g; Sugar: 2.9g; Protein: 101.2g

Spice Chicken Wings with Parmesan Cheese

Prep time: 15 minutes | Cook time: 22 minutes | Serves: 3

¼ cup almond meal

¼ cup flaxseed meal

2 tablespoons butter, melted
6 tablespoons Parmesan cheese, preferably freshly grated

1 tablespoon Ranch seasoning mix
2 tablespoons oyster sauce
6 chicken wings, bone-in

At 370 degrees F, preheat your Air Fryer. In a re-sealable bag, place the almond meal, flaxseed meal, butter, parmesan, Ranch seasoning mix, and oyster sauce. Add the chicken wings and shake to coat on all sides. Arrange the chicken wings in the air fryer basket. Spritz the chicken wings with a nonstick cooking spray. Cook for 11 minutes. Turn them over and cook an additional 11 minutes. Serve warm.
Nutritional information: Calories: 206; Fat: 6.4 g; Total Carbs: 28.9g; Net Carbs: 3g; Fiber: 3.6g; Sugar: 20.4g; Protein: 11g

Seasoned Chicken Legs with Brussels Sprouts

Prep time: 15 minutes | Cook time: 35 minutes | Serves: 2

2 chicken legs
½ teaspoon paprika
½ teaspoon kosher salt

½ teaspoon black pepper
1 pound Brussels sprouts
1 teaspoon dill, fresh or dried

At 370 degrees F, preheat your Air Fryer. Now, season your chicken with paprika, salt, and black pepper. Transfer the chicken legs to the cooking basket. Cook for 10 minutes. Flip the chicken legs and cook an additional 10 minutes. Set aside. Add the Brussels sprouts to the cooking basket; sprinkle with dill. Cook at almost 380 degrees F for almost 15 minutes, shaking the basket halfway through. Serve with the reserved chicken legs. Enjoy.
Nutritional information: Calories: 370; Fat: 10.5 g; Total Carbs: 21.4g; Net Carbs: 3g; Fiber: 3.1g; Sugar: 1.9g; Protein: 46.6g

Rosemary Chicken with Lemon Wedges

Prep time: 15 minutes | Cook time: 25 minutes | Serves: 2

¾ pound chicken
½ tablespoon olive oil
1 tablespoon soy sauce
1 teaspoon fresh ginger, minced

1 tablespoon oyster sauce
3 tablespoons sugar
1 tablespoon fresh rosemary, chopped
½ fresh lemon, cut into wedges

In a suitable bowl, combine the chicken, oil, soy sauce, and ginger, coating the chicken well. Refrigerate for 30 minutes. At 390 degrees F, preheat your Air Fryer for 3 minutes. Place the chicken in the baking pan, transfer to the air fryer and cook for 6 minutes. In the meantime, put the rosemary, sugar, and oyster sauce in a suitable bowl and mix together. Add the rosemary mixture in the air fryer over the chicken and top the chicken with the lemon wedges. Resume cooking for another 13 minutes, turning the chicken halfway through. Serve.
Nutritional information: Calories: 346; Fat: 16.8 g; Total Carbs: 5.7g; Net Carbs: 3g; Fiber: 1g; Sugar: 2.9g; Protein: 42.2g

Garlic Chicken Breast

Prep time: 15 minutes | Cook time: 17 minutes | Serves: 3

1-pound chicken breast, skinless, boneless
1 teaspoon garlic powder
1 teaspoon dried thyme

1 teaspoon salt
½ teaspoon black pepper
½ teaspoon cayenne pepper
2 teaspoons sunflower oil

Sprinkle the chicken breast with garlic powder, dried thyme, salt, black pepper, and cayenne pepper. Then gently brush the chicken with sunflower oil and put it in the air fryer. Cook the chicken breast for almost 17 minutes at 385 degrees F. Slice the cooked chicken into servings.

Nutritional information: Calories: 669; Fat: 43.4 g; Total Carbs: 36.2g; Net Carbs: 3g; Fiber: 14.9g; Sugar: 4.3g; Protein: 38.4g

Ginger Lemon Chicken

Prep time: 15 minutes | Cook time: 24 minutes | Serves: 4

2 tablespoons spring onions, minced	½ cup chicken stock
1 tablespoon ginger, grated	Black pepper and salt to the taste
4 garlic cloves, minced	1 teaspoon olive oil
2 tablespoons coconut aminos	¼ cup cilantro, chopped
8 chicken drumsticks	1 tablespoon lemon juice

Heat up a suitable pan with the oil over medium-high heat, add the chicken drumsticks, brown them for 2 minutes per side and transfer to a pan that fits the air fryer. Add all the other ingredients, toss everything, put the pan in the air fryer and cook at almost 370 degrees F for 20 minutes. Divide the chicken and lemon sauce between plates and serve.

Nutritional information: Calories: 855; Fat: 39.2 g; Total Carbs: 13g; Net Carbs: 3g; Fiber: 3.1g; Sugar: 6.7g; Protein: 109.8g

Healthy Vegetable Patties

Prep time: 15 minutes | Cook time: 10 minutes | Serves: 6

¼ teaspoon black pepper	1 teaspoon onion powder
½ teaspoon paprika	1-pound radish, peeled and grated
¾ teaspoon salt	
1 onion, chopped	3 tablespoons coconut oil
1 teaspoon garlic powder	

At 350 degrees F, preheat your Air Fryer. Place all the recipe ingredients in a suitable mixing bowl. Form patties using your hands and place individual patties in the air fryer basket. Spray with cooking spray before closing the air fryer. Cook for 10 minutes at 350 degrees F or until crispy. When done, serve and enjoy.

Nutritional information: Calories: 467; Fat: 19.8 g; Total Carbs: 2.6g; Net Carbs: 3g; Fiber: 0.1g; Sugar: 2.2g; Protein: 65.7g

Glazed Chicken Drumsticks with Herbs

Prep time: 15 minutes | Cook time: 25 minutes | Serves: 4

½ tablespoon fresh rosemary, minced	drumsticks
	¼ cup Dijon mustard
1 tablespoon fresh thyme, minced	1 tablespoon honey
	2 tablespoons olive oil
4 6-ounces boneless chicken	Black pepper and salt, to taste

At 320 degrees F, preheat your air fryer. and spray its air fryer basket. Mix mustard, honey, oil, herbs, salt, and black pepper in a suitable bowl. Rub the chicken drumsticks with marinade and refrigerate overnight. Arrange the drumsticks into the air fryer basket in a single layer and cook for about 12 minutes. Set the air fryer to 355 degrees F and cook for 10 more minutes. Dish

out the chicken drumsticks onto a serving platter and serve hot.
Nutritional information: Calories: 199; Fat: 7.8 g; Total Carbs: 5.9g; Net Carbs: 3g; Fiber: 1.7g; Sugar: 1.9g; Protein: 25.9g

Seasoned Turkey Meat with Kale

Prep time: 15 minutes | Cook time: 15 minutes | Serves: 4

½ teaspoon garlic powder	shredded
½ teaspoon onion powder	2 cups kale, chopped
1 cup coconut milk	4 eggs, beaten
1-pound leftover turkey,	Black pepper and salt to taste

In a suitable mixing bowl, combine the eggs, coconut milk, garlic powder, and onion powder. Season with black pepper and salt to taste. Place the turkey meat and kale in a suitable baking dish. Pour over the egg mixture. Place in the preheated air fryer. Cook for 15 minutes at 350 degrees F. When done, serve and enjoy.

Nutritional information: Calories: 199; Fat: 7.8 g; Total Carbs: 5.9g; Net Carbs: 3g; Fiber: 1.7g; Sugar: 1.9g; Protein: 25.9g

Crispy Parmesan Chicken Breasts

Prep time: 15 minutes | Cook time: 15 minutes | Serves: 3

2 6-ounces boneless chicken breasts, cut into tenders	required
¾ cup buttermilk	½ cup all-purpose flour
1½ teaspoons Worcestershire sauce, divided	1½ cups panko breadcrumbs
	¼ cup Parmesan cheese, finely grated
½ teaspoon smoked paprika, divided	2 tablespoons butter, melted
Salt and black pepper, as	2 large eggs

In a suitable bowl, mix together buttermilk, ¾ teaspoon of Worcestershire sauce, ¼ teaspoon of paprika, salt, and black pepper. Add in the chicken tenders and refrigerate overnight. In a suitable bowl, mix the flour, remaining paprika, salt, and black pepper. Place the remaining Worcestershire sauce and eggs in a third bowl and beat until well combined. Mix well the panko, Parmesan, and butter in a fourth bowl. Remove the chicken tenders from bowl and discard the buttermilk. Coat the chicken tenders with flour mixture, then dip into egg mixture and finally coat with the panko mixture. At 400 degrees F, preheat your Air Fryer. Oil its air fryer basket. Arrange chicken tenders into the prepared air fryer basket in 2 batches in a single layer. Air fry for about 13-15 minutes, flipping once halfway through. Remove from Air Fryer and transfer the chicken tenders onto a serving platter. Serve hot.

Nutritional information: Calories: 286; Fat: 9.8 g; Total Carbs: 11.9g; Net Carbs: 3g; Fiber: 0.9g; Sugar: 1.2g; Protein: 36.2g

Za'atar Chicken Thighs

Prep time: 15 minutes | Cook time: 35 minutes | Serves: 4

4 chicken thighs	1 lemon juice
2 sprigs thyme	1 lemon zest
1 onion, cut into chunks	¼ cup olive oil
2 ½ tablespoons za'atar	¼ teaspoon black pepper
½ teaspoon cinnamon	1 teaspoon salt
2 garlic cloves, smashed	

Add oil, lemon juice, lemon zest, cinnamon, garlic, black pepper, 2 tablespoon za'atar, and salt in a large zip-lock bag and shake well. Add chicken, thyme, and onion to bag and shake well to coat. Place in refrigerator for overnight. At 380 degrees F, preheat your air fryer. Add marinated chicken in air fryer

basket and cook at 380 degrees F for 15 minutes. Turn chicken to another side and sprinkle with remaining za'atar spice, then cook for 15-18 minutes more. Serve and enjoy.
Nutritional information: Calories: 556; Fat: 37.8 g; Total Carbs: 16.5g; Net Carbs: 3g; Fiber: 0.5g; Sugar: 0g; Protein: 29.8g

Seasoned Chicken Thighs with Italian Herbs

Prep time: 15 minutes | Cook time: 20 minutes | Serves: 4

4 skin-on bone-in chicken thighs
2 tablespoons unsalted butter, melted
3 teaspoons Italian herbs
½ teaspoon garlic powder
¼ teaspoon onion powder

Using a brush, coat the chicken thighs with the melted butter. Combine the herbs with the garlic powder and onion powder, then massage into the chicken thighs. Place the thighs your air fryer's basket. Cook at almost exactly 380 degrees F for 20 minutes, turning the chicken halfway through to cook on the other side. Once the inner temperature has reached 165 degrees F, remove from the fryer and serve.
Nutritional information: Calories: 407; Fat: 11.5 g; Total Carbs: 31.9g; Net Carbs: 3g; Fiber: 1.3g; Sugar: 25.9g; Protein: 42.2g

Paprika Chicken Legs

Prep time: 15 minutes | Cook time: 25 minutes | Serves: 3

1-pound chicken legs
1 teaspoon Himalayan salt
1 teaspoon paprika
½ teaspoon black pepper
1 teaspoon butter, melted
1 turnip, trimmed and sliced

Spritz the sides and bottom of the cooking basket with a nonstick cooking spray. Season the chicken legs with salt, paprika, and black pepper. Cook at 370 degrees F for 10 minutes. Increase the temperature to 380 degrees F. Drizzle turnip slices with melted butter and transfer them to the cooking basket with the chicken. Cook the turnips and chicken for almost 15 minutes more, flipping them halfway through the cooking time. As for the chicken, an instant-read thermometer should read at least 165 degrees F. Serve and enjoy!
Nutritional information: Calories: 880; Fat: 50.8 g; Total Carbs:52.9g; Net Carbs: 3g; Fiber: 2.4g; Sugar: 5.9g; Protein: 53.2g

French Mustard Chicken Thighs

Prep time: 15 minutes | Cook time: 15 minutes | Serves: 4

1-pound bone-in or boneless, skinless chicken thighs
Black pepper and salt to taste
2 garlic cloves, minced
½ cup honey
¼ cup French mustard
2 tablespoons butter
2 tablespoon dill, chopped
Herbs de Provence seasoning, as needed

At 390 degrees F, preheat your Air fryer. Grease its air fryer basket with cooking spray. In a suitable bowl, mix the Herbs de Provence seasoning, salt, and black pepper. Rub the chicken with this mixture. Transfer to the cooking basket. Cook for almost 15 minutes, flipping once halfway through. Meanwhile, melt the butter in a suitable saucepan over medium heat. Add honey, French mustard, and garlic; cook until reduced to a thick consistency, about 3 minutes. Serve the chicken drizzled with the honey-mustard sauce.

Nutritional information: Calories: 386; Fat: 9.8 g; Total Carbs: 6.2g; Net Carbs: 3g; Fiber: 1.7g; Sugar: 3.1g; Protein: 19.2g

Mayo Turkey Breasts

Prep time: 15 minutes | Cook time: 60 minutes | Serves: 4

3 pounds' boneless turkey breast
¼ cup mayonnaise
2 teaspoons poultry seasoning
Black pepper and salt to taste
½ teaspoon garlic powder

At 360 degrees F, preheat your air fryer. Season the turkey with mayonnaise, seasoning, salt, garlic powder, and black pepper. Cook the turkey in the preheated Air Fryer for 1 hour at 360 degrees F. Turning after every 15 minutes. Serve.
Nutritional information: Calories: 722; Fat: 40.8 g; Total Carbs: 7.2g; Net Carbs: 3g; Fiber: 0.9g; Sugar: 5.9g; Protein: 79.2g

Marinated Chicken Breasts

Prep time: 15 minutes | Cook time: 15 minutes | Serves: 4

4 (6 oz. each) Boneless, skinless chicken breast
2 tablespoons BBQ seasoning
Cooking spray

Rub the chicken with BBQ seasoning and marinate in the refrigerator for 45 minutes. At 400 degrees F, preheat your Air Fryer. Grease its air fryer basket with oil and place the chicken. Spray oil on top. Cook for 13 to 14 minutes. Flipping at the halfway through. Serve.
Nutritional information: Calories: 186; Fat: 5.8 g; Total Carbs: 8.1g; Net Carbs: 3g; Fiber: 1.9g; Sugar: 4.3g; Protein: 25.2g

Sweet and Sour Chicken Drumsticks

Prep time: 15 minutes | Cook time: 40 minutes | Serves: 6

6 chicken drumsticks
1 cup water
¼ cup tomato paste
1 cup soy sauce
1 cup white vinegar
¾ cup sugar
¾ cup minced onion
¼ cup minced garlic
Black pepper and salt to taste

Place all the recipe ingredients in a Ziploc bag and refrigerate for 2 hours in the fridge. At 375 degrees F, preheat your Air Fryer. Set a suitable grill pan accessory in the air fryer. Cook the chicken in the preheated air fryer for 40 minutes in total. Turn chicken every 10 minutes for even grilling. Meanwhile, pour the prepared marinade in a suitable saucepan and heat over medium flame until the sauce thickens. Before serving the chicken, brush with the glaze.
Nutritional information: Calories: 562; Fat: 31.2 g; Total Carbs: 1.9g; Net Carbs: 3g; Fiber: 1.1g; Sugar: 0.9g; Protein: 66g

Chicken Burgers with Parmesan Cheese

Prep time: 15 minutes | Cook time: 15 minutes | Serves: 4

1 palmful dried basil
⅓ cup Parmesan cheese, grated
2 teaspoons dried marjoram
⅓ teaspoon ancho chili powder
2 teaspoons dried parsley
flakes
½ teaspoon onion powder
Toppings, to serve
⅓ teaspoon porcini powder
1 teaspoon salt flakes

1-pound chicken meat, ground | crushed
2 teaspoons cumin powder | 1 teaspoon freshly black
⅓ teaspoon red pepper flakes, | pepper

Generously grease an Air Fryer basket with a thin layer of vegetable oil. In a mixing dish, combine chicken meat with all seasonings. Shape into 4 patties and coat them with grated parmesan cheese. Cook chicken burgers in the preheated Air Fryer for almost 15 minutes at 345 degrees F, working in batches, flipping them once. Serve with toppings of choice.
Nutritional information: Calories: 291; Fat: 15.2 g; Total Carbs: 13g; Net Carbs: 3g; Fiber: 0.9g; Sugar: 10.9g; Protein: 26.5g

Dijon Chicken Breasts

Prep time: 15 minutes | Cook time: 24 minutes | Serves: 6

6 (6-oz, each) Boneless, | 3 tablespoons Honey
skinless chicken breasts | 1 tablespoon Dijon mustard
2 tablespoons Fresh rosemary, | Black pepper and salt to taste
minced |

Combine the mustard, honey, black pepper, rosemary and salt in a suitable bowl. Rub the chicken with this mixture. Grease its air fryer basket with oil. Air fry the chicken at 350 degrees F for 20 to 24 minutes or until the chicken' inner doneness reaches 165 degrees F. Serve.
Nutritional information: Calories: 236; Fat: 13.2 g; Total Carbs: 6.3g; Net Carbs: 3g; Fiber: 0.9g; Sugar: 4.4g; Protein: 23.2g

Chicken Wings with Paprika & Parmesan

Prep time: 15 minutes | Cook time: 15 minutes | Serves: 4

2 pounds Chicken wings, cut | 1 teaspoon Herbs de Provence
into drumettes, pat dried | 1 teaspoon Paprika
½ cup plus 6 tablespoons | Salt to taste
Parmesan, grated |

Combine the parmesan, herbs, paprika, and salt in a suitable bowl and rub the chicken with this mixture. At 350 degrees F, preheat your Air fryer. Grease the basket with cooking spray. Cook for almost 15 minutes. Flip once at the halfway through the cooking time. Garnish with parmesan and serve.
Nutritional information: Calories: 433; Fat: 8.7 g; Total Carbs: 4.9g; Net Carbs: 3g; Fiber: 1.1g; Sugar: 1.9g; Protein: 33.2g

Simple Grilled Chicken

Prep time: 15 minutes | Cook time: 35 minutes | Serves: 4

2 pounds' chicken wings | Cooking spray
Black pepper and salt, to taste |

Flavor the chicken wings with black pepper and salt. Grease its air fryer basket with cooking spray. Add chicken wings and cook at 400 degrees F for 35 minutes. Flip 3 times during cooking for even cooking. Serve.
Nutritional information: Calories: 499; Fat: 23.8 g; Total Carbs: 0.9g; Net Carbs: 3g; Fiber: 0.3g; Sugar: 0.1g; Protein: 65.6g

Honey-Mustard Duck Breasts

Prep time: 15 minutes | Cook time: 21 minutes | Serves: 2

1 smoked duck breast, halved | 1 teaspoon honey

1 teaspoon tomato paste | ½ teaspoon apple vinegar
1 tablespoon mustard |

Mix tomato paste, honey, mustard, and vinegar in a suitable bowl. Whisk well. Add duck breast pieces and coat well. Cook in the preheated Air Fryer at about 370 degrees F for almost 15 minutes. Remove the duck breast from the air fryer and add to the honey mixture. Coat again. Cook again at 370 degrees F for 6 minutes. Serve.
Nutritional information: Calories: 642; Fat: 34.3 g; Total Carbs: 12.9g; Net Carbs: 3g; Fiber: 2.9g; Sugar: 9.1g; Protein: 70.8g

Grilled Chicken Legs with Coconut Cream

Prep time: 15 minutes | Cook time: 25 minutes | Serves: 4

4 big chicken legs | Black pepper and salt to taste
5 teaspoons turmeric powder | 4 tablespoons coconut cream
2 tablespoons ginger grated |

In a suitable bowl, mix salt, black pepper, ginger, turmeric, and cream, whisk well. Add chicken pieces, coat and marinate for 2 hours. Transfer chicken to the preheated air fryer and cook at almost 370 degrees F for 25 minutes. Serve.
Nutritional information: Calories: 301; Fat: 11.2g; Total Carbs: 4.7g; Net Carbs: 3g; Fiber: 0.3g; Sugar: 3.5g; Protein: 42.9g

Air-fried Whole Chicken

Prep time: 15 minutes | Cook time: 45 minutes | Serves: 8

1-2 ½ pounds Whole chicken, | 1 teaspoon Salt
washed and pat dried | Cooking spray
2 tablespoons Dry rub |

At 350 degrees F, preheat your Air Fryer. Rub the dry rub on the chicken, then rub with salt. Cook it at 350 degrees F for 45 minutes. After 30 minutes, flip the chicken and resume cooking. Serve.
Nutritional information: Calories: 457; Fat: 28.8 g; Total Carbs: 7.8g; Net Carbs: 3g; Fiber: 2.9g; Sugar: 3.9g; Protein: 42g

Garlic Chicken Tenders with Pork Rinds

Prep time: 15 minutes | Cook time: 20 minutes | Serves: 4

1 pound boneless, skinless | ground
chicken tenders | 1 teaspoon chili powder
¼ cup hot sauce | 1 teaspoon garlic powder
1 ½ ounces pork rinds, finely |

Put the chicken breasts in a suitable bowl and pour hot sauce over them. Toss to coat. Mix ground pork rinds, chili powder and garlic powder in another bowl. Place each tender in the ground pork rinds, and coat well. With wet hands, press down the pork rinds into the chicken. Place the tender in a single layer into the air fryer basket. Cook at almost 375 degrees F for 20 minutes. Flip once at the middle of cooking time. Serve.
Nutritional information: Calories: 391; Fat: 12.3 g; Total Carbs: 23.9g; Net Carbs: 3g; Fiber: 3.7g; Sugar: 13.9g; Protein: 46.2g

Beef, Pork, and Lamb Recipes

Pork Meatballs

Prep time: 10 minutes | Cook time: 17 minutes | Serves: 8

1 ½ lbs. ground pork
2 small onions, chopped
4 garlic cloves, minced
2 tbsps. brie cheese, grated

1 ½ tsp. mustard
1 tsp. cayenne pepper
Pepper
Salt

Add all the recipe ingredients into the bowl and mix well. Make small balls from meat mixture and place into the air fryer basket. Air Fry the meatballs at 375 degrees F for 17 minutes. Serve and enjoy.
Nutritional information: Calories 142; Fat 3.9g; Total Carbs 2.5 g; Sugar 0.8 g; Net Carbs 6g; Protein 23.2 g; Fiber 4 g

Teriyaki Pork

Prep time: 15 minutes | Cook time:45 minutes | Serves: 4

2 lb. pork loin
½ tbsp. onion powder
1 tbsp. ground ginger
2 tbsps. honey

½ cup water
¼ cup soy sauce
1 cup chicken stock
2 tsps. dry garlic

Put and mix all the recipe ingredients in a suitable bowl except main meat and stock. Pour the stock into the Air Fryer. Place meat into the pot then pours bowl mixture over the pork. Air Fry the meat at 370 degrees F for 45 minutes. Turn the meat periodically. After the beep sounds, open the cover. Enjoy.
Nutritional information: Calories 201; Fat: 9g; Total Carbs 2.9g; Net Carbs 2g; Protein: 26.1g; Fiber: 0.1g; Sugar: 0.2g

Bratwurst with Vegetables

Prep time: 15 minutes | Cook time:20 minutes | Serves: 6

1 package bratwurst, sliced into identical pieces
½ tbsp. red chili pepper

¼ cup onion, diced
1 carrot, sliced

Add all the recipe ingredients into the large mixing bowl and toss well. Sprinkle the basket with oil spray. Add vegetable and bratwurst mixture into the sprayed "Air Fryer Basket" and Air Fry them at 370 degrees F for 10 min. Toss well and Air Fry for 10 min more. Enjoy.
Nutritional information: Calories 291; Total Carbs 19g; Net Carbs 15g; Protein 5g; Fat 23g; Sugar 13g; Fiber 4g

Asian Pork

Prep time: 15 minutes | Cook time:15 minutes | Serves: 4

1 lb. pork shoulder, boneless and cut into slices
½ inch sliced
3 tbsps. green onions, sliced
3 garlic cloves, diced
1 tbsp. ginger, diced

2 tbsps. red pepper paste
1 onion, sliced
1 tbsp. sesame seeds
¾ tbsp. cayenne pepper
1 tbsp. sesame oil
1 tbsp. rice wine

Add all the recipe ingredients into the bowl and mix well and place in the refrigerator for 1 hour. Place marinated meat and onion slices into the Air Fryer Basket. Air Fry the food at 380 degrees F for 15 min, flipping halfway through. Serve with sesame seeds and green onions. Enjoy.
Nutritional information: Calories 255; Total Carbs 18g; Net Carbs 16g; Protein 20g; Fat 11g; Sugar 3g; Fiber 2g

Great Garlicky Pork Roast

Prep time: 15 minutes | Cook time:35 minutes | Serves: 2

1 lb. pork roast
1 tbsp. basil
1 ½ tbsp. soy sauce
2 tbsps. honey
3 garlic cloves, diced

½ cup chicken stock
½ tbsp. corn-starch
½ tbsp. olive oil
salt, to taste

Mix all the recipe ingredients into the bowl. Transfer the entire contents of the bowl to the Air Fryer Basket. Air Fry the food at 370 degrees F for 35 minutes. Stir the meat periodically during cooking. Stir and serve.
Nutritional information: Calories 325; Total Carbs 20g; Net Carbs 14g; Protein 5g; Fat 26g; Sugar 10g; Fiber 6g

Air Fried Pork Strips

Prep time: 15 minutes | Cook time:30 minutes | Serves: 2

4 pork loin chops
2 tbsps. honey
1 tbsp. soy sauce

⅛ tbsp. ground ginger
1 garlic clove, minced
½ tbsp. apple sider vinegar

Cut pork into strips. Tenderize meat and season with pepper and salt. In a suitable bowl, mix honey, soy sauce, and vinegar. Add ginger and garlic and set aside. At 360 degrees F, preheat your Air Fryer. Add marinated meat into the Air Fryer Basket and Air Fry them for 15 minutes on each side. Serve with Greek yogurt souse. Enjoy.
Nutritional information: Calories 256; Total Carbs 15g; Net Carbs 10g; Protein 9g; Fat 18g; Sugar 5g; Fiber 5g

Air Fried Pork Loin

Prep time: 15 minutes | Cook time:40 minutes | Serves: 6

3 lbs. pork loin
½ tbsp. dried garlic
¼ tbsp. pepper

½ tbsp. herbs de Provence
1 tbsp. olive oil

Coat meat with olive oil, pepper, garlic salt, and herb de Provence. Place the loin in the Air Fryer Basket and Air Fry at 360 degrees F for 25 minutes. Turn to another side and Air Fry for 15 minutes more. Stir and serve.
Nutritional information: Calories 306; Total Carbs 20g; Net Carbs 15g; Protein 15g; Fat 19g; Sugar 4g; Fiber 5g

Pork Chops with Seasoning marinade

Prep time: 15 minutes | Cook time:12 minutes | Serves: 1

8 oz. pork chops
1 tsp. olive oil
1 tsp. paprika

1 tsp. onion powder
1 tsp. salt
1 tsp. pepper

At 380 degrees F, preheat your Air fryer. Brush pork chops with some olive oil. Mix the pork seasonings together in a suitable bowl and apply to both sides of the pork chops. Place pork chops in Air Fryer Basket and Air Fry them at 380 degrees F for 9 to 12 minutes, turning the chop over halfway, until it reaches a minimum temp of 145 degrees F.

Nutritional information: Calories 117; Total Carbs 4g; Net Carbs 0g; Protein 14g; Fat 5g; Sugar 2g; Fiber 0g

Greek Vegetable Mix

Prep time: 15 minutes | Cook time:19 minutes | Serves: 4

½ lb. 96 percent lean ground beef
2 medium tomatoes, minced
1 onion, minced
2 garlic cloves, diced
2 cups fresh baby spinach

2 tbsps. freshly squeezed lemon juice
⅓ cup low-sodium beef broth
2 tbsp. crumbled low-sodium feta cheese

Crumble the ground beef in the Air Fryer for 3 to 7 minutes at 370 degrees F, stirring once during cooking, until browned. Drain off any fat or liquid. Add the tomatoes, onion, and garlic to the basket. Air-fry for 4 to 8 minutes more, or until the onion is tender. Add the spinach, lemon juice, and beef broth. Air-fry for 2 to 4 minutes more, or until the spinach is wilted. Sprinkle with the feta cheese and serve immediately.

Nutritional information: Calories 239; Total Carbs 20g; Net Carbs 13g; Net Carbs 2g; Protein 4g; Fat 18g; Sugar 4g; Fiber 7g

Beef Chops with Broccoli

Prep time: 15 minutes | Cook time:30 minutes | Serves: 1

8 oz. Beef chops
6 oz. Broccoli
olive oil spray
1 tbsp. olive oil

⅛ tbsp. kosher salt
½ tbsp. black pepper
1 tbsp. dried garlic

Brush the beef chop with olive oil cooking spray; sprinkle with salt and ¼ tablespoon of pepper. Mix beef and broccoli with spices in a suitable bowl. Place the beef chops on one side of the Air Fryer Basket and the marinated Broccoli sprouts on the other. Air Fry the food at 380 degrees F for 20 minutes. Broccoli will be ready in 6 minutes. Serve hot with balsamic sauce.

Nutritional information: Calories 200; Total Carbs 7g; Net Carbs 4g; Protein 3g; Fat 18g; Sugar 2g; Fiber 3g

Honey Mustard Meatballs

Prep time: 15 minutes | Cook time:15 minutes | Serves: 8

2 onions, minced
1 lb. ground beef
4 tsps. fresh basil, minced
2 tsps. chopped garlic

2 tsps. honey
salt and black pepper, to taste
2 tsps. mustard

At 385 degrees F, preheat your Air fryer and grease an Air Fryer basket. Mix all the recipe ingredients in a suitable bowl well.

Shape the prepared mixture into equal-sized balls gently and arrange the meatballs in the Air Fryer Basket. Air Fry the food at 385 degrees F for 15 minutes. Dish out to serve warm with tomato salsa.

Nutritional information: Calories 320; Total Carbs: 10; Net Carbs 1.2g; Protein: 42g; Fat: 8; Sugar: 1g; Fiber: 2g

Adorable Air Fried Steak

Prep time: 15 minutes | Cook time:10 minutes | Serves: 2

2 sirloin steaks
2 tbsps. olive oil
2 tbsps. steak seasoning

pepper
salt

At 350 degrees F, preheat your Air Fryer F. Coat sirloin steaks with olive oil and season with steak seasoning, pepper, and salt. Spray "Air Fryer Basket" with some cooking spray and place steaks in it. Air Fry the steaks for 10 min, turning halfway through. Slice and serve with boiled white rice and tomato salsa.

Nutritional information: Calories 330; Total Carbs: 9g; Net Carbs 2g; Protein: 49g; Fat: 12; Sugar: 1g; Fiber: 2g

Classic Burger

Prep time: 15 minutes | Cook time:12 minutes | Serves: 2

1 lb. (450g) 80/20 ground chuck
¾ tsp. salt
½ tsp. ground black pepper
4 gluten free burger buns

4 slices tomato
1 cup shredded lettuce
4 tbsps. mayonnaise
4 slices cheddar cheese

Crumble the beef into a bowl and sprinkle over the black pepper and salt. Form into 4 evenly sized burger patties by hand or with a burger press. At 350 degrees F, preheat your Air Fryer. Air Fry the food at 350 degrees F for 8-12 minutes, or until the burger patty is cooked to your liking, flip the burger over after 4 minutes of cooking. If you want to add a slice of cheese, simply add it on top of each hot burger after the air fryer has switched off, if it's still on, it may blow the cheese off the burger! Serve while hot and add your preferred burger toppings.

Nutritional information: Calories 300; Total Carbs: 4g; Net Carbs 2g; Protein: 40g; Fat: 12g; Sugar: 1g; Fiber: 2g

Teriyaki Steak

Prep time: 15 minutes | Cook time:10 minutes | Serves: 4

1 lb. (450g) steak, cut into strips
¼ cup brown sugar
¼ cup soy sauce
⅛ cup teriyaki sauce

½ tsp. onion powder
½ tsp. garlic powder
¼ tsp. crushed red pepper
¼ tsp. pepper

Mix all the recipe ingredients the marinade in a suitable bowl. Add steak to bowl, dip in and cover. Marinate the steak for 1 hour in the refrigerator. Place the steak strips in the Air Fryer Basket and Air Fry them at 360 degrees F for 7 minutes on one side and 3 minutes on the other.

Nutritional information: Calories 290; Total Carbs: 22g; Net Carbs 2g; Protein: 34g; Fat:10g; Sugar: 1g; Fiber: 2g

Tasty & Spicy Lamb

Prep time: 15 minutes | Cook time:20 minutes | Serves: 4

1 lb. lamb meat, cut into pieces   2 tbsps. lemon juice

½ cup fresh parsley, minced
2 onions, minced
2 cups chicken stock
1 cup of coconut milk
1 cup grape tomatoes, minced
½ tbsp. cumin powder
2 ½ tbsps. chili powder
1 tsp. salt

Season the lamb meat pieces with black pepper and salt. Transfer the meat pieces to the "Air Fryer Basket" and Air Fry them at 370 degrees F for 5 minutes. When the time is up, add the remaining ingredients and stir, then resume cooking for 15 minutes more. Serve and enjoy.
Nutritional information: Calories 240; Total Carbs: 9g; Net Carbs 1.2g; Protein: 35g; Fat: 10g; Sugar: 1g; Fiber: 2g

Gorgeous Lamb Meatballs

Prep time: 15 minutes | Cook time:8 minutes | Serves: 4

2 eggs, beaten
2 tbsps. pistachios, minced
1 lb. ground lamb
1 tbsp. plain flour
2 tbsps. flat-leaf parsley, minced
1 tsp. chili pepper
2 garlic cloves, diced
2 tbsps. fresh lemon juice
2 tsps. oregano
2 tsps. salt
olive oil
1 tsp. freshly ground black pepper

Preheat the Air Fryer to 355 degrees F and grease an Air Fryer basket. Mix lamb, pistachios, eggs, juice, chili, flour, oregano, parsley, salt, and black pepper in an exceedingly large bowl. Form meatballs, place the meatballs in the "Air Fryer Basket" and Air Fry them for 8 minutes. Enjoy.
Nutritional information: Calories 200; Total Carbs: 12g; Fat: 7; Net Carbs 0.5g; Protein: 41g; Sugar: 1g; Fiber: 2g

Nourishing Lamb with Potatoes

Prep time: 15 minutes | Cook time:20 minutes | Serves: 2

½ lb. lamb meat
2 small potatoes, peeled and halved
½ small onion, peeled and halved
1 garlic clove, crushed
½ tbsp. dried rosemary, crushed
1 tsp. olive oil
salt, pepper

Preheat the Air Fryer to 355 degrees F and arrange a divider in the Air Fryer Basket. Rub the lamb evenly with garlic and rosemary and place on 1 side of Air Fryer Basket. Cut the potatoes into desired pieces, add the onion, olive oil, black pepper and salt. Place the potato pieces on the other side of basket. Air Fry the lamb meat for 20 minutes, but get the potatoes after 10 minutes of cooking time. Cut meat in portions. Serve hot.
Nutritional information: Calories 310; Total Carbs: 20g; Sugar: 3g; Fat: 5g; Net Carbs 2g; Protein: 27g; Sugar: 1g; Fiber: 2g

Roast Lamb with Rosemary

Prep time: 15 minutes | Cook time:15 minutes | Serves: 2

10 oz. (280g) butterflied lamb leg roast
1 tbsp. olive oil
1 tsp. rosemary, fresh or dried
1 tsp. thyme, fresh or dried
½ tsp. black pepper

Preheat the Air Fryer to 360 degrees F. Mix olive oil with rosemary and thyme in a plate Pat lamb roast dry and place into the herb oil mixture. Place lamb in the Air Fryer Basket and Air Fry for 15 minutes at 360 degrees F. Remove roast lamb from air fryer, cover it with foil and leave to rest for 5 minutes before serving. Cut against the grain to serve.
Nutritional information: Calories 250; Total Carbs: 5g; Sugar: 0g; Fat: 10g; Net Carbs 2g; Protein: 40g; Sugar: 1g; Fiber: 2g

Keto Crispy Pork Chops

Prep time: 10 minutes | Cook time: 12 minutes | Serves: 4

Salt and black pepper to taste
1 tbsp. crushed pork rinds
¼ tsp. garlic powder
¼ tsp. onion powder
⅛ tsp. paprika
1 egg
4 small slices cold butter

At 390 degrees F, preheat your Air Fryer. In a suitable bowl, combine all the recipe ingredients except the pork, egg, and butter and mix well. in another bowl, whisk the egg with salt. Dip the pork first in the egg and then coat with the pork rind mixture. Spray with some cooking spray and place them in the "Air Fryer Basket". Air Fry them at 390 degrees F for 12 minutes, flipping once halfway through. Garnish with a slice of butter to serve.
Nutritional information: Calories 193; Fat 15.3 g; Total Carbs 10.9 g; Net Carbs 2g; Protein 5.2 g; Sugar 5.6 g; Fiber 2g

Steak Bites with Mushrooms

Prep time: 10 minutes | Cook time: 18 minutes | Serves: 3

1 lb. steaks, cut into ½-inch cubes
½ tsp. garlic powder
1 tsp. Worcestershire sauce
2 tbsps. butter, melted
8 oz. mushrooms, sliced
Pepper
Salt

Add all the recipe ingredients into the large mixing bowl and toss well. Spray the "Air Fryer Basket" with some cooking spray. At 400 degrees F, preheat your Air Fryer. Add steak mushroom mixture into the "Air Fryer Basket" and Air Fry at 400 degrees F for 15-18 minutes. Shake basket twice during cooking. Serve and enjoy.
Nutritional information: Calories 347; Total Carbs 23g; Net Carbs 11g; Protein 9g; Fat 12 g; Sugar 6g; Fiber 3g

Simple Air Fryer Steak

Prep time: 10 minutes | Cook time: 18 minutes | Serves: 2

12 oz. steaks, ¾-inch thick
1 tsp. garlic powder
1 tsp. olive oil
Pepper
Salt

Coat steaks with oil and season with garlic powder, pepper, and salt. At 400 degrees F, preheat your Air Fryer. Place the prepared steaks in "Air Fryer Basket" and Air Fry them at 400 degrees F for 15-18 minutes, turning halfway through. Serve and enjoy.
Nutritional information: Calories 375; Total Carbs 14g; Net Carbs 4g; Protein 6g; Fat 13g; Sugar 7g; Fiber 2g

Savory Apple Pork Bites

Prep time: 25 minutes | Cook time: 25 minutes | Serves: 10

1 whole egg, beaten
3 ½ oz. onion, chopped
2 tbsps. dried sage
2 tbsps. almonds, chopped
½ tsp. pepper
3 ½ oz. apple, sliced
½ tsp. salt

At 350 degrees F, preheat your Air fryer. In a suitable bowl, mix onion, almonds, sliced apples, egg, pepper and salt. Add the almond mixture and sausage to a Ziploc bag. Mix to coat well and set aside for 15 minutes. Use the prepared mixture to form cutlets. Add them to the Air Fryer Basket and Air Fry them at 350 degrees F for 25 minutes. Serve with heavy cream.

Nutritional information: Calories 409; Total Carbs 20g; Net Carbs 6.7g; Protein 4.3g; Fat 5g; Sugar 1.1g; Fiber 2g

Crisp Pork Chops

Prep time: 10 minutes | Cook time: 12 minutes | Serves: 6

1 ½ lbs. pork chops, boneless
1 tsp. paprika
1 tsp. creole seasoning

1 tsp. garlic powder
¼ cup parmesan cheese, grated
⅓ cup almond flour

At 360 degrees F, preheat your Air Fryer. Add all the recipe ingredients except pork chops in a zip-lock bag. Add pork chops in the bag. Seal this bag and shake well to coat pork chops. Remove pork chops from zip-lock bag and place them in the Air Fryer Basket. Air Fry the pork chops at 360 degrees F for 10-12 minutes. Serve and enjoy.

Nutritional information: Calories 401; Total Carbs 21g; Net Carbs 9g; Protein 5.3g; Fat 7g; Sugar 2.1g; Fiber 2g

Easy Pork & Parmesan Meatballs

Prep time: 10 minutes | Cook time: 10 minutes | Serves: 3

1 lb. ground pork
2 tbsps. tamari sauce
1 tsp. garlic, minced
2 tbsps. spring onions, chopped
1 tbsp. brown sugar

1 tbsp. olive oil
½ cup breadcrumbs
2 tbsps. parmesan cheese, preferably freshly grated

Combine the ground pork, tamari sauce, garlic, onions, and sugar in a mixing dish. Mix until everything is well incorporated. Form the prepared mixture into small meatballs. In a shallow bowl, mix the olive oil, breadcrumbs, and parmesan. Roll the meatballs over the parmesan mixture. Air Fry the meatballs at 380 degrees F for 3 minutes; shake the basket and cook an additional 4 minutes or until meatballs are browned on all sides. Bon appétit!

Nutritional information: Calories 375; Total Carbs 20g; Net Carbs 11g; Protein 7.6g; Fat 11g; Sugar 5g; Fiber 1g

Coconut Butter Pork Chops

Prep time: 10 minutes | Cook time: 15 minutes | Serves: 2

4 pork chops
1 tbsp. coconut oil
1 tbsp. coconut butter
1 tsp. dried parsley
¼ tsp. dried basil

¼ tsp. rosemary
3 garlic cloves, minced
Pepper
Salt

At 350 degrees F, preheat your Air Fryer. In a suitable bowl, mix garlic, coconut butter, coconut oil, parsley, basil, rosemary, pepper, and salt. Rub garlic mixture over pork chops. Place in the refrigerator for 2 hours. Place marinated pork chops into the "Air Fryer Basket" and Air Fry them at 350 degrees F for 7 minutes. Turn pork chops to another side and Air Fry for 8 minutes more. Serve and enjoy.

Nutritional information: Calories 409; Total Carbs 20g; Net Carbs 6.7g; Protein 4.3g; Fat 5g; Sugar 1.1g; Fiber 2g

Beef with Creamed Mushroom Sauce

Prep time: 10 minutes | Cook time: 15 minutes | Serves: 5

2 tbsps. butter

2 lbs. sirloin, cut into 4 pieces

Salt and cracked black pepper, to taste
1 tsp. cayenne pepper
½ tsp. dried rosemary
½ tsp. dried dill
¼ tsp. dried thyme

1 lb. Cremini mushrooms, sliced
1 cup sour cream
1 tsp. mustard
½ tsp. curry powder

Start by preheating your Air Fryer to 395 degrees F. Grease a baking pan with butter. Add the sirloin, salt, black pepper, cayenne pepper, rosemary, dill, and thyme to the baking pan. Air Fry the food at 395 degrees F for 9 minutes. Next, stir in the mushrooms, sour cream, mustard, and curry powder. Continue to cook for 5 minutes or until everything is heated through. Spoon onto individual serving plates. Bon appétit!

Nutritional information: Calories 375; Total Carbs 14g; Net Carbs 4g; Protein 6g; Fat 13g; Sugar 7g; Fiber 2g

Mushrooms Meatballs

Prep time: 10 minutes | Cook time: 20 minutes | Serves: 2

½ lb. ground beef
2 tbsps. onion, chopped
2 mushrooms, diced
¼ tsp. pepper

1 tbsp. parsley, chopped
¼ cup almond flour
½ tsp. salt

In a suitable mixing bowl, combine together all the recipe ingredients well. Make small balls from meat mixture and place into the Air Fryer Basket. Air Fry the balls at 350 degrees F for 20 minutes. Serve and enjoy.

Nutritional information: Calories 389; Total Carbs 21g; Net Carbs 9g; Protein 5.3g; Fat 7g; Sugar 2.1g; Fiber 2g

Mustard Pork Tenderloin

Prep time: 10 minutes | Cook time: 15 minutes | Serves: 2

1 pork tenderloin, cut into pieces
½ tbsp. mustard
1 onion, sliced
1 bell pepper, cut into strips

1 tbsp. oil
2 tsps. herb de Provence
Pepper
Salt

At 390 degrees F, preheat your Air Fryer. In a suitable bowl, mix bell pepper strips, herb de Provence, onion, pepper, and salt. Add ½ tablespoon of oil and mix well. Season pork tenderloin with mustard, pepper, and salt. Coat pork tenderloin with the remaining oil. Place pork tenderloin pieces into the air fryer pan and top with bell pepper mixture. Place pan in the air fryer and Air Fry the food for 15 minutes. Stir halfway through cooking. Serve and enjoy.

Nutritional information: Calories 347; Total Carbs 23g; Net Carbs 11g; Protein 9g; Fat 12 g; Sugar 6g; Fiber 3g

Spanish-style Pork with Padrón Peppers

Prep time: 10 minutes | Cook time: 26 minutes | Serves: 4

1 tbsp. olive oil
8 oz. Padrón peppers
2 lbs. pork loin, sliced
1 tsp. Celtic salt

1 tsp. paprika
1 heaped tbsp. capers, drained
8 green olives, pitted and halved

Drizzle olive oil all over the Padrón peppers; Air Fry them at 400 degrees F for 10 minutes, turning occasionally, until well blistered all over and tender-crisp. Season the pork loin with salt and paprika. Add the capers and Air Fry them at 360 degrees

F for 16 minutes, turning them over halfway through the Cook Time. Serve with olives and the reserved Padrón peppers.
Nutritional information: Calories 415; Total Carbs 21g; Net Carbs 10g; Protein 7g; Fat 14g; Sugar 8g; Fiber 3g

McCormick Pork Chops

Prep time: 40 minutes | Cook time: 15 minutes | Serves: 2

2 pork chops	2 tbsps. arrowroot flour
½ tsp. McCormick Montreal chicken seasoning	1 ½ tbsps. coconut milk
	Salt

Season pork chops with pepper and salt. Drizzle milk over the pork chops. Place pork chops in a zip-lock bag with flour and shake well to coat. Marinate the pork chops for 30 minutes. Place marinated pork chops into the "Air Fryer Basket" and Air Fry them at 380 degrees F for 15 minutes, turning halfway through. Serve and enjoy.
Nutritional information: Calories 375; Total Carbs 20g; Net Carbs 11g; Protein 7.6g; Fat 11g; Sugar 5g; Fiber 1g

Flavorful Kabab

Prep time: 10 minutes | Cook time: 10 minutes | Serves: 2

½ lb. ground beef	1 ½ tbsps. kabab spice mix
1 tbsp. parsley, chopped	½ tbsp. garlic, minced
½ tbsp. olive oil	½ tsp. salt

Add all the recipe ingredients into the bowl and mix well combined. Divide mixture into the two equal portions and give it to kabab shape. Place kababs into the "Air Fryer Basket" and Air Fry them at 370 degrees F for 10 minutes. Serve and enjoy.
Nutritional information: Calories 391; Total Carbs 19g; Net Carbs 5g; Protein 3g; Fat 8g; Sugar 3g; Fiber 1g

Dreamy Beef Roast

Prep time: 10 minutes | Cook time: 50 minutes | Serves: 3

4 lb. top round roast beef	½ tsp. fresh rosemary, chopped
1 tsp. salt	3 lbs. red potatoes, halved
¼ tsp. fresh ground black pepper	Olive oil, black pepper and salt for garnish
1 tsp. dried thyme	

At 360 degrees F, preheat your Air Fryer. In a suitable bowl, mix rosemary, salt, pepper and thyme; rub oil onto beef. Season with the spice mixture. Place the prepared meat in your air fryer's "Air Fryer Basket" and Air Fry them at 360 degrees F for 20 minutes. Give the meat a turn and add potatoes, more pepper and oil. Air Fry the food for 20 minutes more. Take the steak out and set aside to cool for 10 minutes. Air Fry the potatoes in your air fryer for 10 more minutes at 400 degrees F. Serve hot.
Nutritional information: Calories 401; Total Carbs 21g; Net Carbs 9g; Protein 5.3g; Fat 7g; Sugar 2.1g; Fiber 2g

St. Louis-style Pork Ribs with Roasted Peppers

Prep time: 10 minutes | Cook time: 50 minutes | Serves: 2

2 lbs. St. Louis-style pork spareribs, individually cut	1 tbsp. sweet paprika
1 tsp. seasoned salt	½ tsp. mustard powder
½ tsp. ground black pepper	2 tbsps. sesame oil
	4 bell pepper, seeded

Toss and rub the spices all over the pork ribs; drizzle with 1 tablespoon of sesame oil. Air Fry the pork ribs at 360 degrees F for 15 minutes; flip the ribs and cook an additional 20 minutes or until they are tender inside and crisp on the outside. Toss the peppers with the remaining 1 tablespoon of oil; season to taste and Air Fry them at 390 degrees F for 15 minutes. Serve the warm spareribs with the roasted peppers on the side. Enjoy!
Nutritional information: Calories 409; Total Carbs 20g; Net Carbs 6.7g; Protein 4.3g; Fat 5g; Sugar 1.1g; Fiber 2g

Minty Tender Filet Mignon

Prep time: 2 hours 10 minutes | Cook time: 20 minutes | Serves: 4

2 tbsps. olive oil	chopped
2 tbsps. Worcestershire sauce	4 garlic cloves, minced
1 lemon, juiced	salt and black pepper, to taste
¼ cup fresh mint leaves,	2 lbs. filet mignon

In a ceramic bowl, place the olive oil, Worcestershire sauce, lemon juice, mint leaves, garlic, salt, black pepper, and cayenne pepper. Add the fillet mignon and let it marinate for 2 hours in the refrigerator. Air Fry the food at 400 degrees F for 18 minutes, basting with the reserved marinade and flipping a couple of times. Serve warm. Bon appétit!
Nutritional information: Calories 415; Total Carbs 21g; Net Carbs 10g; Protein 7g; Fat 14g; Sugar 8g; Fiber 3g

Spice-coated Steaks

Prep time: 10 minutes | Cook time: 6 minutes | Serves: 2

½ tsp. cayenne pepper	½ tsp. ground paprika
1 tbsp. olive oil	Salt and black pepper to taste

Preheat air fryer to 390 degrees F. Mix olive oil, black pepper, cayenne, paprika, and salt and rub onto steaks. Spread evenly. Put the steaks in the Air Fryer Basket, and Air Fry them at 390 degrees F for 6 minutes, turning them halfway through.
Nutritional information: Calories 375; Total Carbs 20g; Net Carbs 11g; Protein 7.6g; Fat 11g; Sugar 5g; Fiber 1g

Hawaiian Cheesy Meatball Sliders

Prep time: 10 minutes | Cook time: 15 minutes | Serves: 4

1 lb. ground pork	½ cup Romano cheese, grated
2 tbsps. bacon, chopped	1 cup tortilla chips, crushed
2 garlic cloves, minced	1 ½ cups marinara sauce
2 tbsps. scallions, chopped	8 Hawaiian rolls
Salt and ground black pepper, to taste	1 cup Cheddar cheese, shredded

Mix the ground pork with the bacon, garlic, scallions, salt, black pepper, cheese, and tortilla chips. Shape the prepared mixture into 8 meatballs. Add the meatballs to the lightly greased baking pan. Pour in the marinara sauce and lower the pan onto the Air Fryer Basket. Air Fry the meatballs at 380 degrees for 10 minutes. Check the meatballs halfway through the Cook Time. Place one meatball on top of the bottom half of one roll. Spoon the marinara sauce on top of each meatball. Top with cheese and Air Fry them at 370 degrees F for 3 to 4 minutes. Add the other half of the Hawaiian roll on top and serve immediately. Bon appétit!
Nutritional information: Calories 390; Total Carbs 20g; Net Carbs 6.7g; Protein 4.3g; Fat 5g; Sugar 1.1g; Fiber 2g

Smoked Sausage with Sauerkraut

Prep time: 10 minutes | Cook time: 35 minutes | Serves: 4

4 pork sausages, smoked
2 tbsps. canola oil
2 garlic cloves, minced
1 lb. sauerkraut

1 tsp. cayenne pepper
½ tsp. black peppercorns
2 bay leaves

At 360 degrees F, preheat your Air Fryer. Prick holes into the sausages using a fork and transfer them to the Air Fryer Basket. Air Fry the sausages at 360 degrees F for 14 minutes, shaking the basket a couple of times. Set aside. Now, heat the canola oil in a baking pan at 380 degrees F for about 1 minute on Air Fry mode. Add the garlic and Air Fry for 1 minute. Immediately stir in the sauerkraut, cayenne pepper, peppercorns, and bay leaves. Air Fry the food at 380 degrees F for 15 minutes, stirring every 5 minutes. Serve in individual bowls with warm sausages on the side!

Nutritional information: Calories 375; Total Carbs 14g; Net Carbs 4g; Protein 6g; Fat 13g; Sugar 7g; Fiber 2g

Juicy Strip Steak

Prep time: 10 minutes | Cook time: 30 minutes | Serves: 4

1 ½ lbs. strip steak, sliced
¼ cup chickpea flour
⅓ cup Shoyu sauce
2 tbsps. honey
1 tsp. mustard seeds

2 tbsps. champagne vinegar
1 tsp. ginger-garlic paste
½ tsp. coriander seeds
1 tbsp. cornstarch

At 395 degrees F, preheat your Air Fryer. Toss the strip steak slices with chickpea flour. Transfer the steak slices to the Air Fryer Basket. Air Fry the strip steak slices at 395 degrees F for 12 minutes; flip them over and cook an additional 10 minutes. In the meantime, heat the saucepan over medium-high heat. Add the Shoyu sauce, honey, mustard seeds, champagne vinegar, ginger-garlic paste, and coriander seeds. Reduce the heat and simmer until the sauce is heated through. Make the slurry by whisking the cornstarch with 1 tablespoon of water. Now, whisk in the cornstarch slurry and continue to simmer until the sauce has thickened. Pour the prepared sauce over the steak and serve.

Nutritional information: Calories 389; Total Carbs 21g; Net Carbs 9g; Protein 5.3g; Fat 7g; Sugar 2.1g; Fiber 2g

Vienna Sausage with Broccoli

Prep time: 10 minutes | Cook time: 25 minutes | Serves: 4

1 lb. beef Vienna sausage
½ cup mayonnaise
1 tsp. yellow mustard
1 tbsp. fresh lemon juice

1 tsp. garlic powder
¼ tsp. black pepper
1 lb. broccoli

At 380 degrees F, preheat your Air Fryer. Spritz the grill pan with cooking oil. Cut the sausages into serving sized pieces. Cook the sausages for 15 minutes, shaking the basket occasionally to get all sides browned. Set aside. In the meantime, whisk the mayonnaise with mustard, lemon juice, garlic powder, and black pepper. Toss the broccoli with the mayo mixture. Turn up temperature to 400 degrees F. Cook broccoli for 6 minutes, turning halfway through the Cook Time. Serve the sausage with the broccoli on the side. Bon appétit!

Nutritional information: Calories 409; Total Carbs 20g; Net Carbs 6.7g; Protein 4.3g; Fat 5g; Sugar 1.1g; Fiber 2g

BBQ Ribs

Prep time: 10 minutes | Cook time: 30 minutes | Serves: 2

1 lb. pork ribs
½ tsp. five-spice powder
1 tbsp. swerve
4 tbsps. BBQ sauce, sugar-free
3 garlic cloves, chopped

1 tsp. soy sauce
1 tsp. pepper
1 tsp. sesame oil
1 tsp. salt

At 350 degrees F, preheat your Air Fryer. Add all the recipe ingredients into the large bowl and mix well to coat. Place into the fridge for 1 hour. Add marinated ribs into the "Air Fryer Basket" and Air Fry them at 350 degrees F for 15 minutes. Turn ribs to another side and Air Fry for 15 minutes more. Serve and enjoy.

Nutritional information: Calories 375; Total Carbs 20g; Net Carbs 11g; Protein 7.6g; Fat 11g; Sugar 5g; Fiber 1g

Taco Casserole with Cheese

Prep time: 10 minutes | Cook time: 16 minutes | Serves: 4

1 lb. lean ground pork
½ lb. ground beef
¼ cup tomato puree
Salt and black pepper, to taste
1 tsp. smoked paprika
½ tsp. dried oregano

1 tsp. dried basil
1 tsp. dried rosemary
2 eggs
1 cup Cottage cheese, crumbled, at room temperature
½ cup Cotija cheese, shredded

Lightly grease a suitable casserole dish with a nonstick cooking oil. Add the ground meat to the bottom of your casserole dish. Add the tomato puree. Sprinkle with salt, black pepper, paprika, oregano, basil, and rosemary. In a suitable mixing bowl, whisk the egg with cheese. Place on top of the ground meat mixture. Place a piece of foil on top. Air Fry the food at 350 degrees F for 10 minutes; remove the foil and cook an additional 6 minutes. Bon appétit!

Nutritional information: Calories 391; Total Carbs 19g; Net Carbs 5g; Protein 3g; Fat 8g; Sugar 3g; Fiber 1g

Crispy Sweet and Spicy Beef Tenderloin

Prep time: 10 minutes | Cook time: 15 minutes | Serves: 3

2 lbs. beef tenderloin, cut into strips
½ cup flour
Cooking spray
Sauce:
1 tbsp. minced ginger
1 tbsp. minced garlic
½ cup chopped green onions

2 tbsps. olive oil
½ cup soy sauce
½ cup water
¼ cup vinegar
¼ cup sugar
1 tsp. cornstarch
½ tsp. red chili flakes
Black pepper and salt to taste

Pour the flour in a suitable bowl, add in beef strips and mix. Grease the Air Fryer Basket with some cooking spray and arrange the beef strips in it; spray with some cooking spray. Air Fry the beef at 400 degrees F for 4 minutes. Slide-out and shake the basket to toss the beef strips. Cook further for 3 minutes; set aside. To make the sauce, pour the cornstarch in a suitable bowl and mix it with 3 to 4 teaspoons of water until well dissolve; set aside. In a suitable wok, add the olive oil, garlic, and ginger, cook them over medium heat on a stovetop. Stir continually for 10 seconds. Add the soy sauce, vinegar, and remaining water. Stir well and bring to boil for 2 minutes. Stir in the sugar, chili flakes, and cornstarch mixture. Add the beef strips, stir and cook for 3 minutes. Stir in the green onions and cook for 1 to 2 minutes. Season with pepper and salt as desired. Turn off the

heat. Serve with a side of steamed rice.
Nutritional information: Calories 389; Total Carbs 21g; Net Carbs 9g; Protein 5.3g; Fat 7g; Sugar 2.1g; Fiber 2g

Panko Beef Schnitzel

Prep time: 10 minutes | Cook time: 12 minutes | Serves: 1

1 thin beef cutlet	1 tsp. paprika
1 egg, beaten	¼ tsp. garlic powder
2 oz. breadcrumbs	Black pepper and salt, to taste

At 350 degrees F, preheat your Air Fryer. Combine olive oil, breadcrumbs, paprika, garlic powder, and salt, in a suitable bowl. Dip the beef in with the egg first, and then coat it with the breadcrumb mixture completely. Line a baking dish with baking paper and place the breaded meat on it. Air Fry the meat at 350 degrees F for 12 minutes. Serve.
Nutritional information: Calories 347; Total Carbs 23g; Net Carbs 11g; Protein 9g; Fat 12 g; Sugar 6g; Fiber 3g

Cheese Herb Pork Chops

Prep time: 10 minutes | Cook time: 9 minutes | Serves: 2

2 pork chops, boneless	grated
1 tsp. herb de Provence	⅓ cup almond flour
1 tsp. paprika	½ tsp. Cajun seasoning
4 tbsps. parmesan cheese,	

At 350 degrees F, preheat your Air Fryer. Mix almond flour, Cajun seasoning, herb de Provence, paprika, and cheese. Spray pork chops with some cooking spray and coat pork chops with almond flour mixture and place into the Air Fryer Basket. Air Fry the pork chops at 350 degrees F for 9 minutes. Serve and enjoy.
Nutritional information: Calories 409; Total Carbs 20g; Net Carbs 6.7g; Protein 4.3g; Fat 5g; Sugar 1.1g; Fiber 2g

Cheesy Pork Meatballs

Prep time: 10 minutes | Cook time: 15 minutes | Serves: 2

5 oz. pork minced	½ onion, diced
½ tbsp. cheddar cheese, grated	½ tsp. mustard
½ tsp. erythritol	Pepper
½ tsp. garlic, minced	Salt
1 tbsp. fresh basil, chopped	

Add all the recipe ingredients into the large bowl and mix well to combine. Make small balls from meat mixture and place in the Air Fryer Basket. Air Fry the meatballs at 390 degrees F for 15 minutes. Serve and enjoy.
Nutritional information: Calories 409; Total Carbs 20g; Net Carbs 6.7g; Protein 4.3g; Fat 5g; Sugar 1.1g; Fiber 2g

Parmesan Pork Chops

Prep time: 10 minutes | Cook time: 15 minutes | Serves: 4

4 pork chops, boneless	½ tsp. chili powder
4 tbsp. parmesan cheese,	½ tsp. onion powder
grated	1 tsp. paprika
1 cup pork rind	¼ tsp. pepper
2 eggs, lightly beaten	½ tsp. salt

At 400 degrees F, preheat your Air Fryer. Season pork chops with pepper and salt. Add pork rind in food processor and

process until crumbs form. Mix pork rind crumbs and seasoning in a suitable bowl. Place egg in a separate bowl. Dip pork chops in egg mixture then coat with pork crumb mixture and place in the air fryer basket. Air Fry the pork chops at 400 degrees F for 12-15 minutes. Serve and enjoy.
Nutritional information: Calories 401; Total Carbs 21g; Net Carbs 9g; Protein 5.3g; Fat 7g; Sugar 2.1g; Fiber 2g

Cayenne Cumin Lamb

Prep time: 10 minutes | Cook time: 10 minutes | Serves: 4

1 lb. lamb, cut into 1-inch pieces	2 tbsps. ground cumin
2 tbsp. olive oil	2 chili peppers, chopped
1 tsp. cayenne	1 tbsp. garlic, minced
	1 tsp. salt

In a suitable bowl, mix ground cumin, chili peppers, garlic, olive oil, cayenne, and salt. Stir in diced lamb meat and mix well. Place in refrigerator for 1 hour. Place marinated meat into the Air Fryer Basket and Air Fry them at 360 degrees F for 10 minutes. Serve and enjoy.
Nutritional information: Calories 375; Total Carbs 20g; Net Carbs 11g; Protein 7.6g; Fat 11g; Sugar 5g; Fiber 1g

Scotch Fillet with Sweet 'n' Sticky Sauce

Prep time: 10 minutes | Cook time: 30 minutes | Serves: 4

2 lbs. scotch fillet, sliced into strips	2 garlic cloves, minced
4 tbsps. tortilla chips, crushed	½ tsp. dried rosemary
2 green onions, chopped	½ tsp. dried dill
Sauce:	½ cup beef broth
1 tbsp. butter	1 tbsp. fish sauce
	2 tbsps. honey

At 390 degrees F, preheat your Air Fryer. Coat the beef strips with the crushed tortilla chips on all sides. Spritz with some cooking spray on all sides and transfer them to the Air Fryer Basket. Air Fry the food at 390 degrees F for 30 minutes, shaking the basket every 10 minutes. Meanwhile, heat the sauce ingredient in a saucepan over medium-high heat. Cook this sauce to a boil and reduce the heat; cook until the sauce has thickened slightly. Add the steak to the sauce; let it sit for approximately 8 minutes. Serve over the hot egg noodles if desired.
Nutritional information: Calories 389; Total Carbs 20g; Net Carbs 6.7g; Protein 4.3g; Fat 5g; Sugar 1.1g; Fiber 2g

Asian Beef

Prep time: 10 minutes | Cook time: 25 minutes | Serves: 4

1 lb. beef tips, sliced	2 tbsps. coconut aminos
¼ cup green onion, chopped	1 tsp. xanthan gum
2 tbsps. garlic, minced	2 red chili peppers, sliced
2 tbsps. sesame oil	2 tbsps. water
1 tbsp. fish sauce	1 tbsp. ginger, sliced

Spray the "Air Fryer Basket" with some cooking spray. Toss beef and xanthan gum together. Add beef tips into the "Air Fryer Basket" and Air Fry them at 390 degrees F for 20 minutes, tossing halfway through. Meanwhile, in a saucepan, add the remaining ingredients except for green onion and heat over low heat. When sauce begins to boiling, remove from heat. Add cooked meat into the saucepan and stir to coat. Let sit in for 5 minutes. Garnish with green onion and serve.
Nutritional information: Calories 389; Total Carbs 21g; Net Carbs 9g; Protein 5.3g; Fat 7g; Sugar 2.1g; Fiber 2g

Cracker Pork Chops with Mustard

Prep time: 10 minutes | Cook time: 15 minutes | Serves: 3

¼ cup all-purpose flour
1 tsp. turmeric powder
1 egg
1 tsp. mustard
Kosher salt, to taste
¼ tsp. freshly ground black

pepper
2 cups crackers, crushed
½ tsp. porcini powder
1 tsp. shallot powder
3 center-cut loin pork chops

Place the flour and turmeric in a shallow bowl. in another bowl, whisk the eggs, mustard, salt, and black pepper. In the third bowl, mix the crushed crackers with the porcini powder and shallot powder. At 390 degrees F, preheat your air fryer. Dredge the pork chops in the flour mixture, then in the egg, followed by the cracker mixture. Air Fry the pork chops at 390 degrees F for 7 minutes per side, spraying with cooking oil. Bon appétit!
Nutritional information: Calories 347; Total Carbs 23g; Net Carbs 11g; Protein 9g; Fat 12 g; Sugar 6g; Fiber 3g

Mini Meatloaves

Prep time: 10 minutes | Cook time: 25 minutes | Serves: 4

2 tbsps. bacon, chopped
1 small-sized onion, chopped
1 bell pepper, chopped
1 garlic clove, minced
1 lb. ground beef
½ tsp. dried basil

½ tsp. dried mustard seeds
½ tsp. dried marjoram
Salt and black pepper, to taste
½ cup panko crumbs
4 tbsps. tomato puree

Heat a suitable nonstick skillet over medium-high heat. Cook the bacon for 1 to 2 minutes; add the onion, bell pepper, and garlic and cook another 3 minutes or until fragrant. Heat off. Stir in the ground beef, spices, and panko crumbs. Stir well. Shape the prepared mixture into 4 mini meatloaves. At 350 degrees F, preheat your Air fryer. Place the mini meatloaves in the "Air Fryer Basket" and Air Fry them at 350 degrees F for 10 minutes. When the time is up, turn them over, top with the tomato puree and continue to Air Fry for 10 minutes more. Bon appétit!
Nutritional information: Calories 375; Total Carbs 14g; Net Carbs 4g; Protein 6g; Fat 13g; Sugar 7g; Fiber 2g

Chinese Spice Meatballs

Prep time: 10 minutes | Cook time: 15 minutes | Serves: 4

1 lb. minced pork
2 tsps. curry paste
1 tbsp. Worcestershire sauce
1 ½ tsps. garlic paste
1 small onion, chopped
1 tsp. coriander

1 tsp. Chinese spice
1 tsp. mixed spice
½ fresh lime juice
Pepper
Salt

Add all the recipe ingredients into the bowl and mix until combined. Make small balls from the meat mixture and place into the Air Fryer Basket. Air Fry the meatballs for 15 minutes at 350 degrees F. Serve and enjoy.
Nutritional information: Calories 391; Total Carbs 19g; Net Carbs 2g; Protein 3g; Fat 8g; Sugar 3g; Fiber 1g

Pastrami and Cheddar Quiche

Prep time: 10 minutes | Cook time: 10 minutes | Serves: 2

4 eggs
1 bell pepper, chopped

2 spring onions, chopped
1 cup pastrami, sliced

¼ cup Greek-style yogurt
½ cup Cheddar cheese, grated

Sea salt, to taste
¼ tsp. ground black pepper

At 330 degrees F, preheat your air fryer Spritz the baking pan with cooking oil. Combine all the recipe ingredients and pour the prepared mixture into the prepared baking pan. Air Fry the food at 330 degrees F for 7 to 9 minutes or until the eggs have set. Place on a cooling rack and let it sit for 10 minutes before slicing and serving.
Nutritional information: Calories 391; Total Carbs 19g; Net Carbs 6g; Protein 3g; Fat 8g; Sugar 3g; Fiber 1g

Thai Roasted Beef

Prep time: 10 minutes | Cook time: 20 minutes | Serves: 2

½ tsp. salt
2 tbsps. soy sauce
½ tsp. pepper
Thumb-sized piece of ginger, chopped
3 chilies, deseeded and chopped
4 garlic cloves, chopped

1 tsp. brown sugar
Juice of 1 lime
2 tbsps. mirin
2 tbsps. coriander, chopped
2 tbsps. basil, chopped
2 tbsps. oil
2 tbsps. fish sauce
2 lbs. boneless beef, sliced

Place all the recipe ingredients, except the beef, black pepper and salt in a blender; process until smooth. Season the beef slices with black pepper and salt. Place all in a zipper bag and shake to combine. Put in the fridge for 4 hours. At 350 degrees F, preheat your Air fryer. Place the seasoned beef slices in Air Fryer Basket and Air Fry them for 12 minutes, or more if you like it really well done. Let sit for a couple of minutes before serving. Serve with cooked rice and fresh vegies.
Nutritional information: Calories 415; Total Carbs 21g; Net Carbs 10g; Protein 7g; Fat 14g; Sugar 8g; Fiber 3g

Lamb Rack with Lemon Crust

Prep time: 10 minutes | Cook time: 25 minutes | Serves: 5

1.7 lbs. frenched rack of lamb
Salt and black pepper, to taste
0.13-lb. dry breadcrumbs
1 tsp. grated garlic
½ tsp. salt

1 tsp. cumin seeds
1 tsp. ground cumin
1 tsp. oil
½ tsp. Grated lemon rind
1 egg, beaten

Place the lamb rack in a baking tray and pour the whisked egg on top. Whisk rest of the crusting ingredients in a suitable bowl and spread over the lamb. Air Fry the food at 350 degrees F for 25 minutes. Slice and serve warm.
Nutritional information: Calories 427; Fat 5.4 g; Total Carbs 58.5 g; Sugar 1.1 g; Fiber 4 g; Net Carbs 6g; Protein 21.9 g

Braised Lamb Shanks

Prep time: 10 minutes | Cook time: 20 minutes | Serves: 4

4 lamb shanks
1½ tsps. salt
½ tsp. black pepper
4 garlic cloves, crushed

2 tbsps. olive oil
4 to 6 sprigs fresh rosemary
3 cups beef broth, divided
2 tbsps. balsamic vinegar

Place the sham shanks in a baking pan. Whisk rest of the ingredients in a suitable bowl and pour over the shanks. At 360 degrees F, preheat your Air Fryer. Place these shanks in the Air Fryer Basket. Air Fry the shanks at 360 degrees F for 20 minutes. Slice and serve warm.
Nutritional information: Calories 336; Fat 9.7 g; Total Carbs 32.5 g; Net Carbs 6g; Fiber 0.3 g; Sugar 1.8 g; Protein 30.3 g

Za'atar Lamb Chops

Prep time: 10 minutes | Cook time: 10 minutes | Serves: 8

8 lamb loin chops, bone-in
3 garlic cloves, crushed
1 tsp. olive oil

½ fresh lemon
1 ¼ tsp. salt 1 tbsp. Za'atar
Black pepper, to taste

Rub the bone-in lamb chops with oil, Za'atar, salt, lemon juice, garlic, and black pepper. At 400 degrees F, preheat your Air Fryer. Place these lamb chops in the Air Fryer Basket. Air Fry the chops at 400 degrees F for 10 minutes. Flip the chops when cooked halfway through. Serve warm.

Nutritional information: Calories 391; Fat 2.8 g; Total Carbs 36.5 g; Net Carbs 6g; Fiber 9.2 g; Sugar 4.5 g; Protein 6.6

Lamb Sirloin Steak

Prep time: 10 minutes | Cook time: 15 minutes | Serves: 2

½ onion 4 slices ginger
5 cloves garlic
1 tsp. garam masala
1 tsp. fennel, ground

1 tsp. cinnamon ground
½ tsp. cardamom ground
1 tsp. cayenne 1 tsp. salt
1-lb. boneless lamb sirloin steaks

In a blender, jug adds all the recipe ingredients except the chops. Rub the chops with this blended mixture and marinate for 30 minutes. Transfer the chops to the Air Fryer Basket. Air Fry the chops at 330 degrees F for 15 minutes. Flip the chops when cooked halfway through then resume cooking. Serve warm.

Nutritional information: Calories 453; Fat 2.4 g; Total Carbs 18 g; Net Carbs 6g; Fiber 2.3 g; Sugar 1.2 g; Protein 23.2 g

Lemony Lamb Chops

Prep time: 10 minutes | Cook time: 25 minutes | Serves: 2

2 medium lamb chops

¼ cup lemon juice

Rub the lamb chops with lemon juice. Place the lemony chops in the Air Fryer Basket. Air Fry the chops at 350 degrees F for 25 minutes. Flip the chops when cooked halfway through then resume cooking. Serve warm.

Nutritional information: Calories 529; Fat 17 g; Total Carbs 55 g; Net Carbs 6g; Fiber 6 g; Sugar 8 g; Protein 41g

Garlicky Rosemary Lamb Chops

Prep time: 10 minutes | Cook time: 12 minutes | Serves: 4

4 lamb chops
2 tsps. olive oil
1 tsp. fresh rosemary

2 garlic cloves, minced
2 tsps. garlic puree
Salt and black pepper

Rub them with olive oil, rosemary, garlic, garlic puree, salt, and black pepper Place lamb chops in the Air Fryer Basket. Air Fry the chops at 350 degrees F for 12 minutes. Flip the chops when cooked halfway through then resume cooking. Serve warm.

Nutritional information: Calories 297; Fat 14 g; Total Carbs 8 g; Net Carbs 6g; Fiber 1 g; Sugar 3g; Protein 32g

Baked Lamb with Tomato Pasta

Prep time: 10 minutes | Cook time: 40 minutes | Serves: 6

25 oz. potatoes, boiled

14 oz. lean lamb mince

1 tsp. cinnamon
23 oz. jar tomato pasta
Sauce

12 oz. white sauce
1 tbsp. olive oil

Mash the potatoes in a suitable bowl and stir in white sauce and cinnamon. Sauté lamb mince with olive oil in a frying pan until brown. Layer a casserole dish with tomato pasta sauce. Top the sauce with lamb mince. Spread the potato mash over the lamb in an even layer. Cook the food at 350 degrees F for 35 minutes on Bake mode. Serve warm.

Nutritional information: Calories 352; Fat 14 g; Total Carbs 15.8 g; Net Carbs 6g; Fiber 0.2 g; Sugar 1 g; Protein 26 g

Greek Lamb Farfalle

Prep time: 10 minutes | Cook time: 20 minutes | Serves: 4

1tbsp. olive oil
1 onion, chopped
2 garlic cloves, chopped
2 tsps. dried oregano
1 lb. pack lamb mince
¾ lb. tin chopped tomatoes
¼ cup pitted black olives

½ cup frozen spinach, defrosted
2 tbsps. dill, stems removed and chopped
9 oz. farfalle, boiled
1 ball half-fat mozzarella, torn

At 350 degrees F, preheat your Air fryer Sauté onion and garlic with oil in a pan over moderate heat for 5 minutes. Stir in tomatoes, spinach, dill, lamb, and olives, then cook for 5 minutes. Spread the lamb in a casserole dish and toss in the pasta. Top the pasta lamb mix with mozzarella cheese. Cook the food in air fryer at 350 degrees F for 10 minutes on Bake mode. Serve warm.

Nutritional information: Calories 440; Fat 7.9 g; Total Carbs 21.8 g; Net Carbs 6g; Sugar 7.1 g; Fiber 2.6 g; Protein 37.2 g

Minced Lamb Casserole

Prep time: 10 minutes | Cook time: 40 minutes | Serves: 4

2 tbsps. olive oil
1 medium onion, chopped
½ lb. ground lamb
4 fresh mushrooms, sliced
1 cup small pasta shells, cooked

2 cups bottled marinara sauce
1 tsp. butter
4 tsps. flour
1 cup milk
1 egg, beaten
1 cup cheddar cheese, grated

Put a suitable wok on moderate heat and add oil to heat. Toss in onion and sauté until soft. Stir in mushrooms and lamb, and then cook until meat is brown. Add marinara sauce and cook it to a simmer. Stir in pasta then spread this mixture in a casserole dish. Set the sauce by melting butter in a saucepan over moderate heat. Stir in flour and whisk well, pour in the milk. Mix well and whisk ¼ cup sauce with egg then return it to the saucepan. Stir for 1 minute and then pour this sauce over the lamb. Drizzle cheese over the lamb casserole. In the air fryer, cook the food at 350 degrees F for 30 minutes on Bake mode. Serve warm.

Nutritional information: Calories 361; Fat 16.3 g; Total Carbs 19.3 g; Net Carbs 6g; Fiber 0.1 g; Sugar 18.2 g; Protein 33.3 g

Lamb Baked with Tomato Topping

Prep time: 10 minutes | Cook time: 1hr. 47 minutes | Serves: 8

8 lamb shoulder chops, trimmed
¼ cup plain flour
1 tbsp. olive oil
1 large brown onion, chopped
2 garlic cloves, crushed
2 medium carrots, peeled and

diced
2 tbsps. tomato paste
2 ½ cups beef stock
2 dried bay leaves
1 cup frozen peas
2 cups potato gems

Dust the lamb chops with flour and sear it in a pan layered with olive oil. Sear the lamb chops for 4 minutes per side. Transfer the chops to a baking tray. Add onion, garlic, and carrot to the same pan. Sauté for 5 minutes, then stir in tomato paste, stock and all other ingredients. Cook for 4 minutes, then pour this sauce over the chops. In the air fryer, cook the chops at 350 degrees F for 90 minutes. Serve warm.

Nutritional information: Calories 388; Fat 8 g; Total Carbs 8 g; Net Carbs 6g; Fiber 1 g; Sugar 2 g; Protein 13 g

Flavor Beef Ribs

Prep time: 10-15 minutes | Cook time: 12 minutes | Serves: 4

1 cup coriander, finely chopped	1 chipotle powder
1 tablespoon basil leaves, chopped	1 teaspoon fennel seeds
2 garlic cloves, finely chopped	1 teaspoon hot paprika
1 pound meaty beef ribs	Kosher salt and black pepper, as needed
3 tablespoons apple cider vinegar	½ cup vegetable oil

Thoroughly mix all the ingredients in a medium-size bowl and then coat the ribs well. Cover and refrigerate for 3-4 hours. Coat the cooking basket of your air fryer with cooking oil or spray. Once marinated, take the ribs out of the marinade and place on the cooking basket. Cook the ribs at 360 degrees F for 8 minutes. If the meat is not tender, then cook for 3-4 more minutes. Top with the leftover marinade and serve warm!

Nutritional information: Calories: 404; Fat 32.9g; Total Carbs 0.7g; Net Carbs: 0g; Fiber 0.2g; Sugars 0.1g; Protein 25g

Meat Burger with Salad

Prep time: 10-15 minutes | Cook time: 45 minutes | Serves: 4

1 teaspoon garlic puree	1 teaspoon tomato puree
4 bread buns	1 teaspoon mixed herbs
1 teaspoon mustard	4 ounces cheddar cheese
1 onion, diced	1 teaspoon basil
10 ounce mixed mince (beef and pork)	Pepper and salt as required
	Salad of your choice

Thoroughly mix up the seasoning ingredients and coat the meat well in a medium-size bowl. Form the burger patties from the mixture and flatten them. Coat the cooking basket of your air fryer with cooking oil or spray. Place the patties on the basket and then arrange the basket to the air fryer. Cook the patties at 390 degrees F for 20-25 minutes. When the time is up, turn the patties and cook for 20 more minutes. Make burgers using buns, patties, cheese, and salads!

Nutritional information: Calories: 501; Fat 12.2g; Total Carbs 80.2g; Net Carbs: 0g; Fiber 10.8g; Sugars 15.3g; Protein 24.6g

Beef Cubes with Vegetables

Prep time: 10-15 minutes | Cook time: 20 minutes | Serves: 4

1 tablespoon apple cider vinegar	¾ teaspoon cayenne pepper, smoked
1 teaspoon fine sea salt	¼ pound broccoli, make florets
1 pound top round steak, make cubes	¼ pound mushrooms, sliced
2 tablespoons olive oil	1 teaspoon dried basil
½ teaspoon black pepper, ground	½ teaspoon garlic powder
	¼ teaspoon ground cumin
1 teaspoon shallot powder	1 teaspoon celery seeds

To marinate, prepare a zip-lock bag, combine the beef with olive oil, vinegar, salt, black pepper, shallot powder, cayenne pepper,

garlic powder and cumin. Seal and marinate at room temperature for 3 hours. Coat the cooking basket of your air fryer with cooking oil or spray. Place the beef cubes on the basket and then arrange the basket to the air fryer. Cook the beef cubes at 365 degrees F for 12 minutes. When cooked, transfer the cubes to a prepared bowl. Clean the basket, arrange the vegetables in it and sprinkle basil and celery seeds on them. Cook the vegetables at 400 degrees F for 5 to 6 minutes. When done, serve with the reserved meat cubes.

Nutritional information: Calories: 326; Fat 17.5g; Total Carbs 3g; Net Carbs: 1g; Fiber 1.3g; Sugars 1.1g; Protein 37.9g

Delectable Beef with Kale Pieces

Prep time: 5-8 minutes | Cook time: 15-20 minutes | Serves: 4

1 cup kale, make pieces and wilted	4 eggs, beaten
1 tomato, chopped	4 tablespoons heavy cream
¼ teaspoon brown sugar	½ teaspoon turmeric powder
½ pound leftover beef, coarsely chopped	Salt and ground black pepper, as needed
2 garlic cloves, pressed	⅛ teaspoon ground allspice

Make 4 ramekins and lightly oil them. Divide the remaining ingredients among the ramekins. Coat the cooking basket of your air fryer with cooking oil or spray. Place the ramekins on the basket and then arrange the basket to the air fryer. Cook the ramekins at 360 degrees F for 15 minutes. When done, serve warm!

Nutritional information: Calories: 209; Fat 12.6g; Total Carbs 4g; Net Carbs: 2g; Fiber 0.5g; Sugars 1g; Protein 19.5g

Cube Steak

Prep time: 15 minutes | Cook time: 20 minutes | Serves: 4

1 ½ lbs. cube steak	2 scallions, finely chopped
Salt, to taste	2-tablespoon fresh parsley, finely chopped
¼-teaspoon ground black pepper, or more to taste	1 tablespoon fresh horseradish, grated
4 ounces' butter	1 teaspoon cayenne pepper
2 garlic cloves, finely chopped	

Use the kitchen to pat the cube steak dry, then season it with salt and black pepper. Coat the cooking basket of your air fryer with cooking oil or spray. Place the cube steak on the basket and then arrange the basket to the air fryer. Cook the cube steak at 400 degrees F for 14 minutes. While cooking the cube steak, melt the butter in a skillet over a moderate heat. Add the remaining ingredients and simmer them, until the sauce has thickened and reduced slightly. When done, serve the cube steak and drizzle the Cowboy sauce on the top. Serve and enjoy.

Nutritional information: Calories: 447; Fat 20.1g; Total Carbs 1g; Net Carbs: 0g; Fiber 0.4g; Sugars 0.5g; Protein 61.9g

Pork Cutlets

Prep time: 15 minutes | Cook time: 1 Hour 20 minutes | Serves: 2

1 cup water	Sea salt and ground black pepper, to taste
1 cup red wine	
1 tablespoon sea salt	1 egg
2 pork cutlets	¼ cup yogurt
½ cup all-purpose flour	1 teaspoon brown mustard
½ teaspoon shallot powder	1 cup tortilla chips, crushed
½-teaspoon porcini powder	

In a large ceramic dish, combine the water, wine and salt. After adding the pork cutlets, refrigerating the mixture for 1 hour. In a shallow bowl, mix the flour, shallot powder, porcini powder, salt, and ground pepper. In another bowl, whisk the eggs with yogurt and mustard. In the third bowl, place the crushed tortilla chips. Evenly coat the pork cutlets with the flour mixture and egg mixture in order, then, roll them over the crushed tortilla chips. Coat the bottom of the cooking basket with cooking oil. Place the breaded pork cutlets on the basket and cook them at 395 degrees F and for 10 minutes. Flip and cook for 5 minutes more on the other side. Serve warm.

Nutritional information: Calories: 331; Fat 12.1g; Total Carbs 32g; Net Carbs: 12g; Fiber 2.4g; Sugars 2.7g; Protein 10.8g

Air-fried Pork with Wine Sauce

Prep time: 8-10 minutes | Cook time: 20 minutes | Serves: 4

For the Ribs:
½ teaspoon cracked black peppercorns
½ teaspoon Hickory-smoked salt
1 pound pork ribs
2 tablespoons olive oil
1 tablespoon Dijon honey mustard

¼ cup soy sauce
1 clove garlic, minced
For the Sauce:
1 teaspoon brown sugar
1 teaspoon balsamic vinegar
1 ½ cups beef stock
1 cup red wine
¼ teaspoon salt

To marinate, prepare a large dish, add the ingredients and seal and refrigerate for 3-4 hours or overnight. Coat the cooking basket of your air fryer with cooking oil or spray. Place the ribs on the basket and then arrange the basket to the air fryer. Cook the ribs at 320 degrees F for 10 minutes. Add the stock in a deep saucepan and boil over medium flame until half reduces it. Add the remaining sauce ingredients. Cook for 10 minutes over high heat or until the sauce is reduced by half. Serve the air fried pork ribs with the wine sauce.

Nutritional information: Calories: 438; Fat 27.3g; Total Carbs 3g; Net Carbs: 1g; Fiber 0.2g; Sugars 1.5g; Protein 32.2g

Beer Beef

Prep time: 8-10 minutes | Cook time: 15 minutes | Serves: 4-5

1 bottle beer
2-3 cloves garlic, finely minced

1 ½ pounds short loin
2 tablespoons olive oil
2 bay leaves

Use the kitchen towel to pat the beef dry. Thoroughly mix the beef and other ingredients in a medium-size bowl. Set aside for 60-80 minutes. Coat the cooking basket of your air fryer with cooking oil or spray. Place the marinated beef on the basket and then arrange the basket to the air fryer. Cook the marinated beef at 395 degrees F for 7 minutes. After that, turn the meat and cook for another 8 minutes. Serve warm!

Nutritional information: Calories: 163; Fat 12g; Total Carbs 3g; Net Carbs: 1g; Fiber 0g; Sugars 0g; Protein 6g

Creole Pork Chops

Prep time: 15 minutes | Cook time: 12 minutes | Serves: 4

1 ½ lbs. pork chops, boneless
1 teaspoon garlic powder
5-tablespoon parmesan cheese, grated

⅓ cup almond flour
1 ½-teaspoon paprika
1 teaspoon Creole seasoning

Heat the air fryer to 360 degrees F in advance. In a zip-lock bag, in addition to the pork chops, mix the other ingredients well. Add pork chops into the bag and coat it with the mixture well by shaking the bag. Coat the basket of your air fryer with cooking spray. Place pork chops into the air fryer basket and cook for 12 minutes at 360 degrees F. Serve and enjoy.

Nutritional information: Calories: 478; Fat 36.2g; Total Carbs 2g; Net Carbs: 0.5g; Fiber 0.9g; Sugars 0.2g; Protein 34.5g

Delicious Pork Shoulder with Molasses Sauce

Prep time: 2 hours 15 minutes | Cook time: 25 minutes | Serves: 3

1 tablespoon molasses
1 tablespoon soy sauce
2-tablespoon Shaoxing wine
2 garlic cloves, minced
1 teaspoon fresh ginger,

minced
1 tablespoon cilantro stems and leaves, finely chopped
1 lb. boneless pork shoulder
1 tablespoon sesame oil

Thoroughly mix up the molasses, soy sauce, wine, garlic, ginger, and cilantro in a large bowl. Put the pork shoulder in the spice mixture and allow it to refrigerate for 2 hours. Oil the cooking basket with sesame oil, put the pork shoulder in it and reserve the marinade. Cook the pork shoulder at 395 degrees F for 14 to 17 minutes, flipping and basting with the reserved marinade halfway through. While cooking the pork should, heat a skillet and cook the marinade in it over medium heat, until thickened. When the pork shoulder cooked, let it rest for 5 to 6 minutes before slicing and serving. Brush the pork shoulder with the sauce and enjoy!

Nutritional information: Calories: 283; Fat 9.9g; Total Carbs 6.5g; Net Carbs: 1g; Fiber 0.2g; Sugars 3.8g; Protein 40.1

Garlic Beef Meatloaf

Prep time: 15 minutes | Cook time: 15 minutes | Serves: 4

1 lb. ground beef
¼-teaspoon cinnamon
tablespoon ginger, minced
¼ cup fresh cilantro, chopped
1 cup onion, diced
2 eggs, lightly beaten

1 teaspoon cayenne
1 teaspoon turmeric
1 teaspoon garam masala
1 tablespoon garlic, minced
1 teaspoon salt

Prepare a large bowl, mix up all of the ingredients. Place the meat mixture in the cooking pan of your air fryer. Arrange the pan to the air fryer and cook at 360 degrees F for 15 minutes. Slice before serving and enjoying.

Nutritional information: Calories: 265; Fat 9.5g; Total Carbs 5g; Net Carbs: 2g; Fiber 1.2g; Sugars 1.5g; Protein 37.9g

Beef Sausage with Tomato Puree

Prep time: 15 minutes | Cook time: 40 minutes | Serves: 2

1 tablespoon lard, melted
1 shallot, chopped
1 bell pepper, chopped
2 red chilies, finely chopped
1 teaspoon ginger-garlic paste
Sea salt, to taste
¼-teaspoon ground black pepper

4 beef good quality sausages, thinly sliced
½ teaspoon smoked paprika
1 cup beef bone broth
½ cup tomato puree
2 handfuls spring greens, shredded

In a skillet, melt the lard over medium-high flame; sauté the shallots and peppers about 4 minutes or until fragrant. Add the ginger-garlic paste and cook for 1 more minute. After seasoning with salt and black pepper, transfer the food to a lightly sprayed cooking basket. Sauté the sausages and stir occasionally, until brown, working in batches. Add the sausages, smoked paprika,

broth, and tomato puree to the cooking basket. Cook at 325 degrees F for 30 minutes. When the time is up, stir in the spring greens and cook for 5 minutes more. Serve over the hot rice if desired. Bon appétit!
Nutritional information: Calories: 265; Fat 9.5g; Total Carbs 5g; Net Carbs: 2g; Fiber 1.2g; Sugars 1.5g; Protein 37.9g

Pork Tenderloins with Soy Sauce

Prep time: 15 minutes | Cook time: 60 minutes | Serves: 4

1 apple, wedged	1 tablespoon soy sauce
1 cinnamon quill	Salt and black pepper
1 tablespoon olive oil	1 lb. pork tenderloin

Prepare a suitable bowl, mix up the apple, cinnamon, olive oil, soy sauce, salt, and black pepper, then add the pork and coat well. Marinate the pork for 25-35 minutes at room temperature. Place the pork, apples and add a little bit of marinade on the cooking basket. Cook at 380 degrees F for 14 minutes, flipping halfway through. Serve hot!
Nutritional information: Calories: 223; Fat 7.6g; Total Carbs 8g; Net Carbs: 3.5g; Fiber 1.4g; Sugars 5.9g; Protein 30.1g

Liver Muffins

Prep time: 15 minutes | Cook time: 25 minutes | Serves: 2

2 large eggs	1 tablespoon cream
1 tablespoon butter	Salt and black pepper
½-tablespoon black truffle oil	½ lb. beef liver, minced

Heat the air fryer to 320 degrees F in advance. Crack the eggs to separate the whites from the yolks, and put each yolk in a cup. Cut the liver into thin slices and refrigerate for 10 minutes. In a separate bowl, mix up the cream, truffle oil, salt and pepper with a fork. In a small ramekin, arrange half of the mixture. Equally divide the whites equally between ramekins after pouring in. Top with the egg yolks. Use each liver to surround each yolk. Cook for 15 minutes at 320 degrees F. When cooled, serve and enjoy.
Nutritional information: Calories: 316; Fat 18.4g; Total Carbs 1g; Net Carbs: 0g; Fiber 0g; Sugars 0.5g; Protein 34.2g

BBQ Pork Chops with Vegetables

Prep time: 10-15 minutes | Cook time: 20 minutes | Serves: 5-6

6 pork chops	as needed
1 teaspoon onion powder	½ teaspoon cayenne pepper
½ teaspoon garlic powder	1 teaspoon brown sugar
Ground black pepper and salt	⅓ cup all-purpose flour

To marinate, prepare a Ziploc bag, add the ingredients, seal and shake well. Coat the cooking basket of your air fryer with cooking oil or spray. Place the chops on the basket and then arrange the basket to the air fryer. Cook the chops at 375 degrees F for 20 minutes. When done, serve warm with sautéed vegetables!
Nutritional information: Calories: 286; Fat 20g; Total Carbs 6g; Net Carbs: 2.5g; Fiber 0.3g; Sugars 0.7g; Protein 18.8g

Spicy Pork Belly Pieces

Prep time: 15 minutes | Cook time: 50 minutes | Serves: 4

1 ½ lbs. pork belly, cut into 4 pieces	Kosher salt and ground black pepper, to taste

1 teaspoon smoked paprika	1 tablespoon green onions
½-teaspoon turmeric powder	4 cloves garlic, sliced
1 tablespoon oyster sauce	1 lb. new potatoes, scrubbed

Heat your Air Fryer to 390 degrees F in advance. Use the kitchen to pat the pork belly pieces dry and season with the remaining spices. Spray the coated pieces with a non-stick spray on all sides and add the oyster sauce. Cook in the preheated Air Fryer for 30 minutes. Turn them over every 10 minutes. When the time is up, increase the temperature to 400 degrees F. Add the green onions, garlic, and new potatoes and cook for another 15 minutes, shaking regularly. When done, serve warm and enjoy.
Nutritional information: Calories: 581; Fat 30.7g; Total Carbs 13g; Net Carbs: 7g; Fiber 2.1g; Sugars 1g; Protein 53.8g

Festive Pork Fillets

Prep time: 15 minutes | Cook time: 20 minutes | Serves: 3

¼ cup chickpea flour	1 teaspoon cayenne pepper
1 tablespoon Romano cheese, grated	2 pork fillets (1 lb.)
1 teaspoon onion powder	1 Granny Smiths apple, peeled and sliced
1 teaspoon garlic powder	1 tablespoon lemon juice
½-teaspoon ground cumin	1 oz. butter, cold

In a zip-lock bag, mix the flour, cheese, onions powder, garlic powder, cumin, and cayenne pepper well, the add the pork fillets in it and shake to coat on all sides. Spray the cooking basket of your air fryer with cooking spray and then arrange the coated pork fillets to it. Cook the pork fillets at 370 degrees F for 10 minutes. When the time is up, add the apples, drizzle the lemon juice and place the cold butter on the top in order. Cook for 5 minutes more. Once done, serve and enjoy.
Nutritional information: Calories: 325; Fat 18.1g; Total Carbs 19g; Net Carbs: 6.7g; Fiber 4.9g; Sugars 8.2g; Protein 21.4g

Lamb Chops with Mustard Mixture

Prep time: 15 minutes | Cook time: 15 minutes | Serves: 4

8 lamb chops	3 tablespoons Dijon mustard
1 tablespoon lemon juice	Pepper
4 teaspoons tarragon	Salt
½-teaspoon olive oil	

Thoroughly mix up the mustard, lemon juice, tarragon, and olive oil in a small bowl. Coat the lamb chops with the mustard mixture. Arrange the coated lamb chops to the air fryer basket and cook at 390 degrees F for 15 minutes, flipping halfway through. Serve and enjoy.
Nutritional information: Calories: 411; Fat 16.5g; Total Carbs 0.2g; Net Carbs: 0g; Fiber 0.1g; Sugars 0.1g; Protein 61.4g

Pork Meatloaf with Onion

Prep time: 15 minutes | Cook time: 20 minutes | Serves: 4

1 egg, lightly beaten	1 tablespoon almond flour
1 onion, chopped	1 lb. ground pork
½ tablespoon thyme, chopped	Pepper
1 oz. chorizo, chopped	Salt

In a suitable bowl, mix up all of the ingredients, then transfer the mixture to the cooking pan of your air fryer. Cook at 390 degrees F for 20 minutes. When cooked, slice to serve and enjoy.
Nutritional information: Calories: 234; Fat 8.7g; Total Carbs 3g; Net Carbs: 1g; Fiber 1g; Sugars 1.3g; Protein 33.5g

Country-style Pork Ribs

Prep time: 15 minutes | Cook time: 40 minutes | Serves: 4

1 teaspoon salt	and grated
1 teaspoon cayenne pepper	½-teaspoon onion powder
½-teaspoon ground black pepper	½-teaspoon porcini powder
1 teaspoon raw honey	1 teaspoon mustard seeds
2 garlic cloves, minced	1 tablespoon sweet chili sauce
1 (1-inch) piece ginger, peeled	1 tablespoon balsamic vinegar
	1 ½ lbs. pork country-style ribs

Thoroughly mix up the cayenne pepper, honey, garlic, ginger, onion powder, porcini powder, mustard seeds, sweet chili sauce, balsamic vinegar, salt and black pepper in a suitable bowl. Rub the pork ribs with the spice mixture. Cook the ribs in your air fryer at 360 degrees F for 15 minutes. After 15 minutes, flip the ribs and cook for 20 minutes more or until they are tender inside and crisp outside. Garnished with fresh chives if desired. Serve and enjoy.

Nutritional information: Calories: 312; Fat 23.2g; Total Carbs 2g; Net Carbs: 0.5g; Fiber 0.4g; Sugars 1.7g; Protein 21.6g

Spiced Rib Eye Steak

Prep time: 15 minutes | Cook time: 9 minutes | Serves: 3

1 lb. rib eye steak	¼-teaspoon black pepper
½-teaspoon chipotle powder	⅛ teaspoon coffee powder
¼-teaspoon paprika	⅛-teaspoon cocoa powder
¼-teaspoon onion powder	⅛-teaspoon coriander powder
½-teaspoon garlic powder	1 ½-teaspoon sea salt
½ teaspoon chili powder	

In addition to the steak, mix the other ingredients well in a small bowl. Rub the steak with the spice mixture and marinate the steak for 20 minutes. Coat the cooking basket of your air fryer with cooking spray. Cook the marinated steak on the basket in your air fryer at 390 degrees F for 9 minutes. Once done, serve and enjoy.

Nutritional information: Calories: 419; Fat 33.5g; Total Carbs 1g; Net Carbs: 0g; Fiber 0.5g; Sugars 0.3g; Protein 26.9g

Moroccan-style Steak with Salad

Prep time: 15 minutes | Cook time: 20 minutes | Serves: 4

2 lbs. flank steak	½ teaspoon onion powder
¼ cup soy sauce	½ teaspoon garlic powder
1 cup dry red wine	½-teaspoon ground coriander
Salt, to taste	¼-teaspoon ground allspice
½-teaspoon ground black pepper	1 tablespoon olive oil
2 parsnips, peeled and sliced lengthways	½ tablespoon lime juice
1 tablespoon paprika	1 teaspoon honey
	1 cup lettuce leaves, shredded
	½ cup pomegranate seeds

In a suitable bowl, add the soy sauce, wine, salt, black pepper and flank steak, then refrigerate the mixture for 2 hours to marinate the steak completely. Spray the cooking basket with cooking spray and then transfer the marinated steak on it. Sprinkle the parsnips on the top, add the paprika, onion powder, garlic powder, coriander, and allspice. Cook at 400 degrees F for 7 minutes, then turn the steak over and cook for 5 minutes more. To make the dressing, mix up the olive oil, lime juice and honey. In a salad bowl, add the lettuce leaves and roasted parsnip, then toss with the dressing. When the steak cook, slice and place on top of the salad. Sprinkle over the pomegranate seeds and serve. Enjoy!

Nutritional information: Calories: 558; Fat 22.7g; Total Carbs 19g; Net Carbs: 6.7g; Fiber 4g; Sugars 7g; Protein 65.4g

Steak with Onion and Bell Peppers

Cook time: 15 minutes | Serves: 6

1 lb. steak, sliced	gluten-free
1 tablespoon olive oil	½ cup onion, sliced
1 tablespoon fajita seasoning,	3 bell peppers, sliced

Line up the aluminum foil on the cooking basket of your air fryer. In a large bowl, mix up all of the ingredients and toss well until coated. Arrange the fajita mixture to the basket and cook at 390 degrees F for 5 minutes. After 5 minutes, toss well again and cook for 5-10 minutes more. Serve and enjoy.

Nutritional information: Calories: 199; Fat 6.3g; Total Carbs 6g; Net Carbs: 2.5g; Fiber 1g; Sugars 3.4g; Protein 28g

Marinated Beef and Vegetable Stir Fry

Cook time: 35 minutes | Serves: 4

2 lbs. top round, cut into bite-sized strips	Salt and black pepper, to taste
2 garlic cloves, sliced	½ tablespoon olive oil
1 teaspoon dried marjoram	1 red onion, sliced
¼ cup red wine	2 bell peppers, sliced
1 tablespoon tamari sauce	1 carrot, sliced

In a suitable bowl, add the top round, marjoram, red wine, garlic, tamari sauce, salt and pepper in a bowl; cover and marinate for 1 hour. Oil the cooking tray of your air fryer. Take the beef out of the marinade and arrange to the tray. Cook at 390 degrees F for 15 minutes. After that, add the garlic, onion, peppers and carrot, cook for 15 minutes more or until tender. Open the Air Fryer every 5 minutes and baste the meat with the remaining marinade. When done, serve and enjoy.

Nutritional information: Calories: 489; Fat 14.8g; Total Carbs 9g; Net Carbs: 4.3g; Fiber 1.9g; Sugars 5.1g; Protein 73g

Garlic Pork Roast

Cook time: 30 minutes | Serves: 8

2 lbs. pork roast	1 ½ dried thyme
1 ½-teaspoon garlic powder	1 ½-teaspoon dried oregano
1 ½-teaspoon coriander powder	1 ½-teaspoon cumin powder
⅓-teaspoon salt	3 cups water
1 ½-teaspoon black pepper	1 lemon, halved

Mix up the garlic powder, coriander powder, salt, black pepper, thyme, oregano and cumin powder in a suitable bowl. Dry the pork well and then poke holes all around it using a fork. Smear the oregano rub thoroughly on all sides with your hands and squeeze the lemon juice all over it. Set aside for 5 minutes. Cook the pork at 300 degrees F for 10 minutes. Turn the pork and increase the temperature to 350 F and continue cooking for 10 minutes. Once ready, remove it and place it in on a chopping board to sit for 4 minutes before slicing. Serve the pork slices with a side of sautéed asparagus and hot sauce.

Nutritional information: Calories: 240; Fat 10.8g; Total Carbs 1g; Net Carbs: 0g; Fiber 0.3g; Sugars 0.2g; Protein 32.6g

Roasted Garlic Ribeye with Mayo

Cook time: 20 minutes | Serves: 3

1 ½ lbs. ribeye, bone-in	1 tablespoon butter, room

temperature
Salt, to taste
½-teaspoon crushed black pepper
½-teaspoon dried dill
½-teaspoon cayenne pepper
½-teaspoon garlic powder
½-teaspoon onion powder
1 teaspoon ground coriander
1 tablespoon mayonnaise
1 teaspoon garlic, minced

Use the kitchen towel to pat the ribeye dry, then rub it with the softened butter on all sides. Transfer the ribeye to the basket of your air fryer after sprinkling with the seasonings. Cook the ribeye at 400 degrees F for 15 minutes, flipping halfway through. Meanwhile, mix the mayonnaise and garlic well, and refrigerate the mixture until the ribeye cooked. When ready, serve and enjoy!

Nutritional information: Calories: 552; Fat 48.2g; Total Carbs 2g; Net Carbs: 0.5g; Fiber 0.2g; Sugars 0.6g; Protein 24.3g

Pork Chops with Soy Sauce

Prep time: 10 minutes | Cook time: 20 minutes | Serves 2

2 pork chops
1 teaspoon onion powder
½ teaspoon garlic powder
1 tablespoon brown sugar
Salt and pepper, to taste
1 teaspoon paprika
1 tablespoon mustard
2 tablespoons soy sauce
1 teaspoon dried cilantro
2 tablespoons olive oil

In a zip-lock bag, put the olive oil, garlic powder, onion powder, brown sugar, paprika, mustard, soy sauce, dried cilantro, salt, pepper and add the pork chops, then shake up to coat well. When coated, cook the pork chops in your air fryer at 390 degrees F for 15 minutes. When the time is up, serve and enjoy.

Nutritional information: Calories: 438; Fat 35.7g; Total Carbs 9g; Net Carbs: 4.3g; Fiber 1.5g; Sugars 5.7g; Protein 20.8g;

Montreal Steak

Prep time: 10 minutes | Cook time: 7 minutes | Serves: 2

12 oz. steak
½-teaspoon liquid smoke
1 tablespoon soy sauce
½-tablespoon cocoa powder
1 tablespoon Montreal steak seasoning
Pepper
Salt

In a large zip-lock bag, coat the steak well with the liquid smoke, soy sauce, and steak seasonings, then refrigerate the mixture for overnight. Coat the cooking basket of your air fryer with cooking spray. Arrange the marinated steak to the air fryer and cook at 375 degrees F for 7 minutes. After that, turn the steak and cook another side for 5 minutes more. Serve and enjoy.

Nutritional information: Calories: 346; Fat 8.7g; Total Carbs 1g; Net Carbs: 0g; Fiber 0.5g; Sugars 0.2g; Protein 62.2g

Italian-style Honey Pork

Prep time: 10 minutes | Cook time: 50 minutes | Serves: 3

1 teaspoon Celtic sea salt
½-teaspoon black pepper, freshly cracked
¼ cup red wine
1 tablespoon mustard
1 tablespoon honey
2 garlic cloves, minced
1 lb. pork top loin
1 tablespoon Italian herb seasoning blend

Prepare a suitable bowl, mix up the salt, black pepper, red wine, mustard, honey, garlic and the pork top loin, then marinate the pork top loin at least 30 minutes. Spray the cooking basket of your air fryer with the non-stick cooking spray. Sprinkle the Italian herb on the top of the pork top loin after transfer it to the basket. Cook the pork top loin at 370 degrees F for 10 minutes,

flipping and spraying with cooking oil halfway through. When cooked, serve and enjoy.

Nutritional information: Calories: 201; Fat 7.7g; Total Carbs 8.5g; Net Carbs: 4g; Fiber 0.7g; Sugars 6.2g; Protein 20.3g

Garlic Lamb Rack

Prep time: 10 minutes | Cook time: 30 minutes | Serves: 6

1 egg, lightly beaten
½ tablespoon fresh thyme, chopped
1 ¾ lbs. rack of lamb
½ tablespoon fresh rosemary,
chopped
1 tablespoon olive oil
2 garlic cloves, chopped
Pepper
Salt

Mix up the oil and garlic, then brush the lamb rack with the mixture. Season the lamb rack with pepper and salt. After mix the thyme and rosemary well, coat the lamb rack with the egg and the herb mixture. Place lamb rack in the air fryer basket and cook for at 390 degrees F for 30 minutes. After 25 minutes of cooking time, turn the lamb rack and cook for 5 minutes more. Serve and enjoy.

Nutritional information: Calories: 225; Fat 13.2g; Total Carbs 1g; Net Carbs: 0g; Fiber 0.4g; Sugars 0.1g; Protein 24.1g

Delicious Baby Back Ribs

Prep time: 10 minutes | Cook time: 30 minutes | Serves: 4

1 teaspoon cayenne pepper
1 rack baby back ribs, cut into individual pieces
1 teaspoon onion powder
1 teaspoon garlic powder
1 teaspoon pomegranate
molasses
1 teaspoon dried oregano
½ cup barbecue sauce
Salt and black pepper to taste
2 scallions, chopped

In a bowl, mix up the smoked paprika, cayenne pepper, garlic powder, pomegranate molasses, onion powder, oregano, salt, black pepper and ribs, then toss to coat well. Cover and refrigerate for 30 minutes. Spray the cooking basket of your air fryer with cooking spray. Transfer the marinated ribs to the basket in the air fryer and cook at 360 degrees F for 25 minutes, flipping halfway through. While cooking the ribs, in a saucepan, sauté the vegetable broth and gravy mix for 2 minutes or until the sauce thickens. When the ribs cooked, drizzle the sautéed sauce, BBQ sauce and scatter scallions on the top, serve and enjoy.

Nutritional information: Calories: 407; Fat 24.8g; Total Carbs 11g; Net Carbs: 6.7g; Fiber 0.5; Sugars 6.5g; Protein 0.3g

Filet Mignon with Peanut Sauce

Prep time: 10 minutes | Cook time: 25 minutes | Serves: 4

2 lbs. filet mignon, sliced into bite-sized strips
1 tablespoon oyster sauce
1 tablespoon sesame oil
1 tablespoon tamari sauce
1 tablespoon ginger-garlic paste
1 tablespoon mustard
1 tablespoon honey
1 teaspoon chili powder
¼ cup peanut butter
1 tablespoon lime juice
1 teaspoon red pepper flakes
1 tablespoon water

Prepare a large dish, add the oyster sauce, sesame oil, tamari sauce, ginger-garlic paste, mustard, honey, chili powder and beef strips, then cover and refrigerate to marinate completely. Cook the beef strips at 400 degrees F for 18 minutes, flipping them occasionally. To make the sauce, mix up the peanut butter, lime juice, red pepper flakes and water. Serve and enjoy the beef strips with the sauce.

Nutritional information: Calories: 589; Fat 29.6g; Total Carbs 10.3g; Net Carbs: 0g; Fiber 1.7g; Sugars 6.1g; Protein 68.8g

Tender Pork Ribs with BBQ Sauce

Prep time: 10 minutes | Cook time: 25 minutes | Serves 4

1 lb. baby back ribs	1 tablespoon Dijon mustard
3 tablespoons olive oil	⅓ cup soy sauce
½ teaspoon pepper	2 cloves garlic, minced
½ teaspoon smoked salt	½ cup BBQ sauce

Cut the ribs in half after removing their back membrane. To marinate the ribs completely, prepare a large dish, add the olive oil, pepper, salt, Dijon mustard, soy sauce, garlic and ribs, then cover and refrigerate for 2 hours. When ready, cook the pork ribs in your air fryer at 370 degrees F for 25 minutes. With the BBQ sauce on the top, serve and enjoy!
Nutritional information: Calories: 407; Fat 24.6g; Total Carbs 13g; Net Carbs: 7g; Fiber 0.6g; Sugars 8.6g; Protein 31.5g

Simple Pork Chops

Prep time: 40 minutes | Cook time: 12 minutes | Serves 3

3 boneless pork chops	1 tablespoon honey
Salt and pepper, to taste	2 tablespoons olive oil
½ cup all-purpose flour	1 tablespoon Dijon mustard
½ cup breadcrumbs	1 tablespoon soy sauce

In a zip-lock bag, mix up the soy sauce, honey, olive oil, Dijon mustard and pork chops, then seal and refrigerate for 30 minutes. After remove the pork chops from the marinade, season them with salt, pepper and coat them with flour and breadcrumbs. Cook the pork chops in your air fryer at 370 degrees F for 12 minutes. When done, serve and enjoy.
Nutritional information: Calories: 548; Fat 16.8g; Total Carbs 26g; Net Carbs: 13g; Fiber 1.2g; Sugars 5.3g; Protein 69.2g

Spiced Pork Chops with Mushroom

Prep time: 10 minutes | Cook time: 20 minutes | Serves 2

1 tablespoon olive oil	6 large mushrooms, cleaned and sliced
½ lb. pork chops	1 large yellow onion, chopped
½ teaspoon dried oregano	1 ½ tablespoons soy sauce
¼ teaspoon red pepper flakes	2 tablespoons fresh parsley, finely chopped
1 teaspoon dried thyme	
½ teaspoon salt	
½ teaspoon pepper	

In a large bowl, mix the pork chops with the onion, mushrooms, salt, pepper, thyme, soy sauce, oregano, red pepper flakes, and olive oil. When coated, cook the pork chops and clean mushrooms in your air fryer at 390 degrees F for 20 minutes. Sprinkle with the fresh parsley, serve and enjoy!
Nutritional information: Calories: 480; Fat 35.6g; Total Carbs 11.5g; Net Carbs: 5g; Fiber 3.1g; Sugars 4.6g; Protein 29.5g

Unique Beef Cheeseburgers

Prep time: 10 minutes | Cook time: 15 minutes | Serves 4

½ lb. ground beef	⅓ teaspoon pepper
⅓ cup breadcrumbs	4 slices Cheddar cheese
2 tablespoons parsley, finely chopped	4 burger buns
3 tablespoons parmesan cheese, shredded	1 red onion, sliced
½ teaspoon salt	4 romaine lettuce leaves
	4 teaspoons mayonnaise
	1 cup pickles, sliced

Mix the ground beef with breadcrumbs, parmesan cheese, parsley, salt and pepper well in a suitable dish. Form 4 patties from the meat mixture. Cook the patties in your air fryer at 390 degrees F for 13 minutes. After that, place the cheese slices on the top and cook for 1 minute more. When cooked, top with pickles, red onion, lettuce leaves, and mayonnaise. Enjoy!
Nutritional information: Calories: 570; Fat 22.7g; Total Carbs 51g; Net Carbs: 15g; Fiber 3.6g; Sugars 4.3g; Protein 39.8g

Pork Sausages with Mustard Sauce

Prep time: 10 minutes | Cook time: 18 minutes | Serves 2

4 pork sausages	1 tablespoon mayonnaise
Non-stick cooking spray	½ cup Dijon mustard
For the Mustard sauce:	1 tablespoon honey

Make holes in the sausages with toothpick or fork. Cook the processed sausages at 370 degrees F for 18 minutes. While cooking the sausages, mix up the mayonnaise, honey, and Dijon mustard in a sauce bowl. When cooked, serve and enjoy sausages with the mustard sauce.
Nutritional information: Calories: 191; Fat 12.3g; Total Carbs 13g; Net Carbs: 7g; Fiber 2.1g; Sugars 9.6g; Protein 7.9g

Tasty Spaghetti with Beef Meatballs

Prep time: 10 minutes | Cook time: 12 minutes | Serves 3

1 ½ pound ground beef	minced
½ yellow onion, chopped	½ teaspoon salt
5 tablespoons seasoned breadcrumbs	¼ teaspoon pepper
½ teaspoon cumin powder	1 package spaghetti pasta, cooked
1 ½ tablespoon fresh parsley,	

In a large bowl, combine the ground beef with the yellow onion, and finely chopped parsley well, then mix with the breadcrumbs, cumin, salt, and pepper well. Form small balls from the mixture. Cook the meat balls in your air fryer at 370 degrees F for 12 minutes, turning them over halfway through. With the cooked spaghetti, serve and enjoy.
Nutritional information: Calories: 484; Fat: 13.6g; Total Carbs: 45.5g; Net Carbs: 3g; Fiber: 5.6g; Protein: 44.6g;

Flank Steak with Honey and Paprika

Prep time: 2 hours 10 minutes | Cook time: 15 minutes | Serves 4

1 ½ lb. flank steak	3 garlic cloves, minced
1 teaspoon salt	1 ½ teaspoon paprika
½ teaspoon pepper	1 ½ tablespoon fresh rosemary, finely chopped
2 tablespoons fresh thyme, chopped	4 tablespoons olive oil
2 teaspoons honey	

In a sealable bag, coat the flank steak with the honey, thyme, paprika, garlic, rosemary, olive oil, salt and pepper, then refrigerate for at least 2 hours. Cook the coated and marinated flank steak in your air fryer at 390 degrees F for 15 minutes, flipping halfway through. Serve immediately. Bon appétit!
Nutritional information: Calories: 475; Fat 28.6g; Total Carbs 5g; Net Carbs: 2g; Fiber 1.5g; Sugars 3g; Protein 47.8g

Beef Tenderloin Steaks with Marjoram

Prep time: 10 minutes | Cook time: 11 minutes | Serves 4

4 beef tenderloin steaks	1 teaspoon garlic powder
Salt and pepper, to your taste	1 teaspoon dried coriander
1 teaspoon dried oregano	2 tablespoons olive oil
1 teaspoon dried thyme	2 eggs, well-whisked
1 teaspoon marjoram	½ cup seasoned breadcrumbs
1 teaspoon dried sage	

Mix up the olive oil, salt, pepper, thyme, oregano, sage, marjoram, garlic powder, oregano, and coriander in a large-size bowl, then use the spice mixture to season the beef tenderloin steaks. In a shallow bowl, add the whisked egg; in another bowl, add the breadcrumbs. Coat the seasoned beef tenderloin steak with the egg mixture and breadcrumbs in order; coat the left steaks with the same steps. Cook the steaks in your air fryer at 380 degrees F for 11 minutes. When done, serve and enjoy with the fresh salad and potatoes.

Nutritional information: Calories: 310; Fat 16.3g; Total Carbs 9g; Net Carbs: 4.3g; Fiber 1g; Sugars 0.4g; Protein 30.3g

Spiced Lamb Kebabs

Prep time: 10 minutes | Cook time: 60 minutes | Serves: 3

1 ½ pounds lamb shoulder, bones removed and cut into pieces	1 tablespoon Sichuan peppercorns
2 tablespoons cumin seeds, toasted	1 teaspoon sugar
	2 teaspoons crushed red pepper flakes
2 teaspoons caraway seeds, toasted	Salt and pepper

In a suitable bowl, add all of the ingredients, stir well and refrigerate for at least 2 hours to marinate the lamb shoulder pieces completely. Cook the marinated pieces at 390 degrees F for 15 minutes. After 8 minutes, flip the pieces for even grilling and then cook for 7 minutes more. Working in batches is suggested. When done, serve warm and enjoy.

Nutritional information: Calories: 450; Fat 17.9g; Total Carbs 4.5g; Net Carbs: 0.5g; Fiber 1.3g; Sugars 1.6g; Protein 64.8g

Glazed Meatloaf

Prep time: 10 minutes | Cook time:45 minutes | Serves: 8

4 cups ground lean beef	2 eggs beaten
1 cup (soft and fresh) bread crumb	3 tbsp. ketchup
½ cup chopped mushrooms	1 tbsp. Worcestershire sauce
cloves of minced garlic	1 tbsp. Dijon mustard
½ cup shredded carrots	For Glaze
¼ cup beef broth	¼ cup honey
½ cup chopped onions	half cup ketchup
	2-teaspoon Dijon mustard

Stir well the beef broth and breadcrumbs in a large bowl. Set the mixture aside in a food processor, add garlic, onions, mushrooms, and carrots, and pulse at high speed until finely chopped. In a separate bowl, combine well the soaked breadcrumbs, Dijon mustard, Worcestershire sauce, eggs, lean ground beef, ketchup, and salt to make them into a meatloaf. Cook the meatloaf at 390 degrees F for 45 minutes. Mix well the Dijon mustard, ketchup, and brown sugar. After 40 minutes of cooking time, glaze the meatloaf with the mixture. Before serving, rest the cooked meatloaf for 10 minutes.

Nutritional information: Calories: 244; Fat: 13.3 g; Total

Carbs: 3g; Net Carbs: 1g; Fiber: 0.9g; Sugar: 0.7g; Protein: 32.2g

Flank Steak with Tamari Sauce

Prep time: 20 minutes | Cook time:30 minutes | Serves: 2

olive oil spray	half cup tamari sauce
2 pounds flank steak, cut into 6 pieces	3 bell peppers: sliced thinly
	beef broth: ⅓ cup
kosher salt and black pepper	1 tbsp. of unsalted butter
2 cloves of minced garlic	¼ cup balsamic vinegar
4 cups asparagus	

Rub the steak pieces with salt and pepper. In a zip-lock bag, toss the steak pieces well with Tamari sauce and garlic, seal the bag and let the steak pieces marinate for overnight. Top the steak pieces with the bell peppers and asparagus. Roll the steak piece around the vegetables and secure with toothpick. Deal the remaining pieces with the same steps. Transfer the processed steak rolls to the oiled cooking basket and cook at 400 degrees F for 15 minutes. When the time is up, remove the rolls from the air fryer and set aside for 5 minutes. Meanwhile, stir fry the balsamic vinegar, butter, and broth over medium flame. Mix well and reduce it by half. Add salt and pepper to taste. Pour over steaks, serve and enjoy.

Nutritional information: Calories: 471; Fat: 13.3 g; Total Carbs: 3g; Net Carbs: 1g; Fiber: 0.9g; Sugar: 0.7g; Protein: 32.2g

Cajun Spareribs with Coriander

Prep time: 10 minutes | Cook time: 30 minutes | Serves: 4

2 slabs spareribs	1 teaspoon coriander seed powder
2 teaspoons Cajun seasoning	
¼ cup brown sugar	2 tablespoons onion powder
½ teaspoon lemon	1 tablespoon salt
1 tablespoon paprika	

After mixing well the paprika, lemon, coriander, onion, and salt, rub the spareribs with the spice mixture. Cook one sparerib in your air fryer at 390 degrees F for 20 minutes. Cook another sparerib with the same steps. When done, serve and enjoy.

Nutritional information: Calories: 490; Fat: 13.3 g; Total Carbs: 3g; Net Carbs: 1g; Fiber: 0.9g; Sugar: 0.7g; Protein: 32.2g

Steak Kabobs with Vegetables

Prep time: 30 minutes | Cook time:10 minutes | Serves: 4

2 tablespoons light soy sauce	½ onion
4 cups lean beef chuck ribs, cut into one-inch pieces	8 6-inch skewers:
	1 bell peppers
⅓ cup low-fat: sour cream:	

Mix well the soy sauce and sour cream in a suitable bowl, then add the lean beef chunks and coat well. Marinate the chunks for 30 minutes. Soak skewers for 10 minutes in boil water. Cut onion and bell pepper in 1-inch pieces. Add bell peppers, onions and beef chunks on skewers. You can also choose to sprinkle with black pepper. Cook them in air fryer at 400 degrees F for 10 minutes, flipping halfway through. When done, serve with yogurt dipping sauce.

Nutritional information: Calories: 268; Fat: 13.3 g; Total Carbs: 3g; Net Carbs: 1g; Fiber: 0.9g; Sugar: 0.7g; Protein: 32.2g

Delicious Empanadas

Prep time: 10 minutes | Cook time:20 minutes | Serves: 2

8 pieces square gyoza wrappers
1 tablespoon olive oil:
¼ cup white onion, finely diced
¼ cup mushrooms, finely diced
½ cup lean ground beef
2 teaspoons chopped garlic
¼ teaspoon paprika
¼ teaspoon ground cumin
6 green olives, diced
⅛ teaspoon ground cinnamon
½ cup diced tomatoes
1 egg, lightly beaten

In a skillet, sauté the oil, onions, and beef over a medium heat for 3 minutes or until beef turns brown. After that, add mushrooms and cook for 6 minutes until they start to brown. Add paprika, cinnamon, olives, cumin, garlic and cook for 3 minutes more. Put in the chopped tomatoes and cook for 1 minute. When cooked, set aside for 5 minutes. Place the gyoza wrappers on a flat surface, add 1-½ tablespoons of beef filling to each wrapper. To better fold the wrappers and pinch the edges, brush the edges with water or eggs. Cook 4 empanadas in your air fryer at 400 degrees F for 7 minutes, until nicely browned. Cook the left empanadas with the same steps. When done, serve and enjoy.

Nutritional information: Calories: 343; Fat: 13.3 g; Total Carbs: 3g; Net Carbs: 1g; Fiber: 0.9g; Sugar: 0.7g; Protein: 32.2g

Spice Meatloaf

Prep time: 15 minutes | Cook time: 20 minutes | Serves: 8

1-pound ground beef
½ teaspoon dried tarragon
1 teaspoon Italian seasoning
1 tablespoon Worcestershire sauce
¼ cup ketchup
¼ cup coconut flour
½ cup almond flour
1 garlic clove, minced
¼ cup onion, chopped
2 eggs, lightly beaten
¼ teaspoon black pepper
½ teaspoon salt

Add all the recipe ingredients into the mixing bowl and mix until well combined. Make the equal shape of patties from mixture and place on a plate. Place in refrigerator for 10 minutes. Grease its air fryer basket with cooking spray. At 360 degrees F, preheat your air fryer. Place prepared patties in air fryer basket and cook for 10 minutes. Serve and enjoy.

Nutritional information: Calories: 244; Fat: 13.3 g; Total Carbs: 3g; Net Carbs: 3g; Fiber: 0.9g; Sugar: 0.7g; Protein: 32.2g

Lemon Beef Schnitzel

Prep time: 10 minutes | Cook time:15 minutes | Serves: 1

1 lean beef schnitzel
2 tablespoon Olive oil
¼ cup Breadcrumbs
1 egg
1 lemon, to serve

To form a crumbly mixture, mix the oil and breadcrumbs well in a bowl. Coat the beef schnitzel with the whisked egg and breadcrumb mixture in order. Cook the beef schnitzel at 370 degrees F for 15 minutes. When done, serve and enjoy.

Nutritional information: Calories: 521; Fat 36.8g; Total Carbs 19.8g; Net Carbs: 16.6g; Fiber 1.2g; Sugars 2g; Protein 31.4g

Simple Rib-Eye Steak

Prep time: 5 minutes | Cook time: 14 minutes | Serves: 2

2 medium-sized rib eye steaks
Salt & freshly ground black
pepper, to taste

Use the kitchen towels to pat dry the steaks. Season the steaks with salt and pepper well on both sides. Cook the steaks at 400 degrees F for 14 minutes, flipping halfway through. Let the steaks cool for 5 minutes before serving.

Nutritional information: Calories: 180; Fat 9g; Total Carbs 0g; Net Carbs: 0g; Fiber 0g; Sugars 0g; Protein 23g

Flank Steaks with Capers

Prep time: 10 minutes | Cook time: 45 minutes | Serves: 4

1 anchovy fillet, minced
1 clove of garlic, minced
1 cup pitted olives
1 tablespoon capers, minced
2 tablespoons fresh oregano
2 tablespoons garlic powder
2 tablespoons onion powder
2 tablespoons smoked paprika
⅓ cup extra-virgin olive oil
2 pounds flank steak, pounded
Salt and pepper

Season the steaks with salt and pepper. Sprinkle the steaks with onion powder, oregano, paprika, and garlic powder. Cook the steaks in your air fryer at 390 degrees F for 45 minutes, flipping every 10 minutes. Meanwhile, stir well the olive oil, capers, garlic, olives, and anchovy fillets. When done, serve and enjoy.

Nutritional information: Calories: 446; Fat 26.7g; Total Carbs 7g; Net Carbs: 3g; Fiber 2.7g; Sugars 1.8g; Protein 43.7g

Cajun Pork

Prep time: 10 minutes | Cook time: 12 minutes | Serves: 3

1 lb. pork loin, sliced into 1-inch cubes
2 tablespoons Cajun seasoning
3 tablespoons brown sugar
¼ cup cider vinegar

Coat the pork loin well with Cajun seasoning and 3 tablespoons of brown sugar in a suitable dish. Let the pork loin marinate for 3 hours. To baste, mix the brown sugar and vinegar well in a bowl. Thread pork pieces onto skewers, then baste with sauce. Cook at 360 degrees F for 12 minutes, flipping and basting with sauce halfway through. Cooking in batches is suggested. When done, serve and enjoy.

Nutritional information: Calories: 303; Fat 15.8g; Total Carbs 6g; Net Carbs: 2.5g; Fiber 0g; Sugars 6.6g; Protein 31.1g

Homemade Steak

Prep time: 70 minutes | Cook time: 20 minutes | Serves: 6

3 pounds steak
1 cup chimichurri
Salt and pepper

To better marinate, mix up the beef steak with the remaining ingredients in a sealed zip-lock bag and refrigerate for at least 60 minutes. When marinated, cook the steak in your air fryer at 390 degrees F for 20 minutes in batches, flipping halfway through. When done, serve and enjoy.

Nutritional information: Calories: 481; Fat 14.5g; Total Carbs 0.3g; Net Carbs: 0g; Fiber 0g; Sugars 0.1g; Protein 82g

Marinated Beef with BBQ Sauce

Prep time: 1 hour 10 minutes | Cook time: 20 minutes | Serves: 4

2 pounds beef steak, pounded
¼ cup bourbon
1 tablespoon Worcestershire
sauce
¼ cup barbecue sauce
Salt and pepper

Marinate the beef steak with the remaining ingredients in a sealed zip-lock bag for at least 60 minutes. When marinated, cook beef steak at 390 degrees F for 20 minutes in batches. Flip the steak halfway through for even cooking. While cooking the steak, in a saucepan, simmer the marinade until the sauce starts to thicken. With the bourbon sauce, serve and enjoy.

Nutritional information: Calories: 481; Fat 14.2g; Total Carbs 6g; Net Carbs: 2.5g; Fiber 0.1g; Sugars 4.8g; Protein 68.8g

Garlic Beef with Sauce

Prep time: 1 hour 10 minutes | Cook time: 1 hour | Serves: 12

1 ½ tablespoon garlic	1 pound eye of round roast
1 cup beef stock	6 tablespoons extra-virgin
1 teaspoon thyme leaves,	olive oil
chopped	1 teaspoon pepper
3 tablespoons butter	1 teaspoon salt

In a zip-lock bag, mix all of the ingredients, seal and put in the refrigerator to marinate for 60 minutes. Transfer the marinated food to the cooking pan of your air fryer and cook at 400 degrees F for 60 minutes, basting the beef with sauce halfway through. When done, serve and enjoy.

Nutritional information: Calories: 150; Fat 11.5g; Total Carbs 0.5g; Net Carbs: 0g; Fiber 0.1g; Sugars 0g; Protein 11.5g

Garlic Beef with Egg and Bell Pepper

Prep time: 10 minutes | Cook time: 30 minutes | Serves: 4

1 pound ground beef	1 onion, chopped
6 eggs, beaten	3 cloves of garlic, minced
1 green bell pepper, seeded	3 tablespoons olive oil
and chopped	Salt and pepper

Stir the ground beef well with the olive oil, onion, garlic, and bell pepper in the cooking basket of your air fryer. Dress with salt and pepper, then pour in the beaten eggs and mix. Cook at 330 degrees F for 30 minutes. When done, serve and enjoy.

Nutritional information: Calories: 419; Fat 24.3g; Total Carbs 6g; Net Carbs: 2.5g; Fiber 1g; Sugars 3.2g; Protein 43.4g

Spiced Beef Chuck Roast

Prep time: 10 minutes | Cook time: 1 hour | Serves: 6

1 pound beef chuck roast	1 tablespoon Worcestershire
1 onion, chopped	sauce
2 cloves of garlic, minced	1 teaspoon rosemary
2 tablespoons olive oil	1 teaspoon thyme
3 cups water	3 stalks of celery, sliced
1 tablespoon butter	

Stir all of the ingredients and arrange them to the cooking pan of your air fryer. Cook them at 350 degrees F for 60 minutes, braising the meat with its sauce halfway through. When done, serve and enjoy.

Nutritional information: Calories: 345; Fat 27.7g; Total Carbs 3g; Net Carbs: 1g; Fiber 0.7g; Sugars 1.4g; Protein 20.2g

Pork Tenderloins

Prep time: 5 minutes | Cook time: 30 minutes | Serves: 3

1 teaspoon salt	½ teaspoon pepper

1 lb. pork tenderloin	Apricot Glaze Ingredients:
2 tablespoons minced fresh	1 cup apricot preserves
rosemary	3 garlic cloves, minced
2 tablespoons olive oil, divided	4 tablespoons lemon juice
1 garlic cloves, minced	

After mixing the pepper, salt, garlic, oil, and rosemary well, brush the pork with them on all sides. If needed, you can cut pork crosswise in half. Arrange the pork to the sprayed cooking pan and cook at 390 degrees F for 3 minutes on each side. While cooking the pork, mix all of the glaze ingredients well. Baste the pork every 5 minutes. Cook at 330 degrees F and cook for 20 minutes more. When done, serve and enjoy.

Nutritional information: Calories: 569; Fat 15.4g; Total Carbs 71g; Net Carbs: 0g; Fiber 1.5g; Sugars 46.7g; Protein 40.7g

Paprika Pork Chops

Prep time: 15 minutes | Cook time: 12 minutes | Serves: 6

1 ½ pounds pork chops, boneless	1 teaspoon garlic powder
1 teaspoon paprika	¼ cup parmesan cheese, grated
1 teaspoon creole seasoning	⅓ cup almond flour

At 360 degrees F, preheat your Air fryer. Add all the recipe ingredients except pork chops in a zip-lock bag. Add pork chops in the bag. Seal this bag and shake well to coat pork chops. Remove pork chops from zip-lock bag and place in the air fryer basket. Cook pork chops for almost 10-12 minutes. Serve and enjoy.

Nutritional information: Calories: 237; Fat: 12.8 g; Total Carbs: 3.9g; Net Carbs: 1.3g; Fiber: 0.9g; Sugar: 1.9g; Protein: 31.7g

Pork Chops with Parmesan Cheese

Prep time: 15 minutes | Cook time: 15 minutes | Serves: 4

4 pork chops, boneless	½ teaspoon chili powder
4 tablespoons parmesan	½ teaspoon onion powder
cheese, grated	1 teaspoon paprika
1 cup pork rind	¼ teaspoon black pepper
2 eggs, lightly beaten	½ teaspoon salt

At 400 degrees F, preheat your air fryer. Season pork chops with black pepper and salt. Add pork rind in food processor and process until crumbs form. Mix together pork rind crumbs and seasoning in a suitable bowl. Place egg in a separate bowl. Dip the prepared pork chops in egg mixture then coat with pork crumb mixture and place in the air fryer basket. Cook pork chops for 12-15 minutes. Serve and enjoy.

Nutritional information: Calories: 329; Fat: 20.6 g; Total Carbs: 19.4g; Net Carbs: 10g; Fiber: 1.1g; Sugar: 0.4g; Protein: 50.4g

Simple Homemade Steak

Prep time: 15 minutes | Cook time: 7 minutes | Serves: 2

12 oz. steaks	1 teaspoon liquid smoke
½ tablespoon unsweetened	1 tablespoon soy sauce
cocoa powder	Black pepper
1 tablespoon Montreal steak	Salt
seasoning	

Add steak, liquid smoke, and soy sauce in a zip-lock bag and shake well. Season steak with seasonings and place in the refrigerator for overnight. Place marinated steak in air fryer basket and cook at almost 375 F for 5 minutes. Turn steak to another side and cook for 2 minutes more. Serve and enjoy.

Nutritional information: Calories: 324; Fat: 17.8 g; Total Carbs: 8.9g; Net Carbs: 4g; Fiber: 0.5g; Sugar: 1.9g; Protein: 36.6g

Delicious Cheeseburger

Prep time: 15 minutes | Cook time: 12 minutes | Serves: 2

½ pound ground beef
¼ teaspoon onion powder
2 cheese slices
¼ teaspoon black pepper
⅛ teaspoon salt

In a suitable bowl, mix together ground beef, onion powder, black pepper, and salt. Make 2 equal shapes of patties from meat mixture and place in the air fryer basket. Cook patties at 370 degrees F for 12 minutes. Turn patties halfway through. Once air fryer timer goes off then place cheese slices on top of each patty and close the air fryer basket for 1 minute. Serve and enjoy.
Nutritional information: Calories: 292; Fat: 9.4 g; Total Carbs: 2.5g; Net Carbs: 1g; Fiber: 0.4g; Sugar: 1.6g; Protein: 46.6g

Steak Mushroom Bites

Prep time: 15 minutes | Cook time: 18 minutes | Serves: 3

1 pound steaks, cut into ½-inch cubes
½ teaspoon garlic powder
1 teaspoon Worcestershire sauce
2 tablespoons butter, melted
8 oz. mushrooms, sliced
Black pepper
Salt

Add all the recipe ingredients into the suitable mixing bowl and toss well. Grease its air fryer basket with cooking spray. At 400 degrees F, preheat your air fryer. Add steak mushroom mixture into the air fryer basket and cook at almost 400 degrees F for almost 15-18 minutes. Shake basket twice. Serve and enjoy.
Nutritional information: Calories: 388; Fat: 24.8 g; Total Carbs: 4.1g; Net Carbs: 1.7g; Fiber: 0.9g; Sugar: 1.9g; Protein: 58g

Homemade and Delectable Pork Chops

Prep time: 15 minutes | Cook time: 9 minutes | Serves: 4

4 pork chops, boneless
1 teaspoon onion powder
1 teaspoon smoked paprika
½ cup parmesan cheese, grated
2 tablespoons olive oil
½ teaspoon black pepper
1 teaspoon kosher salt

Brush pork chops with olive oil. In a suitable bowl, mix together parmesan cheese and spices. Grease its air fryer basket with cooking spray. Coat pork chops with parmesan cheese mixture and place in the air fryer basket. Cook pork chops at 375 degrees F for 9 minutes. Turn halfway through the cooking time. Serve and enjoy.
Nutritional information: Calories: 291; Fat: 14.8 g; Total Carbs: 5.2g; Net Carbs: 2.3g; Fiber: 0.5g; Sugar: 4.9g; Protein: 33.6g

Beef with Spanish Rice Casserole

Prep time: 10 minutes | Cook time: 50 minutes | Serves: 3

½-pound lean ground beef
2 tablespoons chopped green bell pepper
1 tablespoon chopped fresh cilantro
¼ cup shredded Cheddar cheese
½ teaspoon brown sugar
½ pinch ground pepper
⅓ cup uncooked long grain rice
¼ cup finely chopped onion
¼ cup chile sauce
¼ teaspoon ground cumin
¼ teaspoon Worcestershire sauce
½ (14.5 ounce) can canned
tomatoes
½ cup water
½ teaspoon salt

Spray the cooking pan of your air fryer with cooking spray. Transfer the ground beef to the pan and cook at 360 degrees F for 10 minutes. After 5 minutes of cooking time, mix the crumble beef. After discarding the excess fat, stir in pepper, Worcestershire sauce, salt, chile sauce, rice, cumin, brown sugar, water, tomatoes, green bell pepper, and onion. Use the aluminum foil to cover the pan and cook for 25 minutes more, stirring regularly. Stir at the end, press hard and sprinkle with cheese, then cook at 390 degrees F for 15 minutes more or until the tops are lightly browned. when done, serve with cilantro.
Nutritional information: Cal: 346; Fat: 19.1 g; Total Carbs: 24.9 g; Net Carbs: 11.8g; Fiber: 0.2g; Sugar: 0.2g; Protein:18.5 g

Easy-to-Make Steak

Prep time: 15 minutes | Cook time: 18 minutes | Serves: 2

12 oz. steaks, ¾-inch thick
1 teaspoon garlic powder
1 teaspoon olive oil
Black pepper
Salt

Coat steaks with oil and season with garlic powder, black pepper, and salt. At 400 degrees F, preheat your air fryer. Place steaks in air fryer basket and cook for almost 15-18 minutes. Turn halfway through the cooking time. Serve and enjoy.
Nutritional information: Calories: 325; Fat: 27 g; Total Carbs: 2.2g; Net Carbs: 0.5g; Fiber: 0.2g; Sugar: 0.2g; Protein: 61.7g

Glazed Tender Pork Chops

Prep time: 15 minutes | Cook time: 14 minutes | Serves: 3

3 pork chops, rinsed and pat dry
¼ teaspoon smoked paprika
½ teaspoon garlic powder
2 teaspoons olive oil
Black pepper
Salt

Coat pork chops with paprika, olive oil, garlic powder, black pepper, and salt. Place the prepared pork chops in air fryer basket and cook at almost 380 degrees F for almost 10-14 minutes. Turn halfway through the cooking time. Serve and enjoy.
Nutritional information: Calories: 319; Fat: 21.2 g; Total Carbs: 14g; Net Carbs: 7.4g; Fiber: 3.5g; Sugar: 8.9g; Protein: 19.6g

Garlic Pork Chops with Mushrooms

Prep time: 15 minutes | Cook time: 18 minutes | Serves: 4

1-pound pork chops, rinsed and pat dry
½ teaspoon garlic powder
1 teaspoon soy sauce
2 tablespoons butter, melted
8 oz. mushrooms, halved
Black pepper
Salt

At 400 degrees F, preheat your air fryer. Cut pork chops into the ¾-inch cubes and place in a suitable mixing bowl. Add the remaining ingredients into the bowl and toss well. Transfer pork and mushroom mixture into the air fryer basket and cook for almost 15-18 minutes. Shake basket halfway through the cooking time. Serve and enjoy.
Nutritional information: Calories: 629; Fat: 40.5 g; Total Carbs: 16.9g; Net Carbs: 5g; Fiber: 4.1g; Sugar: 9.3g; Protein: 50.3g

Cajun Seasoned Bratwurst with Vegetables

Prep time: 15 minutes | Cook time: 20 minutes | Serves: 6

1 package bratwurst, sliced ½-inch rounds
½ tablespoon Cajun seasoning
¼ cup onion, diced
2 bell pepper, sliced

Add all the recipe ingredients into the suitable mixing bowl and toss well. Line air fryer basket with foil. Add vegetable and bratwurst mixture into the air fryer basket and cook at almost 390 degrees F for almost 10 minutes. Toss well and cook for almost 10 minutes more. Serve and enjoy.
Nutritional information: Calories: 248; Fat: 11.8 g; Total Carbs: 2.2g; Net Carbs: 1g; Fiber: 0.4g; Sugar: 1.5g; Protein: 33.3g

Beef Burgers with Worcestershire Sauce

Prep time: 15 minutes | Cook time: 15 minutes | Serves: 4

1 ½ pound ground beef
Black pepper and salt to season
¼ teaspoon liquid smoke
2 teaspoons onion powder
1 teaspoon garlic powder
1 ½ tablespoon Worcestershire sauce

Burgers:
4 buns
4 trimmed lettuce leaves
4 tablespoons mayonnaise
1 large tomato, sliced
4 slices Cheddar cheese

At 370 degrees F, preheat your air fryer. In a suitable bowl, combine the beef, salt, black pepper, liquid smoke, onion powder, garlic powder and Worcestershire sauce using your hands. Form 3 to 4 patties out of the mixture. Place the patties in the fryer basket making sure to leave enough space between them. Ideally, work with 2 patties at a time. Close the air fryer and cook for 10 minutes. Turn the beef with kitchen tongs, reduce the temperature to 350 degrees F, and cook further for 5 minutes. Remove the patties onto a plate. Assemble burgers with the lettuce, mayonnaise, sliced cheese, and sliced tomato.
Nutritional information: Calories: 267; Fat: 15.2 g; Total Carbs: 13.9g; Net Carbs: 6g; Fiber: 0.1g; Sugar: 12.9g; Protein: 20.6g

Steak Fajitas with Vegetables

Prep time: 15 minutes | Cook time: 15 minutes | Serves: 6

1-pound steak, sliced
1 tablespoon olive oil
1 tablespoon fajita seasoning,
gluten-free
½ cup onion, sliced
3 bell peppers, sliced

Line air fryer basket with aluminum foil. Add all the recipe ingredients suitable bowl and toss until well coated. Transfer fajita mixture into the air fryer basket and cook at almost 390 degrees F for 5 minutes. Toss well and cook for 5-10 minutes more. Serve and enjoy.
Nutritional information: Calories: 360; Fat: 30.8 g; Total Carbs: 1.3g; Net Carbs: 0.9g; Fiber: 0.5g; Sugar: 0.2g; Protein: 18.6g

Thyme Beef Roast

Prep time: 15 minutes | Cook time: 35 minutes | Serves: 7

2 pounds' beef roast
1 tablespoon olive oil

1 teaspoon thyme
2 teaspoons garlic powder
¼ teaspoon black pepper
1 tablespoon kosher salt

Coat roast with olive oil. Mix together thyme, garlic powder, black pepper, and salt and rub all over roast. Place roast into the air fryer basket and cook at almost 400 degrees F for 20 minutes. Spray roast with cooking spray and cook for 15 minutes more. Slice and serve.
Nutritional information: Calories: 238; Fat: 30.8 g; Total Carbs: 2.4g; Net Carbs: 1g; Fiber: 0.5g; Sugar: 1.3g; Protein: 31.6g

Italian-style Cheeseburgers with Cheese Slices

Prep time: 15 minutes | Cook time: 12 minutes | Serves: 4

1-pound ground beef
4 cheddar cheese slices
½ teaspoon Italian seasoning
Black pepper
Salt

Grease its air fryer basket with cooking spray. In a suitable bowl, mix together ground beef, Italian seasoning, black pepper, and salt. Make 4 equal shapes of patties from meat mixture and place into the air fryer basket. Cook at almost 375 degrees F for 5 minutes. Turn patties to another side and cook for 5 minutes more. Place cheese slices on top of each patty and cook for 2 minutes more. Serve and enjoy.
Nutritional information: Calories: 325; Fat: 20.3 g; Total Carbs: 3.4g; Net Carbs: 1g; Fiber: 1g; Sugar: 1.2g; Protein: 53.4g

Juicy Spiced Rib-Eye Steaks

Prep time: 15 minutes | Cook time: 14 minutes | Serves: 2

2 medium rib-eye steaks
¼ teaspoon garlic powder
¼ teaspoon onion powder
1 teaspoon olive oil
Black pepper
Salt

Coat steaks with oil and season with garlic powder, onion powder, black pepper, and salt. At 400 degrees F, preheat your air fryer. Place steaks into the air fryer basket and cook for 14 minutes. Turn halfway through. Serve and enjoy.
Nutritional information: Calories: 324; Fat: 17.8 g; Total Carbs: 8.9g; Net Carbs: 3g; Fiber: 0.5g; Sugar: 1.9g; Protein: 36.6g

Asian Sirloin Steaks with Worcestershire Sauce

Prep time: 15 minutes | Cook time: 25 minutes | Serves: 2

12 oz. sirloin steaks
1 tablespoon garlic, minced
1 tablespoon ginger, grated
½ tablespoon Worcestershire sauce
1 ½ tablespoon soy sauce
2 tablespoons Erythritol
Black pepper
Salt

Add steaks in a large zip-lock bag along with remaining ingredients. Shake well and place in the refrigerator for overnight. Spray its air fryer basket with cooking spray. Place marinated steaks in air fryer basket and cook at almost 400 degrees F for 10 minutes. Turn steaks to another side and cook for 10-15 minutes more. Serve and enjoy.
Nutritional information: Calories: 602; Fat: 38 g; Total Carbs: 0.3g; Net Carbs: 0g; Fiber: 0.1g; Sugar: 0g; Protein: 61.4g

Juicy Beef Kabobs with Sour Cream

Prep time: 15 minutes | Cook time: 10 minutes | Serves: 4

1-pound beef, cut into chunks	2 tablespoons soy sauce
1 bell pepper, cut into 1-inch pieces	⅓ cup sour cream
	½ onion, cut into 1-inch pieces

In a suitable bowl, mix together soy sauce and sour cream. Add beef into the bowl and coat well and place in the refrigerator for overnight. Thread marinated beef, bell peppers, and onions onto the soaked wooden skewers. Place in your air fryer basket and cook at almost 400 degrees F for almost 10 minutes. Turn halfway through the cooking time. Serve and enjoy.
Nutritional information: Calories: 251; Fat: 8.3 g; Total Carbs: 22.9g; Net Carbs: 10g; Fiber: 0.5g; Sugar: 2g; Protein: 23g

Flavorsome Beef Broccoli with Sauces

Prep time: 15 minutes | Cook time: 15 minutes | Serves: 3

½ pound steak, cut into strips	4 tablespoons oyster sauce
1 teaspoon garlic, minced	1-pound broccoli florets
1 teaspoon ginger, minced	1 tablespoon sesame seeds, toasted
2 tablespoons sesame oil	
2 tablespoons soy sauce	

Add all the recipe ingredients except sesame seeds into the suitable mixing bowl and toss well. Place this bowl in the refrigerator for 1 hour. Add marinated steak and broccoli into the air fryer basket and cook at almost 350 degrees F for almost 15 minutes. Shake basket 2-3 times while cooking. Garnish with sesame seeds and serve.
Nutritional information: Calories: 382; Fat: 32.5 g; Total Carbs: 3.2g; Net Carbs: 1g; Fiber: 0.2g; Sugar: 1.9g; Protein: 19.1g

Cheesy Pork Chops

Prep time: 15 minutes | Cook time: 8 minutes | Serves: 2

4 pork chops	½ teaspoon garlic powder
¼ cup cheddar cheese, shredded	½ teaspoon salt

At 350 degrees F, preheat your air fryer. Rub pork chops with garlic powder and salt and place in the air fryer basket. Cook pork chops for 4 minutes. Turn pork chops over and cook for 2 minutes. Add cheese on top of pork chops and cook for 2 minutes more. Serve and enjoy.
Nutritional information: Calories: 398; Fat: 37.8 g; Total Carbs: 2.5g; Net Carbs: 1g; Fiber: 0.2g; Sugar: 0.5g; Protein: 13.6g

Burgundy Beef Dish with Egg Noodles

Prep time: 15 minutes | Cook time: 25 minutes | Serves: 5

1 package egg noodles, cooked	2 cups mushrooms, sliced
1 oz. dry onion soup mix	1 whole onion, chopped
1 can (14.5 oz.) cream mushroom soup	½ cup beef broth
	3 garlic cloves, minced

At 360 degrees F, preheat your air fryer. Drizzle onion soup mix all over the meat. In a suitable mixing bowl, mix the sauce, garlic cloves, beef broth, chopped onion, sliced mushrooms and mushroom soup. Top the meat with the prepared sauce mixture. Place the prepared meat in the air fryer's cooking basket and cook for 25 minutes. Serve with cooked egg noodles.
Nutritional information: Calories: 368; Fat: 32.8 g; Total Carbs: 0.6g; Net Carbs: 0g; Fiber: 0.1g; Sugar: 1.1g; Protein: 18.5g

Hungarian Air Fryer Stew

Prep time: 15 minutes | Cook time: 65 minutes | Serves: 4

4 tablespoons all-purpose flour	2 bay leaves
Salt and black pepper, to taste	1 teaspoon caraway seeds.
1 teaspoon Hungarian paprika	2 cups roasted vegetable broth
1-pound beef chuck roast, boneless, cut into bite-sized cubes	2 ripe tomatoes, pureed
	2 tablespoons red wine
2 teaspoons sunflower oil	2 bell peppers, chopped
1 medium-sized leek, chopped	2 medium carrots, sliced
2 garlic cloves, minced	1 celery stalk, peeled and diced

Add the flour, salt, black pepper, paprika, and beef to a re-sealable bag; shake to coat well. Heat the oil in a Dutch Air Fryer over medium-high flame; sauté the leeks, garlic, bay leaves, and caraway seeds about 4 minutes or until fragrant. Transfer to a lightly sprayed baking pan. Then, brown the beef, with occasional stirring, working in batches. Add to the baking pan. Add the vegetable broth, tomatoes, and red wine. Lower the pan onto the Air Fryer basket. Air fry at 325 degrees F for 40 minutes. Add the bell peppers, carrots, and celery. Cook an additional 20 minutes. Serve immediately and enjoy!
Nutritional information: Calories: 257; Fat: 17 g; Total Carbs: 13.9g; Net Carbs: 9.5g; Fiber: 4.2; Sugar 5.9g; Protein: 13.6g

Tasty Pork Chops

Prep time: 15 minutes | Cook time: 9 minutes | Serves: 4

4 pork chops, boneless	2 tablespoons olive oil
1 teaspoon onion powder	½ teaspoon black pepper
1 teaspoon smoked paprika	1 teaspoon kosher salt
½ cup parmesan cheese, grated	

Brush pork chops with olive oil. In a suitable bowl, mix together parmesan cheese and spices. Grease its air fryer basket with cooking spray. Coat pork chops with parmesan cheese mixture and place in the air fryer basket. Cook pork chops at 375 degrees F for 9 minutes. Turn halfway through the cooking time. Serve and enjoy.
Nutritional information: Calories: 159; Fat: 5.8 g; Total Carbs: 9.5 g; Net Carbs: 3g; Fiber: 1.1g; Sugar: 7.2g; Protein: 16.6g

Cheese Ground Pork

Prep time: 15 minutes | Cook time: 40 minutes | Serves: 4

1 tablespoon olive oil	1 can (10 ¾-ounces) condensed cream of mushroom soup
1 ½ pounds pork, ground	
Salt and black pepper, to taste	1 cup water
1 medium-sized leek, sliced	½ cup ale
1 teaspoon fresh garlic, minced	1 cup cream cheese
2 carrots, trimmed and sliced	½ cup soft fresh breadcrumbs
1 (2-ounce) jar pimiento, drained and chopped	1 tablespoon fresh cilantro, chopped

At 320 degrees F, preheat your Air Fryer. Spread the olive oil

in a suitable baking dish and heat for 1 to 2 minutes. Add the pork, salt, black pepper and cook for 6 minutes, crumbling with a fork. Stir in the leeks and cook for 4 to 5 minutes, with occasional stirring. Add the garlic, carrots, pimiento, mushroom soup, water, ale, and cream cheese. Gently stir to combine. Turn the temperature to 370 degrees F. Top with the breadcrumbs. Place the stuffed baking dish in the cooking basket and cook approximately 30 minutes or until everything is thoroughly cooked. Serve garnished with fresh cilantro.
Nutritional information: Calories: 826; Fat: 11.3 g; Total Carbs: 154.9g; Net Carbs: 23g; Fiber: 4.5g; Sugar: 3.3g; Protein: 17g

Bacon-wrapped Tater Tots

Prep time: 15 minutes | Cook time: 16 minutes | Serves: 5

10 thin slices of bacon	¼ cup mayo
10 tater tots, frozen	4 tablespoons ketchup
1 teaspoon cayenne pepper	1 teaspoon rice vinegar
Sauce:	1 teaspoon chili powder

Lay the slices of bacon on your working surface. Place a tater tot on 1 end of each slice; sprinkle with cayenne pepper and roll them over. Cook in the preheated Air Fryer at about 390 degrees F for almost 15 to 16 minutes. Whisk all the recipe ingredients for the sauce in a suitable mixing bowl. Serve Bacon-Wrapped Tater Tots with the sauce on the side. Enjoy!
Nutritional information: Calories: 303; Fat: 3.1 g; Total Carbs: 24.9g; Net Carbs: 10g; Fiber: 1.5g; Sugar: 0.9g; Protein: 22.6g

Pork Sausage Bacon Rolls

Prep time: 15 minutes | Cook time: 35 minutes | Serves: 4

8 bacon strips	A pinch of salt
8 pork sausages	A pinch of black pepper
Relish:	2 tablespoons sugar
8 large tomatoes	1 teaspoon smoked paprika
1 garlic clove, peeled	1 tablespoon white wine
1 small onion, peeled	vinegar
3 tablespoons chopped parsley	

Start with the relish; add the tomatoes, garlic, and onion in a food processor. Blitz them for almost 10 seconds until the mixture is pulpy. Pour the pulp into a saucepan, add the vinegar, salt, black pepper, and place it over medium heat. Bring to simmer for almost 10 minutes; add the paprika and sugar. Stir with a spoon and simmer for almost 10 minutes until pulpy and thick. Turn off the heat, transfer the relish to a bowl and chill it for an hour. In 30 minutes after putting the relish in the refrigerator, move on to the sausages. Wrap each sausage with a bacon strip neatly and stick in a bamboo skewer at the end of the sausage to secure the bacon ends. Open the air fryer, place in the wrapped sausages and cook for 12 minutes at 350 degrees F. Ensure that the bacon is golden and crispy before removing them. Remove the relish from the refrigerator. Serve the sausages and relish with turnip mash.
Nutritional information: Calories: 341; Fat: 24.6 g; Total Carbs: 12g; Net Carbs: 5g; Fiber: 0.1g; Sugar: 11.9g; Protein: 18.6g

Grilled Ribs with Soy Sauce

Prep time: 15 minutes | Cook time: 25 minutes | Serves: 2

1 teaspoon soy sauce	3 tablespoon barbecue sauce
Black pepper and salt to season	2 garlic cloves, minced
1 teaspoon oregano	1 tablespoon cayenne pepper
2 tablespoons maple syrup	1 teaspoon sesame oil

Put the chops on a chopping board and use a knife to cut them into smaller pieces of desired sizes. Put them in a suitable mixing bowl, add the salt, soy sauce, oregano, black pepper, 1 tablespoon of maple syrup, barbecue sauce, garlic, cayenne pepper, and sesame oil. Mix well and place the pork in the fridge to marinate in the spices for 5 hours. At 350 degrees F, preheat your air fryer. Open the air fryer and place the ribs in the fryer basket. Slide the air fryer basket in and cook for almost 15 minutes. Open the air fryer, turn the ribs using tongs, apply the remaining maple syrup with a brush, close the air fryer, and continue cooking for almost 10 minutes. Serve.
Nutritional information: Calories: 634; Fat: 19.6 g; Total Carbs: 13.1g; Net Carbs: 6.4g; Fiber: 1.5g; Sugar: 8.6g; Protein: 96g

Homemade Ham Cheese Sandwiches

Prep time: 15 minutes | Cook time: 10 minutes | Serves: 4

4 slices lean pork ham	8 slices tomato
4 slices cheese	

At 360 degrees F, preheat your Air fryer. Spread 4 slices of bread on a flat surface. Spread the slices with cheese, tomato, turkey and ham. Cover with the remaining pork slices to form sandwiches. Add the sandwiches to the air fryer basket and cook for almost 10 minutes. Serve.
Nutritional information: Calories: 324; Fat: 17.8 g; Total Carbs: 8.9g; Net Carbs: 4.1g; Fiber: 0.5g; Sugar: 1.9g; Protein: 36.6g

Cayenne Sirloin Steaks

Prep time: 15 minutes | Cook time: 15 minutes | Serves: 4

1-pound lamb sirloin steaks, boneless	1 teaspoon cayenne
	½ teaspoon ground cardamom
1 teaspoon garam masala	1 teaspoon ground cinnamon
4 garlic cloves	1 teaspoon ground fennel
¾ tablespoon ginger	1 teaspoon salt
½ onion	

Add all the recipe ingredients except steak into the blender and blend until smooth. Place meat into the bowl and pour the blended mixture over meat and coat well. Place in refrigerator for 1 hour. Place marinated meat into the air fryer and cook for almost 15 minutes at 330 degrees F. Turn meat halfway through. Serve and enjoy.
Nutritional information: Calories: 539; Fat: 17.5 g; Total Carbs: 79.2g; Net Carbs: 43g; Fiber: 4.5g; Sugar: 26.9g; Protein: 15.6g

Elegant Pork Chops

Prep time: 15 minutes | Cook time: 25 minutes | Serves: 4

4 pork chops, bone-in	2 cooking apples, peeled and
Salt and black pepper, to taste	sliced
½ teaspoon onion powder	1 tablespoon honey
½ teaspoon paprika	1 tablespoon peanut oil
½ teaspoon celery seeds	

Place the pork in a suitable greased baking pan. Season with black pepper and salt, and transfer the pan to the cooking basket. Cook in the preheated Air Fryer at about 370 degrees F for almost 10 minutes. Meanwhile, in a suitable saucepan, simmer the remaining ingredients over medium heat for about 8 minutes or until the apples are softened. Pour the applesauce over the prepared pork chops. Add to the preheated Air Fryer and air fry for 5 minutes more. Serve

Nutritional information: Calories: 398; Fat: 27 g; Total Carbs: 34.9g; Net Carbs: 13g; Fiber: 6.5g; Sugar: 6.9g; Protein: 11.6g

Italian Seasoned Steak with Garlic Butter

Prep time: 15 minutes | Cook time: 6 minutes | Serves: 2

2 steaks
2 teaspoons garlic butter
¼ teaspoon Italian seasoning

Black pepper
Salt

Season steaks with Italian seasoning, black pepper, and salt. Rub steaks with garlic butter and place into the air fryer basket and cook at almost 350 degrees F for 6 minutes. Serve and enjoy.

Nutritional information: Calories: 399; Fat: 13 g; Total Carbs: 52.9g; Net Carbs: 24; Fiber: 8.8g; Sugar: 3.9g; Protein: 19.6g

Mediterranean-style Beef Steak

Prep time: 15 minutes | Cook time: 12 minutes | Serves: 4

1 ½ pounds beef steak
1-pound zucchini
1 teaspoon dried rosemary
1 teaspoon dried basil
1 teaspoon dried oregano

2 tablespoons extra-virgin olive oil
2 tablespoons fresh chives, chopped

At 400 degrees F, preheat your Air Fryer. Toss the steak and zucchini with the spices and olive oil. Transfer to the cooking basket and cook for 6 minutes. Now, shale the basket and cook another 6 minutes. Serve immediately garnished with fresh chives. Enjoy!

Nutritional information: Calories: 213; Fat: 4.1 g; Total Carbs: 37.9g; Net Carbs: 15g; Fiber: 1.5g; Sugar: 1.9g; Protein: 26.6g

Beef and Chorizo Sausage with Cheese Tart

Prep time: 15 minutes | Cook time: 19 minutes | Serves: 4

1 tablespoon canola oil
1 onion, chopped
2 fresh garlic cloves, minced
½ pound ground beef chuck
½ pound Chorizo sausage, crumbled
1 cup pasta sauce
Salt, to taste

¼ teaspoon black pepper
½ teaspoon red pepper flakes, crushed
1 cup cream cheese, room temperature
½ cup Swiss cheese, shredded
1 egg
½ cup crackers, crushed

At 370 degrees F, preheat your Air Fryer. Grease a baking pan with canola oil. Add the onion, garlic, ground chuck, sausage, pasta sauce, salt, black pepper, and red pepper. Cook for 9 minutes. In the meantime, combine cheese with egg. Place the cheese-egg mixture over the beef mixture. Sprinkle with crushed crackers and cook for almost 10 minutes. Serve warm and enjoy!

Nutritional information: Calories: 685; Fat: 18.3 g; Total Carbs:99.3g; Net Carbs: 51g; Fiber: 6.5g; Sugar: 7.9g; Protein: 27.6g

Jerk Pork Butt Pieces

Prep time: 15 minutes | Cook time: 20 minutes | Serves: 4

1 ½ pounds pork butt, chopped into pieces

3 tablespoons jerk paste

Add meat and jerk paste into the bowl and coat well. Place in the fridge for overnight. Grease its air fryer basket with cooking spray. At 390 degrees F, preheat your air fryer. Add marinated meat into the air fryer and cook for 20 minutes. Turn halfway through the cooking time. Serve and enjoy.

Nutritional information: Calories: 257; Fat: 10.4g; Total Carbs: 20g; Net Carbs: 6g; Fiber: 0g; Sugar: 1.6g; Protein: 21g

Simple & Tasty Pork Sandwiches

Prep time: 15 minutes | Cook time: 50 minutes | Serves: 3

2 teaspoons. peanut oil
1 ½ pounds pork sirloin
Coarse salt and black pepper, to taste

1 tablespoon smoked paprika
¼ cup prepared barbecue sauce
3 hamburger buns, split

At 360 degrees F, preheat your Air Fryer. Drizzle the oil all over the pork sirloin. Sprinkle with salt, black pepper, and paprika. Cook for 50 minutes in the preheated Air Fryer. Remove the prepared roast from the Air Fryer and shred with 2 forks. Mix in the barbecue sauce. Serve over hamburger buns. Enjoy!

Nutritional information: Calories: 249; Fat: 5.7 g; Total Carbs: 23.9g; Net Carbs: 10g; Fiber: 0.9g; Sugar: 1.9g; Protein: 3.6g

Polish Beef Sausage with Worcestershire Sauce

Prep time: 15 minutes | Cook time: 11 minutes | Serves: 4

1 pound smoked Polish beef sausage, sliced
1 tablespoon mustard
1 tablespoon olive oil
2 tablespoons Worcestershire

sauce
2 bell peppers, sliced
2 cups sourdough bread, cubed
Salt and black pepper, to taste

Toss the sausage with the mustard, olive, and Worcestershire sauce. Thread sausage, black peppers, and bread onto skewers. Sprinkle with black pepper and salt. Cook in the preheated Air Fryer at about 360 degrees F for 11 minutes. Brush the skewers with the reserved marinade. Serve

Nutritional information: Calories: 351; Fat: 20.3 g; Total Carbs: 40.9g; Net Carbs: 16g; Fiber: 0.5g; Sugar: 35.5g; Protein: 33.6g

Cheese Beef Roll

Prep time: 15 minutes | Cook time: 15 minutes | Serves: 4

Black pepper and salt to taste
3 tablespoons pesto
6 slices cheese

¾ cup spinach, chopped
3 oz. bell pepper, deseeded and sliced

At 400 degrees F, preheat your air fryer. Top the steak slices with pesto, cheese, spinach, bell pepper. Roll up the steak slices and secure using a toothpick. Season with black pepper and salt accordingly. Place the prepared slices in your air fryer's cooking basket and cook for almost 15 minutes. Serve and enjoy!

Nutritional information: Calories: 416; Fat: 8.3 g; Total Carbs: 22.9g; Net Carbs: 8g; Fiber: 0.5g; Sugar: 19g; Protein: 60.6g

Flavorsome Onion and Sausage Balls

Prep time: 15 minutes | Cook time: 15 minutes | Serves: 4

Black pepper and salt to taste

1 cup onion, chopped

3 tablespoons breadcrumbs   1 teaspoon sage
½ teaspoon garlic puree

At 340 degrees F, preheat your air fryer. In a suitable bowl, mix onions, sausage meat, sage, garlic puree, black pepper and salt. Add breadcrumbs to a plate. Form balls using the mixture and roll them in breadcrumbs. Add onion balls in your air fryer's cooking basket and cook for almost 15 minutes. Serve and enjoy!

Nutritional information: Calories: 297; Fat: 1g; Total Carbs: 35g; Net Carbs: 13g; Fiber: 1g; Sugar: 9g; Protein: 29g

Pork Ratatouille with Butterbean

Prep time: 15 minutes | Cook time: 45 minutes | Serves: 4

For Ratatouille   1-ounce butterbean, drained
1 black pepper, chopped   15 oz. tomatoes, chopped
2 zucchinis, chopped   2 sprigs fresh thyme
1 eggplant, chopped   1 tablespoon balsamic vinegar
1 medium red onion, chopped   2 garlic cloves, minced
1 tablespoon olive oil   1 red chili, chopped

At 390 degrees F, preheat your Air Fryer. Mix black pepper, eggplant, oil, onion, zucchinis, and add to the cooking basket. Roast for 20 minutes. Set aside to cool. Reduce air fryer temperature to 355 degrees F. In a suitable saucepan, mix prepared vegetables and the remaining ratatouille ingredients, and bring to a boil over medium heat. Let the mixture simmer for almost 10 minutes; season with black pepper and salt. Add sausages to your air fryer's basket and cook for almost 10-15 minutes. Serve the sausages with ratatouille.

Nutritional information: Calories: 399; Fat: 16g; Total Carbs: 28g; Net Carbs: 12g; Fiber: 3g; Sugar: 10g; Protein: 35g

Oregano Lamb Patties

Prep time: 15 minutes | Cook time: 20 minutes | Serves: 4

1 ½ pounds ground lamb   ¼ teaspoon black pepper
⅓ cup feta cheese, crumbled   ½ teaspoon salt
1 teaspoon oregano

At 375 degrees F, preheat your air fryer. Add all the recipe ingredients into the bowl and mix until well combined. Grease its air fryer basket with cooking spray. Make the equal shape of patties from meat mixture and place into the air fryer basket. Cook lamb patties for almost 10 minutes, then turn to another side and cook for almost 10 minutes more. Serve and enjoy.

Nutritional information: Calories: 348; Fat: 30g; Total Carbs: 5g; Net Carbs: 1g; Fiber: 0g; Sugar: 0g; Protein: 14g

Pork Burgers with Cheddar Cheese

Prep time: 15 minutes | Cook time: 20 minutes | Serves: 2

1 medium onion, chopped   Assembling:
1 tablespoon mixed herbs   1 large onion, sliced in 2-inch
2 teaspoons garlic powder   rings
1 teaspoon dried basil   1 large tomato, sliced in 2-inch
1 tablespoon tomato puree   rings
1 teaspoon mustard   2 small lettuce leaves, cleaned
Black pepper and salt to taste   4 slices Cheddar cheese
2 bread buns, halved

In a suitable bowl, add pork, chopped onion, mixed herbs, garlic powder, dried basil, tomato puree, mustard, salt, and black pepper. Use hands to mix evenly. Form 2 patties out of the mixture and place on a flat plate. At 370 degrees F, preheat your

air fryer. Place the pork patties in the fryer basket, and cook for almost 15 minutes. Slide-out the basket and turn the patties with a spatula. Reduce its temperature to 350 degrees F and continue cooking for 5 minutes. Once ready, remove them onto a plate and start assembling the burger. Place 2 halves of the bun on a clean flat surface. Add the lettuce in both, then a patty each, followed by an onion ring each, a tomato ring each, and then 2 slices of cheddar cheese each. Cover the buns with their other halves. Serve with ketchup and French fries.

Nutritional information: Calories: 336; Fat: 6g; Total Carbs: 1.3g; Net Carbs: 0g; Fiber: 0.2g; Sugar: 0.4g; Protein: 69.2g

Mayonnaise Tomato Beef Patties

Prep time: 15 minutes | Cook time: 20 minutes | Serves: 4

¾ pound ground beef   4 tablespoons rolled oats
1 smoked beef sausage,   2 tablespoons tomato paste
chopped   Himalayan salt and black
4 scallions, chopped   pepper, to taste
1 garlic clove, minced   8 small pretzel rolls
2 tablespoons fresh coriander,   4 tablespoons mayonnaise
chopped   8 thin slices of tomato

At 370 degrees F, preheat your Air Fryer. In a suitable mixing bowl, thoroughly combine the ground beef, sausage, scallions, garlic, coriander, oats, tomato paste, salt, and black pepper. Knead with the prepared mixture until well combined. Form the mixture into eight patties and cook them for almost 18 to 20 minutes. Place the burgers on slider buns; top with mayonnaise and tomato slices. Serve.

Nutritional information: Calories: 308; Fat: 24g; Total Carbs: 0.8g; Net Carbs: 0g; Fiber: 0.1g; Sugar: 0.1g; Protein: 21.9g

Homemade Toad in the Hole

Prep time: 15 minutes | Cook time: 40 minutes | Serves: 4

6 beef sausages   A pinch of salt
1 tablespoon butter, melted   2 eggs
1 cup plain flour   1 cup semi-skimmed milk

Cook the sausages in your Air Fryer at about 380 degrees F for almost 15 minutes, shaking halfway through the cooking time. Meanwhile, make up the batter mix. Tip the flour into a bowl with salt; make a well in the middle and crack the eggs into it. Mix with an electric whisk; now, slowly and gradually pour in the milk, whisking all the time. Place the sausages in a lightly greased baking pan. Pour the prepared batter over the sausages. Cook in the preheated Air Fryer at about 370 degrees F approximately 25 minutes, until golden and risen. Serve.

Nutritional information: Calories: 351; Fat: 16g; Total Carbs: 26g; Net Carbs: 13g; Fiber: 4g; Sugar: 5g; Protein: 28g

Garlic Steak with Cheese Butter

Prep time: 15 minutes | Cook time: 10 minutes | Serves: 2

2 rib-eye steaks   butter
2 teaspoons garlic powder   1 teaspoon black pepper
2 ½ tablespoons blue cheese   2 teaspoons kosher salt

At 400 degrees F, preheat your air fryer. Mix together garlic powder, black pepper, and salt and rub over the steaks. Grease its air fryer basket with cooking spray. Place trimmed steak in the air fryer basket and cook for 4 -5 minutes on each side. Top with blue butter cheese. Serve and enjoy.

Nutritional information: Calories: 275; Fat: 1.4g; Total Carbs: 31.5g; Net Carbs: 12g; Fiber: 1.1g; Sugar: 0.1g; Protein: 29.8g

Tasty Meatloaf Muffins with Sweet Potato Frosting

Prep time: 15 minutes | Cook time: 58 minutes | Serves: 4

Meatloaf Muffins:
1-pound pork sausage, crumbled
1 shallot, chopped
2 garlic cloves, minced
½ cup oats
½ cup pasta sauce
1 teaspoon dried oregano
1 teaspoon dried basil
Salt and black pepper, to taste
1 egg
Sweet Potato Frosting:
½ pound sweet potatoes, diced
½ teaspoon garlic powder
¼ cup coconut milk
1 tablespoon coconut oil
1 teaspoon salt

Mix all the recipe ingredients for the meatloaf muffins in a suitable bowl. Place the meat mixture in 4 cupcake liners. Air fry at 220 degrees F for 23 minutes. Remove from the cooking basket and reserve keeping warm. Cook the sweet potatoes at 380 degrees F for 35 minutes, shaking the basket occasionally. When the sweet potatoes are cooled enough to handle, scoop out the flesh into a bowl. Add the garlic powder, coconut milk, coconut oil, and salt; mix to combine well. Beat with a hand whisk until thoroughly mixed and fluffy. Pipe the potato mixture onto the sausage muffins using a pastry bag. Enjoy!
Nutritional information: Calories: 275; Fat: 1.4g; Total Carbs: 31.5g; Net Carbs: 14g; Fiber: 1.1g; Sugar: 0.1g; Protein: 29.8g

Seasoned Pork and Mixed Greens Salad

Prep time: 15 minutes | Cook time: 6 minutes | Serves: 4

2 pounds' pork tenderloin, cut sliced
1 teaspoon olive oil
1 teaspoon dried marjoram
⅛ teaspoon freshly black pepper
6 cups mixed salad greens
1 red bell pepper, sliced
1 8-ounce package button mushrooms, sliced
⅓ cup low-fat vinaigrette dressing

In a suitable bowl, mix the pork slices and olive oil. Toss to coat. Sprinkle with the marjoram and black pepper and rub these into the pork. Cook the pork in the air fryer, in batches, for about 4 to 6 minutes. Meanwhile, in a serving bowl, mix the salad greens, red bell pepper, and mushrooms. Toss gently. When the pork is cooked, add the slices to the salad. Drizzle with the vinaigrette and toss gently. Serve immediately.
Nutritional information: Calories: 353; Fat: 5g; Total Carbs: 53.2g; Net Carbs: 22g; Fiber: 4.4g; Sugar: 8g; Protein: 17.3g

Lime Pork Tenderloin

Prep time: 15 minutes | Cook time: 15 minutes | Serves: 4

1 (1-pound) pork tenderloin, cut into 1½-inch cubes
¼ cup minced onion
2 garlic cloves, minced
1 jalapeño black pepper, minced
2 tablespoons lime juice
2 tablespoons coconut milk
2 tablespoons unsalted peanut butter
2 teaspoons curry powder

In a suitable bowl, mix the pork, onion, garlic, jalapeño, lime juice, coconut milk, peanut butter, and curry powder until well combined. Let stand for almost 10 minutes at room temperature. With a slotted spoon, remove the pork from the marinade. Reserve the marinade. Thread the pork onto about 8 bamboo or metal skewers. Air fry for 9 to 14 minutes, brushing once with the reserved marinade. Discard any remaining marinade. Serve immediately.
Nutritional information: Calories: 346; Fat: 16.1g; Total Carbs: 1.3g; Net Carbs: 0g; Fiber: 0.5g; Sugar: 0.5g; Protein: 48.2g

Air Fried Steak with Montreal Seasoning

Prep time: 15 minutes | Cook time: 7 minutes | Serves: 2

12 oz. steaks
½ tablespoon unsweetened cocoa powder
1 tablespoon Montreal steak seasoning
1 teaspoon liquid smoke
1 tablespoon soy sauce
Black pepper
Salt

Add steak, liquid smoke, and soy sauce in a zip-lock bag and shake well. Season steak with seasonings and place in the refrigerator for overnight. Place marinated steak in air fryer basket and cook at almost 375 degrees F for 5 minutes. Turn steak to another side and cook for 2 minutes more. Serve and enjoy.
Nutritional information: Calories: 220; Fat: 1.7g; Total Carbs: 1.7g; Net Carbs: 0g; Fiber: 0.2g; Sugar: 0.2g; Protein: 32.9g

Beer Corned Beef

Prep time: 15 minutes | Cook time: 50 minutes | Serves: 3

1 whole onion, chopped
4 carrots, chopped
12 oz. bottle beer
1½ cups chicken broth
4 pounds corned beef

At 380 degrees F, preheat your air fryer. Cover beef with beer and set aside for 20 minutes. Place carrots, onion and beef in a pot and heat over high heat. Add in broth and bring to a boil. Drain the meat and veggies. Top with beef spice. Place the meat and veggies in air fryer's cooking basket and cook for 30 minutes. Serve.
Nutritional information: Calories: 380; Fat: 29g; Total Carbs: 34.6g; Net Carbs: 1g; Fiber: 0g; Sugar: 0g; Protein: 30g

Marinated Flank Steak

Prep time: 15 minutes | Cook time: 12 minutes | Serves: 4

1 ½ pounds flank steak
½ cup red wine
½ cup apple cider vinegar
2 tablespoons soy sauce
Salt, to taste
½ teaspoon black pepper
½ teaspoon red pepper flakes, crushed
½ teaspoon dried basil
1 teaspoon thyme

Add all the recipe ingredients to a large ceramic bowl. Cover and let it marinate for 3 hours in your refrigerator. Transfer the flank steak to the Air Fryer basket that is previously greased with nonstick cooking oil. Cook in the preheated Air Fryer at about 400 degrees F for 12 minutes, flipping over halfway through the cooking time. Serve and enjoy.
Nutritional information: Calories: 374; Fat: 13g; Total Carbs: 25g; Net Carbs: 10g; Fiber: 1.2g; Sugar: 1.2g; Protein: 37.7g

Parmesan Sausage Meatballs

Prep time: 15 minutes | Cook time: 15 minutes | Serves: 8

1 pound Italian sausage
1-pound ground beef
½ teaspoon Italian seasoning
½ teaspoon red pepper flakes

1 ½ cups Parmesan cheese, grated
2 egg, lightly beaten
2 tablespoons parsley, chopped
2 garlic cloves, minced
¼ cup onion, minced
Black pepper
Salt

Add all the recipe ingredients into the suitable mixing bowl and mix until well combined. Grease its air fryer basket with cooking spray. Make meatballs from bowl mixture and place into the air fryer basket. Cook at almost 350 degrees F for almost 15 minutes. Serve and enjoy.

Nutritional information: Calories: 268; Fat: 10.4g; Total Carbs: 0.4g; Net Carbs: 0g; Fiber: 0.1g; Sugar: 0.1g; Protein: 40.6g

Tomato Pork Burgers

Prep time: 15 minutes | Cook time: 7 minutes | Serves: 4

½ cup Greek yogurt
2 tablespoons mustard, divided
1 tablespoon lemon juice
¼ cup sliced red cabbage
¼ cup grated carrots
1-pound lean ground pork
½ teaspoon paprika
1 cup mixed baby lettuce greens
2 small tomatoes, sliced
8 small whole-wheat sandwich buns, cut in ½

In a suitable bowl, combine the yogurt, 1 tablespoon mustard, lemon juice, cabbage, and carrots; mix and refrigerate. In a suitable bowl, combine the pork, remaining 1 tablespoon mustard, and paprika. Form into 8 small patties. Set the sliders into the air fryer basket and cook for 7 minutes. Make the burgers by placing adding the lettuce greens on a bun. Top it with a tomato slice, the burgers, and the cabbage mixture. Add the bun top and serve immediately.

Nutritional information: Calories: 502; Fat: 25g; Total Carbs: 1.5g; Net Carbs: 0g; Fiber: 0.2g; Sugar: 0.4g; Protein: 64.1g

Broccoli Pork Chops

Prep time: 15 minutes | Cook time: 10 minutes | Serves: 4

2 5 oz. bone-in pork chops
2 garlic cloves
2 tablespoons avocado oil
½ teaspoon paprika
½ teaspoon onion powder
1 teaspoon salt
½ teaspoon garlic powder
2 cups broccoli florets

At 350 degrees F, preheat your air fryer. Spitz basket with cooking spray. Brush 1 tablespoon of oil per side of the ready pork chops. Season the ready pork chops from per side with the paprika, onion powder, garlic powder, and ½ teaspoon of salt. Put pork chops in the preheated air fryer basket and cook for 5 minutes. Meanwhile pork chops are cooking put the broccoli, garlic, remaining ½ teaspoon of salt and remaining tablespoon of oil to a bowl and toss to coat. Put the broccoli to the basket and go back to the air fryer. Now cook for 5 more minutes, stirring the broccoli during cooking. Remove the food from the air fryer and serve.

Nutritional information: Calories: 379; Fat: 19g; Total Carbs: 12.3g; Net Carbs:5g; Fiber: 0.6g; Sugar: 2g; Protein: 37.7g

Glazed Beef with Fruits

Prep time: 15 minutes | Cook time: 11 minutes | Serves: 8

12 ounces sirloin tip steak, thinly sliced
1 tablespoon lime juice
1 cup canned mandarin orange segments, drained
1 cup canned pineapple
chunks, drained
1 teaspoon soy sauce
1 tablespoon cornstarch
1 teaspoon olive oil
2 scallions, white and green parts, sliced

Brown rice, cooked

In a suitable bowl, mix the steak with the lime juice. Set aside. In a suitable bowl, mix 3 tablespoons of reserved pineapple juice, 3 tablespoons of reserved mandarin orange juice, cornstarch and the soy sauce. Drain the marinated beef and transfer it to a medium metal bowl, keep the juice aside. Stir the reserved juice into the mandarin-pineapple juice mixture. Drizzle the olive oil and scallions on the steak. Set the metal bowl in the preheated Air Fryer and cook for 3 to 4 minutes. Add the mandarin oranges, juice mixture and pineapple. Cook for 3 to 7 minutes more. Stir and serve.

Nutritional information: Calories: 352; Fat: 9.1g; Total Carbs: 3.9g; Net Carbs: 0g; Fiber: 1g; Sugar: 1g; Protein: 61g

Mayo Cheeseburgers

Prep time: 15 minutes | Cook time: 12 minutes | Serves: 4

1 garlic clove, minced
1 teaspoon soy sauce
1 tablespoon allspice
4 yellow cheese slices
2 tablespoons mayonnaise
1 teaspoon ketchup
1 dill pickle, sliced
4 bread buns
Black pepper and salt to taste

At 360 degrees F, preheat your air fryer. Grease its air fryer basket with cooking spray. In a suitable bowl, combine the ground meat, soy sauce, garlic, allspice, salt, and black pepper; mix well. Mold the mixture into 4 equal burgers and transfer to the cooking basket. Cook for 12 minutes, flipping once. Serve on bread buns with yellow cheese, mayonnaise, ketchup, and dill pickle slices.

Nutritional information: Calories: 220; Fat: 13g; Total Carbs: 0.9g; Net Carbs: 0g; Fiber: 0.3g; Sugar: 0.2g; Protein: 25.6g

Flavorful Espresso-Grilled Pork Tenderloin

Prep time: 15 minutes | Cook time: 21 minutes | Serves: 4

1 tablespoon packed brown sugar
2 teaspoons espresso powder
1 teaspoon ground paprika
½ teaspoon dried marjoram
1 tablespoon honey
1 tablespoon lemon juice
2 teaspoons olive oil
1 1-pound pork tenderloin

In a suitable bowl, mix the brown sugar, espresso powder, paprika, and marjoram. Add the honey, lemon juice, and olive oil until well mixed. Spread the honey mixture over the pork and let stand for almost 10 minutes at room temperature. Roast the tenderloin in the air fryer basket for 9 to 11 minutes, or until the pork registers at least 145 degrees F on a meat thermometer. Slice the meat to serve.

Nutritional information: Calories: 546; Fat: 33.1g; Total Carbs: 30g; Net Carbs: 10g; Fiber: 2.4g; Sugar: 9.7g; Protein: 32g

Mustard Pork Tenderloin with Ground Walnuts

Prep time: 15 minutes | Cook time: 16 minutes | Serves: 4

3 tablespoons grainy mustard
2 teaspoons olive oil
¼ teaspoon dry mustard powder
1 1-pound pork tenderloin,
excess fat trimmed
2 slices whole-wheat bread, crumbled
¼ cup ground walnuts
2 tablespoons cornstarch

In a suitable bowl, stir together the mustard, olive oil, and mustard powder. Spread this mixture over the pork. On a plate, mix the bread crumbs, walnuts, and cornstarch. Dip the mustard-coated pork into the crumb mixture to coat. Air-fry the pork for 12 to 16 minutes, or until it registers at least 145 degrees F on a meat thermometer. Slice to serve.

Nutritional information: Calories: 223; Fat: 11.7g; Total Carbs: 13.6g; Net Carbs: 6g; Fiber: 0.7g; Sugar: 8g; Protein: 15.7g

Oregano Pork Tenderloin

Prep time: 15 minutes | Cook time: 25 minutes | Serves: 4

2 cups creamer potatoes, rinsed and dried	1 onion, chopped
2 teaspoons olive oil	1 red bell pepper, chopped
1 1-pound pork tenderloin, diced	2 garlic cloves, minced
	½ teaspoon dried oregano
	2 tablespoons chicken broth

In a suitable bowl, toss the potatoes and olive oil to coat. Transfer the potatoes to your air fryer basket. Roast for almost 15 minutes. In a medium metal bowl, mix the potatoes, pork, onion, red bell pepper, garlic, and oregano. Drizzle with the chicken broth. Put the bowl in the air fryer basket. Roast for about 10 minutes more, shaking the basket once during cooking, until the pork reaches at least 145 degrees F on a meat thermometer and the potatoes are tender. Serve immediately.

Nutritional information: Calories: 351; Fat: 11g; Total Carbs: 3.3g; Net Carbs: 1g; Fiber: 0.2g; Sugar: 1g; Protein: 33.2g

Steak and Vegetable Skewers

Prep time: 15 minutes | Cook time: 7 minutes | Serves: 4

2 tablespoons balsamic vinegar	¾ pound round steak, cut into 1-inch pieces
2 teaspoons olive oil	1 red bell pepper, sliced
½ teaspoon dried marjoram	16 button mushrooms
⅛ teaspoon freshly black pepper	1 cup cherry tomatoes

In a suitable bowl, stir together the balsamic vinegar, olive oil, marjoram, and black pepper. Add the steak and stir to coat. Let stand for almost 10 minutes at room temperature. Alternating items, thread the beef, red bell pepper, mushrooms, and tomatoes onto 8 bamboo or metal skewers that fit in the air fryer. Air fry in the preheated Air Fryer for 5 to 7 minutes, or until the beef is browned and reaches at least 145 degrees F on a meat thermometer. Serve immediately.

Nutritional information: Calories: 316; Fat: 12.2g; Total Carbs: 12.2g; Net Carbs: 5g; Fiber: 1g; Sugar: 1.8g; Protein: 25.8g

Grilled Steak with Salsa

Prep time: 15 minutes | Cook time: 10 minutes | Serves: 4

2 tablespoons salsa	vinegar
1 tablespoon minced chipotle pepper	1 teaspoon ground cumin
⅛ teaspoon black pepper	⅛ teaspoon red pepper flakes
1 tablespoon apple cider	¾ pound sirloin tip steak, diced

In a suitable bowl, thoroughly mix the salsa, chipotle pepper, cider vinegar, cumin, black pepper, and red pepper flakes. Rub this mixture into per side of each steak piece. Let stand for almost 15 minutes at room temperature. Cook the steaks in the air fryer, 2 at a time, for 6 to 9 minutes. Slice and serve

Nutritional information: Calories: 336; Fat: 27.1g; Total Carbs: 1.1g; Net Carbs: 3g; Fiber: 0.4g; Sugar: 0.2g; Protein: 19.7g

Vegetable Beef Meatballs with Herbs

Prep time: 15 minutes | Cook time: 17 minutes | Serves: 4

1 medium onion, minced	3 tablespoons (1 percent) milk
2 garlic cloves, minced	1 teaspoon dried marjoram
1 teaspoon olive oil	1 teaspoon dried basil
1 slice whole-wheat bread, crumbled	1-pound (96 percent) lean ground beef

In a 6-by-2-inch pan, combine the onion, garlic, and olive oil. Air-fry for 2 to 4 minutes, or until the vegetables are crisp-tender. Transfer the vegetables to a suitable bowl, and add the bread crumbs, milk, marjoram, and basil. Mix well. Add the ground beef. With your hands, work the mixture gently but thoroughly until combined. Form the meat mixture into about 24 1-inch meatballs. Air fry the meatballs in the preheated Air Fryer basket for 12 to 17 minutes. Serve immediately.

Nutritional information: Calories: 410; Fat: 17.8g; Total Carbs: 21g; Net Carbs:11; Fiber: 1.4g; Sugar: 1.8g; Protein: 38.4g

Roast Beef and Brown Rice

Prep time: 15 minutes | Cook time: 20 minutes | Serves: 4

1 cup cooked brown rice	2 medium beefsteak tomatoes, chopped
1 onion, chopped	
½ cup carrot, grated	1 cup chopped cooked roast beef
4 bell peppers, tops removed	
2 teaspoons olive oil	1 teaspoon dried marjoram

In a 6-by-2-inch pan, toss the chopped bell pepper tops, carrot, onion, and olive oil. Cook for almost 4 minutes, or until the vegetables are crisp-tender. Transfer the vegetables to a suitable bowl. Add the brown rice, tomatoes, roast beef, and marjoram and mix. Stuff the vegetable mixture into the hollow bell peppers. Place the stuffed bell peppers in the air fryer basket. Air fry for almost 16 minutes. Serve immediately.

Nutritional information: Calories: 396; Fat: 23.2g; Total Carbs: 0.7g; Net Carbs: 0g; Fiber: 0g; Sugar: 0g; Protein: 45.6g

Ginger Beef and Vegetables

Prep time: 15 minutes | Cook time: 18 minutes | Serves: 4

2 tablespoons cornstarch	1 onion, chopped
½ cup beef broth	1 cup cremini mushrooms sliced
1 teaspoon soy sauce	
2½ cups broccoli florets	1 tablespoon grated fresh ginger
12 ounces' sirloin strip steak, cubed	
	Brown rice, cooked

In a suitable bowl, stir together the cornstarch, soy sauce and beef broth. Stir in the beef and leave for 5 minutes, Transfer the marinated beef from the broth mixture into a suitable metal bowl. Add the onion, broccoli, ginger and mushrooms to the beef mixture. Set the bowl into the air fryer and cook for almost 15 minutes. Add the reserved broth and cook for almost 2 to 3 minutes more. Serve.

Nutritional information: Calories: 437; Fat: 28g; Total Carbs: 22.3g; Net Carbs: 11g; Fiber: 0.9g; Sugar: 8g; Protein: 30.3g

Dessert Recipes

Divine Apple Pie

Prep time: 15 minutes | Cook time:30 minutes | Serves: 4

2 apples
1 tbsp. sugar
2 sheets of puff pastry
2 tbsps. of melted butter
1 egg yolk

Peel your apples, cut into small pieces. Add your apple on the puff pastry sheets and sprinkle with sugar and cinnamon. In the air fryer, Air Fry the food at 360 degrees F for 30 minutes. With 10 minutes of cooking remaining, wrap the sides and brush with egg yolk. Serve!
Nutritional information: Calories 389; Total Carbs 21g; Net Carbs 9g; Protein 5.3g; Fat 7g; Sugar 2.1g; Fiber 2g

Banana Muffin

Prep time: 15 minutes | Cook time: 20 minutes | Serves: 5

1 banana
½ cup almond flour
1 egg
1 tbsp. sugar
½ tsp. salt
1 tsp. baking powder
1 tbsp. butter

Mash the banana well and mix all the recipe ingredients until smooth. Place the dough in a silicone baking dish. In the air fryer, cook the food for 20 minutes at 340 degrees F on Bake mode. Serve with chocolate if you like. Enjoy.
Nutritional information: Calories 375; Total Carbs 20g; Net Carbs 11g; Protein 7.6g; Fat 11g; Sugar 5g; Fiber 1g

Almond Biscuit

Prep time: 15 minutes | Cook time:35 minutes | Serves: 4

½ cup almond flour
3 tbsps. flour
1 egg
⅓ cup sugar
almond nuts, as desired

Combine sugar, flour and almond flour. Whisk in egg and add to dry ingredients. Shape into small cookies and place almonds on top. Place the cookies in the "Air Fryer Basket" or special molds. Air Fry the cookies for 30-35 minutes at 320 degrees F. Serve and enjoy.
Nutritional information: Calories 415; Total Carbs 21g; Net Carbs 10g; Protein 7g; Fat 14g; Sugar 8g; Fiber 3g

Sweet Cinnamon Donuts

Prep time: 15 minutes | Cook time:6 minutes | Serves:3

½ cup granulated sugar
1 tbsp. ground cinnamon
1 (16.3-oz.) can flaky large biscuits
olive oil spray or coconut oil spray
4 tbsps. unsalted butter, melted

Line a baking pan with baking paper. Mix cinnamon and sugar in a suitable bowl. Place the biscuits on the baking pan. Use a 1-inch round biscuit cutter to cut holes out of the center of each. Lightly coat the Air Fryer Basket with olive or coconut oil spray. Place 3 to 4 donuts in a single layer in the basket. In the air fryer, Air Fry the food at 350 degrees F for 5 to 6 minutes, until the donuts golden-brown. Turn the food halfway through cooking. Transfer donuts place to the baking pan. Repeat with the remaining biscuits. Brush the donuts with melted butter, coat in the cinnamon sugar, and flip to coat both sides. Serve warm.
Nutritional information: Calories 375; Total Carbs 20g; Net Carbs 11g; Protein 7.6g; Fat 11g; Sugar 5g; Fiber 1g

Cardamom Bombs

Prep time: 10 minutes | Cook time: 5 minutes | Serves: 2

2 oz. avocado, peeled
1 egg, beaten
½ tsp. ground cardamom
1 tbsp. Erythritol
2 tbsps. coconut flour
1 tsp. butter, softened

Set the avocado in the bowl and mash it with the help of the fork. Add egg and stir the prepared mixture until it is smooth. Then add ground cardamom, Erythritol, and coconut flour. After this, add butter and stir the prepared mixture well. Make the balls from the avocado mixture and press them gently. At 400 degrees F, preheat your Air Fryer. Put the avocado bombs in the air fryer and Air Fry them at 400 degrees F for 5 minutes.
Nutritional information: Calories 143; Total Carbs 7.5g; Net Carbs 2g; Protein 4.9g; Fat 10.9g; Sugar 2g; Fiber 5g

Lemon Peppermint Bars

Prep time: 15 minutes | Cook time: 16 minutes | Serves: 8

1 tsp. peppermint
1 cup almond flour
⅓ cup peanut butter
½ tsp. baking powder
1 tsp. lemon juice
½ tsp. orange zest, grated

In the bowl, mix up almond flour, peppermint, baking powder, and orange zest. Then add peanut butter and lemon juice. Knead the non-sticky dough. Cut the dough on 8 pieces and roll the balls. Press them gently to get the shape of the bars. At 365 degrees F, preheat your Air Fryer. Layer the "Air Fryer Basket" with baking paper. Put 4 cookies in the basket in one layer. Air Fry them at 365 degrees F for 8 minutes. Remove the cooked bars from the air fryer. Repeat the same steps with uncooked bars.
Nutritional information: Calories 84; Total Carbs 3.1g; Net Carbs 2g; Protein 3.5g; Fat 7.2g; Sugar 2g; Fiber 1.1g

Avocado Cream Pudding

Prep time: 5 minutes | Cook time: 25 minutes | Serves: 6

4 small avocados, peeled, pitted and mashed
2 eggs, whisked
1 cup coconut milk
¾ cup swerve
½ tsp. cinnamon powder
½ tsp. ginger powder

In a suitable bowl, mix all the recipe ingredients and whisk well. Pour the mixture into a pudding mold, put it in the air fryer and Air Fry at 350 degrees F for 25 minutes. Serve warm.

Nutritional information: Calories 192; Total Carbs 5g; Net Carbs 2g; Protein 4g; Fat 8g; Sugar 2g; Fiber 2g

Chocolate Candies

Prep time: 15 minutes | Cook time: 2 minutes | Serves: 4

1 oz. almonds, crushed	2 tbsps. peanut butter
1 oz. dark chocolate	2 tbsps. heavy cream

At 390 degrees F, preheat your Air Fryer. Chop the dark chocolate and put it in the air fryer mold. Add peanut butter and heavy cream. Stir the prepared mixture and transfer in the air fryer. Air Fry the food at 390 degrees F for 2 minutes or until it starts to be melt. Then layer the air tray with parchment. Put the crushed almonds on the tray in one layer. Then pour the cooked chocolate mixture over the almonds. Flatten gently if needed and let it cool. Crack the cooked chocolate layer into the candies.
Nutritional information: Calories 154; Total Carbs 7.4g; Net Carbs 2g; Protein 3.9g; Fat 12.9g; Sugar 2g; Fiber 1.9g

Ginger Lemon Pie

Prep time: 15 minutes | Cook time: 30 minutes | Serves: 6

2 eggs	1 tsp. lemon juice
6 tbsps. coconut flour	½ tsp. ground ginger
½ tsp. vanilla extract	3 tbsps. Erythritol
6 tbsps. ricotta cheese	1 tbsp. butter, melted
½ tsp. baking powder	

Crack the eggs and separate them on the egg whites and egg yolks. Then whisk the egg yolks with Erythritol until you get the lemon color mixture. Then whisk the egg whites to the soft peaks. Add egg whites in the egg yolk mixture. Then add ricotta cheese, baking powder, lemon juice, ground ginger, vanilla extract, Erythritol. Then add butter and coconut flour and stir the pie butter until smooth. Layer the "Air Fryer Basket" with the baking paper. Pour the pie batter inside. At 330 degrees F, preheat your Air Fryer. Put the baking pan with pie in the air fryer and Air Fry the food at 330 degrees F for 30 minutes.
Nutritional information: Calories 97; Total Carbs 5.8g; Net Carbs 2g; Protein 5.2g; Fat 5.9g; Sugar 2g; Fiber 3g

Vanilla Yogurt Cake

Prep time: 5 minutes | Cook time: 30 minutes | Serves: 12

6 eggs, whisked	9 oz. coconut flour
1 tsp. vanilla extract	4 tbsps. stevia
1 tsp. baking powder	8 oz. Greek yogurt

In a suitable bowl, mix all the recipe ingredients and whisk well. Add this prepared batter into a cake pan that fits the air fryer lined with baking paper Put this pan in the air fryer and Air Fry the food at 330 degrees F for 30 minutes.
Nutritional information: Calories 181; Total Carbs 4g; Net Carbs 2g; Protein 5g; Fat 13g; Sugar 2g; Fiber 2g

Cobbler

Prep time: 15 minutes | Cook time: 30 minutes | Serves: 4

¼ cup heavy cream	1 tsp. vanilla extract
1 egg, beaten	2 tbsps. butter, softened
½ cup almond flour	¼ cup hazelnuts, chopped

Mix up heavy cream, egg, almond flour, vanilla extract, and butter. Then whisk the prepared mixture gently. At 325 degrees F, preheat your Air Fryer. Layer the suitable cooking pan with baking paper. Pour ½ part of the batter in the baking pan, flatten it gently and top with hazelnuts. Then pour the remaining batter over the hazelnuts and place the pan in the air fryer. Air Fry the cobbler at 325 degrees F for 30 minutes.
Nutritional information: Calories 145; Total Carbs 2g; Net Carbs 2g; Protein 3g; Fat 14.2g; Sugar 2g; Fiber 0.8g

Almond Pudding

Prep time: 10 minutes | Cook time: 20 minutes | Serves: 6

24 oz. cream cheese, soft	1 tbsp. vanilla extract
2 tbsps. almond meal	½ cup heavy cream
¼ cup erythritol	12 oz. dark chocolate, melted
3 eggs, whisked	

In a suitable bowl mix all the recipe ingredients and whisk well. Divide this into 6 ramekins, put them in your air fryer and Air Fry them at 320 degrees F for 20 minutes. Keep in the fridge for 1 hour before serving.
Nutritional information: Calories 200; Total Carbs 4g; Net Carbs 2g; Protein 6g; Fat 7g; Sugar 2g; Fiber 2g

Lemon Almond Biscotti

Prep time: 15 minutes | Cook time: 40 minutes | Serves: 6

¼ cup almond, crushed	1 tsp. lemon zest, grated
¼ cup butter, softened	½ tsp. baking powder
2 eggs, beaten	1 tsp. lemon juice
1 tsp. of cocoa powder	¼ cup heavy cream
1 tsp. vanilla extract	1 tsp. avocado oil
1 cup almond flour	3 tbsps. Erythritol

In the mixing bowl mix up butter, eggs, cocoa powder, vanilla extract, almond flour, lemon zest, baking powder, lemon juice, heavy cream, and Erythritol. Then add almonds and knead the smooth dough. Brush the "Air Fryer Basket" with avocado oil and put the dough inside. Flatten it well. At 365 degrees F, preheat your Air Fryer. Put this pan with dough inside and Air Fry the food at 365 degrees F for 25 minutes. Then slice the cooked dough on the pieces (biscotti). Place the biscotti in the "Air Fryer Basket" and Air Fry them for 15 minutes at 350 degrees F or until they are light brown.
Nutritional information: Calories 160; Total Carbs 2.7g; Net Carbs 2g; Protein 4g; Fat 15.4g; Sugar 2g; Fiber 1.2g

Plum Almond Cake

Prep time: 10 minutes | Cook time: 30 minutes | Serves: 8

½ cup butter, soft	1 and ½ cups almond flour
3 eggs	½ cup coconut flour
½ cup swerve	2 tsp. baking powder
¼ tsp. almond extract	¾ cup almond milk
1 tbsp. vanilla extract	4 plums, pitted and chopped

In a suitable bowl, mix all the recipe ingredients and whisk well. Add this prepared mixture into a cake pan that fits the air fryer after you've lined it with baking paper. Put this pan in the air fryer and Air Fry the food at 370 degrees F for 30 minutes. Cool the cake down, slice and serve.
Nutritional information: Calories 183; Total Carbs 4g; Net Carbs 2g; Protein 7g; Fat 4g; Sugar 2g; Fiber 3g

Cream Cheese Muffins

Prep time: 15 minutes | Cook time: 11 minutes | Serves: 4

4 tsps. cream cheese	4 tsps. coconut flour
1 egg, beaten	2 tbsps. heavy cream
½ tsp. baking powder	2 tsps. Erythritol
1 tsp. vanilla extract	Cooking spray
4 tsps. almond flour	

Mix up cream cheese, egg, baking powder, vanilla extract, almond flour, coconut flour, heavy cream, and Erythritol. Grease the air fryer muffin molds with some cooking spray. Add the prepared batter in the muffin molds (fill ½ part of every mold). At 365 degrees F, preheat your Air Fryer. Insert the muffin molds in the air fryer and Air Fry the food at 365 degrees F for 11 minutes. Cool the cooked muffins and remove them from the molds.

Nutritional information: Calories 229; Total Carbs 8.3g; Net Carbs 2g; Protein 8.3g; Fat 19.5g; Sugar 2g; Fiber 4g

Cinnamon Fried Plums

Prep time: 5 minutes | Cook time: 20 minutes | Serves: 6

6 plums, cut into wedges	Zest of 1 lemon, grated
1 tsp. ginger, ground	2 tbsps. water
½ tsp. cinnamon powder	10 drops stevia

In a pan that fits the air fryer, combine the plums with the rest of the ingredients. Toss gently. Put this pan in the air fryer and Air Fry at 360 degrees F for 20 minutes. Serve cold.

Nutritional information: Calories 170; Total Carbs 3g; Net Carbs 2g; Protein 5g; Fat 5g; Sugar 2g; Fiber 1g

Creamy Crumble

Prep time: 15 minutes | Cook time: 20 minutes | Serves: 4

4 oz. rhubarb, chopped	1 cup almond flour
¼ cup heavy cream	1 egg, beaten
1 tsp. ground cinnamon	1 tsp. avocado oil
¼ cup Erythritol	4 tsp. butter, softened

In the bowl mix up heavy cream, ground cinnamon, almond flour, egg, and butter. Stir the prepared mixture until you get the crumbly texture. Then mix up rhubarb and Erythritol. Brush the air fryer mold with avocado oil. Separate the crumbled dough on 4 parts. Put 1 part of the dough in the air fryer mold. Then sprinkle it with a small amount rhubarb. Repeat the same steps till you use all the recipe ingredients. Put the crumble in the air fryer. Air Fry the food at 375 degrees F for 20 minutes.

Nutritional information: Calories 124; Total Carbs 4.1g; Net Carbs 2g; Protein 3.4g; Fat 11.4g; Sugar 2g; Fiber 1.9g

Baked Plum Cream

Prep time: 5 minutes | Cook time: 20 minutes | Serves: 4

1 lb. plums, pitted and chopped	1 tbsp. lemon juice
¼ cup swerve	1 and ½ cups heavy cream

In a suitable bowl, mix all the recipe ingredients and whisk really well. Divide this into 4 ramekins, put them in the air fryer and Air Fry at 340 degrees F for 20 minutes. Serve cold.

Nutritional information: Calories 171; Total Carbs 4g; Net Carbs 2g; Protein 4g; Fat 4g; Sugar 2g; Fiber 2g

Blackberries Cake

Prep time: 10 minutes | Cook time: 25 minutes | Serves: 4

2 eggs, whisked	1 cup blackberries, chopped
4 tbsp. swerve	½ tsp. baking powder
2 tbsp. ghee, melted	1 tsp. lemon zest, grated
¼ cup almond milk	1 tsp. lemon juice
1 and ½ cups almond flour	

In a suitable bowl, mix all the recipe ingredients and whisk well until smooth. Add this prepared mixture into a cake pan that fits the air fryer lined with baking paper. Put this pan in your air fryer and Air Fry the cake at 340 degrees F for 25 minutes. Cool the cake down, slice and serve.

Nutritional information: Calories 193; Total Carbs 4g; Net Carbs 2g; Protein 4g; Fat 5g; Sugar 2g; Fiber 1g

Cardamom Coconut Cookies

Prep time: 15 minutes | Cook time: 10 minutes | Serves: 6

3 tbsp. coconut oil, softened	½ tsp. baking powder
4 tbsp. coconut flour	½ tsp. lemon juice
2 tbsp. flax meal	¼ tsp. ground cardamom
2 tbsp. Monk fruit	Cooking spray
1 tsp. poppy seeds	

In the mixing bowl put coconut oil, coconut flour, flax meal, ad Monk fruit. Then add poppy seeds, baking powder, lemon juice, and cardamom. With the help of the fingertips knead the soft but non-sticky dough. Then make the cookies from the dough. At 375 degrees F, preheat your Air Fryer. Place the cookies in the air fryer and Air Fry them at 375 degrees F for 10 minutes.

Nutritional information: Calories 95; Total Carbs 4g; Net Carbs 2g; Protein 1.6g; Fat 8.7g; Sugar 2g; Fiber 2.8g

Butter Plums

Prep time: 5 minutes | Cook time: 20 minutes | Serves: 4

1- ½ tsp. cinnamon powder	4 tbsp. butter, melted
4 plums, halved	3 tbsp. swerve

In a suitable pan, mix the plums with the rest of the ingredients, toss. Put this pan in the air fryer and Air Fry the food at 300 degrees F for 20 minutes. Divide into cups and serve cold.

Nutritional information: Calories 162g; Total Carbs 4g; Net Carbs 2g; Protein 5g; Fat 3g; Sugar 2g; Fiber 2g

Nuts Cookies

Prep time: 15 minutes | Cook time: 10 minutes | Serves: 6

½ cup butter, softened	½ tsp. baking powder
1 cup coconut flour	3 tbsp. Erythritol
3 oz. macadamia nuts, grinded	Cooking spray

In the mixing bowl mix up butter, coconut flour, grinded coconut nuts, baking powder, and Erythritol. Knead the non-sticky dough. Cut the prepared dough into 2 inches' small pieces and roll them into balls. Press every cookie ball gently to get the shape of cookies. At 365 degrees F, preheat your Air Fryer. Put the uncooked cookies in the air fryer and Air Fry them at 365 degrees F for 8 minutes. Air Fry for extra 2 minutes at 390 degrees F to get the light brown crust.

Nutritional information: Calories 331; Total Carbs 14.2g; Net Carbs 2g; Protein 5.3g; Fat 29.4g; Sugar 2g; Fiber 9.2g

Lemon Berries Stew

Prep time: 10 minutes | Cook time: 20 minutes | Serves: 4

1 lb. strawberries, halved	1 tbsp. lemon juice
4 tbsp. stevia	1 and ½ cups water

In a suitable pan, mix all the recipe ingredients, toss, put it in the fryer and Air Fry at 340 degrees F for 20 minutes. Divide the stew into cups and serve cold.

Nutritional information: Calories 176; Total Carbs 3g; Net Carbs 2g; Protein 5g; Fat 2g; Sugar 2g; Fiber 1g

Whipped Cream Cake

Prep time: 15 minutes | Cook time: 25 minutes | Serves: 12

1 cup almond flour	1 tsp. vanilla extract
½ cup coconut flour	1 tsp. cream cheese
¼ cup coconut oil, melted	2 tbsp. Splenda
3 eggs, beaten	½ cup whipped cream
1 tsp. baking powder	

In the mixing bowl mix up almond flour, coconut flour, coconut oil, eggs, baking powder, vanilla extract, and cream cheese. Whisk the prepared mixture well with the help of the immersion blender. Then layer the "Air Fryer Basket" with baking paper. Pour the cake batter in the baking pan. Preheat the air fryer to 355 degrees F. Put the baking pan in the air fryer and Air Fry the food for 25 minutes. Then cool the cake well. Meanwhile, mix up Splenda and whipped cream cheese. Spread the cake with whipped cream mixture.

Nutritional information: Calories 119; Total Carbs 6g; Net Carbs 2g; Protein 3g; Fat 9.3g; Sugar 2g; Fiber 2.3g

Chocolate and Avocado Cream

Prep time: 5 minutes | Cook time: 20 minutes | Serves: 4

2 avocados, peeled, pitted and mashed	4 tbsp. erythritol
3 tbsp. chocolate, melted	3 tbsp. cream cheese, soft

In a pan that fits the air fryer, combine all the recipe ingredients, whisk. Put this pan in the air fryer and Air Fry the food at 340 degrees F for 20 minutes. Divide into bowls and serve cold.

Nutritional information: Calories 200; Total Carbs 4g; Net Carbs 2g; Protein 5g; Fat 6g; Sugar 2g; Fiber 2g

Sweet Coconut Cream Pie

Prep time: 15 minutes | Cook time: 25 minutes | Serves: 4

4 tbsp. coconut cream	1 tsp. vanilla extract
1 tsp. baking powder	½ cup coconut flour
1 tsp. apple cider vinegar	4 tsp. Splenda
1 egg, beaten	1 tsp. xanthan gum
¼ cup coconut flakes	Cooking spray

Put all liquid ingredients in the bowl: coconut cream, apple cider vinegar, egg, and vanilla extract. Stir the liquid until homogenous and add baking powder, coconut flakes, coconut flour, Splenda, and xanthan gum. Stir the ingredients until you get the smooth texture of the batter. Grease the suitable cake mold with some cooking spray. Add the prepared batter in the cake mold. At 330 degrees F, preheat your Air Fryer. Put the cake mold in the "Air Fryer Basket" and Air Fry the food at 330 degrees F for 25 minutes. Then cool the cooked pie completely and remove it from the cake mold. Cut the cooked pie into servings.

Nutritional information: Calories 110; Total Carbs 9.9g; Net Carbs 2g; Protein 2.1g; Fat 6.6g; Sugar 2g; Fiber 3.9g

Cocoa Bombs

Prep time: 5 minutes | Cook time: 8 minutes | Serves: 12

2 cups macadamia nuts, chopped	1 tsp. vanilla extract
4 tbsp. coconut oil, melted	¼ cup cocoa powder
	⅓ cup swerve

In a suitable bowl, mix all the recipe ingredients and whisk well. Shape medium balls out of this mix, place them in your air fryer and Air Fry them at 300 degrees F for 8 minutes. Serve cold.

Nutritional information: Calories 120; Total Carbs 2g; Net Carbs 2g; Protein 1g; Fat 12g; Sugar 2g; Fiber 1g

Cinnamon Squash Pie

Prep time: 15 minutes | Cook time: 35 minutes | Serves: 6

2 tbsp. Splenda	1 tsp. vanilla extract
1 tbsp. Erythritol	1 tsp. butter
5 eggs, beaten	¼ tsp. ground cinnamon
4 tbsp. coconut flakes	4 oz. Kabocha squash, peeled
¼ cup heavy cream	

Grate the Kabocha squash. Then grease the baking mold with butter and put the grated Kabocha squash inside. In the mixing bowl mix up Splenda, Erythritol, coconut flakes, heavy cream, vanilla extract, and ground cinnamon. Then pour the liquid over the Kabocha squash. Stir the prepared mixture gently with the help of the fork. At 365 degrees F, preheat your Air Fryer. Put the mold with pie in the air fryer and Air Fry the food at 365 degrees F for 35 minutes. Cool the cooked pie to the room temperature and cut into the servings.

Nutritional information: Calories 116; Total Carbs 6.7g; Net Carbs 2g; Protein 5.1g; Fat 7.2g; Sugar 2g; Fiber 0.6g

Avocado Cake

Prep time: 10 minutes | Cook time: 30 minutes | Serves: 4

4 oz. raspberries	1 tsp. baking powder
2 avocados, peeled, pitted and mashed	1 cup swerve
1 cup almonds flour	1 tbsp. butter, melted
	4 eggs, whisked

In a suitable bowl, mix all the recipe ingredients, toss. Add this prepared mixture into a cake pan that fits the air fryer after you've lined it with baking paper. Put this pan in the fryer and Air Fry the food at 340 degrees F for 30 minutes. Slice and serve.

Nutritional information: Calories 193; Total Carbs 5g; Net Carbs 2g; Protein 5g; Fat 4g; Sugar 2g; Fiber 2g

Blueberry Cookies

Prep time: 10 minutes | Cook time: 30 minutes | Serves: 2

3 oz. blueberries	½ tsp. avocado oil

Put the blueberries in the blender and grind them until smooth. Layer the "Air Fryer Basket" with baking paper. Brush it with the avocado oil. After this, pour the blended blueberries on the prepared baking paper and flatten it in one layer with the help of the spatula. Air Fry the blueberry leather for 30 minutes at 300 degrees F. Cut into cookies and serve.

Nutritional information: Calories 26; Total Carbs 6.2g; Net Carbs 2g; Protein 0.3g; Fat 0.3g; Sugar 2g; Fiber 1.1g

Cinnamon and Butter Pancakes

Prep time: 10 minutes | Cook time: 12 minutes | Serves: 2

1 tsp. ground cinnamon	½ tsp. vanilla extract
2 tsp. butter, softened	¼ cup heavy cream
1 tsp. baking powder	4 tbsp. almond flour
½ tsp. lemon juice	2 tsp. Erythritol

At 325 degrees F, preheat your Air Fryer. Take 2 small cake mold and line them with baking paper. After this, in the mixing bowl mix up ground cinnamon, butter, baking powder, lemon juice, vanilla extract, heavy cream, almond flour, and Erythritol. Stir the prepared mixture until it is smooth. Then pour the prepared mixture in the prepared cake molds. Put the first cake mold in the air fryer and Air Fry the food at 325 degrees F for 6 minutes. Then check if the pancake is cooked and remove it from the air fryer. Repeat the same steps with the second pancake. Serve.

Nutritional information: Calories 414; Total Carbs 14.7g; Net Carbs 2g; Protein 12.4g; Fat 37.4g; Sugar 2g; Fiber 6.7g

Strawberry Cups

Prep time: 5 minutes | Cook time: 10 minutes | Serves: 8

16 strawberries, halved	2 cups chocolate chips, melted
2 tbsp. coconut oil	

In a suitable pan, mix the strawberries with the oil and the melted chocolate chips, toss gently. Put this pan in the air fryer and Air Fry the food at 340 degrees F for 10 minutes. Divide into cups and serve cold.

Nutritional information: Calories 162g; Total Carbs 5g; Net Carbs 2g; Protein 6g; Fat 5g; Sugar 2g; Fiber 3g

Cardamom Squares

Prep time: 15 minutes | Cook time: 20 minutes | Serves: 4

4 tbsp. peanut butter	½ cup coconut flour
1 tbsp. peanut, chopped	1 tbsp. Erythritol
1 tsp. vanilla extract	½ tsp. ground cardamom

Put the peanut butter and peanut in the bowl. Add vanilla extract, coconut flour, and ground cardamom. Then add Erythritol and stir the prepared mixture until homogenous. At 330 degrees F, preheat your Air Fryer. Layer the "Air Fryer Basket" with baking paper and pour the peanut butter mixture over it. Flatten it gently and Air Fry the food at 330 degrees F for 20 minutes. Then remove the cooked mixture from the air fryer and cool it completely. Cut the dessert into the squares.

Nutritional information: Calories 181; Total Carbs 12.8g; Net Carbs 2g; Protein 7.6 g; Fat 11.7g; Sugar 2g; Fiber 7.2g

Strawberry Cake

Prep time: 10 minutes | Cook time: 35 minutes | Serves: 6

1 lb. strawberries, chopped	1 egg, whisked
1 cup cream cheese, soft	1 tsp. vanilla extract
¼ cup swerve	3 tbsp. coconut oil, melted
1 tbsp. lime juice	1 cup almond flour

2 tsp. baking powder

In a suitable bowl, mix all the recipe ingredients, stir well and add this prepared mixture into a cake pan lined with baking paper. Put this pan in the air fryer, Air Fry the food at 350 degrees F for 35 minutes, cool down, slice and serve.

Nutritional information: Calories 200; Total Carbs 4g; Net Carbs 2g; Protein 6g; Fat 6g; Sugar 2g; Fiber 2g

Butter Crumble

Prep time: 20 minutes | Cook time: 25 minutes | Serves: 4

½ cup coconut flour	1 tbsp. cream cheese
2 tbsp. butter, softened	1 tsp. baking powder
2 tbsp. Erythritol	½ tsp. lemon juice
3 oz. peanuts, crushed	

In the mixing bowl mix up coconut flour, butter, Erythritol, baking powder, and lemon juice. Stir the prepared mixture until homogenous. Then place it in the freezer for 10 minutes. Meanwhile, mix up peanuts and cream cheese. Grate the frozen dough. Layer the air fryer mold with baking paper. Then put ½ of grated dough in the mold and flatten it. Top it with cream cheese mixture. Then put remaining grated dough over the cream cheese mixture. Place the mold with the crumble in the air fryer and Air Fry the food for 25 minutes at 330 degrees F.

Nutritional information: Calories 252; Total Carbs 13.1g; Net Carbs 2g; Protein 8.8g; Fat 19.6g; Sugar 2g; Fiber 7.8g

Stevia Cake

Prep time: 5 minutes | Cook time: 40 minutes | Serves: 6

2 tbsp. ghee, melted	3 tbsp. stevia
1 cup coconut, shredded	1 tsp. cinnamon powder
1 cup mashed avocado	2 tsp. cinnamon powder

In a suitable bowl, mix all the recipe ingredients and stir well. Add this prepared mixture into a cake pan lined with baking paper. Place the pan in the fryer and Air Fry the food at 340 degrees F for 40 minutes. Cool the cake down, slice and serve.

Nutritional information: Calories 192g; Total Carbs 5g; Net Carbs 2g; Protein 7g; Fat 4g; Sugar 2g; Fiber 2g

Cauliflower Rice Pudding

Prep time: 5 minutes | Cook time: 25 minutes | Serves: 4

1 ½ cups cauliflower rice	2 tbsp. ghee, melted
2 cups coconut milk	4 plums, pitted and roughly
3 tbsp. stevia	chopped

In a suitable bowl, mix all the recipe ingredients, toss, divide into ramekins. Put those ramekins in the air fryer, and Air Fry at 340 degrees F for 25 minutes. Cool down and serve.

Nutritional information: Calories 221; Total Carbs 3g; Net Carbs 2g; Protein 3g; Fat 4g; Sugar 2g; Fiber 1g

Sweet Balls

Prep time: 2 hours | Cook time: 5 minutes | Serves: 4

1 tbsp. cream cheese	1 egg, beaten
3 oz. goat cheese	1 tbsp. Splenda
2 tbsp. almond flour	Cooking spray
1 tbsp. coconut flour	

Mash the goat cheese and mix it up with cream cheese. Then add egg, Splenda, and almond flour. Stir the prepared mixture until homogenous. Then make 4 balls and coat them in the coconut flour. Freeze the cheese balls for 2 hours. At 390 degrees F, preheat your Air Fryer. Then place the frozen balls in the Air Fryer Basket, grease them with some cooking spray and Air Fry them at 390 degrees F for 5 minutes or until the cheese balls are light brown.
Nutritional information: Calories 224; Total Carbs 7.7g; Net Carbs 2g; Protein 11.4g; Fat 16.8g; Sugar 2g; Fiber 2.3g

Chia Cinnamon Pudding

Prep time: 10 minutes | Cook time: 25 minutes | Serves: 6

2 cups coconut cream	¼ cup chia seeds
6 egg yolks, whisked	2 tsp. cinnamon powder
2 tbsp. stevia	1 tbsp. ghee, melted

In a suitable bowl, mix all the recipe ingredients. Whisk, divide into 6 ramekins. Place them all in your air fryer and Air Fry at 340 degrees F for 25 minutes. Cool the puddings down and serve.
Nutritional information: Calories 180; Total Carbs 5g; Net Carbs 2g; Protein 7g; Fat 4g; Sugar 2g; Fiber 2g

Seeds and Almond Cookies

Prep time: 15 minutes | Cook time: 9 minutes | Serves: 6

1 tsp. chia seeds	1 tsp. vanilla extract
1 tsp. sesame seeds	1 tbsp. butter
1 tbsp. pumpkin seeds, crushed	4 tbsp. almond flour
1 egg, beaten	¼ tsp. ground cloves
2 tbsp. Splenda	1 tsp. avocado oil

Put the chia seeds, sesame seeds, and pumpkin seeds in the bowl. Add egg, Splenda, vanilla extract, butter, avocado oil, and ground cloves. Then add almond flour and mix up the prepared mixture until homogenous. At 375 degrees F, preheat your Air Fryer. Layer the "Air Fryer Basket" with baking paper. With the help of the scooper make the cookies and flatten them gently. Place the cookies in the basket. Arrange them in one layer. Air Fry the seeds cookies at 375 degrees F for 9 minutes.
Nutritional information: Calories 180; Total Carbs 9.6g; Net Carbs 2g; Protein 5.8g; Fat 13.7g; Sugar 2g; Fiber 3g

Peanuts Almond Biscuits

Prep time: 20 minutes | Cook time: 35 minutes | Serves: 6

4 oz. peanuts, chopped	¼ cup of coconut milk
2 tbsp. peanut butter	2 tsp. Erythritol
½ tsp. apple cider vinegar	1 tsp. vanilla extract
1 egg, beaten	Cooking spray
6 oz. almond flour	

In the bowl mix up peanut butter, apple cider vinegar, egg, almond flour, coconut milk, Erythritol, and vanilla extract. When the prepared mixture is homogenous, add peanuts and knead the smooth dough. Then Grease the cooking mold with some cooking spray and place the dough inside. At 350 degrees F, preheat your Air Fryer. Put the mold with biscuits in the air fryer and Air Fry them for 25 minutes. Then slice the cooked biscuits into pieces and return back in the air fryer. Cook them for 10 minutes more. Cool the cooked biscuits completely.
Nutritional information: Calories 334; Total Carbs 10.8g; Net Carbs 2g; Protein 13.4g; Fat 29.1g; Sugar 2g; Fiber 5.2g

Hazelnut Vinegar Cookies

Prep time: 25 minutes | Cook time: 11 minutes | Serves: 6

1 tbsp. flaxseeds	1 tsp. apple cider vinegar
¼ cup flax meal	3 tbsp. coconut cream
½ cup coconut flour	1 tbsp. butter, softened
½ tsp. baking powder	3 tsp. Splenda
1 oz. hazelnuts, chopped	Cooking spray

Put the flax meal in the bowl. Add flax seeds, coconut flour, baking powder, apple cider vinegar, and Splenda. Stir the prepared mixture gently with the help of the fork and add butter, coconut cream, hazelnuts, and knead the non-sticky dough. Make the big ball from the dough and put it in the freezer for 15 minutes. At 365 degrees F, preheat your Air Fryer. Make the small balls (cookies) from the flax meal dough and press them gently. Arrange the cookies in the "Air Fryer Basket" in one layer and Air Fry them for 11 minutes. (cook 3-4 cookies at a time) Then transfer the cooked cookies on the plate and cool them completely. Repeat the same steps with remaining uncooked cookies. Store the cookies in the glass jar with the closed lid.
Nutritional information: Calories 147; Total Carbs 11.1g; Net Carbs 2g; Protein 4.1g; Fat 10.3g; Sugar 2g; Fiber 6.3g

Sage Cream

Prep time: 5 minutes | Cook time: 30 minutes | Serves: 4

7 cups red currants	1 cup water
1 cup swerve	6 sage leaves

In a suitable pan, mix all the recipe ingredients, toss. Put this pan in the fryer and Air Fry the food at 330 degrees F for 30 minutes. Discard sage leaves, divide into cups and serve cold.
Nutritional information: Calories 171; Total Carbs 3g; Net Carbs 2g; Protein 6g; Fat 4g; Sugar 2g; Fiber 2g

Peanut Butter Cookies

Prep time: 30 minutes | Cook time: 20 minutes | Serves: 4

½ cup almond flour	4 tsp. peanut butter
2 tbsp. butter, softened	1 tsp. Erythritol
1 tbsp. Splenda	Cooking spray
¼ tsp. vanilla extract	

Make the cookies: put the almond flour and butter in the bowl. Add Splenda and vanilla extract and knead the non-sticky dough. Then cut dough on 8 pieces. Make the balls and press them to get the flat cookies. At 365 degrees F, preheat your Air Fryer. Grease the "Air Fryer Basket" with some cooking spray and put the cookies in the air fryer in one layer make 4 flat cookies per one time). Cook them for 10 minutes. Repeat the same steps with remaining cookies. Cool the cooked flat cookies completely. Meanwhile, mix up Erythritol and peanut butter. Then spread 4 flat cookies with peanut butter mixture and cover them with remaining cookies.
Nutritional information: Calories 118; Total Carbs 4.8g; Net Carbs 2g; Protein 2.1g; Fat 10.2g; Sugar 2g; Fiber 0.7g

Clove Crackers

Prep time: 20 minutes | Cook time: 33 minutes | Serves: 8

1 cup almond flour	1 tsp. xanthan gum

1 tsp. flax meal	½ tsp. ground clove
½ tsp. salt	2 tbsp. Erythritol
1 tsp. baking powder	1 egg, beaten
1 tsp. lemon juice	3 tbsp. coconut oil, softened

In the mixing bowl mix up almond flour, xanthan gum, flax meal, salt, baking powder, and ground clove. Add Erythritol, lemon juice, egg, and coconut oil. Stir the prepared mixture gently with the help of the fork. Then knead the prepared mixture till you get a soft dough. Layer the chopping board with parchment. Put the dough on the parchment and roll it up in a thin layer. Cut the thin dough into squares. Cook the crackers in 3 batches. At 360 degrees F, preheat your Air Fryer. Layer the "Air Fryer Basket" with baking paper. Put the prepared crackers in the "Air Fryer Basket" in one layer and Air Fry them for 11 minutes or until the crackers are dry and light brown. Repeat the same steps with remaining uncooked crackers.

Nutritional information: Calories 79; Total Carbs 2.5g; Net Carbs 2g; Protein 1.5g; Fat 7.5g; Sugar 2g; Fiber 1.8g

Chocolate Fudge

Prep time: 15 minutes | Cook time: 30 minutes | Serves:8

½ cup butter, melted	1 tsp. vanilla extract
1 oz. dark chocolate, chopped, melted	2 eggs, beaten
2 tbsp. cocoa powder	3 tbsp. Splenda
3 tbsp. coconut flour	Cooking spray

In the bowl mix up melted butter and dark chocolate. Then add vanilla extract, eggs, and cocoa powder. Stir the prepared mixture until smooth and add Splenda, and coconut flour. Stir it again until smooth. At 325 degrees F, preheat your Air Fryer. Layer the "Air Fryer Basket" with baking paper and spray it with some cooking spray. Pour the fudge mixture in the basket, flatten it gently with the help of the spatula. Air Fry the fudge at 325 degrees F for 30 minutes. Then cut it on the serving squares and cool the fudge completely.

Nutritional information: Calories 177; Total Carbs 8.3g; Net Carbs 2g; Protein 2.6g; Fat 14.8g; Sugar 2g; Fiber 1.6g

Cranberries Pudding

Prep time: 5 minutes | Cook time: 20 minutes | Serves: 6

1 cup cauliflower rice	½ cup cranberries
2 cups almond milk	1 tsp. vanilla extract

In a suitable pan, mix all the recipe ingredients. Whisk a bit, Put this pan in the fryer and Air Fry them at 360 degrees F for 20 minutes. Stir the pudding, divide into bowls and serve cold.

Nutritional information: Calories 211; Total Carbs 4g; Net Carbs 2g; Protein 7g; Fat 5g; Sugar 2g; Fiber 2g

Merengues

Prep time: 15 minutes | Cook time: 65 minutes | Serves: 6

2 egg whites	1 tsp. lime juice
1 tsp. lime zest, grated	4 tbsp. Erythritol

Whisk the egg whites until soft peaks. Then add Erythritol and lime juice and whisk the egg whites until you get strong peaks. After this, add lime zest and carefully stir the egg white mixture. At 275 degrees F, preheat your Air Fryer. Layer the "Air Fryer Basket" with baking paper. With the help of the spoon make the small merengues and put them in the air fryer in one layer. Air Fry the dessert at 275 degrees F for 65 minutes.

Nutritional information: Calories 6; Total Carbs 0.2g; Net Carbs 2g; Protein 1.2g; Fat 0g; Sugar 2g; Fiber 0g

Lemon Coconut Bars

Prep time: 10 minutes | Cook time: 20 minutes | Serves: 12

1 cup coconut cream	Juice of 1 lemon
¼ cup cashew butter, soft	1 tsp. lemon peel, grated
¾ cup swerve	1 tsp. baking powder
1 egg, whisked	

In a suitable bowl, combine all the recipe ingredients gradually and stir well. Spoon balls this on a baking pan lined with baking paper and flatten them. Put the sheet in the fryer and Air Fry them at 350 degrees F for 20 minutes. Cut into bars and serve cold.

Nutritional information: Calories 121; Total Carbs 4g; Net Carbs 2g; Protein 2g; Fat 5g; Sugar 2g; Fiber 1g

Orange Cinnamon Cookies

Prep time: 15 minutes | Cook time: 8 minutes | Serves: 10

3 tbsp. cream cheese	1 cup almond flour
3 tbsp. Erythritol	½ tsp. baking powder
1 tsp. vanilla extract	1 tsp. butter, softened
½ tsp. ground cinnamon	½ tsp. orange zest, grated
1 egg, beaten	

Put the cream cheese and Erythritol in the bowl. Add vanilla extract, ground cinnamon, and almond flour. Stir the prepared mixture with the help of the spoon until homogenous. Then add egg, almond flour, baking powder, and butter. Add orange zest and stir the mass until homogenous. Then knead it with the help of the fingertips. Roll out the prepared dough with the help of the rolling pin into ⅛ inches thickness. Then make the cookies with the help of the cookies cutter. At 365 degrees F, preheat your Air Fryer. Layer the "Air Fryer Basket" with baking paper. Put the cookies on the baking paper and Air Fry at 365 degrees F them for 8 minutes. The time of cooking depends on the cooking size.

Nutritional information: Calories 38; Total Carbs 1g; Net Carbs 2g; Protein 1.4gg; Fat 3.3g; Sugar 2g; Fiber 0.4g

Mini Almond Cakes

Prep time: 10 minutes | Cook time: 20 minutes | Serves: 4

3 oz. dark chocolate, melted	¼ tsp. vanilla extract
¼ cup coconut oil, melted	1 tbsp. almond flour
2 tbsp. swerve	Cooking spray
2 eggs, whisked	

In bowl, combine all the recipe ingredients except the cooking spray and whisk really well. Divide this into 4 ramekins greased with some cooking spray. Put them in the fryer and Air Fry them at 360 degrees F for 20 minutes. Serve warm.

Nutritional information: Calories 161; Total Carbs 4g; Net Carbs 2g; Protein 7g; Fat 12g; Sugar 2g; Fiber 1g

Currant Cream Ramekins

Prep time: 5 minutes | Cook time: 20 minutes | Serves: 6

1 cup red currants, blended	3 tbsp. stevia
1 cup black currants, blended	1 cup coconut cream

In a suitable bowl, combine all the recipe ingredients and stir well. Divide into ramekins. In the air fryer, Air Fry them at 340 degrees F for 20 minutes. Serve the pudding cold.
Nutritional information: Calories 200; Total Carbs 4g; Net Carbs 2g; Protein 6g; Fat 4g; Sugar 2g; Fiber 2g

Chia Bites

Prep time: 15 minutes | Cook time: 8 minutes | Serves: 2

½ scoop of protein powder	1 tsp. Splenda
1 egg, beaten	1 tsp. butter, softened
3 tbsp. almond flour	1 tsp. chia seeds, dried
1 oz. hazelnuts, grinded	¼ tsp. ground clove
1 tbsp. flax meal	

In the mixing bowl mix up protein powder, almond flour, grinded hazelnuts, flax meal, chia seeds, ground clove, and Splenda. Add egg and butter and stir it with the help of the spoon until you get a homogenous mixture. Cut the prepared mixture into pieces and make 2 bites of any shape with the help of the fingertips. At 365 degrees F, preheat your Air Fryer. Layer the "Air Fryer Basket" with baking paper and put the protein bites inside. Air Fry at 365 degrees F them for 8 minutes.
Nutritional information: Calories 433; Total Carbs 15.6g; Net Carbs 2g; Protein 20.2g; Fat 35.5g; Sugar 2g; Fiber 7g

Espresso Cinnamon Cookies

Prep time: 5 minutes | Cook time: 15 minutes | Serves: 12

8 tbsp. ghee, melted	½ tbsp. cinnamon powder
1 cup almond flour	2 tsp. baking powder
¼ cup brewed espresso	2 eggs, whisked
¼ cup swerve	

In a suitable bowl, mix all the recipe ingredients and whisk well. Spread medium balls on a cookie sheet lined baking paper, flatten them. Put the cookie sheet in your air fryer and Air Fry them at 350 degrees F for 15 minutes. Serve the cookies cold.
Nutritional information: Calories 134; Total Carbs 4g; Net Carbs 2g; Protein 2g; Fat 12g; Sugar 2g; Fiber 2g

Turmeric Almond Pie

Prep time: 20 minutes | Cook time: 35 minutes | Serves: 4

4 eggs, beaten	1 tsp. lemon juice
1 tbsp. poppy seeds	1 cup almond flour
1 tsp. ground turmeric	2 tbsp. heavy cream
1 tsp. vanilla extract	¼ cup Erythritol
1 tsp. baking powder	1 tsp. avocado oil

Put the eggs in the bowl. Add vanilla extract, baking powder, lemon juice, almond flour, heavy cream, and Erythritol. Then add avocado oil and poppy seeds. Add turmeric. With the help of the immersion blender, blend the pie batter until it is smooth. Layer the air fryer cake mold with baking paper. Pour the pie batter in the cake mold. Flatten the pie surface with the help of the spatula if needed. At 365 degrees F, preheat your Air Fryer. Put the cake mold in the air fryer and Air Fry the pie at 365 degrees F for 35 minutes. When the pie is cooked, cool it completely and remove it from the cake mold. Cut the cooked pie into the servings.
Nutritional information: Calories 149; Total Carbs 3.8g; Net Carbs 2g; Protein 7.7g; Fat 11.9g; Sugar 2g; Fiber 1.2g

Sponge Cake

Prep time: 5 minutes | Cook time: 30 minutes | Serves: 8

1 cup ricotta, soft	7 tbsp. ghee, melted
⅓ swerve	1 tsp. baking powder
3 eggs, whisked	Cooking spray
1 cup almond flour	

In a suitable bowl, combine all the recipe ingredients except the cooking spray and stir them very well. Grease a cake pan that fits the air fryer with the cooking spray and pour the cake mix inside. Put this pan in the air fryer and Air Fry at 350 degrees F for 30 minutes. Cool the cake down, slice and serve.
Nutritional information: Calories 210; Total Carbs 6g; Net Carbs 2g; Protein 9g; Fat 12g; Sugar 2g; Fiber 3g

Yogurt Treat with Berries

Prep time: 8-10 minutes | Cook time: 6 minutes | Serves: 4-5

1 teaspoon vanilla extract	1 to 2 teaspoon squeeze honey
2 eggs, large	Greek yogurt for serving
2 slices sourdough bread	Your favorite choice of berries
Butter as needed	

On a flat kitchen surface, plug your air fryer and turn it on. Gently coat your air fryer basket with cooking oil or spray. Preheat your air fryer to 355 degrees F for about 4 to 5 minutes. Whisk the eggs and vanilla together in a medium sized bowl. On both sides of the bread, brush with butter. Then soak the bread slices in the egg mixture. Arrange the bread slices onto the air fryer basket. Cook in the preheated air fryer for 3 minutes. When cooked, remove from the air fryer and serve with the berries and yogurt honey on the top. Enjoy!
Nutritional information: Calories:77 Fat:2g; Total Carbs:38.7g; Net Carbs: 30g; Fiber:1.5g; Sugar: 5.6g; Protein:4g

Plum Apple Crumble with Cranberries

Prep time: 10-15 minutes | Cook time: 25 minutes | Serves: 6-7

2 ½ ounces caster sugar	¼ pound plums, pitted and chopped
⅓ cup oats	
⅔ cup flour	¼ pound apples, cored and chopped
½ stick butter, chilled	
1 tablespoon cold water	1 tablespoon lemon juice
1 tablespoon honey	½ teaspoon vanilla paste
½ teaspoon ground mace	1 cup cranberries

On a flat kitchen surface, plug your air fryer and turn it on. Gently coat your cake pan with cooking oil or spray. Before cooking, heat your air fryer to 390 degrees F for about 4 to 5 minutes. Mix the lemon juice, sugar, honey, mace, apples, and plums in a medium sized bowl. Place the fruits onto the cake pan. In a second medium sized bowl, mix thoroughly the rest of the ingredients and add the fruit mixture on the top. Transfer to the cake pan. Bake in the preheated air fryer for 20 minutes. When cooked, remove from the air fryer and serve warm.
Nutritional information: Calories:188 Fat:8g; Total Carbs:27.8g; Net Carbs: 0.16g; Fiber:1.8g; Sugar: 25.84g; Protein:1.6g

Vanilla Banana Puffs

Prep time: 10-15 minutes | Cook time: 10 minutes | Serves: 8

4 ounces instant vanilla	pudding

4 ounces cream cheese, softened	1 cup milk
1 package (8-ounce) crescent dinner rolls, refrigerated	2 bananas, sliced
	1 egg, lightly beaten

On a flat kitchen surface, plug your air fryer and turn it on. Before cooking, heat your air fryer to 355 degrees F for about 4 to 5 minutes. Make 8 squares from the crescent dinner rolls. Mix thoroughly the milk and pudding in a medium sized bowl. Then whisk the cream cheese in the mixture. Divide the mixture onto the squares. Add the banana slices on the top. Fold over and press the edges to seal the filling inside. Brush the whisked egg over each pastry puff. Transfer to the air fryer basket. Cook in the preheated air fryer for 10 minutes. When the cooking time is up, remove from the air fryer and serve warm. Enjoy!
Nutritional information: Calories: 307; Fat:7.2g; Total Carbs:58.65g; Net Carbs: 2.1g; Fiber:4g; Sugar: 37.53g; Protein:5.6g

Chocolate Lava Cake

Prep time: 10 minutes | Cook time: 9 minutes | Serves: 2

1 egg	2 tablespoons erythritol
½ teaspoon baking powder	2 tablespoons water
1 tablespoon coconut oil, melted	2 tablespoons unsweetened cocoa powder
1 tablespoon flax meal	Pinch of salt

Before cooking, heat your air fryer to 350 degrees F. In a bowl, whisk all the ingredients. Then divide the mixture into 2 ramekins. Transfer the ramekins inside the air fryer basket and bake in the preheated air fryer for 8 to 9 minutes. When cooked, remove from the air fryer and set aside to cool for 10 minutes. Serve and enjoy!
Nutritional information: Calories: 119; Fat 11g; Total Carbs 4g; Net Carbs: 2g; Fiber 2.8g; Sugars 0.3g; Protein 4.6g

Vanilla Pineapple Cinnamon Treat

Prep time: 8-10 minutes | Cook time: 8 minutes | Serves: 6

½ teaspoon baking soda	½ cup water
½ teaspoon ground cinnamon	⅔ cup all-purpose flour
¼ teaspoon ground anise star	⅓ cup rice flour
¼ cup flaked coconut, unsweetened	½ teaspoon baking powder
1 pineapple, sliced	1 cup rice milk
A pinch of kosher salt	½ teaspoon vanilla essence
	4 tablespoons caster sugar

On a flat kitchen surface, plug your air fryer and turn it on. Gently coat your air frying basket with cooking oil or spray. Before cooking, hear your air fryer to 380 degrees F for about 4 to 5 minutes. Mix baking soda, ground cinnamon, ground anise star, coconut flakes, kosher salt, water, all-purpose flour, rice flour, baking powder, rice milk, vanilla essence, and caster sugar together in a medium sized bowl to make the batter. Then coat the batter mixture over the pineapple slices. Transfer the slices to the air frying basket. Cook in the preheated air fryer for 8 minutes. When cooked, remove from the air fryer and pour the maple syrup over the pineapple slices. Add a dollop of vanilla ice cream on the top to garnish. Serve and enjoy!
Nutritional information: Calories: 160; Fat 1.7g; Total Carbs 34g; Net Carbs: 18g; Fiber 1.4g; Sugars 11g; Protein 2.3g

Chocolate Cake with Raspberries

Prep time: 10 minutes | Cook time: 3 minutes | Serves: 5-6

| 2 eggs | ⅔ cup all-purpose flour |

5 tablespoons sugar	1 cup chocolate chips, melted
⅔ cup unsalted butter	⅓ cup raspberries
Salt as needed	

On a flat kitchen surface, plug your air fryer and turn it on. Preheat your air fryer for about 4-5 minutes to 355 degrees F. Gently grease 6 ramekins with oil and dust some sugar inside. Whisk the butter and sugar in a medium sized bowl. Then beat the eggs in the mixture till fluffy. Combine together with salt and flour. Then mix in the melted chocolate chips until well combined. Then divide the mixture into the prepared ramekins with ¼ empty. Transfer the ramekins onto the air fryer basket. Cook in the preheated air fryer for 3 minutes. When cooked, remove from the air fryer. Sprinkle the raspberries on the top and serve warm.
Nutritional information: Calories: 443; Fat 30.4g; Total Carbs 38g; Net Carbs: 23.5g; Fiber 1.8g; Sugars 24.9g; Protein 5.7g

Creamy Cheesecake Bites

Prep time: 10 minutes | Cook time: 2 minutes | Serves: 16

8 ounces cream cheese, softened	½ tsp vanilla
2 tablespoons erythritol	4 tablespoons heavy cream
½ cup almond flour	½ cup erythritol

In a stand mixer, mix cream cheese, 2 tbsp. heavy cream, vanilla, and ½ cup erythritol until smooth. Line a plate with parchment paper and spread the cream cheese onto the parchment. Refrigerate for 1 hour. Mix together 2 tbsp. Erythritol and almond flour in a small bowl. Drip the remaining heavy cream over the cheesecake bites and dip in the almond flour mixture to coat. Arrange evenly the cheesecake bites inside the air fryer basket and cook in the air fryer at 350 degrees F for 2 minutes. Halfway cooking, check the cheesecake bites to ensure they are still frozen. Serve with chocolate syrup on the top.
Nutritional information: Calories: 84; Fat 8g; Total Carbs 1g; Net Carbs: 0g; Fiber 0.4g; Sugars 0.1g; Protein 1.9g

Vanilla Cheesecake

Prep time: 10 minutes | Cook time: 10 minutes. |Serves:6

2 eggs	½ teaspoon fresh lemon juice
16 ounces cream cheese, softened	1 teaspoon vanilla
2 tablespoons sour cream	¾ cup erythritol

Before cooking, heat your air fryer to 350 degrees F. In a large bowl, mix the whisked eggs, vanilla, lemon juice, and sweetener together and use a hand mixer to beat until smooth. Then beat in cream cheese and sour cream until fluffy. Divide the batter into 2 4-inch springform pan that fits in your air fryer. Cook in your air fryer at 350 degrees F for 8 to 10 minutes. When cooked, remove from the air fryer and set it aside to cool completely. Transfer in the fridge to reserve. Serve and enjoy!
Nutritional information: Calories: 296; Fat 28.7g; Total Carbs 2g; Net Carbs: 0.5g; Fiber 0g; Sugars 0.4g; Protein 7.7g

Vanilla Coconut Pie

Prep time: 10 minutes | Cook time: 12 minutes | Serves: 6

2 eggs	1 ½ tsp vanilla
½ cup coconut flour	¼ cup butter
½ cup erythritol	1 ½ cups coconut milk
1 cup shredded coconut	

In a large bowl, mix all the ingredients until well combined. Using cooking spray, spray a baking dish that fits in your air fryer. Transfer the batter onto the greased baking dish. Cook in your air fryer at 350 degrees F for 10 to 12 minutes. Before serving, slice into your desired size. Serve and enjoy!
Nutritional information: Calories: 317; Fat 28.9g; Total Carbs 12g; Net Carbs: 7g; Fiber 6.5g; Sugars: 3.1g; Protein 5.1g

Strawberry Muffins with Cinnamon

Prep time: 10 minutes | Cook time: 15 minutes | Serves: 12

3 eggs	⅓ cup heavy cream
1 teaspoon ground cinnamon	1 teaspoon vanilla
2 teaspoons baking powder	½ cup Swerve
2 ½ cups almond flour	5 tablespoons butter
⅔ cup fresh strawberries, diced	

Before cooking, heat your air fryer to 325 degrees F. In a bowl, add the sweetener and butter and use a hand mixer to beat until smooth. Beat in cream, whisked eggs, and vanilla until frothy. Sift the cinnamon, baking powder, salt, and almond flour together in a second bowl. Mix the flour mixture together with the wet ingredients until well incorporated. Then place the strawberries. Fold and press well. Divide the batter into the silicone muffin molds. Cook in batches in your air fryer at 325 degrees F for 15 minutes. Enjoy!
Nutritional information: Calories: 215; Fat 18.2g; Total Carbs 6g; Net Carbs: 2.5g; Fiber 2.8g; Sugars 0.5g; Protein 6.6g

Chocolate Banana Brownie

Prep time: 10 minutes | Cook time: 16 minutes | Serves: 4

1 cup bananas, overripe	cocoa powder
1 scoop protein: powder	½ cup almond butter, melted
2 tablespoons unsweetened	

Before cooking, heat your air fryer to 325 degrees F. Using cooking spray, spray a baking pan that fits in your air fryer. In a blender, mix all the ingredients together until smooth. Spread the better onto the baking pan. Cook in the preheated air fryer for 16 minutes. Serve and enjoy!
Nutritional information: Calories: 52; Fat 1.6g; Total Carbs 10.4g; Net Carbs: 0g; Fiber 2.1g; Sugars 4.7g; Protein 1.4g

Almond Pecan Muffins

Prep time: 10 minutes | Cook time: 15 minutes | Serves: 12

4 eggs	1 tablespoon baking powder
1 teaspoon vanilla	½ cup pecans, chopped
¼ cup almond milk	½ teaspoon ground cinnamon
2 tablespoons butter, melted	2 teaspoons allspice
½ cup swerve	1 ½ cups almond flour
1 teaspoon psyllium husk	

Before cooking, heat your air fryer to 370 degrees F. In a bowl, use a hand mixer to beat the butter, sweetener, almond milk, whisked eggs, and vanilla together until smooth. Mix together the remaining ingredients until well combined. Divide the batter into the silicone muffin molds. Cook in batches in the preheated air fryer for 15 minutes. Serve and enjoy!
Nutritional information: Calories: 142; Fat 11.6g; Total Carbs 5g; Net Carbs: 2g; Fiber 2.5g; Sugars 0.3g; Protein 5g

Blueberry Vanilla Muffins

Prep time: 10 minutes | Cook time: 20 minutes | Serves: 12

3 large eggs	2 ½ cups almond flour
⅓ cup coconut oil, melted	¾ cup blueberries
1 ½ teaspoons gluten-free baking powder	½ teaspoon vanilla
½ cup erythritol	⅓ cup unsweetened almond milk

Before cooking, heat your air fryer to 325 degrees F. Stir together the baking powder, erythritol, and almond flour in a large bowl. Mix vanilla, almond milk, coconut oil, and the whisked eggs in the bowl. Then add in the strawberries and fold together. Divide the batter into the silicone muffin molds. Cook in batches in the preheated air fryer for 20 minutes. Serve and enjoy!
Nutritional information: Calories: 77; Fat 7.4g; Total Carbs 1.5g; Net Carbs: 0g; Fiber: 0.3g; Sugars: 1g; Protein 1.7g

Pumpkin Almond Flour Muffins

Prep time: 10 minutes | Cook time: 20 minutes | Serves: 10

4 large eggs	1 tsp. vanilla
½ cup pumpkin puree	⅓ cup coconut oil, melted
1 tbsp. pumpkin pie spice	½ cup almond flour
1 tbsp. baking powder, gluten-free	½ cup coconut flour
⅔ cup erythritol	½ tsp sea salt

Before cooking, heat your air fryer to 325 degrees F. Add pumpkin pie spice, erythritol, sea salt, almond flour, and coconut flour in a large bowl and stir until well combined. Then combine the mixture with the whisked eggs, pumpkin puree, and coconut oil. Divide the batter into the silicone muffin molds. Cook in batches in your air fryer for 20 minutes. Serve and enjoy!
Nutritional information: Calories: 84; Fat 4.5g; Total Carbs 7g; Net Carbs: 3g; Fiber 3.3g; Sugars 0.6g; Protein 4.3g

Cheese Muffins with Cinnamon

Prep time: 10 minutes | Cook time: 16 minutes | Serves: 10

2 eggs	1 teaspoon ground cinnamon
½ cup erythritol	½ tsp vanilla
8 ounces cream cheese	

Before cooking, heat your air fryer to 325 degrees F. Mix together vanilla, erythritol, eggs, and cream cheese until smooth. Divide the batter into the silicone muffin molds. Top the muffins with cinnamon. In the air fryer basket, transfer the muffin molds. Cook in your air fryer for 16 minutes. Serve and enjoy!
Nutritional information: calories 93; Fat 8.8g; Total Carbs 0.9g; Net Carbs: 0g; Fiber 0.1g; Sugars 0.2g; Protein 2.8g

Yummy Apple Chips

Prep time: 10 minutes | Cook time: 8 minutes | Serves: 6

3 Granny Smith apples, wash, core and thinly slice	1 teaspoon ground cinnamon
	1 pinch of salt

In the air fryer basket, add cinnamon, salt, and apple slices together and rub well. Cook in your air fryer at 390 degrees F for 8 minutes. Flip the apple slices halfway through cooking. When cooked, remove from the air fryer and serve.
Nutritional information: Calories: 59; Fat 0.2g; Total Carbs 15g; Net Carbs: 5.6g; Fiber 2.9g; Sugars 11.6g; Protein 0.3g

Chocolate Peanut Butter Mug Cake

Prep time: 5 minutes | Cook time: 20 minutes | Serves: 1

1 egg, lightly beaten
1 tablespoon heavy cream
¼ teaspoon baking powder
2 tablespoons unsweetened cocoa powder

2 tablespoons Erythritol
½ teaspoon vanilla
1 tablespoon peanut butter
1 teaspoon salt

Before cooking, heat your air fryer to 400 degrees F. Mix the beaten egg, heavy cream, baking powder, cocoa powder, Erythritol, vanilla, peanut butter, and salt together in a bowl until well incorporated. Using cooking spray, spritz a mug. Add the mixture into the mug. Transfer inside your air fryer. Cook in the preheated air fryer at 400 degrees F for 20 minutes. When cooked, remove from the air fryer and serve.
Nutritional information: Calories: 241; Fat 19.5g; Total Carbs 10.6g; Net Carbs: 0g; Fiber 4.6g; Sugars 2.3g; Protein 12g

Almond Cherry Bars

Prep time: 10 minutes | Cook time: 35 minutes | Serves: 12

2 eggs, lightly beaten
1 cup erythritol
½ tsp vanilla
¼ cup water
½ cup butter, softened

¾ cup cherries, pitted
1 ½ cup almond flour
1 tablespoon xanthan gum
½ teaspoon salt

Mix vanilla, butter, salt, almond flour, the beaten eggs, and erythritol together in a bowl to form a dough. Transfer the dough to a baking dish that fits in your air fryer and press the dough to flatten the surface. Bake in your air fryer at 375 degrees F for 10 minutes. While baking, stir together the xanthan gum, water, and cherries in a separate bowl. When the cooking time is up, add the cherry mixture over the dough. Cook again for 25 minutes. Once cooked, cut the dough into your desired size and serve.
Nutritional information: Calories: 206; Fat 15.1g; Total Carbs 13.5g; Net Carbs: 6.5g; Fiber 1.7g; Sugars 0.1g; Protein 4.1g

Berry Pudding

Prep time: 10 minutes | Cook time: 15 minutes | Serves: 6

2 cups coconut cream
1 lime zest, grated
3 tablespoons erythritol

¼ cup blueberries
⅓ cup blackberries

In a blender, add coconut cream, the grated lime zest, erythritol, blueberries, and blackberries and combine together. Using cooking spray, spritz 6 ramekins. Divide the mixture into the ramekins. Transfer the ramekins inside the air fryer basket. Cook in your air fryer at 340 degrees F for 15 minutes. When cooked, remove the ramekins onto a rack to cool. Serve and enjoy.
Nutritional information: Calories: 191; Fat 19.1g; Total Carbs 6g; Net Carbs: 2.5g; Fiber 2.3g; Sugars 3.7g; Protein 2g

Cheese Cake with Strawberries

Prep time: 10 minutes | Cook time: 35 minutes | Serves: 6

1 cup almond flour
3 tablespoons coconut oil, melted
½ teaspoon vanilla
1 egg, lightly beaten

1 tablespoon fresh lime juice
¼ cup erythritol
1 cup cream cheese, softened
1 pound strawberries, chopped
2 teaspoons baking powder

In a large bowl, combine almond flour, the melted coconut oil, vanilla, the beaten egg, fresh lime juice, erythritol, softened cream cheese, chopped strawberries, and baking powder together. Using cooking spray, spray an air fryer cake pan that fits in your air fryer. Spread the batter into the greased pan. Transfer to your air fryer. Cook in your air fryer at 350 degrees F for 35 minutes. When cooked, remove the pan onto a wire rack to cool completely. Then slice the cake into your desired size and serve. Enjoy!
Nutritional information: Calories: 345; Fat 30.1g; Total Carbs 12g; Net Carbs: 7g; Fiber 3.6g; Sugars 4g; Protein 8.4g

Coffee Cookies

Prep time: 10 minutes | Cook time: 15 minutes | Serves: 12

1 cup almond flour
2 eggs, lightly beaten
2 teaspoons baking powder
½ tablespoon cinnamon

¼ cup erythritol
¼ cup brewed espresso
½ cup ghee, melted

In a bowl, combine almond flour, the beaten eggs, baking powder, cinnamon, erythritol, brewed espresso, and the melted ghee together. Then shape the mixture into small cookies. Transfer to an oven-safe cookie sheet. Place the sheet onto the air fryer basket. Then cook in your air fryer at 350 degrees F for 15 minutes. When cooked, remove from the air fryer and serve.
Nutritional information: Calories: 143; Fat 13.7g; Total Carbs 2g; Net Carbs: 0.5g; Fiber 1.2g; Sugars 0.1g; Protein 3g

Sweet Orange Muffins

Prep time: 10 minutes | Cook time: 10 minutes | Serves: 5

5 eggs, beaten
1 tablespoon poppy seeds
1 teaspoon vanilla extract
¼ teaspoon ground nutmeg
½ teaspoon baking powder
1 teaspoon orange juice

1 teaspoon orange zest, grated
5 tablespoons coconut flour
1 tablespoon Monk fruit
2 tablespoons coconut flakes
Cooking spray

After adding the eggs, poppy seeds, vanilla extract, ground nutmeg, baking powder, orange juice, orange zest, coconut flour, Monk fruit and coconut flakes, mix them well until homogenous and have no clumps. Spray the inside of the muffin molds. Pour the mixture batter in the molds and then arrange them to the air fryer. Cook them at 360 degrees F for 10 minutes. When cooked, serve and enjoy.
Nutritional information: Calories: 114; Fat 6.6g; Total Carbs 6g; Net Carbs: 2.5g; Fiber 3.4g; Sugars 0.9g; Protein 7g

Fluffy Cocoa Cupcakes

Prep time: 5 minutes | Cook time: 25 minutes | Serves: 4

⅓ cup coconut flour
½ cup cocoa powder
3 tablespoons stevia
½ teaspoon baking soda
1 teaspoon baking powder
4 eggs, whisked

1 teaspoon vanilla extract
4 tablespoons coconut oil, melted
¼ cup almond milk
Cooking spray

In addition to the cooking spray, whisk the other ingredients well. Spray the cooking pan of your air fryer with the cooking spray, then pour the mixture on it. Cook the mixture at 350 degrees F for 25 minutes. Cool down before serving.
Nutritional information: Calories: 283; Fat 24g; Total Carbs 14g; Net Carbs: 9.5g; Fiber 7.6g; Sugars 1.2g; Protein 9.2g

Lemon Creamy Muffins

Prep time: 15 minutes | Cook time: 11 minutes | Serves: 6

1 cup almond flour	1 egg, beaten
3 tablespoons Erythritol	½ teaspoon baking powder
1 scoop protein: powder	½ teaspoon instant coffee
1 teaspoon vanilla extract	1 teaspoon lemon juice
3 tablespoons coconut oil, melted	2 tablespoons heavy cream
	Cooking spray

After adding the almond flour, Erythritol, protein: powder, vanilla extract, coconut oil, egg, baking powder, instant coffee, lemon juice, and heavy cream in a suitable bowl, use the immersion blender to whisk them until smooth. Spray the muffin molds with cooking spray. Fill half of each muffin mold with muffin batter and arrange them to the cooking basket of your air fryer. Cook them at 360 degrees F for 11 minutes. When done, serve and enjoy.

Nutritional information: Calories: 202; Fat 18.4g; Total Carbs: 4.5g; Net Carbs: 0.5g; Fiber: 2g; Sugars: 0.2g; Protein 5g

Easy-to-Make Almond Cookies

Prep time: 5 minutes | Cook time: 15 minutes | Serves: 8

1 and ½ cups almonds, crushed	¼ teaspoon almond extract
2 tablespoons Erythritol	2 eggs, whisked
½ teaspoon baking powder	

In a bowl, whisk all of the ingredients well. Scoop 8 servings of the mixture and then arrange them to the cooking pan lined with parchment paper. Cook them at 350 degrees F for 15 minutes. Serve cold.

Nutritional information: Calories: 89; Fat 7.3g; Total Carbs 2g; Net Carbs: 0.5g; Fiber 1.6g; Sugars 0.6g; Protein 4g

Coconut Walnuts

Prep time: 5 minutes | Cook time: 40 minutes | Serves: 12

1 and ¼ cups almond flour	1 and ½ cups coconut, flaked
1 cup swerve	1 egg yolk
1 cup butter, melted	¾ cup walnuts, chopped
½ cup coconut cream	½ teaspoon vanilla extract

Stir the flour, half of the swerve and half of the butter well, then press the mixture on the cooking pan of your air fryer. Cook the mixture at 350 degrees F for 15 minutes. While cooking the mixture, heat the rest of the ingredients in a pan for 1 to 2 minutes. Arrange the heated mixture to the air fryer and continue to cook for 25 minutes more. Before serving, cool the food down and cut into bars.

Nutritional information: Calories: 232; Fat: 24.2g; Total Carbs 2g; Net Carbs: 0.5g; Fiber: 1.1g; Sugars: 0.9g; Protein: 3.1g

Cinnamon Butter Muffins

Prep time: 15 minutes | Cook time: 10 minutes | Serves: 2

1 teaspoon of cocoa powder	melted
2 tablespoons coconut flour	¼ teaspoon baking powder
2 teaspoons swerve	1 teaspoon apple cider vinegar
½ teaspoon vanilla extract	¼ teaspoon ground cinnamon
2 teaspoons almond butter,	

After adding the cocoa powder, coconut flour, swerve, vanilla extract, almond butter, baking powder, apple cider vinegar and ground cinnamon, use a spoon to stir them until smooth. Pour the brownie mixture in the muffin molds and let them rest for 10 minutes. Cook the muffins at 365 degrees F for 10 minutes. Cool them completely before serving.

Nutritional information: Calories 135; Fat: 9.9g; Total Carbs: 9g; Net Carbs: 4.3g; Fiber: 5g Sugars: 0.9g; Protein 4.6g

Lemon Nut Bars

Prep time: 15 minutes | Cook time: 30 minutes | Serves: 10

½ cup coconut oil, softened	1 teaspoon vanilla extract
1 teaspoon baking powder	2 eggs, beaten
1 teaspoon lemon juice	2 oz. hazelnuts, chopped
1 cup almond flour	1 oz. macadamia nuts, chopped
½ cup coconut flour	Cooking spray
3 tablespoons Erythritol	

Mix the coconut oil, baking powder, lemon juice, almond flour, coconut flour, Erythritol, vanilla extract and eggs well until smooth. Continue to add the hazelnuts and macadamia nuts and stir the mixture until homogenous. Transfer the nut mixture to the cooking basket and use the spatula to flatten it. Cook the mixture at 325 degrees F for 30 minutes. When done, cool the mixture well and cut it into the serving bars. Enjoy.

Nutritional information: Calories: 135; Fat: 9.9g; Total Carbs: 9g; Net Carbs: 4.3g; Fiber: 5g Sugars: 0.9g; Protein: 4.6g

Enticing Cappuccino Muffins

Prep time: 10 minutes | Cook time: 20 minutes | Serves: 12

4 eggs	1 teaspoon cinnamon
2 cups almond flour	2 teaspoons baking powder
½ teaspoon vanilla	¼ cup coconut flour
1 teaspoon espresso powder	½ cup Swerve
½ cup sour cream	¼ teaspoon salt

Before cooking, heat your air fryer to 325 degrees F. In a blender, mix together vanilla, espresso powder, eggs, and sour cream until smooth. Then blend again with cinnamon, coconut flour, baking powder, salt, and sweetener until smooth. Divide the batter into the silicone muffin molds. Cook in batches in the preheated air fryer for 20 minutes. Serve and enjoy!

Nutritional information: Calories: 150; Fat: 13 g; Total Carbs: 5.3 g; Net Crabs:3.8g; Fiber: 1g; Sugar: 0.8 g; Protein: 6 g

Moist Cinnamon Muffins

Prep time: 10 minutes | Cook time: 12 minutes | Serves: 20

1 tablespoon cinnamon	½ cup almond flour
1 teaspoon baking powder	½ cup coconut oil
2 scoops vanilla protein: powder	½ cup pumpkin puree
	½ cup almond butter

Before cooking, heat your air fryer to 325 degrees F. Combine together cinnamon, baking powder, vanilla protein: powder, and almond flour in a large bowl. Then mix the dry mixture together with the coconut oil, pumpkin puree, and almond butter until well incorporated. Divide the batter into the silicone muffin molds. Cook in batches in your air fryer for 12 minutes. Serve and enjoy!

Nutritional information: Calories: 135; Fat: 9.9g; Total Carbs: 9g; Net Carbs: 4.3g; Fiber: 5g Sugars: 0.9g; Protein: 4.6g

Scones with Cream Cheese

Prep time: 20 minutes | Cook time: 10 minutes | Serves: 4

4 oz. almond flour
½ teaspoon baking powder
1 teaspoon lemon juice
¼ teaspoon salt
2 teaspoons cream cheese

¼ cup coconut cream
1 teaspoon vanilla extract
1 tablespoon Erythritol
1 tablespoon heavy cream
Cooking spray

Mix up the almond flour, baking powder, lemon juice, salt and cream cheese in a suitable bowl and stir well. In another bowl, mix up the vanilla extract, coconut cream and then add this mixture in the almond flour mixture. Stir gently and then knead the dough. Roll the dough up and cut it into scones. Cook the scones on the oiled basket in your air fryer at 360 degrees F for 10 minutes, or until they are light brown. When cooked, cool them to the room temperature, and at the same time, mix up the heavy cream and Erythritol. Brush each scone with the cream mixture, then serve and enjoy.
Nutritional information: Calories: 107; Fat: 9.9g; Total Carbs: 9g; Net Carbs: 4.3g; Fiber: 5g Sugars: 0.9g; Protein: 4.6g

Donuts with Cardamom

Prep time: 20 minutes | Cook time: 6 minutes | Serves: 4

1 teaspoon ground cardamom
½ teaspoon ground cinnamon
½ teaspoon baking powder
½ cup coconut flour
1 tablespoon Erythritol

1 egg, beaten
1 tablespoon butter, softened
¼ teaspoon salt
Cooking spray

Thoroughly mix up the Erythritol, ground cinnamon and ground cardamom in a suitable bowl. In another bowl, mix up the coconut flour, baking powder, egg, salt, and butter. Knead the non-sticky dough. Roll up the dough and use the donut cutter to form 4 donuts. Coat every donut with the cardamom mixture, then place the donuts in a warm place to let it rest for 10 minutes. Spray the cooking basket of your air fryer with cooking spray and transfer the donuts on it. Cook the donuts at 355 degrees F for 6 minutes or until they are golden brown. Sprinkle the remaining cardamom mixture on the hot donuts. Enjoy!
Nutritional information: Calories: 114; Fat: 9.9g; Total Carbs: 9g; Net Carbs: 4.3g; Fiber: 5g Sugars: 0.9g; Protein: 4.6g

Cocoa Nutmeg Cake

Prep time: 20 minutes | Cook time: 40 minutes | Serves: 8

½ cup heavy cream
3 eggs, beaten
3 tablespoons cocoa powder
1 teaspoon vanilla extract
1 teaspoon baking powder

3 tablespoons Erythritol
1 cup almond flour
¼ teaspoon ground nutmeg
1 tablespoon avocado oil
1 teaspoon Splenda

In a bowl, stir the heavy cream, eggs and cocoa powder well until smooth, then add vanilla extract, baking powder, Erythritol, almond flour, ground nutmeg, avocado oil and whisk well. Pour the mixture in the cake mold. Use the toothpick to pierce the foil. Arrange the cake mold to the cooking basket and cook in the air fryer at 360 degrees F for 40 minutes. When cooked, sprinkle the Splenda on the top after cooling completely. Serve and enjoy.
Nutritional information: Calories: 209; Fat: 12.6g; Total Carbs: 4g; Net Carbs: 2g; Fiber: 0.5g; Sugars: 1g; Protein: 19.5g

Simple Donuts

Prep time: 5 minutes | Cook time: 15 minutes | Serves: 4

8 ounces' coconut flour 2 tablespoons stevia
1 egg, whisked

1-½ tablespoons butter, melted
4 ounces' coconut milk
1 teaspoon baking powder

Thoroughly mix up all of the ingredients in a bowl. Form donuts from the mixture. Cook the donuts in your air fryer at 370 degrees F for 15 minutes. When cooked, serve and enjoy.
Nutritional information: Calories: 135; Fat: 9.9g; Total Carbs: 9g; Net Carbs: 4.3g; Fiber: 5g Sugars: 0.9g; Protein: 4.6g

Zucchinis Bars with Cream Cheese

Prep time: 10 minutes | Cook time: 15 minutes | Serves: 12

3 tablespoons coconut oil, melted 6 eggs
3 ounces' zucchini, shredded 2 teaspoons vanilla extract

½ teaspoon baking powder
4 ounces' cream cheese
2 tablespoons erythritol

Whisk all of the ingredients in a bowl, then pour in the cooking pan lined with parchment paper. Cook at 320 degrees F for 15 minutes. Slice and cool down. Serve and enjoy.
Nutritional information: Calories: 211; Fat: 12.6g; Total Carbs: 4g; Net Carbs: 2g; Fiber: 0.5g; Sugars: 1g; Protein: 19.5g

Aromatic Cup with Blondies

Prep time: 10 minutes | Cook time: 15 minutes | Serves: 1

1 egg, beaten
1 tablespoon peanut butter
½ teaspoon baking powder
1 teaspoon lemon juice

½ teaspoon vanilla extract
1 teaspoon Erythritol
2 tablespoons coconut flour

In a cup, thoroughly mix up all of the ingredients until homogenous. Arrange the cup with blondies to your air fryer and cook the mixture at 350 degrees F for 15 minutes. When done, serve and enjoy.
Nutritional information: Calories: 237; Fat: 12.6g; Total Carbs: 4g; Net Carbs: 2g; Fiber: 0.5g; Sugars: 1g; Protein: 19.5g

Vanilla Spread

Prep time: 10 minutes | Cook time: 5 minutes | Serves: 4

2 oz. walnuts, chopped
5 teaspoons coconut oil
½ teaspoon vanilla extract

1 tablespoon Erythritol
1 teaspoon of cocoa powder

Preheat the air fryer to 350F. Put the walnuts in the mason jar, then add the coconut oil, vanilla extract, Erythritol and cocoa powder. Use a spoon to stir the mixture until smooth. Arrange the mason jar with Nutella to your air fryer and cook at 350 degrees F for 5 minutes. Before serving, stir Nutella.
Nutritional information: Calories: 91; Fat: 12.6g; Total Carbs: 4g; Net Carbs: 2g; Fiber: 0.5g; Sugars: 1g; Protein: 19.5g

Tasty Mozzarella Balls

Prep time: 20 minutes | Cook time: 20 minutes | Serves: 8

2 eggs, beaten

1 teaspoon almond butter,

melted
7 oz. coconut flour
2 oz. almond flour
5 oz. Mozzarella, shredded
1 tablespoon butter

2 tablespoons swerve
1 teaspoon baking powder
½ teaspoon vanilla extract
Cooking spray

Mix up butter and Mozzarella in a suitable bowl, then microwave the mixture for 10 to 15 minutes or until it is melted. Add the almond flour, coconut flour, swerve, baking powder and vanilla extract, then stir well. Knead the soft dough. Microwave the mixture for 2-5 seconds more to melt better. In the bowl, mix up almond butter and eggs. Form 8 balls from the mixture and coat them with the egg mixture. Coat the cooking basket of your air fryer with cooking spray. Cook the food at 400 degrees F for 4 minutes. Before serving, cool the food completely and sprinkle with Splenda if desired.
Nutritional information: Calories: 249; Fat: 9g; Total Carbs: 27g; Net Carbs: 19g; Fiber: 2.4g; Sugar: 15g; Protein: 1.3g

Enticing Ricotta Cheese Cake

Prep time: 10 minutes | Cook time: 30 minutes | Serves: 8

3 eggs, lightly beaten
1 teaspoon baking powder
½ cup ghee, melted

1 cup almond flour
⅓ cup erythritol
1 cup ricotta cheese, soft

In a mixing bowl, combine the beaten eggs, baking powder, melted ghee, almond flour, erythritol, and soft ricotta cheese. Gently grease a baking dish that fits in your air fryer. Add the mixture onto the prepared baking dish. Transfer the baking dish inside your air fryer. Cook in the air fryer at 350 degrees F for 30 minutes. When cooked, remove from the air fryer and cool. Then slice the cake into your desired size and serve. Enjoy!
Nutritional information: Calories: 148; Fat: 0.3 g; Total Carbs: 38g; Net Carbs: 23.5g; Fiber: 0.5g; Sugar: 33.9g; Protein: 0.6g

Delicious Walnut Bars

Prep time: 5 minutes | Cook time: 16 minutes | Serves: 4

1 egg
⅓ cup cocoa powder 3 tablespoons swerve
7 tablespoons ghee, melted 1

teaspoon vanilla extract
¼ cup almond flour
¼ cup walnuts, chopped
½ teaspoon baking soda

Thoroughly mix up all of the ingredients in a bowl. Arrange the mixture to the cooking pan lined with parchment paper. Cook at 330 degrees F for 16 minutes. Cool the bars before serving.
Nutritional information: Calories: 182; Fat: 9g; Total Carbs: 27g; Net Carbs: 19g; Fiber: 2.4g; Sugar: 15g; Protein: 1.3g

Pineapple Chips with Cinnamon

Prep time: 5 minutes | Cook time: 20 minutes | Serves: 4

4 pineapple slices
1 teaspoon cinnamon

2 tablespoons erythritol

In a zip-lock bag, add the cinnamon, sweetener, and pineapple slices. Seal the bag and shake. Then cool in the refrigerator for 30 minutes. Before cooking, heat your air fryer to 350 degrees F. In the air fryer basket, arrange the pineapple slices. Cook in the preheated air fryer at 350 degrees F for 20 minutes. Flip the slices halfway through cooking. When cooked, remove from the air fryer and serve.
Nutritional information: Calories: 46; Fat: 9g; Total Carbs: 27g; Net Carbs: 19g; Fiber: 2.4g; Sugar: 15g; Protein: 1.3g

Vanilla Cheese Custard

Prep time: 10 minutes | Cook time: 20 minutes | Serves: 2

5 eggs
2 tablespoons swerve
1 teaspoon vanilla

½ cup unsweetened almond milk
½ cup cream cheese

Using a hand mixer, beat the eggs in a bowl. Then beat in sweetener, almond milk, vanilla, and cream cheese for 2 minutes or until beaten well. Using cooking spray, spray two ramekins. Divide the beaten mixture into the greased ramekins. Before cooking, heat your air fryer to 350 degrees F. Transfer the ramekins inside your air fryer. Then cook the ramekins at 350 degrees F for 20 minutes. When cooked, remove the ramekins onto a wire rack to cool. Now it's time to treat yourself.
Nutritional information: Calories: 374; Fat: 25g; Total Carbs: 7g; Net Carbs: 3g; Fiber: 0g; Sugar: 6g; Protein: 12.3g

Simple Almond Muffins with Blueberries

Prep time: 5 minutes | Cook time: 14 minutes | Serves: 2

1 egg
1 teaspoon baking powder
3 tablespoons butter, melted
¾ cup blueberries

⅔ cup almond flour
2 tablespoons erythritol
⅓ cup unsweetened almond milk

Using cooking spray, spray the silicone muffin molds. In a bowl, combine egg, baking powder, melted butter, blueberries, and almond flour. Add the combined mixture into the muffin molds. Transfer the molds onto the air fryer basket. Cook the muffins in your air fryer at 320 degrees F for 14 minutes. When cooked, remove the muffins onto a wire rack to cool. Now it's time to treat yourself!
Nutritional information: Calories: 374; Fat: 25g; Total Carbs: 7g; Net Carbs: 3g; Fiber: 0g; Sugar: 6g; Protein: 12.3g

Vanilla Berry Cobbler

Prep time: 10 minutes | Cook time: 10 minutes | Serves: 6

1 egg, lightly beaten
1 tablespoon butter, melted
2 teaspoons swerve
½ teaspoon vanilla

1 cup almond flour
½ cup raspberries, sliced
½ cup strawberries, sliced

Before cooking, heat your air fryer to 360 degrees F. Combine the sliced raspberries and strawberries in an air fryer baking dish that fits in your air fryer. Pour the sweetener over the berries. In a separate bowl, combine together vanilla, butter, and almond flour. Combine the almond flour mixture with the beaten egg. Top the sliced berries with the almond flour mixture and then use foil to cover the dish. Then transfer the dish inside your air fryer and cook at 360 degrees F for 10 minutes. When cooked, remove from the air fryer and serve.
Nutritional information: Calories: 157; Fat: 1.3g; Total Carbs: 1g; Net Carbs: 0g; Fiber: 1g; Sugar: 2.2g; Protein: 8.2g

Flavorsome Ricotta Cheese Cake

Prep time: 15 minutes | Cook time: 30 minutes | Serves: 8

3 eggs, beaten
1 teaspoon baking powder
½ cup ghee, melted

1 cup almond flour
⅓ cup Erythritol
1 cup ricotta cheese, soft

Add all the recipe ingredients into the bowl and mix until well combined. Pour batter into the greased air fryer basket and place into the air fryer. Cook at almost 350 degrees F for 30 minutes. Slice and serve.

Nutritional information: Calories: 374; Fat: 25g; Total Carbs: 7.3g; Net Carbs: 3g; Fiber: 0g; Sugar: 6g; Protein: 12.3g

Erythritol Pineapple Slices

Prep time: 15 minutes | Cook time: 20 minutes | Serves: 4

4 pineapple slices	2 tablespoons Erythritol
1 teaspoon cinnamon	

Add pineapple slices, sweetener, and cinnamon into the ziplock bag. Shake well and keep in the refrigerator for 30 minutes. At 350 degrees F, preheat your air fryer. Place pineapples slices into the air fryer basket and cook for 20 minutes. Turn halfway through. Serve and enjoy.

Nutritional information: Calories: 391; Fat: 24g; Total Carbs: 38.5g; Net Carbs: 13g; Fiber: 3.5g; Sugar: 21g; Protein: 6.6g

Simple Blueberry Muffins

Prep time: 15 minutes | Cook time: 14 minutes | Serves: 5

1 egg	⅔ cup almond flour
1 teaspoon baking powder	2 tablespoons erythritol
3 tablespoons butter, melted	⅓ cup unsweetened almond
¾ cup blueberries	milk

Spray silicone muffins molds with cooking spray and set aside. Add all the recipe ingredients into the bowl and mix until well combined. Pour batter into the prepared molds and place into the air fryer basket. Cook at almost 320 degrees F for 14 minutes. Serve and enjoy.

Nutritional information: Calories: 327; Fat: 14.2g; Total Carbs: 47.2g; Net Carbs: 23g; Fiber: 1.7g; Sugar: 24.8g; Protein: 4.4g

Tasty Berry Cobbler

Prep time: 15 minutes | Cook time: 10 minutes | Serves: 6

1 egg, lightly beaten	1 cup almond flour
1 tablespoon butter, melted	½ cup raspberries, sliced
2 teaspoons swerve	½ cup strawberries, sliced
½ teaspoon vanilla	

At 360 degrees F, preheat your air fryer. Add sliced strawberries and raspberries into the air fryer basket. Sprinkle sweetener over berries. Mix together almond flour, vanilla, and butter in the bowl. Add egg in almond flour mixture and stir well to combine. Spread almond flour mixture over sliced berries. Cover dish with foil and place into the air fryer and cook for almost 10 minutes. Serve and enjoy.

Nutritional information: Calories: 192; Fat: 9.3g; Total Carbs: 27.1g; Net Carbs: 14g; Fiber: 1.4g; Sugar: 19g; Protein: 3.2g

Chocolate Cashew Pie

Prep time: 15 minutes | Cook time: 18 minutes | Serves: 8

1 egg	⅓ cup heavy cream
2 oz. cashews, crushed	1 oz. dark chocolate, melted
½ teaspoon baking soda	1 tablespoon butter

1 teaspoon vinegar	1 cup coconut flour

Crack 1 egg in a suitable bowl and beat using a hand mixer. Stir in coconut flour and stir well. Add butter, vinegar, baking soda, heavy cream, and melted chocolate and stir well. Toss in cashews and mix well. At 350 degrees F, preheat your air fryer. Add prepared dough in air fryer basket and flatten it into a pie shape. Cook for almost 18 minutes. Slice and serve.

Nutritional information: Calories: 204; Fat: 9g; Total Carbs: 27g; Net Carbs: 14g; Fiber: 2.4g; Sugar: 15g; Protein: 1.3g

Cinnamon Pumpkin Cookies

Prep time: 15 minutes | Cook time: 8 minutes | Serves: 8

¼ cup almond flour	1 tablespoon coconut flakes
½ cup pumpkin puree	½ teaspoon cinnamon
3 tablespoons swerve	Pinch of salt
½ teaspoon baking soda	

At 360 degrees F, preheat your air fryer. Add all the recipe ingredients into the bowl and mix until well combined. Grease its air fryer basket with cooking spray. Make cookies from bowl mixture and place into the air fryer and cook for 8 minutes. Serve and enjoy.

Nutritional information: Calories: 157; Fat: 1.3g; Total Carbs: 1.3g; Net Carbs: 0g; Fiber: 1g; Sugar: 2.2g; Protein: 8.2g

Erythritol Vanilla Butter Pie

Prep time: 15 minutes | Cook time: 20 minutes | Serves: 8

1 egg	1 cup almond flour
2 tablespoons erythritol	1 teaspoon baking soda
½ cup butter, melted	1 tablespoon vinegar
1 teaspoon vanilla	

Mix almond flour and baking soda in a suitable bowl. In a separate bowl, whisk the egg with sweetener and vanilla. Pour whisk egg, vinegar, and butter in almond flour and mix until dough is formed. At 340 degrees F, preheat your air fryer. Roll dough using the rolling pin in air fryer basket size. Place rolled dough in air fryer basket and cook for 20 minutes. Slice and serve.

Nutritional information: Calories: 258; Fat: 12.4g; Total Carbs: 34.3g; Net Carbs: 3g; Fiber: 1g; Sugar: 17g; Protein: 3.2g

Choco Chips Cookies with Macadamia Nuts

Prep time: 15 minutes | Cook time: 15 minutes | Serves:4

1 egg	crushed
3 tablespoons butter	1 cup almond flour
1 teaspoon vanilla	2 tablespoons unsweetened
¼ teaspoon baking powder	chocolate chips
2 tablespoons macadamia nuts,	Pinch of salt

In a suitable bowl, beat egg using a hand mixer. Stir in almond flour, butter, vanilla, baking powder, and salt and stir well. Add Chocó chips and macadamia nuts and mix until dough is formed. At 360 degrees F, preheat your air fryer. Make cookies from dough and place into the air fryer and cook for almost 15 minutes. Serve and enjoy.

Nutritional information: Calories: 284; Fat: 16g; Total Carbs: 31.6g; Net Carbs: 12g; Fiber: 0.9g; Sugar: 6.6g; Protein: 3.7g

Coconut Cheese Muffins

Prep time: 15 minutes | Cook time: 10 minutes | Serves: 8

1 egg	2 teaspoons erythritol
1 teaspoon baking soda	1 teaspoon vinegar
1 cup almond flour	1 cup cream cheese
2 tablespoons coconut flakes	Pinch of salt

Beat cream cheese and egg in a suitable bowl until well combined. Add almond flour, vinegar, baking soda, coconut flakes, sweetener, and salt and beat until well combined. At 360 degrees F, preheat your air fryer. Pour batter into silicone muffin molds and place into the air fryer. Cook for almost 10 minutes. Serve and enjoy.

Nutritional information: Calories: 116; Fat: 4.3 g; Total Carbs: 32.9g; Net Carbs: 12g; Fiber: 2.5g; Sugar: 29g; Protein: 1.6g

Walnut Banana Split

Prep time: 15 minutes | Cook time: 15 minutes | Serves: 8

3 tablespoons coconut oil	lengthwise
1 cup panko breadcrumbs	3 tablespoons sugar
½ cup of corn flour	¼ teaspoon ground cinnamon
2 eggs	2 tablespoons walnuts,
4 bananas, peeled and halved	chopped

In a suitable skillet, melt the coconut oil over medium heat and cook the breadcrumbs for about 4 minutes or until golden brown and crumbly, stirring constantly. Transfer the breadcrumbs to a shallow bowl and set aside to cool. In a second bowl, place the cornmeal. In a third bowl, beat the eggs. Coat the banana slices with the flour, dip them in the eggs and finally coat them evenly with the breadcrumbs. In a suitable bowl, mix the sugar and cinnamon. Set the cook time to 10 minutes and set the temperature to 280 degrees F on the air fryer. Arrange banana slices in Air Fry Basket and sprinkle with cinnamon sugar. Transfer banana slices to plates to cool slightly. Sprinkle with chopped walnuts.

Nutritional information: Calories: 416; Fat: 8.3 g; Total Carbs: 22.9g; Net Carbs: 8g; Fiber: 0.5g; Sugar: 19g; Protein: 60.6g

Vanilla Chocolate Soufflé

Prep time: 15 minutes | Cook time: 14 minutes | Serves: 2

⅓ cup milk	¼ cup sugar-free chocolate
2 tablespoons butter soft to melted	chips
	2 egg whites
1 tablespoon flour	½ teaspoon of cream of tartar
2 tablespoons Splenda	½ teaspoon of vanilla extract
1 egg yolk	

Grease the ramekins with spray oil or softened butter. Sprinkle with any sugar alternative, make sure to cover them. At 330 degrees F, preheat your air fryer. Melt the chocolate in a microwave-safe bowl. Mix every 30 seconds until fully melted. Or use a double boiler method. Melt the 1 and a ½ tablespoons of butter over low-medium heat in a pan. When the butter has melted, then whisk in the flour. Keep whisking until thickened. Then turn the heat off. Add the egg whites with cream of tartar, with the whisk attachment, in a stand mixer, mix until peaks forms. Meanwhile, combine the ingredients in a melted chocolate bowl, add the flour mixture and melted butter to chocolate, and blend. Add in the vanilla extract, egg yolks, remaining sugar alternative. Fold the egg white peaks gently with the ingredients into the bowl. Add the mix into ramekins about ¾ full of five-ounce ramekins Let it air fry for 12-14 minutes, or until done.

Nutritional information: Calories: 506; Fat: 48.3 g; Total Carbs: 58.9g; Net Carbs: 23g; Fiber: 6.5g; Sugar: 83.9g; Protein: 12.6g

Coconut Butter Cookies

Prep time: 15 minutes | Cook time: 12 minutes | Serves: 30

8 oz. cream cheese	1 cup swerve
1 teaspoon vanilla	¾ cup butter, softened
1 tablespoon baking powder	1 ¼ cup coconut flour
¾ cup coconut flakes	Pinch of salt

At 325 degrees F, preheat your air fryer. Beat cream cheese, butter, and sweetener in a suitable bowl using a hand mixer until fluffy. Add vanilla and stir well. Stir in baking powder, coconut flour, and salt and mix until well combined. Add coconut flakes and mix to combine. Make cookies from mixture and place on a plate. Place cookies in batches in the preheated Air Fryer and cook for 12 minutes. Serve and enjoy.

Nutritional information: Calories: 551; Fat: 29.3 g; Total Carbs: 73.9g; Net Carbs: 23g; Fiber: 3.5g; Sugar: 55.9g; Protein: 5g

Splenda Carrot Cake

Prep time: 15 minutes | Cook time: 40 minutes | Serves: 8

1 ¼ cups all-purpose flour	2 cups carrots, grated
1 teaspoon pumpkin pie spice	2 eggs
1 teaspoon baking powder	½ teaspoon baking soda
¾ cup Splenda	¾ cup canola oil

At 350 degrees F, preheat your Air Fryer. Spray the cake pan with oil spray. Dust flour over that. In a suitable bowl, combine the baking powder, pumpkin pie spice, flour, and baking soda. In another bowl, mix the eggs, oil, and sugar alternative. Now combine the dry to wet ingredients. Add ½ of the dry ingredients first mix and the other ½ of the dry mixture. Add in the grated carrots. Add the prepared cake batter to the greased cake pan. Place the cake pan in the basket of the air fryer. Let it Air fry for ½ an hour, but do not let the top too brown. If the top is browning, add a piece of foil over the top of the cake. Air fry it until a toothpick comes out clean, 35-40 minutes in total. Let the cake cool down before serving.

Nutritional information: Calories 399; Fat: 13 g; Total Carbs: 52.9g; Net Carbs: 18g; Fiber: 8.8g; Sugar: 3.9g; Protein: 19.6g

Low Carb Cheesecake Muffins

Prep time: 15 minutes | Cook time: 30 minutes | Serves: 18

½ cup Splenda	2 eggs
1 ½ cup cream cheese	1 teaspoon vanilla Extract

At 300 degrees F, preheat your air fryer. Spray the muffin pan with oil. In a suitable bowl, add the sugar alternative, vanilla extract, and cream cheese. Mix well. Add in the eggs gently, 1 at a time. Do not over mix the batter. Let it air fry for 25 to 30 minutes, or until cooked. Serve.

Nutritional information: Calories 116; Fat: 2.3 g; Total Carbs: 18.9g; Net Carbs: 7g; Fiber: 4.5g; Sugar: 2.2g; Protein: 6g

Chocolate Donut Holes

Prep time: 15 minutes | Cook time: 12 minutes | Serves: 32

6 tablespoons Splenda	1 cup flour

½ teaspoon baking soda
6 tablespoons unsweetened cocoa powder
3 tablespoon of butter
1 egg

½ teaspoon baking powder
2 tablespoons unsweetened chocolate chopped
¼ cup plain yogurt

In a suitable mixing bowl, combine the baking powder, baking soda, and flour. Then add in the cocoa powder and sugar alternative. In a mug or microwave-safe bowl, melt the butter and the unsweetened chocolate. Mix every 15 seconds and make sure they melt together and combine well. Set it aside to cool it down. In that big mixing bowl from before, add in the yogurt and the egg. Stir in the melted butter and chocolate mixture. Cover the bowl with wrap and let it chill in the refrigerator for 30 minutes. To make the donut balls, take out the batter from the fridge. Scoop out sufficient batter so a donut ball will form with your hands. You can use oil on your hands if the dough is too sticky. Spray the oil on the air fryer basket and sprinkle with flour and let it preheat to 350 degrees F. Work in batches and add the balls in 1 single layer. Let it Air fry for almost 10-12 minutes until they are done. Take out from air fryer, let it cool and serve hot or cold.
Nutritional information: Calories 213; Fat: 4.1 g; Total Carbs: 37.9g; Net Carbs: 17g; Fiber: 1.5g; Sugar: 1.9g; Protein: 6.6g

Low Carb Peanut Butter Cookies

Prep time: 15 minutes | Cook time: 10 minutes | Serves: 24

1 cup peanut butter
1 whisked egg

1 teaspoon Liquid stevia drops
1 cup sugar alternative

Mix all the recipe ingredients into a dough. Make 24 balls with your hands from the combined dough. On a cookie sheet or cutting board, press the dough balls with the help of a fork to form a crisscross pattern. Add six cookies to the basket of air fryer in a single layer. Cook in batches. Let them Air Fry, for 8-10 minutes, at 325 degrees F. Let the cookies cool for 1 minute, then with care, take the cookies out. Keep baking the rest of the peanut butter cookies in batches. Let them cool completely and serve.
Nutritional information: Calories: 175; Fat: 13.1g; Total Carbs: 14g; Net Carbs: 7g; Fiber: 0.8g; Sugar: 8.9g; Protein: 0.7g

Banana Chocolate Muffins

Prep time: 15 minutes | Cook time: 30 minutes | Serves: 8

Wet Mix
3 tablespoons of milk
1 teaspoon of Nutella
4 Cavendish size, ripe bananas
½ cup sugar
1 teaspoon of vanilla essence
2 large eggs
Dry Mix
1 teaspoon of baking powder

1 ¼ cup of whole wheat flour
1 teaspoon of baking soda
1 teaspoon of cinnamon
2 tablespoons of cocoa powder
1 teaspoon of salt
Optional
1 handful chopped walnuts
Fruits, Dried slices
Chocolate sprinkles

With the fork, in a suitable bowl, mash up the bananas, add all the wet ingredients to it, and mix well. Sift all the dry ingredients so they combine well. Add into the wet ingredients. Carefully fold both ingredients together. Do not over mix. Then add in the diced walnuts, slices of dried up fruits, and chocolate sprinkles. Let the air fryer preheat to 250 degrees F. Add the batter into muffin cups before that, spray them with oil generously. Air fryer them for at least ½ an hour, or until a toothpick comes out clean. Serve.
Nutritional information: Calories: 239; Fat: 48.3 g; Total Carbs: 98g; Net Carbs: 44g; Fiber: 2.5g; Sugar: 4.9g; Protein: 7.6g

Butter Cheesecake

Prep time: 15 minutes | Cook time: 28 minutes | Serves: 6

For crust:
2 tablespoons butter, melted
¼ teaspoon cinnamon
1 tablespoon swerve
½ cup almond flour
Pinch of salt

For Cheesecake:
1 egg
½ teaspoon vanilla
½ cup swerve
8 oz. cream cheese

At 280 degrees F, preheat your air fryer. Grease its air fryer basket with cooking spray. Add all crust ingredients into the bowl and mix until combined. Transfer crust mixture into the prepared baking dish and press down into the bottom of the dish. Place dish in the preheated Air Fryer and cook for 12 minutes. In a suitable bowl, beat cream cheese using a hand mixer until smooth. Stir in vanilla, egg, and salt and stir to combine. Pour cream cheese mixture over cooked crust and cook for 16 minutes. Allow to cool completely. Slice and serve.
Nutritional information: Calories: 276; Fat: 2.1 g; Total Carbs: 65.9g; Net Carbs: 23g; Fiber: 4.5g; Sugar: 59g; Protein: 2.6g

Simple & Tasty Brownies

Prep time: 15 minutes | Cook time: 5 minutes | Serves: 2

2 tablespoons of baking chips
⅓ cup of almond flour
1 egg
½ teaspoon of baking powder
3 tablespoons of powdered sweetener sugar alternative

2 tablespoons of cocoa powder unsweetened
2 tablespoons of chopped pecans
4 tablespoons of melted butter

Let the air fryer preheat to 350 degrees F In a suitable bowl, add cocoa powder, almond flour, Swerve sugar substitute, and baking powder, give it a good mix. Add melted butter and crack in the egg in the dry ingredients. Mix well until combined and smooth. Fold in the chopped pecans and baking chips. Take 2 ramekins to grease them well with softened butter. Add the batter to them. Air fry for 10 minutes. Make sure to place them as far from the heat source from the top in the air fryer. Take the brownies out from the air fryer and let them cool for 5 minutes. Serve with your favorite toppings and enjoy.
Nutritional information: Calories: 192; Fat: 9.3g; Total Carbs: 27.1g; Net Carbs: 12g; Fiber: 1.4g; Sugar: 19g; Protein: 3.2g

Coconut Pineapple Bites

Prep time: 15 minutes | Cook time: 10 minutes | Serves: 4

½ of pineapple
¼ cup desiccated coconut
1 tablespoon fresh mint leaves,

minced
1 cup vanilla yogurt

Peel the pineapple and cut into long 1-to 2-inch-thick sticks. In a dish, place the coconut. Coat the pineapple sticks with coconut evenly. Select the "Air Fry" and set the cooking time to 10 minutes. Set the temperature at 390 degrees F. Arrange the pineapple sticks in a lightly greased air fry basket and insert it in the air fryer. Meanwhile, for a dip in a suitable bowl, mix mint and yogurt. Serve pineapple sticks with yogurt dip.
Nutritional information: Calories: 477; Fat: 13.3 g; Total Carbs: 89.5g; Net Carbs: 33g; Fiber: 6.5g; Sugar: 59.2g; Protein: 5.4g

Buttery Shortbread Sticks

Prep time: 15 minutes | Cook time: 22 minutes | Serves: 10

⅓ cup caster sugar
1 ⅔ cups plain flour

¾ cup butter

In a suitable bowl, mix the sugar and flour. Add the butter and stir until it makes a smooth dough. Cut the dough into ten equal-sized sticks. With a fork, lightly prick the sticks. Place the sticks into the lightly greased baking pan. Set the cook time to 12 minutes. At 355 degrees F, preheat your air fryer. Arrange the pan in preheat air fry basket and insert it in the air fryer. Place the baking pan to cool for about 5-10 minutes. Serve.
Nutritional information: Calories: 416; Fat: 8.3 g; Total Carbs: 22.9g; Net Carbs: 8g; Fiber: 0.5g; Sugar: 19g; Protein: 6.6g

Blueberry Muffins

Prep time: 15 minutes | Cook time: 14 minutes | Serves: 8

½ cup of sugar alternative
1 ⅓ cup of flour
⅓ cup of oil
2 teaspoons of baking powder
¼ teaspoon of salt
1 egg

½ cup of milk
8 muffin cups foil with paper liners or silicone baking cups
⅔ cup of frozen and thawed blueberries, or fresh

Let the air fryer preheat to 330 degrees F. In a suitable bowl, sift together baking powder, sugar, salt, and flour. Mix well In another bowl, add milk, oil, and egg mix it well. To the dry ingredients to the egg mix, mix until combined but do not over mix Add the blueberries carefully. Pour the mixture into muffin paper cups or muffin baking tray Put 4 muffin cups in the air fryer basket. Cook for 12-14 minutes, at 330 degrees F, or until when touch lightly the tops, it should spring back. Cook the remaining muffins accordingly. Serve.
Nutritional information: Calories: 391; Fat: 24g; Total Carbs: 38.5g; Net Carbs: 10g; Fiber: 3.5g; Sugar: 21g; Protein: 6.6g

Lemon Cookies

Prep time: 15 minutes | Cook time: 5 minutes | Serves: 24

½ teaspoon of salt
½ cup of coconut flour
½ cup of unsalted butter softened
½ teaspoon of liquid vanilla stevia
½ cup of swerve granular sweetener

1 tablespoon lemon juice
¼ teaspoon lemon extract, it is optional
2 egg yolks
For icing
3 teaspoons of lemon juice
⅔ cup of Swerve confectioner's sweetener

In a stand mixer bowl, add baking soda, coconut flour, salt and Swerve, mix until well combined. Then add the butter softened to the dry ingredients, mix well. Add all the remaining ingredients but do not add in the yolks yet. Adjust the seasoning of lemon flavor and sweetness to your liking, add more if needed. Add the yolk and combine well. Spread a big piece of plastic wrap on a flat surface, put the batter in the center, roll around the dough and make it into a log form. At 325 degrees F, preheat your air fryer. Cut in ¼ inch cookies, place as many cookies in the air fryer basket in 1 single, do not overcrowd the basket. Air fry for 3-5 minutes, or until the cookies' edges become brown. Once all cookies are air fried, pour the icing over. Serve.
Nutritional information: Calories: 327; Fat: 14.2g; Total Carbs: 47.2g; Net Carbs: 23g; Fiber: 1.7g; Sugar: 24.8g; Protein: 4.4g

Berry Tacos

Prep time: 15 minutes | Cook time: 5 minutes | Serves: 2

2 soft shell tortillas
4 tablespoons strawberry jelly
¼ cup fresh blueberries

¼ cup fresh raspberries
2 tablespoons powdered sugar

Spread 2 tablespoons of strawberry jelly over each tortilla. Top each with berries evenly and sprinkle with powdered sugar. Arrange the tortillas in air fry basket and insert it in the air fryer. Cook in your air fryer at 300 degrees F for 5 minutes. Serve.
Nutritional information: Calories: 276; Fat: 2.1 g; Total Carbs: 65.9g; Net Carbs: 14g; Fiber: 4.5g; Sugar: 59g; Protein: 2.6g

Enticing Grain-Free Cakes

Prep time: 15 minutes | Cook time: 4 minutes | Serves: 2

2 large eggs
½ cup of chocolate chips, you can use dark chocolate
2 tablespoons of coconut flour
2 tablespoons of honey as a sugar substitute

A dash of salt
½ teaspoon of baking soda
Butter and cocoa powder for 2 small ramekins
¼ cup of butter or grass-fed butter

At 370 degrees F, preheat your air fryer. Grease the ramekins with soft butter and sprinkle with cocoa powder. It will stick to the butter. Turn the ramekins upside down, so excess cocoa powder will fall out. Set it aside. In a double boiler or microwave, safe bowl, melt the butter and chocolate chips together, stir every 15 seconds. Make sure to mix well to combine. In a suitable bowl, crack the eggs and whisk with either honey or sugar, mix well. Add in the salt, baking soda, and coconut flour. Then add the melted chocolate chip and butter mixture to the egg, flour, and honey mixture. Mix well, so everything combines. Pour the batter in those 2 prepared ramekins. Let them air fry for 10 minutes. Then take them out from the air fryer and let it cool for 3 to 4 minutes. Top with mint leaves and coconut cream, raspberries, if you want. Serve right away and enjoy.
Nutritional information: Calories: 284; Fat: 16g; Total Carbs: 31.6g; Net Carbs: 8g; Fiber: 0.9g; Sugar: 6.6g; Protein: 3.7g

Air Fryer Reduced-Sugar Cookies

Prep time: 35 minutes | Cook time: 15 minutes | Serves: 10

1 teaspoon of baking powder
1 cup of almond flour
3 tablespoons of natural low-calorie sweetener
1 large egg

3-½ tablespoons raspberry reduced-sugar preserves
4 tablespoons of softened cream cheese

In a suitable bowl, add egg, baking powder, flour, sweetener, and cream cheese, mix well until a dough wet forms. Chill the dough in the fridge for almost 20 minutes, until dough is cool enough. And then form into balls. Let the air fryer preheat to 400 degrees F, add the parchment paper to the air fryer basket. Make ten balls from the dough and put them in the prepared air fryer basket. With your clean hands, make an indentation from your thumb in the center of every cookie. Add 1 teaspoon of the raspberry preserve in the thumb hole. Air fry in the preheated Air Fryer for 7 minutes, or until light golden brown to your liking. Let the cookies cool completely in the parchment paper for almost 15 minutes, or they will fall apart.
Nutritional information: Calories: 204; Fat: 9g; Total Carbs: 27g; Net Carbs: 12g; Fiber: 2.4g; Sugar: 15g; Protein: 1.3g

Tasty Cheesecake Bites

Prep time: 15 minutes | Cook time: 2 minutes | Serves: 12

8 ounces cream cheese, softened	4 tablespoons heavy cream, divided
½ cup plus 2 tablespoons sugar, divided	½ teaspoon vanilla extract
	½ cup almond flour

In a stand mixer, mix add cream cheese, ½ cup sugar, vanilla extract and 2 tablespoons of heavy cream. Using a paddle attachment, pour the mixture onto a baking sheet lined with baking paper. Freeze for about 30 minutes. In a suitable bowl, place the remaining cream. In another bowl, add the almond flour and remaining sugar and mix well. Dip each cheesecake bite into the cream and then top with the flour mixture. Set the air frying time to 2 minutes on your air fryer. Set the temperature to 300 degrees F. Place pan in air fry basket and place in the air fryer.

Nutritional information: Calories: 551; Fat: 29.3 g; Total Carbs: 73.9g; Net Carbs: 41g; Fiber: 3.5g; Sugar: 55.9g; Protein: 5g

Chocolate-Almond Candies

Prep time: 15 minutes | Cook time: 2 minutes | Serves: 4

1-ounce almonds, crushed	2 tablespoons peanut butter
1-ounce dark chocolate	2 tablespoons heavy cream

At 390 degrees F, preheat your air fryer. Chop the dark chocolate bar and put it in the preheated air fryer mold. Add peanut butter and heavy cream. Stir the mixture and transfer in the air fryer. Cook it for 2 minutes or until it starts to be melt. Then line the air fryer tray with parchment. Put the crushed almonds on the tray in 1 layer. Then pour the cooked chocolate mixture over the almonds. Flatten gently if needed and let it cool. Crack the cooked chocolate layer into the candies.

Nutritional information: Calories: 398; Fat: 37.8 g; Total Carbs: 2.5g; Net Carbs: 1g; Fiber: 0.2g; Sugar: 0.5g; Protein: 3.6g

Chocolate Oatmeal Cookies

Prep time: 15 minutes | Cook time: 8 minutes | Serves: 8

⅓ cup of tahini	2 tablespoons of almond flour
¼ cup of walnuts	1 teaspoon of vanilla
¼ cup of maple syrup	1 cup of gluten-free oat flakes
¼ cup of chocolate chunks	1 teaspoon of cinnamon
¼ teaspoon of salt	

At 350 degrees F, preheat your air fryer. In a big bowl, add cinnamon, the maple syrup, the tahini, salt, and vanilla. Mix well, then add in the walnuts, oat flakes, and almond meal. Then fold in the chocolate chips gently. Now the mix is ready, take a full tablespoon of mixture, separate into 8 amounts. Wet damp hands, press them on a baking tray or with a spatula. Place 4 cookies, or more depending on your air fryer size, line the air fryer basket with parchment paper in 1 single layer. Let them cook for 5-6 minutes at 350 degrees F, air fry for more minutes if you like them crispy. Serve.

Nutritional information: Calories: 416; Fat: 8.3 g; Total Carbs: 22.9g; Net Carbs: 11g; Fiber: 0.5g; Sugar: 19g; Protein: 60.6g

Eggless & Vegan Cake

Prep time: 15 minutes | Cook time: 10 minutes | Serves: 8

2 tablespoons olive oil	3 tablespoons milk:
¼ cup all-purpose flour	2 drops of vanilla extract
2 tablespoons cocoa powder	4 raw almonds for decoration
⅛ teaspoon baking soda	roughly chopped
3 tablespoons sugar	a pinch of salt
1 tablespoon of warm water	

Let the air fryer preheat to 390 degrees F for at least 2 minutes. In a suitable bowl, add sugar, milk, water, and oil. Whisk until a smooth batter forms. Now add salt, all-purpose flour, cocoa powder, and baking soda, sift them into wet ingredients, mix to form a paste Spray the four-inch baking pan with oil and pour the batter into it. Then add in the chopped up almonds on top of it. Put the baking pan in the preheated air fryer. And cook for 10 minutes. Take out from the air fryer. Let it cool completely before slicing.

Nutritional information: Calories: 351; Fat: 20.3 g; Total Carbs: 40.9g; Net Carbs: 14g; Fiber: 0.5g; Sugar: 35.5g; Protein:3.6g

Honey Donuts

Prep time: 15 minutes | Cook time: 8 minutes | Serves: 8

1 cup coconut flour	⅔ cup apple cider vinegar:
4 eggs	1 teaspoon cinnamon
4 tablespoons coconut oil, melted	3 tablespoons honey
1 teaspoon baking soda	a pinch of salt

Let the air fryer pre-heat to 350 degrees F. Spray oil on a baking tray, spray a generous amount of grease with melted coconut oil. In a suitable bowl, add apple cider vinegar, honey, melted coconut oil, salt mix well, then crack the eggs and mix it all together. In another bowl, sift the coconut flour, baking soda, and cinnamon so that the dry ingredients will combine well. Add the wet ingredients and mix with the dry ingredients until completely combined. Pour the prepared batter into the prepared donut baking pan. And add the batter into cavities. Let it air fry for 10 minutes or 8 minutes at 350 degrees F, or until light golden brown. Serve right away and enjoy.

Nutritional information: Calories: 426; Fat: 36.3 g; Total Carbs: 22.1g; Net Carbs: 10g; Fiber: 2g; Sugar: 10.9g; Protein: 6.6g

Vanilla Chocolate Bites

Prep time: 15 minutes | Cook time: 13 minutes | Serves: 8

2 cups plain flour	1 teaspoon vanilla extract
2 tablespoons cocoa powder	¾ cup chilled butter
½ cup icing sugar	¼ cup chocolate, chopped into
Pinch of ground cinnamon	eight chunks

In a suitable bowl, mix the flour, icing sugar, cocoa powder, cinnamon, and vanilla extract. Cut the butter and mix to make a smooth dough. Divide the dough into 8 equal-sized balls. Insert 1 chocolate chunk in the center of each dough ball and cover with the dough thoroughly. Place the balls into the baking pan. Set the cook time to 8 minutes. Set the temperature at 355 degrees F. Arrange this pan in air fry basket and insert it in the air fryer. After 8 minutes of cook, set the temperature at 320 degrees F for 5 minutes. Place the hot baking pan onto the wire rack to cool before serving.

Nutritional information: Calories: 56; Fat: 4.3 g; Total Carbs:

2.9g; Net Carbs: 1g; Fiber: 0.3g; Sugar: 3.9g; Protein: 0.6g

Greek Apple Fritter

Prep time: 15 minutes | Cook time: 14 minutes | Serves: 3

½ apple peeled, chopped	⅛ teaspoon of ground nutmeg
½ cup of all-purpose flour	3 tablespoon of Greek yogurt
1 teaspoon of baking powder	fat-free
¼ teaspoon of kosher salt	1 tablespoon of butter
½ teaspoon of ground	for the glaze
cinnamon	2 tablespoons of powdered
2 tablespoon of brown sugar or	sugar
sugar alternative	½ tablespoon of water

In a suitable mixing bowl, add baking powder, nutmeg, brown sugar, flour, cinnamon, and salt. Mix it well. With the help of a fork or cutter, slice the butter until crumbly. It should look like wet sand. Add the chopped apple and coat well, then add fat-free Greek yogurt. keep stirring or tossing until everything together, and a crumbly dough forms. Put the prepared dough on a clean surface and with your hands, knead it into a ball form. Flatten the dough in an oval shape about a half-inch thick. Grease the air fryer's basket with cook spray generously. Put the dough in the air fry for 12-14 minutes at 375 degrees F cook until light golden brown. For making the glaze mix, the ingredients, and with the help of a brush, pour over the apple fritter when it comes out from the air fryer. Slice and serve after cooling for 5 minutes.
Nutritional information: Calories: 157; Fat: 1.3g; Total Carbs: 1.3g; Net Carbs: 1g; Fiber: 1g; Sugar: 2.2g; Protein: 8.2g

Yummy Berry Cheesecake

Prep time: 15 minutes | Cook time: 50 minutes | Serves: 8

½ cup raspberries	¼ cup of strawberries
2 blocks of softened cream	2 eggs
cheese, 8 ounce	¼ cup of blackberries
1 teaspoon raspberry or vanilla	1 cup and 2 tablespoons of
extract:	sugar

In a big mixing bowl, whip the sugar-alternative confectioner sweetener and cream cheese, mix whip until smooth and creamy. Then add in the raspberry or vanilla extract and eggs, again mix well. In a food processor, pulse the berries and fold into the cream cheese mix with 2 extra tablespoons of sweetener. Take a springform pan and spray the oil generously, pour in the mixture. Put the pan in the air fryer, let it air fryer, and cook for 10 minutes at 300 degrees F. Lower the air fryer's temperature to 400 degrees F and cook for 40 minutes. Take out from the air fryer and cool a bit before chilling in the fridge. Keep in the fridge for 2-4 hours or as long as you have time. Slice and serve.
Nutritional information: Calories: 258; Fat: 12.4g; Total Carbs: 34.3g; Net Carbs: 12g; Fiber: 1g; Sugar: 17g; Protein: 3.2g

Vanilla Cobbler with Hazelnut

Prep time: 15 minutes | Cook time: 30 minutes | Serves: 4

¼ cup heavy cream	1 teaspoon vanilla extract
1 egg, beaten	2 tablespoons butter, softened
½ cup almond flour	¼ cup hazelnuts, chopped

Mix up heavy cream, egg, almond flour, vanilla extract, and butter. Then whisk the mixture gently. At 325 degrees F, preheat your air fryer. Layer its air fryer basket with baking paper. Pour ½ part of the batter in the baking pan, flatten it gently and top with hazelnuts. Then pour the remaining batter over the hazelnuts and place the pan in the air fryer. Cook the cobbler for 30 minutes.
Nutritional information: Calories: 368; Fat: 32.8 g; Total Carbs: 0.6g; Net Carbs: 0g; Fiber: 0.1g; Sugar: 1.1g; Protein: 8.5g

Vanilla Muffins with Pecans

Prep time: 15 minutes | Cook time: 15 minutes | Serves: 12

4 eggs	1 tablespoon baking powder
1 teaspoon vanilla	½ cup pecans, chopped
¼ cup almond milk	½ teaspoon ground cinnamon
2 tablespoons butter, melted	2 teaspoons allspice
½ cup swerve	1 ½ cups almond flour
1 teaspoon psyllium husk	

At 370 degrees F, preheat your air fryer. Beat eggs, almond milk, vanilla, sweetener, and butter in a suitable bowl using a hand mixer until smooth. Add remaining recipe ingredients and mix until well combined. Pour batter into the silicone muffin molds and place into the air fryer basket in batches. Cook muffins for almost 15 minutes. Serve and enjoy.
Nutritional information: Calories: 404; Fat: 20.3 g; Total Carbs: 3.4g; Net Carbs: 1g; Fiber: 1g; Sugar: 1.2g; Protein: 3.4g

Banana Slices with Cardamom

Prep time: 15 minutes | Cook time: 15 minutes | Serves: 8

4 medium ripe bananas, peeled	½ teaspoon baking powder
⅓ cup rice flour, divided	½ teaspoon ground cardamom
2 tablespoons all-purpose flour	Pinch of salt
2 tablespoons corn flour	Water, as required
2 tablespoons desiccated	¼ cup sesame seeds
coconut	

In a suitable bowl, mix 2 tablespoons of rice flour, all-purpose flour, cornmeal, coconut, baking powder, cardamom and salt. Add the water and mix until a thick, smooth dough forms. In another bowl, place the remaining rice flour. In a third bowl, add the sesame seeds. Cut each banana in ½ and then cut each ½ into 2 pieces lengthwise. Dip the banana into the coconut mixture and then top with the remaining rice flour, followed by the sesame seeds. Select the "Air Fry" mode and set the cooking time to 15 minutes. Set the temperature to 390 degrees F. Arrange banana slices in air fry basket and place in air fryer. Transfer banana slices to plates to cool slightly.
Nutritional information: Calories: 148; Fat: 0.3 g; Total Carbs: 38.9g; Net Carbs: 13g; Fiber: 0.5g; Sugar: 33.9g; Protein: 0.6g

Chewy Donut Holes with Cinnamon

Prep time: 15 minutes | Cook time: 10 minutes | Serves: 6

¼ cup almond milk	1 tablespoon coconut oil,
¼ cup coconut sugar	melted
¼ teaspoon cinnamon	1 teaspoon baking powder
½ teaspoon salt	2 tablespoons aquafaba or
1 cup white all-purpose flour	liquid from canned chickpeas

In a suitable mixing bowl, mix the flour, sugar, and baking powder. Add the salt and cinnamon and mix until combined. Mix the almond milk, coconut oil, and aquafaba. Gently stir in the dry ingredients to the wet ingredients. Mix until well combined or until it forms a dough. Cover and set this dough in the refrigerator to rest for at least an hour. At 370 degrees F, preheat your air fryer. Male small balls of the prepared dough and place inside the air fryer and cook for almost 10 minutes. Do not shake the air fryer. Once cooked, sprinkle with sugar and cinnamon. Serve with your breakfast coffee.

Nutritional information: Calories: 416; Fat: 8.3 g; Total Carbs: 22.9g; Net Carbs: 9g; Fiber: 0.5g; Sugar: 19g; Protein: 1.6g

Chocolate Almond Cake

Prep time: 15 minutes | Cook time: 15 minutes | Serves: 4

1½ tablespoons almond flour	chocolate, chopped
3½ ounces unsalted butter	2 eggs
3½ ounces sugar free dark	3½ tablespoons swerve

At 375 degrees F, preheat your air fryer. and grease 4 regular sized ramekins. Microwave all chocolate bits with butter in a suitable bowl for about 3 minutes. Remove this melt from the microwave and whisk in the eggs and swerve. Add the flour and mix well until smooth. Transfer the mixture into the ramekins and arrange in the air fryer basket. Cook for about 10 minutes and dish out to serve.

Nutritional information: Calories: 398; Fat: 27 g; Total Carbs: 34.9g; Net Carbs: 14g; Fiber: 6.5g; Sugar: 6.9g; Protein: 11.6g

Coconut Cupcakes with Cardamom

Prep time: 15 minutes | Cook time: 5 minutes | Serves: 4

½ cup coconut flour	melted
⅓ cup coconut milk	1 teaspoon vanilla
2 eggs	A pinch of ground cardamom
1 tablespoon coconut oil,	½ cup coconut chips

Mix the flour, coconut milk, eggs, coconut oil, vanilla, and cardamom in a suitable bowl. Let it stand for 20 minutes. Spoon this prepared batter into a greased muffin tin. Cook at almost 230 degrees F for 4 to 5 minutes or until golden brown. Repeat with the remaining batter. Decorate your cupcakes with coconut chips. Serve

Nutritional information: Calories: 539; Fat: 17.5 g; Total Carbs: 79.2g; Net Carbs: 46g; Fiber: 4.5g; Sugar: 26.9g; Protein: 15.6g

Enticing Chocolate Cake

Prep time: 15 minutes | Cook time: 30 minutes | Serves: 6

2 eggs, beaten	1 ½ teaspoons baking powder
⅔ cup sour cream	1 teaspoon vanilla extract
1 cup almond flour	½ teaspoon pure rum extract
⅔ cup swerve	Chocolate Frosting:
⅓ cup coconut oil, softened	½ cup butter, softened
¼ cup cocoa powder	¼ cup cocoa powder
2 tablespoons chocolate chips,	1 cup powdered swerve
unsweetened	2 tablespoons milk

Mix all the recipe ingredients for the chocolate cake with a hand mixer on low speed. Scrape the batter into a cake pan. Air fry at 330 degrees F for 25 to 30 minutes. Transfer the cake to a wire rack Meanwhile, whip the butter and cocoa until smooth. Add the powdered swerve. Slowly and gradually, pour in the milk until your frosting reaches desired consistency. Whip until smooth and fluffy; then, frost the cooled cake. Place in your refrigerator for a couple of hours. Serve well chilled.

Nutritional information: Calories: 267; Fat: 15.2 g; Total Carbs: 13.9g; Net Carbs: 5g; Fiber: 0.1g; Sugar: 12.9g; Protein: 2.6g

Zucchini Bread with Chocolate Chips

Prep time: 15 minutes | Cook time: 15 minutes | Serves: 12

¼ teaspoon salt	squeezed
½ cup almond milk	1 tablespoon flax egg; 1
½ cup maple syrup	tablespoon flax meal + 3
½ cup sunflower oil	tablespoons. water
½ cup unsweetened cocoa	1 teaspoon apple cider vinegar
powder	1 teaspoon baking soda
1 cup oat flour	1 teaspoon vanilla extract
1 cup zucchini, shredded and	⅓ cup chocolate chips

At 350 degrees F, preheat your air fryer. Layer a suitable baking dish that will fit the air fryer with parchment paper. In a suitable bowl, combine the flax meal, zucchini, sunflower oil, maple syrup, vanilla, apple cider vinegar and milk. Add the oat flour, baking soda, cocoa powder, and salt. Mix until well combined. Add the chocolate chips. Pour over the baking dish and cook for almost 15 minutes or until a toothpick inserted in the middle comes out clean.

Nutritional information: Calories: 382; Fat: 32.5 g; Total Carbs: 3.2g; Net Carbs: 1g; Fiber: 0.2g; Sugar: 1.9g; Protein: 9.1g

Fluffy Strawberry Cake

Prep time: 15 minutes | Cook time: 30 minutes | Serves: 12

¼ cup butter, melted	12 egg whites
1 cup powdered erythritol	2 teaspoons cream of tartar
1 teaspoon strawberry extract	A pinch of salt

At 400 degrees F, preheat your air fryer. Beat all the egg whites and cream of tartar. Use a hand mixer and whisk until white and fluffy. Add the rest of the recipe ingredients except for the butter and whisk for another minute. Pour into a suitable baking dish. Place this dish in air fryer basket and cook for 30 minutes at 400 degrees F. Drizzle with melted butter once cooled.

Nutritional information: Calories: 413; Fat: 30.8 g; Total Carbs: 2.4g; Net Carbs: 0.5g; Fiber: 0.5g; Sugar: 1.3g; Protein: 1.6g

Dark Chocolate Soufflé

Prep time: 15 minutes | Cook time: 15 minutes | Serves: 6

3 eggs, separated	2 tablespoons heavy cream
1 teaspoon vanilla	2 tablespoons almond flour
¼ cup swerve	2 oz. dark chocolate, melted
5 tablespoons butter, melted	

Mix together melted chocolate and butter. In a suitable bowl, whisk egg yolk with sweetener until combined. Add almond flour, heavy cream, and vanilla and whisk well. In a separate bowl, whisk egg white s until soft peaks form. Add the egg white to the chocolate mixture slowly and fold well. Pour chocolate mixture into the ramekins and place into the air fryer. Cook at almost 330 degrees F for 12 minutes. Serve and enjoy.

Nutritional information: Calories: 386; Fat: 10.3 g; Total Carbs: 72.9g; Net Carbs: 23g; Fiber: 4.5g; Sugar: 59g; Protein: 2.6g

Fluffy Vanilla Butter Cake

Prep time: 15 minutes | Cook time: 35 minutes | Serves: 8

6 egg yolks
3 cups almond flour
2 teaspoons vanilla
1 egg, lightly beaten

¼ cup erythritol
1 cup butter
Pinch of salt

At 350 degrees F, preheat your air fryer. In a suitable bowl, beat butter and sweetener until fluffy. Add vanilla and egg yolks and beat until well combined. Add remaining ingredients and beat until combined. Pour batter into air fryer cake pan and place into the air fryer and cook for 35 minutes. Slice and serve.

Nutritional information: Calories: 426; Fat: 36.3 g; Total Carbs: 22.1g; Net Carbs: 10g; Fiber: 2g; Sugar: 10.9g; Protein: 6.6g

Fudgy Chocolate Brownies

Prep time: 15 minutes | Cook time: 16 minutes | Serves: 6

3 eggs
½ teaspoon baking powder
¾ cup erythritol
2 oz. dark chocolate

¾ cup butter softened
½ cup almond flour
¼ cup of cocoa powder

At 325 degrees F, preheat your air fryer. Grease its air fryer basket with cooking spray and set aside. In a suitable bowl, mix together chocolate and butter and microwave for 30 seconds or until melted. Stir well. Mix together almond flour, baking powder, cocoa powder, and sweetener. In a suitable bowl, beat eggs using a hand mixer. Add chocolate-butter mixture and beat until combined. Slowly stir in dry recipe ingredients and mix until well combined. Pour batter into the prepared dish and place into the air fryer. Cook for 16 minutes. Slice and serve.

Nutritional information: Calories: 477; Fat: 13.3 g; Total Carbs: 89.5g; Net Carbs: 41g; Fiber: 6.5g; Sugar: 59.2g; Protein: 5.4g

Yummy Peanut Butter Cookies

Prep time: 15 minutes | Cook time: 12 minutes | Serves: 5

1 egg
¼ cup erythritol

1 cup peanut butter

At 325 degrees F, preheat your air fryer. Add all the recipe ingredients into the bowl and mix until well combined. Make cookies from mixture and place into the air fryer and cook for 12 minutes. Serve and enjoy.

Nutritional information: Calories: 148; Fat: 0.3 g; Total Carbs: 38.9g; Net Carbs: 10g; Fiber: 0.5g; Sugar: 33.9g; Protein: 0.6g

Sweet Blackberry Cream

Prep time: 15 minutes | Cook time: 20 minutes | Serves: 6

2 cups blackberries
Juice of ½ lemon
2 tablespoons water

1 teaspoon vanilla extract
2 tablespoons swerve

In a suitable bowl, mix all the recipe ingredients and whisk well. Divide this into 6 ramekins, put them in a preheated air fryer and cook at almost 340 degrees F for 20 minutes. Cool down and serve.

Nutritional information: Calories: 23, Fat 0.2g; Total Carbs: 4.7g; Net Carbs: 1g; Fiber: 2.5g; Sugars: 2.4g; Protein: 0.7g

4 Weeks Meal Plan

Week 1

Day 1

Breakfast: Simple Tomato Cheese Sandwich
Lunch: Cheesy Patties
Snack: Cauliflower Wings with Buffalo Sauce
Dinner: Thyme Catfish
Dessert: Merengues

Day 2:

Breakfast: Cheddar Bacon Frittata
Lunch: Sesame Fennel
Snack: Stuffed Jalapeno Poppers
Dinner: Lemony Lamb Chops
Dessert: Peanut Butter Cookies

Day 3:

Breakfast: Fried Bacon with Pork Rinds
Lunch: Mozzarella Green Beans
Snack: Deviled Eggs with Ricotta
Dinner: Chicken in Bacon Wrap
Dessert: Mini Almond Cakes

Day 4:

Breakfast: Scrambled Eggs with Spinach
Lunch: Vegetarian Quesadillas
Snack: Enticing Jalapeno Poppers
Dinner: Greek Lamb Farfalle
Dessert: Peanuts Almond Biscuits

Day 5:

Breakfast: Tomatoes Hash with Cheddar Cheese
Lunch: Tomato Spinach Frittatas
Snack: Beef Meatballs with Chives
Dinner: Spicy Turkey Breast
Dessert: Cauliflower Rice Pudding

Day 6:

Breakfast: Classical French Frittata
Lunch: Green Bean Casserole
Snack: Mexican Beef Muffins with Tomato Sauce
Dinner: Baked Lamb with Tomato Pasta
Dessert: Butter Crumble

Day 7:

Breakfast: Grilled Butter Sandwich
Lunch: Broccoli and Asparagus
Snack: Eggplant Chips
Dinner: Crunchy Golden Nuggets
Dessert: Nuts Cookies

Week 2

Day 1:

Breakfast: Vanilla French Toast Sticks
Lunch: Carrots with Honey Glaze
Snack: Spicy Cocktail Wieners
Dinner: Cayenne Cumin Lamb
Dessert: Baked Plum Cream

Day 2:

Breakfast: Simple Cheddar-Omelet
Lunch: Asparagus with Almonds
Snack: Pickles with Egg Wash
Dinner: Buttered Roasted Whole Chicken
Dessert: Vanilla Yogurt Cake

Day 3:

Breakfast: Parmesan Spinach Muffins
Lunch: Cheese Spinach
Snack: Air Fried Shrimp & Bacon
Dinner: Cracker Pork Chops with Mustard
Dessert: Enticing Chocolate Cake

Day 4:

Breakfast: Mozzarella Eggs with Basil Pesto
Lunch: Potato-Nut Casserole Dish
Snack: Delicious Mushroom Pizzas
Dinner: Fish Packets
Dessert: Yummy Berry Cheesecake

Day 5:

Breakfast: Classical Eggs Ramekins
Lunch: Buttered Kale Mix
Snack: Salmon Bites with Coconut
Dinner: Easy Ritzy Chicken Nuggets
Dessert: Tasty Cheesecake Bites

Day 6:

Breakfast: Baked Eggs with Mascarpone
Lunch: Garlicky Vegetable Rainbow Fritters
Snack: Simple Pizza Bites
Dinner: Classic No Frills Turkey Breast
Dessert: Coconut Butter Cookies

Day 7:

Breakfast: Yummy Bagel Breakfast
Lunch: Italian Eggplant and Tomato Bites
Snack: Chicken Bites with Coconut
Dinner: Minty Tender Filet Mignon
Dessert: Coconut Cheese Muffins

Week 3

Day 1:

Breakfast: Sausage and Potato Frittata
Lunch: Garlic Provolone Asparagus
Snack: Bacon Pickle Spear Rolls
Dinner: Gorgeous Lamb Meatballs
Dessert: Delicious Walnut Bars

Day 2:

Breakfast: Coconut Muffins with Cinnamon
Lunch: Zucchinis and Arugula Salad
Snack: Squash Chips with Sauce
Dinner: Air Fryer Turkey Breast
Dessert: Fluffy Cocoa Cupcakes

Day 3:

Breakfast: Creamy Broccoli Omelet
Lunch: Cheddar Mushroom Cakes
Snack: Zucchini Chips with Cheese
Dinner: Steak and Vegetable Skewers
Dessert: Chocolate Cake with Raspberries

Day 4:

Breakfast: Flavorful Cheesy Frittata
Lunch: Buttery Mozzarella Eggplants
Snack: Bacon with Chocolate Coating
Dinner: Garlic Steak with Cheese Butter
Dessert: Chocolate Banana Brownie

Day 5:

Breakfast: Dill Eggs in Wonton
Lunch: Zucchini and Potato Polenta
Snack: Delectable Chaffles
Dinner: Air Fryer Chicken Wings
Dessert: Creamy Cheesecake Bites

Day 6:

Breakfast: Bacon Wrapped Eggs
Lunch: Awesome Mushroom Tots
Snack: Potato Pastries
Dinner: Flavorsome Beef Broccoli with Sauces
Dessert: Chocolate Peanut Butter Mug Cake

Day 7:

Breakfast: Baked Pancakes with Caramelized Apples
Lunch: Coconut Brussels Sprouts
Snack: Simple Curried Sweet Potato Fries
Dinner: Cajun Cheese Shrimp
Dessert: Chocolate Lava Cake

Week 4

Day 1:

Breakfast: Home-Made Potatoes with Paprika
Lunch: Flavorful Radish Salad
Snack: Garlicky Eggplant Chips
Dinner: Marinated Chicken Breasts
Dessert: Strawberry Muffins with Cinnamon

Day 2:

Breakfast: Mushroom Frittata with Parmesan
Lunch: Creamy Cauliflower Puree
Snack: Garlicky Cucumber Chips
Dinner: Garlic Pork Chops with Mushrooms
Dessert: Blueberry Vanilla Muffins

Day 3:

Breakfast: Spinach Egg Muffins
Lunch: Green Beans with Parsley
Snack: Barbecue Chicken Wings
Dinner: Paprika Baked Tilapia
Dessert: Vanilla Pineapple Cinnamon Treat

Day 4:

Breakfast: Asparagus Arugula Salad
Lunch: Balsamic Brussels Sprouts
Snack: Zucchini Fritters with Olives
Dinner: Delicious Cheeseburger
Dessert: Plum Apple Crumble with Cranberries

Day 5:

Breakfast: Pesto Gnocchi
Lunch: Roasted Butternut Squash with Cranberries
Snack: Crab Mushrooms
Dinner: Tender Pork Ribs with BBQ Sauce
Dessert: Simple Donuts

Day 6:

Breakfast: Cauliflower Ham Quiche
Lunch: Broccoli with Paprika
Snack: Chicken Jalapeno Poppers
Dinner: Spice Chicken Wings with Parmesan Cheese
Dessert: Erythritol Vanilla Butter Pie

Day 7:

Breakfast: Sunflower Bread
Lunch: Garlic Asparagus with Provolone
Snack: Egg Roll with Prawns
Dinner: Pork Cutlets
Dessert: Chocolate Oatmeal Cookies

Conclusion

The Air Fryer is the best solution for frying without adding oil to your kitchen top. We all want to live a healthy lifestyle but eating boring and tasteless food makes you ill and couldn't satisfy your hunger as well, so tasty food is a must. The question arises of how to get tasty food without compromising health. The new era solution is the Air Fryer. The air-fried food is tasty, full of spices as well as has fewer calories because the cooking procedure requires little or no oil. The air-fried food has the same texture as the fried food, roast or baked.

This amazing cookbook will give you complete guidance about healthy living and air frying. You can have tasty food all-time with less time in the kitchen without compromising taste. You will have all your addiction food with no guilt of being overweight with help of this amazing book and the Air Fryer.

With the guidance of this book, you will organize healthy parties and amaze your friends and family with your cooking. If you are planning for weight loss, it's the right time to grab this cookbook along with the Air Fryer of your choice and enjoy your diet.

MEASUREMENT CONVERSION CHART

VOLUME EQUIVALENTS(DRY)

US STANDARD	METRIC (APPROXIMATE)
1/8 teaspoon	0.5 mL
1/4 teaspoon	1 mL
1/2 teaspoon	2 mL
3/4 teaspoon	4 mL
1 teaspoon	5 mL
1 tablespoon	15 mL
1/4 cup	59 mL
1/2 cup	118 mL
3/4 cup	177 mL
1 cup	235 mL
2 cups	475 mL
3 cups	700 mL
4 cups	1 L

VOLUME EQUIVALENTS(LIQUID)

US STANDARD	US STANDARD (OUNCES)	METRIC (APPROXIMATE)
2 tablespoons	1 fl.oz.	30 mL
1/4 cup	2 fl.oz.	60 mL
1/2 cup	4 fl.oz.	120 mL
1 cup	8 fl.oz.	240 mL
1 1/2 cup	12 fl.oz.	355 mL
2 cups or 1 pint	16 fl.oz.	475 mL
4 cups or 1 quart	32 fl.oz.	1 L
1 gallon	128 fl.oz.	4 L

TEMPERATURES EQUIVALENTS

FAHRENHEIT(F)	CELSIUS(C) (APPROXIMATE)
225 °F	107 °C
250 °F	120 °C
275 °F	135 °C
300 °F	150 °C
325 °F	160 °C
350 °F	180 °C
375 °F	190 °C
400 °F	205 °C
425 °F	220 °C
450 °F	235 °C
475 °F	245 °C
500 °F	260 °C

WEIGHT EQUIVALENTS

US STANDARD	METRIC (APPROXIMATE)
1 ounce	28 g
2 ounces	57 g
5 ounces	142 g
10 ounces	284 g
15 ounces	425 g
16 ounces (1 pound)	455 g
1.5 pounds	680 g
2 pounds	907 g

Appendix 2 Recipes Index

© Copyright 2021 – All rights reserved.

The content contained within this book may not be reproduced, duplicated or transmitted without direct written permission from the author or the publisher.

Under no circumstances will any blame or legal responsibility be held against the publisher, or author, for any damages, reparation, or monetary loss due to the information contained within this book, either directly or indirectly.

Legal Notice:

This book is copyright protected. It is only for personal use. You cannot amend, distribute, sell, use, quote or paraphrase any part, or the content within this book, without the consent of the author or publisher.

Disclaimer Notice:

Please note the information contained within this document is for educational and entertainment purposes only. All effort has been executed to present accurate, up to date, reliable, complete information. No warranties of any kind are declared or implied. Readers acknowledge that the author is not engaged in the rendering of legal, financial, medical or professional advice. The content within this book has been derived from various sources. Please consult a licensed professional before attempting any techniques outlined in this book.

By reading this document, the reader agrees that under no circumstances is the author responsible for any losses, direct or indirect, that are incurred as a result of the use of the information contained within this document, including, but not limited to, errors, omissions, or inaccuracies.

Printed in Great Britain
by Amazon

10303458R00119